INTRODUCTIONS TO OLDER LANGUAGES

W. P. Lehmann
FOUNDING EDITOR

Marcabru, *Dire vos vuelh ses duptansa* (reading 14). Paris, Bibliothèque Nationale de France, fonds français 22543 (ms. *R*), fol. 5v. Reproduced by permission.

AN INTRODUCTION TO
Old Occitan

William D. Paden

THE MODERN LANGUAGE ASSOCIATION OF AMERICA
NEW YORK
1998

For information about obtaining permission to reprint material from
MLA book publications, send your request by mail (see address below),
e-mail (permissions@mla.org), or fax (646 458-0030).

Library of Congress Cataloging-in-Publication Data
Paden, William D. (William Doremus), 1941–
    An introduction to Old Occitan / William D. Paden.
       p.   cm. — (Introductions to older languages ; 4).
    Includes bibliographical references.
    ISBN 0-87352-293-1
    1. Provençal language—Grammar.   I. Title. II. Series.
  PC3221.P33   1998
  449′.82421—dc21   97-24074
ISSN 1099-0313
Printed on recycled paper

Published by The Modern Language Association of America
26 Broadway, New York, New York 10004-1789
www.mla.org

Contents

PART 2 HISTORICAL PHONOLOGY

Preface

This book aims at providing the student with the means to learn Old Occitan either independently or in a class. Students approach Old Occitan from many perspectives—literary or linguistic, with or without a background in Latin or other Romance languages—and need a textbook flexible enough to satisfy their individual interests. I have attempted to make this book adaptable to different patterns of use, while necessarily opting for one presentation that I believe will be appropriate for many, perhaps most, readers.

Each of the thirty-two chapters contains two components, the exposition of a subject in the study of the language and a reading. The first ten readings are presented in an approximate order of increasing difficulty, from three easy prose pieces to poems selected for their relative ease of translation. The remaining readings are presented chronologically, from the earliest text we have in literary Old Occitan through the halcyon days of the twelfth and thirteenth centuries to one example of fourteenth-century verse and, as an epilogue, one text representative of the twentieth-century language. Since all the texts are provided with explanatory notes and since the Glossary includes reference to every occurrence of every word in the texts, the student may take up the readings in any order; yet I suggest the order as given, for the sake of the easy start.

Traditional grammars, such as the excellent and still valuable ones by Grandgent or Anglade, assume considerable familiarity with Latin. They begin with the study of historical phonology (examining how the sounds of Latin became those of Old Occitan) and proceed to morphology (the declension of nouns and conjugation of verbs), seen against assumed familiarity with corresponding Latin structures—and give scant attention to anything else. The cultural perspective of such grammars, profoundly imbued with reverence for classical antiquity, has undergone a fundamental change by the present time, the end of the twentieth century. We can no longer assume that all students taking up Old Occitan will have pored for years over the texts of canonical Latin authors or that they will have internalized an extensive Latin vocabulary, the myriad forms of Latin morphology, and the patterns of Latin syntax. Nevertheless, it remains true that among those with an interest in Old Occitan, more will bring to it a background in Latin than there are, proportionally, in today's population as a whole.

Faced with this complex pedagogical situation, I have opted to introduce Old Occitan with descriptive morphology—that is, the ways verbs, nouns, and demonstratives (a distinct morphological class in Old Occitan) change their form to express different meanings (chs. 2–10). Such descriptive study, assuming no background in Latin, puts non-Latinists and Latinists on equal footing. While it does not allow the Latinists to take advantage at first of their prior training, it offers them the advantage that they will begin by considering Old Occitan in itself, as a functioning linguistic system in its own time, and not as a distorted prolongation of the older language. It offers both non-Latinists and Latinists immediate access to the most informative element in sentence structure, which is the verb. By learning to read the highly variable form of a verb, the less complicated form of a noun, and the particular form of a demonstrative, the student will recognize the relations among words that communicate meaning.

After descriptive morphology I turn to historical phonology (chs. 11–19), which will enable the Latinist to multiply his or her recognition of Occitan words by learning the processes through which they developed from Latin. (Students with Latin may wish to read these chapters first, to gain immediate understanding of more Occitan vocabulary.) To enable non-Latinists to develop recognition of vocabulary by activating their passive knowledge of Latin elements in languages they know (Italian, Spanish, French, or English), I provide cognates in these languages at the end of entries in the Glossary. Thus students with or without Latin will learn to read relationships among words in descriptive morphology and to recognize words themselves in historical phonology.

For Latinists, the next step is a logical one: by applying principles of historical phonology to the materials of descriptive morphology, Latinists can advance to historical morphology, studying the development of Latin conjugations and declensions into the Old Occitan systems with which we began (chs. 20–23). Here a Latin background enables the student to gain particular insight into the development of the language. For non-Latinists, however, it may seem difficult to appreciate the development from the unknown morphology of Latin into the distinct morphology of Old Occitan. Those without Latin may wish to pass over the grammatical components of these chapters.

Finally, a series of chapters on syntax (24–29) analyzes patterns of word order; the usage of verbs in the indicative, subjunctive, and conditional moods; the usage of nouns in the case system; and the usage of demonstratives, including personal pronouns. Concluding chapters investigate the historical composition of the Old Occitan lexicon, discuss tools available for research in the field, and add an epilogue on the subsequent history of the language down to the twentieth century. These chapters may interest the linguist as discursive analyses of aspects of Occitan or serve as reference for any student wishing to understand a reading in terms of its immanent syntactic patterns.

In addition to the readings and the grammatical exposition, there are exercises at the end of chapters 1–19 and 30, designed to help the student assimilate the topics being studied. Exercises are dispensed with in the other chapters, which are more discursive and less concerned with solving problems. The backmatter includes morphological tables summarizing the descriptive morphology of verbs, nouns, and demonstratives. As a further aid, especially for students working independently, translations of all the readings are included.

Throughout the book the grammatical analysis derives from the readings, which have been edited from the manuscripts to ensure that the analysis will be faithful in detail to actual records of the language. The editorial method is conservative. Each text is based on one manuscript version, with notation of any readings, in the base manuscript, rejected from this edition, selected variants from other versions preserved, and variations in stanza order. For policy on emendation for case, see chapter 28.

The Glossary lists every occurrence of every word in the readings and occasional interesting variants. After the head form, each entry gives the meaning or meanings and then a classified list of forms. Square brackets enclose the etymon of the word, with reference to sources for further information. Cognates are listed in Italian, Spanish, French, occasionally German, and English.

The backmatter also includes the melodies of ten reading selections; the sources of the melodies are noted after each reading. The compact disk that accompanies this book includes performance of five songs, as well as pronunciation of the first four readings. To understand the art of the troubadours as fully as possible, there is no substitute for singing their songs, or at least hearing them sung; even students without musical training will gain a powerful impression of what this art was like, and those who understand music will hear the poetry in its true artistic context.[1]

---

[1] For a study of troubadour music, see Aubrey; Switten and Chickering provide cassette recordings of performances of a number of songs in this book. For a history of medieval music, see Hoppin, *Medieval Music*; for a collection of texts, see Hoppin, *Anthology*.

However the student chooses to make use of it, this book will introduce the language and provide an initial, extensive reading experience. It should ideally be followed by further reading in some chosen area or areas, with the intention of going on to original interpretation and research.

For the student with little prior experience of medieval languages, Old Occitan will represent something new because its status was and remains different from that of modern languages. Before the normalization of language on various levels—before the publication of dictionaries, before the foundation of academies in France, Spain, and Italy, before the invention of a concept of linguistic correctness in the vernacular, before the development of national mentalities with their linguistic ramifications—Old Occitan prospered in an atmosphere of relative freedom. The medieval vernacular corresponded in some ways to our more relaxed, unself-conscious usage, while medieval Latin corresponded more closely to our canons of self-consciously correct language. The manuscripts may spell a given word two ways in the same line, and we have no warrant to correct them. Verb forms sometimes proliferate unexpectedly. Tenses combine in ways that may surprise us, conditioned as we are to expecting specific patterns in modern languages or in Latin. If we pay close attention to medieval texts, however, we learn that they make perfectly good sense; if they seem at times to confuse tenses, or what have you, the confusion is ours, not theirs. Medieval study can expand our modern horizons.

It is a pleasure to acknowledge the advice of friends and colleagues, including F. R. P. Akehurst, Keith Busby, Joseph J. Duggan, M. Roy Harris, Hans-Erich Keller, Richard Laurent, Deborah Nelson, Rupert T. Pickens, and Elizabeth Poe. Joe Duggan and Beth Poe used versions of the book in the classroom and sent me their students' reactions, which have been very useful. None of these friends, of course, are responsible for the faults of the finished book. F. Gregg Ney provided invaluable assistance in preparing a concordance. Evelyna Donnelly drew the map. The compact disk was produced by Professor Lowell Cross, Director of the Recording Studios, University of Iowa, as recording engineer, with assistant engineers Bradley Brummett and Chris Poma.

Members of the MLA staff have been very helpful. I wish to thank Martha Evans, Elizabeth Holland, Judith Altreuter, and Paul Banks for their patience and their expertise.

For her generous help and support, I am grateful to Frances Freeman Paden.

I learned about Old Occitan from my teacher, Thomas G. Bergin, and from my students as I taught them and collaborated with them in research. I wish to thank my students for all I have learned from them.

Occitan words and letters are printed in boldface (**cantar**), except in reading selections. Headwords in the Glossary are standardized by the principles used in Levy's *Petit dictionnaire*, including the distinction between close and open stressed vowels; for an explanation of these principles, see the headnote to the Glossary. These standardized forms are preferred in discussion except in reference to specific textual occurrences. An acute accent (**cantár**) indicates the stressed syllable when it is useful to do so. The texts follow the orthography of the manuscripts except for punctuation, which has been provided; the manuscripts indicate neither the distinction between close and open stressed vowels nor the stressed syllable (except occasionally in the *Boeci*, reading 11).

Latin etyma of all periods are printed in small capitals (CANTĀRE); the variety of Latin in question is identified when useful (CL, VL, ChL, LL, ML: see Abbreviations). Vulgar Latin forms are generally provided in classical orthography; when changes specific to VL are pertinent, the form is given in broad phonemic notation (/kantáre/). Words referred to as words in other languages are italicized (Fr. *chanter*). Symbols from the International Phonetic Alphabet are given in square brackets ([p], [t], [k]).

Abbreviations

abl.:	ablative (in Latin)
acc.:	accusative (in Latin)
adj.:	adjective
adv.:	adverb
art.:	article
B-W:	Bloch, Oscar, and Walther von Wartburg. *Dictionnaire étymologique de la langue française* (1968).
CGr.:	Classical Greek
ch.:	**canso** (Fr. *chanson*); see chapter 2.
ch. crois.:	crusade song (Fr. *chanson de croisade*); see chapter 2.
ChL:	Church Latin
CL:	Classical Latin
cond.:	conditional
1st cond.:	first conditional
2nd cond.:	second conditional
conj.:	conjunction
Ctc.:	Celtic
d:	*coblas doblas*; see chapter 2.
dat.:	dative (in Latin)
Dauzat:	Dauzat, Albert. *Dictionnaire étymologique des noms de famille et prénoms de France* (1980).
def.:	definite
dem.:	demonstrative
E.:	English
Ekwall:	Ekwall, Eilert. *The Concise Oxford Dictionary of English Place-Names* (1960).

em.:	emended by
fem.:	feminine
FEW:	Wartburg, Walther von. *Französisches etymologisches Wörterbuch* (1928–).
fig.:	figuratively
fol.:	folio
Fr.:	French (Modern)
Frank:	Frank, István. *Répertoire métrique de la poésie des troubadours* (1953–57).
fut.:	future
G.:	German (Modern)
gen.:	genitive (in Latin)
Germ.:	Germanic
Gk.:	Greek
imper.:	imperative
imperf.:	imperfect
indef.:	indefinite
indic.:	indicative
inf.:	infinitive
interj.:	interjection
intrans.:	intransitive
It.:	Italian
LGr.:	Late Greek
lit.:	literally
LL:	Late Latin
LR:	Raynouard, François-Just-Marie. *Lexique roman: ou, Dictionnaire de la langue des troubadours* (1844).
L & S:	Lewis, Charlton T., and Charles Short. *A Latin Dictionary* (1879).
masc.:	masculine
MFr.:	Middle French
ML:	Medieval Latin
ModOc:	Modern Occitan
ms.:	manuscript reading
n.:	noun
Nègre:	Nègre, Ernest. *Toponymie générale de la France* (1990–91).
nom.:	nominative
num.:	numeral

obl.:	oblique
OED:	*Oxford English Dictionary* (1989).
OFr.:	Old French
OHG:	Old High German
OIt.:	Old Italian
om.:	omitted
ONorse:	Old Norse
OOc:	Old Occitan
Oxf.:	Glare, P. G. W. *Oxford Latin Dictionary* (1982).
part.:	participle
past.:	pastourelle
P-C:	Pillet, Alfred, and Henry Carstens, eds. *Bibliographie der Troubadours* (1933).
PD:	Levy, Emil. *Petit dictionnaire provençal-français* (1909; 4th ed. 1966).
perf.:	perfect
pl.:	plural
pp.:	past participle
prep.:	preposition
pres.:	present
pret.:	preterit
pron.:	pronoun
refl.:	reflexive
rel.:	relative
relig.:	religious
REW:	Meyer-Lübke, W. *Romanisches etymologisches Wörterbuch* (1935).
s:	**coblas singulars**; see chapter 2.
sg.:	singular
sirv.:	**sirventes** (satire)
Sp.:	Spanish
st.:	stanza
subj.:	subjunctive
S-W:	Levy, Emil, and Carl Appel. *Provenzalisches Supplement-Wörterbuch* (1894–1924).
tens.:	**tenso** (song in dialogue)
T-L:	Tobler, Adolf, and Erhard Lommatzsch. *Tobler-Lommatzsch altfranzösisches Wörterbuch* (1925–).

trans.:	transitive
u:	**coblas unissonans**; see chapter 2.
v.:	verse; vv.: verses
var.:	variant
vb.:	verb
VL:	Vulgar Latin

Sources of the Texts

MANUSCRIPTS

The sigla are those of P-C except for K', Y, Z, d, and y, which were proposed by Zufferey (*Recherches*), and M^h, V^a. Note that d in P-C, the appendix to D, is merely a copy from K and so has been disregarded, following the argument of Zufferey (7–8). I have consulted the manuscripts in Paris, Venice, Milan, Modena, Florence, and Rome in the original; for the others I have used photographs, except for K', M^h, and y, for which I have relied on the editions noted.

A Rome, Biblioteca Apostolica Vaticana, latini 5232.
   Contains nos. 5, 6, 7, 12, 13, 14, 15, 16, 17, 18, 19, 20, 21, 22, 23.
   Base of nos. 6, 7, 15, 18, 20, 22.

B Paris, Bibliothèque Nationale, fonds français 1592.
   Contains nos. 5, 6, 15, 19, 21.

C Paris, Bibliothèque Nationale, fonds français 856.
   Contains nos. 2, 4, 9, 10, 12, 13, 14, 15, 16, 18, 19, 20, 21, 22, 24, 27, 28, 29.
   Base of nos. 2, 4, 9, 28, 29.

D Modena, Biblioteca Nazionale Estense, Estero 45 (α. R.4.4).
   Contains nos. 2, 6, 7, 10, 14, 15, 16, 17, 18, 19, 20, 21, 22, 24.
   Base of nos. 10, 16, 17, 24.

E Paris, Bibliothèque Nationale, fonds français 1749.
   Contains nos. 5, 15, 17, 18, 21, 22.

F Rome, Biblioteca Apostolica Vaticana, Chigiani L.IV. 106.
   Contains nos. 18, 20, 21, 22.

F^b Milan, Biblioteca Ambrosiana, D 465 inferiore (item 25).
   Contains no. 3.

G Milan, Biblioteca Ambrosiana, R 71 superiore.
   Contains nos. 16, 17, 18, 19.

H Rome, Biblioteca Apostolica Vaticana, latini 3207.
   Contains nos. 6, 19.

I   Paris, Bibliothèque Nationale, fonds français 854.
Contains nos. 1, 2, 3, 5, 6, 7, 10, 12, 13, 14, 15, 16, 17, 18, 19, 20, 21, 22, 23, 24, 26, 27.
Base of nos. 1, 3, 5, 21, 26, 27.

K   Paris, Bibliothèque Nationale, fonds français 12473.
Contains nos. 1, 2, 3, 5, 6, 7, 10, 12, 13, 14, 15, 16, 17, 18, 19, 20, 21, 22, 23, 24, 26, 27.

K'   Udine, Biblioteca Arcivescovale, codici fragmentari I, 265 (ed. Suttina).
Contains no. 18.

L   Rome, Biblioteca Apostolica Vaticana, latini 3206.
Contains nos. 17, 18.

M   Paris, Bibliothèque Nationale, fonds français 12474.
Contains nos. 14, 15, 18, 20, 24.

M^h   Madrid, Real Academia de la Historia, 9-24-6/4579 (ed. Pellegrini).
Contains nos. 15, 21.

N   New York, Pierpont Morgan Library, 819.
Contains nos. 8 (twice), 9 (twice), 10 (twice), 13, 18, 19, 20, 23.
Base of nos. 8, 23.

O   Rome, Biblioteca Apostolica Vaticana, latini 3208.
Contains no. 18.

P   Florence, Biblioteca Medicea Laurenziana, Plut. 41.42.
Contains nos. 16, 18, 24.

Q   Florence, Biblioteca Riccardiana, 2909.
Contains nos. 18, 19.

R   Paris, Bibliothèque Nationale, fonds français 22543.
Contains nos. 5, 10, 12, 13, 14, 15, 18, 19, 24, 27.
Base of nos. 12, 13, 14, 19.

S   Oxford, Bodleian Library, Douce 269.
Contains nos. 15, 18.

T   Paris, Bibliothèque Nationale, fonds français 15211.
Contains nos. 6, 13, 24, 26, 27.

T^a   Toulouse, Académie des Jeux Floraux, 500.010.
Base of no. 31.

U   Florence, Biblioteca Medicea Laurenziana, Plut. 41.43.
Contains no. 18.

V   Venice, Biblioteca Nazionale Marciana, 278 (fr. App. cod. XI).
Contains nos. 9, 18, 19.

V^a   Barcelona, Biblioteca de Cataluña, 7 (P-C *Ve. Ag. I*).
Contains no. 18.

W   Paris, Bibliothèque Nationale, fonds français 844.
Contains nos. 12, 15, 17, 18.

X   Paris, Bibliothèque Nationale, fonds français 20050.
Contains nos. 15, 18.

Y   Copenhagen, Kongelige Bibliotek, Thott 1087 (P-C *Kp*).
Contains no. 4.

Z   Barcelona, Biblioteca de Cataluña, 146 (P-C *Sg*).
Contains nos. 5, 15, 19, 31.

a   Florence, Biblioteca Riccardiana, 2814.
      Contains nos. 6, 16, 18, 19.

a¹   Modena, Biblioteca Nazionale Estense, Càmpori Appendice 426, 427, 494 (formerly γ.N.8.4.11–13).
      Contains nos. 8 (twice), 10, 12, 13, 14, 15.

d   Berlin, Staatsbibliothek, Phillipps 1910 (P-C *N²*).
      Contains nos. 1, 16, 18, 19.

e   Rome, Biblioteca Apostolica Vaticana, Barberiniani 3965.
      Contains no. 15.

f   Paris, Bibliothèque Nationale, fonds français 12472.
      Contains nos. 26, 27.

y   Sondrio, Archivio Statale, Romegialli (ed. Rajna 1924).
      Contains no. 22.

Carcassonne, Bibliothèque Municipale 34 (anc. 2703).
      Base of no. 30.

Orléans, Bibliothèque Municipale 444 (anc. 374).
      Base of no. 11.

Paris, Bibliothèque Nationale, fonds français 25425 (anc. La Vallière 91).
      Base of no. 25.

QUOTATIONS

α   In Matfre Ermengaud, *Breviari d'amor*. See Richter; Ricketts.
      Contains nos. 14, 16, 18.

β¹   In Raimon Vidal, *So fo e·l temps c'om era iays*. See Cornicelius.
      Contains no. 18.

β³   In Raimon Vidal, *Razos de trobar*. See Marshall.
      Contains no. 18.

ε   In Jean Renart, *Le roman de la rose ou de Guillaume de Dole*. See Lecoy.
      Contains nos. 15, 18.

κ   In Barbieri.
      Contains nos. 15, 19.

μ   In Terramagnino da Pisa, "Doctrina d'Acort." See Marshall 27–53.
      Contains no. 18.

In Gerbert de Montreuil, *Le roman de la violette ou de Gérart de Nevers*. See Buffum.
      Contains no. 18.

Claude Martí, "Cridarai." See Pécout (82).
      Contains no. 32.

AN INTRODUCTION TO

Old Occitan

Introduction

NAME OF THE LANGUAGE

Occitan refers to a Romance language spoken in southern France since the Middle Ages in which the affirmative particle *yes* is expressed by the word **oc**.[1] The troubadours, who flourished during the twelfth and thirteenth centuries and remain the most renowned users of this language, did not call it Occitan. It was known at the time by several names. It was called **proensal**, '(the language) of Provence,' especially in the region of that name east of the Rhône and among Italians who were interested in the troubadours. West of the Rhône and in Catalonia, where troubadours from the western area were particularly admired, it was called **lemozin**, '(the language) of Limoges.' The first troubadour called it simply **romans**, 'vernacular (language)' (see reading 10.24).[2]

In the Latin of administrative documents composed in the 1290s, the expression LINGUA DE OC referred not to the language but to the people of the region where the language was spoken.[3] The Latin form LINGUA OCCITANA appeared in 1302, modeled on LINGUA

---

[1] The major Romance languages include Italian, Spanish (Castilian), Portuguese, French, and Romanian; less familiar are Catalan (spoken in the region around Barcelona and as far north as Perpignan, in southern France), Franco-Provençal (around Lyon), Sardinian, Rheto-Romansh in Switzerland, and the extinct Dalmatian, formerly spoken along the eastern Adriatic coast. Although Occitan regionalists sometimes consider Catalan a form of Occitan, "from the standpoint of the linguist there can be no doubt concerning its status" as an independent language (Elcock 448).

[2] The notation "10.24" refers to the reading in chapter 10, line 24. See also Bec, *Langue occitane* 64–67; Gonfroy; Barthès 17–78; Paterson 3.

[3] See the articles "Oc," "Occitan" in the *Trésor de la langue française* 12: 377, 385–86. For LINGUA in the sense 'nation,' see Du Cange 5: 116.

AQUITANA 'the region of Aquitaine.' Dante applied the concept to the language itself in his treatise *De vulgari eloquentia* (c. 1305), in which he distinguished among three interrelated languages according to the affirmative particle, **oc** in Occitan, *oïl* in French (Modern French *oui*), and *si* in Italian (1.viii.6).[4] It is unclear whether the Occitan term **lenga d'oc**, first attested in 1323, referred to the region or to the language.

The noun **occitan** was introduced into both Occitan and French by the poet Frédéric Mistral (see ch. 32) in 1886 and was first recorded in English as late as 1940 (*OED*). Despite its air of neologism, *Occitan* is clearly superior to the traditional but misleading term *Provençal*, attested in English since 1642, since *Provençal* unavoidably suggests a language specific to Provence, the region lying to the east of the Rhône. *Occitan* enjoys increasing acceptance in all the languages of scholarship on the subject (despite the resistance of Provençal partisans)[5] and will be adopted here.

OCCITAN IN THE MIDDLE AGES

Old Occitan (OOc) refers to the stage of this language during the Middle Ages—that is, from the earliest traces around A.D. 1000 down to about 1500. The language employed in the poetry of the troubadours does not represent the dialect specific to any one area of the broader linguistic domain. Instead, like the language of Homer in the *Iliad* and the *Odyssey*, it is a koine, or common language, incorporating features of various regional dialects yet identifiable with none (CGk. *koinē* [*dialektos*] 'common [dialect]'; Elcock 403–05). Such a koine was the goal Dante sought for Italian in *De vulgari eloquentia*, as he struggled to found a poetry that would not be limited to local expression. Like Italian before Dante, Old French was strongly marked by dialectal features; such features in French retained their currency throughout the medieval period and keep the reader of medieval French texts constantly alert (Kibler 3).

In the more standardized language of the troubadours, the koine was already established by the time of Guilhem, seventh count of Poitou and ninth duke of Aquitaine to bear the name, the first troubadour whose works we have. It is a striking fact that Guilhem was born and lived most of his life in Poitiers—which was probably not then part of the Occitan-speaking area, as it is not

---

[4] Dante called Occitan *il provenzale* in *Convivio* (1.vi.8).

[5] "Only among specialists outside France has Occitan come to be the generally accepted term for the language" (Field 233). As outspoken a critic of the term as Barthès nevertheless employs it himself in the title of his book *Etudes historiques sur la "langue occitane"* (1987), while enclosing it in ironic quotation marks.

now.[6] If this is true, the first troubadour may have adopted a foreign language for the purpose of lyric expression, as other poets in Spain and Italy would adopt Occitan later on.[7] The Occitan koine became an international language for lyric expression, comparable to the Italian of Mozart's *Don Giovanni* (in the libretto by Lorenzo Da Ponte), which was first performed in Prague, or to English as the language of lyric song around the globe at the end of the twentieth century (Paden, "Old Occitan").

STUDY OF OLD OCCITAN

Serious study of OOc began in the early nineteenth century with the publication of two collections of texts, the *Choix des poésies originales des troubadours (1816–21)*, edited by François-Just-Marie Raynouard, and *Le Parnasse occitanien* (1819), by Henri-Pascal de Rochegude.[8] In an interview at Jena in 1818, Goethe, the poet and sage, recommended Raynouard's collection to a young scholar named Friedrich Diez, who took the advice to heart and went on to found the modern study of Occitan and of the Romance languages in *Die Poesie der Troubadours* (1826).[9] The concept that the Romance languages share a common descent from a form of Latin— the idea that gave rise to university departments of Romance languages—was not demonstrated systematically until the nineteenth century. It did not occur to Dante, who had no concept of a historical evolution out of Latin and into what we now recognize as its eventual descendants, from Romanian to Portuguese.

Then and now, the strongest attraction of OOc lies in the poetry of the troubadours, who composed songs on the theme of love— **fin'amors**, in their own words—that is, 'true love'; *amour courtois*, in the words of Gaston Paris (1883); *courtly love* for generations of English and American scholars.[10] The word *troubadour* has a useful specificity, referring as it does to a lyric poet in Occitan during

---

[6] "La limite oc/oïl . . . ne semble pas avoir beaucoup varié depuis le Moyen Age" (Bec, *Langue occitane* 11). Some linguists, however, believe that during the Middle Ages the Occitan region extended as far north as the Loire, including Poitiers (Kremnitz 9).

[7] Duby suggests that Guilhem did so out of a political motive, to emphasize the cultural singularity of the lands he held, in relation to the lands of his suzerain, the king of France ("Modèle courtois" 264). A similar motive, it is believed, led Alfonso II of Aragon (ruled 1162–96) to compose poetry in Occitan in order to win the sympathy of his Provençal subjects (Paterson 95).

[8] For background, see Körner.

[9] See Mölk, *Trobadorlyrik* 11–22 (Italian trans. 13–23); Gumbrecht; Jeanroy, *Poésie lyrique* 1.1–44.

[10] See Boase; Ferrante.

two centuries, the twelfth and the thirteenth. The cognate *trouvère*, in French, refers to those who wrote similar poetry, largely inspired by the troubadours, in northern France, beginning somewhat later (about 1180). After about 1300, language and culture evolved in both northern and southern France so significantly as to suggest a new period. Students of French recognize a distinction between Old French, with literary texts dating from the ninth century through the thirteenth, and Middle French, which dates from the fourteenth through the sixteenth—that is, from Machaut to Montaigne. In Occitan, too, a similar discontinuity may be observed around 1300 (or perhaps 1350), suggesting that the OOc period may be considered as essentially the twelfth and thirteenth centuries, followed by Middle Occitan.[11]

Scholars of the nineteenth and early twentieth centuries regarded troubadour poetry as the earliest vernacular expression of the theme of love in Europe, subsequently imitated in French by the *trouvères*, in Italian by the Sicilian school, and later by the poets of the *dolce stil nuovo*, in German and in English. C. S. Lewis's *Allegory of Love* (1936) was an influential expression of this powerful synthesis. Some, unaware of nonliterary texts such as the Strasbourg Oaths in both Old French and Old High German (A.D. 842), considered Occitan the oldest recorded Romance language, or even the first of the modern European languages to have left records—ignoring Old High German, Old English, and Gothic, with its records from as early as the fourth century. Raynouard regarded the language of the troubadours (which he called "la langue romane") as the source of all other Romance languages. We know today that it was not their source; rather, all the major vernaculars evolved from Vulgar Latin: Italian grew most slowly, French most rapidly, Occitan and Spanish at middling rates. Furthermore, we now know, since the discovery in 1948 of a body of love poetry written in Spain, in a form of Romance heavily influenced by Arabic, that Occitan was not the first Romance language to leave poetry of love. These *kharjas*, or Romance envois to Arabic love poems, typically in the voice of the beloved, were written from the tenth century onward.[12]

For today's student, OOc offers a brilliant and diverse body of poetry on love and other themes. The poetry includes some 2,500 lyric compositions, including about 1,000 **cansos**, or love songs; about 500 **sirventes**, or satires; about 500 dialogues of various kinds; and about 500 **coblas**, or isolated stanzas. Some ten percent of troubadour lyrics have come down to us with melodic transcriptions, and the remaining ninety percent are generally assumed to have been

---

[11] See Zufferey, *Bibliographie*; Jeanroy, *Poésie lyrique* 2: 347–64. The Old Occitan period extended to the middle of the fourteenth century, according to Bec, *Langue occitane* 89.

[12] Stern; see also Hitchcock.

meant to be sung. There are also narrative and historical compositions and an extensive corpus of religious, scientific, and cultural
texts.[13] As critics of this literature become more cognizant of its variety, the sometimes disproportionate emphasis on courtly love will
yield to a fuller understanding of medieval Occitan culture.

For someone beginning the study of OOc now, the time is op-
portune. In recent years the field has been renewed by rapid progress on several fronts. New editions and instruments for research
have appeared at such a rate that a convenient bibliography of the
subject, first published in 1977 (Taylor), became outdated in fifteen
years and will soon appear in its second edition. Major troubadours have reappeared in editions that represent new readings,
differing significantly from the older ones. More generally, the field
cannot fail to be renewed, as it already has been to a significant degree, as the effects of evolving attitudes about sexuality and gender
make themselves increasingly felt. New methodologies in history
have altered our perception of the situation of medieval women,
and necessarily of the situation of men as well; and we are only beginning to understand better the distinctive nature of urbanization
and feudalism in the south of France (Paterson, 1993). Musicolo-
gists now understand more fully the nature of troubadour performance, and the complete corpus of troubadour melodies has been
published in two independent editions—Fernández de la Cuesta
and Lafont (1979); van der Werf and Bond (1984).

Precisely because the art of the troubadours is a lyric art, it demands to be studied in the original language. The student who ap-
proaches the subject having an acquaintance with modern
Romance languages such as Italian, Spanish, or French (not to
mention the source of these vernaculars, in Latin) can extend his
or her prior knowledge into a fascinating new domain. Anyone
who undertakes the study of OOc will find in it a language of undis-
puted cultural significance as well as linguistic interest.

BIBLIOGRAPHICAL NOTE

Concise introductory treatments of troubadour poetry include
Marrou; Riquer 1: 9–102; Mölk, *Trobadorlyrik* (and Italian trans.);
and Di Girolamo. It is typical of the cosmopolitan quality in troubadour scholarship that these works have appeared in French,
Spanish, German, and Italian.

For further bibliographical orientation, see chapter 31, "Research Tools."

---

[13] Brunel, *Bibliographie*. On individual troubadours and works, see the *Dictionnaire des lettres françaises: Le Moyen Age.*

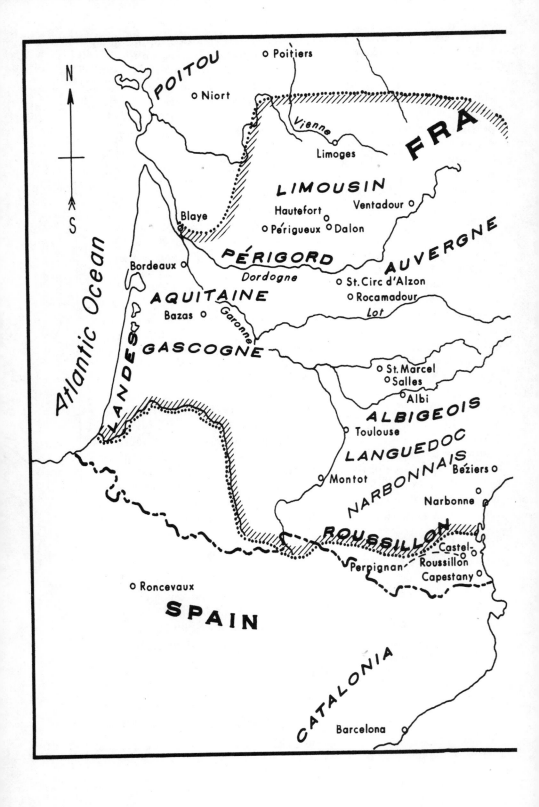

NCE

Saône

Loire

Rhône

Isère

o Vienne

Milan o

ITALY

LOMBARDY

Die o

Rhône

o Le Caire

o Orange

Avignon o

Durance

Nimes o

Montpellier o

Arles o

Aix-en-Provence

Nice o

PROVENCE

Vence o

o Marseille

Mediterranean Sea

Map of Occitania

SCALE:

.... Approximate linguistic boundary

0 —   150 km

E. Donnelly

0   100 miles

CHAPTER 1

Prologue: Getting Started

PRONUNCIATION

Vowels

In general, Occitan vowels are pronounced in the "Continental" manner. The general values of the letters **a**, **e**, **i**, and **o** are like those in Italian, Spanish, French, or Latin, while Old Occitan **u** is pronounced like French *u* or German *ü*:

> **a** as in E. *father*
>
> **e** as in E. *met*
>
> **i** as in E. *marine*
>
> **o** as in E. *note* (but a single vowel timbre, as in Fr. *beau*, not a diphthong as in E.)
>
> **u** as in Fr. *tu*, *plume*, *pur*; German *dünn* 'thin'

Note that in English the names of these vowels have become diphthongs (combinations of two vowel qualities in one syllable) or triphthongs (combinations of three vowel qualities in one syllable): the name of the English letter *a* is pronounced [ej], *e* [ij], *i* [aj], *o* [ow], and *u* [juw].

Three of these vowels occur in Occitan in two distinct varieties when in the stressed syllable of a word. The vowels **e** and **o** may be either open or closed, as in French—that is, the tongue may be positioned relatively lower, so as to produce the open vowel, or higher to produce the closed one. These distinctions are noted in the headword of each entry in the Glossary:

> Open **e**, symbolized **ẹ**, as in E. *met*, Fr. *mettre*: OOc **mẹu** 'my'
>
> Close **e**, symbolized **ẹ**, as in Fr. *été*: OOc **mẹ** 'me'

Open **o**, symbolized **ǫ**, as in Fr. *botte*: OOc **mǫl** 'soft'

Close **o**, symbolized **ọ**, as in Fr. *beau*: OOc **mọlt** 'much'

In Modern Occitan close **o** has shifted to [u], as in It. *tutto*, Fr. *toute*, E. *toot*; the shift may have occurred as early as the troubadours.

The pronunciation of OOc **a** is usually front and open, symbolized **ạ**, as in Fr. *patte* 'paw,' almost as far front as in E. *pat*; however, when followed by a nasal consonant under certain conditions (see ch. 12), it shifts to a back and closed form, symbolized **ạ**, as in Fr. *pâte* 'pasta,' almost as far back as in E. *pot*. Back closed **ạ** in Old Occitan has yielded an open [ǫ] in some Modern Occitan dialects:

> **mạns** or **mạs**, oblique (objective) plural of **maṇ** 'hand,' ModOc [mǫ]; in contrast to **mạs**, feminine oblique plural of **mon** 'my'

Old Occitan open **ę** and **ǫ** may produce diphthongs, **ę** becoming **ię** and **ǫ** becoming **uọ́** or **uę́**. The scribes of troubadour manuscripts employed these alternative forms in seemingly random fashion:

> **męlhs** 'better,' diphthongized form **mię́lhs**
>
> **colhir** 'to receive,' present indicative, third person singular **cǫlh**, **cuọ́lh**, or **cuę́lh**

Further discussion will be found in chapter 12.

Semivowels

Occitan possessed two semivowels (or semiconsonants, since they are midway between vowels and consonants): [j] in front position, pronounced like E. *y* in *you*, and [w] in back position, pronounced like E. *w* in *we*. The former is commonly referred to as *yod*, the name of the corresponding letter in the Hebrew alphabet; the latter will here be called *waw*, by the same logic. Unlike vowels, semivowels cannot constitute syllables, nor can they bear stress; rather they form diphthongs in combination with vowels. Yod combined with the various vowels as follows:

> vowel + yod: **ái** (**paire** 'father'); **ę́i** (**sęis** 'six'); **ę́i** (**vęi** 'I see'); **ọ́i** (**pọis** 'then'); **ǫ́i** (**conǫiser** 'to know'); **úi** (**cuid** 'I believe'); exceptionally [íj] (**diịre**, form of **dire** 'to say')
>
> yod + vowel: **ię́** (**mię́lhs** 'better')

Waw formed these combinations:

> vowel + waw: **áu** (**autre** 'other'); **ę́u** (**bręu** 'short'); **ę́u** (**bęure** 'to drink'); **íu** (**estiu** 'summer'); **ǫ́u** (**mǫu** 'it moves'); **ọ́u** (**dọus** 'sweet')

waw + vowel: **uǫ́** (**cuǫlh** 'he receives'); **uę́** (**cuęlh** 'he receives')

When open **ę́** and **ǫ́** occur as diphthongs, they may combine with following semivowels to produce triphthongs:

ę́i becomes **ię́i**, pronounced [jęj]: **lię̂is** 'her'

ę́u becomes **ię́u**, pronounced [jęw]: **ię̂u** 'I'

ǫ́i becomes **uǫ́i**, pronounced [wǫj]: **nuǫit** 'night,' or **uę́i**, pronounced [węj]: **puę̂is** 'then'

ǫ́u becomes **uǫ́u**, pronounced [wǫw]: **uǫ̂u** 'egg,' or **uę́u**, pronounced [węw]: **buę̂u** 'ox'

In pronunciation of OOc triphthongs, the stress falls on the middle element: **ię́i, ię́u, uǫ́i, uę́i, uǫ́u, uę́u**.

Consonants

Most Old Occitan consonants are pronounced as in English.

OOc **c** and **g** have two basic values. Their pronunciation is "hard" before **a**, **o**, or **u**:

[k] in **cantar** 'to sing,' **cortęs** 'polite,' **cuidar** 'to believe'

[g] in **gai** 'joyous,' **gonęla** 'cloak,' **gu-**; note that in the texts in this book, **gu-** occurs before a vowel only as a digraph for "hard" **g**, as in **guęrra**, pronounced [gęrra]; that is, **gu-** never represents "hard" **g** + the vowel **u**[1]

The pronunciation is "soft" before **e** or **i**:

c = [ts] in the twelfth century, but simplified during the thirteenth to [s], in **cęla** 'that one' (fem.), **cinc** 'five'

g = [dž] in **gelǫs** 'jealous,' **gitar** 'to throw'

Ch- is often supposed to represent an affricate, as in **chantar** [tšantar] (cf. E. *church*). But since this orthography alternates freely with **cantar**, it seems possible that **ch-** could also correspond to [k], as in Italian *chi* 'who,' *che* 'what.' In final position, **g** may represent [tš]: **plag** 'conflict' [platš], also spelled **plaich**; **gaug** 'joy' [gawtš], also spelled **gauch**.

Qu- before a vowel represents [k], as in **quan**, **can** 'when,' Fr. *quand*, not [kw] as in It. *quando*, Sp. *cuando*.

Lh and **nh**, called "liquid" or "palatal," represent distinct consonants contrasted with the more familiar dental varieties. They are similar to the medial consonants in E. *million, canyon*, and to the sounds spelled in Castilian Spanish *ll* and *ñ*, or in Italian *gl* and *gn*:

---

[1] The *PD* lists a few words in which **gu-** is followed by a consonant, such as **gustamęn** 'taste.'

melhor 'better,' similar to It. *migliore*; also spelled **meillor**, where **ill** represents palatal l (the **i** is part of the spelling of the liquid **l**, and not a distinct vowel)

senhor 'lord,' pronounced like Sp. *señor*; also spelled **seignor**, in which the **i** is not a distinct vowel; the range of spellings may be illustrated further in nominative singular **sénher, séigner, séingner, ségner** (for the use of **g**, compare It. *signore*, Fr. *seigneur*)

Aside from these combinations, **h** is silent.[2]

A particular form of the nasal is called "**n**-mobile," symbolized in this book **ṇ**, which occurs at the end of numerous words such as **paṇ** 'bread' and less conspicuously at the end of internal syllables, as in **coṇselh** 'counsel.' This consonant was freely omitted or included by scribes: **pa, coselh**. In most Modern Occitan dialects it has disappeared. Etymologically, **n**-mobile represents a single N in Latin that became final through loss of the last syllable, as in CL PĀNEM 'bread' > **paṇ**. The Latin cluster NT produced stable **n**, as in CL FRŎNTEM > **froṇ** 'forehead.'

S is normally unvoiced in initial or final position, as in E. *song*; between vowels it may be voiced like the *z* in E. *razor*. Double **s** represents intervocalic voiceless [s], as in **fassa**, present subjunctive of **faire**. **Z** between vowels represents the voiced sound (**azirar** 'to hate' [azirar]) or the affricate (**razón** 'reason' [radzón]; cf. E. *adze*); in final position, **z** represents [ts], as in the second person plural, present indicative of **aver**, spelled either **avetz** or **avez**. In the headword of each entry in the Glossary, **s** is used to represent the voiceless sibilant [s], and **z** to represent the voiced sibilant [z].

J may represent either the affricate [dž] (cf. E. *judge*) or the semivowel [j] (cf. E. *you*):

> **jǫrn** [džǫrn] 'day'

> **aja** or **aia**, pronounced like Sp. *haya*; present subjunctive, third person singular of **aver**

Double **r**, pronounced as a trill, is generally distinguished from the single flap **r** as in Spanish, but exceptions occur, such as **guera** for **guerra** 'war.' Other double consonants are pronounced as single.

Word Stress

In general, Occitan words ending in a consonant are stressed on the final syllable:

---

[2] Do not pronounce an English *h* in **melhor, senhor,** producing [mel-hor], [sen-hor].

cantár 'to sing,' **partír** 'to leave'

cantátz 'you sing,' **partítz** 'you leave'

Words ending in a vowel are stressed on the penult, or next-to-final syllable (CL ᴘᴀᴇɴᴇ ᴜ̆ʟᴛ̆ɪᴍᴜᴍ 'almost last'):

cánta 'he sings' (present indicative), **párta** 'that he leave' (present subjunctive)

dǫ́mna 'lady,' **páire** 'father,' **glázi** 'sword'

The position of stress in Occitan almost always corresponds to the CL etymon or its reflexes in other Romance languages (cf. ch. 11).

A syllable may, however, be inherently stressed or unstressed in defiance of this generalization. Stressed final vowels occur in words such as **aisí**, **enaisí** 'here, thus,' **acǫ́** 'that,' **Jaufrę́** (a man's name; Fr. *Geoffroi*, E. *Geoffrey*). Words ending in **n**-mobile are naturally stressed on the final syllable, as in **certáṇ** 'certain'; when the **n**-mobile is not marked, the vowel retains its stress (**certá**). Unstressed final syllables ending in consonants occur in words in **-er** such as nominative singular **mólher** 'wife' and **sénher** 'lord,' infinitive **plánher** 'to lament,' and in other words such as **ávol** 'bad,' **jóven** 'young.' Such stresses are indicated in the headwords of the Glossary.

Morphology comes into play in nouns ending in a vowel plus declensional **-s** for the plural, or for the nominative singular masculine, which does not alter the position of stress on the penult: **dǫ́mna**, plural **dǫ́mnas**; **páire**, alternative nominative singular **páires**. Verbs may have unstressed final syllables ending in a consonant (present indicative, second person singular **cántas**, third person plural **cántan**; preterit, third person plural **vénguen**), or stressed final vowels (future **cantará**, preterit **morí**), where stress is determined by the system of verb morphology.

FIRST ELEMENTS OF MORPHOLOGY

Old Occitan was an inflected language. Most masculine nouns possessed distinct forms for two cases, the nominative and the oblique. The nominative case was used to express the subject of the sentence; the oblique case could express the direct object or the object of a preposition, less frequently the indirect object or a genitive (for a possessor). These two cases represent a simplification of the Latin system of five cases: the Latin nominative survives in Old Occitan, but the Latin accusative (for the direct object), dative (for the indirect object), genitive (for a possessor), and ablative (expressing manner) have merged into the OOc oblique, which continues the functions of them all. Old French, like Old Occitan, also had these two cases. Nouns of address, which took the vocative in Latin (a sixth case), normally took the nominative in Old Occitan.

The most striking example of the two-case system in Old Occitan is that of regular masculine nouns such as **jọrn** 'day.' These nouns exhibit forms in the oblique case that correspond to the forms of Modern French or Spanish, with no ending (signified in this book by -zero) in the singular and **-s** in the plural:

Obl. sg. **jọrn**, pl. **jọrns**

But in the nominative case, the distribution of **-s** and -zero is reversed:

Nom. sg. **jọrns**, pl. **jọrn**

That is, as the subject of a sentence, **jọrns** is singular, **jọrn** plural. This pattern may be noted in four slots, as follows:

	Sg.	Pl.
Nom.	**jọrns**	**jọrn**
Obl.	**jọrn**	**jọrns**

The pattern of four declensional slots will be used throughout this book. Feminine nouns, such as **dọmna** 'lady,' inflect as in modern French or Spanish—singular **dọmna**, plural **dọmnas** (for both cases).

The definite article **lo** 'the' is also inflected. In the masculine:

	Sg.	Pl.
Nom.	**lo**	**li**
Obl.	**lo**	**los**

and in the feminine:

	Sg.	Pl.
Nom.	**la**	**las**
Obl.	**la**	**las**

The pattern for a basic masculine noun phrase is therefore as follows:

	Sg.	Pl.
Nom.	**lo jọrns**	**li jọrn**
Obl.	**lo jọrn**	**los jọrns**

Notice that in this pattern, the combination of definite article and masculine noun expresses case and number with no ambiguity. Basic feminine noun phrases, in contrast, do not distinguish case:

	Sg.	Pl.
Nom.	**la dọmna**	**las dọmnas**
Obl.	**la dọmna**	**las dọmnas**

OOc verbs are inflected in patterns that depend, in most tenses, on whether the infinitive ends in **-ar** or in some other form. The **-ar** group is the largest, corresponding to -ĀRE in Classical Latin, *-are* in Italian, *-ar* in Spanish, *-er* in French: OOc **cantar** 'to sing,' CL CANTĀRE, It. *cantare*, Sp. *cantar*, Fr. *chanter*. Expression of the pronoun subject is optional and infrequent in Old Occitan, as in Italian or Spanish, whereas in Modern French the pronoun subject is obligatory (*je vais, tu vas, il va*, etc.) except in imperatives. The subject is expressed in the ending of the verb, as in the present indicative of **cantar**:

	Sg.	Pl.
1st	cánt	cantám
2nd	cántas	cantátz
3rd	cánta	cántan or cánton

Other infinitive types end in **-ír**, like **partír** 'to leave'; in stressed **-ér**, like **tenér** 'to hold'; in unstressed **-er**, like **conóiser** 'to know'; in unstressed **-re**, like **recébre** 'to receive'; and in the single consonant **-r**, as in the forms **far** 'to do,' **dir** 'to say.'

READING 1

Vida of Jaufre Rudel

*The prose **vidas** (or 'lives' of the troubadours) and **razos** (or 'reasons' for the composition of individual songs) were probably composed around 1220–50. We have **vidas** and **razos** concerning 101 troubadours. Most of them, like this one, are anonymous.*

The troubadour Jaufre Rudel, lord of Blaye, north of Bordeaux, signed a legal document in 1125, participated in the Second Crusade, in 1147–48, and had probably died by 1164. As lord he was styled PRINCEPS *in Latin (**princes** in the text of the **vida** given here). We have six poems by him. Scholars have debated whether the love story in the **vida** has any historical foundation or was invented on the basis of an imaginative reading of Jaufre's poetry (see ch. 15).*

[1] Jaufres Rudels de Blaia si fo mout gentils hom, e fo princes de Blaia. [2] Et enamoret se de la comtessa de Tripoli ses vezer, per lo bon qu'el n'auzi dire als pelerins que venguen d'Antiocha. [3] E fez de leis mains vers ab bons sons, ab paubre motz. [4] E per voluntat de leis vezer, el se croset e se mes en mar; e pres lo malautia en la nau, e fo condug a Tripoli en un alberc per mort. [5] E fo fait saber a la comtessa, et ella venc ad el, al son leit, e pres lo antre sos bratz. [6] E saup qu'ella era la comtessa, e mantenent recobret l'auzir e·l flairar, e lauzet Dieu, que l'avia la vida sostenguda tro qu'el l'agues vista; et enaissi el mori entre sos braz.

[7] Et ella lo fez a gran honor sepellir en la maion del Temple; e pois en aquel dia ella se rendet morga, per la dolor qu'ella n'ac de la mort de lui.

Major editions: Boutière and Schutz 16–19; Riquer 154; Pickens 53–59; Wolf and Rosenstein 95–101; Chiarini 51–53. For pronunciation of the reading, refer to the accompanying compact disk.

Three manuscripts: *I* fol. 121v; *K* fol. 107v; *d* fol. 19. Base *I.* There is a longer version in mss. *AB.*

Rejected readings in the base manuscript: (3) delleis. (4) delleis.

Selected variants: (1) molt *d;* princeps *(Lat.) Kd.* (2) Tripol *Kd;* ben *Kd.* (3) paubre *IK,* paubres *d.* (4) e mes se *Kd.* (6) et el saub *d.* flairar] flazar *Kd.* (7) maison *K,* mason *d;* monga *d.*

Notes

(1) **Jaufrés Rudels**] Masc. nom. sg. **-s. gentils hom**] The **-s** of **gentils** represents masc. nom. sg., modifying **hom. Hom** belongs to another type of declension, called shifting because the syllabic or accentual structure shifts from form to form (see ch. 23). In this word the syllabic structure varies but the accent does not move:

	Sg.	Pl.
Nom.	**hóm**	**hóme**
Obl.	**hóme**	**hómes**

A similar contrast in Old French has produced Modern French *on* (from the nom., like OOc **hom**) and *homme* (from the obl., like OOc **home**). **prínces**] Stressed in accordance with obl. sg. **prínce**.

(2) **enamorét**] Preterit 3rd sg. **Trípoli**] Proparoxytone (stressed on the third syllable from the end), as in CL nom. Trĭpŏlis, acc. Trĭpŏlem. **ses vezer**] 'Without seeing [her],' 'sight unseen.' It is not necessary to posit an ellipsis of the feminine object. **als pelerins**] 'The good that he heard told by the pilgrims' or 'the good that he heard the pilgrims tell.' The preposition introduces the agent of the infinitive **dire. vénguen**] Preterit 3rd pl.; **g** marks a set of three tenses, the preterit, the past subjunctive (**vengués**), and the second conditional (**véngra**).

(3) **fez**] Pronounced the same as **fetz**; preterit 3rd sg. **vers**] Since the root **vers** (CL vĕrsus; cf. E. *verse*) has a final **-s**, the word is invariable in declension. **ab bons sons, ab paubre motz**] Masc. obl. pl. **-s**. The sentence contains three key terms of troubadour poetry: **vers** 'song' (including both words and melody), **son** 'melody,' **motz** 'words.' **paubre**] The **au** was a diphthong (E. *cow*) in CL paupĕrem, and remained one in Old Occitan and in Modern Occitan, whereas it monophthongized in It. *povero*, Sp. *pobre*, Fr. *pauvre* [pǫvrə]. Pronounce as a diphthong. **paubre motz**] Obl. pl. noun phrase with declension on the noun only (**paubre** for **paubres**; see ch. 28).

(4) **crosét**] Preterit 3rd sg., cf. **enamorét**. **mes**] Pret. 3rd sg. of **metre**; **-s** marks the set of three tenses including the preterit. **pres**] Pret. 3rd sg. of **prendre**; **-s** marks the set of three tenses. **malautía**] Stressed as in Fr. *maladie*; subject of **pres**. **fo**] Fr. *fut*, Sp. *fue*. **per mort**] 'As good as dead,' 'as though he were a dead man.'

(5) Contrary to what the **vida** says, Hodierna, the historical countess of Tripoli at this time, was kept in a state of seclusion by her husband, Count Raymond II. **fo fait**] The subject is the preceding narrative. **venc**] Pret. 3rd sg. of venir; [k] marks the set of three tenses.

(6) **saup**] Pret. 3rd sg. of **saber**; the marker for the set of tenses takes the form of an infix waw, spelled **u**. The meaning 'to know' becomes 'to realize' in the preterit, as in Spanish. **recobrét**] Pret. 3rd sg.; cf. **crosét**, **enamorét**, etc. **que l'avia la vida sostenguda**] Proclitic ('forward-leaning') **l'**, for **li**, expresses the indirect object of inalienable possession: 'who had sustained his life.' **agués**] Past subjunctive 3rd sg., marked as past subjunctive by **-s**; subjunctive after **tro que** 'until' dependent on a verb in the past. **morí**] Pret. 3rd sg.

(7) **ella lo fez a gran honor sepellir**] Causative **faire**; 'she caused him to be buried with great honor' or 'she caused (someone) to bury him with great honor.' **del Temple**] The Knights Templars were a religious and military order founded at Jerusalem early in the twelfth century for the protection of pilgrims and the Holy Sepulcher. They were so named because they occupied an apartment of the palace of Baldwin II in Jerusalem near the temple. **en aquel dia**] Note that **dia** is here masc.; cf. Glossary. **rendét**] Cf. **lauzét**, **recobrét**, **crosét**, **enamorét**. **morga**] CL MŎNĂCHAM; CL N has become OOc **r** by the effect of dissimilation from nasal M. OOc **monga**, without dissimilation, also occurs (see Glossary). **n'**] **En** (2) in the Glossary, equivalent in meaning to **de** + object pronoun; CL ĬNDE, It. *ne*, Fr. *en*. Here **n'** anticipates the phrase **de la mort de lúi**, redundantly for the modern reader.

Exercise

After you read through the **vida** of Jaufre Rudel, analyze the position of stress in each word, study the pronunciation of the entire text, and pronounce it aloud.

Descriptive Morphology

CHAPTER 2

Verbs: Present Set (Section 1)

SETS OF TENSES: PRESENT SET

An overview of the entire conjugation of a verb such as **cantár** 'to sing,' in the Morphological Tables (pp. 349–52), shows that the forms of the eight tenses fall into three clusters, or sets. Most distinctive is the future set, comprising the future tense (3rd sg. **cantará**) and the first conditional (3rd sg. **cantaría**), because both these tenses are evidently built on the infinitive. In the past set, comprising the preterit (3rd sg. **cantę́t**), past subjunctive (3rd sg. **cantę́s**), and second conditional (3rd sg. **cantę́ra**), all or nearly all the forms are visibly based on the root **cant-** plus the ending **ę́**. In contrast, the present set, comprising the present indicative (3rd sg. **cánta**), the present subjunctive (3rd sg. **cant**), and the imperfect (**cantáva**), is based on the root **cant-** alone, with modifications for some individual tenses. These three sets of tenses will provide the foundation for our analysis of OOc verb morphology. We shall begin with the present set.

PRESENT INDICATIVE TENSE AND PRESENT SUBJUNCTIVE TENSE

The forms of the present indicative and subjunctive are as follows, for **cantar** 'to sing' and **partir** 'to leave,' model verbs of the **-ar** and non-**ar** types:[1]

---

[1] See chapter 25 for usage of the indicative mood and chapter 26 for the subjunctive.

| | *Present Indicative* | | *Present Subjunctive* | |
	Column 1	Column 2	Column 3	Column 4
1st sg.	**cant**	**part**	**cant**	**párta**
2nd sg.	**cántas**	**partz**	**cantz**	**pártas**
3rd sg.	**cánta**	**part**	**cant**	**párta**
1st pl.	**cantám**	**partém**	**cantém**	**partám**
2nd pl.	**cantátz**	**partétz**	**cantétz**	**partátz**
3rd pl.	**cántan, -on**	**párton**	**cánton**	**pártan**

Two general observations concerning these forms will serve as the basis of the following analysis. First, there appears to be a set of nearly uniform endings for the various persons; and second, preceding these endings for person, there appears to be a fairly regular alternation in the presence or absence of the vowel **a**, according to tense (present indicative or subjunctive) and infinitive type.

To make these observations more systematic, we shall adopt a model for the analysis of verb forms:

Verb = root + set + tense + person.[2]

Applying this model to the forms given above, we posit that the infix vowel **a**, absent from columns 2 and 3 but present throughout column 4 and in all but one form in column 1, marks the tense of the verb according to its infinitive type. Its distribution is chiastic: that is, **a** marks the present indicative of **-ar** verbs but not that of non-**ar** verbs; it marks the present subjunctive of non-**ar** verbs but not that of **-ar** verbs.

TENSE MARKERS

Present Indicative	Present Subjunctive
a for **-ar** verbs	zero for **-ar** verbs
zero for non-**ar** verbs	**a** for non-**ar** verbs

The reader who knows the infinitive type of a given verb (which is not difficult to remember, because it is either **-ar** or non-**ar**) can read the tense of a verb by recognizing these markers.

In column 1, however, the first person singular is not ***canta**, as we would expect, but **cant**. This effacement of a hypothetical tense marker occurs throughout the system in this slot—that is, in all first person singular forms of **-ar** verbs in the present tense, without exception.

---

[2] As we have already suggested, the set marker for all tenses in the present set is zero; we include "+ set" in the model now as preparation for subsequent analysis of the future and past sets.

We shall also posit a set of person markers: subjonctif

    1st person sg.: -zero

    2nd person sg.: **-s**

    3rd person sg.: -zero

    1st person pl.: **-ę́m** in general; **-ám** after unstressed **a**

    2nd person pl.: **-ę́tz** in general; **-átz** after unstressed **a**

    3rd person pl.: **-on**

The assumption of these regular markers for tense and person makes for clarity in understanding, retaining, and recognizing verb forms. These person markers, in particular, are found throughout seven of the eight tenses of OOc (all except the preterit, which uses its own person markers) in all verbs of all infinitive types. However, the simplicity of this analysis must be purchased at the price of certain refinements. We shall now reconsider the given forms in order to develop some of these refinements.

In column 3, as will be seen, the given forms represent exactly the combination of the root **cant-** with the set and tense markers zero and the appropriate person markers.

In column 2 the analysis works equally well except for the second person plural, **partę́tz**, where we expected to find ***partę́tz**. This anomaly in the system, which recurs in all non-**ar** verbs in the present indicative, second person plural, has been explained as the result of influence of the individual, very frequent verb **ętz** 'you are,' second person plural of **éser**. Historically, **ętz** represents the normal development of the OOc vowel **ę** from the ĕ of CL ĔSTIS (see ch. 12).

In column 4 the person markers in the plural have combined with the tense marker we have proposed. To explain such forms in this and other tenses, we must postulate an underlying form that generates the surface form by certain regular changes. The most important such change is elision, or vowel deletion.

ELISION OF PERSON MARKERS

When the underlying verb form has two vowels in a row (that is, in hiatus):

    1. If only one vowel is stressed, elide the unstressed vowel.

    2. If both vowels are stressed, elide the first vowel.

    3. If both vowels are unstressed, the second one is usually elided, but the first may be instead.

Elision rule 1 applies to **partir** in the subjunctive (column 4 above), first person plural and second person plural:

> **part- + a + -ám > partám**
>
> **part- + a + -átz > partátz**

Rule 3 applies to **partir**, third person plural, present subjunctive, and to **cantar**, third person plural, present indicative:

> **part- + a + -on > pártan**
>
> **cant- + a + -on > cántan** or **cánton**

(As we shall see in ch. 4, rule 2 applies to a form such as the future, first person plural: **cant- + ar + á + -ę́m > cantarę́m.**)

This analysis suggests that in the form **partám**, the **á** reflects the present subjunctive **a** (in the absence of which, the person marker would have been **-ę́m**) and the stress expresses the first person plural—similarly in the second person plural. In the third person plural, **partan**, the **a** signifies the present subjunctive, in contrast to the indicative **parton** (except for the possibility, under rule 3, that the subjunctive could be **parton** as well).

Unusual person markers in the present indicative and present subjunctive include the following:

The first person singular, present indicative may be marked by a sporadic [-k], as in **dic** (**dire**) and **tenc** (**tenér**), or by [-wk], as in **fauc** (root **fa-**, infinitive **faire**) and **vauc** (root **va-**, infinitive **anar**; first person singular **vau** also occurs).

The first person singular, present indicative may be marked by a sporadic yod. This yod combines with a vowel—as in **ai** (**avér**); **sui**, **soi** (**ę́ser**); **sai** (**sabér**)—or with a consonant—as in **tenh**, **teing** (**tenér**). It becomes syllabic, but unstressed, in **ámi** 31.8 var. (**amar**); **dópti** 18.23 ms. (**doptar**); **láuzi** 31.33 (**lauzar**), perhaps influenced by the support vowel **-e** (see below).

The second person plural ending **-tz** commonly reduces to **-s** by simplification (ch. 16), as in **ęs** beside **ętz** (**ę́ser**), **devę́s** beside **devę́tz** (**devér**), subjunctive **siás** for **siátz** (**ę́ser**). Rarely the ending is represented as **-t**, as in **cosselhát** 19.6 var., beside **cosselhátz** 19.6.

The third person plural marker may be reduced to **-en**, as in present indicative **blásmen** (**blasmar**), **sáben** (**saber**), or in present subjunctive **ónren** (**onrar**), **préguen** (**pregar**). It may appear as **-o**, as though the normal **-n** were an **n**-mobile (although etymologically it is not), as in **mánjo** (**manjar**), **deféndo** (**defendre**). It may occur as **-nt**, as in **sunt** (= CL sŭnt; inf. **ę́ser**), **fant** (**faire**). In a very few cases elision may not function at all, producing **aun** 21.24 var. beside **an** (root **a-** + **-on**, inf. **avér**), present subjunctive **vengau** (**ven- + ga + -on**, inf. **venir**).

A final **-e** sometimes occurs where we expect to find a zero ending (first person singular and third person singular, present indicative and subjunctive). This **-e** may appear to be a person marker but is in fact a support vowel needed after certain consonant clusters that cannot occur word-finally in OOc. Thus we have present indicative, third person singular **óbre** (**obrir**) and present subjunctive, first person singular **tracte** (**tractar**) and **menbre** (**membrar**), which would otherwise end in the unpronounceable clusters **-br**, **-ct**, or **-nbr**. In present indicative, first person singular **esclaire** (**esclairar**), as in the identical form for present subjunctive, third person singular, the support was necessary because the group [-ajr] required it, being pronounceable in OOc only as [-ajre]. The support function was necessary at an earlier stage of the language in present, first person singular **cossire** (**consirar**), CL CONSĪDĔRŌ > [konsid're], [konsiðre]. Some final clusters could be pronounced without a support vowel but nevertheless attracted one at times, as in present subjunctive **guarde** 24.8 var. beside **gart** 12.71 (**gardar**); **laisse** 18.32 beside **lais** 8.23 (**laisar**); **passe** (**paisar**). When the support vowel was extended to present subjunctive forms that did not require it for phonetic reasons, it became a sporadic marker for that tense, as in present subjunctive **done** (**donar**), **mire** (**mirar**). On support vowels in historical phonetics, see chapter 13.

OTHER UNUSUAL MARKERS FOR
PRESENT SUBJUNCTIVE

> **-ga**: **diga** (**dire** 'to say'); **tenga** (**tener** 'to hold'); **vengan** (**venir** 'to come')
>
> [-ja]: **aia** (root **a**, inf. **aver**); **preigna** (= **prenha**, inf. **prendre** 'to take'); **teigna**, **teingna** (= **tenha**, inf. **tener**); **valha** (**valer** 'to be worth'); **venha** (**venir**)
>
> **-sa**: **fasa** (root **fa**, inf. **faire** 'to do'); **plasa** (root **pla**, inf. **plazer** 'to please')

READING 2

Peire Vidal, *Ab l'alen tir vas me l'aire*

*Peire Vidal of Toulouse (fl. 1183–1204) left more than forty poems, principally **cansos**, or love songs. He served in the courts of Toulouse, Aragon, León, Marseille, and Monferrato, in northern Italy, and traveled as far as to Hungary and Malta.*

1

Ab l'alen tir vas me l'aire
qu'ieu sen venir de Proensa;
tot quant es de lai m'agensa,
si que quan 'n'aug ben retraire
ieu m'o escout en rizen,
e·n deman per un mot cen;
tan m'es bel quan n'aug ben dire.

2

Qu'om no sap tan dous repaire
cum de Rozer tro c'a Vensa,
si cum clau mars e Durensa,
ni on tant fins joys s'esclaire;
per qu'entre la franca gen
ai layssat mon cor jauzen
ab lieys que fa·ls iratz rire.

3

Qu'om no pot lo jorn mal traire
qu'aja de lieys sovinensa;
qu'en liey nays joys e comensa,
e qui qu'en sia lauzaire,
de be que·n digua no·i men.
Mielhers es (e ses conten!)
e genser qu'e·l mon se mire.

4

E s'ieu sai ren dir ni faire,
ylh n'aia·l grat, que scïensa
m'a donat e conoissensa;
per qu'ieu sui guays e chantaire.
E tot quan fauc d'avinen
ai del sieu belh cors plazen,
neis quan de bon cor cossire.

Note on Meter

The forms of OOc lyric songs have been cataloged by István Frank in his *Répertoire métrique de la poésie des troubadours*. Frank formulated the rhyme scheme for each song, here *a b b a c c d*, and systematized his catalog of all the songs by the simple expedient of putting the rhyme schemes in alphabetical order. The present rhyme scheme figures in Frank as number 571.

Under each rhyme scheme, Frank further classified each song according to the number of syllables in the line corresponding to each rhyme. The pattern for the present song is as follows:

a	b	b	a	c	c	d
7'	7'	7'	7'	7	7	7'

The apostrophe symbolizes a feminine ending—that is, an un-stressed final syllable that is not counted. By consulting Frank, item 571:14, we find that this song is the only one in the trouba-dour repertory constructed on this rhyme scheme and this syllabic formula. It is typical of the OOc **canso** to be composed in a unique metrical form.

In this song not only does the abstract rhyme scheme remain uniform throughout; the concrete rhyme sounds remain constant as well. That is, rhyme *a* remains **-aire** in all stanzas; *b* remains **-ensa**; *c* remains **-on**; and *d* remains **-ire**. The technical term desig-nating a song in which the rhyme sounds remain constant is **coblas unissonans** 'one-sounding stanzas.' **Coblas unissonans** also occur in readings 4, 15, 16, 18, 20, 21, 22, 23, 24, 26, and 27.

This term and many other useful terms derive from a codifica-tion of troubadour metrical practice that was drawn up in the four-teenth century by the founders of the **Consistòri del Gai Saber**, or 'Consistory of the Gay Knowledge,' an academy founded at Tou-louse. The consistory intended "gay knowledge" as equivalent to the knowledge of what we call courtly love, itself equivalent to the knowledge of how to write poetry. Its founders called themselves **mantenedors** 'sustainers,' since they saw their task as the mainte-nance of honored practice; accordingly, they commissioned Gui-lhem Molinier to formulate elaborate regulations for annual poetry competitions in which the goal was to imitate the best prac-tice of established tradition. The resulting treatise, called the *Leys d'amors*, or *Laws of Love* (in which **amors**, literally 'love,' refers to love poetry), multiplied technical terms and distinctions with diz-zying ingenuity.

Unlike **coblas unissonans**, other songs employ given rhyme sounds for only two stanzas while maintaining the same rhyme scheme throughout; this structure is called **coblas doblas** 'double stanzas,' as in the readings in chapters 6, 7, 8, 13, 17, and 19. The opposite to **coblas unissonans** is **coblas singulars**, or 'single coblas,' in which the given rhyme sounds are maintained for only one stanza, as in the readings in chapters 9, 10, 14, 28, 29, and 31.

Frank gives this abbreviated description of the metrical form of Peire's song (item 571:14):

> *a*   *b*   *b*   *a*   *c*   *c*   *d*
> 7'   7'   7'   7'   7   7   7'
> Ch. 4 u 7 **-aire, -ensa, -on, -ire.**

That is, in this rhyme scheme, with this syllabic formula, a **canso** ("ch." for Fr. *chanson*) of four stanzas, **coblas unissonans** ("u"), with seven lines in each stanza, on the rhyme sounds **-aire, -ensa, -on, -ire**.

P-C 364,1. Major editions: Avalle, *Peire Vidal*, no. 20; Riquer, no. 169. For pro-nunciation of the reading, refer to the accompanying compact disk.

Four manuscripts: *C* fol. 43; *D* fol. 24; *I* fol. 43; *K* fol. 30v. Base *C*.
Stanza order: Uniform.
Rejected reading in the base manuscript: (2) veni *C*, venir *DIK*.
Selected variants: (9) Rozer *C*, Roine *DIK*. (13) jauzen *CIK*, jazen *D*. (25) per
qu'ieu sui *C*, q'eu sia *IK*, q'eu sui *D* (*hypometric—i.e., lacking a syllable*).

Notes

(1) **tir**] Pres. 1st sg. of **tirar**.

(3) **tot quant**] Neuter nom. sg., 'all that'; cf. It. *tutto quanto*.

(4) **aug**] Pronounce [autš], CL Auदĭo, Pres. 1st sg. of **auzir**. **n'aug ben retraire**] 'I hear [someone] speak well of it' or 'I hear it well spoken of.'
The agent of **retraire** is not expressed; cf. expression of the agent with
a in 1.2: **lo bon qu'el n'auzi dire als pelerins** 'the good that he heard
tell of it by the pilgrims' or 'the good that he heard the pilgrims tell of
it.' Cf. also 1.7 note.

(5) **m'o**] **O** is the neuter pronoun 'it,' referring back to the sense of verse 4
(cf. redundant pronoun construction, **n'** in 1.7). **M'** is the "ethical dative," which expresses a person concerned or influenced by the verb.
escout] Pres. 1st sg. of **escoutar**.

(6) **e·n**] Enclisis ('backward-leaning'); cf. proclisis in **l'alen** 1, etc. **deman**]
Pres. 1st sg. of **demandar**, with normal deletion of hypothetical final **-t**
(**demant**).

(7) **es bel**] The subject is an implicit neuter (hence **bel**, neuter nom. sg.)
referring to the clause **quan n'aug ben dire**: 'it is so beautiful to me
when I hear. . . . ' **n'aug ben dire**] 'I hear [someone] speak well of it' or
'I hear it well spoken of.'

(8) **sap**] Pres. 3rd sg. of **saber**, with unvoicing of **b** in final position. **dous**]
Invariable; **-s** is part of the root. **tan . . . cum . . . si cum**, **ni on**] 'As
(sweet) as . . . or as . . . , or where.'

(10) **clau**] Pres. 3rd sg. of **claure**, singular because the verb agrees with the
nearer element (**mars**) in the compound subject (**mars e Durensa**).
mars] Fem. nom. sg., of feminine declension 2 (ch. 9).

(11) **fins joys**] Masc., nom. sg. **esclaire**] Pres. subj. 3rd sg. of **esclairar**. See
discussion of the support vowel **-e**, above.

(14) **ab lieys que fa·ls iratz rire**] 'With her who makes the sad [ones]
laugh.' In the embedded sentence, 'sad [ones]' is the subject of 'to
laugh.' To embed it, 'sad [ones]' is made the direct object of **fa**. In contrast, consider 1.2: **lo bon qu'el n'auzi dire als pelerins**, where the
embedded sentence is 'pilgrims spoke well of her.' Since embedding is
accomplished by taking **bon** as the object of **auzi**, the agent of **dire**
must be expressed with a preposition (**a**).

(15) **lo jorn**] Adverbial, 'on the day.'

(16) **ája**] Pres. subj. 3rd sg. of **aver**. Root **a-**, as in pres. 3rd sg. **a** 'he has'; **-ja**
is an unusual marker for the present subjunctive; see above. Cf. pres.
subj. 1st pl. **aiám**, 3rd pl. **áian**.

(17) **nays**] Pres. 3rd sg. of **náiser** (infinitive in unstressed **-er**), root **nais-** +
zero (tense) + -zero (3rd sg.).

(18) **sía**] Pres. subj. 3rd sg. of **éser**; root (for pres. subj. only) **sí-** + **a** (tense) + -zero. Cf. 1st sg. **sía**, 2nd pl. **siátz**, 3rd pl. **sían**. Note that the pres. subj. **-a** is not etymological (CL sĭт) but analogical (CL HABĔAT). **lauzaire**] Nom. **lauzaire**, obl. **lauzador**; shifting declension (see ch. 23). The agentive suffix **-ador** also occurs in **trobador** (nom. **trobaire**), **cantador** (nom. **cantaire**), etc. With **éser**, the agentive suffix functions as a periphrasis for the simple verb: **eser lauzaire de** = **lauzar**.

(19) **digua**] Pres. subj. 3rd sg. of **dire**; root **di-** + **ga** (tense) + -zero. **Ga** is another unusual marker for present subjunctive (see above). Pres. subj. 1st sg. **diga**, 2nd sg. **digas**, 3rd sg. **diga** or **dia** (with basic tense marker **-a**), 2nd pl. **diátz**.

(20) **miélhers**] Fem. nom. sg.; cf. **mars** 2.10. The **-s** is an optional nominative singular marker for feminine nouns and adjectives ending in a consonant or semivowel, etymological in **naus** 'ship' (CL nom. NAVIS, acc. NAVEM) but analogical in **mélhers** (CL nom. MĔLĬOR, acc. MĔLĬŌREM), **mars** (CL MAR). 'She is better . . . and nobler than may be seen in the world.'

(21) **génser**] Fem. nom. sg. like **miélhers**, but without the optional **-s**. **mire**] Pres. subj. 3rd sg., subjunctive because subordinate to a comparative (**genser**); cf. the subjunctive with a superlative in Modern Fr. (*le meilleur que je connaisse*). The **-e** is the support vowel; cf. **esclaire** 11, **cossire** 28.

(22) **sai**] Pres. 1st sg. of **saber**: the root is **sa-**, the final **-i** (yod) is an unusual 1st sg. person marker. Cf. **aver** 'to have,' **a** 'he has,' **ai** 'I have'; **éser** 'to be,' **son** 'they are,' **soi** 'I am'; **vezér** 'to see,' **ve** 'he sees,' **vei** 'I see.' **dir**] Note absence of **-e**; the implicit root is **di-**, not **dij-** (as in the infinitive **dire**).

(23) **ylh**] 'She,' nom., with the feminine marker **i**; see chapter 10.

(26) **fauc**] Pres. 1st sg. of **faire**, roots **fai**, **faz**, **fa**. The [-wk] is an unusual marker for 1st sg.; cf. **vau**, **vauc** 'I go,' from **anar**. Not to be confused with the end of **aug** [autš] 'I hear,' in which the **g** is part of the root.

(27) **cors**] Invariable; CL cŏRPUS, neuter, hence identical in nominative and accusative. Note the overlap of **cor** 'heart' and **cors** 'body, person, self':

'Heart'		'Body'	
cors	**cor**	**cors**	**cors**
cor	**cors**	**cors**	**cors**

The two words are distinct in oblique singular (as here) and nominative plural.

(28) **cossire**] The **-e** is the support vowel; cf. **mire** 21, **esclaire** 11.

Exercise

Using the person markers, tense markers, elision rule, and special considerations studied in this chapter, derive the six forms for the present indicative and present subjunctive of **cantar** and **partir** without consulting the forms tabulated at the head of this chapter. Then compare what you have written with the forms listed.

CHAPTER 3

Verbs: Present Set (Section 2)

IMPERFECT TENSE

The imperfect tense expresses ongoing or background action in the past, seen as unconnected to the present time (see ch. 25).

The forms of the imperfect tense are as follows:

	-ar verbs	non-**ar** verbs
1st sg.	**cantáva**	**partía**
2nd sg.	**cantávas**	**partías**
3rd sg.	**cantáva**	**partía**
1st pl.	**cantavám**	**partiám**
2nd pl.	**cantavátz**	**partiátz**
3rd pl.	**cantávan, -on, -en**	**partían, -on, -en**

Markers for the imperfect tense are **áva** for **-ar** verbs and **ía** for non-**ar** verbs. The person markers are the same as for the present indicative and subjunctive.

Elision functions in the same way as for the present indicative and subjunctive. Thus in the first person plural, where the vowels in hiatus are unstressed and then stressed, we delete the unstressed vowel (elision rule 1, ch. 2). When the underlying form implies two stressed syllables, only the one nearer the end of the word actually receives stress:

> **cant-** + zero (set) + **áva** + **-ám** > **cantavám**
>
> **part-** + zero (set) + **ía** + **-ám** > **partiám**

Similarly for the second person plural:

> **cant-** + zero (set) + **áva** + **-átz** > **cantavátz**
>
> **part-** + zero (set) + **ía** + **-átz** > **partiátz**

In the third person plural, two unstressed vowels are in hiatus, so the second one is usually elided but the first may be instead (elision rule 3):

cant- + áva + -on > cantávan, cantávon

part- + ía + -on > partían, partíon

Note that first person singular **cantáva** and **partía** express the whole tense marker, unlike first person singular **cant** in the present, where the underlying tense marker **a** is effaced (ch. 2).

The third person plural ending **-on** occurs among texts in this book in the forms **avion** (aver 'to have') and **plasion** (plazer 'to please'). The ending **-en** occurs in **apellaven** (apelar 'to call'), **solíen** (soler 'to be accustomed'), and **tenien** (tener 'to have'). A variant **-ent** occurs in **solient** (soler).

The verb **éser** forms its imperfect on the etymological root **ęr-** (CL imperf. 1st sg. ĔRAM, etc.). We may analyze the forms into this root plus a unique marker for the imperfect, **a**, plus the person markers: 1st sg. **éra**, 2nd sg. **éras**, 3rd sg. **éra**, 1st pl. **erám**, 2nd pl. **erátz**, 3rd pl. **éran, éron**.[1] The unusual second person plural form **eravás** (= **eravátz**), 21:18 var., represents the root **er-** with the tense marker **áva**, as though the infinitive ended in **-ar**: er- + zero (set) + áva + -átz > **eravátz**.

READING 3

Vida of Guilhem de Cabestanh

*Guilhem de Cabestanh, a knight from Capestany, near Perpignan, perhaps fought in the Battle of Las Navas de Tolosa (1212). He has left us seven **cansos**. The **vida** is anonymous. The story of the eaten heart has many analogues in literature and folklore.*[2]

[1] Guillems de Capestaing si fo uns cavalliers de L'encontrada de Rossillon, que confinava con Cataloingna e con Narbones. [2] Molt fo avinenz e prezatz d'armas e de servir e de cortesia. [3] Et avia en la soa encontrada una domna que avia nom ma dompna Sermonda, moiller d'en Raimon del Castel de Rossillon, qu'era molt rics e gentils e mals e braus et orgoillos. [4] E Guillems de Capestaing si l'amava, la domna, per amor, e cantava de leis e fazia sas chansos d'ella. [5] E la domna, qu'era joves e gentil e bella e plaissenz, si·l volia be major que a'rè del mon. [6] E fon dit a Raimon del Castel de Rossiglon, et el, com hom iratz e gelos, enqueri lo fait, e sap que vers era, e fez gardar la moiller fort.

---

[1] The texts in this book contain only the third person singular **éra** and second person plural **erátz**.

[2] For references, see the anonymous *Novellino* 62 (Lo Nigro 149, note 1) and Boccaccio's *Decameron*, fourth day, ninth story (Branca 1: 548–49).

[7] E quant venc un dia, Raimon del Castel Rossillon troba paissan Guillem senes gran compaingnia, et ausis lo e trais li lo cor del cors; e fez lo portar a un escudier a son alberc; e fez lo raustir e far peurada, e fes lo dar a manjar a la muiller. [8] E quant la domna l'ac manjat, lo cor d'en Guillem de Capestaing, en Raimon li dis o que el fo. [9] Et ella, quant o auzi, perdet lo vezer e l'auzir. [10] E quant ela revenc si dis, "Seingner, ben m'avez dat si bon manjar que ja mais non manjarai d'autre." [11] E quant el auzi so qu'ella dis, el coret a sa espaza e volc li dar sus en la testa; et ella s'en anet al balcon e se laisset cazer jos, e fo morta.

Major editions: Långfors 31; Boutière and Schutz 530–31. For pronunciation of the reading, refer to the accompanying compact disk.

Three manuscripts: *F^b* fol. 8v; *I* fols. 105v–105 bis; *K* fol. 89v. Base *I*. There is another version in mss. *ABd*.

Rejected readings in the base manuscript: (4) delleis. (5) Ella domna; si·l] si *IK*, si·l *F^b*. (7) Raimon] R. (8) Raimon] R; o que] a que *F^bIK*. (11) coret *F^bK*, comenzet *I*.

Selected variants: (3) Seremonda *F^bK*, Soremonda *ABN²*; braus e fers et orgoillos *F^bK*. (7) una dia *K*.

Notes

(3) The historical Saurimunda de Peiralada married Raimon del Castel de Rossillon (today, Castel-Roussillon, near Perpignan) in 1197; their marriage contract is reproduced by Långfors (51–52). **en la sóa encontrada**] Note use of definite article, as in **del sieu bel cors** 2.27, **al son leit** 1.5.

(4) **amáva . . . cantáva . . . fazía**] Imperf. 3rd sg.

(5) **gentil**] Note the absence of flexional **-s** (*F^bIK*). **si·l**] **·l** is the enclitic form of **li**, indirect object of either gender, here masculine. **volia be major**] Cf. It. *voler bene ad alcuno* 'to love someone.' The comparative ('loved him better than') is expressed here through the synthetic comparative adjective **majór** 'greater,' modifying **be**.

(6) **enquerí . . . sap . . . fez**] Enquerí and **fez** are preterit 3rd sg. **Sap** is, morphologically, present indicative 3rd sg., but semantically represents a continuation of the preterit reference established by **enquerí** and continued by **fez**. "Vicarious" present, in which the present represents the preterit ("vicar," representative); cf. chapter 25. **la moillér**] Clearly means 'his wife'; the definite article expresses possession.

(7) **venc un dia**] May be interpreted as an impersonal verb with adverbial complement ("there came on a day") or, more plausibly, as an oblique used as nominative ("one day came"). On the gender of **dia**, see Glossary; ms. *K* reads **venc una dia**, feminine. **Venc**] Pret. 3rd sg. of **venir**; [-k] marks the past set. **venc . . . troba . . . ausis . . . trais**, etc.] All the verbs are preterit 3rd sg. except **troba**, which is a vicarious present, like **sap** 6. **ausis . . . trais**] Pret. 3rd sg. with **-s** past-set marker. **paissan**] All the mss. in both versions read **paissan**, apparently the present

participle of a verb **paissar**, with substitution of infinitive **-ar** for normal unstressed **-er**, as in **páiser**, from CL PASCĔRE; the substitution is further evidenced in **apaisar** (see Glossary). **far peurada**] Thus mss. *FᵇIK* and Boutière and Schutz, **far a pebrada** in *AB*; both meaning 'to prepare with a pepper sauce'; in **far peurada** the word **peurada** is used adverbially.

(8) **ac**] Pret. 3rd sg. with [-k] marker for the past set (for the root **a**, cf. **a** 'he has'), as in **venc** 7. **dis**] Pret. 3rd sg. of **dire**, with **-s** marker for the past set, as in **ausis** 7, **trais** 7.

(9) **auzí**] Pret. 3rd sg.; cf. **enquerí** 6. **perdét**] Pret. 3rd sg., the regular ending for verbs with infinitives in **-re** (**perdre**) or in **-ar**.

(10) **revenc**] Pret. 3rd sg. with [-k] marker for the past set, as in **ac** 8, **venc** 7.

(11) In fact, Saurimunda de Peiralada outlived Raimon del Castel de Rossillon and married again. **corét**] Pret. 3rd sg. of **corre**, as in **perdét** 9, from **perdre**. **volc**] Pret. 3rd sg. of **voler**, with [-k] marker for the past set, as in **venc** 7, **ac** 8, **revenc** 10. **a sa espaza**] The other version reads **ab** 'with' (CL APUD, mss. *AB*) or **ad** 'to' (ms. *d*); thus the sense here may be either 'ran to his sword' or 'ran (up) with his sword.' **anét . . . laissét**] Regular pret. 3rd sg. ending of **-ar** verbs; the same ending as for **-re** verbs such as **perdét** 9, **corét** 11.

Exercise

Reread the **vida** of Guilhem de Cabestanh and identify all the verbs in the imperfect. Give all six forms of the following verbs in the imperfect:

1. **era** 3.3
2. **amava** 3.4
3. **volia** 3.5

Check your answers against the forms given in this chapter.

CHAPTER 4

Verbs: Future Set

FUTURE TENSE AND
FIRST CONDITIONAL TENSE

Forms of the future set are built on the infinitive—that is, the set marker added to the root is the infinitive ending (with occasional modifications; see below). The set comprises two tenses, the future and the first conditional.[1] These are the forms for **-ar** and non-**ar** verbs:

	Future		First Conditional	
	Column 1	Column 2	Column 3	Column 4
	-ar verbs	non-**ar** verbs	**-ar** verbs	non-**ar** verbs
1st sg.	**cantarái**	**partirái**	**cantaría**	**partiría**
2nd sg.	**cantarás**	**partirás**	**cantarías**	**partirías**
3rd sg.	**cantará**	**partirá**	**cantaría**	**partiría**
1st pl.	**cantar̨ém**	**partir̨ém**	**cantariám**	**partiriám**
2nd pl.	**cantar̨étz**	**partir̨étz**	**cantariátz**	**partiriátz**
3rd pl.	**cantarán**	**partirán**	**cantarían**	**partirían**

The marker specific to the future tense is stressed **á**; the one specific to the first conditional is **ía**.

---

[1] On the usage of the future tense, see chapter 25. On the first conditional, as in the artificial sentence **Si sabia**, *cantaria* 'If I knew how, *I would sing*,' see chapter 27.

The person markers in the future and the first conditional are the same as those already studied, with one exception. This is the first person singular in the future, which uniformly adds a yod throughout all verb classes to produce the ending **-ái** (Fr. *chanterai*, Sp. *cantaré*, but cf. It. *canterò*; VL */cantare ajo/*, from CL CANTĀRE . . . HABĒO, 'I have . . . to sing').

Elision in the future, first and second persons plural involves a sequence of two stressed vowels, the first of which is elided, as stated by elision rule 2 (ch. 2):

> **cant- + ar + á + -ę́m > cantarę́m**
>
> **cant- + ar + á + -ę́tz > cantarę́tz**

Therefore, the ending for the first person plural in the future is **-ę́m**, not **-ám**, as in present indicative **cantám** (where the underlying person marker follows unstressed **a**: **cant- + zero + a + -ám**).[2] For the same reason, the ending for the second person plural is **-ę́tz**, not **-átz**, as in the present indicative **cantátz** (with the underlying **cant- + zero + a + -átz**). In the future, third person plural, one underlying stressed vowel is stressed and another is unstressed, so the unstressed vowel is elided, according to elision rule 1:

> **cant- + ar + á + -on > cantarán**

Occasionally the infinitive ending is modified in the future and first conditional. Thus **-ar** verbs occur with **er**:

> **laisserai** 10.7; cf. normal **laissarai** 10.7 var. (inf. **laisar**)[3]

Verbs in **-ir** frequently reduce the marker to **r**:

> **partrai** (**partir**)
>
> **venra, venran** (**venir**)
>
> **morria** (**morir**)

but the **ir** marker is preserved in **auziretz** (**auzir**), **chausirai** (**causir**), **gauzirai** (**jauzir**), and so on. In the texts in this book, verbs in **-ę́r** always reduce the marker to **r**:[4]

> **aver**: fut. 1st sg. **aurai**, 3rd sg. **aura**, 1st pl. **aurem**, 2nd pl. **auretz**, 3rd pl. **auran**; 1st cond. 1st sg. **auria**, 2nd pl. **auriaz**, 3rd pl. **auríen**
>
> **dever**: 1st cond. 3rd sg. **deuria**, 1st pl. **deuriam**
>
> **tener**: fut. 1st sg. **tenrai**, 3rd sg. **tenra**
>
> **valer**: fut. 1st sg. **valray**; 1st cond. 3rd sg. **valria**

---

[2] Recall from chapter 2 that the underlying person markers are **-ę́m** and **-ę́tz** generally, but **-ám** and **-átz** after unstressed **a**.

[3] Conversely, the marker for **-er** verbs may occur as **-ar**: thus **ę́ser** has the normal first conditional **seria**, but **saria** at 13.52 var.

[4] But cf. **temeretz**, from **temę́r** 'to fear' (Appel, *Provenzalische* xxx).

Likewise, verbs in **-re** reduce the marker to **r**:

> **dire**: fut. 1st sg. **dirai**, 3rd pl. **diran**; 1st cond. 1st sg. **diria**
>
> **faire**: fut. 1st sg. **farai, ferai** (like an **-ar** verb substituting **-er-**), 3rd sg. **fara**, 2nd pl. **farez**, 3rd pl. **faran**; 1st cond. 2nd pl. **fariatz**

Occasionally the future, first person singular appears with **-ei** instead of **-ai**, in a partial assimilation of **a** to yod: **irei** beside **irai** (**anar**), **farei** beside **farai** (**faire**), **veirei** beside **veirai** (**vezer**).[5] In exceptional cases, the final **-a** in the first conditional **ía** becomes **-e**, as **a** becomes schwa in Old French when final: 1st cond. 1st sg. **aurie** 23.31 var., 3rd pl. **auríen** 11.25 (**aver**).

The infinitive and the ending in future forms may be used separably, reflecting the origin of the future tense in Vulgar Latin: **dir vos ay** 31.7 'I shall tell you.' The first conditional could also be used in separable form, but rarely was: **emendar vos ía** 'I would compensate you' in a legal document (Brunel, *Plus anciennes chartes* 194.28; cf. Grafström, *Morphologie*, par. 49a).

REVIEW OF PRESENT AND FUTURE SETS

The five tenses studied so far are shown in table 4.1. Note the structural similarities among the tenses of the present set, all of which distinguish between **-ar** and non-**ar** verbs, and between the tenses of the future set, both of which use a single marker for all verbs.

TABLE 4.1. *Two Sets of Verbs*

Present Set	Future Set
marker = zero	marker = infinitive ending
Present Indicative Tense **a** for **-ar** zero for non-**ar**	Future Tense **á**
Present Subjunctive Tense zero for **-ar** **a** for non-**ar**	—
Imperfect Tense **áva** for **-ar** **ía** for non-**ar**	First Conditional Tense **ía**

---

[5] Grandgent explains this variation on dialectal grounds (par. 152, note 1).

Gaucelm Faidit (?), *Us cavaliers si jazia*

*The following **alba**, or dawn poem, may be the work of the prolific*
Gaucelm Faidit (fl. 1172–1203), from the Limousin (the region around
Limoges). Its authorship must remain uncertain, however, in view of the
conflicting attributions in the two manuscripts. The characters of the
lover, his beloved, and the watchman are recurrent elements in the genre,
as is the refrain word that gives the genre its name.

1
Us cavaliers si jazia
ab la re que plus volia.
Soven baizan li dizia,
"Doussa res, ieu que farai?
Que·l jorns ve e la nueytz vai,　　　　5
　　　ay!
Qu'ieu aug que li gaita cria,
'Via! Sus! Qu'ieu vey lo jorn
　　　venir apres l'alba.'

2
"Doussa res, s'esser podia　　　　10
que ja mais alba ni dia
no fos, grans merces seria,
al meyns al luec on estai
fis amicx ab so que·l plai.　　　　15
　　　Ay!
Qu'ieu aug que li guaita cria,
'Via! Sus! Qu'ieu vey lo jorn
　　　venir apres l'alba.'

3
"Doussa res, que qu'om vos dia,
no cre que tals dolors sia　　　　20
cum qui part amic d'amia,
qu'ieu per me mezeys o sai;
ai las, quan pauca nueyt fai!
　　　Ay!
Qu'ieu aug que li guaita cria,　　　　25
'Via! Sus! Qu'ieu vey lo jorn
　　　venir apres l'alba.'

4
"Doussa res, ieu tenc ma via.
Vostres suy on que ieu sia;
per Dieu, no m'oblidetz mia,　　　　30
que·l cor del cors reman sai,
ni de vos mais no·m partrai.
　　　Ay!

Qu'ieu aug que li guaita cria,
'Via! Sus! Qu'ieu vey lo jorn   35
   venir apres l'alba.'

5
"Doussa res, s'ieu no·us vezia
breumens, crezatz que morria,
que·l gran dezirs m'auciria;
per qu'ieu tost retornarai,   40
que ses vos vida non ai.
     Ay!
Qu'ieu aug que li gaita cria,
'Via! Sus! Qu'ieu vey lo jorn
   venir apres l'alba.'"   45

Meter

a	a	a	b	b	b	a	c	d
7'	7'	7'	7	7	1	7'	7	5'

5 u 9. **-ia, -ai, -ǫrn, alba.**
Verses 6–9: refrain.
Cf. Frank 69:1 (erroneous; should be listed as Frank 70 bis).

P-C 76, 23. Major editions: Mouzat, no. 68; Riquer, no. 294. For pronunciation
of the reading, refer to the accompanying compact disk.
Two manuscripts: *C* fol. 266v; *Y* fol. 108v. Base *C*.
Attributions: Bertran d'Alamanon *C*, Gauselm Faiditz *Y*. See Mouzat 557.
Stanza order:
   C 1   2   3   4   5
   Y 1   2   3 —   5
Rejected readings in the base manuscript: (5) jorn *CY*; nueyt *C*, nuog *Y*.
Selected variants: (18, 27) aprop *Y*.

Notes

(1) **Us cavaliers**] Masc. nom. sg. **jazia**] Imperf. 3rd sg. of **jazer**.

(2) **volia**] Imperf. 3rd sg. of **voler**.

(3) **dizia**] Imperf. 3rd sg. of **dire** on the root **diz-**, as in pres. indic. 3rd pl.
dizon, 3rd sg. **ditz**, etc.

(4) **farai**] Fut. 1st sg. of **faire** on the root **far-**, as in other persons in the future, **fariatz** 1st cond. 2nd pl., and infinitive **far** (beside **faire**). **ieu que
farai**] The pronoun **ieu** has been moved forward by prolepsis (anticipation; see ch. 24); the corresponding expression in Modern French
would be *Moi, que ferai-je?*

(5) **ve**] Pres. indic. 3rd sg. of **venir**; the root ends in **n**-mobile (also **ven**).
nueytz] Fem. nom. sg. in **-s**, like **mars** 2.10; cf. obl. sg. **nueyt** v. 23. The
form **nueytz** corresponds to the Glossary entry **nǫch**; the open vowel **ǫ**
in stressed position optionally diphthongizes to **úo, úe**, or (when in a

triphthong, as here) [uój, uéj]. The **-ytz** is a variant on the affricate **-ch. vai**] Pres. indic. 3rd sg. of **anar** on the root **vai-**, as in 2nd sg. **vais** and pres. subj. 3rd sg. **vaia** (Appel, *Provenzalische* xl).

(6–9) The use of a refrain, with its suggestion of a folkloric quality, is exceptional in the generally more aristocratic art of the troubadours. The refrain word **alba** (v. 9) constitutes one of the identifying marks of the genre of the **alba** in OOc.

(7) **li gaita**] Definite article **li**, fem., distinctively nom. sg. (see Glossary); fem. **i**, as in **ylh** 2.23.

(8) **Via! Sus!**] 'Away! Up!' The order is counter to common sense: hysteron proteron (Greek: 'the second first'), a natural means of expressing urgency or haste. **vey**] Pres. indic. 1st sg. of **vezer** on the root **vei-**, as in pres. subj. 1st sg. **veia**.

(10) **podia**] Imperf. 3rd sg. of **poder**.

(12) **fos**] Past subj. 3rd sg. of **ęser** on the root **fo**; the **-s** is the tense marker, with person marker zero. **grans merces**] Fem. nom. sg., with **-s**, as in **nueytz** 5. The adj. **gran** is one of a class that does not change the masc. forms to produce fem. forms, except by occasional analogy, as in **granda** (see ch. 9). **seria**] 1st cond. 3rd sg. of **ęser** on the root **ser-**, as in fut. 1st sg. **serai**, etc.

(13) **estai**] Pres. indic. 3rd sg. of **estar** on the root **estai-**, as in 2nd pl. **estaitz** and imperative 2nd pl. **estaitz** (Appel, *Provenzalische* xxiv). **luec**] Diphthongized form of **lǫc** (see Glossary; cf. **nueytz** 5). On diphthongization, see chapter 12.

(14) **plai**] Pres. indic. 3rd sg. of **plazęr** on the root **plai-**; cf. pres. subj. 1st sg. **plaia** (Appel, *Provenzalische* xxxvii).

(19) **dia**] Pres. subj. 3rd sg. of **dire** on the root **di-**, as in pres. indic. 1st sg. **di**, 3rd sg. **di**, pres. subj. 2nd pl. **diatz**.

(20) **cre**] Should be interpreted as 1st sg. by continuity from **vey** 17 and not as imperative 2nd sg.; the lover addresses his lady in the second person plural (**vostres** 4.29, etc.). From the infinitive **creire**, root **cre-**, as in imperf. 3rd pl. **creyan** (Appel, *Provenzalische* xxvi), pronounced **creían. tals dolors**] Fem. nom. sg. in **-s**, as in **grans merces** 4.12; **tal** is another adjective, like **gran**, that does not change its form for gender. **sia**] Pres. subj. 3rd sg. of **ęser** on the root **si-**, as in pres. subj. 2nd pl. **siatz**.

(23) **nueyt**] Object of **fai**, which is used impersonally in expressions concerning the weather and the time of day (S-W 3: 384): 'How little night is left!'

(28) **tenc**] Pres. indic. 1st sg. of **tenir** with [-k] person marker; cf. **fauc** 2.26.

(29) **vostres**] Nom. sg. masc.; the **-s** is analogical, as in nom. sg. **paire**, analogical **paires**.

(30) **oblidetz**] Subjunctive form as imperative 2nd pl.

(31) **cor**] Nom. sg. masc., in violation of the normal form in **-s**, as in **jorn**, nom. sg. **jorns**; but in this case the violation is etymological, since CL cŏʀ is neuter. Nom. sg. **cor**, as here, may therefore be regarded as a survival of the neuter gender into OOc. Cf. chapter 28 on the neuter gender.

(37) **s'ieu no·us vezia**] The imperfect in the conditional clause expresses neutrality, neither likelihood nor unlikelihood (see ch. 27). **vezia**] Imperf. 1st sg. of **vezẹr** on the root **vez-**.

(38) **breumens**] Modifies **vezia** 4.37: 'If I didn't see you soon . . . ': syntactic enjambment. **crezatz**] Pres. subj. 2nd pl. of **creire** on the root **crez-**. Subjunctive used as imperative; cf. **oblidetz** 30. **morria**] First conditional, first person singular of **morir**, with reduction of **-ir** to **r**.

(39) **·l gran dezirs**] Nom. sg., with declension on the noun only; cf. **paubre motz** 1.3. The definite article expresses possession; cf. **la moiller** 'his wife' 3.6.

Exercise

Give all six forms for the following first person verbs in the tenses in question:

1. **manjarai** 3.10
2. **farai** 4.4
3. **trobaria** 17.42 var.
4. **morria** 4.38

Compare your forms with the conjugations at the beginning of this chapter.

CHAPTER 5

Verbs: Past Set (Section 1)

The preterit expresses past events considered as unrelated to the present time (see ch. 25). It corresponds to the perfect in Latin (CANTĀVIT), the *passato remoto* in Italian (*cantò*), the *pretérito* in Spanish (*cantó*), and the *passé simple* in French (*chanta*).

The past set differs from the present set in that its patterns do not vary according to the simple distinction between **-ar** verbs and non-**ar** verbs. The past set shows greater variety; it may be marked, according to the verb, by either of two vowels (**ę́** or **í**), either of two consonants ([k] or **s**), or a semivowel (waw or yod, the latter seen implicitly in its effects). The preterit with vowel markers will be treated in this chapter; preterits marked by a semivowel or consonant will be treated in chapter 6.

PRETERIT TENSE FORMS WITH VOWEL MARKERS (ę́ OR í)

Preterits marked by **ę́** occur in all **-ar** verbs and in some **-re** verbs. Model forms for the preterit in these two types are the following:

	cantar 'to sing'	**perdre** 'to lose'
1st sg.	cantę́i	perdę́i
2nd sg.	cantę́st	perdę́st
3rd sg.	cantę́t	perdę́t
1st pl.	cantę́m	perdę́m
2nd pl.	cantę́tz	perdę́tz
3rd pl.	cantę́ron	perdę́ron

As may be seen, the **ę́** marker runs throughout the preterit of these verbs except for the first person plural, where underlying **ę́** closes to **ę́** under the influence of the following **m** by the general phenomenon of nasal raising (ch. 12). The preterit tense appears to have a zero marker, since there is no element common to these forms except the set marker and the root.

These preterit forms in Old Occitan derive from the Classical Latin reduplicated perfect DĔDĪ 'I gave.' In a reduced version, -ĔĪ, this type of preterit ending not only survived in **perdę́i** (from recomposed VL PER-DĔDĪ, stressed PER-DÉDI; CL PĔRDĬDĪ) but spread to **-ar** verbs and replaced the ending in -AI (CL CANTĀVĪ, Fr. *chantai*). For more on historical evolution, see chapter 21.

Most verbs with infinitives in **-ir** show **í** as a marker for the past set of tenses. These endings result from contraction of CL -ĪVĪ to -Ī, etc.

	partir 'to leave'
1st sg.	**partí**
2nd sg.	**partíst**
3rd sg.	**partí, partít, partíc**
1st pl.	**partím**
2nd pl.	**partítz**
3rd pl.	**partíron**

PERSON MARKERS FOR THE PRETERIT AFTER A VOWEL

We are obliged to recognize distinctive markers for four persons in the preterit: the three singular forms and the third person plural. The remaining two, the first and second persons plural, would create difficulty for the elision rule as constituted if we attempted to analyze them into person markers of the basic type. We shall therefore posit an entire new set of six person markers. Following a vowel, the person markers for the preterit are these:

1st sg. -yod
2nd sg. **-st**
3rd sg. **-t, -c**; zero after **i**
1st pl. **-m**
2nd pl. **-tz**
3rd pl. **-ron**

The preterit of **cantar** is therefore analyzed as follows:

1st sg. **cant-** + **ę́** (set) + zero (tense) + -yod > **cantę́i**
2nd sg. **cant-** + **ę́** (set) + zero (tense) + **-st** > **cantę́st**
3rd sg. **cant-** + **ę́** (set) + zero (tense) + **-t** > **cantę́t**

1st pl. **cant-** + **ę́** (set) + zero (tense) + **-m** > **cantę́m**

2nd pl. **cant-** + **ę́** (set) + zero (tense) + **-tz** > **cantę́tz**

3rd pl. **cant-** + **ę́** (set) + zero (tense) + **-ron** > **cantę́ron**

Since no preterit person markers begin in a vowel, they involve no elision. And since none of them bear stress, preterit forms will not vary in the position of stress, as do other tenses.

The set marker **ę́** may diphthongize to **ię́** in the first person singular under the influence of the following yod, as in **mirię́i** 'I looked' (**mirar**), **perdię́i** 'I lost' (**perdre**).

The preterit forms of **partir** take the same person markers:

1st sg. **part-** + **í** (set) + zero (tense) + **-yod** > **partí**

2nd sg. **part-** + **í** (set) + zero (tense) + **-st** > **partíst**

3rd sg. **part-** + **í** (set) + zero (tense) + **-t, -c** > **partít, partíc**

1st pl. **part-** + **í** (set) + zero (tense) + **-m** > **partím**

2nd pl. **part-** + **í** (set) + zero (tense) + **-tz** > **partítz**

3rd pl. **part-** + **í** (set) + zero (tense) + **-ron** > **partíron**

In the first person singular, yod combines with the preceding **í**. In the third person singular, we also find the type **partí**.

Unusual endings include third person singular **-c** with **-ar** verbs, as in **comtec** 'he told' (**comtar**), **intrec** 'he entered' (**entrar**), **tirec** 'he drew' (**tirar**).[1] In the third person plural, **-ron** may be reduced to **-ro**, as in **menero** 'they led' (**menar**) and **perdero** 'they lost' (**perdre**), or to **-ren**, as in **falíren** 'they failed' (**falhir**) and **mesdren** 'they put' (**metre**).

READING 5

Vida of Bernart de Ventadorn

*Bernart de Ventadorn is considered by many readers as the greatest love poet among the troubadours (see readings 16–18). In his poetry he seems to say that he learned his art from Eble II of Ventadorn (died c. 1147), viscount and troubadour, whose poems are no longer extant. Bernart is mentioned by Peire d'Alvernhe in a satire written c. 1170. Although the poet's activity is usually dated on these grounds to c. 1147–70, he may be identical to a Bernardus, son of Eble III of Ventadorn (hence Bernart de Ventadorn), who became abbot of Tulle and died around 1237 (Paden, "Bernart"). If so, the **vida** is fictional through and through; even if not, its historicity remains problematic.*

---

[1] Note that this **-c**, the alternative person marker for the third person singular (**partíc**, **comtéc**), echoes words such as **ac** 'he had' (**aver**) and so on (see ch. 6); but in words such as **ac**, the [k] marks the entire past set of tenses, not just the third person singular.

[1] Bernartz de Ventedorn si fo de Limozin, del castel de Vente- dorn. [2] Fo de paubra generacion; fils fo d'un sirven qu'era forniers, qu'esquaudava lo forn a coszer lo pan del castel. [3] E venc bels hom et adreichs, e saup ben chantar e trobar, e venc cortés et enseing- natz. [4] E lo vescons, lo seus seingner, de Ventedorn, s'abelli mont de lui e de son trobar e de son cantar, e fez li gran honor.

[5] E·l vescons de Ventedorn si avia moiller joven e gentil e gaia. [6] E si s'abelli d'en Bernart e de soas chansos, e s'enamora de lui et el de la dompna, si qu'el fetz sas chansons e sos vers d'ella, de l'amor qu'el avia ad ella e de la valor de leis. [7] Lonc temps duret lor amors anz que·l vescons ni l'autra gens s'em apercebes. [8] E quant lo vescons s'en aperceup, si s'estranjet de lui, e la moillier fetz serar e gardar. [9] E la dompna si fetz dar comjat a·n Bernart, qu'el se partis e se loingnes d'aquella encontrada.

[10] Et el s'en parti e si s'en anet a la duchesa de Normandia, qu'era joves e de gran valor e s'entendia en pretz et en honor et en bendig de lausor. [11] E plasion li fort las chansos e·l vers d'en Bernart, et ella lo receup e l'acuilli mout fort. [12] Lonc temps estet en sa cort, et enamoret se d'ella et ella de lui, e fetz mantas bonas chansos d'ella. [13] Et estan cum ella, lo reis Enrics d'Engletera si la tols per moiller e si la trais de Normandia e si la menet en Angleterra. [14] En Barnartz si remas de sai tristz e dolentz, e venc s'en al bon comte Raimon de Tollosa, e com el estet tro que·l coms mori. [15] Et en Bernartz per aquella dolor si s'en rendet a l'ordre de Dalon, e lai el definet.

[16] Et ieu, n'Ucs de Saint Circ, de lui so qu'ieu ai escrit si me con- tet lo vescoms n'Ebles de Ventedorn, que fo fils de la vescomtessa qu'en Bernartz amet. [17] E fetz aquestas chansos que vos auzirez aissi desotz escriptas.

Major editions: Appel, *Bernart* xi–xv; Boutière and Schutz 20–23; Nichols et al. 29–31; Lazar 54–58; Riquer 1: 351–52.

Seven manuscripts: *A* fol. 86; *B* fol. 55; *E* p. 190; *I* fol. 26v; *K* fol. 15; *R* fol. 1–v; *Z* fol. 101v–102. Base *I*. There is another version in ms. *d*.

Rejected readings in the base manuscript: (3) venc b.] ven b. *IK*, venc *AB*, era *ERZ*. (4) abelli *IK*, s'abeli *EZ*, s'abellic *ABR*. (6) dellui; della d.; dellamor; della volor delleis *I*, valor *ABEKRZ*. (8) ella moillier. (9) Ella. (10) essi; alla; Lormandia *IK*, Normandia *ABERZ*. (12) dellui. (13) silla; ennangleterra. (15) talon *IK*, Dalon *ABERZ*; ellai. (16) della.

Selected variants: (2) a coszer *IKEZ*, per c. *AB*, de c. *R*. (4) mont] mōt *I*, mont *K*, mout *AB*, molt *EZ*, om. *R*; fez *IKABR*, fazia *EZ*. (6) s'abelli *IKEZ*, abellic se *ABR*; de soas *IKZ*, de sas *R*, de las soas *ABE*; s'enamora *IK*, s'enamoret *EZ*, enamoret se *ABR*. (7) apercebes *I*, aperceubes *KERZ*, aperceubessen *AB*. (8) s'en aperceup *IKBERZ*, s'en fo aperceubutz *A*; s'estranjet *IKBZ*, se trachet *R*, estraigniet . . . de si *A*; serar *I*, serrar *ABEK*, om. *RZ*. (10) parti *IKR*, partic *AB*, partit *EZ*; s'en anet *IKE*, anet s'en *ABR*. (11) acuilli *IKR*, acuillic *AB*, acuillit *E*, om. *Z*. (13) tols *I*, tolc *BK*, pres *AERZ*. (14) com el *IK*, ab el *ER*, ab lui *AB*, om. *Z*. (15) Bernartz *IABE*, Bernatz *K*, om. *Z*, B. *R*; ordre *IZ*, orde *KER*, orden *AB*.

(1) The Limousin, or region around Limoges, corresponds to the modern departments of Corrèze and Haute-Vienne. There are ruins of the castle of Ventadorn near the village of Moustier-Ventadour (canton of Egletons, arrondissement of Tulle, Corrèze). **fo**] Pret. 3rd sg. of **éser**, root zero-, set marker **fo**, person marker -zero (see ch. 19).

(2) **fils fo d'un sirven**] The **vida** agrees with the satire by Peire d'Alvernhe. **esquaudava**] Imperfect 3rd sg. of **escaldar**: **escald-** + zero (set) + **áva** + -zero.

(3) **venc**] Preterit 3rd sg. of **venir**, with [k] marking the set (ch. 6); on the sense 'became,' cf. Fr. *de-venir*, E. *be-come*.

(4) Viscount Eble III of Ventadorn, son of Eble II, married twice and died in 1169. Either his first or second wife may have been the poet's love, unless the whole story is fictional. **s'abelli**] Preterit 3rd sg. of **abelir**: **abel-** + **í** (set) + zero (tense) + -zero. **mont**] CL MŬLTUM, usually OOc **molt**, **mout**. But *S-W* (5: 303) recognizes the unusual form **mon**, perhaps due to influence of **maint**, **mant** 'many a' (OFr. *maint*); or there may be influence from **mon** 'mountain, pile' (*PD* 251). Hence **mont** cannot be summarily dismissed as a scribal misreading of **n** for **u** (**mout > mont**). Cf. variants.

(5) **avía**] Imperf. 3rd sg. of **aver**: **av-** + zero (set) + **ía** + -zero. **moillér**] Shifting declension, since the accent shifts:

	Sg.	Pl.
Nom.	**mólher**	**molhérs**
Obl.	**molhér**	**molhérs**

(6) **s'enamora**] Pres. indic. 3rd sg.; a historical present, since it expresses the dramatic change that motivates the following verbs in the preterit (**fetz**, **duret**, etc.). **sas chansos e sos vers**] 'His songs.' The two nouns are approximate synonyms, with a possible distinction between **vers** as songs in an older style, and **chansos** as more stylish love songs.

(7) **durét**] Pret. 3rd sg. of **durar**: **dur-** + **é** (set) + zero (tense) + **-t**. **apercebés**] Past subj. 3rd sg. from **apercebre**: **aperceb-** + **é** (set) + **s** (tense) + -zero (person).

(8) **aperceup**] Pret. 3rd sg. with past-set marker waw (ch. 6). **estranjet**] Pret. 3rd sg. of **estranjar**.

(9) 'And he [the viscount] made the lady give leave to Sir Bernart, [saying] that he must leave. . . . ' This interpretation is preferable to 'And the lady made [someone] give leave. . . . ' **partis . . . loingnes**] Past subjunctive 3rd sg.: **part-** + **í** (set) + **s** (tense) + -zero; **lonh-** + **é** (set) + **s** (tense) + -zero. In **loingnes** the graphy **ingn** spells **nh**.

(10) The duchess of Normandy must be Eleanor of Aquitaine (c. 1122–1204), although, contrary to what the **vida** says, Eleanor acceded to the title by her marriage in 1152 to Henry II Plantagenet. Henry

became king of England in 1154; Bernart may have traveled to England, perhaps in 1154–55 (Appel, *Bernart* liii–lix).

(11) **plasion**] Imperf. 3rd pl. of **plazer**: **plaz-** + zero (set) + **ía** (tense) + **-on**. **receup**] Pret. 3rd sg. of **recebre**, with past-set marker waw. **acuilli**] Pret. 3rd sg. of **acolhir**: **acolh-** + **í** (set) + zero (tense) + -zero; the **o** closes to **u**, as in **morir**, **murir** 'to die' (see ch. 13); **ill** spells **lh**.

(13) **estan**] Pres. part., undeclined. The logical subject is not the noun **lo reis**; rather, **estan** is an absolute construction: 'While he [Bernart] was staying .⁙.' **tols**] Pret. 3rd sg. of **tolre**: **tol-** + **s** (set) + zero (tense) + -zero; see chapter 6. **trais**] Pret. 3rd sg. of **traire**.

(14) **remas**] Pret. 3rd sg. of **remaner** 'to remain.' **Raimon de Tollosa**] Count Raymond V of Toulouse (1148–94). The information that Bernart served Raymond may have been deduced from several of his poems. **coms**] Shifting declension:

	Sg.	Pl.
Nom.	coms	comte
Obl.	comte	comtes

Cf. **om, ome** (1.1 note).

(15) **rendet, definet**] Pret. 3rd sg. of **redre, definar**. **l'ordre de Dalon**] Dalon (commune of Sainte-Trie, canton of Hautefort, Dordogne) was the site of a Cistercian abbey to which the troubadour Bertran de Born (readings 20–22) retired in 1196. It is not certain that Bernart de Ventadorn retired there; we know the names of nearly sixty monks of Dalon during the twelfth century, but his name is not among them (Paden, "Identité" 219). The **vida**'s statement that Bernart retired to Dalon may have been borrowed from the **vida** of Bertran de Born; Bertran's retirement is confirmed by records from the abbey.

(16) Uc de Saint-Circ (fl. 1217–53) also identified himself as the author of **razos** on Savaric de Malleo (Boutière and Schutz 224,11). According to Uc's own **vida** (Boutière and Schutz 239,4), he collected stories about worthy men and noble ladies. On the basis of this evidence, Uc has sometimes been credited with the composition of many of the anonymous **vidas**, including Jaufre Rudel's. It is not even certain, however, that he is the true author of a signed **vida** such as the present one, since the author claims to have been in direct contact with Eble IV of Ventadorn, who is attested as early as 1169–84 (Stroński 167), over thirty years before our earliest evidence for the activity of Uc. Between the last evidence for the activity of Eble IV, in 1184, and the last evidence for the activity of Uc de Saint-Circ, in 1253, there intervened sixty-nine years. Boutière and Schutz (25) ask if Uc's name might have been interpolated into the text of the **vida**. **Ucs**] Shifting declension: nom. **Ucs** or **Uc**, obl. **Ugó**. Cf. **coms** v. 14 note.

(17) **auzirez**] Future 2nd pl. of **auzir** 'to hear': **auz-** + **ir** (set) + **á** (tense) + **-étz**.

Exercise

Analyze the components of these verbs from the **vida** of Bernart de Ventadorn into their roots and the markers for set, tense, and person:

    1. **duret** 5.7
    2. **acuilli** 5.11

Provide all six forms of the following verbs in the preterit:

    3. **anet** 5.10
    4. **mori** 5.14

Check your answers against the models in this chapter.

CHAPTER 6

Verbs: Past Set (Section 2)

PRETERIT TENSE WITH SEMIVOWEL MARKERS (WAW OR IMPLICIT YOD)

Model verbs showing the use of waw and implicit yod as markers for the preterit tense include **saber** 'to know' and **vezer** 'to see.' **Saber** forms the preterit on the root **sab-**; **vezer**, on the root **ve-**, as in present indicative, third person singular **ve**.[1]

	Waw	Yod
1st sg.	*saup, saubí	vi
2nd sg.	*saubíst	*vist
3rd sg.	saup	vi, *vit, *vic
1st pl.	*saubém	*vim
2nd pl.	*saubétz	*vitz
3rd pl.	*saubron	*viron

If we posit underlying forms beginning with a root and set marker, **sab-** + waw and **ve-** + yod, we see that the two semivowels have been absorbed into the preceding syllable: the waw has become part of the diphthong **au**, and the yod has caused the vowel **ę** to close to **i**, as occurs historically in metaphony (see ch. 12).

The person markers in the preterit of **vezer** are added to a vowel and are identical to the person markers for the preterit with vowel markers (see ch. 5): -yod (absorbed into **vi**, as into pret. 1st sg. **partí**); -st; -zero, -t, -c (as in 3rd sg. **partí, partit, partic**); -m; -tz; -ron.

---

[1] The asterisk marks forms not attested in the texts of this book but found in Appel, *Provenzalische* xxviii, xxxiv.

The preterit with waw shows distinctive treatment of person markers that follow a consonant. Comparing the forms of **saber**, in the conjugation above, with the forms of **vezer**, to the right, we note that in the first person singular, the -yod has either been effaced, in **saup**, or has given rise to a stressed **-í**, in **saubí**, influenced by preterit, first person singular **partí**. The second person singular intercalates **í** before **-st**, resembling **partíst**; the third person singular shows -zero, one of the three alternative markers in **vezer**; the first and second persons plural intercalate **ę́** before **-m** and **-tz**, resembling preterit **cantę́m** but not resembling preterit **cantę́tz** because of the open vowel. Only the third person plural remains unchanged. These endings are normal in the preterit after a consonant:

> 1st sg. -zero, **-í**
> 2nd sg. **-íst**
> 3rd sg. -zero
> 1st pl. **-ę́m**
> 2nd pl. **-ę́tz**
> 3rd pl. **-ron**

Other verbs that show waw for the past set include **apercebre** 'to notice,' preterit, third person singular **apercéup**; **recebre** 'to receive,' preterit, third person singular **recéup**, third person plural **recéubron**. Another verb showing implicit yod, or metaphony, is **faire** 'to do,' root **fai-**, as in the present indicative, third person singular **fai**; one form of the preterit, third person singular is **fei** (with metaphony).

PRETERIT TENSE WITH
CONSONANT MARKERS ([k] OR s)

Model verbs showing the use of [k] and **s** as markers for the past set include **aver** 'to have' and **prendre** 'to take':

1st sg.	**aic, aguí**	**pris, pres**
2nd sg.	**aguíst**	**presíst**
3rd sg.	**ac**	**pręs**
1st pl.	**aguę́m**	**presę́m**
2nd pl.	**aguę́tz**	**presę́tz**
3rd pl.	**agron**	**prę́iron, presę́ron**

The consonantal marker effaces certain final consonants in the root:

av- + [k] > 3rd sg. **ac**

pren- + **s** > 3rd sg. **pres**

Similarly, in **poder** 'to be able,' **pod-** + [k] yields preterit 3rd sg. **poc**; in **metre** 'to put,' **met-** + **s** yields preterit 3rd sg. **mes**. But consonants in other roots remain, as in **tener** 'to hold,' preterit 3rd sg. **tenc**; **venir** 'to come,' **venc**; **voler** 'to want,' **volc**.

Person markers in the preterits of **aver** and **prendre** are like those of **saber**, above, in the forms for the second and third persons singular, first and second persons plural. In the first person singular, yod has been anticipated in **aic** (without metaphony), and has caused metaphony in **pris**; **pres** shows a zero person marker, while **aguí** shows influence of **partí**. In the third person plural, **agron** has the normal ending; in **préiron**, **preséron**, the juncture of the root **pres-** and the ending **-ron** has produced two alternative solutions to the unacceptable consonant cluster **sr**, either by reducing the **s** to yod (**préiron**), by yodicism (ch. 16), or by intercalating the transitional vowel **é** (**preséron**, influenced by **cantéron**).

REDUNDANT PAST-SET MARKERS

Some non-**ar** verbs show redundant marking in the past set, combining two or more of the markers of other verbs:

vezer, pret. 3rd sg. **vic** (both metaphony and [k])

prendre, pret. 3rd sg. **pris** (both metaphony and **s**)

ESER IN THE PAST SET

The verb **eser** uses the set marker **fo-** in the preterit and the other tenses of the past set: 1st sg. **fuy** (where the yod closes the vowel); 3rd sg. **fo**, **fon**; 2nd pl. **foz**, **fos**; 3rd pl. **foro**, **foren**.[2] Since we recognize that **fo-** marks the past set (preterit **fo**, past subjunctive **fos**, second conditional **fora**), it follows that the root preceding the set marker is zero.

[2] The preterit 3rd sg. form, **fon**, reflects the final **-n** in 3rd pl. **foron**, **foro**, supported by alternations in adj. **bon**, possessive adj. **mon**, etc. (Grandgent 141; Schultz-Gora 93).

Comtessa de Dia, *Ab joi et ab joven m'apais*

*We have four **cansos** by the Comtessa de Dia, as she is called in the chansonniers. She may perhaps be identified as Beatrix, who enjoyed the title of countess as the eldest daughter of the count of Die, near Valence in the département of Drôme. This Beatrix witnessed a donation in 1212.*[3]

1
Ab joi et ab joven m'apais
  e jois e jovens m'apaia,
que mos amics es lo plus gais,
  per q'ieu sui coindet'e gaia;
  e pois eu li sui veraia,   5
be·is taing q'el me sia verais;
c'anc de lui amar no m'estrais,
  ni ai cor que m'en estraia.

2
Mout mi plai car sai que val mais
  sel q'ieu plus desir que m'aia,   10
e cel que primiers lo m'atrais
  Dieu prec que gran joi l'atraia;
  e qui que mal l'en retraia,
no·l creza fors so qu'ie·l retrais;
c'om cuoill maintas vetz los balais   15
  ab q'el mezeis se balaia.

3
E dompna q'en bon pretz s'enten
  deu ben pausar s'entendenssa
en un pro cavallier valen,
  pois qu'ill conois sa valenssa.   20
  Que l'aus amar a presensa,
que dompna pois am'a presen
ja pois li pro ni li valen
  no·n dirant mas avinenssa.

4
Q'ieu n'ai chausit un pro e gen
  per cui pretz meillur'e genssa,   25
larc et adreig e conoissen,
  on es sens e conoissenssa.
  Prec li qe m'aia crezenssa,
ni hom no·il puosca far crezen   30

---

[3] See Monier. Riquer finds no cogent grounds for any specific date (2: 791–93). Rieger leans toward the second half of the twelfth century (614).

q'ieu fassa vas lui faillimen— *pas laya*
sol non trob en lui faillensa. *in s, i d é l i t é*

5

Amics, la vostra valenssa
saben li pro e li valen; *de valeur*
per q'ieu vos qier de mantenen,   35
si·us plai, vostra mantenensa. *soutenance*

Meter: The poem is composed in **rims derivatius,** in which pairs of rhymed
 words are derived from the same lexical root. The derivative pairs are ar-
 ranged, in this song, into couplets: **apais** 1–**apaia** 2, **gais** 3–**gaia** 4, and so on.
 The derivative pairs link words in contrasting rhyme sounds **(-ais, -aia).** The
 tornada, or short final stanza, conventionally replicates the corresponding
 rhymes of the preceding full stanza from the last rhyme backward. See also
 tornadas in the readings in chapters 8, 10, 13, 15–22, 24, 27, 29, and 31.

> *a   b   a   b   b   a   a   b*
> 8   7'   8   7'   7'   8   8   7'
> Ch. 4 d 8, 1–4 **Rims derivatius:** 1/2, 3/4, 5/6, 7/8.
> *a* = **-ais, -ęn;** *b* = **-aja, -ęnsa.**
> Frank 295:8.

P-C 46, 1. Major editions: Kussler-Ratyé, no. 1; Riquer, no. 153; Rieger, no. 34;
 Bruckner, Shepard, and White, no. 1; Bec, *Chants d'amour,* no. 8.
Eight manuscripts: *A* fol. 167vD–168rA; *B* fol. 104vC–D; *D* fol. 85vC; *H* fol.
 49vD; *I* fol. 141rA–B; *K* fol. 126vD–127rA; *T* fol. 197v; *a* p. 232. Base *A.*
Divergent attribution: N'Uc de San Sir *T.*
Stanza order: Uniform.
Rejected readings in the base manuscript: (4) coindeta e. (14) so qu'ie·l] qui cel
 A, qu'ie·l *Ba,* cho que·ill *D,* so q'ie·l *HIK,* so cil *T.* (22) ama a. (26) meillura e.
Selected variants: (33) Amics *ABa,* Floris *DHIKT.*

Notes

(1) **apais,** (2) **apaia**] Alternation of root. Inf. **apaisar** 'to nourish'; 1st sg.
 apais represents root **apais-** + **a** (tense, deleted for 1st sg.) + -zero (person); 3rd sg. **apaia** represents root **apai-** + **a** (tense) + -zero (person).
 The alternation of the roots **apais-** and **apai-** is like that of roots **vez-**
 and **vei-** in **vezer,** or that of roots **av-** and **au-** in **aver.** See chapter 19.
 joven] The noun ('youth') is stressed **jovén** (CL JŬVĔNTUM); the adjective ('young') is stressed **jóven** (CL JŬVĔNEM).

(2) **jois e jovens**] Compound subject; the verb agrees with the closer element (**jovens**), and hence is singular.

(6) **taing**] The **ing** spells **nh;** infinitive **tanher** 'to be fitting,' root **tanh-** +
 zero (tense) + -zero (person).

(7) **estrais**] Pret. 1st sg. of inf. **estraire** (refl., 'to cease'): root **estrai-** + **s**
 (past set) + zero (tense) + -zero (person).

(8) **estraia**] Pres. subj. 1st sg.

(10) **aia**] Pres. subj. 1st sg. of **aver.**

(11) **atrais**] Pret. 3rd sg. of **atraire** 'to bring'; cf. **estrais** 7.

(11–12) The independent verb is **prec** 12, from **pregar** 'to pray.' The subordinate clause **cel que primiers lo m'atrais** is in apposition to the indirect object **l'** 12 (= **li**): 'I pray God to bring great joy to the one who first brought him to me.' Example of prolepsis (Greek: 'anticipation')—that is, the moving forward of an element of the sentence to conspicuous initial position; cf. chapter 24.

(13–14) **Qui que** 'whoever' introduces an absolute clause. The independent verb is **creza** 14 (optative): 'Whoever tells him (**l'** = **li**) evil about the matter (**en**), he should not believe it, except what I told him.' **retraia**] Pres. subj. 3rd sg. of **retraire** 'to tell'; cf. **atraia** 12, **estraia** 8.

(14) **retrais**] Pret. 1st sg. of **retraire** with past marker **s**; cf. **atrais** 11, **estrais** 7.

(15) **cuoill**] Pres. indic. 3rd sg. of **colhir** 'to gather': root **colh-**, with palatal **l** spelled **ill**; zero (tense), -zero (person); diphthongization of **o** to **uo**, as in **luoc**, etc.

(15–16) The stanza ends with a veiled threat: if her beloved believes gossip about the speaker, she will believe gossip about him. The proverbial image of the **balais** 'rod, switch' suggests the punishment of a child.

(17) **dompna**] The zero article expresses the sense of the E. indefinite article ('a lady').

(18) **deu**] Pres. 3rd sg. of **dever** 'to have to,' with alternation of root: **dev-**, as in pres. 1st pl. **devem**; **deu-** before **r** (fut. **deura**) or word-final, as here; also **de-**, as in pres. 1st sg. **dei**, with -yod for 1st sg.

(20) **ill**] Feminine **i** ('she').

(21) **aus**] Optative subj. 3rd sg., from **ausar**, expressing a wish or a command. The direct object pronoun **l'** (= **lo**) precedes the independent verb, not the complementary infinitive of which it is the object.

(22) **dompna**] A mild prolepsis, since **dompna** is the subject of the clause introduced by **pois**: 'A lady, once she loves openly . . . ,' as prolepsis of 'Once a lady loves openly . . .'

(23–24) **ja pois** . . . **non**] 'Never again.'

(24) **dirant**] Fut. 3rd pl. of **dire** 'to say.'

(25) **ieu n'ai chausit un**] 'I have chosen one of them'; Fr. *j'en ai choisi un.* The **n'** is a form of **en**, not a negation.

(31) **fassa**] Pres. subj. 1st sg. of **faire** 'to do': root **fa-**, unusual tense marker **sa**, person marker -zero.

(32) **sol non**] 'Provided that I not find . . .': another veiled threat, as at the end of stanza 2. He must not believe that she would do him wrong—as long as he does not wrong her.

(33) **Amics**] Nominative singular as vocative. On the variant **Floris**, see 7.14 note.

(36) **mantenensa** 'support'] Taken by Cropp (*Vocabulaire* 478) as a feudal

metaphor denoting an obligation of the lord; but Rieger considers it simply amorous (591).

Exercise

Analyze these preterit, third person singular verbs from the **vidas** into their roots and various markers:

1. **ac** 1.7, **volc** 3.11, **venc** 5.3
2. **ausis** 3.7, **trais** 3.7, **remas** 5.14 *re mandre*
3. **saup** 5.3, **receup** 5.11
4. **fez** 5.4 (root **faz**; see ch. 19)

Verbs: Past Set (Section 3)

PAST SUBJUNCTIVE TENSE AND
SECOND CONDITIONAL TENSE
WITH VOWEL MARKERS

The form of the past subjunctive in Old Occitan derives from the Classical Latin pluperfect subjunctive (CANTĀVISSET 'he might have sung'), which is also the source of the Spanish imperfect subjunctive in -s- (*cantase, debiese*).

OOc had a tense called the "second conditional," close in meaning to the first conditional.[1] The second conditional derives from the CL pluperfect indicative (CANTĀVĔRAT 'he had sung' > **cantę́ra** 'he would have sung'), which also survives in Spanish imperfect subjunctive forms of the type *cantara* (beside *cantase*) and *debiera* (beside *debiese*).

The forms of the past subjunctive and second conditional tenses for verbs that take vowel markers for the past set are the following:

	Past Subjunctive		*Second Conditional*	
	-ar verbs	non-**ar** verbs	**-ar** verbs	non-**ar** verbs
1st sg.	cantę́s	partís	cantę́ra	partíra
2nd sg.	cantę́sses	partísses	cantę́ras	partíras
3rd sg.	cantę́s	partís	cantę́ra	partíra
1st pl.	cantessę́m	partissę́m	canterám	partirám
2nd pl.	cantessę́tz	partissę́tz	canterátz	partirátz
3rd pl.	cantę́ssoṇ, -en	partíssoṇ, -en	cantę́ran	partíran

[1] The first conditional is used in neutral hypotheses (neither likely nor unlikely) when **si** 'if' introduces the imperfect indicative (**Si sabia, cantaria** 'If I knew how, I would sing'). The second conditional occurs in unlikely hypotheses when **si** introduces the imperfect subjunctive (**Si saubes, cantera** 'If I had known how, I would have sung'). See chapter 27.

Perdre is also conjugated like **cantar**.

The past set is marked by **ę́** in the forms of **cantar** and by **í** in those of **partir**. The tenses are marked as follows:

Past subjunctive: **s** after a vowel (otherwise **ęs**; see below)

Second conditional: **ra**

Person markers in these two tenses are of the basic type. One apparent exception is the past subjunctive, second person singular, where a support vowel is inserted between the **ess** and the person marker **-s**; the support vowel is necessary to avoid reduction of the person marker (**cant-** + **ę́** [set] + **s** [tense] + **-s** [person] yields not *__*cantęs__, which would be identical to first person singular and third person singular, but **cantę́sses**). This is the first case we have come across in which a support vowel is necessary to ensure that a given form remains distinctive.

The past subjunctive is constructed as follows, for example, in the first person plural:

cant- + **ę́** + **s** + **ę́m** > **cantessę́m**

part- + **í** + **s** + **-ę́m** > **partissę́m**

And the second conditional is constructed as follows:

cant- + **ę́** + **ra** + **-ám** > **canterám**

part- + **í** + **ra** + **-ám** > **partirám**

In **cant-** + **ę́** + **ra** + **-ám**, the person marker **-ám** is normal after unstressed **a** (ch. 2). Elision functions here according to the usual pattern. So does accent reduction: when the underlying form posits two stressed syllables (**cant-** + **ę́** + **s** + **-ę́m** or **cant-** + **ę́** + **ra** + **-ám**), only the one closer to the end of the word receives stress. Hence **cantessę́m**, **canterám**, like imperfect **cant-** + **áva** + **-ám**, which produces **cantavám** (ch. 3).

In the second conditional, **-ar** verbs rarely substitute **ara** for the expected **era**: 2nd pl. **cujarátz** 19.36 for normal **cujerátz**. We have noted the same alternation in the first conditional form **saría** for normal **sería**, and the opposite pattern in the future form **laisserái** for normal **laissarái** (ch. 4).

PAST SUBJUNCTIVE TENSE AND
SECOND CONDITIONAL TENSE WITH
SEMIVOWEL OR CONSONANT MARKERS

The conjugation of **aver** 'have' is as follows:[2]

---

[2] The asterisk marks forms not attested in the texts of this book but found in Appel, *Provenzalische* xxxiii–xxxiv.

	Past Subjunctive	Second Conditional
1st sg.	**aguę́s**	**ágra**
2nd sg.	***aguę́sses**	***ágras**
3rd sg.	**aguę́s**	**ágra**
1st pl.	***aguessę́m**	***agrám**
2nd pl.	**aguessę́tz, acsę́s**	**agrátz, agrás**
3rd pl.	***aguę́sson, -en**	**ágran**

The past subjunctive of **aver** shows the set marker [k], here vocalized as **g**, and the tense marker **ę́s**. This tense marker occurs also after underlying [k] in **tenguę́s (tenir)**, **volguę́s (voler)**; after **s** in **fezę́s (faire)**; and after waw in **aperceubę́s (apercębre)**. It combines normally with the basic person markers.

In the second conditional, these forms represent the root **av-** with the past-set marker [k]. The consonant **v** at the end of the root is effaced, as in preterit **ac**, and [k] is voiced to **g** between a vowel and **r** (which is a voiced consonant). The tense marker **ra** combines normally with the basic person markers; final **-tz** may simplify to **-s**, as we have observed.

Analyze the various markers in the following forms, which use [k] for the past set:

> **dever**: 2nd cond. 1st sg. **degra**, 3rd sg. **degra**, 2nd pl. **degratz**, 3rd pl. **degran**
>
> **poder**: 2nd cond. 3rd sg. **pogra**, 2nd pl. **pogratz**, **pogras**
>
> **tener**: past subj. 1st sg. **tenguę́s**: 2nd cond. 3rd sg. **tengra**
>
> **venir**: past subj. 3rd sg. **venguę́s**
>
> **voler**: past subj. 1st sg. **volguę́s**, 3rd sg. **volguę́s**; 2nd cond. 1st sg. **volgra**

And these, using waw for the past set:

> **saber**: past subj. 3rd sg. **saubę́s**; 2nd cond. 3rd sg. **saubra**
>
> **apercebre**: past subj. 3rd sg. **aperceubę́s**; 2nd cond. 3rd sg. **aperceubra**

And this form, which uses implicit yod:

> **vezer** (root **ve-**, as in pres. 3rd sg. **ve**): pret. 3rd sg. **vi**; past subj. 3rd sg. **vis**; 2nd cond. 3rd sg. **vira** (Appel, *Provenzalische* xxviii)

Eser uses the marker **fǫ-** for the past set: preterit, third person singular **fǫ** (see ch. 6); past subjunctive, first person singular **fǫs** (with past subjunctive **s** after a vowel), third person singular **fǫs**, second person plural **fossę́tz**; second conditional, first person singular **fǫra**, third person singular **fǫra**, second person plural **forátz**, third person plural **fǫron**.

On the ModOc form **ajudèsse** for past subjunctive, third person singular (**ajudar**), see 32.1 note.

REVIEW OF PRESENT, FUTURE, AND PAST SETS

We may expand our earlier diagram of the tenses to include new information, as shown in table 7.1.

TABLE 7.1. *Three Sets of Verb Forms*

Present Set	Future Set	Past Set
marker = zero	marker = infinitive ending	marker = **ę, i**; [k], **s**; [w], [j]
Present Indicative Tense **a** for **-ar** zero for non-**ar**	Future Tense **á**	Preterit Tense zero
Present Subjunctive Tense zero for **-ar** **a** for non-**ar**	(see ch. 8)	Past Subjunctive Tense **s** after vowel **ęs** otherwise
Imperfect Tense **áva** for **-ar** **ía** for non-**ar**	First Conditional Tense **ía**	Second Conditional Tense **ra**

READING 7

Comtessa de Dia, *Estat ai en greu cossirier*

1
Estat ai en greu cossirier
per un cavallier q'ai agut,
e vuoil sia totz temps saubut
cum eu l'ai amat a sobrier;
    ara vei q'ieu sui trahida   5
car eu non li donei m'amor,
don ai estat en gran error
    en lieig e qand sui vestida.

2

9

Ben volria mon cavallier ~~soir~~
tener un ser e mos bratz nut,
q'el s'en tengra per ereubut *remplir de passion*   10
sol q'à lui fezes cosseillier. *oreiller, conseiller*
Car plus m'en sui abellida *plaire / je suis plus amoureux*
no fetz Floris de Blanchaflor, *de lui*
eu l'autrei mon cor e m'amor, *je lui donne*
mon sen, mos huoills, a ma vida. *yeux* X   15

3
Bels amics avinens e bos, *charmant / bons*
cora·us tenrai e mon poder? *pouvoir*
E que jagues ab vos un ser *gesir soir*
e qe·us dès un bais amoros! *baiser*   20
Sapchatz gran talan n'auria *saber (impers.)*
qe·us tengues en luoc del marit, *place*
ab so que m'aguessetz plevit *promis, juré*
de far tot so qu'eu volria.

Meter:

a	b	b	a	c	d	d	c
8	8	8	8	7'	8	8	7'

Ch. 3 d 8.
a = **-ier, -os;** *b* = **-ut, -er;** *c* = **-ida, -ia;** *d* = **-or, -it.**
Frank 624:57.

P-C 46,4. Major editions: Kussler-Ratyé, no. 4; Riquer, no. 155; Rieger, no. 36; Bruckner, Shepard, and White, no. 3; Bec, *Chants d'amour,* no. 10.
Four manuscripts: *A* fol. 168–v; *D* fols. 85v–86; *I* fol. 141; *K* fol. 127. Base *A.*
Stanza order: Uniform.
Rejected readings in the base manuscript: None.
Selected variants: (7) on *IK.* (11) erebut *D,* errebut *IK.* (14) fis *IK.* (16) a ma *A,* e ma *DIK.* (17) avenenz *D.* (23) avessez *D.*

Notes

(2) **ai agut**] The sense of erotic possession is inescapable even though it seems to be an exaggeration, if we take verse 6 (**non li donei m'amor**) as true. Riquer paraphrases **q'ai agut** as "who has been my knight," "who has been at my service."

(3) **vuoil**] Root **vol-,** from **voler,** with -yod as first person singular marker; yod combines with l as palatal **lh,** spelled **il,** and the **o** diphthongizes to **uó. vuoil sia**] Ellipsis of the subordinating conjunction **que.**

(6) **donei**] Root **don-** + past-set marker **é** + preterit zero + first person singular marker -yod.

(8) That is, night and day, all the time, with an erotic overtone.

9

Chapter 7.
Verbs: Past Set
(Section 3)

(9) **volria**] First cond. 1st sg. of **voler** 'to want': **vol-** + **r** + **ía** + -zero.

(10) **e mos**] That is, **en mos**. **nut**] Modifies **cavallier** 9 (not **bratz**).

(11) **tengra**] Root **ten-** + past-set marker [k] + 2nd cond. **ra** + -zero marker for third person singular.

(12) **fezęs**] Root **faz-** (as in pres. 1st pl. **fazem**) + implicit yod (**fez-**); past subj. **ęs** after a consonant; -zero marker for first person singular.

(14) **no**] Pleonastic (redundant) in a comparison. **fetz**] Root **faz-** (see **fezes** 7.12) + implicit yod + zero tense marker + -zero person marker. In meaning, **fetz** represents a repetition of **sui abellida**: 'than did' (i.e., than was pleased). **Floris**] Recurs as a **senhal** for the comtessa's lover in 6.33 var. The romance of *Floire et Blanchefleur* is extant in two Old French versions of the twelfth and thirteenth centuries, and in numerous versions in other languages, but not in OOc. The lovers are separated, reunited, and finally married (compare v. 22 note).

(15) **autrei**] Present 1st sg. from **autreiar**; the **ei** is part of the root; not a preterit 1st sg. like **cantei**, where the root is **cant-**.

(16) **a ma vida**] 'For my life'; cf. *LR* 2: 6. Other manuscripts read **e ma vida**, creating a triplet of mind, eyes, and life (see variants).

(18) **e mon**] That is, **en mon**.

(19) **jaguęs**] Root **jaz-**, as in **jazer**; past-set marker [k], here voiced to **g**; past subj. **ęs** after a consonant; -zero marker for first person singular. Note the use of the subjunctive in an independent clause to express a wish ('I wish that I could lie').

(20) **dęs**] Root **d-** from **dar**; past-set marker **ę́**; past subj. **s** after a vowel; -zero marker for first person singular.

(21) **sapchatz**] Root **sab-** from **saber**; pres. subj. **ja**; 2nd pl. **-átz**. The underlying **sapjatz** produces **sapchatz** by assibilation (see ch. 18).

(22) **tenguęs**] Root **ten-** from **tener** 'to hold'; past-set marker [k], here voiced to **g**; past subjunctive **ęs** after a consonant; -zero marker for third person singular. **en luoc del marit**] The definite article **·l** (in **del**) expresses the possessive 'my' (husband); the sense may be either 'in the place of my husband' (a husband to whom I am married), or 'as my husband' (whether such a husband is real or hypothetical). For the expression **en luoc de** meaning 'as,' see *S-W* 4. 419. Whether the comtessa is married or not, she expresses the wish to make her lover into her husband. (Note that according to the identification proposed by Monier, she had the title **comtessa** from her father, not by marriage.)

(23) **aguessetz**] Root **av-** from **aver**; past-set marker [k], voiced to **g**; past subjunctive **ęs**; 2nd pl. **-ętz**.

Exercise

Close this book and write out the past subjunctive and the second conditional for **cantar**, **partir**, and **aver**. Then compare what you have written with the forms given above.

Other Verb Forms

IMPERATIVES

The imperative formulates a command in the second person singular, the second person plural, or the first person plural. Normally the subject is not expressed (**escotatz!** 'Listen!'), but compare **vos o crezatz** 'You believe it!' 19.14. A noun of address may name the person who is the implicit subject of the imperative (**Doussa res, s'ieu no·us vezia / breumens, crezatz que morria** 'Sweet creature, if I didn't see you soon, believe that I would die' 4.37–38).

The imperative is expressed in OOc by a variety of means, depending on the type of imperative and the type of the verb, including forms from three distinct sources.[1]

Present indicative forms: first person plural of non-**ar** verbs (***partem** 'let us part'); second person plural of -**ar** verbs (**escotatz!**) and some non-**ar** verbs (***metetz**)

Present subjunctive forms: second person singular of certain verbs (**diguas**); first person plural of -**ar** verbs (**parlem**); second person plural of many non-**ar** verbs (**aujatz, crezatz, sapchatz, siatz, vejatz**); negative imperatives of all verbs, either -**ar** (**no m'oblidetz mia** 'Don't forget me' 4.30) or non-**ar** (**s'amor no la·us tolatz!** 'Don't deprive yourself of her love' 19.68)

Etymological imperatives from imperative forms in Classical Latin: second person singular of most verbs (***canta** 'Sing!,' CL CANTA; **acapta, bada, met**). Note the absence of the second person singular marker -**s**.

---

[1] The asterisk is used in this chapter to mark forms not attested in the texts of this book but found in Appel, *Provenzalische*.

The tendency resulting from these patterns is to produce imperatives in the first person plural with **-em**, regardless of verb type (**parlem**, **partem**), and in the second person plural with **-atz**, regardless of verb type (**escotatz**, **sapchatz**). However, the exception ***metetz** remains.

In ***metetz vos**, the reflexive imperative, the **-tz** may be deleted to produce **mete·us** (28.72).

PRESENT PARTICIPLES

The present participle has two markers:

> **-an**(**t**) for **-ar** verbs, as in **estan** or **estant** 'being' (**estar**),
> **parlan** 'speaking' (**parlar**)

> **-en**(**t**) for all others, as in **jauzen** 'enjoying' (**jauzir**), **dolen**
> 'grieving' (**doler**), **conoissen** 'knowing' (**conoiser**),
> **crezen** 'believing' (**creire**)

Since participles are verbal adjectives, the present participle is declined like an adjective for gender, case, and number. See "Masculine Declension" and "Second Feminine Declension" in chapter 9.

PAST PARTICIPLES

The past participle has the following markers:

> **-át** for **-ar** verbs, as in **amat** 'loved' (**amar**), **dat** 'given' (**dar**)

> **-ít** for some **-ir** verbs, as in **fenit** 'ceased' (**fenir**)

> **-út**, with or without a past-set marker, for some **-ir** verbs,
> some **-ér** verbs, some **-er** verbs, and some **-re** verbs:

>> no past-set marker: **vezut** 'seen' (**vezer**), **batut** 'beaten'
>> (**batre**), **perdut** 'lost' (**perdre**)

>> [k] past-set marker: **agut** 'had' (**aver**; also **avut**, **aüt**),
>> **begut** 'drunk' (**beure**), **vengut** 'come' (**venir**),
>> **vencut** 'conquered' (**vénser**)

>> s past-set marker: **remazut** 'remained' (**remaner**)

>> waw past-set marker: **saubut** 'known' (**saber**, also
>> **sabut**)

> **-t** for some **-ir** verbs, some **-ér verbs**, some **-er** verbs, and
> some **-re** verbs:

>> no past-set marker: **dit** 'said' (**dire**), **fait** 'done' (**faire**),
>> **mort** 'died' (**morir**), **nat** 'born' (**naiser**; also
>> ***nascut**)

>> implicit yod: **vist** 'seen' (**vezér**)

-s for some verbs that use the same -s for the past set (some
-ér verbs, some -re verbs):

> mes 'put' (**metre**; cf. pret. 3rd sg. **mes**)
>
> pres 'taken' (**prendre**; cf. pret. 3rd sg. **pres**)

Since participles are verbal adjectives, the past participle may be
declined like an adjective for gender, case, and number. See "Masculine Declension" and "First Feminine Declension" in chapter 9.

INFINITIVES

A number of infinitives show variable endings, especially among
non-**ar** verbs: **estre** or **éser** 'to be'; **querre** or **querẹr** or **querir** 'to
seek' (*PD*); **tenẹr** or **tenir** 'to hold' (*PD*); **vezẹr** or **veire** or **vezir** 'to
see' (*PD*) (see, further, ch. 19). The phenomenon occurs rarely
among -**ar** verbs: **páiser** 'to feed' or **paisár** 'to eat' (*Glossary*); **finar**
or **finir** 'to cease' (*PD*); **tradar** or **tradir** 'to betray' (*PD*). Infinitives
such as **dir** 'to say' (beside **dire**) and **far** 'to do' (beside **faire**) show
evidence for the ending -**r** that could be posited as underlying the
ending -**re**, with addition of a support vowel; see the discussion of
support vowels in chapters 2 and 13.

The infinitive may be substantivized—that is, treated as a noun,
with nominalized meaning and masculine declension (like **jorn**):
departir 'departure,' nom. sg. **departirs**; **dormir** 'sleeping'; **parlar**
'speech'; **plazer** 'pleasure'; **saber** 'wisdom, knowledge, skill'; **bel**
viure 'living well.'

Some infinitives show optional closing of **o** to **u** in the initial
syllable (see ch. 13): **morir**, **murir** 'to die'; **sofrir**, **sufrir** 'to suffer.'

Final -**r** of the infinitive is deleted in occasional manuscript
variants, as in ModOc pronunciation since the late fifteenth century (Lafont 57): **veni** 'to come,' variant of **venir** (2.2).

FUTURE SUBJUNCTIVE TENSE

To complete the study of verb forms in OOc, we observe that the
pattern of the eight tenses tabulated at the end of chapter 7 implies
a vacant box in the middle. This vacant function was perhaps filled
by a future subjunctive tense, which Roncaglia has detected in ex-
tremely rare traces ("Valore" 60–62; see also "Cortesamen" 956).
One trace occurs in a passage by Marcabru:

> Cortesamen vuoill comensar
> un vers, si es qui l'escoutar
>
> > Courteously I wish to begin
> > a song, if there is anyone who will [be willing to] listen to it.

Escoutar, as an OOc future subjunctive, third person singular, would correspond to the Spanish future subjunctive *cantare* and to its sources, the CL future perfect indicative CANTĀ(VĚ)RIT and the CL perfect subjunctive, identical in all forms but the first person singular (future perfect indicative CANTĀVERO, perfect subjunctive CANTĀVERIM). There are also vestiges of the future subjunctive in Old Italian (Roncaglia, "Valore" 61). The OOc form would be identical to the infinitive—that is, it would take the infinitive ending, as is normal in the future set, with a zero marker for the future subjunctive tense and zero for third person singular. An earlier editor of Marcabru had read **escout'ar**, present indicative **escouta** followed by the adverb **ar**: 'if there is anyone who is listening now.'[2] Though this simpler reading is not indefensible, Roncaglia's analysis of the form and its meaning is subtler and more elegant.

REVIEW OF VERB FORMS

Including the hypothetical future subjunctive, we may summarize the verb tenses of OOc in table 8.1.

TABLE 8.1. *Verb Forms in Old Occitan*

Personal Forms

Verb = Root + Set + Tense + Person

Present Set	Future Set	Past Set
marker = zero	marker = infinitive ending	marker = ẹ, i; [k], s; [w], [j]
Present Indicative Tense	Future Tense	Preterit Tense
a for **-ar**	**á**	
zero for non-**ar**		zero
Present Subjunctive Tense	(Future Subjunctive Tense)	Past Subjunctive Tense
zero for **-ar**	(zero)	**s** after vowel
a for non-**ar**		**ẹs** after consonant
Imperfect Tense	First Conditional Tense	Second Conditional Tense
áva for **-ar**	**ía**	**ra**
ía for non-**ar**		

[2] A second trace reads **forsar** or **fors'ar** in Arnaut de Comminges, **Be·m plai us usatges que cor** (P-C 28, 1), v. 5.

TABLE 8.1. *(cont.)*

65

*Chapter 8.
Other Verb
Forms*

Nonpersonal Forms

Verb = Root + Tense

Present Set	Future Set	Past Set
marker = zero	marker = infinitive ending	marker = ę, i; [k], s; [w], [j]
Present Participle -**án** for -**ar** -**ę́n** for non-**ar**	Infinitive -**ár**, -**ír**, -**ę́r**, ´-**er**, -**re**, -**r**	Past Participle -**át** for -**ar** -**ít**, -**út**, -**t**, -**s** for non-**ar**

The person markers used in verb forms may be summarized as follows:

	Basic Type 1	Preterit Type 2	Systematic Type 3	Sporadic Type 4
1st sg.	-zero	-yod	-yod (fut.)	-yod (pres. **ai**, **sai** . . .); [k] (pres. **dic** etc.)
2nd sg.	**-s**	**-st**		
3rd sg.	-zero	**-t**, **-c**		**-ṇ** (pret. **foṇ**)
1st pl.	**-ę́m** **-ám** after **a**	**-m**		**-mes** (pres. **ésmes**)
2nd pl.	**-ę́tz** **-átz** after **a**	**-tz**	**-ę́tz** (pres. ind. non-**ar**)	**-ę́t** (fut. **auret**)
3rd pl.	**-on**[3]	**-ron**[4]		

READING 8

Guilhem IX, *Ab la dolchor del temps novel*

Guilhem, ninth of the name as duke of Aquitaine and seventh as count of Poitiers, was born in 1071 and died in 1126. At age fifteen he inherited lands more extensive than those of the king of France, his nominal lord.

[3] Reduced forms **-o**, **-en**; also **-ont**.

[4] Reduced forms **-ro**, **-ren**; also **-ront**.

*He is the first troubadour whose works are extant. They include eleven
songs represented here in their range from amorous (ch. 8) to bawdy (ch.
9) to meditative (ch. 10).*

1

Ab la dolchor del temps novel
foillo li bosc, e li aucel
chanton, chascus en lor lati,
segon lo vers del novel chan;
adonc esta ben c'om s'aisi
d'acho dont hom a plus talan.

2

De lai don plus m'es bon e bel
non vei mesager ni sagel,
per que mon cor non dorm ni ri
ni no m'aus traire adenan
tro qu'eu sacha ben de la fi,
s'el'es aissi com eu deman.

3

La nostr'amor va enaissi
com la branca de l'albespi,
qu'esta sobre l'arbr'entrenan
la nuoit ab la ploi'ez al gel
tro l'endeman, que·l sol s'espan
per la fueilla vert e·l ramel.

4

Enquer me menbra d'un mati
que nos fezem de guera fi
e que·m donet un don tan gran,
sa drudari'e son anel.
Enquer me lais Dieus viure tan
c'aia mas mans soz so mantel!

5

Qu'eu non ai soing de lor lati
que·m parta de mon bon vezi;
qu'eu sai de paraulas, com van
ab un breu sermon que s'espel;
que tal se van d'amor gaban,
nos n'avem la pess'e·l coultel.

Meter

a	a	b	c	b	c
8	8	8	8	8	8

Ch. 4 d 6, 1–6.

a = -elh, -i; b = -i, -an; c = -an, -elh.

In the second pair of stanzas the original *b*-rhyme becomes the *a*-rhyme, the original *c*-rhyme becomes the *b*-rhyme, and the original *a*-rhyme becomes the *c*-rhyme. Frank's analysis of stanza 5 as a tornada enables him to classify the structure as **coblas doblas**; it is unusual, however, to find a tornada as long as a regular stanza, as here, so it is perhaps more straightforward to think of the poem as five stanzas with one set of rhymes in stanzas 1–2 and a rotated set in stanzas 3–5. The shift in rhymes puts stanza 3 in relief (Frank 190: 2).

P-C 183,1. Major editions: Pasero, no. 10; Riquer, no. 2; Bond, no. 10.

Four manuscript transcriptions: $N_1 = N$ fols. 228v–229; $N_2 = N$ fol. 235; $a^1_1 = a^1$ p. 463; $a^1_2 = a^1$ p. 499. Base N_1.

Divergent attribution: Jaufre Rudel a^1_2.

Stanza order: Uniform.

Rejected readings in the base manuscript: (1) *The initial letter of each stanza is omitted in N_1N_2 and supplied here from $a^1_1a^1_2$ (but see note to 19).* (11) que eu $N_1a^1_2$, qu'eu N_2, qe a^1_1; de fi N_1N_2, de la fi a^1_1, la fi a^1_2. (16) ploia ez. (18) par N_1N_2, per $a^1_1a^1_2$; verz $N_1N_2a^1_2$, vert a^1_1. (19) Nquer N_1N_2, Anqar a^1_1, Ancar a^1_2. *S-W (1: 63) lists* anquer *in the* Chanson de la Croisade albigeoise, *but it is an unusual form;* enquer *is more frequent; cf. v. 23.* (21) que·n N_1N_2, qe·m a^1_1, qi a^1_2. (27) pauralas N_1, paraulas $N_2a^1_1a^1_2$. (30) pessa e.

Selected variants: (9) mon cor N_1N_2, mos cors $a^1_1a^1_2$. (15) arbr'entrenan N_1N_2, arbre tremblan a^1_1, arbre treman a^1_2. (17) sol $N_1N_2a^1_1$, sols a^1_2. (20) guera N_1N_2, guerra $a^1_1a^1_2$. (25) de lor N_1N_2, d'estraing $a^1_1a^1_2$.

Notes

(2) **foillo**] Pres. 3rd pl. of **folhar**: root **folh-**, with palatal l spelled **ill. li bosc e li aucel**] Masc. nom. pl.

(3) **lati**] Latin is understood to be the model of language in general.

(5) **s'aisi**] Pres. subj. 3rd sg. of **aizinar**; root **aiziṇ-** (the **-n** is mobile, as in the root adj. **aisiṇ**) + zero tense marker + -zero person marker.

(6) **hom**] Nom. sg. in shifting declension; obl. sg. **ome**.

(7) **bon e bel**] Neuter (see "Neuter Gender" in ch. 28).

(9) **mon cor**] Neuter nom. sg. **cor**; cf. nom. sg. **cor** 4.31. **Mon** may be regarded as neuter or as unmarked, an oblique form used as nom. (see ch. 28).

(10) **m'aus traire**] The object pronoun **m'** precedes the independent verb **aus**, not the subordinate infinitive **traire**, even though the pronoun is the object of the infinitive; such order is normal.

(11) **de la fi**] Prolepsis from the following clause: lit., 'Until I know well about the pact, if it is as I ask' = 'Until I know for sure if our pact is as I ask' (cf. ch. 24).

(13) **amor**] Nom. sg. without **-s**, which is etymological (CL nom. AMOR). See "Absence of **-s** in the Nominative Singular" in chapter 9.

(15) **entrenan**] With a static verb such as **estar**, **entrenar** means 'to resist, to remain standing'; see Pfister 414 note 31, and cf. variants.

(16) **al** (introducing **gel**) = **ab lo**, parallel to **ab la ploi**.' Cf. **als** 23.28, meaning **ab los**, parallel to **ab**.

(17) **sol s'espan**] Declensional final **-s** may fall before initial **s-**; see Grafström, *Graphie* 78.5.b., and cf. variants.

(18) **la fueilla vert**] **Vert** is an adjective of type 2, as it was also in Old French. Modern French fem. *verte* is an analogical formation on type 1. See "Adjectives" in chapter 9. The form **fueilla** = **fǫlha**, with palatal l spelled **-ill-** and diphthongization of **ǫ** to **ué**.

(20) **guera**] The form **rr** sometimes reduces to **r**.

(23) **lais**] Optative subj.

(23–24) **tan / que**] 'Until.'

(24) **mantel** 'cloak'] Considered by some scholars as a feudal metaphor for protection (Pasero 263) but by others as erotic (Bond 77); cf. **mantelh** 9.19. The same range of interpretations has been applied to **mantenensa** 6.36 (see note).

(25) **de lor lati**] Prolepsis from the following clause: 'I have no care about their speech, that would part me from . . . ' = 'I have no care that their speech would part me from . . . '

(26) **mon bon vezi**] Masc. as an abstract term referring to a woman; or a **senhal**, in which case the expression could be capitalized: **mon Bon Vezi**.

(27) **de paraulas**] Prolepsis: 'I know about words, how they go' = 'I know how words go.'

(29) **tal**] Masc. nom. pl.

(30) **la pess'e·l coultel**] Everything we need to eat well, categorized as a piece (of meat? of bread?) and a knife, with an erotic suggestion. Cf. **en lieig e . . . vestida** 7.8.

Exercise

Reread text 8, isolating and identifying all forms of person markers.

CHAPTER 9

Nouns and Adjectives

DECLENSION OF THREE TYPES: STABLE, INVARIABLE, AND SHIFTING

Most Old Occitan nouns and adjectives are declined with a stable stress pattern throughout the declension. Forms are distinguished by the presence or absence of final **-s** in three patterns: one for masculine nouns, two for feminine nouns (ending in **-a** or not). Adjectives fall into two types (adding **-a** for the feminine or not); each type follows the suitable pattern for nouns.

Nouns and adjectives with stable stress and with roots ending in **-s** are invariable, since the root masks the presence or absence of declensional **-s**.

In a smaller class of nouns and adjectives that we shall call the shifting declension, stress moves forward (to the left) for the nominative singular, as in oblique singular **senhór** 'lord,' nominative singular **sénher**.

STABLE DECLENSION

This chapter will present stable declension synchronically, as constituted in Old Occitan. After the study of sound changes from Classical Latin to OOc in chapters 11–19, chapter 22 will present diachronic study of stable declension. Chapter 23 will analyze shifting declension, which requires both synchronic and diachronic perspectives.

Masculine Declension

Stable masculine substantives (nouns and adjectives) are declined in this pattern:

	Sg.	Pl.
Nom.	**-s**	-zero
Obl.	-zero	**-s**

Most masculine nouns end in consonants, like **jǫrn** 'day,' declined as follows:

	Sg.	Pl.
Nom.	**jorns**	**jorn**
Obl.	**jorn**	**jorns**

Some masculine nouns end in diphthongs, like **rẹi** 'king,' and are declined like **jorn**:

	Sg.	Pl.
Nom.	**reis**	**rei**
Obl.	**rei**	**reis**

Substantives ending in unstressed **-e** are all masculine, like **paire** 'father,' with the single exception of **maire** 'mother.' They are usually declined in the same pattern as **jorn** and **rei** (but see below, "Absence of **-s** in the Nominative Singular"):

	Sg.	Pl.
Nom.	**paires**	**paire**
Obl.	**paire**	**paires**

The same pattern applies to masculine adjectives, whether they end in consonants (like **bǫṇ** 'good,' **fǫl** 'foolish,' **mal** 'bad,' **nul** 'any,' **pauc** 'little,' **saṇ** 'healthy') or in unstressed **-e** (like **paubre** 'poor'). The same pattern applies to present participles (masc. **dolen** 'grieving,' **gauzen** 'rejoicing,' **rizen** 'laughing'). After **t-**, declensional **-s** is often spelled **-z**, as in past participles such as masculine nominative singular **amatz** 'loved,' **faitz** 'done,' **mortz** 'died.'

Note 1. A small number of masculine paroxytonic nouns end in unstressed **-i**, from Latin -ĭᴜᴍ (neuter); see chapter 11. They are declined like **glázi** 'sword':

	Sg.	Pl.
Nom.	**glázis**	**glázi**
Obl.	**glázi**	**glázis**

In this book this group includes the nominative singular forms **martíris** 'slaughter,' **sétis** 'siege'; the oblique singular **ávi** 'grandfather,' **círi** 'candle,' **empéri** 'empire,' **gramávi** 'teacher,' **ofíci** 'office,' **óli** 'olive oil,' **sacrifíci** 'sacrifice,' **sautéri** 'psalter'; proper nouns **Boéci, Capitóli, Marsíli**. Proparoxytones with this ending include **cálici** 'chalice' and **Trípoli**.

Note 2. Exceptional masculine nouns ending in unstressed **-a** are treated either in the masculine pattern (nom. sg. **uns sols dias** 'one single day' 16.49) or in the feminine declension (nom. sg. **·l papa** 'the pope' 31.39).

Note 3. Masculine nouns ending in stressed vowels include **di** 'day,' **pę** 'foot,' **brǫ** 'broth.'

Note 4. This declension includes nouns ending in **n**-mobile, which is omitted in a form such as nominative singular **capellás** 'chaplain' beside **capellans**, or **vilás** 'peasant' beside **vilans**. The **-a** of the final syllable is stressed whether or not the **n**-mobile is present.

First Feminine Declension (**in** -a)

By far the largest class of feminine nouns and adjectives, comprising those that end in unstressed **-a**, is declined in this pattern:

	Sg.	Pl.
Nom.	-zero	-s
Obl.	-zero	-s

For example, **dǫmna** 'lady':

	Sg.	Pl.
Nom.	domna	domnas
Obl.	domna	domnas

This pattern is also used in feminine adjectives (**bǫna** 'good,' **paubra** 'poor') and past participles (**amada** 'loved').

Second Feminine Declension (Not in -a)

Feminine nouns that do not end in **-a** are declined in this pattern:

	Sg.	Pl.
Nom.	-s	-s
Obl.	-zero	-s

Most such nouns end in a consonant, like **part** 'part, share':

	Sg.	Pl.
Nom.	partz	partz
Obl.	part	partz

This declension also includes **dolǫr** 'grief,' **flǫr** 'flower,' **lausǫr** 'praise,' **paǫr** 'fear'; **beutat** 'beauty,' **bontat** 'goodness,' **foudat** 'folly,' **vertut** 'power'; **cǫrt** 'court,' **sǫrt** 'fate'; **regiǫn** 'region,' **reṇ** 'creature'; **cárcer** 'prison,' **carn** 'flesh,' **fam** 'hunger,' **man** 'hand,' **mar** 'sea,' **nǫch** 'night.' Other feminine nouns end in a stressed vowel, like **fę** 'faith,' **mercę** 'mercy'; in a diphthong, like **lęi** 'law,' **nau** 'ship,' **nęu** 'snow'; or in an unstressed vowel, like **maire** 'mother.'

Amor 'love,' feminine, which takes **-s** in the nominative singular and in both plural forms by the second feminine declension, is occasionally treated as an invariable with **-s** in the oblique singular:

> Diray vos d'amors com minha,   14.19
>
> I shall tell you about love, how it eats

In the selections in this book, invariable **amors** occurs only in ms. *R* (see Glossary). For nominative singular **amor**, see below, "Absence of **-s** in the Nominative Singular."

Feminine adjectives that do not end in **-a**, such as **gentil** 'noble,' are declined the same way:

	Sg.	Pl.
Nom.	**gentils**	**gentils**
Obl.	**gentil**	**gentils**

Other feminine adjectives in this group are **ávol** 'bad,' **brẹu** 'short,' **cal** 'which,' **egal** 'equal,' **fọrt** 'strong,' **gran** 'large,' **jóven** 'young,' **par** 'like,' **sotil** 'subtle,' **tal** 'such,' **vẹrt** 'green,' **vil** 'vile.' Feminine present participles in the oblique singular include **gardan** 'watching,' **plazen** 'pleasing,' **auvẹnt** (**auvent la gent** 'in the hearing of the people' 11.23); the oblique plural appears in **sas armas trespassans** 'his [i.e., God's] dying souls' 27.16.

Absence of -s in the Nominative Singular, Masculine or Feminine

Final **-s** marks the nominative singular in the masculine declension and in the second feminine declension. This final **-s** is occasionally omitted, however, in forms called "asigmatic" (that is, 'lacking final **-s**'), for specific etymological reasons.

A small number of masculine nouns and adjectives ending in **-re** may occur in the nominative singular without **-s** because they had no final **-s** in Classical Latin, but rather a final -ʀ, which, because of a preceding consonant, came to require a support vowel in OOc. The list includes nominative singular **paire** 'father,' from CL ᴘᴀᴛᴇʀ; nominative singular **pẹbre** 'pepper,' from CL ᴘĭᴘᴇʀ (neuter); nominative singular **autre** 'other,' from CL ᴀʟᴛᴇʀ; nominative singular **nọstre** 'our,' from CL ɴŏsᴛᴇʀ. Usually, however, the support vowel takes the normal final **-s** in the masculine nominative singular, as in **evẹsques** 'bishop' (CL ᴇᴘĭsᴄŏᴘᴜs), **ọstes** 'innkeeper' (VL ʜŏsᴘĭᴛɪs), **princes** 'prince' (CL ᴘʀīɴᴄᴇᴘs), **sẹgles** 'world' (CL sᴀᴇᴄŭʟᴜᴍ, neuter, with masculine **-s** added in OOc).

Similarly, feminine nouns that ended in -ʀ in Classical Latin sometimes occur in OOc without the normal **-s** of the second feminine declension; witness nominative singular **amor**, from CL ᴀᴍᴏʀ, beside normal **amors** (see 8.13 note).

Stable nouns and adjectives with roots ending in **-s** (written **-s**, or **-z** in **-tz** and **-nz**) are invariable, since stable declension is based entirely on the play of final **-s**. Properly speaking, the final **-s** is not declensional at all but the termination of the root.

	Sg.	Pl.
Nom.	s-	s-
Obl.	s-	s-

The invariable declension includes masculine nouns such as **cọrs** 'body, person, self'; **tẹmps** 'time'; **prẹtz** 'merit'; **solatz** 'company'; feminine nouns such as **patz** 'peace,' **vẹtz** 'time, occasion,' **vọtz** 'voice'; masculine adjectives such as **cortẹs** 'courtly,' **gelọs** 'jealous'; and masculine past participles such as **aprẹs**, from **aprendre** 'to learn'; **mẹs**, from **metre** 'to put'; **prẹs**, from **prendre** 'to take.'

Note. OOc **bratz** 'arm,' masculine, was normally invariable; but the insertion of a support vowel between the **-tz** of the root and the **-s** of declension produced oblique plural **braces** 25.12, following the standard masculine declension (see below). In ModOc such forms are frequent; cf. **sagnoses** 32.14 var., from OOc **sagnọs** 'bloody.'[1]

ADJECTIVES

OOc adjectives fall into two classes, depending on whether they show a distinctive marker for feminine gender. Those that do show a feminine marker (type 1) add unstressed **-a** to the root of the masculine and are, accordingly, declined in the first feminine pattern. The masculine forms follow the masculine type appropriate to the root, either stable, like **jọrn**, or invariable, like **cọrs**. Such adjectives include stable masculines, like **bọn/bọna** 'good,' **clar/clara** 'bright,' **fọl/fọla** 'foolish,' **lọnc/lọnga** 'long,' **tant/tanta** 'so much,' and invariable masculines, like **cortẹs/cọrteza** 'courtly,' **dous/doussa** 'sweet,' **fals/falsa** 'false.' In **paubre/paubra** 'poor' the masculine shows a support vowel, and feminine **-a** is added to the underlying root **paubr-**. Example declensions:

	Masc.			*Fem.*	
	Sg.	Pl.		Sg.	Pl.
Nom.	**bọns**	**bọn**	Nom.	**bọna**	**bọnas**
Obl.	**bọn**	**bọns**	Obl.	**bọna**	**bọnas**

---

[1] We have encountered such morphologically motivated support vowels before in the past subjunctive, second person singular: **cant-** + **ẹ́** (set) + **s** (tense) + **s** (person) > **cantẹ́sses** (not ***cantẹ́s**). Cf. chapter 7.

	Masc.				*Fem.*	
	Sg.	Pl.			Sg.	Pl.
Nom.	**fals**	**fals**		Nom.	**falsa**	**falsas**
Obl.	**fals**	**fals**		Obl.	**falsa**	**falsas**

In a smaller number of adjectives (type 2) there is no feminine marker, and the two genders show an identical oblique singular form. Since the roots of these words end in a consonant, the feminine forms are declined in the second feminine; the masculine forms are declined in the standard masculine declension. For example, **tal** 'such':

	Masc.				*Fem.*	
	Sg.	Pl.			Sg.	Pl.
Nom.	**tals**	**tal**		Nom.	**tals**	**tals**
Obl.	**tal**	**tals**		Obl.	**tal**	**tals**

READING 9

Guilhem IX, *En Alvernhe part Lemozi*

1
En Alvernhe part Lemozi
m'en aniey totz sols a tapi;
trobey la moler d'en Guari
 e d'en Bernart;
saluderon me francamen
 per Sanh Launart.

2
Aujatz ieu que lur respozi:
anc fer ni fust no·y mentaugui,
mas que lur dis aital lati:
 "Tarrababart,
marrababelio riben
 saramahart."

3
So dis n'Agnes e n'Ermessen:
"Trobat avem qu'anam queren!
Alberguem lo tot plan e gen
 que ben es mutz,
e ja per el nostre secretz
 non er saubutz."

La una·m pres sotz so mantelh, ~~soup sor~~ *et me faisait bon*

et a mi fon mout bon e belh; 20

meneron m'en a lur fornelh, *foyer*

   e·l focs fo·m bos, *feu était bon*

et ieu calfei me voluntiers *et je me chauffait*

   als gros carbos. *par les gros morceaux de charbon*

5

A manjar me deron capos, *donnèrent de chapons* *capon*

et ieu dirney me volentos; 25 *nourriture (de dîner) me plaisait*

e·l pans fon cautz, e·l vins fon bos, *chaud*

   fortz e espes; *abondant* *j'avais même*

et anc sol no·y ac coguastro, *garçon qui fait la cuisine*

   mas quan nos tres. 30

6 *cel* *trompeur*

"Sor, aquest hom es enginhos, *décevoir*

e laissa son parlar per nos. *ne parle pas*

Aportatz lo nostre cat ros

   tost e corren, *tôt et vite*

que li·n fara dir veritat, 35

   si de res men." *s'il ment du tout*

7

Quant ieu vi vengut l'enujos *horrible créature)*

(grans ac los pels, fers los guinhos, *faroûche les moustaches*

ges son solas no mi fon bos!) *compagnie ne me faisait pas bien*

   totz m'espaven;) *j'avais peur* 40

ab pauc no perdiey mas amors *avec un peu je perdais mon amour*

   e l'ardimen. *courage*

8

Quan aguem begut e manjat, *bu* *elles m'ont*

despulley·m a lur voluntat; *déshabiller*

derreire m'aportero·l cat 45

   mal e fello, *cruel*

et escorgeron me del cap *la peler de la tête*

   tro al talo. *jusqu'au talon*

9 *gratter*

Per la coa·l pres n'Ermessen

e tira, e·l catz escoyssen; *gratta des* *blessure*

plaguas me feyron mays de cen *frappèrent* 50

   aquella ves; *sois*

coc me, mas ieu per tot aquo *cela*

   no·m mogui ges. *bouger*

10
Ni o feyra qui m'aucizes,
entro que pro fotut agues
ambedos; qu'ayssi fon empres
   a mon talen,
ans vuelc mais sufrir la dolor
   e·l greu turmen.

11
Aitan fotey cum auziretz:
cen e quatre vint e ueit vetz!
Ab pauc no·m rompet mos corretz
   e mos arnes,
e venc m'en trop gran malaveg,
   tal mal me fes.

12
Monet, tu m'iras al mati,
mo vers portaras e·l borssi
dreg a la molher d'en Guari
   e d'en Bernat,
e diguas lor que per m'amor
   aucizo·l cat!

Meter:

a a a b c b
8 8 8 4 8 4
12 s 6.
a = -i, -i, -ęn, -ęlh, -ǫs, -ǫs, -ǫs, -at, -ęn, -ęs, -ętz, -i.
b = -art, -art, -utz, -ǫs, -ęs, -ęn, -ǫ, -ęs, -ęn, -ęs, -at.
c = -ęn, -ęn, -ętz, -iers, -ǫ, -at, -ǫrs, -ap, -ǫ, -ǫr, -ęch, -ǫr.
Cf. Frank 62:1.

P-C 183, 12. Major editions: Pasero, no. 5; Riquer, no. 7; Bond, no. 5.
Four manuscript copies: C fol. 232; N_1 = N fol. 228–v; N_2 = N fol. 235–236; V
fol. 148v. Base C. I have chosen C as base because V is largely illegible,
while $N_1 N_2$ give a text of poor linguistic quality, and despite the fact that
$N_1 N_2 V$ include four stanzas (and a tornada in V) lacking in C, while omitting
two stanzas included there. For variants from V, I have relied to a great extent
on the transcription made by Crescini in 1890 ("Canzoniere"). In my own direct consultation of V (1 Oct. 1987), the text was so faint that I could neither
confirm nor deny Crescini's readings in a number of passages. See the facsimile of V in Bond (159).
Stanza order:

C	—	—	1	—	2	3	4	5	6	7	8	9	10	11	12
V	A	B	1	C	(2)	3	4	5	6	7	8	9	D	11	E
$N_1 N_2$	A	B	1	C	(2)	3	4	5	8	6	7	9	D	11	—

Rejected readings in the base manuscript: (17) secret C, conseill $N_1 N_2 V$. (22) foc
CV, fog N_1, focs N_2; bo C, bon $N_1 N_2$, bos V. (24) al C, au $N_1 N_2$, als V; carbo
C, carbon $N_1 N_2$, carbos V. (26–27) *Reversed in C, which leaves v. 28 incom-*

prehensible. (27) pan CN_1N_2, pans *V*; vin CN_1N_2V. (28) fort *C*, lo peur'espes N_1N_2V. (39) son s. *C, om.* N_1N_2V. (50) cat *C*, pilleron lo gat ez escoisen N_1N_2V. (62) .c. e quatre .xxviii. *C*, c.xx.iiii.viii. N_1N_2, .c. & iiij vint & viij *V*. Selected variants: (18) saubutz *C*, saipuz N_1N_2, sabutz *V*. (41) amors *C*, amor *V*, valors N_1N_2. (63) ronpei N_1N_2. (65) gran *C*, lo N_1N_2V.

Notes

(1) 'In Auvergne beyond the Limousin,' implying Guilhem's perspective from Poitiers.

(3) **moler**] Shifting declension, stressed **molhér** in oblique singular.

(4) **e d'en Bernart**] 'And [the wife] of Sir Bernart.'

(7) **ieu**] Subject of **respozi** in proleptic (anticipatory) position. On prolepsis, see chapter 24.

(8) **fer ni fust**] I.e., nothing at all, with alliterative pairing.

(10–12) Perhaps pseudo-Arabic in humorous usage. Attempts to treat the passage as real Arabic have produced conflicting translations (Bond 84; cf. Pasero 145–47).

(15) **plan e gen**] Neuter adjectives used adverbially.

(16) **mutz**] Does not mean 'mute' in the sense 'unable to utter a sound' but rather 'unable to utter coherent speech.'

(17–18) **ja . . . non**] 'Never.'

(19) **mantelh**] Cf 8.24 note.

(20) **fon**] Sg.; pl. **foron. bon e belh**] Neuter adjectives.

(29) **anc sol**] 'Even.'

(31) **Sor**] Shifting declension, using nom. sg. form for vocative function.

(33) **lo nostre**] 'Our'; cf. use of definite article with possessive in **lo seus seingner** 5.4, etc.

(39) **son solas**] Final **-s** may be elided before initial **s-**; cf. 8.17 note.

(40) **m'espaven**] Historical present, in meaningful contrast to the preterits **vi** 37, **perdiey** 41.

(41–42) **mas amors e l'ardimen**] Def. art. **l'** corresponds to **mas**, and so means 'my.'

(46) **felló**] Shifting declension.

(47–48) These lines anticipate the narrative events developed more fully in the following stanza.

(50) **tira . . . escoyssen**] Historical presents.

(53) **coc me**] 'He [the cat] seared me,' 'gave me a searing pain'; the root meaning of **cóire** 'to cook' relates to the foods in stanza 5 and the absence of a **coguastró** 'scullion.'

(55) **feyra**] "I would [not] have done" (2nd cond.). **qui m'aucizes**] "Conditional **qui**" (cf. ch. 27) followed by a past subjunctive: 'Even if someone had killed me.'

(57) **fon empres**] 'It happened.'

(65) **gran**] Object form for nominative function, possibly influenced by the invariable noun **malaveg** ending in an affricate; cf. **ta gran dolors** 11.41 (eleventh-century ms.), in which the form of **gran** is possibly influenced by the adverb **ta** (**tan**).

(67–68) The jussive future tense expresses a command.

(68) **e·l borssi**] The definite article means 'your.' If the meaning is literal, Monet will carry a written document in his pouch; but if the pouch is a metaphor for memory, Monet will carry an orally transmitted song.

Exercise

Rehearse the four forms of the following stable nouns, adjectives, and phrases:

1. **fust** 9.8
2. **nostre secretz** 9.17
3. **totz sols** 9.2
4. **la una** 9.19
5. **aquella ves** 9.52
6. **la dolor** 9.59

CHAPTER 10

Demonstratives

→ Review stable declension (ch. 9).

PARAMETERS OF
DEMONSTRATIVE MORPHOLOGY

Demonstrative morphology in OOc derives from three degrees of proximity in Classical Latin:

ʜīc, acc. ʜŏc 'this, what is near me, the speaker'

ĭsᴛᴇ, acc. ĭsᴛᴜᴍ 'that, what is near you, the addressee'

ĭʟʟᴇ, acc. ĭʟʟᴜᴍ 'yonder, what is near him, the person spoken about'

In CL these degrees correspond to the first, second, and third persons in the verb. In OOc the first of these degrees of proximity evolved into a series of neuter pronouns used as syntactic links between elements of the sentence, leaving the second and third degrees to refer to 'this, what is near the speaker' and 'that, what is far from the speaker.' Each degree of proximity could be expressed with three degrees of demonstrative force: weak, introductory (requiring completion), or strong, as shown in table 10.1.

TABLE 10.1 *Proximity and Force in Demonstrative Morphology*

Proximity		Force		
CL	OOc	Weak	Introductory	Strong
		root	s-/c- + root	ais-/aic-/ac- + root
ʜŏc	neuter	ǫ	sǫ	aisǫ́, acǫ́
ĭsᴛᴜᴍ	near	ęst	cęst	aicę́st, aquę́st
ĭʟʟᴜᴍ	far	ęl/lo	cęl	aicę́l, aquę́l

Unlike the morphology of the verb and the noun, which vary in suffixes only, demonstrative morphology in OOc uses both suffixes and prefixes. An abstract model of a demonstrative would be this:

Demonstrative = prefix + root + suffix

The prefix expresses demonstrative force, either weak (zero prefix, the root alone), introductory (the prefix **s-/c-** + root), or strong (the prefix **ais-/aic-/ac-** + root). The root expresses either a neuter syntactic link or proximity in two degrees, near and far. The suffix expresses gender, case, and number, except in the neuter pronouns, which are indeclinable, like other neuters.

The words involved in demonstrative morphology include pronouns, adjectives, and the definite article. The personal pronoun **ęl** 'he' is closely bound up, both synchronically and diachronically, with the definite article **lo** 'the.' As a pronoun it represents normal development of CL ĭLLE; the definite article represents an aphetic ('headless') development in unstressed position, since the article was treated as an unstressed initial element in the following noun.

This chapter discusses the expression of gender, case, and number in the suffix of demonstratives. For the expression of variable demonstrative force in the prefix, see chapter 23; for the syntax of demonstratives, see chapter 29.

DECLENSION OF THE SUFFIX FOR GENDER, CASE, AND NUMBER

The near and far demonstratives form their feminine root, as do adjectives of type 1 (see ch. 9), by adding **-a** to final consonants:

> **ęl > ęla**
>
> as **bęl > bęla**

or by replacing final unstressed **-o** with final **-a**:

> **lo > la**
>
> similar to **paubre > paubra**

Thus the feminine demonstrative forms are as follows:

Weak	Introductory	Strong
ęst > ęsta	cęst > cęsta	aicęst > aicęsta
ęl > ęla	cęl > cęla	aicęl > aicęla
lo > la		

Case and number are expressed in ways similar but not identical to the variations in stable declension of nouns and adjectives. Feminine demonstratives, which all end in unstressed **-a**, are declined exactly like the first feminine declension (**domna**):

	Sg.	Pl.
Nom.	ẹ́sta	ẹ́stas
Obl.	ẹ́sta	ẹ́stas

cẹ́sta, aicẹ́sta, etc.

	Sg.	Pl.
Nom.	ẹ́la	ẹ́las
Obl.	ẹ́la	ẹ́las

cẹ́la, aicẹ́la, etc.

	Sg.	Pl.
Nom.	la	las
Obl.	la	las

The declension of masculine demonstratives differs from that of masculine nouns because, for etymological reasons, they lack the nominative singular **-s** (as does **paire**, but the demonstratives do not have the characteristic **r** of most asigmatic nouns and adjectives) and because they show an implicit yod (metaphony) in the nominative plural:

	Sg.	Pl.
Nom.	ẹst	ist
Obl.	ẹst	ẹstz

cẹst, aicẹst, etc.

	Sg.	Pl.
Nom.	ẹl	il
Obl.	ẹl	ẹls

cẹl, aicẹl, etc.

	Sg.	Pl.
Nom.	lo	li
Obl.	lo	los

This metaphony results from the influence of the final vowel in CL nominative plural ĭstī, ĭllī, which causes the stressed vowel to become **i** instead of **ẹ** in **ist**, **il**; the final vowel remains in **li**. (For more on metaphony, see ch. 12.)

There are also exceptional forms in the masculine nominative singular with metaphony: **il** instead of **ẹl**, **cil** instead of **cẹl**. These forms should probably not be regarded as Gallicisms produced by influence of French nominative singular **il** but as results of the same factors that produced **il** independently in French—that is, the analogy of masculine nominative singular and plural **qui** (CL quī) and masculine nominative plural **il**, where the metaphony is etymological (CL ĭllī).

Another unusual form in the masculine nominative singular is **le** instead of **lo**, from CL nominative singular ĭlle, and resembling **paire**, **paubre** in its masculine unstressed **-e**.

The vowel **i**, in final or stressed position, functions as an alternative marker for the feminine nominative singular, beside final **-a**, in a number of demonstratives.

Personal pronoun, nominative singular **il, ilh** 'she' (beside **ela**):

> S'**ela** m'a trag may de cen vetz premeyra   19.34

>> If she has lured me more than a hundred times first

> qu'**il** m'a mentit   19.34 var.

>> for she has lied to me

Definite article, nominative singular **li** 'the' (beside **la**):

> Religïons fon **li** premieir'enpresza   26.25

>> The first religious order was founded

Nominative singular **cist** 'this' (beside **césta**):

> **Cist** fabla est az aquest mon
> semblans   Appel, *Provenzalische* 111.49

>> This fable resembles this world.

Nominative singular **aquist** 'this' (beside **aquésta**):

> **Aquist** verge vellava en oracion.   Appel, *Provenzalische* 119.30

>> This virgin would stay awake in prayer.

Nominative singular **cil** 'that one' (beside **céla**):

> que **cil** que plus en degr'aver
> no n'a jes   18.27–28

>> For she who should have had the most [love]
>> has none at all.

Nominative singular **aquil** 'that' (beside **aquéla**):

> **Aquilh** guerra es pieitz que de vezi   Appel, *Provenzalische* 78.12

>> That war [between husband and wife] is worse than with a
>> neighbor.

The origin of OOc **il** 'she' has been traced to a hypothetical VL *ĭLLĪ, nominative singular, masculine, from CL ĭLLE, with influence of QUĪ, the origin of OOc nominative singular, masculine **il** (see above), on the supposition that this *ĭLLĪ, like QUĪ, might have served in the feminine as well. Presumably the marker generalized from **il** to the other demonstratives that have it. This suggestion notwithstanding, however, Grandgent admitted that these forms are "hard to explain" (118.3; cf. 125.2).

Guilhem IX, *Pos de chantar m'es pres talenz*

In 1119, Guilhem fell ill and took steps to arrange for his burial; he recovered, however, and joined a crusade the following year against the Moors in Spain. Fear of death during his sickness may have led to the composition of this song, which blends overtones of pilgrimage or crusade, monastic retreat, and death (Bond li–lii). Another hypothesis suggests that the poem was composed in 1111 or 1112, when Guilhem's son was about twelve years old and Foulque of Anjou about twenty-two (Riquer 139).

1
Pos de chantar m'es pres talenz,
farai un vers don sui dolénz;
mais non serai obedíenz
en Peitau ni en Lemozi.

2
Qu'era m'en irai en eisil;
en gran paor, en gran peril,
en guerra laisserai mon fil,
e faran li mal siei vezin.

3
Lo departirs m'es aitan grieus
del seignorage de Peitieus;
en garda de Folcon d'Angieus
lais la terra e·l son cozi.

4
Si Folcos d'Angieus no·l socor
e·l reis de cui ieu tenc m'onor,
faran li mal tut li plusor
felon Gascon et Angevi.

5
Si ben non ès savis ni pros,
cant ieu serai partiz de vos,
vias l'auran tornat en jos,
car lo veiran jov'e mesqui.

6
Per merce prec mon compaignon;
s'anc li fi tort, q'il m'o perdon,
et il prec en Jezu del tron
en romans et en son latin.

7
De proeza e de joi fui, 25
mais ara partem ambedui;
et eu irai m'en a scellui
on tut peccador troban fi.

8
Mout ai estat cuendes e gais,
mas nostre seigner no·l vol mais.
Ar non puesc plus soffrir lo fais,
tant soi aprochatz de la fi.

9
Tot ai guerpit cant amar sueill,
cavalaria et orgoill,
e pos Dieu platz, tot o acueill,
e prec li que·m reteng'am si.

10
Toz mos amics prec a la mort
que·i vengan tut e m'onren fort;
qu'eu ai avut joi e deport
loing e pres et e mon aizi.

11
Aissi guerpisc joi e deport
e vair e gris e sembeli.

Meter:

    a   a   a   b
    8   8   8   8
    Ch. relig. 10 s 4, 1–2.
    a = **-enz, -il, -ieus, -or, -os, -on, -ui, -ais, -olh, -ort**
    b = **-in**.
    Frank 44:7.

P-C 183,10. Major editions: Pasero, no. 11; Riquer, no. 8; Bond, no. 11.

Music: For transcription, see page 561. The fragmentary melody, perhaps from this song, is recorded in the unique manuscript of a fourteenth-century Occitan religious play with lyric insertions, the *Jeu de sainte Agnès* (Rome, Vatican Library, Chigiani, C.V. 151, fol. 84b). A stage direction in Latin and Occitan accompanying the song reads: MODO SURGUNT OMNES ET TENDUNT IN MEDIO CAMPI ET FACIUNT OMNES SIMUL PLANCTUM IN SONU DEL COMTE DE PEYTIEU ('Now all rise and go to the middle of the field and all at once perform a lament to the melody of the count of Poitou'). Among the surviving songs of Guilhem IX, this one is most like a planctus, or lament. On the following folio the scribe failed to continue notating the melody. Facsimile in Bond 144. Editions: Fernández de la Cuesta and Lafont 48; van der Werf and Bond 151*; Switten and Chickering 1. 41–43 and cassette 1.

Eight transcriptions: *C* fol. 230–v; *D*ᵃ fol. 190v; *I* fol. 142v; *K* fol. 128; *N₁* = *N* fol. 230; *N₂* = *N* fols. 234v–235; *R* fol. 8; *a¹* pp. 463–64. Base *D*ᵃ. See the facsimile of ms. *D* (*Canzoniere,* vol. 2).

Stanza order:

D^aIK	1	2	3	4	5	6	7	8	9	10	11
N_1N_2	1	2	3	4	5	6	7	8	9	10	—
a^1	1	3	4	2	5	7	9	6	10	8	—
C	1	3	4	2	5	7	9	6	10	11	—
R	1	9	3	4	2	6	10	7	—	—	—

Rejected readings in the base manuscript: None.

Selected variants: (5) irei $N_1N_2a^1$. (7) laisserai $D^aN_1N_2a^1$, laissarai *CIKR*. (12) ·l son D^a, son IKN_1Ra^1, mon *C*. (28) on merce clamon pellegri *C*. (36) li D^a, lui *IK*. (39) agut $N_1N_2a^1$.

Notes

(1) **es pres**] When used intransitively, **prendre** means 'to befall' and forms the present perfect tense (Fr. *passé composé*) with **eser**. See "Present Perfect Tense" in chapter 25.

(2) **farai**] 'I shall make' the present song, implying that he has not made it yet when he begins to sing; a fictional effect of spontaneity. **don**] 'About what (I am sad) about.'

(3) **obedïenz**] 'Obedient,' implying 'I will no longer be able to serve God and the king' (Roncaglia, "Obediens" 612).

(7) **laisserai**] On the vowel **e** instead of **a** (**laissarai**), see chapter 4. **mon fil**] The troubadour's son would succeed him as Guilhem X of Aquitaine, the father of Eleanor of Aquitaine.

(11) **Folcon d'Angieus**] Foulque V, count of Anjou (1108–44), cousin of Guilhem's son after a marriage in 1109 (Bond 79).

(14) **e·l reis de cui ieu tenc m'onor**] Louis VI of France, "the Fat," Guilhem's nominal overlord.

(19) **viás**] 'Quickly'; CL vɪvācĭus adv.

(20) The poet's son Guilhem, born in 1099, would have been twenty years old if this poem was written in 1119; not, perhaps, too old to be considered **jov'e mesqui** 'young and weak' by his father.

(21) **mon compaignon**] Perhaps the troubadour's wife, Philippa-Mathilde, in 1119 a nun at Fontevrault, wronged by Guilhem for the sake of his mistress Maubergeonne (Bond 80); or perhaps Foulque of Anjou (v. 11). The forms **li** 22 and **il** 22, 23 may be either masculine or feminine.

(23) **il prec**] Optative without **que** (ch. 26).

(24) **son latin**] Latin seen as the language of Christ—i.e., the church.

(26) **ambedui**] The poet on one hand, **proeza** and **joi** on the other.

(28) **tut peccador**] Nom. pl. masc., shifting declension.

(33) **sueill**] From **solẹr**; root **sọl-** + -yod (1st sg.); **ill** spells **lh**, diphthongization of **ọ >ué**. Rhymes with **orgoill**, **acueill**; the underlying rhyme is **-ọlh**, whether diphthongized or not.

(34) **cavalaria**] "Almost entirely devoid of ethical and ideological connotations. . . . In the twelfth century it most often designates the horse-

manship, skill, agility and effectiveness of the knight as a warrior. It also commonly means simply 'cavalry', and occasionally, 'deeds of arms'" (Paterson 64).

(35) **o**] Refers to the preceding idea of renunciation of worldly goods. **acueill**] From **acolhir**; cf. **sueill** 33.

(36) **reteng'**] Pres. subj. 3rd sg. of **retener** 'to retain,' 'to appoint as a retainer.' On the feudal metaphor, see Cropp, *"Retener."*

(37) Guilhem may have had in mind a ritual of dying similar to that recorded at the death of William Marshal in 1219; see Duby, *Marshal*, ch. 1. **a la mort**] The definite article means 'my.'

(41) **guerpisc**] On the ending, see "Roots Ending in -[sk], -[j]s" in chapter 19.

(42) Furs used in trimming luxurious garments.

Exercise

Interpret the expression of gender, case, and number in the following passages:

1. en **esta** terra 25.85
2. e formet **cest**'amor de loing 15.37
3. Sor, **aquest** hom es enginhos 9.31
4. E fetz **aquestas** chansos 5.17
5. **ilh** no podon sufrir **los** perilhs 25.9
6. Amics, la vostra valenssa / saben **li** pro e **li** valen 6.33–34
7. (Love is truly lost,) que **cil** que plus en degr'aver / no n'a jes 18.27–28
8. Plaguas me feyron mays de cen / **aquella** ves 9.51–52

PART 2

Historical Phonology

CHAPTER 11

Production of Vowels; Vowels in Latin

PRODUCTION OF VOWELS

Vowel sounds may be described by the positions of the organs in the mouth that produce them. The most important of these organs is the tongue, which may be moved horizontally to a position in the front, the center, or the back of the mouth, and vertically to a high, middle, or low position. The lips may be either spread or rounded.

The highest point of the tongue takes the various positions indicated in figure 11.1, to produce the vowels of Latin, Italian, and Spanish.

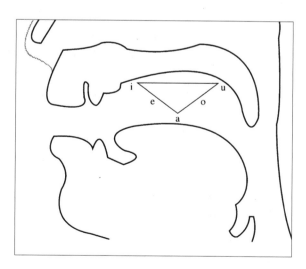

FIG. 11.1. *The vowel triangle showing the tongue in position to pronounce* [a]

89

If the highest point of the tongue assumes a high front position in the mouth, the vowel produced is [i]; the high back position produces [u]. The mid-front vowel is [e], and the back is [o]. The low central vowel is [a]. The lips are rounded for [u] and [o], but spread for [a], [e], and [i].

The vowel of OOc **tu** (like Fr. *tu*), which will be written here with the phonetic symbol [y], is produced with the tongue in the high front position, as for [i], and the lips rounded, as for [u]. If, while pronouncing [i], one rounds the lips, the sound produced becomes [y]. One may also arrive at [y] by moving the tongue forward while pronouncing [u], keeping the lips rounded.

The vowel triangle in figure 11.1 will underlie subsequent figures showing the vowel system in CL, VL, and OOc.

VARIETIES OF LATIN

Like all living languages, Latin varied in pronunciation and in other ways from place to place, from time to time, and among speakers in a given place at a given time. The term *Classical Latin* (abbreviated CL) refers to the formal language of written texts that have become canonical, like Vergil's *Aeneid* or the philosophical treatises of Cicero, and presumably to the spoken language of formal usage, as in Cicero's orations before the Senate.

The term *Vulgar Latin* (abbreviated VL) refers to more informal usage, principally in spoken language. For our understanding of VL we depend on the eventual development of the Romance languages out of spoken Latin, and we find support in scattered written but informal texts, such as inscriptions at Pompeii and elsewhere, and the comedies of Plautus. In his informal letters Cicero shows traces of VL usage.

The validity of the distinction between CL and VL has been debated.[1] It is neither rigorous nor exact, and yet it is useful for understanding the development of Romance languages such as Occitan. CL and VL were contemporary phases of Latin; because CL provides a well-documented point of departure, however, we shall trace the development of the language from CL through VL, as though it were an intermediary stage, and into OOc.

In citing etyma of OOc words in the Glossary, we shall also refer to *Late Latin* (LL), *Church Latin* (ChL), and *Medieval Latin*

---

[1] See Väänänen 3–6. Väänänen uses the term *Vulgar Latin* to refer to "toutes les particularités et les tendances plus ou moins vivaces, propres à la langue populaire et familière, et qui se soustraient à la norme classique et, en général, littéraire" (6). For an overview of recent work showing that Latin remained comprehensible to Romance speakers longer than was formerly believed, see Banniard.

(ML). *LL* refers to the language of written texts compiled from the second to about the sixth century A.D.; *ChL,* to the distinctive language of ecclesiastical discourse, either written or oral (as in the liturgy); and *ML,* to texts written in Latin as the high language in contrast to the vernacular, from about the ninth century through the thirteenth.

VOWELS AND POSITION OF STRESS IN CLASSICAL LATIN

Classical Latin had five vowel positions: [a, e, i, o, u]. Each of these could be either long or short.[2] A long vowel is conventionally indicated with the mark ¯, as in Ā, Ē, Ī, Ō, Ū, and a short one with the mark ˘, as in Ă, Ĕ, Ĭ, Ŏ, Ŭ.

CL also had the diphthongs AE, AU, OE, UI, which were intrinsically long.

CL stress in words of two syllables always fell on the first syllable, or penult (from PAENE ULTĬMA 'almost last'):

CŎRPUS > **cọrs** 'body, person, self' (It. *corpo,* Sp. *cuerpo,* Fr. *corps,* E. *corps, corpse, corpus*)

PĂTREM > **paire** 'father' (It. *padre,* Sp. *padre,* Fr. *père*; cf. E. *paternal*)

RĒGEM > **rẹi** 'king' (It. *re,* Sp. *rey,* Fr. *roi*; cf. E. *royal*)

In words of three or more syllables, CL stress fell on the penult if the penult was a long syllable—that is, if it contained a long vowel or ended in a consonant.

The penult contained a long vowel in words such as these:

CANTĀRE > **cantar** 'to sing' (It. *cantare,* Sp. *cantar,* Fr. *chanter,* E. *to chant*)

PARTĪRE > **partir** 'to share' (It. *partire,* Sp. *partir,* Fr. *partir,* E. *to part*)

AMŌREM > **amọr** 'love' (It. *amore,* Sp. *amor,* Fr. *amour*)

The penult ended in a consonant, which created a long syllable:

ĬNFAN-TEM 'not speaking' > **enfan** 'child' (It. *infante,* Sp. *infante,* Fr. *enfant,* E. *infant*)

CABAL-LUM 'inferior horse, nag' > **caval** 'horse' (It. *cavallo,* Sp. *caballo,* Fr. *cheval*; cf. E. *cavalry*)

DĬŬR-NUM 'daily' (three syllables) > **jọrn** 'day' (It. *giorno,* Fr. *jour*; cf. E. *journal*)

[2] There was no qualitative difference in CL between long and short [a], but in the other vowels length correlated with relative closeness, and shortness with relative openness; see Sturtevant, par. 114, 119, 125.

Otherwise, stress receded to the antepenult (from ANTE PAENE ULTIMA 'before almost last'):

PĔRDĔRE (stressed pérdere) > **pęrdre** 'to lose' (It. *pérdere*, Sp. *perdér* [with change of conjugation], Fr. *perdre*; cf. E. *perdition*)

ĂRBŎREM (stressed árborem) > **arbre** 'tree' (It. *álbero*, Sp. *árbol*, Fr. *arbre*; cf. E. *arbor*)

GLĂDĬUM (stressed gládium) > **glázi** 'sword' (Fr. *glaive*, E. *glaive*)

HŎMĬNEM (stressed hóminem) > **ǫ́me** 'man' (It. *uómo*, Sp. *hombre*, Fr. *homme*)

DŎMĬNAM (stressed dóminam) > **dǫmna** 'lady' (It. *donna*, Sp. *dueña*, Fr. *dame*, E. *dame*)

A word stressed on its last syllable is termed an oxytone; on the penult, a paroxytone; on the antepenult, a proparoxytone.

STRESSED VOWELS IN VULGAR LATIN

In Vulgar Latin, vowels ceased to be distinguished into long versus short, as they had been in CL, and came to differ in four degrees of openness of the passage through the mouth (i.e., vertical tongue position) instead of three. In VL the vertical tongue positions range from high [i, u] to high-mid [ẹ, ọ] to low-mid [ę, ǫ] to low [a].

To the CL system of ten vowels, there succeeded the VL system of seven (see fig. 11.2).

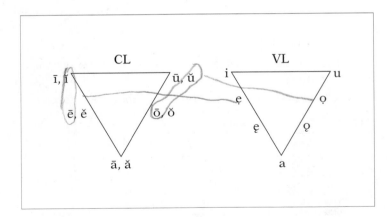

FIG. 11.2. *The vowel systems of CL and VL*

In the process of transition from one system to the other, three mergers took place:

1. CL short ĭ and long ē merged as close [ẹ];
2. CL short ŭ and long ō merged as close [ọ];
3. CL long ā and short ă became indistinguishable.

The CL diphthong AE became a monophthong, open [ę], while
OE became close [ẹ]. The diphthongs AU and UI remained unchanged.

CHANGES IN STRESS POSITION
IN VULGAR LATIN

VL retains the stress distribution of CL except for certain limited
cases.

1. In hiatus (that is, immediately before another vowel), VL
[ẹ], produced from CL short ĭ and long ē, could no longer bear
stress. VL [ẹ] in hiatus was therefore reduced to yod as stress ad-
vanced to the following vowel:

> CL MŬLĬĔREM 'woman' (in the accusative, stressed
> mulíerem) > VL MULIĘREM > **molhę́r** 'wife' (Sp. *mujér*)

> CL MŬLĬĔR (nominative form, stressed múlier) > **mǫ́lher**
> (It. *móglie*)

This shift in stress position underlies the shifting declension of the
word in OOc (cf. ch. 23).

2. The consonant cluster formed of a stop (voiceless [p, t, k];
voiced [b, d, g]; see ch. 14) plus a liquid [l, r], which in CL formed
the onset of the following syllable, came, in VL, to have the syllabic
break between the two consonants, and so closed the preceding
syllable:

> CL ĬNTĔGRUM (stressed ínte-grum; cf. E. *integer*) > VL
> /ęntę́g-ro/ > **entier** 'whole' (It. *intero*, Sp. *entero*, Fr.
> *entier*, E. *entire*)

> CL ĂLĂCREM (stressed ála-crem) > VL *ALĔCREM (stressed
> /alę́c-rem/; with dissimilation of the vowel) > **alę́gre**
> 'joyful'

3. By a process called recomposition, CL words compounded
of simpler elements were felt once again as separable units and
stressed accordingly:

> CL CŎNVĔNIT 'it comes together,' stressed as one word, cón-
> venit; it is a compound of CUM 'with, together' + VĔNIT 'it
> comes.' By recomposition the word became VL /con-
> véne/ > **conve** (It. *conviene*, Sp. *conviene*, Fr. *convient*),
> stressed like the simple verb **ve** (It. *viene*, Sp. *viene*,
> Fr. *vient*)

Boeci

The fragmentary Occitan paraphrase of Boethius's Consolation of Philosophy *is regarded as the oldest literary text preserved in the language, having been written, perhaps, around A.D. 1000. Only 258 lines long, the fragment narrates Boethius's imprisonment, as here, and then describes the visit of Lady Philosophy, as in book 1 of the* Consolation.

1
Nos jove omne   quandius que nos estam,
de gran follia   per folledat parllam,
quar no nos membra   per cui viur' esperam,
qui nos soste   tan quan per terr' annam
e qui nos pais   que no murem de fam,
per cui salv esmes   per pur tan que·ll clamam.

2
Nos jove omne   meham ta mal jovent
qu'us hon o preza   si·s trada son parent,
senor ni par   si·ll mena malament,
ni l'us vel l'aitre   si·s fai fals sacrament.
Quant o a fait,   miia no s'en repent,
enivers Deu   no·n fai emendament.
Pro non es gaigre,   si penedenza·n pren:
dis que l'a presa,   miia nonqua la té,
qu'eps los forfaizc   sempre fai epsamen.
E laisa·n Deu,   lo grant omnipotent,
ki·l mort et vius   tot a in jutjamen.
Eps li satan   son en so mandamen:
ses Deu licencia   ja non faran torment.

3
En anzs en dies   foren ome fello;
mal omе foren,   aora sunt peior.
Volg i Boecis   metre quastiazo;
auvent la gent   fazi'en so sermo,
creessen Deu   qui sostenc passio,
per lui aurien   trastút redemcio.
Molt s'en penét,   quar no i mes foiso;
anz per eveia   lo mesdren e preiso.

4
Donz fo Boecis,   lo corps ag bo e pró,
cui tan amet   Torquator Mallios.
De sapiencia   no fo trop nüallos;
tant en retenc   que de tót no·n fo blos.
Tan bo essemple   en laiset entre nos
no cuid qu'e Roma   om de so saber fos.

5
Cóms fo de Roma   e ac ta gran valor
aprob Mallio,   lo rei emperador,
el era·l meler   de tota la onor;   35
de tót l'emperi·l   tenien per senor.
Mas d'una causa   nom avia genzor:
de sapiencia   l'apellaven doctor.

6
Quan veng la fis   Mallio Torquator,
donc venc Boeci   ta gran dolors al cor: 40
no cuid aprob   altre dols li demor.

7
Morz fo Mallios   Torquator dunt eu dig.
Ec vos e Roma   l'emperador Teiric;
del fiel Deu   no volg aver amig.   45

8
No credet Deu,   lo nostre creator.
Per zo no·l volg   Boecis a senor,
ni gens de lui   nó volg tener s'onor.

9
Eu lo chastia   ta bé ab so sermo,
e Teiríx col   tot e mal sa razó;   50
per grant evea   de lui volg far fello.
Fez u breu faire   per grán decepcio,
e de Boeci   escriure fez lo nóm,
e si·l tramét   e Grecia la regio.
De part Boeci   lor manda tal raizó:
que passen mar   guarnit de contenço,   55
eu lor redrá   Roma per traazo.
Lo sénz Teiric   miga no fo de bo:
fez sos mes segre,   si·lz fez metr'e preso.

10
E·l Capitoli,   l'endema al di clar,
lai o solíen   las altras leis jutjar,   60
lai veng lo reis   sà felni'a menár;
lai fo Boecis   e foren i soi par.
Lo reis lo pres   de felni'a reptar,
qu'el trametía   los breus ultra la mar,
Roma volia   a óbs los Grécx tradár.   65
Pero Boeci   anc no venc e pesat.
Sál en estánt   e cuidet s'en salvar;
l'om no·l laiset   a salvament annár.
Cil li falíren   qu'él solí'aiudar;
fez lo lo reis   e sa charcer gitar.   70

11

Ec vos Boeci   cadegut en afan,
e granz kadenas   qui l'están apesant;
reclama Deu,   de cel lo rei, lo grant:
"Domine pater,   e te·m fiav'eu tant,
e cui marce   tuit peccador estant!
Las mias musas,   qui ant perdut lor cánt,
de sapiencia   anava eu ditan;
plor tota dia,   faz cosdumna d'efant,
tuit a plorár   repairen mei talant,"

Meter: Decasyllabic lines with caesura after the fourth syllable, grouped together
  in assonating (frequently rhyming) laisses. Either the first or the second half
  line, or both, may be feminine—that is, may have an unstressed and un-
  counted final syllable or (infrequently) two such syllables. The same form is
  found in the Oxford *Chanson de Roland* and other chansons de geste.
Major editions: Lavaud and Machicot, vv. 1–80; Schwarze, vv. 1–80.
Manuscript: Orléans, Bibliothèque Municipale 444 (anc. 374), pp. 269–71.
  Written in the eleventh century in the Limousin.
Rejected readings in the base manuscript: (3) viuri. (4) terra. (8) que us. (11) a *om.*
  in ms.; supplied. (14) bresa. (15) que eps; lor forfarzc. (16) E *supplied.* (20)
  Ensanzs. (23) fazia en. (26) Mas molt. (28) lo *supplied by Schwarze.* (38) u
  nom. (56) contenco. (59) metre e. (60) dia. (66) a óbs los Grécx   Roma vo-
  lia tradár. (68) Sál él en. (70) solient. (73) kdenas.

Notes

(1) **Nos jove omne**] Proleptic (anticipatory) position. The clause is introduced by the subordinating conjunction **quandius**; the subject **nos** is
  emphatically expressed twice, once in the prolepsis and once with the
  verb (cf. verbs without overt subjects in the following lines, **parllam**,
  esperam, **annam**, etc.). **Jove omne** is the predicate nominative: 'As
  long as we are young men.' Hiatus in **jove / omne**. For more on prolepsis, see chapter 24.

(5) **murem**] Indicative: 'who nourishes us so that we do not die,' not 'so
  that we should not die.'

(6) **esmes**] CL sŭmus; It. *siamo*, Sp. *somos*, Fr. *sommes*. In **esmes** the **-mes**
  represents the end of the etymological form, with substitution of the
  root **es-** (as in 3rd sg.) for sŭ-. The normal OOc form is **em**.

(7) **Nos jove omne**]: 'We, (as) young men,' not necessarily implying that
  the narrator is young at the time he speaks.

(8) **o**] Anticipates the clause in the second half line. **si·s**] The **·s** is an "ethical dative" that may be omitted in translation.

(9) **senor ni par**] Proleptic, represented redundantly by **·ll** in the second
  half line.

(10) **vel**] Contraction of **vas**, **ves** 'toward' with the article (*S-W* 8: 591).
  aitre] Emended by earlier editors to **altre**, but the unusual form ap-

pears to be an instance of yodicism (see ch. 16). **l'us vel l'aitre**] Proleptic; **l'us** is the subject of **fai**; **vel l'aitre** is the complement.

(11) **o**] Refers to the idea expressed in **fai fals sacrament**. **miia**] The spelling perhaps indicates the reduction of the c in MĪCAM to a yod by accelerated lenition; cf. **miga** 11.58, with normal lenition. On lenition, see chapter 15.

(13) **Pro**] Neuter adj.

(14) **té**] The acute accent occurs in the ms. here and elsewhere in *Boeci*. It appears tó mark stressed syllables or words (Avalle, *Letteratura* 29–31).

(15) **eps, epsamen**] The **p** is etymological (CL ĬPSUM), normally a yod in troubadour manuscripts (**eis, eissamen**).

(17) **·l mort et vius**] 'The dead [man] and living men.'

(19) **Deu**] Obl. sg. with gen. meaning: 'the permission of God.'

(20) **dies**] Perhaps a Latinism, acc. pl. DĬĒS. **ome, fello**] Both words of the shifting declension.

(22) **volg**] In troubadour manuscripts, **volc**. **Boecis**] Boethius (c. 480–524), author of the *Consolation of Philosophy* and other works. The OOc author depicts him as more strongly Christian than he was (vv. 24–25), but medieval tradition adopted him as a Christian author. **metre quastiazo**] 'To chastise.'

(23) **auvent**] CL AUDĪRE, OOc **auzir**, gives **auvir** in Limousin dialect (Lavaud and Machicot 49).

(24) **creessen**] Past subj., paraphrasing Boethius's sermon.

(26) **mes**] OOc **medre, meire**, from CL MĔTĔRE 'to harvest,' rather than OOc **metre**, from CL MĬTTĔRE 'to send' (Schwarze 163 n.).

(28) **ag**] Cf. **volg** 22.

(29) **Torquator Mallios**] The emperor Manlius Torquator is a fiction created by the OOc poet. Apparently he misunderstood the beginning of the *Life* of Boethius, which declares that he was of the 'family of Manlius Torquator' (Schwarze 44), meaning the biological family of this illustrious ancestor; but the poet took 'family' as 'following, retainers, servants' and assumed that Boethius's lord must have been an emperor. The historical predecessor of Theodoric (**Teiric** 44) was Odoacer, who deposed Romulus Augustulus, emperor of Rome, in A.D. 476, which marks the traditional date for the end of antiquity and the beginning of the Middle Ages. Odoacer ruled as king of Italy until 493. **Mallios**] Three syllables, stressed on the penultimate: **Mallíos**. The final syllable is treated as unstressed at the caesura and hence is not counted, in vv. 35 and 43. In v. 29 the unstressed final syllable provides assonance and is counted; such usage may be regarded as a Latinism, since, in Medieval Latin, rhyme could be based exclusively on unstressed syllables.

(32–33) **Tan** . . . **(que)**] 'Such a good example . . . [that] . . . '

(33) **cuid**] Intervention of the narrator (1st sg.). **fos**] Subjunctive after a negative verb of belief.

(34–36) **ta(n)** . . . **(que)**] 'He had such great merit . . . [that] he was the most highly regarded.'

(36) **méler**] Shifting declension, masc. nom. sg.

(40) **veng**] Cf. **ag** 28, **volg** 22; but also **venc** 41. **Mallio Torquator**] Oblique expressing possession ('the end of M. T. came') or dative ('the end came to M. T.').

(41) **ta gran dolors**] On the case forms, cf. 9.65 note. Case marked only on the noun. **ta** . . . **(que)**] 'Such great grief . . . [that] . . . '

(44) **Teiric**] Theodoric the Great (A.D. 455–526), king of the Ostrogoths, later king of Italy.

(45) **Deu**] Obl. sg., indicating possession ('God's faithful man') or dative ('the man faithful to God'); cf. **Deu licencia** 19, **la fis Mallio Torquator** 40: 'He did not want to make [to begin to have, **aver** inchoative] a friend of the man faithful to God.'

(46) **credét**] Pret. 3rd sg., from the infinitive **creire** (here the root **cred-**, as in CL CRĒDĔRE), like **vendet** (**vendre**), **cantet** (**cantar**).

(49) **Eu lo**] El lo, with reduction of the first **l** to [w] by wawicism (ch. 16).

(49–59) The present tense forms in laisse 9 (**chastia** 49, **col** 50, **tramét** 54, **manda** 55) are interspersed among preterits (**volg** 51, **fez** 52, **fez** 53, **fo** 58, **fez** 59, **fez** 59). They seem to be the present of indirect discourse— that is, in paraphrase of a discourse that was originally in the present, except for **col** 50.

(53) **de Boeci**] Proleptic: **lo nóm de Boeci**.

(55) **Boeci**] Oblique singular with genitive meaning.

(57) **eu**] = **el**.

(58) **Teiric**] Oblique singular with genitive meaning.

(61) **leis**] 'Punishments,' '(Geld-)Busse, Strafe' *S-W* 4: 357. The sense of **altras**, 'other (than the one in the story),' is close to 'ordinary.'

(65) **trametía**] The imperfect for background of a preterit (**pres** . . . **a reptar** 64) is tantamount to a pluperfect (cf. "Imperfect Tense" in ch. 25).

(68) **sál**] Historical present for dramatic relief (cf. "Present Tense in Past Narrative" in ch. 25).

(73) **e** = **en**.

(75) DOMINE PATER] 'O Lord father' (Latin vocative).

(76) **e** = **en**. **tuit**] Masc. nom. pl.

(77) **musas**] Two meanings: 'muses' who have lost their song, but also 'poems' that Boethius would formerly write.

1. Describe the articulatory position of the vowels [a, e, i, o, u].

2. Describe the vowels in Fr. *tu* 'thou' and *tout* 'all.' What is the phonological difference between them? between the stressed vowels of Fr. *tu* and Fr. *type* (Sp. *tipo*, It. *tipo*)?

3. How many distinct vowel sounds did CL have?

4. What are the two front vowels of CL? the two back vowels? the two mid-vowels? the central vowel?

5. State the conditions required in CL for a paroxytone and for a proparoxytone.

6. Describe the three vowel mergers of VL.

Stressed Vowels

Stressed vowels and diphthongs in Vulgar Latin remained mostly unchanged in OOc, with the exceptions of VL /u/ and /ǫ/ (see "Unconditioned Changes" below) and developments conditioned by specific contexts.

CL	VL	OOc	
Ă, Ā >	/a/ >	**a**	RĂDĬUM 'ray' > **rai**; GRĀTUM 'pleasing' > **grat**
Ĕ >	/ę/ >	**ę**	ĬNFĔRNUM 'Hell' > **enfęrn**
Ē, Ĭ >	/ẹ/ >	**ẹ**	HĂBĒRE 'to have' > **avẹr**; ChL MĬSSAM 'Mass' > **mẹsa**
Ī >	/i/ >	**i**	TRĪSTEM 'sad' > **trist**
Ŏ >	/ǫ/ >	**ǫ**	FŎRTEM 'strong' > **fǫrt**
Ō, Ŭ >	/ọ/ >	**ọ** > [u]	FLŌREM 'flower' > **flọr** [flur]; BŬCCAM 'cheek' > **bǫca** [buka] 'mouth'
Ū >	/u/ >	**u** > [y]	PLŪS 'more' > **plus** [plys]
AE >	/ę/ >	**ę**	CAELUM 'sky' > **cęl**
OE >	/ę/ >	**ę**	POENAM 'punishment' > **pęna**
AU >	/au/ >	**au**	PAUPĔRUM 'poor' > **paubre**
UI >	/ui/ >	**ui**	CUI 'to whom' > **cui**, obl. sg. of **qui** (1), (2) (see Glossary)

UNCONDITIONED CHANGES

Fronting of CL ū to OOc [y]

Classical Latin ū became Vulgar Latin /u/, which became OOc [y], as in French, but not in Italian or Spanish. This change is difficult to detect in many words: Did the vowel of **luna** sound like French [y] in *lune*, or like Italian and Spanish [u] in *luna*? However, the change seems to have left a trace in spellings where the alternation of **u** and **i** implies a front rounded [y]:

> **onchura** or **onchira** 'seasoning' (CL ŪNCTŪRAM)
>
> **cominal** or **comunal** 'common' (CL COMMŪNĀLEM)

It has left a more subtle trace in a word such as **piusela** 'maiden,' from VL *PŪLLICELLAM, where the VL /u/ came to be followed by the semivowel [u̯], or [w], as a result of the vocalization of [l]; the group [uu̯] must have passed through a stage [yu̯], in order to produce the recorded [iu̯] by dissimilation (see **despieuselatge** in the Glossary).

The change of /u/ to [y] must have begun after the eighth century, when Occitan and Catalan started to become distinct, since this change did not occur in Catalan. Some scholars hold that it was completed by the tenth or eleventh century, while others claim that it was not completed until the thirteenth.[1]

Raising of VL /ọ/ to OOc [u]

Vulgar Latin close /ọ/ was raised to OOc [u], but the spelling was unaffected until the fourteenth century, when *o* came to be written *ou*, as in French. The change may well have been in process during the twelfth and thirteenth centuries.[2] Pronounce **Tọlọsa** like French *Toulouse*, except for the final vowel.

> FLŌREM 'flower' > **flọr** [flur]
>
> BŬCCAM 'cheek' > **bọca** [buka] 'mouth'; cf. Fr. *bouche* [buš]

Note that these two changes must have occurred one after the other, first /u/ > [y], then /ọ/ > [u]. If /ọ/ had become [u] before [u] shifted to [y], the vowels in **luna** and **flor** would have become identical.

Both these changes are difficult to detect, and philologists are not unanimous regarding their chronology. For speakers of Modern Occitan, in which both shifts have occurred, it seems natural to suppose that the changes were already present in the language of the troubadours. For scholars less familiar with Modern Occitan than with Classical Latin or with modern languages in which these changes have not taken place, such as Italian or Spanish, it is more

---

[1] For support of the early date, see Rohlfs 44 and note 119 (with references); for the late date, see Lafont 27. See also Grafström, *Graphie*, par. 3. Doubt that the palatalization of [u] occurred in OOc at all has been expressed by Cremonesi 38–39.

[2] Thus Grandgent 20; according to Lafont 27, it occurred by the fourteenth century. Spelling changed in the fourteenth century (Anglade, *Grammaire* 77–78).

congenial to consider the language of the troubadours without them. The view adopted in this book takes a slight risk of modernizing OOc on the basis of the slender evidence available.

CONDITIONED CHANGES

Diphthongization

Stressed open /ę/ and open /ǫ/ diphthongized under the influence of a following semivowel (yod or waw). Stressed open /ę/ produced **ié**, while stressed open /ǫ/ produced **uó** or **ué**.

/ę́/ + yod > **ié**

> MĔLĬUS > **mélhs, miélhs** 'better'; the yod produced from the ĭ with the loss of syllabic value (ch. 13) has combined with the consonant that intervenes between it and the stressed vowel.

> The preterit 1st sg. ending **-ęi** becomes **-ięi** in **miriéi, perdiéi**, etc.; the yod is in hiatus.

/ę́/ + waw > **ié**

> VL GRĔVEM > **gréu, griéu**; the waw represents CL v, made final by the fall of the last syllable.

> ĔGO 'I' > **éu, iéu**; the waw is in hiatus after loss of intervocalic G and change of final -o into waw.

/ǫ́/ + yod > **uó, ué**

> VL vŏLĔo 'I want' > **vólh, vuólh, vuélh**; the yod, produced by reduction of the unstressed penult, combines with **l** to form palatal **l**; synchronically, yod is a sporadic marker for the first person singular (ch. 2).

> ŏCŬLUM 'eye' > **ólh, uólh, uélh**; the yod, produced from the c by simplification (ch. 16), combines with the L to form palatal **lh**.

> NŏCTEM 'night' > **nuóit, nuéit, nóch**; the yod, produced from the [k] by simplification, combines with the T to produce **-ch** (assibilation, ch. 18).

/ǫ́/ + waw > **uó, ué**

> BŏVEM 'ox' > **bóu, buóu, buéu**; the waw derives from CL v, made final.

> FŏCUM 'fire' > **fóc, fuóc, fuéc**; the waw, produced by reduction of the final syllable (VL /fǫcu/), has perhaps combined with the [k]; or perhaps the velar [k] is capable itself of triggering diphthongization.

Diphthongization does not occur generally in the *Boeci*, c. A.D. 1000 (see ch. 11), but is found commonly in the earliest troubadours.[3]

DĔUM 'God' > **Deu** in *Boeci* (11.12, etc.), but **Dieu** in Guilhem IX (**Dieus** 8.23, **Dieu** 10.35)

MĔĪ 'my' nom. pl. masc. > **mei** in *Boeci* (11.80), but *SĔĪ 'his' nom. pl. masc. > **siei** in Guilhem IX (10.8)

CŎLLĬGIT 'he receives' > **col** in *Boeci* (11.50) but **cuelh** in Marcabru (12.59)

However, the undiphthongized forms continued to be used commonly throughout the troubadour period—for example, **Deu** beside **Dieu** in Peire Cardenal (26.8, 26.16). Perhaps the troubadours pronounced either the simple vowel or the diphthong indifferently; a more satisfactory explanation, although it complicates the task of reading OOc aloud, would suggest that undiphthongized spellings were perhaps intended to represent the diphthong. In either case, the student may feel satisfied to pronounce the diphthong only when it is written.

Although diphthongization in OOc resembles phenomena in Italian, Spanish, and French, the former must be distinguished from the latter because, in OOc, diphthongization was triggered by the specific influence of a semivowel. Stressed /ę/ and /ǫ/ in Vulgar Latin produced diphthongs in Italian and French when in an open syllable—that is, a syllable that ends in the vowel, regardless of any semivowel: PĔDEM 'foot' > It. *piede*, Fr. *pied* (compare OOc **pę**; no diphthong). In Spanish, diphthongization occurred regardless of any semivowel and regardless of whether the syllable was open or blocked: TĔRRAM 'earth' > It. *terra*, Fr. *terre*, OOc **tęrra**, but Sp. *tierra*; FŎRTEM 'strong' > It. *forte*, Fr. *fort*, OOc **fǫrt**, but Sp. *fuerte*.

Nasal Raising

The three most open vowels (open /ę/, open /ǫ/, and, under certain conditions, /a/) were closed one degree by the influence of a following nasal consonant:

/ę/ > ẹ

BĔNE 'well' (adverb) > VL /bęne/ > **bẹṇ**

/ǫ/ > ọ

BŎNUM 'good' > VL /bǫno/ > **bọṇ**

---

[3] On the chronology of diphthongization in OOc, see Grafström (*Graphie*, par. 6.5), who shows evidence from charters (legal documents) that diphthongization was in process during the eleventh and twelfth centuries. Grafström mentions a single case of diphthongization in the *Boeci*: CL ŏcŭlĭ 'eyes,' masc. nom. pl., > **uel**.

Normal open ạ followed by a nasal plus **s** became a new vowel, close ạ, which rhymed only with itself:

ᴍᴀ̆ɴᴜ̄s 'hands,' acc. pl. > **mạs**, obl. pl. 30.6, rhyming with
capellạs, nom. sg. (ML ᴄᴀ̆ᴘᴇ̆ʟʟᴀ̄ɴᴜs)

This distinction did not occur in the absence of the following **s**: oblique singular **capellạ́** 30.99 rhymes with **vạ** (CL ᴠᴀᴅɪᴛ) in the following line.[4]

Stressed Vowels in Old Occitan

As a result of these changes, OOc had the system of stressed vowels shown in figure 12.1.

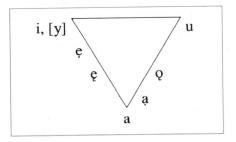

FIG. 12.1. *The vowel system of OOc*

SPORADIC CHANGES

Metaphony

In metaphony (also called umlaut or vowel mutation), the VL vowel /i/ or the corresponding semivowel, yod, caused a close /ẹ/ in the preceding syllable to become /i/, or a close /ọ/ to become /u/. The /u/ produced by metaphony then became [y] by the unconditioned change discussed above. In either case, the mechanism is essentially an assimilation, a raising of the tongue to the high position of the /i/ or yod. (Compare the vowel triangle, fig. 11.1.) Metaphony commonly occurs during reduction of an unstressed final syllable.

/ẹ/ > **i**, influenced by /i/ in the final syllable:

VL (ᴇ̆ᴄ)ᴄᴇ̆ ɪ̆ʟʟɪ̄ > **cil** 'they'; metaphony serves as a distinctive marker of the masculine nominative plural in demonstrative morphology (ch. 10).

---

[4] Close ạ may have extended to other contexts; see Smith and Bergin 29–30.

CL ꜰēcꜱ 'I made' (ꜰᴀcꜱŏ, ꜰᴀcĕʀᴇ; cf. E. *factory*) > **fis** (pret. 1st sg. of **faire**); the CL -ī also causes assibilation of the c (ch. 18), later simplified from /ts/ to /s/.

/ọ́/ > **u** > [y], influenced by /i/ in the final syllable:

LL ᴛōᴛᴛī > **túit, tut, túich**; the yod remains (**túit**), or disappears (**tut**), or causes assibilation of the final **t** (**túich**; see ch. 18). Metaphony identifies the masculine nominative plural, in contrast to other forms (nom. sg. **totz**, obl. sg. **tot**, obl. pl. **totz**); cf. chapter 10.

CL ꜰŭī 'I was' > **fui** (pret. 1st sg. of **ẹser**).

Contrariwise, by dissimilation VL /a/ may also cause preceding close /ẹ/ to become /i/:

CL sĭᴛ, pres. subj. 3rd sg. of ĕssᴇ 'to be' > VL *sĭᴀᴛ, */sẹa/ (cf. Sp. *sea*) > **sia**

CL vĭᴀᴍ (cf. E. *viable*) > VL */vẹa/ > **via** 'road'

Note that this infrequent change involves vowels in hiatus.

Analogical Substitutions

Occasionally, one vowel replaced another by the effect of analogy between words of related meaning:

CL sĭɴĭsᴛʀᴜᴍ > **senẹstre** 'left,' with **ẹ** by analogy to CL ᴅĕxᴛʀᴀᴍ 'right (hand)' > **dẹstra**

CL sĭɢĭʟʟᴜᴍ > **sagẹl** 'seal,' with **ẹ** by substitution of the CL diminutive -ĕʟʟᴜᴍ (OOc -**ẹl**)

CL ɢʀᴀ̆ᴠᴇᴍ > VL ɢʀĕᴠᴇᴍ (influenced by CL ʟĕᴠᴇᴍ 'light') > **grẹu, grieu** 'heavy'

CL ĭʟʟᴀ̄c > **lai** 'there' by aphaeresis (loss of the initial syllable; see ch. 13) and influence of **i** 'there' (CL ʜīc 'here,' ĭʙī 'there') to produce the diphthong

Classical Latin -ᴀ̄ʀĭᴜᴍ

The CL suffix -ᴀ̄ʀĭᴜᴍ corresponds to the frequent endings -**ier**, -**er** in OOc:

CL ᴘʀīᴍᴀ̄ʀĭᴜᴍ > **primier, primer** 'first'

LL cᴀʙᴀʟʟᴀ̄ʀĭᴜᴍ 'horseman' > **cavalier, cavaler** 'knight'

CL vĭʀĭᴅĭᴀ̄ʀĭᴜᴍ 'pleasure garden' > **vergier, verger** 'orchard'

For more examples, see -**ier** in the Glossary: Prefixes, Infixes, Suffixes.

Explanations that have been proposed for this correspondence have generally neglected OOc -**er** in order to focus on the relation between -ārĭum and **-ier**. Perhaps CL -ārĭum was replaced by CL -ĕrĭum, VL /-érjo/, and the stressed /ẹ/ was then diphthongized, as would have been normal, under the influence of the following yod. It is true, in any case, that some OOc words in **-ier** have -ĕrĭum in their etyma:

CL mĭnĭstĕrĭum > **mestier, mester** 'trade, craft'

ChL mŏnăstĕrĭum > **mostier** 'church'

VL *tĕmpĕrĭum > **tempier** 'storm'

However, no satisfactory reason has been suggested for the substitution of -ĕrĭum for -ārĭum.

Fouché has proposed a phonological explanation, assuming that, by anticipation of the yod, -ārĭum produced [-ai̯rjo], then [-ei̯rjo], by the double effect of the two semivowels on the [a]; then normal diphthongization, hence [-ie̯i̯ro]; then [-iei̯r], with the loss of the final vowel, and simplification of the final cluster to **-ier**.[5]

Any such hypothesis is upset, however, by evidence from early charters that -ārĭum produced first **-er**, and only later **-ier**, during the eleventh and twelfth centuries. This sequence of events seems to rule out any normal diphthongization as an explanation for **-ier**, since no semivowel is apparent in **-er**.[6] The problem remains unsolved.

READING 12

Marcabru, *Pax in nomine Domini!*

*The activity of Marcabru has been dated by allusions in his works to the period 1130–49. There are two **vidas** of Marcabru; according to them, he was a minstrel and mercenary from Gascony. He left about thirty moral and satirical **vers**, two crusade songs, two **tensos**, two romances, and a **pastorela**. Our selections include a crusade song (called a **vers**, 12.2), the **pastorela** (reading 13), and a satirical **vers** (see 14.2).*

Rubric in ms. R:

Aisi comensa so de Marcebru, que fo lo premier trobador que fos.

1

Pax in nomine Domini!
Fes Marcebrus lo vers e·l so.

---

[5] Fouché, *Phonétique* 2: 413–14. For earlier discussion, see Adams 207–10.

[6] Grafström, *Graphie*, par. 6.5. Grafström made no attempt to explain how -ārĭum can have produced **-er**. He suggested that **-er** can have led to **-ier** if the graphy **-er** actually represented the diphthong already, as **Deu** in late texts perhaps represented the same pronunciation as **Dieu**. The change of **-er** to **-ier** would then be a change in the graphic system, not in the vowel system of the language.

Enlindez que je dis

Aujatz que di *que je dis*
com nos a fat, per sa dossor, *douceur*
lo senher reys celestials *seigneur*
probet de nos un lavador *près* *endroit pour laver*
c'anc sal d'otra mar no fo tals *telle qu'il n'y en a pas sauf*
—o de say—en vas Jozafat; *ici — ou vers J. Josafat — mémé*
e d'aquest de say vos conort. *et de celui-ci je vous conforte*

2
Lavar de ser e de mati
nos deuriam segon razo, *raison*
  so vos afi. *assure*
Cascus a de lavar lezor; *chacun — occasion*
dementre qu'el es sas e sals *en bonne santé*
deuri'anar al lavador *doit aller*
que·ns es veray medicinals.
E si ans anam a la mort,
d'aut de sus aurem alberc bas. *autre de sus nous aurons une auberge basse*

3
Mas eschasetatz e no-fes *avarice. manque de fidélité*
part joven de son companhon.
  Aquel dols es
que tug volon lai li pluzor *tout*
don lo gazanhs er ifernaus, *gagne d'enfer*
s'ans no correm al lavador;
qui la boca te ni·l uelh claus, *entoure*
no y a un d'orguelh tan gras
c'al murir non truep contrafort. *trouve ennemi*
quand il meurt

4
Que·l senher que sap tot cant es
e sap tot cant er ni anc fo *jamais été*
  nos i promes
honor e nom d'emperador;
e·l beutatz sera (sabetz cals?) *beauté* *quoi*
de sels qu'iran al lavador.
pus que l'estela guauzinaus, *matin*
ab sol que venguem Dieu del tort
que·l fan payan lay ves Domas. *vers* *Damascus*

5 *Près de*
Probet del linhatje Caï, *lignage*
del primairan home felo,
  a tans aysi
c'us a Dieu no porta honor.
Veyrem qui l'er amics coraus,
c'ap la vertut del lavador
nos sera Jhesus cominaus; *commun*

e tornem los garsos atras
qu'en agurs crezon et en sort!   45

6
Si·l luxurios corno-vi,
coytat del dinnar al tuzo,
    com e·l cami,
remanran en fera pudor,
Dieus vol los arditz e·ls süaus
assajar a son lavador;
e sil guararan los ostaus,
e trobaran fort contrafort.
Per dreg venran ad aytal cas!

7
En Espanha say lo marques   55
e sels del temple Salamo;
    sofron los pes
e·l fays de l'orguelh payanor,
per que jovens cuelh avol laus.
E Crist, per aquest lavador,   60
venra sobre·ls pus rics chaptaus,
fraitz, falhitz, de proeza las,
que non amon joi ni deport.

8
Desnaturat son li Franses
s'al fag de Dieu dizon de no,   65
    qu'ieu say com es
d'Antiocha. Pretz ab valor
say plora Vian'e Peitaus;
Dieus senher, al tieu lavador
l'arma del comte met en paus,   70
e sai gart Peitieus e Niort
lo senher que resors del vas!

Meter

a	b	a	c	d	c	d	e	f
8	8	4	8	8	8	8	8	8

a = **-i** in st. 1, 2, 5, 6; = **-ęs** in st. 3, 4, 7, 8.
b = **-ǫ(n)**.
c = **-ǫr**. Verse 6: **lavador.**
d = **-als /-aus.**
e = **-as /-at** in st. 1, 3, 5, 7; = **-ǫrt** in st. 2, 4, 6, 8.
f = **-ǫrt** in st. 1, 3, 5, 7; = **-as** in st. 2, 4, 6, 8.
The rhyme sounds in the first four stanzas recur in the same pattern in
the second four (1 = 5, 2 = 6, 3 = 7, 4 = 8).
Ch. crois. 8 (2 fois 4) alternées 9.
Frank 456:1.

P-C 293,35. Major editions: Dejeanne, no. 35; Ricketts and Hathaway; Riquer, no. 21.

109

Chapter 12.
Stressed Vowels

Music: For transcription, see pages 561–63; from *W* fol. 194. Editions: Fernández de la Cuesta and Lafont 68–69; van der Werf and Bond 227*.

Seven manuscripts: *A* fol. 29; *C* fol. 177v; *I* fol. 117v; *K* fol. 103v; *R* fol. 5; *W* fol. 194v; *a¹* p. 293. Base *R*.

Divergent attribution: Anonymous *W*.

Stanza order

RACIK	1	2	3	4	5	6	7	8
a¹	1	2	4	3	5	6	7	8
W	1	2	—	—	—	—	—	—

Rejected readings in the base manuscript: (4) fatz *RCa¹*, fait *AIKW*. (5) senhor rey *R*, senhor reys *C*, seingnorius *AIKa¹*, seignoris *W*. (14) ql *R*, q'el *A*, qu'el *IK*, que *C*, qu'il *W*, q'estam *a¹*. (22) lai *AIKa¹*, om. *RC*. (23) gazanh *R*, gazains *ACIKa¹*. (25) si te *R*, sian *C;* c'aiam la bocha ni·ls huoils claus *AIKa¹*. (26) us *R*, un *ACIKa¹*; gray *R*, gras *AIKa¹*, guay *C*. (30) i] om. *R*, hi *C*, a *AIKa¹*. (32) beutat *Ra¹*, beutatz *ACIK*. (34) guaurinaus *RC*, gauzignaus *AIKa¹*. (36) payas *RC*, sai e *AIKa¹*. (37) cani *RC*, Caï *AIK*, Caïm *a¹*. (59) joven *R*, jovens *ACIKa¹*. (62) iratz *R*, frait *A*, fraich *IK*, francs *a¹*, quals *C;* proera *R*, proeza *ACIKa¹*. (71) et ab grat penan de la mort *R*, et ab grat li valha la mort *C*, e sai gart Peitieus e Niort *AIK*, sel conceilh Peiteus e Niortz *a¹*. (72) al senhor *R*, lo seigner *AIK*, del senhor *C*, per qe *a¹*.

Selected variants: (8) Jozafat *RAIKW*, Jozafatz *C*, vizitaz *a¹*. (16) veray *R*, verais *ACIKa¹*, vrais *W*. (46) cor-no-vi *RC*, corna-vi *AIKa¹*. (47) coytat del dinnar al tuzo *RC*, coita-disnar, bufa-tizo *AIK*, bufa-nizo *a¹*. (48) com el cami *RC*, crup-en-cami *AIK*, trop en cozi *a¹*. (49) en fera pudor *RC*, inz e·l folpidor *AIK*, aqueil felpidor *a¹*. (68) Vian' e *R*, Vianae *C*, Guiana e *A*, Gian' e *a¹*, Giama e *I*, Guiama e *K*.

Notes

Rubric] The misinformation in the rubric of ms. *R* implies a deliberate attempt to place a moral and religious voice at the source of troubadour lyric poetry. Note the violations of declension in the rubric: **so** and **trobador** are both object forms in subject functions.

(1) **Pax in nomine Domini**!] The salutation echoes liturgy and the Bible. In the Mass, "Pax Domini sit semper vobiscum" expresses solemn greeting (Blaise 206). "In nomine Domini" occurs frequently in the Bible, including Luke 19.38, where a multitude of disciples praise Jesus Christ, saying, "Benedictus, qui venit rex in nomine Domini, pax in caelo, et gloria in excelsis" 'Blessed be the king who cometh in the name of the Lord! Peace in heaven and glory on high!'

(6) **lavador**] Refers variously to crusade in the Holy Land (35–36), to crusade in Spain (55), and to Santiago de Compostela (70 note). *PD* provides a range of meanings, including 'lavoir' ('washhouse' or 'washing and rinsing board by riverside'); 'lieu où l'on lave' ('place where people wash'); 'piscine' ('fishpond,' 'piscina' = 'a basin with a drain, near the altar of a church, for the disposal of water used for sacred purposes'); 'cuvette' ('washbasin'). "Lavatorium, ubi manus lavant Monachi,

priusquam eant ad refectorium" 'Lavatorium, where monks wash their hands before they go to refectory' (Du Cange 5: 39).

(7–9) 'such that there has never been one like it except across the sea toward Jehoshaphat, or here'—that is, in the Holy Land or Spain. The use of **sai** 'here' to refer to Spain in contrast to Palestine is not so specific as to locate the speaker in Spain, since **sai** refers to France in vv. 68, 71.

(8) **Jozafat**] "The valley of Jehoshaphat (Joel 3.2), thought of as the scene of the Last Judgment" (Chambers, *Proper Names* 162). The phrase **en vas Josafat** modifies **otra mar** 7, not **de say** 8.

(16) **veray medicinals**] Nom. sg., with declension only on the noun (**veray** for **verays**).

(18) 'We shall have a low dwelling' (in Hell) 'instead of a high one on high' (in Paradise).

(20) **joven**] Lit., 'young people.' Translated 'Jeunesse,' 'Youth,' by Dejeanne; 'libéralité,' 'generosity,' by Ricketts and Hathaway.

(22) **volon**] Ellipsis of **anar**: 'So everyone wants [to go] where . . . '

(25) **qui**] 'Whoever.' **claus**] Past participle of **claure**; modifies both **boca** and **uelh**, masculine like the nearer of the two. Sinners close their eyes to the decadence around them, and close their mouths, since they do not cry out like Maracabru.

(31) Cf. Wisdom 3.7–8: "The just . . . shall judge nations, and rule over people"; Apocalypse 5.9–10: "Thou . . . hast made us to our God a kingdom and priests. And we shall reign on the earth."

(34) **guauzinaus**] 'Of cockcrow, of early dawn'; GALLĬCĬNĬUM 'cock-crow, early dawn' (*Oxf.*) + -ĀLIS.

(36) **Domas**] Damascus was never conquered by the crusaders (Ricketts and Hathaway). The pagans wrong God in Damascus because they worship false gods.

(42) **vertut**] 'Virtue, power'; also 'miracle' (*PD* 382).

(46) **Si** 'even if': 'Wenngleich, wenn auch, obgleich; und wenn auch, selbst wenn' (*SW* 7: 642–43). **corno-vi**] 'They toot wine,' like the singular variant **corna-vi** 'He toots wine': 'qui corne le vin, qui donne le signal de boire? ou crieur public qui au son du cor, annonce la vente du vin?' (*PD* 96–97).

(47) Perhaps an allusion to Guilhem IX, "En Alvernhe part Lemozi" (9.21–30).

(49) **fera pudor**] The reading in mss. *RC* is lucid and satisfactory. Other editors have read **inz e·l folpidor** with *AIK*, possibly 'in the ragbag, in the place for discarded refuse' (see Glossary), or 'in the place of ruin' (see *S-W* 3: 526). Ms. *a¹* reads **aqueil felpidor**, perhaps 'those dandies' (see Glossary).

(52) **sil**] 'Those ones'—i.e., the **corno-vi**.

(55) **say**] 'I know the marquis [is] in Spain.' **lo marques**] Raimond-Bérenger IV; he was count of Barcelona and marquis of Provence from 1131 to 1162.

(56) **sels del temple Salamo**] The Knights Templars.

(67) **Antiocha**] Reference to the defeat in 1136 of Raymond, prince of Antioch and younger son of Guilhem IX of Aquitaine (the troubadour), at the hands of the Saracen Sévar. **Pretz**] Invariable; must be the direct object of **plora** because the subject is **Vian'e Peitaus**, with nom. sg. **-s** in **Peitaus**.

(68) **Vian'**] The Vienne River, which gives its name to the department of Vienne. **Peitaus**] Poitou, the region around Poitiers (**Peitieus**, v. 71); **Peitaus** has the nom. sg. **-s**, in contrast to obl. sg. **Peitau** (see Glossary of Proper Names), and so the phrase **Vian'e Peitaus** must be the subject of **plora**, while **Pretz ab valor** is the object.

(70) **comte**] Guilhem, son of the first troubadour, died in 1137 on pilgrimage to Saint James of Compostela, the **lavador** of v. 69. The song must have been composed soon thereafter.

(71) **Peitieus**] The name of the city is an invariable noun; the **-s** is the final consonant of the root (see Glossary of Proper Names). **Niort**] In the department of Deux-Sèvres, west of Poitiers. The subject of **gart** is **lo senher** 72.

Exercise

Explain the development of the following etymologies, specifying the articulation of the stressed vowels in OOc.

1. ămīcum > **amic** 'friend'
2. ChL mīrăbĭlĭa > **meravelha, meravilha** 'wonder'
3. pĕndĕre > **pendre** 'to hang'
4. CL frīgĭdum 'cold,' VL *frĭgĭdum (influenced by CL rĭgĭdum 'stiff') > **freg** 'cold'
5. hĕri 'yesterday' > **ier**, (**l'autr)ier** 'the other day'
6. crăssum 'thick' (influenced by grŏssum 'fat') > **gras** 'fat'
7. grānum > **graṇ** PD, obl. pl. **gras** 'grain'
8. cŏrpus 'body' > **cors** 'body, person, self'
9. sŏlĕō 'I am accustomed' > **suolh, suelh**, pres. 1st sg. of **soler**
10. dŏlōrem > **dolor** 'sadness'
11. pŏntem > **pon** 'bridge'
12. nūdum > **nut** 'nude'

Vowels in Initial and Unstressed Syllables

INITIAL SYLLABLES

Classical Latin vowels in initial syllables carried secondary stress. They evolved from Vulgar Latin into OOc much as stressed vowels did, but with two differences:

They were more subject to sporadic changes.

The distinction between the close and open mid-vowels (ẹ versus ę, ọ versus ǫ) was not made in this position, so no diphthongization could occur.

Examples of regular development:

CL hībĕrnum 'of winter' (adj.) > **ivẹrn** 'winter' (n.)

CL ĭnfantem > **enfan** 'child'

CL dēbēre > **devẹr** 'ought, should'

CL mĕlĭōrem > **melhọr** 'better'

CL caballum > **caval** 'horse'

CL vĕlle > VL *vǒlēre > **volẹr** 'to want'

CL sōlācĭum > **solatz** 'solace'

CL sŭbĭnde > **sovẹn** 'often'

CL hūmānum > **umaṇ** [ymaṇ] 'human'

An initial **e-** was regularly added before a consonant group comprising an initial **s-** + stop [p, t, k]:

CL (from Gk.) spătham > **espaza** 'sword'

CL stāre 'to stand' > **estar** 'to be'

CL scrībĕre > **escriure** 'to write'

This change may be called prosthesis, since it resembles the addition of a prosthetic limb. In one sense, it is the opposite of aphaeresis, or loss of an etymological initial vowel (see below), except that prosthesis is regular, whereas aphaeresis is sporadic. In another sense, prosthesis is the mirror image of the addition of a support vowel in the final position following certain consonant groups (see below, "The Final Syllable").

113

*Chapter 13.
Vowels in
Initial and
Unstressed
Syllables*

The mid-vowels (**e**, **o**) often closed to high position (**i**, **u**) in the initial syllable:

> Initial **e** > **i**
>
>> CL SERVĬĔNTEM > **serven, sirven** 'servant'
>>
>> CL ĬNTRĀRE > **entrar, intrar** 'to enter'
>
> Initial **o** > **u**
>
>> CL SŬFFĔRRE > VL *SŬFFĔRĪRE > **sofrir, sufrir** 'to suffer'
>>
>> CL MŎRĪ > LL MŎRĪRE > **morir, murir** 'to die'

Assimilation affected the vowel in the initial syllable in LL or OOc:

> /ẹ-a/ > **a-a**
>
>> CL SĬLVĂTĬCUM 'of the wood' > LL SALVĀTĬCUM > **salvatge** 'wild'
>
> /ę-a/ > **a-a**
>
>> VL *MEDANTĀRE > **mazantar** 'to shake'
>
> /ọ-ę/ > **e-ę**
>
>> VL *DUM INTĔRIM > **demęntre** 'while'

Dissimilation affected the vowel in the initial syllable in VL or OOc:

> /i-i/ > **e-i**
>
>> CL FĪNĪRE > VL *FENĪRE > **fenir** 'to cease'
>>
>> CL VĪCĪNUM > VL *VĒCĪNUM > **veziṇ** 'near'
>
> /ọ-ọ/> **e–ọ**:
>
>> CL SŎRŌREM > **serọr** 'sister'
>>
>> CL RŎTŬNDUM > VL *RĔTŬNDUM > **redọn** 'round'

Aphaeresis, or loss of the initial syllable, also occurred:

> Celtic *alauda* + **-ęta** > **alauzęta, l'alauzęta, la lauzęta** 'lark'
>
> AQUĪTĀNĬAM > **Guiana** 'Aquitaine'

The vowel in the initial syllable sometimes fell if it was between a stop and a liquid or in hiatus:

> CL DĪRĒCTUM > **dręch** 'right'
>
> CL QUĬRĪTĀRE > VL *CRĪTĀRE > **cridar** 'to shout'
>
> VL *DĒ ŬNDE > **dọn** 'about that which'

In normal usage CL ᴅᴏ̆ᴍĬɴᴜᴍ produced **dǫn** 'lord.' As a title in address ('sir'), however, the vocative form, CL ᴅᴏ̆ᴍĬɴᴇ, came to be used as a proclitic—that is, in dependence on the stress of the following name. Consequently, it lost its independent stress and with it the entire first syllable, and so was reduced to **ne**. Then **ne** before a vowel was reduced to **n**, which, in combinations such as **de n**, **que n**, came to be understood as **d'en**, **qu'en**; and so was produced the title **en** 'sir' (Grandgent 25).

UNSTRESSED SYLLABLES

The Unstressed Penult

By the principle of stress position in CL, a penult ending in a short vowel was unstressed, since stress reverted to the antepenult (see ch. 11). The vowel of an unstressed penult dropped in VL, if it had not already done so in CL. This change normally preceded the reduction of a vowel in the final syllable:

> CL ᴅᴏ̆ᴍĬɴᴀᴍ or ᴅᴏ̆ᴍɴᴀᴍ > **dǫmna** 'lady'
>
> CL ᴄᴏ̆ᴍĬᴛᴇᴍ 'companion' > **cǫmte** 'count'
>
> CL ᴏ̆ᴘᴇ̆ʀᴀ 'works,' neuter pl. > **ǫbra** 'work,' fem. sg.
>
> CL ᴘᴇ̆ʀᴅᴇ̆ʀᴇ > **pęrdre** 'to lose'
>
> CL ꜱᴀᴇᴄᴜ̆ʟᴜᴍ > **sęgle** 'world'

The Final Syllable

All vowels except **a** in the final syllable fell:

> CL ᴛᴇ̆ʀʀᴀᴍ > **tęrra** 'land'
>
> CL ʜᴀ̆ʙᴇ̄ʀᴇ > **avęr** 'to have'
>
> CL ꜰᴇ̄ᴄĪ > **fis** 'I did'
>
> CL ǫᴜᴀɴᴅᴏ̄ > **can** 'when'
>
> CL ꜰᴇ̆ʀʀᴜᴍ > **fęr** 'iron'

Note that in Italian, all final vowels remain, as in *terra, avere, feci, quando, ferro*. In Spanish, some do: *tierra, haber, hice, cuando, hierro*. In French, only /a/ remains in the reduced form of the "mute e," or schwa: *terre, avoir, fis, quand, fer*.

However, final /i/ or /u/ joins an immediately preceding vowel to form a diphthong:

> CL ᴍᴇ̆Ī > **męi** 'my,' masc. nom. pl.
>
> CL ᴅᴇ̆ᴜᴍ > **Dęu** 'God'

A final /e/ may be retained or created as support for pronunciation of a consonant group, as noted in chapter 2:

> CL ᴇxᴇ̆ᴍᴘʟᴜᴍ > **eisęmple** 'example'
>
> CL ꜱᴇ̆ᴍᴘᴇʀ > **sęmpre** 'still, always'

115

*Chapter 13.
Vowels in
Initial and
Unstressed
Syllables*

CL ᴅŬᴘʟᴜᴍ > **dǫble** 'double'

CL ᴀ̆ʀʙŏʀᴇᴍ > **arbre** 'tree'

CL ᴛʀᴀᴄᴛᴇᴍ > **tracte** 'that I negotiate,' pres. subj. 1st sg.

ChL ᴍīʀᴀ̆ᴄŭʟᴜᴍ > **miracle** 'miracle'

CL ꜱᴀᴇᴄŭʟᴜᴍ > **sęgle** 'world'

CL ꜱᴇ̆ǫᴜᴇ̆ʀᴇ > **sęgre** 'to follow'

Consonant groups consisting originally of a stop + a liquid that became in OOc a semivowel + a liquid, by yodicism or wawicism (ch. 16), still required support:

CL ᴘᴀ̆ᴛʀᴇᴍ > **paire** 'father'

CL ᴘĭᴘᴇʀ > **pębre, pęure** 'pepper'

In some cases a consonant group requiring support simplified, but the support vowel remained:

ChL ᴇᴘĭꜱᴄŏᴘᴜᴍ > */evęskve/ > **evęsque** 'bishop'

CL ʜŏꜱᴘĭᴛᴇᴍ > */ǫspte/ > **ǫste** 'innkeeper'

CL ŏʀᴅĭɴᴇᴍ > */ǫrdne/ > **ǫrde** '(monastic) order'

CL ʜŏᴍĭɴēꜱ nom. pl. > VL *ʜŏᴍĭɴī > **ǫmne** (*Boeci* 11.1, 11.7) > **ǫme**

An infinitive in **-re**, such as **recébre**, may be recognized as having the root **recęb-** with the infinitive marker **r**, and as therefore requiring the support vowel **-e**. In **ęstre** the root is **es-**, with the infinitive marker **r**, requiring a transitional **-t** and a support vowel; cf. **ęser**, with the infinitive marker **-er**. Just as the final cluster of a semivowel (yod or waw) + **r** required support in **paire** 'father' and **pęure** 'pepper,' so it did in infinitives:

faire < root **fai-** + **r** + support vowel; cf. **far** < **fa** + **r**

cręire < root **cręi-** + **r** + support vowel

bęure < root **bęu-** + **r** + support vowel

Infinitives ending in **-íre** imply a latent yod at the end of the root, which may be absorbed into the preceding vowel, as in alternative forms in **-ir**:

dire < **dij-** + **r** + support vowel; an infinitive form **diire** is attested (25.31). Cf. **dir** < **di-** + **r**.

Similarly **rire**, **aucire**. For more on alternate roots, see chapter 19.[1]

---

[1] One could go further, positing **r** as the infinitive marker for all verbs, preceded by the theme vowel **á** in many verbs (**-ar**), by **í** in many others (**-ir**), by **é** in some (**-ér**), by zero in two infinitive types with support vowels (either **-er** or **-re**), or by zero with no support (**dir**, **far**).

Final unstressed **-i** may be retained in semilearned forms:

> CL ĭmpĕrĭum > **empęri** 'empire'

Cf. the suffix **-i** in the Glossary: Prefixes, Infixes, Suffixes.

Intertonic Syllables

An intertonic vowel is one that occurs between the stressed syllable and the initial syllable. Like final vowels, intertonic vowels, with the exception of **a**, fall:

> CL bŏnĭtātem > **bontat** 'goodness'
>
> CL cŏllŏcāre 'to place together' > **colgar** 'to lay down'
>
> ChL mīrābĭlĭa > **meravęlha** 'wonder'

Retention of Unstressed Syllables

It follows from what has been said that only the stressed syllable and the initial syllable in CL naturally remain in OOc. There are, however, numerous exceptions to this generalization, which are due to effects of analogy, composition, or learned retention.

Analogy

> CL ădjūtāre > **ajudar** 'to help' (instead of hypothetical
> ***aidar**; cf. Fr. *aider*), by analogy to forms in which the
> vowel **u** is stressed, such as pres. 3rd sg. **ajuda**.
>
> VL *ămōrōsum > **amorǫs** (instead of hypothetical ***am-**
> **bros**): the VL represents a composition of the noun and
> the suffix -ōsum, but the intertonic vowel is retained by
> analogy to **amǫr** 'love.'

Composition

a- + **bel** 'beautiful' (CL bĕllum) + **-ir** > **abelir** 'to please'

ome(n) (CL hŏmĭnem) + **-atge** (CL -ātĭcum) > **omenatge**
'homage'

Learned retention

> CL augŭrāre, VL *agŭrāre > **aürar** 'to prophesy'
>
> CL ĭmpĕrātōrem > **emperadǫr** 'emperor'

READING 13

Marcabru, *L'autrier just'una sebissa*

*This poem may be regarded as the prototype of the **pastorela** in Occitan,*
the pastourelle in French, the serranilla in Castilian, and related forms in
other medieval languages and in later folk song. As a prototype, however,

117

*Chapter 13.
Vowels in
Initial and
Unstressed
Syllables*

it did not become a member of the eventual genre until the genre grew up around it; that is, in its own time it was not a member of the genre not yet constituted. Rather it may be seen in relation to Marcabru's predecessor Guilhem IX, and in particular to the cat poem (in ch. 9). Critics have suggested that the cat poem may be a parody of the pastourelle; but in view of elementary chronology, it seems more plausible to see Marcabru's pastourelle as a response to the cat poem. Marcabru's narrator bears resemblance to the narrator of the cat poem, and to the persona of Guilhem IX in other poems as well.

1
L'autrier just'una sebissa
trobey pastora mestissa
de joi e de sen massissa,
e fon filha de vilaina;
cap'e gonela, pelissa,   5
vest e camiza treslissa,
sotlars e causas de laina.

2
Ves lieys vau per la planissa;
"Toza," fi m'ieu, "re faytissa,
dol ay gran del ven que·us fissa."   10
"Senher," so dis la vilayna,
"merce Dieu e ma noirissa,
pauc m'o pres si·l vens m'erissa,
c'alegreta soi e sayna."

3
"Toza," fi m'ieu, "cauza pia,   15
destoutz me soy de la via
per far a vos companhia,
car aytal toza vilayna
non pot ses parelh paria
pastorjar tanta bestia   20
en aytal loc, tan soldayna."

4
"Don," fay sela, "qui que sia,
ben conosc sen o fulia;
la vostra parelhayria,
senher," so dis la vilaina,   25
"lay on se tanh si s'estia,
que tals la cuj'en baylia
tener, no n'a mays l'ufayna."

5
"Toza de gentil afayre,
cavayers fo vostre payre
que·us engenret, e la mayre   30

tan fon corteza vilayna.
Com pus vos gart, m'es belayre,
e pel vostre joi m'esclaire;
si fossetz un pauc humayna!"   35

6

"Senher, mon genh e mon ayre
vey revertir et retrayre
al vezoich et a l'arayre,
senher," so ditz la vilayna;
"mays tal se fay cavalgayre   40
c'atretal deuria fayre
lo seis jorns de la semayna!"

7

"Toza," fi m'ieu, "gentil fada
vos adastrec can fos nada
d'una beutat esmerada   45
sobre tot'autra vilayna;
e seria·us be doblada,
si·m vezi'una vegada
sobiran e vos sotraina."

8

"Senher, tan m'avetz lauzada   50
pus en pretz m'avetz levada
qu'ar vostr'amor tan m'agrada,
senher," so dis la vilayna,
"per tal n'auret per soldada
al partir, 'Bada, fol, bada!'   55
e la muz'a meliayna."

9

"Toza, fel cor e salvatje
adomesg'om per uzatje;
ben conosc al trespassatje
c'ap aital toza vilayna   60
pot om far ric companatje
ab amistat de coratje,
can l'us l'autre non enjaina."

10

"Don, hom cochat de folatje
e·us promet e·us plevisc gatje;   65
si·m fariatz omanatge,
senher," so dis la vilayna,
"mays ges per un pauc d'intraje
non vuelh mon despieuselatje
camjar per nom de putaina!"   70

11

"Toza, tota criatura
revert segon sa natura.
Parlem ab paraula pura,"
fi m'ieu, "tozeta vilayna,
a l'abric lonc la pastura,
que mels n'estaretz segura *sure*   75
per far la cauza dossayna." *Charmant*

12

"Don, oc—mas segon drechura *droit*
serca fol sa folatura,
cortes cortez'aventura,   80
e·l vilas ab la vilayna;
'E mans locs fay sofraytura
que no·y esgardo mezura,' *moderation*
so dis la gens ansiayna." *veille, arcienne*

13

"Bela, de vostra figura
non vi autra pus tafura *méchante*   85 *coquine*
ni de son cor pus trefayna." *trompeuse*

14

"Don, lo cavecs nos aüra *chouette*
que tals bad'en la penchura *peinture*
c'autre n'espera la mayna." *Manna* 90

Meter:

a	*a*	*a*	*b*	*a*	*a*	*b*
7'	7'	7'	7'	7'	7'	7'

Past. 12 d 7, 2–3 [1?].[2]

a = **-issa, -ia, -aire, -ada, -atge, -ura.**
b = **-ana.** Verse 4 ends in a refrain word: **vilana.**
Frank 51:5.

P-C 293,30. Major editions: Dejeanne, no. 30 ("graphie de *A*"); Audiau, no. 1 (base *C*); Riquer, no. 14; Paden, *Medieval Pastourelle,* no. 8 (Base *C*).
Music: For transcription, see pages 564–66; from *R* fol. 5. For sung performance of the reading, refer to the accompanying compact disk. Editions: Fernández de la Cuesta and Lafont 65; van der Werf and Bond 226*; Switten and Chickering 1: 51–53 and cassette 1.
Eight manuscripts: *A* fol. 33–v; *C* fol. 176v–177; *I* fol. 120v; *K* fol. 106–v; *N* fol. 169v–170; *R* fol. 5; *T* fol. 205; *a¹* pp. 310–11. Base *R*.
Attributions: Uniform.

[2] Frank must mean that stanzas 13 and 14 might be taken as one tornada 6 lines long.

Stanza order

| RACIKNa[1] | 1 | 2 | 3 | 4 | 5 | 6 | 7 | 8 | 9 | 10 | 11 | 12 | 13 | 14 | — |
| T | 1 | 2 | 3 | 4 | 5 | 6 | 7 | 8 | 9 | 10 | 11 | 12 | 13 | 14 | 15 |

Rejected readings in the base manuscript: (13) ven *R*, vens *CIK*, venz *ANa*[1], freg *T*. (21) el *R*, en *ACIKNTa*[1]. (27) tal *R*, tals *ACIKNa*[1], ome *T*. (30) savayers *R*, cavalliers *ACIKNa*[1], cavalier *T*. (37) reverdir *R*, revertir *Ta*[1], revenir *AIKN*, il-legible *C*; atrayre *R*, retraire *AIKNTa*[1], illegible *C*. (38) a la via de *R*, illegible *except for* via *C*, al vezoich et a *AIKNTa*[1]. (41) artetal *R*, atretal *AIKa*[1], atrestal *C*, altretal *N*, altrestal *T*. (48) vezia una *RC*, ab sol una tropellada *AIKNTa*[1]. (49) sobiras *RC*, ieu sobran *T*, mi sus *A*, mi sobra *Na*[1], mi sobre *IK*; sotiraina *R*, sotrayna *CNa*[1], sotana *IKT*, soteirana *A*. (51–52) *reversed in AIKNTa*[1]. (52) que tota·n soi enoiada *AIKNa*[1], tuta en saria enveada *T*. (52–53) *om. R, supplied from C*. (66) faziatz *R*, fariatz *CIKN*, fariartç *T*, *om. Aa*[1]. (84) gen *RNT*, gens *ACIK*, genz *a*[1]. (89) lo m'avetz nossatura *R*, lo cavecs nos aüra *KIN*, lo chavecs vos ahura *A*, lo chavetz nos aüra *a*[1], l'orjavetz non s'atura *C*, lo canuc taus aiura *T*.

Selected variants: (8) planissa *RC*, chambissa *A*, chamina *IK*, chamisa *N*, calmissa *Ta*[1]. (18) aytal *RCT*, aitals *AIKNa*[1]. (19) parelh *RAIKNTa*[1], plazen *C*. (23) fulia *R*, foillia *ACIKNTa*[1]. (40) tal se *R*, tals se *ACIKNa*[1], tals es *T*. (43) gentil *RCT*, gentils *AIKNa*[1]. (44) fos *RNTa*[1], foz *AIK*, *illegible C*. (54) auret *R*, aurez *IKa*[1], auretz *ACT*, *om. N*. (64) cochat *RC*, coitatz *AIKT*, cujatz *Na*[1]. (72) revert segon sa *R*, revertis a sa *AIKT*, revert eissa *Na*[1], reverta assa *C*. (73) parlem ab paraula pura *RC*, pareillar pareillatura *AIKNa*[1], perigliar pareglia pura *T*. (79) fol sa *R*, fols sa *Aa*[1], sols sa *IKN*, folh la *CT*. (91–92) *T adds a third tornada:* Gies non gara la pintura / cel ce n'espera la mana.

Notes

(15) **cauza pia**] in reference to **merce Dieu** 12.

(18) **aytal toza vilayna**] Declension on heavy elements (not on **aytal**).

(20) **béstia**] Rhymes as **-ía**, possibly with influence of the abstract suffix **-ía** (see Glossary: Prefixes, Infixes, Suffixes).

(24) **parelhayria**] Perhaps a coinage by the shepherdess, mocking or sarcastic (cf. the suffix **-aria** in the Glossary: Prefixes, Infixes, Suffixes).

(26) **lay on**] 'There where,' with reference to the narrator's lady, who is also referred to by **tals** 27. **estia**] The form shows influence of **sia**, present subjunctive of **eser**.

(27) **la**] Refers to **parelhayria** 24.

(28) **no n'a**] Ellipsis of the relative pronoun **que**: '(Who) has only . . . '

(30) **cavayers fo vostre payre**] Is this why the narrator introduced the girl as **mestissa** in v. 2?

(31) **e la mayre**] e *RT*, en *ACIKNa*[1]. With *RT* it is possible to read: 'A knight was [must have been] your father who engendered you, and your mother was [must have been] such a courtly peasant-woman'; with *ACIKNa*[1], 'A knight was your father who engendered you on your mother, such a courtly peasant-woman came of it' (**fon** inchoative; cf. **aver** inchoative 'got'; see Glossary). The reference of **corteza vilayna**

121

Chapter 13.
Vowels in
Initial and
Unstressed
Syllables

32 changes from the girl's mother (in *RT*) to the girl herself (in *ACIKNa*[1]). But of course **e** in *RT* may be a form of **en**. The reading of **e** as 'and' saves the strain of inchoative **fon**; and the compliments to the girl's two parents are parallel, **fon** 32 like **fo** 30.

(33) **com**] 'Lorsque' *PD* 84.

(34) **joi**] Cf. **joi** 3; the character uses the same word as the narrator.

(40) **tal se**] Omission of final -s before initial **s-**; **tal se** = **tals se**. **caval-gayre**] The man uses the currently fashionable term **cavayers** 'knight' 30; the girl, more conservative, uses 'horseman.' Perhaps she is skeptical about the pretentions of the entire knightly class.

(42) **lo seis** = **los seis** (cf. v. 40).

(43) **gentil fada**] Nominative singular, with declension on the noun (**gentil**, not normal **gentils**); **gentil** also occurs as feminine, nominative singular, at 3.5.

(44) **fos** = **fotz** (-s for -tz passim).

(52) **amor**] Nom. sg., the etymological form from CL nom. sg. AMOR, without the analogical -s in the alternative nom. sg. **amors**; cf. Glossary.

(54) **auret**] For the ending without -z, cf. Appel, *Provenzalische* xxiii.

(61) **ric companatje**] Interpreted by the girl in the following stanza as an offer of prostitution.

(64) **hom cochat**] Nominative singular, with declension on the noun. The zero article is equivalent to the indefinite article: 'a man.'

(65) **e·us . . . e·us**] The **·us** is the object form of the impersonal, as in Fr. *vous* used as the object form of *on*.

(73) **paraula pura**] The fastidious hypocrite finds the girl's straightforward language distasteful (**intraje, despieuselatge, putana**).

(78) **Don, oc**] She pretends to agree, as earlier in stanza 8.

(79) **fol sa** = **fols sa** (cf. v. 42).

(80) Ellipsis for **cortes [serca] cortez'aventura.**

(81) Ellipsis for **e·l vilas [serca aventura] ab la vilayna.**

(88) **lo cavecs**] Allusion to the owl as a figure of folk wisdom (cf. v. 84).

(89) **penchura**] 'Painting,' that is, mere appearance.

(90) **mayna**] Reality. The Old Testament reference perhaps echoes from **trefayna** 87, from a Hebrew etymon.

Exercise

For each of the following etymologies, locate the CL stress, identify the stressed vowel in OOC, and explain the developments in syllabic structure:

1. AUDĬĀTĬS > **aujatz** 'hear' (imperative)
2. CŬRRĔRE > **corre** 'to run'

3. FĪLĬAM > **filha** 'daughter'
4. LŬXŬRĬŌSUM > **luxurios** 'lecherous' 12.46 (four syllables)
5. SCŪTUM > **escut** 'shield'
6. SPĒRĀRE > **esperar** 'to wait for'
7. STĂBĬLĪRE > **establir** 'to found'
8. VĔRĒCŬNDĬAM > **vergonha** 'shame'

CHAPTER 14

Production of Consonants

Figure 14.1 depicts the organs of speech used in the production of consonants, and table 14.1 presents the consonants necessary to understanding the historical phonology of OOc.

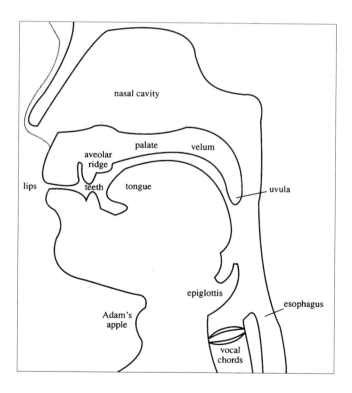

FIG. 14.1. *Organs of speech*

TABLE 14.1. *Consonants in OOc*

	Bilabial	Labio-dental	Inter-dental	Dental	Palatal	Velar
Stops						
Voiceless	p			t		k
Voiced	b			d		g
Fricatives						
Voiceless		f	θ	s	š	χ
Voiced	β	v	ð	z	ž	ɣ
Nasals	m			n	ɲ	
Liquids						
Flaps				r		
Laterals				l	ʎ	
Semi-consonants					j	w

Symbols:

β Sp. *caballo* [kaβaʎo]

θ E. *thin* [θɪn]

ð E. *then* [ðɛn]

š E. *she* [šij]

ž Fr., E. *rouge* [ruž]

ɲ Sp. *señor* [seɲor], Fr. *seigneur* [sɛɲœr], It. *signore* [siɲore]

ʎ Sp. *calle* [kaʎe], It. *figlio* [fiʎo]

j E. *you* [ju]

χ E. *hat* [χæt]

ɣ Sp. *haga* [aɣa]

The production of consonants may be described in terms of their manner of articulation, point of articulation, and voicing. Manner of articulation varies from a momentary arrest of the flow of air up from the lungs through the mouth, through various types of obstruction, to the minimal channeling that produces vowels. If the flow of air is arrested, the consonant produced is a stop: [p, t, k, b, d, g]. If just enough air is allowed to pass to produce a rubbing sound, the consonant is a fricative (Latin FRĬCĀRE 'to rub'): [f, s, š, v, z, ž]. A subclass of the fricatives is that of the sibilants (Latin SĪBĬLĀRE 'to whistle'): [s, š, z, ž]. If the uvula (Latin 'little grape,' visible in a mirror) and velum (Latin 'sail') are lowered so as to direct air into the nose, the consonant is a nasal [m, n, ɲ]. If the air flows around the tongue tip, the consonant is called a liquid; a liquid may be either a flap (if the tongue tip strikes the alveolar ridge, as in Spanish and Italian [r]) or a lateral (if it is held there: [l, ʎ]). If the air is directed with only slightly more restriction than that which produces vowels, the result is called either a semiconsonant or a semivowel [j, w].

Point of articulation varies from the front of the mouth to the back. If the upper and lower lips are brought together, the result is a bilabial, which may be a stop, either voiceless [p] or voiced [b]; a fricative, voiced [β]; or a nasal [m]. If the lower lip touches the upper teeth, the result is a labiodental, which may be a voiceless fricative [f], or a voiced fricative [v]. If the tongue tip is placed between the teeth, the consonant is an interdental, which may be a voiceless fricative [θ] or a voiced fricative [ð]. If the blade of the tongue is brought to the alveolar ridge just behind the teeth, the result is a dental, which may be a stop, either voiceless [t] or voiced [d]; a fricative, voiceless [s] or voiced [z]; a nasal [n]; or a liquid [r, l]. If the blade is brought to the forward region of the hard palate, the result may be a palatal fricative, voiceless [š], voiced [ž]; a nasal [ɲ]; a liquid [ʎ]; or a semiconsonant [j]. If the back of the tongue is raised toward the velum, or soft palate, the result may be a velar stop, voiceless [k] or voiced [g]; a fricative, voiceless [χ] or voiced [ɣ]; or a semiconsonant [w].

Voicing is a vibration produced by tension in the vocal cords below the epiglottis; the alternative relaxation of the vocal cords produces no sound. The voiceless stops [p, t, k] correspond to voiced [b, d, g]. The voiceless fricatives [f, s, š, χ] correspond to voiced [v, z, ž, ɣ]. Nasals, liquids, and semiconsonants are all voiced, as are vowels.

The semiconsonant (or semivowel) [j] corresponds in point of articulation to the vowel [i], as the semiconsonant [w] corresponds to the vowel [u].

In this book the affricates (as in E. *church* and *judge*) are treated as combinations of stop and fricative: [tš] and [dž].

READING 14

Marcabru, *Dire vos vuelh ses duptansa*

1
Dire vos vuelh ses duptansa
d'aquest vers la comensansa;
li mot fan manta semblansa.
    Escotatz!
Qui ves proeza balansa
semblansa fay de malvatz.

2
Jovens falh e franh e briza,
et amors es d'aytal guizad
que pus al saut s'es empriza;
    escotatz!
Quecx en pren a sa deviza,
e pueys non er endeutatz.

3
Amors vay com la beluia
que se mescla en la suia,
art lo fust e la festuia
    (escotatz!)
e no sap vas cal part fuia
sel que del foc es gastatz.

4
Diray yos d'amors com minha:
a vos canta, seluy guinha,
a vos parla, l'autre cinha,
    escotatz!
Pus sera dreita que linha
ans que siatz sos privatz.

5
Amors soli'esser drecha,
mas er es torta e brecha,
e aculhid'a tal decha
    (escotatz!)
que can no pot mordre, lecha
pus aspramen no fay chatz.

6
Anc pueys amor no fo vera
que triet del mel la cera,
ans sap si parar la pera
    (escotatz!)
dosa·us er com chans de lera,
si sol la coa·l tocatz.

7
Qui ab amors pren barata
ab diable s'acoata;
no·l cal c'autra verga·l bata.
    Escotatz!
No·y a cosselh mas que·s grata
tro que s'es vieus escorjatz.

8
Amors es mot de mal avi;
trops homes a mortz ses glavi.
Dieus no fes tan bon gramavi
   (escotatz!)   45
que fol no fasa·l pus savi,
si tant es que·l teng'al latz.

9
Amors a usatje d'egua
que tot jorn vol c[om la sega   50
e que pueg de legu'en lega.
   Escotatz!
E no·us demandara tregua
siatz dejus o dinnatz.

10
Cujatz que ieu non conosca   55
d'amors s'es orba o losca?
Sos fatz aplana e tosca
   (escotatz!),
e punh pus süau de mosca—
e pus greu n'es hom sanatz.   60

11
Marcebrus, filhs Marcebruna,
fon engenratz en tal luna
que sap amors com degruna.
   Escotatz!
C'anc de cor non amet una,   65
ni d'autra non fo amatz.

12
Qui per sen de femna renha
dretz es que mals li·n avenha,
si com la letra ensenha.
   Escotatz!
Mal'aventura vos venha,   70
si tug no vos en gardatz!

Meter:

    a   *a*   *a*   *b*   *a*   *b*
    7' 7' 7' 3   7' 7
    Sirv. 12 s 6
    a = **-ansa, -iza, -uja, -inha, -echa, -era, -ata, -avi, -ega, -osca,**
    -una, -enha; *b* = **-atz;** verse 4: **escotatz.**
    Frank 55:9.

P-C 293,18. Major editions: Dejeanne, no. 18 ("graphie de A"); Riquer, no. 15; Hamlin, Ricketts, and Hathaway, no. 9.

Music: For transcription, see pages 566–68; from *R* fol. 5. Editions: Fernández de la Cuesta and Lafont 63; van der Werf and Bond 225*; Switten and Chickering 1: 48–50 and cassette 1.

Eight manuscripts: *A* fol. 29; *C* fol. 174v–175v; *D*ᵃ fol. 189; *I* fol. 117v; *K* fol. 103v; *M* fol. 142–v; *R* fol. 5v; *a*¹ pp. 309–10. Three stanzas in α 28231–28246–29607. Base *R*. See frontispiece.

Divergent attributions: Raimbaut d'Aurenga *M* (Marcabru *M* index).

Stanza order

R	1	2	3	4	5	6	7	8	9	10	11	12			
AIK	1	2	3	4	5	6	7	8	A	9	10	12	11		
*D*ᵃ	1	2	3	4	5	6	7	8	A	10	12	11	Tornada=11¹		
M	1	2	B	C	5	7	D	E	9	10	F	3	11		
C	1	2	B	C	5	G	8	H	7	D	E	9	10 F	3	11 I
	K	L	M	N	12	6									
*a*¹	1	2	11	10	F	6	7	B	9	8	0	5	3	4	A
	Tornada=A¹														
α	—	—	B	11	M	—	—	—	—	—	—	—	—		

Rejected readings in the base manuscript: (19) tricha *R*, migna *AIKD*ᵃ, sinha *MC*, tigna *a*¹. (20) guincha *R*, gigna *ACD*ᵃ*IKM*, ligna *a*¹. (21) sincha *R*, cigna *AD*ᵃ*IKa*¹, reqinha *MC*. (53) deman/dar *R*, demandara *A*, demandera *IK;* que no·l dara t. *a*¹. (54) o sias *R*, siatz *IK*, si·us etz *A*, se·us es *a*¹, sia *C*, si·s vol *M;* dinnat *R*, disnatz *ACIKMa*¹. (55) Aujatz *R*, Cujatz *ACD*ᵃ*IKMa*¹. (61) filh *RCD*ᵃ, filhs a, fils *IKa*¹, fills *AM*. (67) p *R*, per *C*, ab *AD*ᵃ*IK*.

Selected variants: (19) amors *R*, amor *ACD*ᵃ*IKMa*¹. (31) amor *R*, amors *ACD*ᵃ*IKa*¹. (37) amors *R*, amor *AD*ᵃ*IKa*¹. (43) mot de *RC*, molt *D*ᵃ, mout de *AIK*, de tan *a*¹, *stanza om. M*. (51) pueg] fota *IK*. (56) amors *R*, amor *ACD*ᵃ*IKMa*¹.

Notes

(3) **manta semblansa**] 'Many a semblance, appearance'; *PD* gives 'apparence extérieure, figure; ressemblance, image; parabole.' Possibly 'Many comparisons' (suggested by Terence O'Connell), as in the song.

(9) **s'es empriza**] 'Is begun'; but cf. the sense 'to catch (fire)' in **fuec ab grais fort leumen s'es enpres** 'fire catches very easily with grease' 26.52, in relation to **Amors vay com la beluia** 14.13.

(12) **endeutatz**] **endeudar, -tar**, 's'endetter' *PD* 145: 'Each one takes of love as he wishes, [thinking that] then he will not incur any debt.'

(19) If **minha** is a form of **manjar**, from CL ᴍᴀɴᴅᴜᴄᴀʀᴇ, 'to eat,' the root vowel may reflect Gascon influence (Anglade, *Grammaire* 96; see also *FEW* 6, pt. 1: 176). Another interpretation that has been suggested by Ruth Harvey (*Modern Language Review* 95.3 [2000]: 824–25) would derive **minha** from a root **miñ-** expressing affection, as in French *mignon* (*FEW* 6, pt. 2: 139–42). The line would then mean "I'll tell you how love caresses."

(30) **chatz**] Cf. Guilhem IX (reading 9).

(33–35) **si . . . (que)**] 'It knows so well how to peel the pear (listen!) [that] . . . '

(36) 'If only you touch your tail to it' (cf. **acoata**, v. 38). Or: 'If only you caress its tail' (cf. the image of the cat, v. 30).

(39) 'Love, like a devil, does not care if another (phallic) rod beats it'—i.e., love is like a prostitute.

(41–42) Cf. 9.59–66.

(43) **mot**] Modifies **mal**: 'Love is of very wicked lineage.'

(45–48) 'God has not created a grammarian so good (Listen here!) that [love] can't make a fool of the wisest, if it is true that [love] can catch him in his trap.' Is there an allusion to the grammarian, philosopher, and lover Peter Abelard, who died in 1142?

(51) **pueg**] For the meaning, cf. the variant **fota**.

(53) **demandara tregua**] 'Will ask for a truce'—i.e., will say, "Uncle."

(54) **dejus o dinnatz**] The two words of opposite meaning derive from the same etymon, VL *dĭsjējūnāre, from CL jējūnĭum 'fast.' The paradox is explained by the two meanings of the prefix, VL dĭs- or OOc **de-**, which may be either intensive, as in **dejus** ('fasting'), or privative, as in **dinnatz** ('no longer fasting'); see Prefixes, Infixes, Suffixes, and Adams 423–24.

(69) "Let women be subject to their husbands, as to the Lord: Because the husband is the head of the wife, as Christ is the head of the church. He is the savior of his body. Therefore as the church is subject to Christ: so also let the wives be to their husbands in all things" (Eph. 5.22–24, Douai version).

Exercise

1. The following are voiced stops: [g], [b], [d]. Provide the voiceless stop corresponding to each one.

2. What is the difference between a fricative and a stop?

3. Provide the voiced fricative corresponding to each of the following voiceless fricatives: [s], [f], [θ], [š], [χ].

4. What is a sibilant?

5. Have you ever seen your uvula?

6. Can you move your velum? What can you do with it?

7. Can you flap?

8. Make a bilabial voiced fricative. What language has such a sound?

9. Can you feel your alveolar ridge?

10. What is the relation between the hard palate and the velum?

CHAPTER 15

Consonants (Section 1)

F

LENITION

In lenition (which means 'making smooth,' from CL LENIS 'smooth'), a single consonant in a vocalic context becomes more like a vowel—that is, the consonant is assimilated to its context.[1] The changes caused by lenition may be traced in table 14.1:

The voiceless stops [p, t, k] become voiced stops [b, d, g].

The voiced stops [b, d, g] become voiced fricatives [β, z, ɣ], and may develop further to a semivowel [yod, waw] or zero.

The voiceless sibilant [s] becomes voiced [z].

The context involved is usually two vowels, but it may be one vowel and one liquid (l or r, both of which are voiced), with the liquid usually following the consonant.

Voiceless stops [p, t, k] become voiced [b, d, g].

Intervocalic [p] > **b**:

VL *TRŎPĀRE 'to compose a liturgical trope' > **trobar** 'to find; to compose poetry'

CL APRĪLEM > **abril** 'April'

CL DŬPLUM > **doble** 'double'

Intervocalic [t] > **d**:

CL AMĀTŌREM > **amador** 'lover'

CL COGĬTĀRE > **cuidar** 'to believe'

CL MĔTĔRE > **medre** 'to reap'

---

[1] All vowels are voiced. Consonants differ from vowels because in consonants the air column rising from the lungs is more strongly impeded (stopped, made to rub, etc.).

Intervocalic [k] > **g**:

> LL PRĔCĀRE > **pregar** 'to pray'

> ChL CLĒRĬCUM > **clęrgue** 'cleric, clerk'

> CL ĂLĂ-CREM > VL *ĂLĔC-REM > **alęgre** 'cheerful'

The voiceless sibilant [s] becomes voiced [z]:

> CL CAUSAM > **cauza** 'reason'

> Germ. *wīsa > **guiza** 'kind, manner'

Voiced stops [b, d, g] become voiced fricatives [β, z, ɣ]. The voiced fricatives may remain (β [spelled **v**], z), be reduced to a semivowel, or pass to zero.

The intervocalic [b] becomes [β], [w], or zero.

> [β] between vowels in OOc:

> — CL CABALLUM > **caval** 'horse'

> CL DĒBĒRE > **devęr** 'should, ought'

[w] before a consonant in OOc:

> CL BĬBĔRE > **bęure** 'to drink'

> CL PARABŎLAM > **paraula** 'word'

zero before or after a lip-rounded vowel that absorbs the labial [β]:

> CL ĂBŬNDĀRE > **aondar** 'to help'

> CL PRŎBĀRE > **proar** 'to test'

The intervocalic [d] becomes **z** or zero.[2]

> **z**:

> CL AUDĪRE > **auzir** 'to hear'

> CL VĬDĒRE > **vezęr** 'to see'

zero:

> CL CAUDAM > **cǫa** 'tail'

> CL HŎDĬĒ > **ǫi** 'today'

The intervocalic [g] becomes [ɣ], which becomes [j] and then zero, the [j] absorbed into a high front vowel, **i** or **u** [y]:

> CL LĬGĀRE > **li̇ar** 'to sew'

> CL NŪGĀLEM 'useless' > **nualh** 'laziness'

Lenition in the onset of the final syllable in CL may be masked in OOc by the reduction of the final vowel.

---

[2] It is frequently the case that CL D becomes **z** before stress (as in **auzir, vezer**) and zero after stress (as in **coa, oi**), but not always—for example, the future tense of **fizar** (from VL *FĪDĀRE) is either **fisarai** or **fiarai**.

[b] becomes [w] at the end of the word in OOc:

> CL dēbet > **dęu** 'he, she, it must'

[d] becomes zero at the end of the word in OOc:

> CL fĭdem > **fę** 'faith'

[g] becomes [ɤ], then [j] at the end of the word in OOc:

> CL lēgem > **lęi** 'law'

Accelerated Lenition

Sometimes the voiceless stops and sibilant [p, t, k, s] become voiced [b, d, g, z] so soon that they participate in the further lenition of the originally voiced sounds.

[p] becomes [b], then [β]:

> ChL epĭscŏpum > **evęsque** 'bishop'

[t] becomes [d], then [z]:

> CL (from Gk.) spătham > **espaza** 'sword'
>
> VL mět ĭpsum > **mezęis** 'oneself'
>
> LL flātāre > **flazar** 'power to draw breath'

[k] becomes [g], then [ɤ], then [j], then zero:

> CL mīcam 'crumb' > **miga** (by normal lenition), **miia**
> 11.11 note, **mia** (by accelerated lenition) '(not) at all'
>
> CL dīcat > **diga, dia** 'that he say' (pres. subj. 3rd sg.)

[s] becomes [z], then zero:

> CL mănsĭōnem > **maizǫn** (by normal lenition), **maiǫn**
> (by accelerated lenition) 'house'
>
> Germ. *wīsa > **guiza**, also **guia** *PD*, 'kind, manner'

Lenition in Composition

The alternations of consonants produced diachronically by lenition may be duplicated synchronically in composition.

Intervocalic **p** > **b**:

> **sęp** 'hedge' + **-ęnc** > **sebęnc** 'one conceived under the
> hedge, bastard'

Intervocalic **t** > **d**:

> **a-** + **grat** 'pleasing' + **-ar** > **agradar** 'to please'

Intervocalic [k] > **g**:

> **cǫc** 'cook' + **-astrǫn** > **cogastrǫn** 'scullion'

Intervocalic **s** > **z**:

> **tǫs** 'young man, shaver' + **-a** > **tǫza** 'girl'

By definition, lenition does not affect consonants that were originally double:

> CL ăppĕllāre > **apelar** 'to call'
>
> CL ăttĕndĕre > **atẹndre** 'to hope for'
>
> CL bŭccam 'cheek' > **bọca** 'mouth'
>
> CL ĕsse, VL ĕssĕre > **ẹser** 'to be'

Nor does lenition affect learned words, especially words in the vocabulary of the church, such as these.

p remains:

> CL ŏmnĭpŏtĕntem > **ọmnipotẹnt** 'all-powerful'
>
> ChL pāpam > **papa** 'pope'
>
> CL sapĭĕntĭam > **sapiẹncia** 'wisdom'

t remains:

> CL carĭtātem > **caritat** 'love'
>
> CL creatōrem > **creatọr** 'creator'
>
> CL lătīnum > **latiṇ** 'language, words, Latin'
>
> CL nătūram > **natura** 'inborn character'
>
> ChL patĭnam > **patẹna** 'paten, the plate holding the bread in the Eucharist'
>
> CL pĭĕtātem > **pïetat** 'pity'
>
> ChL satanas > **satan** 'devil'

[k] remains:

> CL sacrămĕntum > **sacramẹnt** or **sagramẹn** 'oath'
>
> CL sēcrētārĭum 'hiding place' > **secretari** 'secret'

b remains:

> ChL dĭăbŏlum > **diable** 'devil'
>
> CL lĭbĕrtātem > **libertat** 'liberty'

d remains:

> CL ŏboedĭentem > **obedïẹn** 'obedient'

g remains:

> CL fīgūram > **figura** 'face'

Lenition does not affect consonants that were felt as initial or final by composition: **re-pairar** 'to return' (CL rĕpătrĭāre), **de-portar** 'to amuse' (LL dēpŏrtāre); **re-tener** 'to keep' (CL rĕtĭnēre); **de-cazer** 'to decline' (LL dēcădĕre, VL *dēcădēre), **re-cobrar** 'to recover' (CL rĕcŭpĕrāre); **a-batre** 'to knock down' (LL ăbăttŭĕre); **ambe-dos** 'both' (CL ămbōs dŭōs); **duc-at** 'duchy' (CL dŭcātum).

Lenition may not affect words borrowed from languages other than Latin:

> Gothic *wīdan* + **-ar** > **guidar** 'to guide,' but also **guizar** by lenition (cf. the noun **guida** 'guide'; also **guia** by lenition)

> Persian *tabīr* + **-or** > **tabọr** 'drum,' borrowed in the eleventh century (?)

> Byzantine Greek *tapition* > **tapi** '(pilgrim's) cloak'

FINAL CONSONANTS IN CLASSICAL LATIN

Final consonants in Classical Latin were generally deleted, except for -R and -S.

Final -M in words of more than one syllable fell:

> CL TĔRRAM > **tẹrra** 'land'

> CL FŎRTEM > **fọrt** 'strong'

In monosyllables, final -M became **n**-mobile, the final [n] symbolized in this book by **ṇ**, which may or may not be noted by scribes:

> CL RĔM > **rẹṇ** 'creature'

> CL SŬUM > **sọṇ** 'his, her, its, their'

But **ja** 'now' (CL IAM) does not occur with **n**-mobile.

Final -N fell in words of more than one syllable:

> CL NŌMEN > **nọm** 'name'

In monosyllables, final -N might remain or become **n**-mobile:

> CL ĬN > normally **ẹn;** the form **e** occurs before **m** (**e mos bratz** 'in my arms,' etc.), before **l** (**e·l mon** 'in the world,' etc.), and rarely before other consonants (**e preiso** 'in prison,' etc., in *Boeci*)

> CL NŎN > **nọṇ** (**non manjarai, no sap**), **n'** (**n'an**)

Final -T and -D fell:

> CL ĂMAT > **ama** 'he loves'

> CL ĔT > **e** 'and'; **ez** + vowel, **es** + vowel (lenition); **et** (Latinate spelling)

> CL ĂD > **a** 'to'; **az** + vowel (lenition); **ad** + vowel

In CL final -NT, the -T usually fell; the -N normally developed into a regular **n**, not **n**-mobile:

> CL TĂNTUM > **tant, tan, tam** (**tam bas**); but **ta** in *Boeci*, rarely elsewhere

> The verbal ending -ŬNT > **-ọn**, but **-ọ** in **defendo** (non-**ar** verb) and by analogical extension in **-ar** verbs: **esgardo, foillo, manjo**

li

Final -sᴛ becomes **-s**:

> CL ᴇ̆sᴛ > **e̥s**

Final [-k] fell:

> CL sɪ̄c 'thus' > **si** 'so'
>
> CL ʜŏc > **o̥** 'it'

CL final -s and -ʀ remained:

> CL vō̆s > **vo̥s** 'you'
>
> CL ᴅŏᴍɪ̆ɴᴀs acc. pl. > **do̥mnas** 'ladies'
>
> CL ᴀᴍɪ̄cᴜs nom. sg. > **amics** 'friend'
>
> CL sŭᴘᴇʀ > **so̥r** 'upon'
>
> Cf. Armenian *thaphur* > **tafur** 'rascally'

FINAL DEVOICING

By a process that may be thought of as the opposite of lenition, voiced consonants that came into final position in OOc became voiceless:

> CL ŏʀʙᴜᴍ masc. > **o̥rp** 'blind,' ŏʀʙᴀᴍ fem. > **o̥rba**
>
> CL ɴū̆ᴅᴜᴍ masc. > **nut** 'naked,' ɴū̆ᴅᴀᴍ fem. > **nuda**[3]
>
> CL ʟŏɴɢᴜᴍ masc. > **lo̥nc** 'long,' ʟŏɴɢᴀᴍ fem. > **lo̥nga**

n-MOBILE

Single intervocalic ɴ, made final in OOc by the reduction of the final syllable, became **n**-mobile, which scribes arbitrarily indicate or not:

> CL ʀᴀ̆ᴛɪ̆ōɴᴇᴍ > **razo̥n, razo̥** 'reason' (cf. E. *rational*)

As we have noted, **n**-mobile may also be produced from final -ɴ or -ᴍ in a monosyllable (**no̥n̥** 'no'; **re̥n̥** 'creature'). Classical Latin ɴ supported by another consonant did not normally produce **n**-mobile:

> CL ᴛᴀ̆ɴᴛᴜᴍ > **tan;** see above
>
> the verbal ending -ŭɴᴛ > **-o̥n**, but also **-o̥;** see above
>
> CL ɪ̄ɴᴅᴇ > **e̥n, ne, n', ·n** 'from it, of it, etc.' (not ***e̥**)

---

[3] **Nuda** does not derive directly from the CL feminine form, a process that would require that the **d** resist lenition; rather it derives from masculine **nut**, with alternation of **t/d** in **nut/nuda** by lenition in composition (see above).

READING 15

Jaufre Rudel, *Lanqan li jorn son lonc en mai*

*As lord of Blaye (Gironde), near Bordeaux, Jaufre Rudel was naturally the vassal of the duke of Aquitaine. The duke was Guilhem, the first troubadour, until his death in 1126. We know that Jaufre was active from 1125 to 1147, when he went on crusade to the Holy Land, and that he probably died by 1164. (Cf. the **vida** in reading 1.)*

One may consider the present song in its historical context as a response to Guilhem and Marcabru. Through textual echoes, Jaufre distances himself from both the libertine Guilhem and the misogynist Marcabru in order to create a new, more sublime love.

1
Lanqan li jorn son lonc en mai
m'es bels doutz chans d'auzels de loing;
e qand me sui partitz de lai,
remembra·m d'un'amor de loing.
Vau de talan embroncs e clis,   5
si que chans ni flors d'albespis
no·m platz plus que l'iverns gelatz.

2
Ja mais d'amor non gauzirai
si no·m gau d'est'amor de loing,
que gensor ni meillor non sai   10
vas nuilla part, ni pres ni loing.
Tant es sos pretz verais e fis
qe lai e·l renc dels Sarrazis
fos ieu per lieis chaitius clamatz.

3
Iratz e gauzens m'en partrai   15
qan veirai cest'amor de loing;
mas non sai coras la veirai,
car trop son nostras terras loing.
Assatz hi a portz e camis,
e per aisso no·n sui devis;   20
mas tot sia cum a Dieu platz.

4
Be·m parra jois qan li qerrai,
per amor Dieu, l'alberc de loing;
e s'a lieis platz, albegarai
pres de lieis, se be·m sui de loing.   25
Adoncs parra·l parlamens fis,
qand, drutz loindas, er tant vezis
c'ab bels digz gauzirai solatz.

5
Ben tenc lo seignor per verai
per qu'eu veirai l'amor de loing.
Mas per un ben que me n'eschai
n'ai dos mals, car tant m'es de loing.
Ai, car me fos lai pelleris
si que mos fustz e mos tapis
fos pels sieus bels oills remiratz!

6
Dieus qui fetz tot cant ve ni vai
e formet cest'amor de loing
mi don poder, que·l cor ieu n'ai,
q'en breu veia l'amor de loing
veraiamen en locs aizis,
si que la cambra e·l jardis
mi resembles totz temps palatz.

7
Ver ditz qui m'apella lechai
ni desiron d'amor de loing,
car nuills autre jois tant no·m plai
cum gauzimens d'amor de loing.
Mas so qu'eu vuoill m'es tant aïs
qu'enaissi·m fadet mos pairis
q'ieu ames e non fos amatz.

8
Mas so q'ieu vuoill m'es tant aïs . . . ;
totz sia mauditz lo pairis
qe·m fadet q'ieu non fos amatz!

Meter:

a	b	a	b	c	c	d
8	8	8	8	8	8	8

Ch. 7 u 7, 1–3.
-ai, -ǫnh, -is, -atz.
Verses 2 and 4: **loing.**
Frank 376:8.

P-C 262,2. Major editions: Riquer, no. 12; Pickens, no. 5, version 1; Wolf and
    Rosenstein, no. 6; Chiarini, no. 4.
Music: For transcription, see pages 568–69; from *X* fol. 81; also notated in *R* and
    W. For sung performance of the reading, refer to the accompanying compact
    disk. Editions: Fernández de la Cuesta and Lafont, 52–54; van der Werf and
    Bond 215*–19*; Switten and Chickering 1: 54–63 and cassette 1.
Sixteen manuscripts: *A* fol. 127–v; *B* fol. 77–v; *C* fol. 215v; *D* fol. 88–v; *E* p. 149;
    I fol. 121v–122; *K* fol. 107v; *M* fol. 165; *M^h* 4–v; *R* fol. 63–v; *S* pp. 182–83;
    W fol. 189v–190; *X* fol. 81v–82; *Z* fol. 108; *a^1* pp. 498–99; *e* pp. 186–90.
    Quotations in ε 1299 (st. 1), κ 72 (Mussafia 215 = vv. 33–35). Base *A*.

Divergent attributions: Gaucelm Faidit *W*, Anonymous *X*.
Stanza order (cf. Pickens 150):

AB	1	2	3	4	5	6	7	8
EIK	1	2	3/5	6	4	—	—	—
D	1	2	3/6	4	—	—	—	—
S	1	2	4	3	—	6	—	—
Z	1	2	3/5	6	4	—	7	—
X	1	4	2/5	5/2	—	—	—	—
W	1	5	4	2/3	—	—	—	—
C	1	5	4	3	2	6	7	—
e	1	5	4	3	2	6/7	—	—
R	1	5/6	6	3	2	—	7	—
a¹	1	6/3	5	4	2	3	—	—
M	1	6	4	3	7/5	2	—	—
Mʰ	1	6	4	5/2	X/3	3/5/7	—	—

Rejected readings in the base manuscript: (8) guizarai *A*, gauzirai *BCDEIKMR-WXZa¹e*, chausirai *S*. (22) jois *BCDEIKMMʰSWXZa¹e*, jocs *A*. (40) loncs *A*, locs *BMʰ*, luec *C*, luoc *R*, tal *DEIKZ*, tals *M*; veraiamen in palazins *S*. (44) amon *A*, amor *BCMZ*, amors *R*.

Selected variants: (23) l'alberc *ADIK*, l'amor *BE*, l'ostal *CMMʰSWXZa¹e*. (24) albegarai *A*, albergarai *BCDEIKMMʰZa¹e*, albergerai *S*, herbergerai *WX*. (28) bels digz *ADEIKS*, bels only *B*, cortes ditz *a¹*, cortes ginh *CMe*, cortes joy *MʰWZ*, corteis geu *X*. (37) fermet *BMS*. (44) desiran *BZ*. (47) tant/ais *A*, tant ahis *B*, tant/ahis *C*, tot taïs *e (trans. 'tutto negato')*, es trays *Mʰ*, aital *R*. (50) tant ais *A*, tant ahis *B*.

Notes

(2) Compare the refrain word **loing** with the refrain word **vilaina** in Marcabru's **pastorela** (13.4, etc.).

(6) **flors d'albespis**] Cf. **la branca de l'albespi**, Guilhem IX (see 8.14).

(14) **fos**] Optative subjunctive, 'I wish I were.'

(22) **jois**] On the erotic qualities in **joc**, the reading in ms. *A*, see Calzolari 147.

(27) **drutz loindas**] In apposition to the implicit subject of **er**, 1st sg.: 'when I, a distant lover, shall be . . . '

(33) **car me fos**] Optative subjunctive with **car**, 'I wish I were' (ch. 26).

(34) **mos tapis**] Cf. **a tapi**, Guilhem IX (see 9.2).

(41–42) Cf. **a l'abric lonc la pastura** 13.75.

(47, 50) **aïs**] Attested only in this passage (see variants). From **aïr** 'to hate' (Frankish **hatjan* 'to hate') + **-is** (CL -ĭcĭum); the context requires the meaning 'full of hatred, which hates me' (not 'hateful, odious, which I hate'). Cf. Pickens 169 note; Wolf and Rosenstein 167; Chiarini 98–99.

(48–49) Allusion to popular belief that children's lives are influenced by the personal destiny of their godfathers and godmothers; perhaps with reference to Guilhem IX, who might have been Jaufre's godfather (Lejeune, *Chanson* 432–36). Cf. Marcabru 14.65–66: inexperience in love, for Marcabru, authorizes his preaching; for Jaufre Rudel, it is a curse.

Exercise

Explain the following etymologies.

1. LL ĂBĂNTE > **avan** 'first'
2. Ctc. *alauda* + **-ęta** > **lauzęta** 'lark' (cf. aphaeresis, ch. 13)
3. AUGŬRĬUM > **agur**, **aür** 'augury' (the **u** [y] by metaphony, ch. 12)
4. LL CABALLICĀRE > **cavalgar** 'to ride a horse'
5. LĂRGUM > **larc** 'generous'
6. MĔDĬCĪNĀLEM > **medicinal** 'remedy'
7. QUĬRĪTĀRE > VL *CRĪTĀRE > **cridar** 'to shout'
8. RĔPŌNĔRE > **rebǫndre** 'to bury'
9. SUCCŬRSUM > **socǫrs** 'help'

CHAPTER 16

Consonants (Section 2) *Sat*

In the position immediately before another consonant (sometimes called "implosive" position, because the following consonant impedes full release), a consonant may simply be deleted, or it may produce a semivowel, either yod or waw. To maintain our focus on the results of sound change in OOc rather than on input from CL or from other sources, we shall call these three changes simplification, yodicism, and wawicism.[1]

SIMPLIFICATION

Simplification of double consonants (except **rr**) is the rule in OOc:

LL CAPPAM > **capa** 'cape'

CL MĀTŪTĪNUM > VL */mattino/ > **matiṇ** 'morning'

CL PĔCCĀTUM > **pecat** 'sin'

CL ĂBBĀTEM > **abat** 'abbot'

VL AD ĬD ĬPSUM (TĔMPUS) 'at the same time' > */addęs/ > **adęs** 'always' (the vowel influenced by **apręs** 'after')

VL *PASSĀRE > **pasar** 'to pass'

CL SŬFFĔRRE > VL *SŬFFĔRĪRE > **sofrir**, **sufrir** 'to suffer'

CL BALLĬSTAM > **balęsta** 'crossbow'

CL FLAMMAM > **flama** 'flame'

VL *ĀFĂNNĀRE > **afanar** 'to suffer'

---

[1] The term *yodicism* is modeled on *rhotacism*, the production of an [r] (Greek *rho*) in classical philology; *wawicism* is modeled, in turn, on *yodicism*.

Double **r** normally remains:

> Frankish *werra > **guẹrra** 'war,' sporadically **guera**

Simplification also occurs in a wide variety of consonant groups, either as constituted in CL or as resulting from later changes. Some illustrative groups in CL:

> [bt] > **t**: CL sŭbtus > **sọtz** 'under'
>
> [ks] > **s**: CL dĕxtram > **dẹstra** 'right hand'
>
> [ns] > **s**: CL mēnsūram > **mezura** 'moderation' (**z** by lenition)
>
> [rs] > **s**: CL vĕrsus > **vas** 'toward'
>
> [mn] > **n**: CL dămnum > **dan** 'loss'

Some later groups:

> [t'p] > **p**: CL antĕpărāre > **amparar** 'to protect' (**m** by assimilation to **p**)
>
> [d-p] > **p**: LL ad prēssum > **aprẹs** 'afterward'
>
> [d't] > **t**: VL *assĕdĭtāre > **asetar** 'to place'
>
> [d-s] > **s**: VL *ad sătis > **asatz** 'quite'
>
> [sb] > **b**: Frankish *halsberg > **albẹrc** 'hauberk'
>
> [t'm] > **m**: VL *blăstĕmāre (ChL blăsphēmāre + CL aestĭmāre) > **blasmar** 'to criticize'
>
> [d'r] > **r**: CL dēsĭdĕrāre > **dezirar** 'to desire'

The alternations created by simplification could be extended to create the reverse effect. Thus, by simplification:

> [nv] > **nv/v**: CL convenīre > **convenir, covenir** 'to befit'

The alternation **nv/v** could be extended by analogy to **v** arising from a different source:

> [b] > **v** (by lenition) /**nv**: CL hībĕrnum (tĕmpus) > **ivẹrn, envẹrn** 'winter'

YODICISM

A consonant (most often [k] or [g], but also [t] or [d], sometimes [p] or [b]) that is before another consonant, in CL or in a later stage, may become yod. The yod thus produced may combine with a vowel to form a diphthong; with a dental [n] to produce palatal **nh**; or with a dental [l] to produce palatal **lh**.

Groups in CL:

consonant + T

CL ʟᴇ̆ᴄᴛᴜᴍ > **lęit** 'bed'

consonant + R

CL ᴘᴀ̆ᴛʀᴇᴍ > **paire** 'father'

CL ᴅɪ̄ᴄᴇ̆ʀᴇ > ***dijre** > **dire** 'to say'

CL ᴀ̆ɢʀᴜᴍ 'field' > **aire** 'family, origin'

consonant + S

CL ʟᴀ̆xᴀ̄ʀᴇ > **laisar** 'to let'

consonant + N

CL ᴄᴏ̆ɢɴɪ̆ᴛᴜᴍ > **cǫinde** 'charming'

Later groups:

CL ғᴀᴄᴇ̆ʀᴇ > */fak're/ > **faire** 'to do'

CL ᴄʀᴇ̄ᴅᴇ̆ʀᴇ > */kręd're/ > **creįre** 'to believe'

VL *ᴄᴀᴘsᴇ̆ᴜᴍ > **cais** 'jaw'

VL *ǫᴜᴀᴅʀᴇ̆ʟʟᴜᴍ > **cairęl** 'bolt for crossbow' *Carreau*

Germ. *wahta (cf. E. *watch*) > **gaita** 'watchman'

Production of **nh** and **lh**:

CL ᴀɢɴᴇ̆ʟʟᴜᴍ > **anhęl** 'lamb'

CL ᴏ̆ᴄᴜ̆ʟᴜᴍ > */ǫk'lo/ > **ǫlh** 'eye'

WAWICISM

A consonant in the position before another consonant or at the end of a word may become waw, especially if it is the lateral [l] or a bilabial [p, b, m], or if there is a bilabial element in the context:

CL ᴀ̆ʟᴛᴇ̆ʀᴜᴍ > **autre** 'other'

CL ᴅᴜ̆ʟᴄᴇᴍ > **dǫus, dǫls** 'sweet'

VL ᴍᴇ̆ᴛ ɪ̆ᴘsᴜᴍ > **mezęis, mezęus** 'self'

CL ᴍᴀ̆ʟᴇ̆ ʜᴀ̆ʙɪ̆ᴛᴜᴍ > **malaut** 'sick'

LL sᴀɢᴍᴀ̄ʀɪ̆ᴜᴍ > **saumier** 'packhorse'

Bernart de Ventadorn,
Chantars no·m pot gaires valer

le meilleur poète de l'amour

*See headnote to the **vida** in chapter 5.*

1

peut guère vaut bien

Chantars no·m pot gaires valer
si dinz dal cor no mou lo chantz; *le chant vient du cœur*
ni chanz non pot dal cor mover *ne peut pas venir*
si no·i es fin'amors coraus. *s'il n'y a pas de fin'amors sincère*
Per so es mos chantars cabaus *distingué*
q'en joi d'amor ai et enten *qu'en la joie d'amour j'ai et je comprends*
la boch'e·ls oillz e·l cor e·l sen. *la bouche, les yeux, le cœur, et le sens*

2

un tel pouvoir

Ja Deus no·m don aqel poder *là*
qe d'amor no·m prenda talanz; *que si ne désire plus l'amour*
si ja ren no·n sabi'aver *si je ne savais rien avoir*
mas chascun jorn m'en vengues maus, *douleur me vient*
toz temps n'aurai bon cor sivaus; *j'aurai un bon cœur au moins*
e n'ai molt mais de jauzimen *et j'ai plus de joie*
car n'ai bon cor e m'i aten. *parce que j'ai un bon cœur, je m'y attends*

3

Amor blasmen per non-saber, *Ils blâment l'amour par*
fola genz, mas lei no n'es danz; *il n'y a pas de mal* *inqualle connaissance, là dedans*
c'amors no pot ges dechader *parce qu'amour ne peut pas diminuer*
si non es amors cominaus. *si l'amour n'est pas partagé*
Aqo non es amor; aitaus *ce n'est pas l'amour, ce qu'on nomme*
no n'a mais lo nom e·l parven, *n'a que le nom et l'air,*
que re non ama si non pren. *qui n'aime rien s'il n'en tire un profit*

4

S'eu en volgues dire lo ver, *si je voulais dire la vérité,*
eu sai ben de cui mou l'enganz: *je sais bien de qui vient la tromperie:*
d'aqelas c'amon per aver, *de celles qui aiment pour avoir,*
e son marchaandas venaus. *et elles sont des marchandes corrompues*
Mensongers en fos eu e faus! *Je serais menteur et faux!*
Vertat en dic vilanamen, *Je dis la vérité en langage grossier,*
e pesa me car eu no men. *et je regrette que je ne mente pas*

5

En agradar et en voler *en plaire et en vouloir*
es l'amors de dos fins amanz; *est l'amour de deux fins amants;*
nuilla res no·i pot pro tener *rien ne peut assez tenir*
se·l voluntaz non es egaus. *si la volonté n'est pas égale*
E cel es ben fols naturaus *Et celui est bien un fou-né*
qi de so que vol la repren *qui fait les reproches de ce qu'elle veut*
e·ill lauza so que no·ill es gen. *et la loue pour ce qui n'est pas*

6

Molt ai ben mes mon bon esper
quant cela·m mostra bel semblanz
q'eu plus dezir e voill vezer,
franch'e dolza, fin'e leiaus,
en cui lo reis seria saus.
Bell'e coind'ab cors covenen,
m'a fait ric home de neien.

7

Ren mais non am ne sai temer,
ne ja res no·m seri'afanz
sol midonz vengues a plazer,
c'aqel jornz me sembla nadaus,
c'ab sos bels oillz esperitaus
m'esgarda—mais so fai tan len
c'uns sols dias me dura cen.

8

Lo vers es fins e naturaus,
e bos celui qui ben l'enten;
e meiller es qe·l joi aten.

9

Bernarz del Ventador l'enten,
e·l di e·l fai, e·l joi n'aten!

Meter:

a   b   a   c   c   d   d
8   8   8   8   8   8   8
Ch. 7 u 7, 2–3, 2.
-er, -ans, -als, -en.
Frank 447:3.

P-C 70,15. Major editions: Appel, *Bernart,* no. 15; Nichols et al., no. 15; Lazar, no. 2; Riquer, no. 55.

Eight manuscripts: *A* fol. 94–v; *C* fol. 55–v; *Dª* fol. 161v–162; *G* fol. 12v–13; *I* fol. 32v; *K* fol. 21; *P* fol. 14–v; *a* p. 82. Quotations in *d* no. 32, α 33290 (st. 2). Base *Dª.* See the facsimile of ms. *D* (*Canzoniere,* vol. 2).

Stanza order: Uniform.

Rejected readings in the base manuscript: (5) cho *DªG,* so *ACIKPa.* (7) bocha els. (8) aqel *ACGIKPa,* om. *Dª.* (10) sabia aver. (13) en nai. (23) l'engaz *Dª,* l'engans *ACGIKPa.* (27) vila- *(illegible superscript)* men *Dª,* vilanamen *ACGIKPa.* (34) cho *DªG,* so *ACIKa,* co *P.* (35) cho *DªG,* so *ACIKPa.* (39) francha e; fina e. (41) bella e coinda ab. (44) seria afanz. (48) cho *DªG,* so *ACIKPa.*

Selected variants: (10) quan . . . sabri'aver *CP,* si . . . sabia *AIKa,* si . . . sabria *G.* (17) decazer *ACIKP,* deschaer *a,* om. *G.* (18) comunaus *AGKP,* comunals *Ia.* (19) amor *DªG,* amors *ACIKPa.* (25) mercadeiras *AC,* merchadanz *a,* marchaandas *IK,* merhaandas *G.* (32) si·l *Aa,* si·lh *CP,* se·l *GIK.* (37) ela *CP,* cella *AGIKa.* (41) covinen *ACGP,* covenen *IK,* avinent *a.* (45) midonz

Notes

(1–7) Note the syllogistic style.

(5) **cabaus**] Lenition in synchronic morphology: **cap** + **-al**.

(7) The definite articles are equivalent to possessive pronouns.

(8) **aqel**] Strong demonstrative force; see ch. 29. **poder**] VL *ᴘᴏᴛᴇ̄ʀᴇ, by lenition.

(8–9) Contrast Bernart's wish never to resist love with Marcabru's boast that he has never felt it (14.61–66).

(10) **sabi'**] **Saber** < VL *ꜱᴀᴘᴇ̄ʀᴇ, CL ꜱᴀᴘᴇʀᴇ, by lenition.

(10–12) On the sequence of tenses in **sabi'**, **vengues**, **aurai**, see "Complex Structures" in chapter 27.

(13) **jauzimen**] **Jauzir** < CL ɢᴀᴜᴅᴇ̄ʀᴇ; lenition with change of conjugation.

(14) **aten**] **Atendre** < CL ᴀ̆ᴛᴛᴇ̆ɴᴅᴇ̆ʀᴇ, with simplification of the double consonant.

(17) **dechader**] LL ᴅᴇ̄ᴄᴀ̆ᴅᴇ̆ʀᴇ produces **dechader** by semilearned retention, if the intervocalic **d** is not merely a Latinate graphy; the form **decazer** shows **z** by normal lenition, while **deschaer** shows reduction of the **d** to zero. Change of conjugation.

(19) **aitaus**] Fem. adjective type 2; cf. chapter 9.

(25) **marchaandas**] The ᴛ in the root, CL ᴍᴇ̆ʀᴄᴀ̄ᴛᴜᴍ, becomes **d** by normal lenition in **mercadan**; here it becomes zero by accelerated lenition. On the theme of prostitution, cf. Marcabru's **pastorela** (13.61).

(29) **agradar**] CL ɢʀᴀ̆ᴛᴜᴍ > **grat**; lenition in synchronic morphology.

(33) **naturaus**] Semilearned form, because of the lack of lenition; cf. **naturaus** 50.

(34–35) 'Who chides her for what she wants / and advises her what is not fitting.'

(35) **lauza**] From CL ʟᴀᴜᴅᴀᴛ; ᴅ > **z** by lenition.

(37) **bel semblanz**] Final **-s** (**bels**) is omitted before initial **s-**.

(38) **vezer**] From CL ᴠɪ̆ᴅᴇ̄ʀᴇ; by lenition ᴅ > **z**.

(45) **midonz**] Invariable for case, here obl.

(46) **nadaus**] Christmas as the season of rejoicing for the birth of Christ; not because of Christmas presents, which have never been customary in France (cf. *étrennes* 'New Year's Day gifts'), nor because of the Christmas tree, an English innovation of the Victorian era.

(49) **uns sols dias**] Masc.; cf. Sp. *buenos días*; see further in Glossary.

Explain the following etymologies:

1. ARBĪTRĬUM > /arbijre/ > **albire** 'opinion'
2. BĔLLUM > **bẹl, bẹlh** 'beautiful'
3. BĬBIT > **bẹu** 'he drinks'
4. CAPTĪVUM 'prisoner' > VL *CACTĪVUM > **caitiu** 'wretched'
5. ĪPSUM > **ẹps, ẹis, ẹus** 'self'
6. MŬLTUM > **mọlt, mọut** 'very'
7. OBSCŪRUM (cf. E. *obscure*) > **oscur** 'dark'
8. SCRĪPTUM > **escrit, escriut** 'written'
9. SĔX > **sẹis** 'six'

CHAPTER 17

Consonants (Section 3) ℒᵤₘ .

DEVELOPMENT OF YOD

Classical Latin had a semiconsonant (or semivowel), yod, spelled either I or J, as in words like ĬAM / JAM 'now.'[1] In the position before a vowel (hiatus), unaccented CL short ĭ and short ĕ lost syllabic value with the general reduction of unstressed syllables, and became yod.[2] Yod was also produced from a consonant in implosive position by the process of yodicism (ch. 16). Whatever its origin, a yod once produced could develop in the following ways.

1. Yod combined with [l] and [n] to produce **lh** and **nh**, the palatal versions of these consonants.

Yod produced from CL ĭ or ĕ in hiatus:

    lh: CL MĔLĬŌREM (cf. E. *meliorate*) > **melhọr** 'better'

           CL FĪLĬAM > **filha** 'daughter'

    nh: CL SENĬŌREM 'older' (cf. E. *senior*) > **senhọr** 'sir'

           CL LĪNĔAM > **linha** 'straight line'

Yod from other vocalic sources:

    lh: Ctc. **galia* 'strength' + **-art** > **galhart** 'outrageous'

    nh: CL LŎNGĒ > **lọnh, lọnh** 'far' (adv.)

Yod from yodicism:

    lh: CL PĔRĪCŬLUM > */pẹrik'lo/ > **perilh** 'peril'

           CL VĬGĬLĀRE > /vẹg'lar/ > **velhar** 'to remain awake'; cf. **revelhar** 'to awaken'

---

[1] "It is quite clear that in early and classical Latin consonantal *i* was similar to Eng. *y* in *yet* and *yoke*, namely [j]" (Sturtevant, par. 164).

[2] Recall that in VL, the close /ẹ/ produced from CL short ĭ and long ĕ could no longer bear stress when in hiatus, as in CL MŬLĬĔREM > **molhẹr** (ch. 11).

lh: CL fǎllĕre + **-ir** > **falhir** 'to fail' (by yodicism in the double l, unlike more frequent simplification of double consonants)

nh: CL planctum > **planh** 'plaint, lamentation'

CL rĕgnāre > **renhar** 'to live, to rule'

2. Otherwise, yod at the beginning of a word or a syllable developed to [dž] (as in E. *judge*):

CL ĭam > **ja** 'now,' pronounced like It. *già*; cf. Fr. *(dé)jà* or E. *déjà vu*, where [dž] has simplified to [ž];

CL ĭocum > **jǫc** 'game'

CL maĭōrem 'greater' > **majǫr** (cf. E. *majority*)

3. If the following vowel was reduced, yod combined with a preceding vowel to form a diphthong:

CL mǎĭum > **mai** 'May'

4. If the following vowel was reduced and yod followed a consonant, it could be anticipated across the consonant and so appear in the preceding syllable:

CL bǎsĭum > **bais** 'kiss'

VL *pǒstĭus (CL pǒst, pǒstĕa influenced by mĕlĭus) > **pǫis** 'then'

CL vǎrĭum 'variegated' > **vair** 'vair, fur of a gray-and-white squirrel'

CL sanctum > **saint** 'saint, saintly, holy' (the yod was produced from [k] by yodicism, and was then anticipated: /sankto/ > /sanjto/ > /sajnt/)

5. Yod could also be anticipated across a consonant when preceding the stressed vowel:

CL fŭsĭōnem > **foizǫn** 'abundance'

CL mānsĭōnem > **maizǫn** 'house'

ChL mōrtārĭŏlum > **mortairǫl** 'type of gravy' (with stress shift in VL; see ch. 11)

DEVELOPMENT OF WAW

Classical Latin consonantal v was pronounced like the semiconsonant [w].[3]

---

[3] "It is clear that in classical Latin consonantal *u* was similar to English *w*. The beginnings of a spirant pronunciation led to a confusion with *b* as early as the first century A.D. No doubt the sound at first was a bilabial spirant [β]" (Sturtevant, par. 155).

1. Normally, CL [w] at the beginning of a word or a syllable became [β] (the sound of *b* in Sp. *caballo*, written **v** in OOc):

> CL vīnum > **viṇ** 'wine' (E. preserves the initial consonant of the Latin word, which entered Germanic by early borrowing)
>
> CL vōcem > **voṭz** 'voice'
>
> CL sĕrvīre > **servir** 'to serve'
>
> CL nŏvĕllum > **noveḷ** 'new'

But CL [w] could be absorbed into a lip-rounded vowel, [o] or [u]:

> CL pavōrem > **paoṛ** 'fear'
>
> CL provĭncĭam 'province' > **Proẹnsa** 'Provence'

2. Word-initial Germanic *w* became **g**:

> Germ. **wahta* (cf. E. *watch*) > **gaita** 'watchman'
>
> Frankish **werra* > **guẹrra** 'war'
>
> Germ. **wīsa* > **guiza** 'kind, manner'

Sometimes word-initial VL v was influenced by Germanic *w*:

> CL vastāre 'to ruin' (cf. E. *to devastate*), influenced by Germ. **wōstjan* 'to lay waste' > **gastar** (cf. Fr. *gâter*)

3. VL [w] after [k] or [g] normally disappeared in OOc:

> CL quandō [kwando] > **can** 'when'; [kw] is preserved in It. *quando*, Sp. *cuando*, but becomes [k] in Fr. *quand*
>
> CL sanguĭnem (cf. E. *sanguine*) > sanguem > **sanc** 'blood'

4. At the end of a word or a syllable in OOc, [w] remained:

> CL vīvit > **viu** 'he lives'
>
> CL lĕvem > **lẹu** 'easily'
>
> CL năvem > **nau** 'ship'
>
> CL vīvĕre > **viure** 'to live'
>
> CL mĕnte hăbēre 'to have in mind' > **mentaure** 'to mention'

SPORADIC CONSONANT CHANGES

Assimilation

One consonant may become more like another in its context:

> [b-t] > **pt**, unvoicing of the [b] by influence of voiceless [t]
>
> > CL dŭbĭtāre > **doptar** 'to fear'
>
> [m'l] > [mn] by assimilation, then [mn] simplifies to **n**

CL ămbŭlāre 'to walk' > /am'lare/ > /amnare/ > **anar** 'to go'[4]

Dissimilation

One consonant may become less like another in its context:

[r-r] > **l–r**

CL arbītrĭum > **albire** 'opinion'

Germ. **haribergōn* > **albergar** 'to lodge'

[l-l] > **r–l**

VL *lŭscĭnĭŏlum > **rosinhọl** 'nightingale'

[n-m] > **rm**

CL ănĭmam > **arma** 'soul'

[m-n] > **m–r**

LL dīem dŏmĭnĭcum > **dimẹngue, dimẹrgue** 'Sunday'

[pr-r] > **p–r**

LL (from Gk.) presbŷtĕrum > **pẹstre** 'priest'

Metathesis

A consonant may appear in a new position in its word, or two consonants may exchange positions:

[g-lt] > **gl–t**

CL sĭngŭltum 'sigh,' VL *sĭnglŭtum (influenced by glŭttīre 'to swallow') > OFr. *sanglot* (necessarily OFr. for the change of the vowel from [ẹ] to [a] under the influence of the following nasal) > **sanglọt** 'sigh'

[θ-rp] > **tr–p**

Frankish *thorp* 'village,' later 'herd' > **trọp** 'much, very, too much'

[n-l] > **l–n**

CL ănhēlāre, LL ălēnāre > **alenar** 'to breathe'

[gn] > *[ng] > **nc**

CL rĕgnum > **rẹnc** 'kingdom'

---

[4] Thus Corominas and Pascual 1: 257. Cf. Glossary for another explanation from the *FEW*: VL *ambĭtāre 'to go around' > /amb'tare/ > /andar/ > **anar**. Here [m-t] becomes [n-d] by another type of assimilation. The step /andar/ > **anar** remains difficult to understand.

Some Greek sounds entered Vulgar Latin by borrowing in ways that require mention:

χ (chi) > VL /k/

> Gk. χορδα 'rope' > VL CORDA > **corda** 'rope'; cf. **acordar** in Glossary

θ (theta) > VL /t/

> Gk. σπαθα > VL SPATA > **espaza** 'sword' (by accelerated lenition); see chapter 15

φ (phi) > VL /p/ (early), or /f/ (late)

> LL (from Gk.) STĔPHĂNUM > STĔPĂNUM > **Estęve** 'Stephen'

> LL (from Gk.) PHLĔGMA > **flęgma** 'phlegm' (*PD*)

ζ (zeta) > VL /dj/ > OOc [dž]

> LL (influenced by Gk.) ZĔLŌSUM > VL /djęlǫsum/ > **gelǫs** 'jealous'

κ (kappa) > VL /k/, /g/

> LL (from Gk.) CATA > **cada** 'by'; cf. **cascuṇ** in Glossary

Some Germanic sounds entered Vulgar Latin by borrowing in ways that require mention:

ð (eth) (as in *then*) > VL /d/

> Frankish **waiðanjan* > VL /wadanjare/ > **gazanhar**, It. *guadagnare* 'to win'

θ (thorn) (as in *thin*) > **t** (cf. Gk. θ > /t/, above)

> Germ. *θrescan* > VL /trescare/ > **trescar** 'to dance, to jump' (*PD*)

hh > VL /kk/ > OOc /k/

> Germ. **jehhjan* > VL /jekkire/ > **gequir** 'to leave.' Note that CL H was unstable, as is shown by Vergilian metrical practice, in which it is not regarded as a consonant: CL HŎNŌREM > **onǫr** 'honor.'[5]

---

[5] "From the time of our earliest documents . . . , Lat. *h* was an unstable sound. . . . Clear evidence that *h* was a weak sound is presented by its regular lack of prosodic effect in all periods. . . . In popular Latin *h* seems to have been completely lost in Pompeii in the first century A.D., and not much later everywhere in the empire" (Sturtevant, par. 180–180b).

READING 17

Bernart de Ventadorn and Peire,
Amics Bernarz del Ventadorn

1

Amics Bernarz del Ventadorn,
com vos podez del chan soffrir
qant aissi auzez esbaudir
lo rosignolet nuoit e jorn?
    Aujaz lo joi qe demena; 5
tota nuoch chanta soz la flor.
Miellz s'enten qe vos en amor!

2

Peire, lo dormir e·l sojorn
am mais que rosignol auzir;
ni ja tant no·m sabriaz dir 10
q'eu mais en la follia torn.
    Dieu lau, fors sui de cadena,
e vos e tuich ll'autr'amador
es remazut en la follor.

3

Bernarz, greu er pros ni cortes
qui ab amor no·s sap tener;
ni ja tan no·us fara doler
qe mais non vailla c'autre bes,
    car si fai mal, puois abena. 20
Greu a hom gran ben ses dolor,
mais ades venz lo jois lo plor.

4

Peire, si fos dos anz o tres
lo segles faiz al mieu plazer,
de domnas vos dic eu lo ver:
non foron mais pregadas ges, 25
    anz sostengran tan gran pena
q'ellas nos feron tant d'onor
q'anz nos pregueran que nos lor.

5

Bernarz, so es desavinen
qe domnas preguen; anz cove 30
c'om las prec e lor clam merce.
Et es plus fols, mon escïen,
    qe cel qe semn'en l'arena
qui las blasma ni lor valor;
e mou de mal enseingnador. 35

6

Peire, molt ai lo cor dolen
qan d'una falsa mi sove
qe m'a mort e no sai per que,
mais car l'amava finamen.
Fach ai longa carantena,
e sai, si la fezes loignor,
ades la trobera peior.

7

Bernarz, foudaz vos amena
car aissi vos partez d'amor,
per cui a hom prez e valor.

8

Peire, qui ama desena,
car las trichariz entre lor
an tout joi e prez e valor.

Meter:

a	b	b	a	c	d	d
8	8	8	8	7'	8	8

Tens. 6 d 7, 2–3.

a = **-orn, -es, -en.**
b = **-ir, -er, -e.**
c = **-ena.** d = **-or.**
Frank 621:7.

P-C 323,4 = 70,2. Major editions: Zenker 790–92; Appel, *Bernart,* no. 2; Nichols et al., no. 2; Lazar, no. 28; Riquer, no. 48.

Music: For transcription, see pages 570–71; from *W* fol. 190. Editions: Fernández de la Cuesta and Lafont 102; van der Werf and Bond 230*; Switten and Chickering 1.71–72 and cassette 1.

Eight manuscripts: *A* fol. 177v–178; *D^a* fol. 143v–144; *E* p. 212; *G* fol. 100v–101; *I* fol. 155–v; *K* fol. 141–v; *L* fol. 51v–52; *W* fol. 190–v. Base *D.* See the facsimile of ms. *D* (*Canzoniere,* vol. 2).

Attributions: Bernart de Ventadorn *AIK*; Bernart *L*; Peire *L*; Peire Vidal *W*; Peirol *ADIK.* Perhaps Peire d'Alvernhe (fl. 1149–68).

Stanza order

DAEGL 1	2	3	4	5	6	7	8
IK	1	2	3	4	5	—	7	8
W	1	2	—	—	—	—	—

Rejected readings in the base manuscript: (14) remazuz *DGIKL,* remasut *AE,* remasu *W.* (15–16) *inverted DAIKL, as here EG.* (22–23) Peire, si fos al mieu plazer / lo segles faiz dos anz o tres *DAGIKL, as here E.* (33) om. *D,* qe cel qe semna en l'arena *GL,* . . . semena arena *A,* . . . semena l'arena *E,* . . . semen en arena *IK.* (41) ssi *D;* loignor *AEGL,* lo jorn *D, om. IK.* (44) vos *AEGIKL,* nos *D.* (46) qui ben ama *DAIK,* ben om. *EGL.*

Selected variants: (6) soz *DAEL,* sor *GIK,* sur *W.* (26) greu p. *AEGL,* gran *DIK.* (35) del *IK,* di *DAEGL.* (42) trobava *A,* trobaria *E,* trobera *DGL, om. IK.* (48) valor *DAEG,* amor *IKL.*

(4) **rosignolet**] From VL *lŭscĭnĭŏlum by dissimilation (see above). **nuoit**] CL nŏctem; yodicism, then the yod combines with the preceding vowel to form a diphthong (**noit**) or a triphthong, as here; by an alternative development the yod produces assibilation in the [t] (see ch. 18), hence the dictionary form **nǫch, nuoch** in v. 6.

(7) **miellz**] From CL mĕlĭus 'better' (adverb). Syncope of the unstressed penult produces yod, which combines with the [l] to produce **lh**, while also producing the diphthongization of the preceding vowel.

(12) **Dieu lau**] From CL dĕum, laudem; in both words, waw, made final, remains. **cadena**] From CL catēnam, by lenition.

(13) **tuich**] From VL *tōttī; the final syllable is reduced to yod, which produces assibilation of the preceding [t] and metaphony of [ǫ] to [u], and is anticipated to produce **ui**. **ll'autr'amador**] CL nom. pl. ĭllī is reduced to an aphetic (headless) form by attraction to the headword; the final syllable is reduced to yod, which combines with [l] to produce **lh**, spelled **ll**.

(14) **es** = **etz. remazut**] Nom. pl. masc.

(18) **vailla**] From CL valĕat; syncope produces yod, which combines with [l], producing **lh**, spelled **ill**.

(23) **mieu**] From CL mĕum; final -m falls; final [u] becomes waw, which joins the stressed vowel and produces diphthongization.

(24) **eu**] From CL ĕgo; by lenition and reduction of [o] to waw, which joins the stressed vowel and produces optional diphthongization in the form **ieu**.

(26) **sostengran**, (27) **feron**, (28) **pregueran**] Second conditionals.

(38) **m'a mort**] **Morir** used with **aver** is transitive.

(41) **loignor**] From CL lŏngĭōrem, with reduction of the unstressed internal syllable to yod, which combines with [n] to produce **nh**, spelled **ign**.

(41–42) **si la fezes . . . la trobera**] By definition the second conditional accompanies conditions in the past subjunctive, as here (ch. 27).

Explain the following etymologies:

1. Campānĭam 'a province of Italy' > **campanha** 'field'
2. consĭlĭum > **conselh** 'counsel'
3. extrānĕum > **estranh** 'foreign'
4. făctĭōnem > **faison** 'manner'
5. fĭngĕre > /fegner/ (by metathesis) > **fenher** 'to pretend'
7. VL mīrăcŭlum 'marvel' > /mirak'lo/ > **miralh** 'mirror'
8. pēĭōrem > **pejor** 'worse'
9. pŭgnum > **ponh** 'fist'
10. Frankish *ŭrgōlī > **orgolh** 'pride'

CHAPTER 18

Consonants (Section 4) ~~Mon~~

TRANSITIONAL CONSONANTS

Between two consonants, a new one may arise that has some features of the first and some features of the second:

> CL ĕsse, VL ĕssĕre (by analogy to regular infinitives in -ĕre) > ẹser, ẹstre 'to be'; cf. It. *essere*, Fr. *être*. Transitional [t] is dental, like both [s] and [r]; as a stop, [t] anticipates the flap [r].

> CL rĕpōnĕre > **rebọndre** 'to bury.' Transitional [d] is dental, like both [n] and [r]; not nasal, like [n], but oral, like [r]; as a stop, [d] anticipates flap [r].

> LL sĭmĭlāre > **semblar** 'to seem'; cf. Fr. *sembler*, E. *to resemble*. Transitional [b] is bilabial, like [m], but oral (nonnasal), like [l].

ASSIBILATION

The term *assibilation* refers to the creation of a sibilant: palatal [ž] or [š], dental [z] or [s]. *Assibilation* will be preferred in this book to the more customary term *palatalization*, which refers less precisely to the process of movement toward the palate.

Assibilation occurred in OOc as a transition between a consonant and a following yod, front vowel [i, ẹ, ę], or central vowel [a]; the sibilant functions as a transitional consonant. The fundamental element is the normal evolution of yod at the beginning of a word or syllable into [dž], as in CL ĭam > **ja**, It. *già* (see ch. 17). Accordingly, the sibilant usually produced is palatal [ž] or its unvoiced counterpart, [š]. Under some circumstances, however, the result is, instead, dental [z] or unvoiced [s]. Such circumstances involve transition between an original consonant [t], which is dental like [s], or a [k] that becomes a [t], and a specifically front vocalic element [j, i, ę, ę̧], which is closer to the dental position than is the central vowel [a].

The concept of assibilation gathers together phenomena that are often treated separately: the evolution of yod, the "palatalization" of [k] and [g], and the development of certain consonant clusters. As will be seen, however, the various forms of assibilation represent the same essential process.

Assibilation of a Voiced Stop Followed by Yod

Assibilation of a voiced stop [b, d, g] followed by yod is not really a separate phenomenon. Vulgar Latin yod at the beginning of a word or a syllable normally became [dž] (see ch. 17). When the onset of the syllable comprised a voiced stop followed by yod, the yod developed normally to [dž], creating an implosive position for the voiced stop, and the stop disappeared by simplification (see ch. 16):

[bj > bdž > dž]

> CL RŬBĔUM > /rǫbjo/ > / rǫbdže/ > /rǫdže/ > **rǫge** 'red'; cf. **enrogir** in Glossary

[dj > ddž > dž]

> CL DĬŬRNUM 'daily' (adj.) > **jǫrn** 'day' (n.); cf. It. *giorno*

[gj > gdž > dž]

> ChL RĔLĬGĬŌNEM > **religïǫn** [relidžiǫn] 'religious order'; for the pronunciation of the sibilant, cf. It. *religione*, E. *religion*, in contrast to Fr. *religion*

Assibilation in Consonant Groups

Assibilation in the consonant groups [kt, tk, dk] may be analyzed as yodicism of the first consonant (see ch. 16), followed by metathesis (ch. 17) yielding consonant plus yod, and finally assibilation by yod:

[kt > *jt > *tj > tš]

> CL FĂCTUM > /fakto/ > /fajto/, /fatjo/ > **fait** or assibilated **fach** /fatš/ 'done' (past participle), 'deed'

> CL NŎCTEM > **nǫit** or **nǫch** 'night'

> CL DĬCTUM > **dit** or **dich** 'said' (past participle), 'word'

[tk > *jk > *kj > tš]

> suffix -ĀTĬCUM > /-at'ko/ > **-atge** as in **salvatge**, **coratge**, etc. (see Glossary: Prefixes, Infixes, Suffixes)

[dk > *jk > *kj > tš]

> CL MĒDĬCUM > **mętge** 'doctor' (*PD*)

Alternative forms such as **fait** and **noit**, in which assibilation did not occur, provide supporting evidence for the assumption of yodicism. In **dit** the vowel represents a closing of CL ĭ, VL /ẹ/ (cf. It. *detto*), under the influence of a yod, produced by yodicism and then absorbed into the vowel.

Assibilation of [g] and [k] by a Front or Central Vowel

The front vowels [i, ẹ, ę] and central [a] may cause assibilation of [g] and [k]:

> [g (+ i, ẹ, ę, a) > dž]
>> CL SAGĬTTAM > **sagęta** 'arrow'
>> CL GAUDĒRE > **jauzir** [džawdzir] 'to enjoy'
> [k (+ a) > tš]
>> CL CANTĀRE > **cantar** [ka-] or **chantar** [tša-] 'to sing'

All the forms of assibilation presented so far produce the palatal sibilant [ž] or [š]. However, when [k] is followed by a front vowel, the result is a dental:

> [k (+ i, ẹ, ę) > ts > ss > s]
>> CL ŏCCĪDĔRE, VL *AUCĪDĔRE > **aucire** [awtsire] 'to kill'
>> CL ĬACĒRE > **jazęr** 'to lie' [džadzęr] ([ts] > [dz] by lenition)
>> CL CAELUM > **cęl** [tsęl] 'sky'
>> CL QUĪNDĔCĬM > **quintze**, **quinze** 'fifteen'

The two factors favoring production of the dental sibilant in this development are the passage of [k] to dental [t], as evidenced in the resulting forms, and the front position of the vowel.

Assibilation of a Voiceless Stop Followed by Yod

After the voiceless stop [p], yod produced the palatal sibilant:

> [pj > ptš > tš]
>> CL SAPĬAT 'that he know' (subjunctive) > **sapcha** [saptša], **sacha** [satša]

However, after the voiceless stops [t] and [k], the result was the dental sibilant:

> [tj > tts > ts] at the end of the word; within the word, [ts > s]:

CL prĕtĭum 'price' > **prętz** 'merit'

CL cantĭōnem > **cansoṇ** 'song'

CL rătĭōnem > **razoṇ** 'reason' (s > **z** by lenition).

[kj > kts > ts] at the end of the word; within the word, [ts > s]:

CL brăchĭum > **bratz** 'arm'

CL facĭat > **fasa** 'that he do' (subjunctive of **faire**)

VL *ĕccĕ hŏc > **so** 'it, that, what'; cf. It. *ciò*, Fr. *ce*; by aphaeresis (ch. 13).

Again, the factors favoring production of the dental sibilant are the dental [t] (original or produced from velar [k]) and the front position of the yod.

READING 18

Bernart de Ventadorn,
Qan vei la lauzeta mover

1

Qan vei la lauzeta mover
de joi sas alas contra·l rai,
que s'oblid'e·is laissa cazer
per la doussor c'al cor li vai,
ai! Tant grans enveia m'en ve
de cui que veia jauzion,
meravillas ai car desse
lo cors de desirier no·m fon.

2

Ai las, tant cujava saber
d'amor, e qant petit en sai!
Car ieu d'amar no·m puosc tener
celei don ja pro non aurai,
tolt m'a mon cor e tolt m'a se
e mi meteus e tot lo mon,
e qan si·m tolc no·m laiset re
mas desirier e cor volon.

3

De las dompnas mi desesper;
ja mais en lor no·m fiarai,
c'aissi cum las suoil captener,
enaissi las descaptenrai.
Pois vei c'una pro no m'en te

vas lieis qe·m destrui e·m cofon,
totas las dopt'e las mescre,
car ben sai c'atretals si son.

4

Amors es perduda per ver, 25
et ieu non o saubi anc mai;
que cil que plus en degr'aver
no n'a jes, et on la qerrai?
Ai, cum mal sembla qui la ve
c'az aquest caitiu desiron, 30
que ja ses lieis non aura be,
laisse morir que no·il aon.

5

Puois ab midonz no·m pot valer
Dieus ni merces ni·l dreitz q'ieu ai,
ni a lieis no ven a plazer 35
qu'il m'am, ja mais no lo dirai;
e si·m part de lieis e·m recre,
mort m'a e per mort li respon;
e vau m'en, s'ella no·m rete,
caitius, en issill, no sai on. 40

6

Anc non agui de mi poder,
ni non fui mieus de l'or'en sai
qe·m laisset en sos huoills vezer
en un miraill que mout mi plai.
Miraills, pois me miriei en te, 45
m'ant mort li sospir de prion,
c'aissi·m perdei cum perdet se
lo bels Narcisus en la fon.

7

D'aisso·s fai ben femna parer
ma dompna, per q'ieu lo retrai 50
car non vol so que deu voler
e so c'om li deveda, fai.
Cazutz sui e mala merce,
et ai ben faich co·l fols e·l pon;
e non sai per que m'esdeve, 55
mas car pojei trop contr'amon.

8

Tristan, no·n auretz jes de me,
que vau m'en, marritz, no sai on.
De chantar mi lais e·m recre,
e de joi e d'amor m'escon. 60

Meter:

a	*b*	*a*	*b*	*c*	*d*	*c*	*d*
8	8	8	8	8	8	8	8

Ch. 7 u 8, 1–4.
-ęr, -ai, -ę, -ǫn.
Frank 407:9.

P-C 70,43. Major editions: Appel, *Bernart,* no. 43; Nichols et al., no. 43; Lazar, no. 31; Riquer, no. 60.

Music: For transcription, see pages 571–73; from *W* fol. 190; also notated in *G* and *R.* For sung performance of the reading, refer to the accompanying compact disk. Editions: Fernández de la Cuesta and Lafont 152–55; van der Werf and Bond 62*–71*; Switten and Chickering 1.64–70 and cassette 1.

Twenty-three manuscripts: *A* fol. 90–v; *C* fol. 47–v; *D* fol. 16–v; *E* p. 102; *F* fol. 22; *G* fol. 10–v; *I* fol. 28; *K* fol. 16v; *K'*; *L* fol. 19v–20; *M* fol. 39–v; *N* fol. 140–v; *O* pp. 60–61; *P* fol. 16v–17; *Q* fol. 25v–26; *R* fol. 56v–57; *S* pp. 53–55; *U* fol. 89v–90; *V* fol. 55–v; *V*ᵃ pp. 169–171; *W* fol. 190v; *X* fol. 148v; *a* pp. 91–92. Quotations in α 29675 (st. 3); *β¹* 402; *β³* ms. B 402 (=v. 23); ε 5198 (st. 1–2); μ 263 (=v. 17), 547 (=v. 1), 548–49 (=vv. 49–50), 560–61 (=vv. 22–23); *d* no. 6; Gerbert de Montreuil, *Le roman de la violette ou de Gérart de Nevers* 4187 (st. 1). Base *A.*

Divergent attributions: Peire Vidal *W;* Anonymous *O, V*ᵃ*, X,* ε, *Le roman de la violette.*

Stanza order

AGLPS	1	2	3	4	5	6	7	8
D	1	2	3	4	5	6	—	—
N	1	2	3	(4)	6	7	5	—
IKK¹	1	2	3	6	4	5	7	—
V	1	2	3	6	5	7/4	4/7	—
O	1	2	3	6	7	5	4	8
MR	1	2	3	6	7	5	4	—
a	1	2	3	6	7	5	—	—
E	1	2	3	7	4	5	6	8
*CV*ᵃ	1	2	6	3	5	7	4	8
QU	1	2	6	3	7/4	4/7	5	8
WX	1	2	—	—	—	—	—	—
F	1	5	—	—	—	—	—	—

Rejected readings in the base manuscript: (3) oblida e. (12) cellui *A,* celei *DELPS,* celleis *IKK'N,* cella *GMOQUV*ᵃ*a,* cele *W,* celi *X*ε, de lieys *CRV.* (21) vei *CDEGIKK'LMNOPQRSUV*ᵃ*a,* om. *A.* (23) dopti e. (27) degra aver. (43) de mos huoills *AGLPSVV*ᵃ*,* en sos oillz *IKK'Oa,* e sos oillz *D,* sos hueils *EQU,* a sos bels oils *N,* a mos huelhs *C.* (49) ·s *CELQR,* se *GM,* ayso . . . femna·s μ, om. *AIKK'NOPSUVV*ᵃ*a.* (56) contra amon. (57) avetz *AG,* aurez *U,* aures *EO,* Tristeza non ave *PQS,* Tristesa non hay *V*ᵃ*.*

Selected variants: (2) sas] las *CDE.* (13–14) se / e mi meteus] me e si mezeus *DEK'LPS*ε*, . . .* meteissa *G.* (18) fierai *DSU.* (25) Amors] merces *CGIKK'LNOPQRSUV*ᵃ*.* (26) saubi] sabia *Q,* conuc *MV.* (32) murir *ER.* (34) Dieus] precs *CRUVV*ᵃ*a.* (36) qu'il m'am] qu'ieu l'am *CIKK'NPRUV*ᵃ*a.* (59) lais] giec *EO,* tuoill *GLPQSU.*

(1) **la lauzeta**] Or **l'alauzeta**; cf. Fr. *alouette*; Appel (*Bernart* 255) prefers the aphetic form by analogy to modern Limousin *lauseto*.

(2) **Sas alas**] Since **lauzeta** is feminine, one could translate as 'When I see the lark beat her wings . . . that forgets herself, 'etc. But the parallel with the poet suggests 'his wings.'

(6) 'Of anyone I see rejoicing.' **veia**] Subjunctive after indefinite relative **cui que** (cf. ch. 26).

(16) **volon**] 'Yearning,' with a punning overtone, perhaps, on the root **vol-**, as in **volar** 'to fly,' like the lark.

(21) **una . . . no**] 'Not a one.'

(26) **saubí**] Preterit 1st sg.: root **sab-** + past-set marker waw + tense marker zero + person marker **-í**, as in **partí**, **aguí** (ch. 6).

(32) **aon**] **Aondar** from CL ăbŭndāre, by lenition. **Laisse** and **aon** are subjunctive because of the expression of judgment **mal sembla qui la ve** 29 (see ch. 26).

(29) **qui la ve**] 'To anyone who sees her.'

(35) **plazer**] From CL placēre; assibilation of [k] by a front vowel.

(36) **am**] Subjunctive because of the (negative) expression of desire in **no ven a plazer** 35. **lo**] Refers to **·l dreitz q'ieu ai** 34.

(42) **non fui mieus**] 'I was not my own' because she took me (13–14).

(45) **me miriei en te**] Cf. Jaufre Rudel:

> Ai, car me fos lai pelleris
> si que mos fustz e mos tapis
> fos pels sieus bels oills remiratz! 15.33–35

(48) **Narcisus**] In Ovid's *Metamorphoses* (3.339–510), the handsome youth Narcissus flees the nymph Echo, falls in love with his reflection in a pool, then falls into the pool, drowns, and is metamorphosed into a narcissus growing on the shore, while Echo withers away into a mere echo of her former cries. Bernart's narcissistic lover looked into his lady's eyes and saw himself; Jaufre Rudel wished to do the same (15.35).

(49–52) By reproaching his lady, Bernart falls under his own censure, from 17.34.

(51) **so**] VL *ĕccĕ hŏc, with assibilation of [k] by the front vowel -ĕ, which is then deleted.

(53) **e**] = **en. merce**] CL mĕrcēdem, with assibilation of [k] by the front vowel.

(54) **co·l fols e·l pon**] According to a proverb, the wise man dismounts when crossing a bridge but the fool does not, and so falls into the river. See Paden, *"Et ai be faih."*

(57) **Tristan**] **Senhal** for someone who might have been a joglar, a patron, or a friend; allusion to the hero of romance, who died for love.

Exercise

Analyze the following etymologies:

1. LL ᴀᴘᴘʀŏᴘꞮᴀʀᴇ > **aprochar** 'to approach'
2. Germ. **burg-* + *-ᴇɴsᴇᴍ* (influenced by Germ. *-isk*) > **borgęs** 'town dweller, bourgeois'
3. CL ᴄᴀʟᴄĕᴜᴍ, VL ᴄᴀʟᴄĕᴀᴍ > **causa** 'stocking'; cf. Fr. *chausse*, E. *Chaucer*
4. CL ᴄᴀᴍʙꞮᴀʀᴇ 'to change' > **cambiar** (three syllables), **camjar** (two syllables) 'to change'; cf. Fr. *changer*
5. CL (from Gk.) ᴄᴀᴍĕʀᴀᴍ 'arched ceiling' > **cambra** 'bedroom'; cf. E. *camera, chamber*
6. CL ᴅꞮʀēᴄᴛᴜᴍ > **dręit, dręch** 'right, what is right'
7. CL ꜰʀꞮɢĭᴅᴜᴍ, VL *ꜰʀĭɢĭᴅᴜᴍ (influenced by ʀĭɢĭᴅᴜᴍ 'stiff') > **fręg** [frętš] 'cold'
8. CL ɢᴀᴜᴅꞮᴜᴍ > **gauch** 'joy'
9. CL ᴍăʀᴛꞮᴜᴍ > **martz** 'the month of March'
10. CL ᴠꞮᴄīɴᴜᴍ, VL *ᴠēᴄīɴᴜᴍ > **veziṇ** [vedziṇ] 'near'

CHAPTER 19

Alternation of Verb Roots

A number of verbs in OOc show more than one root in the various forms of the conjugation. For example:

vezẹr 'to see'

vez-	**vei-**	**ve-**
imperf. **vezia**	fut. **veirai**	pres. 3rd sg. **vẹ**

avẹr 'to have'

av-	**au-**	**a-**
pres. 1st pl. **avẹm**	fut. 1st sg. **aurai**	pres. 3rd sg. **a**

Vezẹr and **avẹr** show roots ending in these patterns:

z-	yod-	zero-
v-	waw-	zero-

Such series have a basis in historical phonological change, since the three phases correspond to lenition in the intervocalic position (CL vĭdēbam > **vezia**; CL habēmus > **avẹm**); in the implosive position, to yodicism (VL vĭdēre habēo, /vedr'ajo/ > **veirai**) or wawicism (VL habēre habēo, /abr'ajo/ > **aurai**); and in word-final position, to deletion (CL vĭdĭt > **vẹ**; CL hăbet > **a**). If series of roots such as these corresponded fully to series of phonological contexts, we could regard the changes they go through as an elaborate form of elision.

However, such series of roots cannot be fully explained in phonological terms and must be recognized as properly morphological, because phonological context does not account for all the alternations. Roots ending in **-z** occur not only with a following vowel but also in word-final position (as **-tz**), as in present, third person singular **ditz** (**dire** 'to say') and **platz** (**plazẹr** 'to please'), and present, first person singular **fatz** (**faire** 'to do'). Roots ending in yod or waw occur not only with a following consonant but also in final position, as in present, third person singular **plai** (**plazẹr**), **fai** (**faire**). Roots ending in zero occur not only in final position but also before a consonant, as in present subjunctive, first person singular **diga** (**dire**), or before a vowel, as in present subjunctive, third person singular **ria** (**rire** 'to laugh').

The alternation of verb roots is in part phonologically conditioned, and in part morphological. The alternate forms of the root are allomorphs—that is, they are alternative versions of the same root morpheme. It is striking that their distribution frequently overlaps, as in present, third person singular **platz** or **plai**, **ditz** or **di**, **fai** or **fa**, and so on.

Analysis of the forms occurring in the texts in this book shows that variations in root that seem baffling at first sight actually express meaningful patterns in the language. The apparent irregularities in verbs such as **anar** 'to go,' **avẹr** 'to have,' **ẹser** 'to be,' **estar** 'to stand, to be,' **faire** 'to do,' **podẹr** 'to be able' turn out to be in large measure regular—or at least their irregularities can be clearly defined.

SERIES Z—YOD—ZERO

An infinitive in **-ẹr**: **vezẹr** 'to see' (cf. **plazẹr** 'to please')

vez-	vei-	ve-
imperf. 1st sg. **vezia** inf. **vezẹr**	fut. **veirai**, etc.	pres. 3rd sg. **vẹ** pres. 1st sg. **vẹi** = **ve-** + yod pres. subj. **veia** = **ve-** + **ja** **ve-** > **vi-** in past set:[1] pret. 3rd sg. **vi** past subj. **vis**

[1] By metaphony as a past tense marker.

*(cont.)*An infinitive in **-re**: **faire** 'to do' (cf. **creire** 'to believe')

faz-	**fai-**	**fa-**
pres. 1st sg. **fatz**	pres. 3rd sg. **fai**	pres. 3rd sg. **fa**
	pres. 2nd pl. **faitz**[2]	pres. 3rd pl. **fan**[3]
		pres. 1st sg. **fauc**[4]
		pres. subj. 1st sg. **fasa**[5]
imperf. 3rd sg. **fazia**		fut. 1st sg. **farai**
		= **fa-** + **r** + **á** + -yod
		1st cond. 2nd pl. **fariátz**
		= **fa-** + **r** + **ía** + -**átz**
pret. 3rd sg. **fẹtz**[6]	pret. 3rd sg. **fẹi**	pret. 3rd sg. **fẹ**
pret. 1st pl. **fezem**		pret. 1st pl. **fẹm**
	pret. 3rd pl. **fẹyron**	
pret. 1st sg. **fis**[7]		pret. 1st sg. **fi**
past subj. 1st sg. **fezẹ́s**[8]		
	2nd cond. 1st sg. **fẹira**	2nd cond. 3rd sg. **fẹra**
		2nd cond. 3rd pl. **fẹro**
	inf. **faire**[9]	inf. **far**
	pp. **fait**	pp. **fat**

[2] = **fai-** + zero + -**ẹ́tz**. Note that elision functions to efface the stressed vowel in order to preserve the diphthong.

[3] = **fa-** + zero + -**on**, with normal elision of the second, unstressed vowel.

[4] = **fa-** + zero + -[wk]; as in **vauc**, root **va-** (inf. **anar**).

[5] = **fa-** + zero + -**sa**; as in pres. subj. **plasa**, root **pla-** (inf. **plazẹr**).

[6] Metaphony marks the past set in all three roots.

[7] The root **fẹtz-** becomes **fis** by (double) metaphony, the effect of the normal yod person marker for 1st sg.; likewise, the root **fẹ-** becomes preterit 1st sg. **fi**.

[8] Metaphonized root **fẹz-** (that is, root **fatz-**, with metaphony as a past-set marker) + past subj. **ẹ́s** (after nonvowel) + person marker -zero.

[9] Inf. **faire** represents root **faj-** with the infinitive marker **r** and a support vowel. In **aucire**, **dire**, **rire**, roots ending in **-z** and zero are overt: pres. 3rd pl. **dizon**,

An infinitive in **-ẹr**: **avẹr** 'to have' (cf. **devẹr** 'ought, should')

av-	au-	a-
pres. 1st pl. **avẹm**		pres. 3rd sg. **a**
pres. 2nd pl. **avẹtz**		pres. 1st sg. **ai** = **a-** + -yod
		pres. 3rd pl. **an** = **a-** + zero + **-on**
		pres. subj. 3rd sg. **aia** = **a-** + **ja**
imperf. 3rd sg. **avia**		
	fut. 1st sg. **aurai**	
	1st cond. 1st sg. **auria**	
pret. 3rd sg. **ac**[10]		
past subj. 3rd sg. **aguẹs**[11]		
2nd cond. 3rd sg. **agra**		

ROOTS ENDING IN -[sk], -[js]

Some verbs have roots ending in -[sk] or -[js] in the present indicative, first person singular, and throughout the present subjunctive. The endings -[js] and **s** represent reductions of the final -[k] in -[sk] because of final position, followed by anticipation of the yod across the consonant (cf. ch. 17 on the development of yod) to produce [-js], or **-s** by absorption of the yod into a preceding vowel. The origin is the "inchoative" infix sc in CL, which adds a nuance of beginning action in verbs such as SENESCŌ 'I grow old' (cf. SENEŌ 'I am old') and which was normally used only in the same two tenses.

pres. 3rd sg. **di**, and so on. Latent roots ending in yod would explain the support vowel in the infinitives: **dij-re**, **rij-re**, **aucij-re**; the latent yod is absorbed into the preceding vowel of identical position. The infinitive form **diire** is attested at 25.31.

[10] Pret. 3rd sg. **ac** = **av-** + past-set marker [k] + pret. marker zero + person marker -zero.

[11] Past subjunctive tense marker **ẹs** is normal after a consonant, **s** after a vowel; cf. chapter 7.

Verbs with infinitives in **-ir** may take **-isc** / **-is** in the present tense, first, second, and third persons singular and third person plural, and throughout the present subjunctive, but such forms are infrequent. Appel (*Provenzalische* xviii–xix) provides a hypothetical model conjugation of **florir** 'to bloom,' which combines forms derived from CL FLŌRĒRE 'to be in flower' and FLŌRESCĔRE 'to begin to flower,' with change of conjugation to *FLŌRĪRE, *FLŌRĪSCĔRE:

Present	
1st sg.	**florisc**
2nd sg.	**floris, florisses**
3rd sg.	**floris**
1st pl.	**florẹm**
2nd pl.	**florẹtz**
3rd pl.	**floriscon**
present subjunctive 1st sg.	**florisca**, etc.

Fenir 'to cease' is attested in present, first person singular **fenisc** (Appel, *Provenzalische* 36.47), and also **fenis** in this book (21.1). Other forms in **-isc**, **-is** are listed in the Glossary under **guerpir** 'to give up,' **plevir** 'to pledge,' **revertir** 'to go back.'

Such forms occur with an infinitive in **-er**: **conọiser** 'to know' (CL COGNŌSCĔRE, VL *CONŌSCĔRE):

> root **conọsk-**
>> pres. 1st sg. **conọsc**
>> pres. subj. 3rd sg. **conọsca**
> root **conọis-**
>> pres. 3rd sg. **conọis**
>> imperf. 3rd sg. **conoyssia**
>> inf. **conọiser**

And with an infinitive in **-ẹr**: **podẹr** 'to be able':

> root **pọsc-**
>> pres. 1st sg. **puosc, puesc** (diphthongization of **ọ́**)
>> pres. subj. 3rd sg. **puosca**, 1st pl. **poscam**

Other forms of **podẹr** show the roots **pọd-** (pres. 3rd sg. **pọt**, 3rd pl. **pọdon**), **pọi-** (1st cond. 3rd sg. **poiria**), **pọ-** (1st cond. 3rd sg. **poria**).

Two frequent verbs, **anar** 'to go' and **estar** 'to stand, be,' are treated
as **-ar** verbs in some forms of the conjugation and as non-**ar** verbs
in others.

1. Anar treated as an **-ar** verb:[12]

root **an-**

---

pres. 1st pl. **anám** = **an-** + tense marker **a** (for **-ar** verb) + **-ám**
(after unstressed **a**), with elision

pres. subj. 3rd sg. **an** = **an-** + tense marker zero (for **-ar** verb) +
person marker -zero (3rd sg.)

imperf. 1st sg. **anava** = **an-** + tense marker **áva** (for **-ar** verb) +
person marker -zero (1st sg.)

fut. 1st sg. **anarai**, 2nd sg. **anaras**, 3rd sg. **anara**, 2nd pl.
*anarẹtz

pret. 1st sg. **aniẹy** = **an-** + past-set marker **ẹ́** (for **-ar** verb) +
pret. marker zero + person marker -yod (1st sg.), with
diphthongization

past subj. 3rd sg. **anẹs** = **an-** + past-set marker **ẹ́** (for **-ar** verb)
+ past subj. marker **s** + person marker -zero

inf. **anar** = **an-** + inf. **-ar**

2. Anar treated as a non-**ar** verb:

root **vai-**	root **va-**	root **i-**
	pres. 1st sg. **vauc**[13]	fut. 1st sg. **irai**
	pres. 1st sg. **vau**	
pres 2nd sg. **vais**		1st cond. 1st sg.
pres. 3rd sg. **vai**	pres. 3rd sg. **va**	**iria**
	pres. 3rd pl. **van**	
pres. subj. 1st sg. **vaia**		

---

[12] Asterisks mark forms attested in Appel (*Provenzalische* xl).

[13] Root **va-** + tense marker zero (for non-**ar** verb) + person marker -[wk] (1st sg.;
cf. **fauc**); variant person marker -waw in **vau**.

3. Estar treated as an **-ar** verb:

root **est-**

pres. 1st pl. **estam** = **est-** + tense marker **a** (for **-ar** verb) + **-ám**
(after unstressed **a**)

pret. 3rd sg. **estęt** = **est-** + past-set marker **ę́** (for **-ar** verb) +
pret. marker zero + person marker **-t** (3rd sg.)

inf. **estar** = **est-** + inf. **-ar**

fut. 2nd pl. **estarętz** = **est-** + **ar** + **-ętz**

4. Estar treated as a non-**ar** verb:

root **estai-**	root **está-**	root **estí-**
pres. 3rd sg. **estai**	pres. 3rd sg. **está**	pres. subj. **estía**
	pres. 3rd pl. **están**	

ESER

The verb **ęser** 'to be' displays six different roots, ranging from a syllable (vowel and consonant) to a single vowel to zero. It also shows
some exceptional markers for set, tense, and person. All the roots
are treated as non-**ar** verbs.

root **ęs-**

pres. 2nd sg. **ęst** = **ęs-** + tense marker zero (for non-**ar**
verb) + person marker **-st** (as in preterit **cantęst**)

pres. 3rd sg. **ęs** = **ęs-** + tense marker zero (for non-**ar**
verb) + person marker -zero (3rd sg.); the vowel perhaps results from confusion in phrases such as ***mę
ęs** 'for me it is' > **mę's, m'ęs** (Grandgent, par. 28.5)

pres. 1st pl. **ęsmes** = **ęs-** + tense marker zero (for non-**ar**
verb) + person marker **-́mes** (unique to this verb)

inf. **ęser, ęstre** (alternative inf. endings)[14]

root **sǫ-**

pres. 1st sg. **sǫi** = **sǫ-** + tense marker zero (for non-**ar**
verb) + person marker -yod (sporadic)

pres. 3rd pl. **sǫn** = **sǫ-** + tense marker zero (for non-**ar**
verb) + person marker **-on** (3rd pl.)

root **si-**

pres. subj. 3rd sg. **sia** = **si-** + tense marker **a** (pres. subj.,
non-**ar** verb) + person marker -zero (3rd sg.)

---

[14] Root **ę́s-** takes either inf. **-́er**, producing **ę́ser**, or inf. **-r**, which produces the
transitional consonant **t** and a support vowel: **ę́stre**.

fut. 1st sg. **serai** = **se-** + inf. **r** + tense marker **á** + person
marker -yod (1st sg.)

1st cond. 3rd sg. **seria** = **se-** + inf. **r** + tense marker **ía** +
person marker -zero (1st sg.)

root **ę-**

fut. 1st sg. and 3rd sg. **ęr** = **ę-** + inf. **r** + tense marker
zero (unlike normal **á**) + person marker -zero (1st
sg., 3rd sg.)

imperf. 3rd sg. **ęra** = **ę-** + tense marker **ra** (unlike normal **ía**) + person marker -zero (3rd sg.)

root zero-

pres. 1st pl. **ęm** = zero- + tense marker zero (for non-**ar**
verb) + person marker **-ém** (not after **a**)

pres. 2nd pl. **ętz** = zero- + tense marker zero (for non-**ar**
verb) + person marker **-ętz** (not after **a**), as in
partętz[15]

root zero + past-set marker **fǫ-**

pret. 3rd sg. **fǫ** = zero- + set marker **fǫ** + tense marker
zero + person marker -zero

pret. 3rd sg. **fǫn** = zero- + set marker **fǫ** + tense marker
zero + person marker **ŋ** (unique to this verb)

pret. 1st sg. **fui** = zero- + set marker **fǫ** + tense marker
zero + person marker -yod (normal for preterit 1st
sg.), with metaphony

past subj. 3rd sg. **fǫs** = zero- + set marker **fǫ** + tense
marker **s** (after vowel) + person marker -zero (3rd
sg.)

2nd cond. 3rd sg. **fǫra** = zero- + set marker **fǫ** + tense
marker **ra** + person marker -zero (3rd sg.)

In **ęser** two tenses have unusual markers, the future (normal **á**
in **serai**, but zero in **ęr**) and the imperfect (**ra** in **ęra**). Both tenses
substitute markers that are normal for another tense. **Ęser** is
unique in having a marker common to the tenses of the past set, **fǫ**,
which contrasts sharply with its roots and other set markers.

---

[15] That is, in synchronic analysis the verb **ętz** 'you are' is constituted entirely of
the personal ending, as in the conjugation of non-**ar** verbs. Historically it was
CL ĚSTIS that produced the OOc personal ending -**ętz**. See chapter 2.

READING 19

Giraut de Bornelh,
S'ie·us quier cosselh, bel'ami'Alamanda

Giraut de Bornelh, active about 1162–99, was born in Exideuil (canton de Chabanais, Charente). He engaged in a debate poem with Alfonso II of Aragon, perhaps in 1170, and traveled to the Holy Land during the Third Crusade (1191). Giraut left over seventy songs, among them about fifty **cansos**, *fifteen* **sirventes**, *two crusade songs, two* **planhs**, *one* **pastorela**, *one* **alba**, *and three* **tensos**, *including the present one. His* **vida** *calls him the* **maestre dels trobadors** *'master [or teacher?] of the troubadours.'*

In this poem the speaker, identified by his interlocutor as **Giraut** *9, 26, 41, and as* **Senher amics** *57, speaks to a* **donzela** *18, 33, whom he calls his* **bel'ami'Alamanda** *1. He tells her about his troubled relation with her lady,* **vostra domna** *3, whom he calls* **truanda** *'treacherous' because the two are having a lovers' quarrel. He appeals to Alamanda for help. Perhaps because their exchange is so lively, it has seemed theatrical, and therefore fictional, to many readers; but others consider it a true dialogue between the troubadour and a historical trobairitz. The manuscripts attribute the song to Giraut alone.*

1
"S'ie·us quier cosselh, bel'ami'Alamanda,
no·l me vedetz, c'om cochatz lo·us demanda;
qu'eras m'a dig vostra domna truanda
c'alhons fuy, fors yssitz de sa comanda;
pus so que·m det, er m'estra e·m demanda.
    Que·m cosselhatz?
C'a pauc lo cor d'ira dins no m'abranda,
    tant fort en soi iratz."

2
"Per Dieu, Giraut, jes aysi tot a randa
volers d'amic no·s fay ni no·s guaranda;
car si l'us falh, l'autre cove que blanda,
que lur destreg no cresca ni s'espanda.
Pero si·eus ditz d'aut pueg que sia landa,
    vos o crezatz
e plassa vos lo bes e·l mals que·us manda,
    c'aysi seretz amatz."   15

    10

3
"Non puesc sofrir que contr'erguelh non gronda,
ja siatz vos donzela bel'e blonda;
pauc d'ira·us notz e pauc joys vos aonda,
mas ges non es premieira ni segonda!
Mas yeu que tem de l'ira que·m cofonda,
    que m'en lauzatz?
Si tem murir, que·m traga pueys vas l'onda?
    Mal cug que·m capdelatz."

    20

4

"Si m'enqueres d'aital razo preonda,   25
per Dieu, Giraut, no say que·us mi responda;
pero si·eus par c'ap pauc fos jauzionda,
may vuelh pelar mon prat c'autre·l mi tonda.
Vos selaray, del plag far desironda?
    Ja l'essercatz
com so bo cors non esduy', en segonda!   30
    Ben par que n'es cochatz."

5

"Donzel', ueymay no siatz trop parleyra!
S'ela m'a trag may de cen vetz premeyra,
lauzatz me doncx que tostemps lo·y sofieyra?   35
No·us cujaratz o fezes per nessieyra
d'autr'amistat? Ar ay talan que·us fieyra;
    co no·us calatz?
Melhor cosselh dera na Berenguieira
    que vos no mi donatz."   40

6

"L'ora vey ieu, Giraut, qu'ela·us o meyra
car l'apelatz camjairitz ni leugeyra;
pero cujatz que del plag no·us enquieyra?
Mas ieu non cug que sia tan manieyra,
ans er hueymais sa promesa derieira,   45
    que que·us diatz,
si s'en destrenh tan qu'ela ja vos quieira
    hueymay treva ni patz."

7

"Bela, per Dieu no perda vostr'aiuda,
que be sabetz co me fon covenguda;   50
s'ieu ay falhit per l'ira c'ay avuda,
no·m tenga dan; s'o sentis c'a leu muda
cor d'om irat amoros, s'anc fos druda,
    del patz pessatz,
que be vos dic, mort soi si l'ai perduda—   55
    may no lo·y descobratz!"

8

"Senher amics, ja n'agr'ieu fi volguda,
mas ela·m ditz c'a dreg s'es yrascuda,
c'autra·n pregetz, com fol, tot a saupuda,
que non la val ni vestida ni nuda.   60
No fara doncs, si no·us giec, que vencuda
    s'autra·n pregatz?
Be·us en valray, si tot l'ay mantenguda,
    sol mays no·us i mesclatz."

9
"Bela, per Dieu, si d'ela n'es crezuda,
per mi lo·y afiatz." *rassurez*   63

10
"Ben o faray, mays can vos er renduda, *cédes*
s'amor no la·us tolatz!" *tu es privez de son amour*

Meter:

> *a   a   a   a   a   b   a   b*
> 10' 10' 10' 10' 10' 4   10' 6
> Tens. 8 d 8, 2-2.
> *a* = **-anda**, **-onda**, **-éra**, **-uda**; *b* = **-atz**.
> Frank 19:2.

P-C 242,69. Major editions: Kolsen, no. 57; Riquer, no. 88; Sharman, no. 57; Rieger, no. 4.

Music: For transcription, see pages 573–75; from *R* fol. 8. For sung performance of the reading, refer to the accompanying compact disk. Editions: Fernández de la Cuesta and Lafont 171–72; van der Werf and Bond 165*.

Fifteen manuscripts: *A* fol. 18v–19; *B* fol. 18v–19; *C* fol. 8v–9; *D* fol. 11v–12; *G* fol. 70v–71v; *H* fol. 37v–38; *I* fol. 23–v; *K* fol. 12–v; *N* fol. 182–v; *Q* fol. 87–v; *R* fol. 8; *R²* = *R* fol. 8, column B, with music; *V* fol. 74–v; *Z* fol. 64v–65; *a* pp. 41–42. Quotations: κ 135 (Mussafia 242 = vv. 1–2), *d* no. 36. Base *R*.

Attributions: Unanimous.

Stanza order

> *RABCDHIKNQVZa* 1   2   3   4   5   6   7   8   9   10
> *G*   1   2   3   4   5   6   7   8   —   —
> *R²*   1   —   —   —   —   —   —   —   —   —

Rejected readings in the base manuscript: (4) yssit *R*, issitz *R²ABCDGHIKNVZa*, isies *Q*. (6) cosselhat *R*, cosselhatz *R²ABCDGHIKNQVZa*. (10) voler *RCNV*, volers *ABDHIKQZa*, volerz *G*. (15) los bes e·ls mals *RCGZ*, lo bes e·l mals *ABDHIKa*, lo ben e·l mal *NV*, los bes e·l mal *Q*. (20) mas que *RHa*, mas jes *ABCG*, e . . . jes *Z*, fors que *V*, pero *IKNQ*. (31) sabacor *R*, son bon cor *HNQVa*, son bel cors *AB*, sos bels cors *G*, sen bel cors *D*, ·l sieu bel cors *IK*, ·l sieus bels cors *Z*, sos gens cors *C*. (33) Donzela *R*. (34) cen] .c. *R*. (44) sia tals sa *R*, sia tan *ABCDGHIKNQVZa*. (45) proesa *RCDGV*, promessa *ABHIKNZa*, pmessa *Q*. (57) Sen n'amic *R*, Senher amics *CDHZa*, Seign'en Giraut *ABIKN*, Segner Giraut *Q*, Per Deu *GV*. (59) assa saupuda *R*, a saubuda *ABCDGHIKNQVZa*. (65) si ela *R*, si d'ela *CDQ*, si d'ella *IKN*, si de lai *ABHZa*, si de lui *V*.

Selected variants: (4) c'alhons *RZ*, que loing *ABCNQ*, c'aillors *DGIK*, que fort *HV*, que totz *a*. (5) pus *RR²QV*, que *ABDGNZa*, quar *C*, mas *H*, en *IK*; estra *RR²*, estrai *ABCDGHIKNVZa*. (19) paucs jois *ABDHIKN*, pauts jois *V*, paucs lois *a*. (34) s'ela m'a trag *R*, si m'a mentit *IKV*, si mal mentit *Q*, qu'il m'a mentit *ABCDGN*, m'a ja mentit *H*, ja m'a mentit *Z*. (36) cujaratz *R*, cujariatz *CV*, creriaz *DIK*, creziatz *Z*. (38) co *R*, si *ABCDGHIKNQVZa*. (51) avuda *RHIKN*, aguda *ABCDGQZa*, aüda *V*. (53) cor *RCGHIKVZ*, cors *ABDQa*. (54) del patz *R*, del plaich *ABCDGHIKNQVZa*. (55) mort *RGV*, mortz *ABCDHIKNQZa*. (68) s'amor *RNVZ*, s'amors *ABCDHIKQa*.

(7) **lo cor**] 'My heart,' neuter nom. sg.

(12) **lur**] May be indeclinable, as here (Appel, *Provenzalische* xv).

(19–20) 'A little anger upsets you' (like the anger I showed in stanza 1) 'and joy affects you little' (you are a cold fish), 'but you are neither the first nor the second' (all women are like you—especially your lady).

(20) **es**] Simplified form of **etz**, second person plural.

(23) Giraut criticizes Alamanda for advising him to accept with pleasure his lady's bad as well as her good (v. 15).

(27–28) 'But if it seems to you that I should be joyful with a little' (that I should be more receptive to trifling joy than you said I ám, v. 19), 'I do very well by myself, thank you.'

(28) Proverbial; cf. Cnyrim 873.

(29–31) 'Shall I conceal you' [your infidelity; cf. 34–37, 51–53, 59] 'out of desire to make a pact? Now you are seeking a way for her not to remove her good self, though she is second in your affection!'

(32) **cochatz**] Reference to v. 2.

(36) **cujarátz**] Second conditional; see chapter 7: 'Would you not have thought . . . '

(39) **na Berenguieira**] Has not been securely identified. Perhaps a person as real as Alamanda, but unknown to us; or possibly there is an allusion to the *Roman de Renart*, where a she-donkey named Berengier may have been a teller of improbable tales:

> Ainz par l'anesse Berengier
> N'oï mes si tres grant merveille.
>
> > Never from the she-donkey Berengier
> > Did I ever hear such a very great marvel.

But the OFr. name *Berengier* is masculine, so the passage may mean 'the she-donkey of Berengier,' a man. See Fukumoto, Harano, and Suzuki, branch 24, vv. 778–79 (= 13322–23). Branch 24 was dated about 1178 by Bossuat (1957, 186).

(53) **cor**] Subject form, neuter. **fos**] For **fotz**, second person plural.

(54) **del**] Fem., as in **del vielha** (Appel, *Provenzalische* 65.16). Cf. the personal pronoun **·l** 14.48 (= **la**).

(55) **mort soi**] Loss of final **-s** before initial **s-**.

(56) **y**] = **li** (cf. Appel, *Provenzalische* 263).

(57) **Senher**] On the by-form **sen** (variant), see *S-W* 7: 579–82.

(59) **com fol**] For **com** as preposition, 'like'; cf. **con els** 26.9.

(60) **ni vestida ni nuda**] Cf. the Comtessa de Dia, **en lieig e qand sui vestida** 7.8.

(65) **si d'ela n'es crezuda**] Lit., 'If you are believed by her'—i.e., 'If she believes you'; redundant **n'** = **d'ela**.

Exercise

1. Analyze the forms of **plazęr** 'to please,' **cręire** 'to believe,' **devęr** 'ought, should,' and **cręiser** 'to grow' given in the Glossary.

2. Explain why we say that the following forms are treated as those of a non-**ar** verb: pres. subj. 1st sg. **vaia**; pres. 3rd pl. **están**.

3. Explain the alternative infinitive forms **cǫire** 'to cook,' **cózer** (spelled **coszer** 5.2); **vezę́r** 'to see,' **veire** (*PD*). (Cf. support vowels, ch. 13.)

PART 3

Historical Morphology

CHAPTER 20

Verbs (Section 1)

The next four chapters will analyze the derivation of OOc conjugations and declensions from Classical Latin. Students without Latin may find the derivation from an unfamiliar point of departure difficult to follow and so may wish to pass over this material.

For this chapter, review the forms of the present indicative and subjunctive, the imperfect, the future, and the first conditional tenses (chs. 2–4).

SETS OF TENSES

In synchronic analysis we have categorized the tenses of the OOc verb, by study of its markers, into three sets:

> a present set, comprising the present indicative, the present subjunctive, and the imperfect, with the set marker zero

> a future set, comprising the future and the first conditional, with the infinitive ending as set marker (sometimes modified)

> a past set, comprising the preterit, the past subjunctive, and the second conditional, with a set marker consisting of a vowel (é or í), a consonant ([k] or s), or a semivowel (waw or implicit yod)

We shall study the historical development of the present and future sets in this chapter and that of the past set in chapter 21.

Of the eight tenses in OOc (setting aside the hypothetical future subjunctive), four continue corresponding tenses in Classical Latin, while the other four represent innovations in form or function. The four showing continuity with CL are the present indicative, the present subjunctive, the imperfect, and the preterit. The future replaces the established future forms of CL with innovative forms compounded of the infinitive with CL ʜᴀʙᴇ̄ʀᴇ 'to have' in the present (e.g., ᴄᴀɴᴛᴀ̄ʀᴇ ʜᴀʙᴇᴏ̄—lit., 'I have to sing' > **cantarai** 'I shall sing'). The past subjunctive in OOc replaces the forms of the CL imperfect subjunctive with new forms derived from the CL pluperfect subjunctive (ᴄᴀɴᴛᴀ̄ᴠɪ̆ssᴇᴍ > **cantęs**). The two conditional tenses of OOc, corresponding to nothing in CL, innovate in form and function. The first conditional compounds forms of the infinitive with CL ʜᴀʙᴇ̄ʀᴇ in the imperfect (ᴄᴀɴᴛᴀ̄ʀᴇ ʜᴀʙᴇ̄ʙᴀᴍ—lit., 'I had to sing' > **cantaria** 'I would sing'). The second conditional adopts the forms of the CL pluperfect indicative (ᴄᴀɴᴛᴀ̄ᴠᴇ̆ʀᴀᴍ 'I had sung' > **cantęra** 'I would have sung').

PRESENT SET

Present Indicative

	OOc -ar	CL	OOc non-**ar**	CL
	cantar	ᴄᴀɴᴛᴀ̄ʀᴇ	**tener**	ᴛᴇ̆ɴᴇ̄ʀᴇ
	Column 1	Column 2	Column 3	Column 4
1st sg.	**cant**	ᴄᴀɴᴛᴏ̄	**tenc, tenh**	ᴛᴇ̆ɴᴇᴏ̄
2nd sg.	**cántas**	ᴄᴀɴᴛᴀ̄s	**tens**	ᴛᴇ̆ɴᴇ̄s
3rd sg.	**cánta**	ᴄᴀɴᴛᴀᴛ	**tęn**	ᴛᴇ̆ɴᴇᴛ
1st pl.	**cantám**	ᴄᴀɴᴛᴀ̄ᴍᴜs	**tenę́m**	ᴛᴇ̆ɴᴇ̄ᴍᴜs
2nd pl.	**cantátz**	ᴄᴀɴᴛᴀ̄ᴛɪs	**tenę́tz**	ᴛᴇ̆ɴᴇ̄ᴛɪs
3rd pl.	**cántan, -on**	ᴄᴀɴᴛᴀɴᴛ	**ténon**	ᴛᴇ̆ɴᴇɴᴛ

Column 1 derives from column 2 straightforwardly, except for two forms:

> The ending of **cantám** lacks the expected final **-s** from ᴄᴀɴᴛᴀ̄ᴍᴜs, which came to be limited to, and hence distinctive of, the second person singular (**cántas**) and plural (**cantátz**). The same change occurs in the first person plural of all tenses.

> The ending of **cántan** represents the normal result of CL ᴄᴀɴᴛᴀɴᴛ, but the alternative form **cánton** shows influence of CL -ŭɴᴛ, as does **ténon**. The ending -ŭɴᴛ came from the CL third conjugation, which developed normally in ʙɪ̆ʙŭɴᴛ > **bevon**, ᴄŭʀʀŭɴᴛ > **corron**, ᴄʀᴇ̄ᴅŭɴᴛ > **crezon**, ᴅɪ̄ᴄŭɴᴛ > **dizon**, ᴘʀᴇ̆ʜᴇ̆ɴᴅŭɴᴛ > **prenon**. The unusual ending of **defendo** (CL ᴅᴇ̄ғᴇ̆ɴᴅŭɴᴛ) shows dialect influence.[1]

---

[1] "In some dialects the n fell after o, u (vęndo, au); -*on* and -*o* were used concurrently by the poets" (Grandgent, par. 83).

In columns 3 and 4, straightforward results of CL endings occur in **tens**, **teṇ**, **teném** (with loss of final **-s**, as in **cantám**). The vowel in **tenętz** has been influenced by the corresponding form of **ęser** 'to be,' OOc **ętz** from CL ĕstis, a change that happened only in the present indicative. The ending of **ténon** shows the same substitution already noted in **cánton**.

In **tenh** we see the normal result of CL tĕneō, by reduction of the unstressed penult to yod and combination of the yod with the preceding consonant to form the palatal. The alternative **tenc** has the sporadic first person singular marker [k], which arose from forms in which the [k] was part of the etymological root, such as **dic** 'I say' (CL dīcō), **prec** 'I pray' (LL prĕcō), **fenc** 'I feign' (CL fĭngō), **planc** 'I lament' (CL plangō). This [k] became distinctive of the first person singular because in the other five forms it was deleted under influence from surrounding sounds—for example, 2nd sg. dīcis > **dis**; 3rd sg. dīcit > **di**, **ditz**; 1st pl. dīcimus > **dizęm**; 2nd pl. dīcĭtis > **dizętz**; 3rd pl. dīcunt > **dizon** (where the **z** was modeled on **dizęm**, **dizętz**).

The marker of the present tense for **-ar** verbs, which we have identified in chapter 2 as **a**, occurred in the five forms as early as Classical Latin, as may be seen in column 2 above. It has been posited for the first person singular in Proto-Indo-European, where -ā- ran consistently throughout all six forms (Kent 96). The zero marker for non-**ar** verbs in the present represents a normal loss of the vowel -e- in the final unstressed syllable of CL second and third persons singular and third person plural, and in the unstressed penult of the first person singular; where this vowel was stressed (first and second persons plural), it became part of the person marker.

The basic person markers that were proposed in chapter 2 may be understood diachronically as follows:

1st sg.   -zero   Loss of final -ō in cantō, tĕneō. Sporadic [k] as in **tenc**, or sporadic -yod, as in **tenh** (see above)

2nd sg.   **-s**   Retention of final -s in cantās, tĕnēs

3rd sg.   -zero   Loss of final -t in cantat, tĕnet

1st pl.   **-ám** for **-ar** verbs, as in cantāmus > **cantám**, explained above; **-ém** for non-**ar** verbs, as in tĕnēmus > **teném**

2nd pl.   **-átz** for **-ar** verbs, as in cantātis > **cantátz**; **-ętz** for non-**ar** verbs in other tenses (present subjunctive **cantętz**, etc.) where the influence of CL ĕstis, present indicative, did not apply; the normal result of -ētis

3rd pl.   **-on** from CL -ŭnt, as above; sporadic **-en**, as in **saben**, VL *sapent, from the remodeled infinitive *sapēre (CL sapĕre)

	OOc	CL	OOc	CL
	-ar		non-**ar**	
	cantar	CANTĀRE	**tener**	TĔNĒRE
	Column 1	Column 2	Column 3	Column 4
1st sg.	**cant**	CANTEM	**ténga, ténha**	TĔNEAM
2nd sg.	**cantz**	CANTĒS	**téngas, ténhas**	TĔNEĀS
3rd sg.	**cant**	CANTET	**ténga, ténha**	TĔNEAT
1st pl.	**cantém**	CANTĒMUS	**tengám, tenhám**	TĔNEĀMUS
2nd pl.	**cantétz**	CANTĒTIS	**tengátz, tenhátz**	TĔNEĀTIS
3rd pl.	**cánton**	CANTENT	**téngan, ténhan**	TĔNEANT

Column 1 derives from column 2, with the sole substitution of **-on**
in **canton** (see "Present Indicative"). Column 3 shows two roots,
teng- and **tenh-**. **Tenh-** represents the normal result of CL TĒNE- in
all six forms. **Teng-** has adopted the tense marker that is natural in
a verb such as 3rd sg. **diga**, infinitive **dire**, from DĪCĔRE by lenition
(DĪCAM, DĪCAS, DĪCAT, DĪCĀMUS, DĪCĀTIS, DĪCANT). Otherwise, column
3 derives from column 4 without difficulty.

The tense marker zero for **-ar** verbs in the present subjunctive
results from the loss of unstressed E in the final syllable and its
amalgamation into the person marker when stressed. The tense
marker **-a** for non-**ar** verbs was already present in all six CL forms.
The unusual tense markers **-ga**, **-[ja]** have been seen in **tenga**,
diga, **tenha**; the form **-sa** in 3rd sg. **fasa**, infinitive **faire**, derives
from FACĬAT by assibilation.

Imperfect

	OOc	CL	OOc	CL
	-ar		non-**ar**	
	cantar	CANTĀRE	**tenęr**	TĔNĒRE
	Column 1	Column 2	Column 3	Column 4
1st sg.	**cantáva**	CANTĀBAM	**tenía**	TĔNĒBAM
2nd sg.	**cantávas**	CANTĀBĀS	**tenías**	TĔNĒBĀS
3rd sg.	**cantáva**	CANTĀBAT	**tenía**	TĔNĒBAT
1st pl.	**cantavám**	CANTĀBĀMUS	**teniám**	TĔNĒBĀMUS
2nd pl.	**cantavátz**	CANTĀBĀTIS	**teniátz**	TĔNĒBĀTIS
3rd pl.	**cantávan,**	CANTĀBANT	**tenían,**	TĔNĒBANT
	-on, -en		**-on, -en**	

From column 2 to column 1, -ĀBAM became **-áva** by lenition. The
-ía ending of non-**ar** verbs shows the influence of the imperfect of

HABĒRE 'to have,' 1st sg. HABĒBAM, etc., which produced VL /aβẹa/ by dissimilation of the two B's and lenition of the first one. The form then became **avía** when [ẹ] in hiatus closed to [i], as in CL vĭAM > **via** (ch. 12).

These three tenses (the present indicative, present subjunctive, and imperfect) are built on the root of the verb, which is followed by elements marking the particular tense and person. Since there is no element distinctive of the forms of all three tenses, we say that the set marker is zero.

FUTURE SET

Future

In Classical Latin the future showed two general patterns, one in the first and second conjugations, another in the third and fourth.

CLASSICAL LATIN

	-ĀRE	-ĒRE	-ĔRE	-ĪRE
	Column 1	Column 2	Column 3	Column 4
1st sg.	CANTĀBŌ	DOCĒBŌ	PŌNAM	MŪNĬAM
2nd sg.	CANTĀBIS	DOCĒBIS	PŌNĒS	MŪNĬĒS
3rd sg.	CANTĀBIT	DOCĒBIT	PŌNET	MŪNĬET
1st pl.	CANTĀBĬMUS	DOCĒBĬMUS	PŌNĒMUS	MŪNĬĒMUS
2nd pl.	CANTĀBĬTIS	DOCĒBĬTIS	PŌNĒTIS	MŪNĬĒTIS
3rd pl.	CANTĀBUNT	DOCĒBUNT	PŌNENT	MŪNĬENT

The future forms of the first and second conjugations resembled the imperfect (fut. CANTĀBIT, imperf. CANTĀBAT; fut. DOCĒBIT, imperf. DOCĒBAT), and those of the first also resembled the perfect, especially as lenition changed /b/ to /β/ (fut. CANTĀBIT, perf. CANTĀVIT). In the third and fourth conjugations the future was much like the present (fut. PŌNET, pres. PŌNIT; fut. MŪNĬET, pres. MŪNIT); the first person singular was identical to the present subjunctive (PŌNAM, MŪNĬAM), and the other forms were similar to the subjunctive (PŌNĀS, etc.; MŪNĬAS, etc.). The tendency to reduce the final syllable in VL made the distinctions among all these forms more difficult to sustain.

The lack of distinctive form for this synthetic future in CL contributed to its replacement with periphrastic expressions. VL had future periphrases such as DĒBEŌ CANTĀRE—lit., 'I must sing' (Sardinian *depo kantare* 'I shall sing') and VOLŌ CANTĀRE—lit., 'I want to sing' (Romanian *voi cînta* 'I shall sing'). The most widespread such periphrase was CANTĀRE HABEŌ—lit., 'I have to sing,' which entered Church Latin in the writings of Tertullian, Saint Jerome, and Saint Augustine.

	OOc	VL	OOc	VL
	-ar		non-**ar**	
	cantar	CANTĀRE	**tenẹr**	TĔNĒRE
		HABĒRE		HABĒRE
	Column 1	Column 2	Column 3	Column 4
1st sg.	**cantarái**	CANTĀRE	**tenrái**	TĔNĒRE
		HABEŌ		HABEŌ
2nd sg.	**cantarás**	CANTĀRE	**tenrás**	TĔNĒRE
		HABĒS		HABĒS
3rd sg.	**cantará**	CANTĀRE	**tenrá**	TĔNĒRE
		HABET		HABET
1st pl.	**cantarẹ́m**	CANTĀRE	**tenrẹ́m**	TĔNĒRE
		HABĒMUS		HABĒMUS
2nd pl.	**cantarẹ́tz**	CANTĀRE	**tenrẹ́tz**	TĔNĒRE
		HABĒTIS		HABĒTIS
3rd pl.	**cantarán**	CANTĀRE	**tenrán**	TĔNĒRE
		HABENT		HABENT

As the present forms of HABĒRE came to be considered part of the preceding word (though still separable; see below), they were reduced, as seen in forms of **avẹr.**

	CL	VL	OOc present	OOc future
1st sg.	HABEŌ	/ajo/	**ai**	**-ai**
2nd sg.	HABĒS	/as/	**as**	**-as**
3rd sg.	HABET	/at/	**a**	**-a**
1st pl.	HABĒMUS	/aβẹm/	**avẹm**	**-ẹm**
2nd pl.	HABĒTIS	/aβẹtz/	**avẹtz**	**-ẹtz**
3rd pl.	HABENT	/ant/	**an**	**-an**

The letter H was not pronounced in VL. The VL forms led directly to the present indicative forms of OOc **avẹr** 'to have' except for **avẹtz,** which was influenced by present **ẹtz** 'you are' (CL ĔSTIS). In the future, first and second persons plural, the **av-** was dropped to create a uniform series of monosyllabic endings. The vowel in the future, second person plural ending, **-ẹtz,** shows that this form branched from the development of HABĒTIS before the influence of ĔSTIS produced the open vowel of **avẹtz.**

In **cantarái** the full infinitive ending marks the set, whereas in **tenrái** the infinitive ending (as in **tenẹr**) has had its vowel deleted. The tendency to reduce this vowel also occurs in forms such as **laisserai** beside **laissarai** (exceptional in **-ar** verbs) and **partrai** beside **partirai**; in infinitives in **-ẹr** and **ʹre** the deletion is normal

(**tenrai** from **tener**; **dirai** from **dire**). In historical terms this reduction is explained by the intertonic position of the vowel in the
future tense; recall that intertonic vowels normally fall, with the
exception of **a** (ch. 13).

Ẹser retains etymological forms in the future singular.

	CL	OOc etymological	OOc periphrastic
1st sg.	ĔRŌ	ẹr	serái
2nd sg.	ĔRIS	ẹrs	serás
3rd sg.	ĔRIT	ẹr	será
1st pl.	ĔRĬMUS		serẹ́m
2nd pl.	ĔRĬTIS		serẹ́tz
3rd pl.	ĔRUNT		serán

The periphrastic forms are aphetic (headless) developments of the
VL infinitive ĔSSĔRE, regularized from CL ĔSSE: ĔSSĔRE HABEŌ, etc.

First Conditional

The first conditional became necessary as a past form of the new
periphrastic future tense. Therefore, as the future combined an infinitive with endings from HABEO in the present, so the first conditional combined an infinitive with endings from HABEO in the
imperfect. Grandgent (par. 142.2) cites VL constructions such as
these, showing the function of the first conditional as a future in
the past.

> Present–Future:
>> "Dīcit quod venīre habet," 'He says that he will come.'
>
> Past–First Conditional:
>> "Dīxit quod venīre habēbat," 'He said that he would
>> come.'

Or these, showing the first conditional in a hypothetical sentence:

> If (present), then (future):
>> "Sī pŏssum, venīre habeo," 'If I can, I shall come.'
>
> If (imperfect), then (first conditional):
>> "Si potĕram, venīre habēbam," 'If I could, I would
>> come.'

Such constructions are documented as early as the third century
A.D.

Since the first conditional tense was created as an extension of
the periphrastic future, it is not surprising that its forms developed
as an extension of future forms.

	OOc	VL	OOc	VL
	-ar		non-**ar**	
	cantar	CANTĀRE HABĒRE	**tenẹr**	TĔNĒRE HABĒRE
	Column 1	Column 2	Column 3	Column 4
1st sg.	**cantaría**	CANTĀRE HABĒBAM	**tenría**	TĔNĒRE HABĒBAM
2nd sg.	**cantarías**	CANTĀRE HABĒBAS	**tenrías**	TĔNĒRE HABĒBAS
3rd sg.	**cantaría**	CANTĀRE HABĒBAT	**tenría**	TĔNĒRE HABĒBAT
1st pl.	**cantariám**	CANTĀRE HABĒBĀMUS	**tenriám**	TĔNĒRE HABĒBĀMUS
2nd pl.	**cantariátz**	CANTĀRE HABĒBĀTIS	**tenriátz**	TĔNĒRE HABĒBĀTIS
3rd pl.	**cantarían**	CANTĀRE HABĒBANT	**tenrían**	TĔNĒRE HABĒBANT

The first conditional endings of **avẹr** derive from the imperfect of HABĒRE.

	CL	VL	OOc Imperfect	OOc First Conditional Endings
1st sg.	HABĒBAM	/aβéβa/	**avía**	**-ía**
2nd sg.	HABĒBAS	/aβéβas/	**avías**	**-ías**
3rd sg.	HABĒBAT	/aβéβa/	**avía**	**-ía**
1st pl.	HABĒBĀMUS	/aβeβám/	**aviám**	**-iám**
2nd pl.	HABĒBĀTIS	/aβeβátz/	**aviátz**	**-iátz**
3rd pl.	HABĒBANT	/aβéβant/	**avían**	**-ían**

From VL to OOc the second /b/ was deleted by dissimilation, and /ę́/ in hiatus closed to **í**. In contrast to the imperfect forms of **avẹr**, the first conditional endings lost the initial syllable **av-** throughout, as in the future, first and second persons plural.

READING 20

Bertran de Born,
D'un sirventes no·m cal far loignor ganda

*Bertran de Born (fl. 1159–1215), lord of the castle of Autafort in Dordogne and vassal of the king of England (first Henry II Plantagenet, then his son Richard Lionheart), sustained the tradition of political and moralizing **sirventes** between Marcabru and Peire Cardenal. In late 1182 he* was actively involved in an uprising of the barons of Aquitaine against then Duke Richard and King Henry, an uprising led by the oldest surviving son of Henry II and elder brother of Richard. This Prince Henry was known as the "Young King" because Henry II had had him crowned king of England to ensure succession in the event of his own demise. Although he had conspired with the rebels against Richard, the Young King—unexpectedly for Bertran—swore fidelity to his father on January 1, 1183.

In this poem Bertran complains bitterly of the Young King's tergiversation, while adopting the form and rhymes of a song by Giraut de Bornelh (see reading 19; Bertran refers to his source overtly in 20.25). This is the earliest sure case of contrafacture using the rhyme sounds as well as the stanzaic pattern of the model, a practice that would become standard in the later **sirventes**.

1

D'un sirventes no·m cal far loignor ganda,
tal talan ai qe·l dig'e qe l'espanda;
car n'ai razon tant novell'e tant granda
del joven rei q'a fenit sa demanda
son frair Richartz, pois sos paire·l comanda.
    Tant es forsatz!   5
Pois n'Aenrics terra non ten ni manda,
    sia reis dels malvatz!

2

Que malvatz fai, car aissi viu a randa
de liurazon a comt'et a garanda.
Reis coronatz que d'autrui pren liuranda   10
mal sembl'Arnaut, lo marques de Belanda,
ni·l pro Guillem que conquis Tor Mirmanda.
    Tant fon presatz!
Pos en Peitau lor ment e lor truanda,
    no·i er mais tant amatz.   15

3

Ja per dormir non er de Coberlanda
reis dels Engles, ni conquerra Yrlanda,
ni tenr'Angieus ni Monsaurel ni Canda,
ni de Peiteus non aura la miranda,   20
ni sera ducs de la terra normanda,
    ni coms palatz
ni de Bordels ni dels Gascos part Landa,
    seigner ni de Basatz.

4

Conseill vuoill dar e·l son de n'Alamanda
lai a·n Richart, si tot no lo·m demanda: 25
ja per son frair mais sos homes non blanda.

Nonca·is fai el, anz asetg'e·ls aranda,
tol lor chastels e derroc'et abranda
         devas totz latz!
E·l reis tornei lai ab cels de Guarlanda
    e l'autre, sos coignatz.

5
Lo coms Jaufres cui es Bersilianda
    volgra fos primiers natz,

6
car es cortes, e fos en sa comanda
    regesmes e·l duchatz.

Meter:

      a   a   a   a   a   b   a   b
      10' 10' 10' 10' 10' 4   10' 6
      Sirv. 4 u 8, 2-2, 2. **-anda, -atz.**
      Frank 19:1.

P-C 80,13. Major editions: Gouiran, *L'amour,* no. 11; Paden, Sankovitch, and
    Stäblein, no. 11; Gouiran, *Seigneur,* no. 11.
Music: Set to the melody of the model, Giraut de Bornelh, "S'ie·us quier cosselh,
    bel'ami'Alamanda," from *R* fol. 8. See chapter 19. For sung performance of
    the reading, refer to the accompanying compact disk.
Eight manuscripts: *A* fol. 195v; *C* fol. 138v; *D* fol. 123v–124; *F* fol. 78–v; *I* fol.
    181v; *K* fol. 166–167; *M* fol. 240; *N* fol. 250–v. Base *A.*
Divergent attribution: Miraval *M.*
Stanza order

ACFIKN	1	2	3	4	5	6
D	1	2	3	4	—	—
M	1	2	4	3	5	6

Rejected readings in the base manuscript: (2) diga e. (3) novella e. (5) sos frair
    Richartz *AIK,* sos frairs Richarz *DN,* sos frairs rich. *F,* son frair Richart *C,*
    fraire Richart *M.* (7) n'Aimerics *A,* n'Aenrics *DIKNR,* n'Ainrics *M,* Enrics *C,*
    nai Henrics *F.* (10) comte et. (12) sembla Arnaut. (13) tor *CDFIKMNR,* tost *A.*
    (19) tenra Angieus *A;* Canda *CFMN,* Ganda *ADIK,* Glanda *R.* (22) palaitz *A,*
    pallatz *FMN,* parlatz *R,* apellatz *C,* om. *DIK.* (28) asetga e. (29) derroca et.
    (31) Guarlanda *CDFIKMNR,* Guislanda *A.*
Selected variants: (15) Pos *ACDFIKN,* mas *M.* (24) senhers *C.* (35) for' [= fora]
    CN, fora *M.*

Notes

(4) **joven rei**] The "Young King" Henry.

(5) **son frair Richartz**] Dative function: 'The Young King, who has
    dropped his claim on his brother Richard.' The base manuscript reads
    sos frair Richartz, nominative form in oblique function, as a result of
    confusion over the historical circumstances in question. Perhaps this
    confusion was set off by the nominative form of **Richartz**; proper

nouns were indifferent to case (see ch. 28). But Bertran must have used the possessive adjective in the oblique, if we may judge by contemporary usage in the charters such as **per Ricardz so-fil** 'for his son Richard' (Brunel, *Plus anciennes chartes*, no. 503.49; vers 1190, Rouergue), where **Ricardz** is the nominative form, but **so-fil** is correctly oblique following the preposition **per**.

(7–8) Young Henry held no lands in his own name, even though he bore the title of a king.

(9–10) **viu . . . de liurazon**] 'He lives by allowance': Young Henry became a paragon of generosity and the embodiment of the chivalric ideal but remained dependent on his father for the means to finance his extravagance.

(12–13) **Arnaut . . . ni·l pro Guillem**] Arnaut de Beaulande and his grandson Guillaume d'Orange, chief character in the cycle of chansons de geste known by his name. Guillaume captured the city of Orange and with it the castle called Mirmanda Tower.

(15) **en Peitau**] Richard was count of Poitou, where Young Henry had attempted to stir up conflict.

(17–24) England, Ireland, Anjou, Poitou, Normandy, and Aquitaine were all parts of the far-flung holdings of Henry II. Bertran taunts Young Henry that he will never rival his father, even though he is already crowned king of England.

(25) **Alamanda**] The heroine of the song that provided the model for contrafacture; see reading 19.

(28–30) Richard had already shown his mettle and soon came to be regarded as one of the greatest warriors of his time.

(31) **·l reis**] The Young King. **Guarlanda**] A fief situated in Paris, today the rue Galande in the Latin Quarter. The circumlocution expresses insignificance.

(32) **sos coignatz**] The Young King's brother-in-law was Philip Augustus, king of France, whom Bertran disdains to name. Subject case; not in apposition to **autre**, which is the object of **ab**, but rather a predicate nominative in an elliptical construction: **l'autre [que es] sos coignatz**.

(33) **lo coms Jaufres**] Geoffrey, count of Brittany, the third son after Henry and Richard. **Bersilianda**] The forest of Brocéliande, setting of Arthurian romance; synecdoche for Brittany.

(36) **regesmes e·l duchatz**] That is, the kingdom of the Young King and the duchy of Duke Richard.

Verbs (Section 2)

✦ Review the forms of the preterit, past subjunctive, and second conditional tenses (chs. 5–7).

PAST SET

The past set of tenses is identified synchronically by its distinctive marker: **ę́** in the third person singular, preterit, as in **cantę́t**; past subjunctive, **cantę́s**; and second conditional, **cantę́ra**, or corresponding markers in other verbs.

Infinitive	Set marker	Preterit	Past subjunctive	Second conditional
cantar	**ę́**	**cantę́t**	**cantę́s**	**cantę́ra**
partir	**í**	**partí**	**partís**	**partíra**
avęr	**[k]**	**ac**	**aguę́s**	**agra**
dire	**s**	**dis**	**dissę́s**[1]	**dissęra**[2]
saber	waw	**saup**	**saubę́s**	**saubra**
vezęr	implicit yod	**vi**	**vis**	**vira**[3]

In this chapter we shall trace the development of these tenses from Classical Latin.

[1] Appel, *Provenzalische* xxxi.

[2] Bartsch 520.

[3] Appel, *Provenzalische* xxviii.

Preterit forms with the vowel marker **ę́** (**cantę́t**) or **í** (**partí**) (ch. 5) are described historically as weak, meaning that the accent always falls on the ending (that is, the stressed set marker), never on the root. Since nonvowel markers ([k], **s**, waw, implicit yod) cannot bear stress, forms that use them will necessarily be stressed on the root whenever the person marker is unstressed, as happens regularly in the first and third persons singular and the third person plural (see "Person Markers for the Preterit after a Consonant," ch. 6). A verb is said to be strong in the preterit if any of its forms bears accent on the root.

Chapter 21.
Verbs
(Section 2)

WEAK PRETERITS

Weak preterit endings originated not in the frequent -ARE verbs but in a more obscure type exemplified by CL PĔRDĔRE.

	OOC **cantar** Column 1	VL Column 2	CL CANTĀRE Column 3
1st sg.	**cantę́i**	CANTAI	CANTĀVĪ
2nd sg.	**cantę́st**	CANTASTI	CANTĀVĬSTĪ
3rd sg.	**cantę́t**	CANTAUT	CANTĀVIT
1st pl.	**cantę́m**	*CANTAMMUS	CANTĀVĬMUS
2nd pl.	**cantę́tz**	CANTASTIS	CANTĀVĬSTĬS
3rd pl.	**cantę́ron**	CANTARUNT	CANTĀVĔRUNT

	OOc **pędre** Column 4	VL Column 5	VL Recomposed Column 6	CL PĔRDĔRE Column 7
1st sg.	**perdę́i**	*PERDĘI	per-dédi	PĔRDĬDĪ
2nd sg.	**perdę́st**	*PERDĘSTE	per-dĕdístī	PĔRDĬDĬSTĪ
3rd sg.	**perdę́t**	*PERDĘT	per-dédit	PĔRDĬDIT
1st pl.	**perdę́m**	*PERDĘMOS	per-dédĭmus	PĔRDĬDĬMUS
2nd pl.	**perdę́tz**	*PERDĘSTES	per-dĕdístĭs	PĔRDĬDĬSTĬS
3rd pl.	**perdę́ron**	*PERDĘRONT	per-dédĕrunt	PĔRDĬDĔRUNT

The OOc endings in column 1 (**cantę́i** etc.) are identical to those in column 4 (**perdę́i** etc.). Their etymology is to be found not in the earlier forms of CANTĀRE, in columns 2 and 3, but in the forms of **perdre**, which developed from the VL forms in columns 5 and 6 and originally from the CL forms in column 7.

The perfect forms of ᴘᴇ̆ʀᴅᴇ̆ʀᴇ, in column 7, were recomposed (see recomposition, ch. 11), as in column 6, and became the VL forms of column 5. By recomposition the CL ending -ᴅᴇ̆ᴅɪᴛ in ᴘᴇ́ʀᴅᴇ̆ᴅɪᴛ and other verbs (ᴄʀᴇᴅᴇ̆ᴅɪᴛ, ᴠᴇ̄ɴᴅᴇ̆ᴅɪᴛ, ʀᴇɴᴅᴇ̆ᴅɪᴛ) became VL -ᴅᴇ̆ᴅɪᴛ, influenced by ᴅᴇ̆ᴅɪᴛ, the preterit of the verb ᴅᴀ̄ʀᴇ 'to give.' The accent was regularized to the syllable -ᴅᴇ̆- except where the accent fell on the ending. The second ᴅ disappeared by dissimilation from the first (cf. CL ʜᴀʙᴇ̄ʙᴀᴛ > /aβea/) to produce, in column 5, the forms *ᴘᴇʀᴅᴇ́ɪ, *ᴘᴇʀᴅᴇ́ᴛ, and *ᴘᴇʀᴅᴇ́ʀᴏɴᴛ. (In OOc **perdét**, the final **-t** survived because it had been supported by the second ᴅ before dissimilation.)

The vowel ᴇ̧, present in column 5 in the four forms in which the ᴇ̆ of -ᴅᴇ̆ᴅɪᴛ bore stress, generalized to the remaining two. From column 5 to column 4, we need add only that in *ᴘᴇʀᴅᴇ̧ᴍᴏs > **perdém**, the final -s dropped, as in the present indicative (see ch. 20) and that the stressed vowel was raised by the following nasal. In *ᴘᴇʀᴅᴇ̧sᴛᴇs > *ᴘᴇʀᴅᴇ̧sᴛᴇs > **perdétz**, the final cluster -sᴛs simplified to **-ts**.

The preterit endings of **perdre** extended to **-ar** verbs on the basis of their etymological origin in the preterits of **dar** 'to give' (CL ᴅᴀ̄ʀᴇ)—first person singular **diey** (CL ᴅᴇ̆ᴅɪ̄), third person singular **det** (CL ᴅᴇ̆ᴅɪᴛ), third person plural **deron** (CL ᴅᴇ̆ᴅᴇ̆ʀᴜɴᴛ)—and the similar development of **estar** 'to be' (CL sᴛᴀ̄ʀᴇ), preterit, first person singular **estey** (CL sᴛᴇ̆ᴛɪ̄), third person singular **estet** (CL sᴛᴇ̆ᴛɪᴛ). By the working of analogy, **dar** is to **det** as **cantar** is to X; X = **cantet**.

The set marker **ᴇ̧** may diphthongize to **iᴇ̧**, as in **diey** versus **estey** (ch. 12).

	OOc	VL	CL
	partir		ᴘᴀʀᴛɪ̄ʀᴇ
	Column 8	Column 9	Column 10
1st sg.	**partí**	ᴘᴀʀᴛɪ̄	ᴘᴀʀᴛɪ̄ᴠɪ̄
2nd sg.	**partíst**	ᴘᴀʀᴛɪ̄sᴛɪ̄	ᴘᴀʀᴛɪ̄ᴠɪ̆sᴛɪ̄
3rd sg.	**partí, -ít, -íc**	ᴘᴀʀᴛɪ̄ᴛ	ᴘᴀʀᴛɪ̄ᴠɪᴛ
1st pl.	**partím**	*ᴘᴀʀᴛɪ̄ᴍᴍᴜs	ᴘᴀʀᴛɪ̄ᴠɪ̆ᴍᴜs
2nd pl.	**partítz**	ᴘᴀʀᴛɪ̄sᴛɪs	ᴘᴀʀᴛɪ̄ᴠɪ̆sᴛɪ̆s
3rd pl.	**partíron**	*ᴘᴀʀᴛɪ̄ʀᴜɴᴛ	ᴘᴀʀᴛɪ̄ᴠᴇ̆ʀᴜɴᴛ

Weak preterits of OOc verbs in **-ir**, such as **partir**, developed from the CL forms of column 10 to VL in column 9 by loss of the infix -v-.[4] From column 9 to column 8, *ᴘᴀʀᴛɪ̄ᴍᴍᴜs > **partím** by the usual loss of -s; ᴘᴀʀᴛɪ̄sᴛɪs > **partítz** by simplification, as in **perdétz**.

---

[4] Fouché, *Morphologie* 244–71; Grandgent, par. 174–75.

In the third person singular, **partí** represents the normal development from VL ᴘᴀʀᴛɪ̄ᴛ; the final [k] in **partíc** developed from strong preterits like **ac** (CL ʜᴀʙᴜ̆ɪᴛ, see below); the final -t in **partít** generalized from **perdét**.

These historical developments yielded the synchronic pattern set forth in chapter 5. The set marker **é** originated in the root vowel of CL ᴅᴇ̄ᴅɪ̄, sᴛᴇ̆ᴛɪ̄, etc., and spread to include the entire class of **-ar** verbs, as well as those ending in **-re**. The set marker **-í** originated in the thematic vowel ɪ̄ of ᴘᴀʀᴛɪ̄ᴠɪ̄, etc. We recognize these as set markers in OOc, and not as tense markers, because they run through the preterit, the past subjunctive, and the second conditional.

Person markers distinctive of the preterit developed as follows:

1st sg. -yod From -ɪ̄ in CL ᴅᴇ̄ᴅɪ̄, which was not deleted but formed a diphthong with the preceding vowel after the loss of the second ᴅ by dissimilation

2nd sg. **-st** From -ɪ̆sᴛɪ̄ in CL ᴄᴀɴᴛᴀ̄ᴠɪ̆sᴛɪ̄, ᴘᴇ̆ʀᴅɪ̆ᴅɪ̆sᴛɪ̄, ᴘᴀʀᴛɪ̄ᴠɪ̆sᴛɪ̄

3rd sg. **-t** From -dit, -tit in CL ᴅᴇ̄ᴅɪᴛ, sᴛᴇ̆ᴛɪᴛ

-[k] From OOc strong preterit **ac**

1st pl. **-m** From -ɪ̄mus in CL ᴄᴀɴᴛᴀ̄ᴠɪ̆mus, ᴘᴇ̆ʀᴅɪ̆ᴅɪ̆mus, ᴘᴀʀᴛɪ̄ᴠɪ̆mus after loss of the final -s

2nd pl. **-tz** From -ɪ̆sᴛɪ̆s in CL ᴄᴀɴᴛᴀ̄ᴠɪ̆sᴛɪ̆s, ᴘᴇ̆ʀᴅɪ̆ᴅɪ̆sᴛɪ̆s, ᴘᴀʀᴛɪ̄ᴠɪ̆sᴛɪ̆s by simplification of the final cluster

3rd pl. **-ron** From -ᴇ̆ʀᴜɴᴛ in CL ᴄᴀɴᴛᴀ̄ᴠᴇ̆ʀᴜɴᴛ, ᴘᴇ̆ʀᴅɪ̆ᴅᴇ̆ʀᴜɴᴛ, ᴘᴀʀᴛɪ̄ᴠᴇ̆ʀᴜɴᴛ

STRONG PRETERITS

Strong preterits use four different markers for the past set: [k], **s**, waw, and implicit yod.

Past-set marker [k] appears as **g** by lenition:

	OOc **avér** Column 1	Analogical stress Column 2	CL Stress Column 3	CL ʜᴀʙᴇ̄ʀᴇ Column 4
1st sg.	**aic, aguí**		hábui	ʜᴀʙᴜ̆ɪ
2nd sg.	**aguíst**		habuísti	ʜᴀʙᴜ̆ɪsᴛɪ̄
3rd sg.	**ac**		hábuit	ʜᴀʙᴜ̆ɪᴛ
1st pl.	**aguém**	habuímus	habúimus	ʜᴀʙᴜ̆ɪmus
2nd pl.	**aguétz**		habuístis	ʜᴀʙᴜ̆ɪsᴛɪs
3rd pl.	**agron**	hábuerunt	habúerunt	ʜᴀʙᴜ̆ᴇ̆ʀᴜɴᴛ

In the stress patterns of CL (column 3), two forms are stressed on ʜᴀʙ-, two on -ʙᴜ-, and two on -ɪsᴛ-. When vowels in hiatus become unable to bear stress (cf. MŬLĬĔREM, stressed /mulíerem/ in CL > **molhẹr**; ch. 23), the forms stressed on -BU- shifted their accent, depending on the closest available models: in the first person plural, the accent aligned with the second person plural and singular; in the third person plural, it aligned with the third person singular and first person singular.

With the reduction of intertonic vowels, the sequence -BŬ- lost syllabic value and so developed into the eventual consonantal set marker [k]. In HABŬIT, for example, B became /β/ by lenition and influenced the following sound—CL ŭ reduced to /w/—so that the back /w/ became a velar stop, /g/, as in the development of word-initial Germanic *w* (Germ. *wahta* > **gaita**; ch. 17). The result was either voiced **g** before a vowel or **r**, or voiceless [k] when word-final, as in **ac**. In **aic** the yod is probably the result, historically, of analogy: present, third person singular **a** is to present, first person singular **ai** as preterit, third person singular **ac** is to *X*; *X* = **aic**. **Aguíst** shows metaphony under the influence of CL final -ī.

By the same process we have **poc** (POTŬIT) from **poder**, **tenc** (TENŬIT) from **tener**, **volc** (VOLŬIT) from **voler**. The process has extended to **venc** (CL VĒNIT, VL *VĒNŬIT) from **venir**.

Past-set marker **s**:

	OOc **dire** Column 1	CL DĪCĔRE Column 2
1st sg.	**dis**	DĪXĪ
2nd sg.	**disíst**	DĪXĬSTĪ
3rd sg.	**dis**	DĪXIT
1st pl.	**disẹm**	DĪXĬMUS
2nd pl.	**disẹtz**	DĪXĬSTIS
3rd pl.	**disẹ́ron**, **diron**	DĪXĔRUNT

In the CL root, x was of course pronounced [ks]; the [k] fell by simplification, leaving the set marker throughout the conjugation. The second person singular shows metaphony. The third person plural shows two ways of resolving the sequence /sr/, created by the fall of the unstressed penult in DĪXĔRUNT. In **disẹ́ron** the set marker **s** is preserved by insertion of another set marker, redundant **ẹ́**, as in **cantẹ́ron**; in **diron** the /s/ drops, simplifying the sequence and leaving the apparent past-set marker **í**, as in **partíron**.

	OOc **saber** Column 1	Analogical stress Column 2	CL Stress Column 3	CL SAPĔRE Column 4
1st sg.	**saup**		sápui	SAPŬĪ
2nd sg.	**saupíst**		sapuísti	SAPŬĬSTĪ
3rd sg.	**saup**		sápuit	SAPŬIT
1st pl.	**saubém**	sapuímus	sapúimus	SAPŬĬMUS
2nd pl.	**saubétz**		sapuístis	SAPŬĬSTIS
3rd pl.	**saubron**	sápuerunt	sapúerunt	SAPŬĔRUNT

The CL origin of this conjugation resembles that of HABEŌ, above, and shows the same shifts of accent. The result in OOc differs because the sequence -PŬ-, instead of developing as -BŬ- did into the set marker [k], underwent metathesis (ch. 17), becoming -ŬP-, and so yielded the infix set marker waw. By the same metathesis PERCĬPŬIT became **apercéup**, RECĬPŬIT became **recéup**.

Past-set marker implicit yod in **vezer**:

	OOc **vezer**	CL VĬDĒRE
1st sg.	**vi**	VĪDĪ
2nd sg.	**vist**	VĪDĬSTĪ
3rd sg.	**vi**	VĪDIT
1st pl.	**vim**	VĪDĬMUS
2nd pl.	**vitz**	VĪDĬSTIS
3rd pl.	**viron**	VĪDĔRUNT

The yod is implicit in the synchronic derivation of these preterit forms from the OOc root **ve-**, as in the infinitive. As is apparent from the conjugation shown here, the same relation of infinitive to preterit forms already obtained in CL (cf. Kent 115–16).

Past-set marker implicit yod in **faire**:

	OOc **faire** Column 1	Analogical stress Column 2	CL Stress Column 3	CL FACĔRE Column 4
1st sg.	**fi, fis**		féci	FĒCĪ
2nd sg.	**fezíst**		fecísti	FĒCĬSTĪ
3rd sg.	**fe, fei, fetz**		fécit	FĒCIT
1st pl.	**fem, fezem**	fecímus	fécimus	FĒCĬMUS
2nd pl.	**fezetz**		fecístis	FĒCĬSTIS
3rd pl.	**feiron**		fécerunt	FĒCĔRUNT

As we said in chapter 19, **faire** shows three roots: **faz-**, **fai-**, and **fa-**. In synchronic terms, metaphony of the root **faz-** by the set marker implicit yod produces **fez-**, as in **fezíst, fẹtz, fezẹm, fezẹtz**. Metaphony of the root **fai-** produces **fẹi, fẹiron**. Metaphony of the root **fa-** produces **fẹ, fẹm**. A second metaphony by another yod, this one the marker for the first person (type 2), produces **fi** from the root **fẹ** and **fis** from the root **fẹz**.

The origin of the yod marking the past set of **faire** lies in the final -ī of FĒCĪ, FĒCĬSTĪ, which by historical metaphony produced **fis, fezíst**. **Fi** may be the result of the analogy of **vi** from VĪDĪ (above). Normal development from CL appears in **fẹtz, fezẹm, fezẹtz**. **Fẹiron** shows yodicism of the -c- in FĒCĔRUNT, after the fall of the unstressed penult. **Fẹi** may be regarded as analogous to **fẹiron** (**ac/agron** = *X*/**fẹiron**; *X* = **fẹi**). This leaves third person singular **fẹ**, which may derive from **fis** by subtraction of metaphony (**aic/ac** = **fi**/*X*; *X* = **fẹ**). **Fẹm** may derive from **fẹ**, with the addition of the preterit person marker **-m**.

The multifarious preterit forms of **faire** permit simpler analysis by the synchronic approach than by the diachronic one.

Past Subjunctive

As we have noted, the past subjunctive in OOc continues the pluperfect subunctive in CL (CANTĀVĬSSEM > **cantẹs**) and the OOc second conditional continues the CL pluperfect indicative (CANTĀVĔRAM > **cantẹra**). Why did these two tenses change their functions as they did? In part, no doubt, for formal reasons: the CL pluperfect subjunctive CANTĀVĬSSEM supplanted the imperfect subjunctive CANTĀREM because, with normal sound changes, the latter became indistinguishable from the infinitive in some forms. The replacement occurred for expressive reasons as well, since OOc invented the second conditional tense for functions that had hitherto not existed (see ch. 27). It is striking that in both these cases a pluperfect (of either mood) assumed the function of a past, as though to strengthen the distinctive reference to events far removed from the speaker.

Weak past subjunctive forms:

	OOc Column 1	CL Column 2	OOc Column 3	CL Column 4
1st sg.	**cantẹs**	CANTĀVĬSSEM	**partís**	PARTĪVĬSSEM
2nd sg.	**cantẹsses**	CANTĀVĬSSĒS	**partísses**	PARTĪVĬSSĒS
3rd sg.	**cantẹs**	CANTĀVĬSSET	**partís**	PARTĪVĬSSET
1st pl.	**cantessẹm**	CANTĀVĬSSĒMUS	**partissẹm**	PARTĪVĬSSĒMUS
2nd pl.	**cantessẹtz**	CANTĀVĬSSĒTIS	**partissẹtz**	PARTĪVĬSSĒTIS
3rd pl.	**cantẹsson, -en**	CANTĀVĬSSENT	**partísson, -en**	PARTĪVĬSSENT

As in the weak preterits (see above), VL deleted -vĭ- from the forms in column 2. The CL theme vowel -ā- was replaced throughout with -ę́-, as in the weak preterit (**cantę́i**, etc.). Since these two changes together transform -āvĭss- into -ę́s, they account essentially for the change from column 2 to column 1. The deletion of -vĭ- accounts for the change from column 4 to column 3.

Strong past subjunctive forms with set marker [k] or **s**:

	OOc **avę̣r** [k] Column 1	CL -BŬ- Column 2	OOc **dire** s Column 3[5]	CL -X- Column 4
1st sg.	**aguę́s**	HABŬĬSSEM	**dissę́s**	DĪXĬSSEM
2nd sg.	**aguę́sses**	HABŬĬSSĒS	**dissę́sses**	DĪXĬSSĒS
3rd sg.	**aguę́s**	HABŬĬSSET	**dissę́s**	DĪXĬSSET
1st pl.	**aguessę́m**	HABŬĬSSĒMUS	**dissessę́m**	DĪXĬSSĒMUS
2nd pl.	**aguessę́tz**	HABŬĬSSĒTIS	**dissessę́tz**	DĪXĬSSĒTIS
3rd pl.	**aguę́sson̦, -en**	HABŬĬSSENT	**dissę́sson̦, -en**	DĪXĬSSENT

The past-set marker [k] arose from -BŬ-, as in the preterit (see above), and **s** arose by simplification of -X-.

Strong past subjunctive with set marker waw or implicit yod:

	OOc **sabę̣r** waw Column 1[6]	CL -PŬ- Column 2	OOc **vezę̣r** yod Column 3[7]	CL -D- Column 4
	saubę́s	SAPŬĬSSEM	**vis**	VĪDĬSSEM
	saubę́sses	SAPŬĬSSĒS	**vísses**	VĪDĬSSĒS
	saubę́s	SAPŬĬSSET	**vis**	VĪDĬSSET
	saubessę́m	SAPŬĬSSĒMUS	**vissę́m**	VĪDISSĒMUS
	saubessę́tz	SAPŬĬSSĒTIS	**vissę́tz**	VĪDISSĒTIS
	saubę́sson̦, -en	SAPŬĬSSENT	**vísson̦, -en**	VĪDĬSSENT

Column 2 gives column 1 by metathesis of the -ŭ- and lenition of the P, as in the preterit. In column 3 the full series on **vis** implies the loss of -Dĭ- in column 4, like the loss of -vĭ- in CANTĀVĬSSEM, etc.

[5] First and third persons singular are supplied from Appel (*Provenzalische* xxxi); for third person plural, Bartsch gives **dizessan** (520). The remaining forms are hypothetical.

[6] Appel (*Provenzalische* xxxiv) gives the first and third persons singular and the second and third persons plural. Other forms are hypothetical.

[7] Appel (*Provenzalische* xxviii) gives the first and third persons singular and the third person plural. Other forms are hypothetical.

Weak second conditional forms are shown in the following chart.

	OOc	CL	OOc	CL
	Column 1	Column 2	Column 3	Column 4
1st sg.	**cantéra**	CANTĀVĚRAM	**partíra**	PARTĪVĚRAM
2nd sg.	**cantéras**	CANTĀVĚRĀS	**partíras**	PARTĪVĚRĀS
3rd sg.	**cantéra**	CANTĀVĚRAT	**partíra**	PARTĪVĚRAT
1st pl.	**canterám**	CANTĀVĚRĀMUS	**partirám**	PARTĪVĚRĀMUS
2nd pl.	**canterátz**	CANTĀVĚRĀTIS	**partirátz**	PARTĪVĚRĀTIS
3rd pl.	**cantéran**	CANTĀVĚRANT	**partíran**	PARTĪVĚRANT

From column 2 to column 1, -vě- was deleted, as -vǐ- was in the preterit and the past subjunctive. The theme vowel ā was replaced with ę́, following the preterit as the past subjunctive followed the same model. From column 4 to column 3, -vě- was deleted.

Strong second conditional forms with set marker [k] or **s**:

	OOc	CL	OOc	CL
	avęr		**dire**	
	[k]	-BŬ-	**s**	-X-
	Column 1	Column 2	Column 3[8]	Column 4
1st sg.	**ágra**	HABŬĚRAM	**disséra, dira**	DĪXĚRAM
2nd sg.	**ágras**	HABŬĚRĀS	—	DĪXĚRĀS
3rd sg.	**ágra**	HABŬĚRAT	—	DĪXĚRAT
1st pl.	**agrám**	HABŬĚRĀMUS	—	DĪXĚRĀMUS
2nd pl.	**agrátz**	HABŬĚRĀTIS	—	DĪXĚRĀTIS
3rd pl.	**ágran**	HABŬĚRANT	—	DĪXĚRANT

From column 2 to column 1 we see the fall of the unstressed penult, the development of -BŬ-, as in the preterit, and shift of stress in the three singular forms and in the third person plural, as in the first and third persons singular of the preterit. In the first and second persons plural, stress remains on the ending. From column 4 to column 3 we see two ways of resolving the sequence /sr/, as in the third person plural preterit **disséron** or **diron**.

Strong second conditional forms with set marker waw or implicit yod are shown on the opposite page.

[8] Forms from Bartsch (520); none occur in Appel (*Provenzalische*) or in the texts of this book.

	OOc	CL	OOc	CL
	sabẹr		**vezẹr**	
	waw	-PŬ-	yod	-D-
	Column 1[9]	Column 2	Column 3[10]	Column 4
1st sg.	**saubra**	SAPŬĔRAM	**vira**	VĪDĔRAM
2nd sg.	**saubras**	SAPŬĔRĀS	**viras**	VĪDĔRĀS
3rd sg.	**saubra**	SAPŬĔRAT	**vira**	VĪDĔRAT
1st pl.	**saubrám**	SAPŬĔRĀMUS	**virám**	VĪDĔRĀMUS
2nd pl.	**saubrátz**	SAPŬĔRĀTIS	**virátz**	VĪDĔRĀTIS
3rd pl.	**saubran**	SAPŬĔRANT	**viran**	VĪDĔRANT

We have seen all these changes before.

READING 21

Bertran de Born, *Mon chan fenis ab dol et ab maltraire*

The revolt of spring 1183 in which Bertran de Born participated came to a sudden end when the Young King died of a fever on June 11. In this **planh**, *or funeral lament, Bertran forgets the inconstancy of which he had complained before (see reading 20) and joins the nearly universal expression of grief at the premature death of a paragon of the chivalric ideal.*

1
Mon chan fenis ab dol et ab maltraire
per totz temps mais e·l tenc per romazut,
car ma rason e mon gaug ai perdut
e·l meillor rei que anc nasqes de maire,　　5
　　larc e gen parlan
　　e gen cavalgan,
　　de bella faiso
　　e d'umil senblan
　　per far grans honors.
　　Tant cre que·m destreingna　　10
　　lo dols que m'esteingna,
　　car en vauc parlan.
　　A Dieu lo coman,
qe·l met'en loc San Joan.

[9] Bartsch gives 3rd sg. **saubra**, 2nd pl. **saupratz** (628).

[10] Appel (*Provenzalische* xxviii) gives the first and third persons singular and the second person plural.

2

Reis dels cortes e dels pros emperaire   15
foratz, seingner, si acses mais vescut;
que "Reis Joves" avias nom agut
e de joven eras capdels e paire.
    Et auberc e bran
    e bel bocaran,   20
    elm e gonfanon
    e perpon e pan
    e jois et amors
    non an que·ls manteingna
    ni qui ja·ls reveingna.   25
    Mas lai vos sigran,
    c'ab vos s'en iran
  e tut ric faig benestan.

3

Gent acuillir e donar ses cor vaire
e bel respos e "Ben sias vengut!"   30
e gran hostal pagat e gen tengut,
dons e garnirs et estar ses tort faire,
    manjar ab mazan
    de viol'e de chan
    e maint compaingnon   35
    ardit e poissan
    de totz los meillors—
    tot voill c'ap vos teingna,
    qu'om ren non retenha
    al segle truan   40
    pel malastruc an
  que nos mostret bel senblan.

4

Seingner, qu'en vos non era res a faire,
qe totz lo mons vos avi'elegut
pel meillor rei que anc portet escut   45
e·l plus ardit e·l meillor torneiaire.
    Deus lo temps Rolan
    de lai ni denan
    non vi hom tan pro
    ni tan guerreian,   50
    ni don sa lausors
    tant pel mon s'enpreingna
    ne si lo reveingna,
    ni que l'an sercan
    per tot agaran
  del Nill tro·l soleill colgan.   55

5
Seingner, per vos mi voill de joi estraire, *renonce*
e tut aqil que·us avion vezut *qui vous avaient vu*
devon estar per vos irat e mut— *mutets*
e ja mais jois la ira no m'esclaire— *maintenont joie me m'eclaire peu?* 60
  Breton e Irlan,
  Engles e Norman,
  Guian e Gasco. *quitaine*
  E Peitou a dan *souffre*
  e·l Maines e Tors. *jours* 65
  Fransa tro Compeingna *les français jusqu'à*
  de plorar no·s teingna,
  e Flandres de Gan
  d'aqui a Guizan.
  Ploron neis li Aleman. 70

6 *esens de Touraine et Brabançon*
  Loirenc e Braiman
  qan torneiaran *ils joue dans un tournoi*
  auran dol quan no·us veiran.

7 *car about un sou*
  No pretz un besan
  ni·l colp d'un'aglan 75
  lo mon, ni cels que·i estan,

8
  per la mort pesan
  del bon rei presan
  on tuit devem aver dan.

Meter

a	b	b	a	c	c	d	c	e	f	f	c	c	c
10'	10	10	10'	5	5	5	5	5	5'	5'	5	5	7

Planh. 5 u 14, 3-3, 3, 3.
-aire, -ut, -an, -on, -ors, -enha.
Frank 576:1.

P-C 80,26. Major editions: Riquer, no. 131; Gouiran, *L'amour,* no. 13; Paden,
  Sankovitch, and Stäblein, no. 15; Gouiran, *Seigneur,* no. 13.
Nine manuscripts: *A* fol. 189v–190; *B* fol. 113v–114; *C* fol. 144v–145; *D* fol.
  122v; *E* pp. 99–100; *F* fol. 97–98; *I* fol. 183v; *K* fol. 169; *Mh* 2. Base *I.*
Divergent attribution: Anonymous *Mh.*
Stanza order

CDEFIK	1	2	3	4	5	6	7	8
Mh	—	—	3	4	5	6	7	8
AB	1	3	2	4	5	6	7	8

Rejected readings in the base manuscript: (14) menten *IK,* met'en *DF,* meta en
  AB, met al *C,* meta *E,* om. *Mh.* (17) angut *IK,* agut *ABDEF,* avut *C,* om. *Mh.*

(22) *perponz IACDEK*, ppoinz *B*, escut *F, om. M^h.* (30) siais *IK*, sias *E*, siatz *ABCDF, om. M^h.* (39) *om. IDK*, qu'om ren non retenha *C*, que hom re non retenha *E*, qe hom re non teigna *F*, c'om çay non reteyna *M^h*, que ren non reteigna *AB*. (40) a *IK*, al *ABCDEFM^h*. (43) affaire *IK*. (44) q'en tot lo mon *IK*, qe tot lo mon *E*, car tot lo mon *M^h*, qe totz lo mons *ABDF*, que tot lo mons *C*. (46) torneiare *IK*, torneiaire *ABDE*, torneiarre *C*, torniar *F*, tor negre *M^h*. (48) dellai *IK*. (50) nid *I*, ni *ABCDEKM^h, om. F*; guerrian *I*, guerreyan *CDEKM^h*, gerreians *AB*, tan prezan *F*. (53) sillo *IK*. (54) ni aqels an *IK*, ni que l'an *C*, ni qels an *DF*, ni quels aus *E*, q'aisi·l van *AB*, . . . vay en *M^h*. (56) tro lo *I*, tro·l *CDEFK*, tro a *M^h*, troc al *AB*. (62) e iau pre e chan *IK*, Engles e Norman *ABCEM^h*, Ançaup e Norman *F*, ei audir e chan *D*. (63) Giena *IDK*, Guian *AC*, Guians *B*, Guiana *E*, German *F*, Vianes *M^h*. (66) canpaingna *I*, campaingna *DEK*, Compeigna *ABC*, Campeyna *M^h*, tensa·n preigna *F*. (71) Loairenc *IK*, Loiarenc *F*, Loirenc *DE*, Lorench *C*, Lorenchs *M^h*, Loier *AB*. (77) pensan *IDK*, pesan *ABCEFM^h*.

Selected variants: (2) remasut *ABCEF*. (16) aguessetz *AB*. (18) eravas *E*. (24) aun *E*; qui *ABCDEF*. (36) prezan *ABF*. (45) portes *ABCDEF*.

Notes

(1) **dol**] Cf. **dols** 11, **dol** 73, **dan** 79.

(2) **romazut**] Perhaps **ro-** < **re-** by assimilation to lip-rounded **m**.

(14) **en loc San Joan**] Saint John the Apostle accompanied Jesus on several occasions when the Savior took with him only three disciples. Several troubadours expressed the belief that Saint John enjoyed a privileged place in Paradise (see also 27.48).

(16) **foratz . . . si acses**] The second conditional, with the *if* clause in the past subjunctive, expresses an intrinsically unlikely or impossible condition (see ch. 27).

(17) **avias**] = **aviátz**.

(18) **eras**] = **erátz**.

(26) **sigran**] Close vowel in first syllable, from the infinitive **sęgre** (see ch. 13).

(29–38) The multiple subjects of **teingna** ('I want all hospitality, largesse, . . . and bold companions to go with you') are in the oblique case, perhaps because the long list presents itself as an absolute construction; it enters the syntax of the sentence almost as an afterthought.

(39) Note that **om** = 'we.'

(42) The year had begun well, for Bertran, because of his hopes for the success of the revolt.

(46) **torneiaire**] Object function, subject form.

(51) **don sa**] Redundant.

(78) **presan**] Passive meaning: 'esteemed, excellent.'

CHAPTER 22

Nouns and Adjectives (Section 1)

→ Review the synchronic presentation of stable declension in chapter 9.

STABLE DECLENSION

Masculine Declension

In OOc the most frequent masculine type ends in a consonant:

	OOc Sg.	OOc Pl.		CL Sg.	CL Pl.
Nom.	**jǫrns**	**jǫrn**	Nom.	DĬŬRNUS	DĬŬRNĪ
			Gen.	DĬŬRNĪ	DĬŬRNŌRUM
			Dat.	DĬŬRNŌ	DĬŬRNĪS
Obl.	**jǫrn**	**jǫrns**	Acc.	DĬŬRNUM	DĬŬRNŌS
			Abl.	DĬŬRNŌ	DĬŬRNĪS

(Note that in Classical Latin, DĬŬRNUS was an adjective meaning 'daily,' not a noun; in VL the adjective replaced CL DĪĒS, of the unusual fifth declension.) As may be seen, the presence or absence of **-s**, on which the OOc declension depends, represents a direct historical continuity from CL, where -s was present or absent in the corresponding slots. In the CL singular, nominative DĬŬRNUS lost its unstressed final vowel (ch. 13) but final -s remained—thus **jǫrns**. With the loss of unstressed final vowels, the four nonnominative singular forms became identical (DĬŬRNĪ, DĬŬRNŌ, DĬŬRNUM, DĬŬRNŌ > **jǫrn**), a merger that underlay the change from five cases to two. The same sound change occurred in the nominative plural (DĬŬRNĪ > **jǫrn**). The nonnominative plural forms became identical to the accusative by normal sound changes (dat. DĬŬRNĪS, acc. DĬŬRNŌS, abl. DĬŬRNĪS > **jǫrns**) or by analogical leveling (gen. DĬŬRNŌRUM > **jǫrns**). Henceforth the genitive, dative, and ablative will not generally be considered.

In CL, declension of the DĬŬRNUS type is called the second declension, the most common declension of masculine nouns and adjectives. The CL third declension also contains masculine nouns as well as feminine and neuter ones—for example, PĂTREM 'father,' illustrating the OOc masculine type with final **-e**:

	OOc				CL	
	Sg.	Pl.			Sg.	Pl.
Nom.	**paire(s)**	**paire**		Nom.	PATER	PATRĒS, VL *PATRĪ
Obl.	**paire**	**paires**		Acc.	PATRĔM	PATRĒS

The evolution of the root may be seen most clearly in the accusative PĂTREM, which became oblique **paire**: final -M drops, and CL T before R becomes yod by yodicism (ch. 17). In nominative singular PATER, the vowel of the final syllable falls, but a support vowel becomes necessary for pronunciation of the consonant cluster: PATER > /patre/, by yodicism /pajre/. Analogy to nominative singular **jorns** adds final **-s**, making nominative singular **paires** the usual form in OOc (see "Masculine Declension" in ch. 9), although etymological **paire** continues (see "Absence of **-s** in the Nominative Singular" in ch. 9).

In the plural, accusative PATRĒS gives **paires** by the same processes. Nominative plural PATRĒS becomes VL *PATRĪ by analogy to the second declension (DĬŬRNĪ), as the entire third declension is assimilated to the second in VL; /patri/ becomes OOc **paire**. Thus in OOc the oblique singular and plural are both etymological, while the nominative singular and plural are both affected, in different ways and to different degrees, by analogy.

OOc **rei** 'king,' representing the OOc masculine type ending in a diphthong, derives from another type of third-declension noun in CL:

	OOc				CL	
	Sg.	Pl.			Sg.	Pl.
Nom.	**rẹis**	**rẹi**		Nom.	REX, VL*REGIS	RĒGĒS, VL *REGĪ
Obl.	**rẹi**	**rẹis**		Acc.	RĒGEM	RĒGĒS

In RĒGEM the G becomes yod by lenition (ch. 15), whereas CL REX lengthened to VL *REGIS by analogy to the oblique case, as in CL genitive REGIS. As in **paire**, the nominative plural is influenced by analogy from the second declension (CL RĒGĒS > VL /regi/ > **rẹi**).

Adjectives replicate the processes already seen in nouns. From the CL second declension, **bọṇ** 'good':

	OOc			CL	
	Sg.	Pl.		Sg.	Pl.
Nom.	**bọṇs**	**bọṇ**	Nom.	BŎNUS	BŎNĪ
Obl.	**bọṇ**	**bọṇs**	Acc.	BŎNUM	BŎNŌS

Classical Latin ŏ became VL /ọ/ by nasal raising (ch. 12), and final -N in a monosyllable became **n**-mobile (ch. 15).

An example of an adjective from the second declension with the nominative singular ending -ER is **paubre** 'poor' (third in CL, acc. sg. PAUPĔREM, but second in VL):

	OOc			CL	
	Sg.	Pl.		Sg.	Pl.
Nom.	**paubres**	**paubre**	Nom.	PAUPER	PAUPĔRĪ
Obl.	**paubre**	**paubres**	Acc.	PAUPĔRUM	PAUPĔRŌS

In PAUPĔRUM the intervocalic P becomes **b** by lenition; the unstressed penult of a proparoxytone falls (ch. 13), as does the final syllable, and a support vowel becomes necessary for pronunciation of the final cluster, hence the oblique **paubre**. Nominative singular **paubres** shows analogical **-s** from **bons** (as obl. **bon** to nom. **bons**, so obl. **paubre** to nom. **paubres**), just as **paires** shows analogical **-s** from **jorns**. The etymological nominative singular type **paubre**, without analogical **-s**, also occurs.

First Feminine Declension (in -a)

Feminine nouns and adjectives ending in **-a** derive from the CL first declension, the most numerous feminine type:

	OOc			CL	
	Sg.	Pl.		Sg.	Pl.
Nom.	**dọmna**	**dọmnas**	Nom.	DŎMĬNA	DŎMĬNAE, VL *DŎMĬNAS
Obl.	**dọmna**	**dọmnas**	Acc.	DŎMĬNAM	DŎMĬNĀS

The nominative and oblique singular form **dọmna** shows the fall of the penult in a proparoxytone and nasal raising; the loss of final -M effaces the distinction between the two cases. CL nominative plural DŎMĬNAE becomes VL *DŎMĬNĀS under influence of the CL third declension, source of the OOc second feminine declension (see below), in which the feminine nominative plural and oblique plural both end in **-s**. This analogical change in the plural effaces the distinction in case just as in the singular. The first feminine declension distinguishes only number.

This analogical change in the nominative plural of the first feminine declension, which becomes identical to the oblique plural, is contrary to the analogical change in the masculine nominative plural (see above), whereby CL PATRĒS becomes VL /patri/. In the masculine declension the nominative plural vocalic ending of DĬŬRNĪ extends to replace the consonantal ending of PATRĒS, whereas in the feminine declension the nominative plural consonantal ending of PARTĒS (see below) extends to replace the vocalic ending of DŎMĬNAE. By these contrary analogies, the nominative plural gains a uniform ending in **-s** for the feminine and in -zero for the masculine, whereas CL showed both types of ending for both genders.

The same patterns hold true for adjectives:

	OOc			CL	
	Sg.	Pl.		Sg.	Pl.
Nom.	**bǫna**	**bǫnas**	Nom.	BŎNA	BŎNAE, VL *BŎNĀS
Obl.	**bǫna**	**bǫnas**	Acc.	BŎNAM	BŎNĀS

	OOc			VL	
	Sg.	Pl.		Sg.	Pl.
Nom.	**paubra**	**paubras**	Nom.	PAUPERA	PAUPĔRAE, *PAUPERĀS
Obl.	**paubra**	**paubras**	Acc.	PAUPĔRAM	PAUPĔRĀS

Second Feminine Declension (not in -a)

OOc feminine nouns and adjectives that do not end in **-a** derive from the CL third declension, the source of masculine nouns such as **paire** and **rei**. Feminine **part** 'share' was declined as follows:

	OOc			CL	
	Sg.	Pl.		Sg.	Pl.
Nom.	**partz**	**partz**	Nom.	PARS, VL *PARTIS	PARTĒS
			Gen.	PARTĬS	PARTUM
			Dat.	PARTĪ	PARTĬBUS
Obl.	**part**	**partz**	Acc.	PARTEM	PARTĒS
			Abl.	PARTE	PARTĬBUS

The CL nominative singular was remodeled as VL *PARTIS (on the basis of the gen.) to regularize the singular forms into two syllables.[1]

---

[1] Thus CL nom. sg. AMOR became VL *AMORIS, producing OOc nom. sg. **amors**.

The feminine adjective **tal** 'such' had these forms:

	OOc			CL	
	Sg.	Pl.		Sg.	Pl.
Nom.	**tals**	**tals**	Nom.	TĂLIS	TĂLĒS
Obl.	**tal**	**tals**	Acc.	TĂLEM	TĂLĒS

Adjectives: Gender and Declension

OOc adjectives have two types, one that shows a distinction for gender and another that does not. The distinctive type originates in the CL first declension for feminine forms, and in the second declension for masculine forms. The feminine root adds final **-a** to the masculine root:

	OOc			CL	

Masculine:

	Sg.	Pl.		Sg.	Pl.
Nom.	**bọns**	**bọṇ**	Nom.	BŎNUS	BŎNĪ
Obl.	**bọṇ**	**bọns**	Acc.	BŎNUM	BŎNŌS

Feminine:

	Sg.	Pl.		Sg.	Pl.
Nom.	**bọna**	**bọnas**	Nom.	BŎNA	BŎNAE, VL *BŎNĀS
Obl.	**bọna**	**bọnas**	Acc.	BŎNAM	BŎNĀS

The nondistinctive type derives from the CL third declension, which does not show gender in adjectives:

	OOc			CL	

Masculine:

	Sg.	Pl.		Sg.	Pl.
Nom.	**tals**	**tal**	Nom.	TĂLIS	TĂLĒS, VL *TĂLĪ
Obl.	**tal**	**tals**	Acc.	TĂLEM	TĂLĒS

Feminine:

	Sg.	Pl.		Sg.	Pl.
Nom.	**tals**	**tals**	Nom.	TĂLIS	TĂLĒS
Obl.	**tal**	**tals**	Acc.	TĂLEM	TĂLĒS

These declensions highlight the effect of contrary analogies in clarifying the gender of the nominative plural: masculine **tal** was influenced by **bon**, both ending in -zero, while feminine **bonas** was influenced by **tals**, both ending in **-s**.

The invariable declension, which had no model in CL, arose as a result of the convergence of two developments: the reduction of declensional distinctions to the single marker **-s** (or -zero) and the creation by normal sound change of individual words with roots ending in **-s**. Roots ending in **-s**, which are therefore invariable for case and number, derive from various sources in CL. For example, **cǫrs** 'body, person, self,' from a third-declension neuter noun in CL:

	OOc			CL	
	Sg.	Pl.		Sg.	Pl.
Nom.	**cǫrs**	**cǫrs**	Nom.	cŏrpus	cŏrpŏra
Obl.	**cǫrs**	**cǫrs**	Acc.	cŏrpus	cŏrpŏra

In the CL accusative singular, the unstressed final vowel fell, and the resulting cluster -rps was simplified to **-rs** (see ch. 16 for discussion of simplification). The plural forms in OOc do not represent development of the corresponding plurals in CL but have been generated from the OOc oblique and nominative singular.

Prętz 'merit' comes from a second-declension neuter in CL:

	OOc			CL	
	Sg.	Pl.		Sg.	Pl.
Nom.	**prętz**	**prętz**	Nom.	prĕtĭum	prĕtĭa
Obl.	**prętz**	**prętz**	Acc.	prĕtĭum	prĕtĭa

When CL prĕtĭum, a proparoxytone, lost its final consonant, final vowel, and penult, the original -ĭ- was reduced to a yod that produced assibilation of the т (ch. 18). Again the OOc plurals (which occur infrequently) have been generated from the singular forms.

Similar developments occurred in feminine **patz** 'peace,' from third-declension CL pācem by assibilation, and in the masculine adjective **gelǫs** 'jealous,' from LL zēlōsum, which already had a root ending in -s.

OTHER DECLENSIONAL CATEGORIES IN CLASSICAL LATIN

The neuter gender in CL, which included nouns such as second-declension fŏlĭum 'leaf' and third-declension cŏrpus 'body,' disappeared in OOc except for neuter pronouns (**o, so aiso, lo**), adjectives, and perhaps sporadic usage of normally masculine nouns such as **cǫr** 'heart' (see chs. 28 and 29). Most CL neuter nouns joined the masculine declension, which many of them resembled in the accusative singular ending -um:

DŎNUM > **dọn** 'gift'

suffix -ĀTĬCUM > **-atge**

suffix -ĬUM > **-i**

CŎR > **cọr** 'heart'

CŎRPUS > **cọrs** 'body'

PĬPER > **pẹbre** 'pepper'

Some words of collective meaning passed from the neuter plural of the second declension, which ended in -A, to a new feminine singular. Thus neuter singular FŎLĬUM 'leaf' produced masculine **fọlh** 'leaf,' while plural FŎLĬA 'leaves' produced feminine **fọlha** 'leaves (*collective*), foliage.'

The CL fourth declension, comprising mostly masculine nouns in nominative -US, genitive -ŪS, accusative -UM (and differing from the second declension in other endings), joined the second declension in VL and so entered the regular masculine declension in OOC, like **jọrn**. Thus nominative PŎRTUS, genitive PORTŪS 'harbor' became OOc **pọrt**. Fourth-declension nominative CĀSUS, genitive CĀSŪS, accusative CĀSUM 'a falling' became invariable because of its root in -S: **cas** 'case, pass, (bad) situation.'

Nouns in the CL fifth declension, which were feminine with the nominative -IĒS, accusative -IEM, could be reformulated as members of the feminine first declension in -A, -AM and so could join the OOc first feminine declension. Thus CL nominative DĬĒS, accusative DĬEM 'day' became VL *DIA, *DIAM, then OOc **dia**, as in **tota dia** 'all day' 11.79. But CL DĬEM also developed by normal sound changes, switched gender, and produced masculine **di**: **al di clar** 'at dawn' 11.60.[2]

READING 22

Bertran de Born, *Ges de far sirventes no·m tartz*

In the aftermath of the revolt of spring 1183, Richard Lionheart besieged Autafort, captured it after a week's resistance, and gave it to Bertran's brother Constantine. Henry II soon returned it to the troubadour, however, and Richard confirmed his father's grant. In this song Bertran gloats over his triumph and defies his enemies. The poem's form would be imitated, and its ethics rebutted, by Peire Cardenal (reading 24).

[2] **Dia** may also be treated as a masculine: **uns sols dias** 'just one day' 16.49, **en aquel dia** 'on that day' 1.7. **En anzs en dies** 'in earlier days' 11.20 perhaps represents a Latinism (CL acc. pl. DIĒS).

1
Ges de far sirventes no·m tartz,
anz lo fauc senes totz affans,
tant es sotils mos geins e m'artz.
Que mes m'en sui en tal enans
    e sai tant de sort   5
    qe ve·us m'en estort,
    qe comte ni rei
    no·m forssan ni grei.

2
E pois lo reis e·l coms Richartz
m'ant perdonat lor maltalans,   10
ja mais n'Azemars ni n'Amblarz
no·m don tregas ni·n Talairans,
    Ni ja d'Autafort
    no·il laissarai ort.
    Qui·s vol m'en gerrei,   15
    pois aver lo dei!

3
Tant sui fortz devas totas partz
q'en mi resta de gerra·l pans.
Pustell'en son huoill qui m'en partz!
Si tot m'o comenssiei enans,   20
    patz no·m fai conort.
    Ab gerra m'acort,
    q'ieu non teing ni crei
    negun'autra lei!

4
E no·i gart diluns ni dimartz
ni setmanas, ni mes, ni ans,   25
ni·m lais per abril ni per martz
q'ieu non tracte cum veigna dans
    a celz qe·m fant tort.
    Mas ja per nuill sort
    non conquerran trei   30
    lo pretz d'un correi!

5
Qui que fassa de bocs issartz,
eu me sui totz temps mes en grans
cum puosc'aver cairels e dartz,
elms et aubercs, cavals e brans.   35
    C'ab aisso·m conort
    e·m teing a deport—
    gerra e tornei,
    donar e dompnei.   40

Mos parsoniers es tant gaillartz
q'el vol la terra mos enfans,
et eu la·il vuoill dar, tant sui gartz.
Pois diran tuich, "Flacs en Bertrans!"
   Mas sal tot lo tort,
cre q'a malvatz port
venra, so·us autrei,
anz c'ab mi plaidei.

7

No·m cal d'Autafort
mais far dreich ni tort,
qe·l jutgamen crei
mon seignor, lo rei.

Meter:

a	b	a	b	c	c	d	d
8	8	8	8	5	5	5	5

Sirv. 6 u 8, 1–4.
-artz, -ans, -ọrt, -ẹi.
Frank 382:89.

P-C 80,20. Major editions: Gouiran, *L'amour,* no. 18; Paden, Sankovitch, and
Stäblein, no. 19; Gouiran, *Seigneur,* no. 18.

Eight manuscripts: *A* fol. 190–v; *C* fol. 139v; *D* fol. 119–v; *E* pp. 100–01; *F* fol.
96–v; *I* fol. 183v–184; *K* fol. 169–v; *y.* Base *A.*

Stanza order

ACE	1	2	3	4	5	6	7
DIK	1	2	6	3	5	4	7
F	1	2	4	6	3	5	7

(Stanza 1 alone occurs in *y.*)

Rejected readings in the base manuscript: (11) Richartz ni n'Aguirans *A,* n'Azemars ni n'Amblarz *F,* n'Aimars ni n'Aicharz *DIK,* Guirautz ni n'Audoartz *CE,*
om. y. (19) pustella en. (26) ni ans ni mes *A,* ni mes ni ans *CDEFIK.* (33) bos
ACEF, bels *DIK, om. y.* (35) puosca aver.

Selected variants: (3) sotils *ADIK,* subtils *C,* soptils *E,* suptils *F.* (6) vec vos *DIK.*
(23) teing *AC,* tenc *E,* tem *DIK,* voill F. (30) mas ja per nuill sort *A,* e ja·us per
fort *CE,* et jab mi per fort *DFIK;* mas ja mais per fort *Gouiran, L'amour* and
Seigneur.

Notes

(7) **comte ni rei**] Plural in form, but alluding to **lo reis e·l coms** 9—that is,
Count Richard and King Henry.

(11–12) **Azemars, Amblarz, Talairans**] Aimar V, viscount of Limoges;
Amblardus d'Ans, a castellan and vassal of Bertran de Born; Elias VI
Talairan, count of Périgord.

(19) Anacoluthon, or syntactic blend: 3rd sg. **son,** 2nd sg. **partz.** Lit., 'A sty
in his eye, if you part me from it [war].'

(24) **autra lei**] Allusion to the Truce of God, by which the church, in a series of councils, called on knights to renounce combat on holy days, sometimes as many as 285 days in the year.

(25–27) **diluns ... dimartz ... setmanas ... mes ... ans ... abril ... martz**] Times when the Truce of God forbade combat.

(31) **trei**] Refers to vv. 11–12.

(33) **bocs**] Obl. pl.; simplification of **boscs**.

(41) **Mos parsoniers**] The troubadour's brother Constantine.

(42) **mos enfans**] Oblique case expressing possession: 'of my children.'

(52) **mon seignor**, **lo rei**] Henry II Plantagenet, who returned Autafort to Bertran.

Nouns and Adjectives (Section 2);
Demonstratives

SHIFTING DECLENSION

We speak of shifting declension in describing nouns that show a shift of stress for a distinctive nominative singular form.[1] Stress shifts away from the end of the word, as in the oblique singular **senhór**, nominative singular **sénher**. The plural forms are based on the oblique singular: nominative plural **senhór**, oblique plural **senhórs**.

The shifting declension may be regarded as a divergence from the stable pattern in the direction of asigmatic nouns ending in **-r(e)**, such as masculine **paire**, feminine **amor**, neuter **cor**. Many shifting words, though not all of them, also have final **-r** in the oblique singular.

Like asigmatic declension, shifting declension diverges from the general pattern because of anomalous etymological factors. These factors come into play in only one slot, the nominative singular, which may be considered from either of two perspectives: synchronically, as formed from the oblique singular in OOc, or dia-

---

[1] The types of declension here called "stable" and "shifting" have often been called "parisyllabic" and "imparisyllabic," meaning that a given word in CL had the same number of syllables throughout its declension (parisyllabic) or a varying number of syllables (imparisyllabic). These terms are less satisfactory for OOc, however, because in OOc the number of syllables is a secondary feature dependent on stress position and because some nouns with shifting stress in fact have the same number of syllables in the various forms. For example, obl. sg. **abát**, nom. sg. **ábas**; obl. sg. **senhór**, nom. sg. **sénher**; obl. sg. **amadór**, nom. sg. **amáire** (three syllables); obl. sg. **molhér**, nom. sg. **mólher**; obl. sg. **Eblón**, nom. sg. **Eble**. In words such as obl. sg. **óme** (nom. sg. **om**), the accent remains on the same internally constituted syllable but nevertheless shifts its position from the penult in **óme** to the final (and only) syllable in **om**. There are fewer words such as **óme** than there are of so-called imparisyllabics with the same number of syllables in the two cases.

chronically, as formed from the etymological nominative singular in CL.[2] The synchronic approach provides an adequate explanation of vowel structure in the nominative singular, but etymological considerations become necessary to understand consonant structure.

Although shifting declension involves only a small number of nouns and adjectives, all of them are relatively frequent. Almost all the nouns are names of people, and the adjectives tend to be those used to describe people. There are only two feminine shifting nouns, **molhęr** 'wife' and **serǫr** 'sister.'

When stress shifts away from the end of the word, the shift causes reduction of the final syllable. Stressed **-á** is reduced to unstressed **-a**; other vowels, whether stressed or unstressed, are deleted. Consonants are adjusted in several ways.

Reduction of Stressed -á to Unstressed -a

If the vowel of the final syllable in the oblique singular is stressed **-á**, the stress shifts to the penult for the nominative singular, but the vowel remains otherwise unchanged:

> Obl. sg. **abát** 'abbot' > nom. sg. **ábas**

> Obl. sg. **enfán** 'child' > nom. sg. **énfas**

This synchronic retention of unstressed final **-a** corresponds to diachronic retention of CL A in the final syllable, as in TĔRRAM > **tęrra** (ch. 13).

The appearance of final **-s** in the nominative singular of these two words reflects the standard declension of masculine nouns (nom. sg. **jorns**). The **-s** is also etymological:

	OOc			CL	
	Sg.	Pl.		Sg.	Pl.
Nom.	**ábas**	**abát**	Nom.	ABBAS	ABBĀTĒS, VL *ABBĀTĪ
Obl.	**abát**	**abátz**	Acc.	ABBĀTEM	ABBĀTĒS

Double B simplifies (ch. 16).

Nom.	**énfas**	**enfánt**	Nom.	ĬNFANS	ĬNFANTĒS, VL *ĬNFANTĪ
Obl.	**enfán**	**enfántz**	Acc.	ĬNFANTEM	ĬNFANTĒS

(Cf. OFr. obl. sg. *enfánt*, nom. sg. *énfes*.)

---

[2] Nouns of the shifting declension in OOc derive from the third declension in CL.

In two masculine paroxytones, unstressed **-e** in the final syllable of the oblique singular is deleted in the nominative singular. No stress shift is possible, since these are words of two syllables:

Obl. sg. **ǫ́me** 'man' > nom. sg. **ǫm**

Obl. sg. **cǫ́mte** 'count' > nom. sg. **cǫms**

The nominative singular forms are etymological:

	OOc				CL	
	Sg.	Pl.			Sg.	Pl.
Nom.	**ǫm**	**ǫme**	Nom.		HŎMŌ	HŎMĬNĒS, VL *HŎMĬNĪ
Obl.	**ǫme**	**ǫmes**	Acc.		HŎMĬNEM	HŎMĬNĒS

The CL letter H was unstable (ch. 17). In the accusative singular, the fall of the unstressed penult (ch. 13) produced **omne** (nom. pl. in *Boeci* 11.1, 11.7), where the final **-e** is preserved as a support vowel. The consonant cluster then reduced (perhaps by way of metathesis to *****onme**, then by simplification of the implosive consonant), but the former support vowel remained. The nominative plural became VL *HŎMĬNĪ by the same substitution of endings as in PATRĒS > *PATRĪ (ch. 22). The analogical nominative singular **oms** shows influence of the regular masculine declension.

	OOc				CL	
	Sg.	Pl.			Sg.	Pl.
Nom.	**cǫms**	**cǫmte**	Nom.		COMES	CŎMĬTĒS, VL *COMĬTĪ
Obl.	**cǫmte**	**cǫmtes**	Acc.		CŎMĬTEM	CŎMĬTĒS

Similarly, oblique singular **vescomte** 'viscount' became nominative singular **vescoms**.

Deletion of Other Vowels and Reduction of Consonant Clusters

Other stressed vowels in the oblique singular are deleted when stress shifts to the penult for the nominative singular, just as, in diachrony, final vowels other than **-a** are dropped. The vowel in question is almost always **o**, rarely **e** (in feminine **molhér** 'woman').

Deletion of the last vowel frequently brings surrounding consonants into contact, with various results. Certain consonants brought into potential clusters by the reduction of the final syllable are deleted. The most frequent of these is **n-mobile**:

Obl. sg. **barón** 'baron' > nom. sg. **bar** (not ***barn**)

Obl. sg. **felón** 'wicked' > nom. sg. **fel**

Obl. sg. **Ugón** 'Hugo' > nom. sg. **Uc, Ucs**

Obl. sg. **garsón** 'rascal' > nom. sg. **gártz**

The diachronic situation underlies these changes:

	OOc			VL (from Germanic)	
	Sg.	Pl.		Sg.	Pl.
Nom.	**bar**	**barón**	Nom.	BARŌ	BARŌNĪ
Obl.	**barón**	**baróns**	Acc.	BARŌNEM	BARŌNĒS
Nom.	**gartz**	**garsón**	Nom.	*WRAKKJO	*WRAKKJŌNĪ
Obl.	**garsón**	**garsóns**	Acc.	*WRAKKJŌNEM	*WRAKKJŌNĒS

The appearance of the **-t-** in **gartz** is explained diachronically as the result of assibilation (ch. 18).

A similar case involves simplification of the potential double **r** in **seror**:

Fem. obl. sg. **serór** > nom. sg. **sor**

In nominative singular **sor**, we may understand the synchronic process **serór** > ***sér'r** > ***ser** (by stress shift) > **sor**; the substitution of the vowel **-o-** in the nominative singular reflects the etymon, CL SŎRŎR. Diachronically the two forms are explained thus:

	OOc			CL	
	Sg.	Pl.		Sg.	Pl.
Nom.	**sor**	**serórs**	Nom.	SŎRŎR	SŎRŌRĒS
Obl.	**serór**	**serórs**	Acc.	SŎRŌREM	SŎRŌRĒS

Diachronically the **o** in the OOc nominative singular underlies the oblique, becoming **e** by dissimilation when not stressed, whereas synchronically the **e** of the oblique underlies the **o** of the nominative.

Support Vowels

If the consonants brought into contact can be neither pronounced as a final cluster nor reduced, a support vowel (unstressed **e**) is inserted between them.

/ˊnh'r/ > ˊ**nher**

OOc obl. sg. **senhór** 'lord' > nom. sg. **sénher**

OOc obl. sg. **lonhór** 'longer' > nom. sg. **lónher**

217

*Chapter 23.
Nouns and
Adjectives
(Section 2);
Demonstratives*

'/-lh'r/ > ꞉lher

    OOc obl. sg. **melhǫ́r** 'better' > nom. sg. **mę́lher**

    OOc obl. sg. **molhę́r** 'woman' > nom. sg. **mǫ́lher**

'/-ns'r/ > ꞉nser

    OOc obl. sg. **gensǫ́r** 'nobler' > nom. sg. **gę́nser**

'/-dž'r/ > /꞉džər/

    OOc obl. sg. **majǫ́r** 'bigger' > nom. sg. **májer**

    OOc obl. sg. **pejǫ́r** 'worse' > nom. sg. **pę́ger, pę́ire** (*PD*)

These words include a masculine noun (**senhǫr**), a feminine noun (**mǫlher**), and synthetic comparative adjectives in both genders (**gensǫr, lonhǫr, majǫr, melhǫr, pejǫr**).

Support vowels also appear in proper nouns:

    Obl. sg. **Carlǫ́n** 'Charles' > nom. sg. **Carle, Carles**

    Obl. sg. **Eblǫ́n** 'Eble' (viscount of Ventadorn) > nom. sg.
    Eble, Ebles

The development of such support vowels may also be seen diachronically:

	OOc				CL	
	Sg.	Pl.			Sg.	Pl.
Nom.	**sę́nher**	**senhǫ́r**		Nom.	sĕnĭor	sĕnĭōrēs, VL *sĕnĭōrī
Obl.	**senhǫ́r**	**senhǫ́rs**		Acc.	sĕnĭōrem	sĕnĭōrēs

	OOc				CL	
Nom.	**mǫ́lher**	**molhę́rs**		Nom.	mŭlĭer	mŭlĭĕrēs
Obl.	**molhę́r**	**molhę́rs**		Acc.	mŭlĭĕrem	mŭlĭĕrēs

In CL the accent on mŭlĭĕrem falls on the antepenult, /mulíerem/, but in VL it shifts to the penult because a vowel in hiatus (directly before another vowel) can no longer bear stress: hence /muliérem/. In nominative singular **mǫ́lher**, the **e** is retained as a support vowel. Note that the spelling of **molher** is the same in the nominative and the oblique, although the shift in stress produces markedly different pronunciations.

Reduction of -adór to -áire, etc.

When a noun with the agentive suffix **-adǫ́r**, such as **amadǫ́r** 'lover,' was reduced in the shifting declension, it became a hypothetical /-adr/, which by yodicism became /-ajr/ (ch. 16) and required a support vowel, yielding **-aire**. This synchronic analysis corresponds to the diachronic development:

OOc   CL

	Sg.	Pl.		Sg.	Pl.
Nom.	**amáire**	**amadǫ́r**	Nom.	AMĀTOR	AMĀTŌRĒS, VL *AMĀTŌRĪ
Obl.	**amadǫ́r**	**amadǫ́rs**	Acc.	AMĀTŌREM	AMĀTŌRĒS

This suffix is found in the following words:

    Obl. sg. **amadǫr** 'lover' > nom. sg. **amaire**

    Obl. sg. **cantadǫr** 'singer' > nom. sg. **cantaire**

    Obl. sg. **emperadǫr** 'emperor' > nom. sg. **emperaire**

    Obl. sg. **trobadǫr** 'troubadour' > nom. sg. **trobaire**

And in the same way, **cavalgadǫr** 'rider'; **ensenhadǫr** 'teacher'; **lauzadǫr** 'praiser'; **lavadǫr** 'washing place'; **pecadǫr** 'sinner'; **torneiadǫr** 'tourneyer.' This suffix accounts for most of the words in the shifting declension.

    Similar in structure to agentive **-adǫr** is the comparative suffix **-azǫr**:

    Obl. sg. **belazǫr** 'more beautiful' > nom. sg. **belaire**

Seen diachronically:

OOc   VL

	Sg.	Pl.		Sg.	Pl.
Nom.	**belaire**	**belazǫr**	Nom.	*BELLĀTĬOR	*BELLATĬŌRĪ
Obl.	**belazǫr**	**belazǫrs**	Acc.	*BELLATĬŌREM	*BELLATĬŌRES

In the nominative plural, masculine **belazǫr** corresponds to feminine **belazǫrs**.

DEMONSTRATIVES

For synchronic declension of the suffix of demonstratives, which expresses gender, case, and number, see chapter 10. For the syntax of demonstratives, see chapter 29.

    The demonstrative prefix shows three degrees of force (weak, introductory, and strong), and the root shows three degrees of proximity (neuter or null proximity, near, and far). Two words, **ęl** 'he' and **lo** 'the,' share the weak–far slot (see table 23.1).

TABLE 23.1

219

*Chapter 23.
Nouns and
Adjectives
(Section 2);
Demonstratives*

Proximity		Force		
CL	OOc	Weak	Introductory	Strong
		root	s/c + root	ais/aic/ac + root
нŏс	neuter	ǫ	sǫ	aisǫ, acǫ
ĭsтuм	near	ęst	cęst	aicęst, aquęst
ĭLLUM	far	ęl/lo	cęl	aicęl, aquęl

Prefixes

The prefix expressing introductory force, symbolized as **s/c** because it may be spelled either way, represents the assibilation of an etymological [k] in CL ĕссĕ 'behold,' used to strengthen the effect of the demonstrative (see "Assibilation of a Voiceless Stop Followed by Yod" in ch. 18):

sǫ < VL *ĕссĕ нŏс, lit., 'behold this'

cęst < VL ĕссĕ ĭsтuм, lit., 'behold that'

cęl < VL ĕссĕ ĭLLUM, lit., 'behold yonder'

In all three words the final vowel of ĕссĕ was reduced to yod by agglutination (when the two words joined into one) and then caused the assibilation of [k] before being effaced entirely. The first syllable of ĕссĕ was lost by aphaeresis (ch. 13).

The prefix expressing strong force, symbolized as **ais/aic/ac**, represents a further reinforcement of CL ĕссĕ by influence of ATQUE 'and also' in VL, an influence that averted aphaeresis:

aisǫ < VL *ăссĕ нŏс < CL ĕссĕ нŏс

aicęst < VL *ăссĕ ĭsтuм < CL ĕссĕ ĭsтuм

aicęl < VL *ăссĕ ĭLLUM < CL ĕссĕ ĭLLUM

acǫ < VL *ăссu нŏс

aquęst < VL *ăссu ĭsтuм

aquęl < VL *ăссu ĭLLUM

The first three of these forms show assibilation by the same mechanism as in **sǫ**, **cęst**, **cęl**; the remaining three do not show it, because ĕссĕ became *ĕссu under the influence of ATQUE and so did not develop a yod.

The neuter demonstratives (**ǫ**, **sǫ**, **aisǫ/acǫ**) do not inflect. In the near series, masculine **ęst** 'this' declines as follows:

	OOc			CL	
	Sg.	Pl.		Sg.	Pl.
Nom.	ęst	ist	Nom.	ĭste	ĭstī
Obl.	ęst	ęstz	Acc.	ĭstum	ĭstōs

Nominative plural **ist** shows metaphony of the vowel under the influence of the final /i/ in VL. Similar to **ęst** are **cęst**, from ĕccĕ ĭstum, and **aicęst**, from *ăccĕ ĭstum. Feminine **ęsta** declines in this way:

	OOc			CL	
	Sg.	Pl.		Sg.	Pl.
Nom.	ęsta	ęstas	Nom.	ĭsta	ĭstae, VL *ĭstās
Obl.	ęsta	ęstas	Acc.	ĭstam	ĭstās

The nominative plural gains analogical **-s** as in regular feminine declension (nom. pl. **domnas**). Similarly **cęsta**, from ĕccĕ ĭstam, and **aicęsta**, from *ăccĕ ĭstam.

In the far series, the masculine personal pronoun **ęl** is declined as follows:

	OOc			CL	
	Sg.	Pl.		Sg.	Pl.
Nom.	ęl	ilh	Nom.	ĭlle	ĭllī
Obl.	ęl	ęls	Acc.	ĭllum	ĭllōs

In the nominative plural the final -ī is reduced to yod, which both causes metaphony of the stressed vowel and combines with /l/ to produce the palatal. Similarly **cęl**, from ĕccĕ ĭllum, and **aicęl**, from *ăccĕ ĭllum. Feminine **ęla** shows these forms:

	OOc			CL	
	Sg.	Pl.		Sg.	Pl.
Nom.	ęla	ęlas	Nom.	ĭlla	ĭllae, VL *ĭllās
Obl.	ęla	ęlas	Acc.	ĭllam	ĭllās

Similarly **cęla**, from ĕccĕ ĭllam, and **aicęla**, from *ăccĕ ĭllam.

The masculine definite article developed by attraction to the following noun, hence lost independent stress and the first syllable with it, and developed secondary stress on the last syllable:

221

Chapter 23.
Nouns and
Adjectives
(Section 2);
Demonstratives

	OOc			CL	
	Sg.	Pl.		Sg.	Pl.
Nom.	**lo**	**li**	Nom.	ĬLLE	ĬLLĪ
Obl.	**lo**	**los**	Acc.	ĬLLUM	ĬLLŌS

The nominative singular was generated from the OOc oblique singular, not from the nominative singular in CL. The feminine definite article looks like this:

	OOc			CL	
	Sg.	Pl.		Sg.	Pl.
Nom.	**la**	**las**	Nom.	ĬLLA	ĬLLAE, VL *ĬLLĀS
Obl.	**la**	**las**	Acc.	ĬLLAM	ĬLLĀS

For additional forms of the personal pronoun, see chapter 29.

READING 23

Castelloza, *Amics, s'ie·us trobes avinen*

With three **cansos** *of certain attribution and a probable fourth, Castelloza joins the Comtessa de Dia as one of the two most prolific trobairitz. Castelloza was perhaps active during the first quarter of the thirteenth century.*[3]

1
    Amics, s'ie·us trobes avinen,
humil e franc e de bona merce,
be·us amera—cant era m'en sove
qu'ie·us trop ves mi mal e sebenc e ric,
e·n fatz chansons per tal que fass'ausir   5
vostre bon prez; don eu no·m puesc sofrir
qu'eu no·us fasa lausar a tota gen
on plus mi faitz mal ez asiramen.

2
    Ja mais no·us tenrai per valen,
ni·us amarai de bon cor ni per fe;   10
per ver veirei si ja·m valria re
s'ie·us mostrava cor felon ni enic.
—Non farei ja, qu'eu non vueill puscaz dir

[3] Rieger 562; Bruckner, Shepard, and White 147; the first third of the century for Bec 75; the first half for Riquer 3: 1325.

qu'eu anc ves vos agues cor de faillir;
c'auriaz i qualque razonamen   15
s'ieu avia ves vos fait faillimen.

3

Eu sai ben qu'a mi esta gen,
si ben dison tuig que mout descove
que dompna prec ja cavalier de se
ni que·l tenga totz tems tam lonc pressic.   20
Mas cil c'o diz non sap gez gen chausir,
qu'ieu vueil prejar ennanz que·m lais morir,
qu'e·l prejar ai maing douz revenimen
can prec sellui don ai gran pessamen.

4

Asatz es fols qui m'en repren   25
de vos amar, pos tan gen me conve;
e cel c'o diz no sap co s'es de me,
ni no·us vi ges als uels ab qu'ieu vos vi,
quan me dissez que non agues consir,
que calc'ora pori endevenir   30
que n'auria enquera jausimen.
De sol lo dig n'ai eu lo cor jausen.

5

Tot'autr'amor teing a nïen—
e sapchaz ben que mais jois no·m soste,
mas lo vostre que m'alegr'e·m reve   35
on mais m'en ven d'afan e de destric.
E·m cug ades per plain e lais jausir
de vos, amics, qu'eu no·m puesc convertir;
ni joi non ai, ni socors non aten,
mas sol aitan can n'aurai en durmen.   40

6

Oimais non sai que·us me presen,
que saiat ai ez a mal ez a be
vostre dur cor—don lo mieus no·s recre.
E no·us o man, qu'eu meseisa·us o dic:
e morai me si no·m volez jausir   45
de qualque joi. E si·m laissatz morir
farez pecat, e serez n'en turmen,
e serai mos quesid'a·l jutjamen.

Meter:

a	b	b	c	d	d	a	a
8	10	10	10	10	10	10	10

Ch. 6 u 8.

-ęn, -ę, -ic, -ir.

Frank 742:1.

223

Chapter 23.
Nouns and
Adjectives
(Section 2);
Demonstratives

P-C 109,1. Major editions: Paden with Hayes et al., no. 1; Rieger, no. 29; Bruckner, Shepard, and White, no. 6; Bec, no. 3.

Four manuscripts: *A* fol. 168v–169; *I* fol. 125; *K* fol. 110v; *N* fol. 227v–228. Base *N.*

Attributions: Na Castelloza *AIK,* Anonymous *N.*

Stanza order: Uniform.

Rejected readings in the base manuscript: *The scribe of N omitted the first letter of every stanza in the poem; these letters are here supplied from the other mss.* (2) humils *NIK,* humil *A.* (4) mi *AIK, om. N;* seben *N,* fellon *A,* fol *IK.* (12) s'ieu vos *N,* si·us *AIK.* (16) faitz *N,* nuill *AIK.* (22) prezar *N,* pregar *IK,* proar *A.* (28) abs suels *N,* ab suels *IK,* aras *A.* (31) aurie *NIK,* auria *A.* (36) oi *N,* on *AIK;* ez *N,* e *AIK.* (37) per plam es les *N,* per plainessa e *IK,* alegrar e *A.* (44) meteisia·us *N,* meseiseu *I,* meseiseou *K,* mezeussa·us *A.*

Selected variants: (4) e ric *N,* e tric *AIK.* (24) gran *N,* greu *AIK.* (42) saiat *N,* cercat *AIK.* (45) qu'enoia me *A.* (47) serai *A.* (48) seretz ne blasmatz vilanamen *AIK.*

Notes

(1–3) **s'ie·us trobes . . . amera**] The past subjunctive in the *if* clause, with the second conditional in the result, depicts an unlikely or impossible hypothesis (see ch. 27).

(13) **vueill puscaz**] For **vueill que puscaz**; zero subordinating conjunction.

(14) **faillir**] In legal usage, 'to fail to appear when summoned'; likewise **faillimen** 16.

(15) **razonamen**] In legal usage, 'defense.'

(25–26) Cf. Bernart de Ventadorn's view that only a fool reproaches his lady for her wishes (16.33–35).

(44) The line seems to suggest direct personal performance, instead of performance by an emissary such as a joglar.

(47–48) A lover's view of the Last Judgment.

PART 4

Syntax

CHAPTER 24

Word Order

MAJOR ELEMENTS OF THE SENTENCE

For the purpose of analyzing word order, we shall consider a sentence to be constituted of three major elements: an independent verb or verb phrase, its subject or subject phrase, and its complement or complements, which may include the direct object, indirect object, adverb, predicate nominative, participle, modifying phrases or clauses, and so on.

Such a sentence does not always correspond to the sentence as punctuated in texts. For example (verbs in **boldface**):

> E **venc** bels hom et adreichs, e **saup** ben chantar e trobar, e **venc** cortes et enseingnatz. 5.3

> > And he became a handsome man and clever, and learned how to sing well and to compose, and became courtly and educated.

This single sentence as punctuated constitutes three sentences as just defined (the double slash indicates a sentence break):

> E **venc** bels hom et adreichs,//
> e **saup** ben chantar e trobar,//
> e **venc** cortes et enseingnatz.//

The verb phrase includes unstressed object pronouns but not stressed subject pronouns, which constitute the subject phrase. It may also include adverbs, if they are closely bound to the verb. We shall divide the subject phrase, verb phrase, and complements with single slashes:

> Bernartz de Ventedorn / si **fo** / de Limozin 5.1
> Subject / Verb / Complement

> > Bernart de Ventadorn was from the Limousin. **227**

But the verb phrase does not include strong independent adverbs or adverbial phrases, which will be considered as complements:

> Ladoncs / se **leva** / ·l setis   25.101
> Complement / Verb   / Subject
>
>> Then the siege is raised.

> Lonc temps / **duret** / lor amors.   5.7
> Complement / Verb   / Subject
>
>> Their love lasted a long time.

Examples of usage in this chapter will be chosen from various linguistic registers: prose (the **vida** of Bernart de Ventadorn, ch. 5), epic (*Chanson de la Croisade albigeoise*, ch. 25), and lyric.

DECLARATIVE STATEMENTS

Word order in declarative statements permits the following generalizations:

1. When the subject phrase, the verb phrase, and a complement are all present, the verb tends to occupy the second position in the sentence.

2. The subject tends to precede the complement.

The first generalization is stronger than the second.

It follows that the usual order of the three major elements in a declarative sentence is subject, verb, complement (SVC):

> Bernartz de Ventedorn / si **fo** / de Limozin   5.1
>
>> Bernart de Ventadorn was from the Limousin.

> E·l coms / **venc** / a so fraire   25.60
>
>> The count came to his brother.

However, the subject and complement may be reversed, leaving the verb phrase in second position (CVS):

> En agradar et en voler /
> **es** / l'amors de dos fins amanz   16.29–30
>
>> In pleasing and in yearning
>> is the love of two true lovers.

> E laïns en Toloza /   **intrec** / us messatgers.   25.89
>
>> And a messenger entered Toulouse.

The tendency for the verb to take second position may be overridden by considerations of versification or style. Thus the verb phrase may take first position (VCS):

> E **venc** / tot dreit / la peira   25.69
>
>> And the stone came straight

where the subject **peira** must be at the caesura so that the final **-a** will be a feminine ending in versification and not count as one of the six syllables in the half line. The verb may also take third position (CSV):

> e lai / el / **definet**.   5.15
>> And there he died.

where the position creates a stylistic effect of finality.

When two or more complements occur together with a subject phrase, the verb normally retains second position, as here (C_1VSC_2):

> De sol lo dig / n'**ai** / eu / lo cor jausen.   23.32
>> From your mere word I have a rejoicing heart.

But it may move elsewhere (SC_1VC_2):

> E·l coms / devant les autres /   **venc** / abrivatz primers 25.35
>> And the count came swiftly, first before the others.

When the sentence includes only two major elements, their order is usually predictable from the normal SVC pattern. Thus when there is no subject phrase—as occurs frequently, since the subject pronoun is not usually expressed—the order is usually VC:

> **Fo** / de paubra generacion   5.2
>> He was of poor birth.

> Que l'**aus** amar a presenssa.   6.21
>> Let her dare to love him openly.

> e **devenc** / trist e ners   25.28
>> And he became sad and somber.

Less frequently we find CV:

> Ren mais / non **am**   16.43
>> Nothing else do I love.

If there is a subject phrase but no complement, the order is either SV:

> Bernarz del Ventador / l'**enten**   16.53
>> Bernart de Ventadorn understands it.

or VS:

> e **tiravan** la / donas,   e tozas e molhers.   25.68
>> And ladies, both girls and wives, were shooting it.

Here **molhers** rhymes, a consideration that may have moved it to final position.

The verb phrase may stand alone, with neither subject phrase nor complement (V):

e·l **di**/ /
e·l **fai**/ / 16.54

    and says it and makes it

If the verb is omitted by ellipsis, the order is either SC:

e s'**enamora** / de lui/ /
et el / de la dompna 5.6

    And she fell in love with him,
    and he [fell in love] with the lady.

or CS:

e bos / celui qui ben l'*enten* 16.51

    And good [is] he who understands it well.

SUBORDINATE CLAUSES

Position in the Sentence

The distinction between independent verbs and dependent, or subordinate, ones is often delicate, since the ubiquitous subordinating conjunction **que** may function with very weak subordinating effect, becoming tantamount to the coordinating conjunction *for* or even to no conjunction at all (see Glossary).

    A subordinate clause used as one of the major sentence elements (subject, verb, complement) is placed as that element would be if it were a word or a phrase. For example (main verbs are in **boldface**, subordinate verbs are *italicized*, and curly brackets {} enclose subordinate clauses):

eu / **sai** ben / {de cui *mou* l'enganz} SV{C} 16.23

    I know well from whom the deception comes.

{so qu'ieu *ai* escrit} / si me **contet** / lo vescoms {C}VS 5.16

    The viscount told me what I have written.

When a subordinate clause modifies a major sentence element, it will tend to follow that element (especially relative clauses and result clauses) but may also precede it.

Relative clauses follow the noun modified:

E **fetz** / aquestas chansos / {que vos *auzirez*} 5.17

    And he made these songs that you will hear.

Result clauses usually follow the main verb:

so **fai** / tan len /
{c'uns sols dias me *dura* cen}. 16.48–49

    She does it so slowly
    that just one day lasts a hundred to me.

Adverbial clauses either follow or precede the element modified:

com el / **estet** / {tro que·l coms *mori*} 5.14

He stayed with him until the count died.

{E quant lo vescons s'en *aperceup*,} / si **s'estranjet** de lui 5.8

And when the viscount became aware of it, he became aloof from him.

Conditions either precede or follow the main clause:

{S'eu / en *volgues* dire / lo ver,} /
eu / **sai** ben . . . 16.22–23

If I wanted to tell the truth,
I know well . . .

nuilla res / no·i **pot** / pro tener /
{se·l voluntaz non *es* egaus} 16.31–32

Nothing can do any good
unless the desire is mutual.

Internal Order

Subordinate clauses are connected to the rest of the sentence by either a subordinating conjunction or a relative pronoun. Within subordinate clauses introduced by a conjunction, the order of elements shows the same variety as in main clauses. The most frequent order is SVC:

si qu'el / *fetz* / sas chansos e sos vers d'ella 5.6

so that he made his songs about her

s'ie / ·us *mostrava* / cor felon ni enic. 23.12

if I showed you a cruel and hostile heart

que pes e punhs e braces /   hi *volan* / a cartiers 25.12

that feet and fists and arms flew in pieces

But the order CVS also occurs frequently, often under the influence of factors such as rhyme:

si dinz dal cor / no *mou* / lo chantz 16.2

unless the song comes from the heart

que dedins la carn nuda /   l'*es* remazutz / l'acers 25.58

so that the steel remained in his naked flesh

More unusual orders also turn up—for example, VCS:

don / *fo* / grans / lo dampnatges 25.108

in whom our loss was great

The position of **dampnatges** at the caesura makes it possible for the final unstressed syllable not to count as one of the six syllables of the half line. An example of SCV:

> car tu / la mort del comte   ni·l dampnatge / *sofers*   25.80
>> since you have allowed the death of the count and this loss

Here the final position of the verb may have been influenced by rhyme.

When no complement is present, the order may be SV:

> anz que·l vescons . . . / s'em *apercebes*.   5.7
>> before the viscount became aware of it

> E cant le cavals / *vira*   25.55
>> And when the horse turned

or VS:

> si ben *dison* / tuig   23.18
>> even though everyone says

> si qu'en *trembla* / la vila   25.42
>> so that the town trembled

When no subject is present, the order may be VC:

> car *n'ai* / bon cor   16.14
>> for I have a good heart from it

> que *sembla* / vens o ploja   25.51
>> that it seemed like wind or rain

or CV:

> c'ab sos bels oillz esperitaus /
> m'*esgarda*   16.47–48
>> when she looks at me with her pretty, spirited eyes

> E mas los teus mezeiches /   *deglazïas* e *fers*   25.84
>> And since you cut to pieces and strike your very own men

The conjunction may introduce only a verb phrase:

> si non *pren*   16.21
>> unless it takes [profit]

When the subordinate clause is introduced by a relative pronoun, the pronoun both introduces the clause and plays a role in its internal syntax. The pronoun may serve within the clause as the subject, as an object, or as an element of a modifying phrase. Therefore, the subject, object, or modifying phrase will be in introductory position.

If the relative pronoun is the subject, the order of the remaining elements may be VC (noting the pronoun subject as "s," the pronoun complement as "c"):

> qu' / *esquaudava* / lo forn   sVC 5.2
>> who would heat the furnace

or CV:

> que / re / non *ama*   sCV 16.21
>> that loves nothing

If the relative pronoun is the object, the remaining elements may take the order SV:

> qu' / en Bernartz / *amet*.   cSV 5.16
>> whom Sir Bernart loved

> q' / eu / plus *dezir*   cSV 16.38
>> whom I most desire

or VS:

> que / *fe* / us carpenters   cVS 25.66
>> that a carpenter made

(**Carpenters** is at the rhyme.) If the relative pronoun is in a modifying phrase, the order may be SVC:

> en cui / lo reis / *seria* / saus.   cSVC 16.40
>> with whom the king would be blessed

or VS:

> de cui *mou* l'enganz   cVS 16.23
>> from whom the deception comes

The pronoun may introduce only a verb phrase:

> que m'*alegr'* / /
> e·m *reve*   sV 23.35
>> that delights me
>> and heals me

WISHES AND COMMANDS

In wishes with expressed subjects, the order may be SVC:

> Ja Deus / no·m **don** / aqel poder . . .   16.8
>> May God never give me such power . . .

or CVS:

> Mensongers / en **fos** / eu   16.26
>> [I wish] I were a liar.

In commands, the subject is normally not expressed, and the order is VC:

> e **sapchaz** ben / {que mais jois no·m soste}   23.34
>> So know well that joy no longer sustains me.

> **Dem** lor / als taverners!   25.1
>> Let's give [it] to these drunkards!

But the occasional exception occurs (CV):

> del patz **pessatz**   19.54
>> Think about this peace.

QUESTIONS

In questions, the verb takes first position among the major elements. We find the order verb, complement, subject:

> **Poiriam** far / acordansa /
> amdos . . . ?   28.61–62
>> Could we reach an agreement
>> together [both of us] . . . ?

or verb, complement:

> **sabetz** / cals?   12.32
>> Do you know what?

> **Cujatz** / {que ieu non conosca
> d'amors s'es orba o losca}?   14.55–56
>> Do you think that I don't know
>> if love is blind or one-eyed?

or verb, subject:

> **falh** vos / connoyssensa?   28.23
>> Is your memory failing?

The verb in a question is frequently introduced by an interrogative. Thus we find the order interrogative, verb, complement:

> cora / ·us **tenrai** / e mon poder?   7.18
>> When shall I hold you in my power?

> ab qui / **etz** / parieira
> en l'efant?   28.55–56
>> With whom are you a partner in this child?

que / m'en **lauzatz**?   19.22

What do you advise me?

NOUNS OF ADDRESS

Frequently in questions, and occasionally in commands or other types of sentence, a noun of address precedes all the major elements of the sentence (subject, verb, complement) and, in questions, the interrogative.

In questions, we find the order address, interrogative, verb, complement:

Amics Bernarz del Ventadorn, /
com / vos **podez** / del chan soffrir . . . ?   17.1–2

Friend Bernart de Ventadorn,
how can you keep yourself from song?

Toza, / quo / ·us **giec** / en ribeira?   28.59

Girl, why does he leave you on a riverbank?

The order address, verb, subject:

Toza, / **falh** vos / connoyssensa?   28.23

Girl, is your memory failing?

In a command, we find the order address, complement$_1$, verb, complement$_2$:

Jhesu Crist dreiturers, /
huei / me **datz** / mort en terra   25.29–30

Righteous Jesus Christ,
grant me death today on earth.

In a command with ellipsis of the verb, we find the order address, complement:

Cavaler, / a las armas!   25.2

Knights, to arms!

The noun of address may also take other positions:

Poiriam far / acordansa /
amdos, / toza plazenteira?   28.61–62

Could we reach an agreement
together [both of us], charming girl?

An element of the sentence may be moved to the beginning of the clause or sentence by prolepsis (Greek, 'anticipation'). Prolepsis commonly involves nouns or noun phrases that are moved forward and marked with the preposition **de** 'about, concerning, in regard to.' Normally prolepsis displaces other sentence elements and leaves the verb in the expected position.

Prolepsis usually occurs in a subordinate clause. We find prolepsis of the subject followed by the conjunction, then the verb phrase (the proleptic phrase is <u>underlined</u>, and its expected position indicated with ˎ):

> Mas yeu que tem {<u>de l'ira</u> / que / ˎ·m cofonda}   19.21
>> But as for me, who fear that sadness will overwhelm me . . .

Prolepsis of the subject may be followed by the conjunction, verb, complement:

> qu'eu sai {<u>de paraulas</u>, com ˎ van
> ab un breu sermon}   8.27–28
>> I know about words, how they go
>> with a short insinuation

or:

>> I know how words go . . .

Again, prolepsis of the subject, followed by the conjunction, verb, complement:

> si·eus ditz {<u>d'aut pueg</u> que ˎ sia landa}   19.13
>> If she tells you that a high hill is a plain . . .

Prolepsis of the subject may be followed by the conjunction, pronoun holding the place of the subject, complement:

> tro qu'eu sacha ben {<u>de la fi</u>,
> s'el' ˎ es aissi com eu deman}.   8.11–12
>> until I know for sure about our pact,
>> if it is as I ask

or:

>> until I know for sure
>> if our pact is as I ask

When the subject comes first in a main clause (SVC), as is most common, prolepsis cannot affect it. But elements modifying the subject may be anticipated, as here (prolepsis, verb, subject), displacing the subject itself to third position:

> <u>Dels brans e de las lansas   e dels cairels grossiers</u>
> recomensa / la guerra ˎ   25.3–4
>> The battle of swords and of lances and heavy bolts
>> begins again.

Prolepsis, verb, complement (here a predicate adjective), subject:

> De sagetas menudas   e de cairels dobliers
> e de peiras redondas   e de grans colps marvers
> d'entrambas las partidas   es / aitals / lo flamers ‿   25.48–50

> Of slender arrows and thick quarrels
> and round stones and great, rapid blows
> on both sides there was such a blaze

Prolepsis may also occur without the conspicuous marker **de**. The next example shows prolepsis, conjunction, verb:

> Marcebrus . . . sap {amors com ‿ degruna}.   14.61–63

> Marcabru . . . knows how love falls from the husk.

In the following passage, the subject **ieu** has an appositive, **n'Ucs de Saint Circ**. Prolepsis has moved the appositive into initial position and tagged it with a repetition of the subject pronoun:

> Et {ieu, n'Ucs de Saint Circ, / de lui so qu' / ieu ‿ / ai escrit ‿}
>   5.16

> And what I, Sir Uc de Saint Circ, have written about him

(The complement **de lui** has been anticipated twice: the first switch is from **ai escrit de lui** to **de lui ai escrit**; then it is linked to the subject and moved again.)

The same tagging with a subject pronoun introduces a proleptic predicate nominative:

> Nos jove omne   quandius que nos / estam ‿   11.1

> As long as we are young men . . .

In a question, prolepsis has moved the subject ahead of the interrogative:

> ieu / que / farai? ‿   4.4

> What shall I do?

SUMMARY OF WORD ORDER

Assuming three basic positions, as in the order SVC, we may say that the verb usually comes second. The alternative CVS occurs less frequently, as do orders in which the verb is first (normal for questions) or third (unusual when both subject and complement are also present).

A prefatory element (a subordinating conjunction or a relative pronoun) introduces subordinate clauses; similarly, an interrogative may introduce a question. A noun of address may occur in a position before such a prefatory element.

Thus a model of all the positions, in the usual order, would look like this:

a	b	1	2	3
Noun of address	Preface	Subject	Verb	Complement

When fewer major sentence elements are present, they usually occur in the order implied by SVC but may also occur in the order implied by CVS.

The order SVC and its reduced forms (SV, VC, SC) seem to be normal—that is, stylistically unmarked. The order CVS and its reduced forms (CV, VS, CS) often seem to reflect stylistic or formal constraints.[1]

READING 24

Peire Cardenal,
Per fols teing Poilhes e Lombartz

Peire Cardenal, the longest-lived troubadour, *composed poetry from around 1205 to 1272. One of the most prolific, he left about sixty-five moral and political* **sirventes**, *a crusade song, a song to the Virgin, and a fable. He excoriated the unworthy clergy of the Midi during the period of the Albigensian Crusade, although he never referred explicitly to the crusade itself and professed an orthodox Catholic faith.*

In this **sirventes**, *written in 1212, Peire Cardenal counsels Frederick Hohenstaufen, who was a candidate for the throne of the Roman Empire, against excessive violence in war. Peire imitates the form of one of Bertran de Born's poems on war (ch. 22), the better to refute Bertran's political message.*

1
Per fols teing Poilhes e Lombartz
e Longobartz ez Alamanz
si volon Frances ni Picartz
a seignors ni a drogomanz,
   qe murtrir e tort
   tenon a deport,
   ez eu non lau rei
   qi non garda lei.

2
Ez aura·ill ops bos estendartz
e qe fera meillz qe Rotlanz

---

[1] Renzi (267–75) has argued that in medieval Romance languages the initial position is generally accorded to whatever element occupies the focal point of the sentence, either the subject or a complement. Although this view has the attraction of freeing our reading from an assumption that may be anachronistic—that the subject normally comes first—OOc texts seem to support precisely that assumption.

e qe sapcha mais qe Renartz *a savoir plus que Renard*
ez aia mais qe Corberanz *et aura plus que Coberans*
e tema menz mort *et craingeit moins l'amour*
qe·l cons de Monfort, *que le comte de Monfort*
si vol q'ab barrei *s'il veut avec violence*
le monz li sopplei. *faire lui soumettre le monde.*

3

E sabez qals sera sa partz *Et savez vous ce que sera sa part*
de las guerras e dels mazanz? *des guerres et de la bruit (tumulte)*
Lo cels e·l paors e·l regartz *la crainte et la peur et le danger*
q'el aura fait e·l dols e·l danz *qu'il aura fait et la douleur et le dommage*
seran sei per sort; *seront les siens par la sort*
d'aitan lo conort, *de cela je le conseille*
q'ab aital charrei *qu'avec un tel charroi (butin)*
venra del tornei. *il viendra du tournoi*

4

Hom, petit val tos senz ni t'artz *Homme, de petite valeur tes sens et*
si perz t'arma per tos enfanz, *si tu perds ton âme pour tes enfants*
per l'autrui charbonada t'arz *si tu te brûle pour la grillade d'un autre*
e l'autrui repaus t'es affanz *et le repos d'un autre devient ton chagrin*
don ves a tal port *de que tu va là une telle destination*
don crei q'us qecs port *dont je crois que chacun porte*
l'engan e·l trafei *la tromperie et l'intrigue*
e·l tort faich q'anc fei. *et la tort qu'il a jamais fait*

5

Anc Charles Martels ni Girartz *Jamais ni Charles Martel ni Girart*
ni Marcilis ni Agolanz *ni Marsili ni Agolant (dans Roland)*
ni·l reis Gormonz ni Insebartz *ni le roi Gormont ni Insebart*
non auciceron d'omes tanz *ne tuent tant d'hommes*
qe n'aian estort *qu'ils ont fait sortir*
lo valen d'un ort, *la valeur d'un jardin*
ni non lor enyei *ni je leur envie*
aver ni arneï. *les possessions ni la parure*

6

Non crei q'a la mort *Je ne crois pas qu'à la mort*
nuls hom plus enport *nul homme n'emporte plus*
aver ni arnei *de possessions ou parure*
mas so qe sai fei. *que il a fait ici.*

Meter:

a	b	a	b	c	c	d	d
8	8	8	8	5	5	5	5

Sirv. 5 u 8, 1–4.
-artz, -ans, -ǫrt, -ei.
Frank 382:90.

P-C 335,40. Major edition: Lavaud, no. 20.

Eight manuscripts: *C* fol. 279; *D*^{b} fol. 232v–233; *I* fol. 166; *K* fol. 151; *M* fol. 208v–209; *P* fol. 65 (tornada only); *R* fol. 69v; *T* fol. 104 (incipit: Je pros dels pros me plazezia). Base *D*^{b}. See the facsimile of ms. *D* (*Canzoniere,* vol. 2).

Divergent attribution: Anonymous *P.*

Stanza order

D^b*CIKRT*	1	2	3	4	5	6
M	1	2	3	5	4	6
P	—	—	—	—	—	6

Rejected readings in the base manuscript: (1) Toscans *D*^{b}*M,* Poilhes *IK,* Polles *CR,* pros me *T.* (4) drogomaz *D*^{b}, droguomanz *T,* drugomanz *M,* drogomans *CIKR.* (5) mur rir *D*^{b}, murtriers *CIKR,* mordrir *M,* moric *T.* (18) dellas *D*^{b}, de las *CIKMRT.* (25) ta artz *D*^{b}, t'artz *CIKMRT.* (26) toz *D*^{b}, tos *CIKMRT.* (32) ·l tort faich *D*^{b}*M,* ·l tortz faitz *R,* ·ls tortz faitz *CIKT.* (34) Marcilius *D*^{b}, Marsilis *CIK,* Marsili *R,* Marsilles *M,* Marseles *T.*

Selected variants: (8) guarde *CIK.* (13) temia *RT.* (15) si *D*^{b}*M,* qui *CIK,* que *R.* (20) fait *D*^{b}, faitz *IK,* fatz *T,* fach *M,* fagz *C,* fag *R.*

Notes

(1) **Poilhes**] Apulians, subjects of Frederick Hohenstaufen, king of Sicily (known as *puer Apuliae* 'the son of Apulia'). In 1212, Frederick became a candidate for the throne of Roman emperor. His cause was supported by Italians of the north (**Lombartz,** v. 1) and south (**Longobartz,** v. 2), by Pope Innocent III, by some Germans (**Alamanz,** v. 2), and by King Philip Augustus of France (**Frances,** v. 3). Peire Cardenal declares that the Apulians, Italians, and Germans are fools if they want the French as their lords. He advises Frederick not to become a pawn of Philip Augustus, nor to imitate the excesses of the French in the Albigensian Crusade. In December, Frederick was elected emperor.

(2) **Frances ni Picartz**] Allusion to the crusading army of Simon de Montfort (see reading 25), which included men from Picardy. The crusaders had perpetrated the massacre at Béziers in 1209 and subsequent episodes of ruthless cruelty, perhaps following a deliberate policy of terrorism.

(7) **rei**] A generality expressing Peire's counsel to Frederick, the indirect object of v. 9 (·ill).

(9) **estendartz**] Synecdoche for 'army.'

(10) **Rotlanz**] The hero slain at Roncevaux.

(11) **Renartz**] The wily fox, protagonist of the *Roman de Renart.*

(12) **Corberanz**] A Persian king, commander in the battle before Antioch, according to the *Chanson d'Antioche.*

(14) **·l cons de Monfort**] "Simon was one of the greatest generals of the Middle Ages. Few other men accomplished as much with as small forces; few other men had his eye for an enemy weakness, his ability to make quick decisions, his courage and his tenacity. But while Simon was a great soldier, he was a mediocre politician" (Strayer 115).

(15) **ab barrei**] "If he wants [to make] the world submit to him by means of his violence."

(20) **fait**] Singular; agrees with the nearest element (**regartz**, sg.) in the compound noun phrase.

(23) **charrei**] Elsewhere in the sense 'wagon train, wagon'; here the booty carried on wagons (Lavaud 108).

(26) **per tos enfanz**] Cf. Bertran de Born, 22.42.

(33) **Charles Martels ni Girartz**] Characters in *Girart de Roussillon*, a chanson de geste composed in an artificial blend of Occitan and French around 1150.

(34) **Marcilius ni Agolanz**] Saracen rulers in the chanson de geste. Marsile bribes Ganelon in the *Song of Roland*. Agolant is defeated and slain by Charlemagne in the *Chanson d'Aspremont*. In the *Vida de Sant Honorat* (c. 1300), Marsile and Agolant are brothers who rule the kingdom of Castile together.

(35) **·l reis Gormonz ni Insebartz**] Isembart, nephew of the king of France, converts to paganism and allies himself with the pagan king Gormond, but they both are slain in battle, in the fragmentary French chanson de geste *Gormond et Isembart*.

(38) **ort**] Cf. Bertran de Born, 22.14.

CHAPTER 25

Indicative Mood

✦   Review the forms of the present, future, preterit, and imperfect tenses (chs. 2–6).

The tenses in the indicative mood state actions without qualifying them with doubt, uncertainty, or subjectivity, as in the subjunctive, or with a condition, as in the conditional. Since the indicative lacks any such qualification, it may be called unmarked, in contrast to the marked moods.

The present, future, preterit, and imperfect may be called simple tenses, since they are expressed in OOc by single words. The compound tenses, by contrast, are expressed by more than one word. Any one of the eight simple tenses may combine with a past participle to form a compound structure. We shall be concerned with the present perfect (**ai cantat**, E. 'I have sung'; cf. Fr. *passé composé*), combining a main verb in the present indicative with a past participle.

PRESENT TENSE

The present expresses an action or event simultaneous with the enunciation of the verb. Such simultaneity may be felt as embracing a time span either short or long. The range of possibilities is illustrated by Peire Vidal:

> Ab l'alen **tir** vas me l'aire   2.1–10
> qu'ieu **sen** venir de Proensa;
> tot quant **es** de lai m'**agensa**,
> si que quan n'**aug** ben retraire
> ieu m'o **escout** en rizen,   5
> e·n **deman** per un mot cen;
> tan m'**es** bel quan n'**aug** ben dire.

Qu'om no **sap** tan dous repaire
cum de Rozer tro c'a Vensa,
si cum **clau** mars e Durensa

10

> With my breath I draw towards myself the breeze
> that I feel coming from Provence;
> whatever is from there pleases me,
> so that when I hear [people] speaking well of it
> I hear it with a smile,
> and in exchange for one word I ask for a hundred;
> I am so happy when I hear [people] speak well of it.

> No one knows so sweet a place
> as from the Rhône to Vence,
> [or] as the sea and the Durance enclose.

In **tir** (v. 1) and **sen** (v. 2), present time is felt as the instant in which one draws a breath or feels a breeze. In contrast, the present embraces all the time of the poet's love in **es** and **agensa** (v. 3). The present verbs in vv. 4–7 describe repeated, habitual actions in that expanded present. The present expands once more in **sap** (v. 8), which refers to the present age, and yet again in **clau** (v. 10), referring to geological time.

In performative verbs, the present tense expresses the exact time of the verbal action:

> A Dieu lo **coman**   21.13

> I commend him to God [by saying the word **coman**].

At the opposite extreme, the present is used in making generalizations:

> res e·l mon tan non **delecha**
> tot fin aman con cel jois **fa**
> que **ven** de lai on son cor **ha**.   30.80–82

> Nothing in the world so delights
> every true lover as does the joy
> that comes from the place where he has his heart.

The present tense refers to past time in expressions with the verb **a**, from **aver** (as in Modern French *il y a deux jours* 'two days ago'):

> tant **a** que·us **am** ses falcia.   28.20

> I have loved you for so long without infidelity.

The present of the verb **soler** 'to be accustomed' also refers to past time:

> tot quan **sol** donar lauzor
> es al pus del tot oblidat   29.22–23

> Everything that used to give praise
> has been forgotten as much as possible.

The present of **anar** used as an auxiliary has a similar function:

> Trobat avem qu'**anam queren!** 9.14
>> We have found what we have been seeking!

The present tense may refer to future time if present time is felt to extend forward:

> tro qu'eu sacha ben de la fi,
> s'el'**es** aissi com eu deman. 8.11–12
>> until I know for sure about our pact,
>> if it is as I ask

This usage is related to the present in *if* clauses with the main verb in the future (cf. ch. 27). Historically, the present tense of **aver** joined the infinitive of another verb to form the future tense (ch. 21) and could still occur separably, as in **dir vos ay** 'I shall tell you' (31.7).

The present tense also functions together with other tenses in past narrative and combines with a past participle to form the present perfect (see below). On the present in hypothetical sentences, see chapter 27.

FUTURE TENSE

The future tense, too, refers to a range of times, from the next lines of the song itself:

> **Diray** vos d'amors com minha 14.19
>> I'll tell you how love destroys.

to the near future:

> Qu'era m'en **irai** en eisil 10.5
>> For now I shall go into exile.

to the rest of a life:

> Ja per dormir non **er** de Coberlanda
> reis dels Engles, ni **conquerra** Yrlanda 20.17–18
>> Never by sleeping will he be king
>> of the English of Cumberland, or conquer Ireland.

to the Last Judgment:

> Un sirventes novel voill comensar
> que **retrarai** al jorn del jutgamen 27.1–2
>> I want to begin an unusual sirventes
>> that I shall perform on the day of judgment.

or to eternity:

> d'aut de sus **aurem** alberc bas. 12.18
>> We shall have a low dwelling instead of a high one on high.

 Monet, tu m'**iras** al mati,
 mo vers **portaras** e·l borssi

> Monet, you will go for me in the morning,
> and carry my song in your pack.

PAST NARRATIVE

Narrative in the past is usually conveyed by the preterit tense, which expresses past events considered as unrelated to the present time. The imperfect tense, used less frequently in OOc than in Modern French, also expresses events unrelated to the present but emphasizes their duration or repetition. The present perfect expresses past events in relation to the present. As often in OOc, however, these distinctions are far from airtight; they permit frequent instances of overlapping functions and meanings.

The present tense often enters past narrative in alternation with the preterit. This usage ranges in meaning between two poles. It may serve as a "vicarious present," equivalent in meaning to the preterit, a means of avoiding unnecessary repetition of a distinctive preterit form; it then carries no difference in meaning from a preterit and is properly translated as though it were a preterit. At the other pole is the "historical present," which depicts a vivid past event as though it were happening before the listener's eye; this form may properly be translated with a present.[1]

These patterns result in two procedures for foregrounding in past narrative: either background events are expressed in the imperfect and the foreground in the preterit, or background events are in the preterit and the foreground in the historical present.

Preterit Tense

The primary role of the preterit in conveying past narrative may be seen in the range of its possible meanings:

> (1) Jaufres Rudels de Blaia si **fo** mout gentils hom, e **fo** princes de Blaia. (2) Et **enamoret** se de la comtessa de Tripoli ses vezer, per lo bon qu'el n'**auzi** dire als pelerins que **venguen** d'Antiocha. (3) E **fez** de leis mains vers ab bons sons, ab paubre motz. (4) E per voluntat de leis vezer, el se **croset** e se **mes** en mar. . . .
>
> 1.1–4

---

[1] On the vicarious present, see Paden, "L'emploi vicaire." "When scattered in among past tenses, [the present] seems merely to take on their connotations" (Smith and Bergin 197). See also Fleischman; Boutière and Schutz xxxix–xliv.

(1) Jaufre Rudel of Blaye was a very noble man, and he was lord of Blaye. (2) He fell in love with the countess of Tripoli sight unseen, because of the good that he had heard tell of her by the pilgrims who were coming back from Antioch. (3) And he made about her many songs with good melodies, [but] with poor words. (4) And out of desire to see her he took the cross and set to sea.

Here the preterit expresses description ("si **fo** mout gentils hom"), a past before the past ("el n'**auzi** dire"), a progressive past ("pelerins que **venguen** d'Antiocha"), and even repeated action ("**fez** de leis mains vers"), as well as more punctual events ("**enamoret** se . . . se **croset** e se **mes** en mar") that form the backbone of the narrative.

Here is another example of the preterit in description, where we would find the imperfect in Modern French:

> Diabol **semblet** de la testa   30.16
>
> He looked like a devil with his head.

And the preterit for repeated action:

> tot jorn nos **bayzem** d'amor fina   31.10
>
> All day we kissed with true love.

The separation of the preterit tense from present time may be seen when Bertran de Born curses the "malastruc an / que nos **mostret** bel senblan" (21.41–42)—the 'ill-starred year that showed us an agreeable prospect' of revolt but that then brought the death of the Young King.

In a sample of the language of the selections in this book (the letters *A*, *E*, and *F* in the Glossary, including **aver**, **eser**, and **faire**), the ratio of preterit tense forms to forms of the imperfect is more than three to one.

Imperfect Tense

Used alone, the imperfect expresses a range of actions in the past:

> Us cavaliers si **jazia**
> ab la re que plus **volia**.
> Soven baizan li **dizia** . . .   4.1–3
>
> A knight was lying
> with the creature he most loved;
> often kissing [her], he was saying to her . . .

Here **jazia** is a past progressive; **volia** describes a continuing emotional relation in the past; **dizia** expresses repeated action, as in the repetition of the refrain. Another example of repeated action:

> ac dins una peireira . . .
> e **tiravan** la donas,   e tozas e molhers.   25.66–68

Inside there was a catapult . . .
and ladies, both girls and wives, were shooting it.

In tandem with the preterit, the imperfect describes the background to the preterit's foreground:

Guillems lo sauteri **tenia**
e **fes** parer los salms i vis   30.86–87

Guilhem was holding the psalter
and made it appear that he was looking at the psalms.

The background–foreground relation can suggest a chronological relation between pluperfect and past:

Lo reis lo **pres**   de felni'a reptar,
qu'el **trametía**   los breus ultra la mar   11.64–65

The king began to accuse him of treachery,
that he had sent the letters across the sea.

The imperfect for background can describe timeless conditions in a past context:

Guillems de Capestaing si **fo** uns cavalliers de l'encontrada de Rossillon, que **confinava** con Cataloingna e con Narbones.   3.1

Guilhem de Cabestanh was a knight from the region of Roussillon, which bordered on Catalonia and the region of Narbonne.

The suggestion of background in the imperfect may override the fact that an action occurred only once in the past:

Ni parton ges lur dapraria
aissi com Saint Martin **fazia**   26.37–38

Nor do they part their garment,
as Saint Martin did.

In the familiar anecdote, Saint Martin of Tours divided his cloak with a beggar just once.

The imperfect marks a contrast with the present:

Ai las, tant **cujava** saber
d'amor, e qant petit en **sai**!   18.9–10

Alas, I thought I knew so much
of love, and how little I know!

The imperfect of **soler** 'to be accustomed' confers on the complementary infinitive either a durative past (i.e., imperfect) meaning, just as the present of **soler** does (see above), or a durative pluperfect meaning (because imperfect **solia** gives background to a preterit foreground):

Amors **soli'**esser drecha   14.25

Love used to be straight.

Cil li falíren   qu'el **soli**'aiudar   11.70

   Those whom he had aided before failed him.

On the imperfect in hypothetical sentences, see chapter 27.

Present Perfect Tense

The present perfect typically shows a palpable link from past to present time:

   eu non li donei m'amor,
   don **ai estat** en gran error
      en lieig e qand sui vestida.   7.6–8

      I did not give him my love,
         which is why I have been in great bewilderment
         in bed and when I am dressed.

The comtessa's distress began in the past (**non . . . donei**) and continues into the present (**sui vestida**)—hence **ai estat**. Another example:

   ma rason e mon gaug **ai perdut**
   e·l meillor rei que anc nasqes de maire   21.3–4

      I have lost my subject and my joy
         and the best king who was ever born of a mother.

Because of the recent death of the Young King, Bertran feels grief as he sings.

But in other occurrences very little distinction in meaning between the preterit and the present perfect can be felt:

   De l'aiga·l **donet** a las mas
   et **an** lur prima **comensada**   30.6–7

      He gave him some water for his hands
         and they began their prime.

The giving of the water and the beginning of the office seem to be analogous past events.

The present perfect usually combines the present of **aver** with a past participle. The past participle may agree in gender and number with a direct object, whether the object precedes the participle, as in "**an** lur prima **comensada**," above, or in

   mi e mos companhers
   ha Dieus **gitatz** en ira   25.62–63

      Me and my companions
         God has visited with wrath.

or follows it, as in "**ai preza** venjansa" 'I have taken vengeance' (28.53). But the participle also may not agree, as in "**Fach ai** longa carantena" 'I have done a long penance' (17.40), or in "scïensa m'**a donat**" 'She has given me knowledge' (2.23–24).

The present of **eser** is used in the present perfect of certain verbs, typically verbs of motion:

soi aprochatz (10.32) 'I have approached.'

cazutz sui (18.53) 'I have fallen.'

suy vengutz (29.16) 'I have come.'

es gandida (28.35) 'You [fem.] have escaped.'

or lack of motion:

es remazut (17.14) 'You [masc. pl.] have remained.'

The past participle agrees with the subject.

Eser is also used with reflexive verbs, with subject agreement:

m'en sui abellida (7.13) 'I [fem.] am fond of him.'

destoutz me soy de la via (13.16) 'I have turned off the road.'

mes m'en sui en tal enans (22.4) 'I got such a head start.'

me sui partitz de lai (15.3) 'I have gone away from there.'

The alternation of **aver** and **eser** in the present perfect corresponds to the distinction between transitive and intransitive in the past participle. When **morir** is intransitive, meaning 'to die,' it takes **eser**:

e lai **es mortz** Wilelmes   25.22

And there Wilelme died.

When **morir** is transitive, meaning 'to kill,' it takes **aver** in the present perfect:

trops homes **a mortz** ses glavi.   14.44

[Love] has slain many men without a sword.

When intransitive, **prendre** means 'to befall' and takes **eser**:

Pos de chantar m'**es pres** talenz   10.1

Since a desire to sing has come over me . . .

As an (infrequently) intransitive verb, **aver** means 'to be' and takes **eser** in the present perfect:

Toza, Belhs Deportz m'enansa
que·us **es** tres vetz **aütz** guida.   28.43–44

Girl, Good Conduct brings me forward,
who has been your guide three times.

Present Tense in Past Narrative

The alternative structures of the vicarious present and the historical present have been presented above (under "Past Narrative"). Though their recognition may be delicate, clear examples of each can be found. The historical present occurs in Guilhem IX:

> Per la coa·l **pres** n'Ermessen
> e **tira**, e·l catz **escoyssen**;
> plaguas me **feyron** mays de cen   9.49–51

> > Lady Ermessen took it by the tail
> > and yanks, and the cat scratches;
> > they gave me more than a hundred wounds.

Tira and **escoyssen** communicate a dramatic high point that is set in relief by the use of an expressive present tense, in contrast to the preceding and following preterits (**pres**, **feyron**). Compare, however, Guilhem's near contemporary Marcabru:

> L'autrier just'una sebissa
> **trobey** pastora mestissa
> de joi e de sen massissa,
> e **fon** filha de vilaina;
> cap'e gonela, pelissa,
> **vest** e camiza treslissa   13.1–6

> > The other day beside a hedge
> > I found a half-breed shepherdess
> > brimful of joy and wit,
> > and she was a daughter of a peasant woman;
> > cape and skirt, fur-lined cloak
> > she wore, and a shirt of canvas.

Vest scarcely expresses a contrast to the preceding preterits (**trobey**, **fon**); rather it should be recognized, and translated, as a vicarious present form representing a preterit meaning.

Earlier yet, the *Boeci* offers examples of both uses. Emperor Theodoric plants false evidence against Boethius:

> **Fez** u breu faire   per grán decepcio,
> e de Boeci   escriure **fez** lo nóm,
> e si·l **tramét**   e Grecia la regio.
> De part Boeci   lor **manda** tal raizó   11.52–55

> > He had a letter made with great deception,
> > and had the name of Boethius written [as signature],
> > and sent it to the region of Greece.
> > On Boethius's behalf he told them this message.

No enhanced dramatic effect appears in **tramét** or **manda**, which should be recognized as vicarious and translated as though they were preterits. But only a few lines later:

> Pero Boeci   anc no **venc** e pesat.
> **Sál** en estánt   e **cuidet** s'en salvar   11.67–68

> > But [treason] had never come into Boethius's mind.
> > He leaps to his feet and tried to defend himself.

Here **sál** possesses dramatic relief, and so requires translation as a historical present.

> E quant **venc** un dia, Raimon del Castel Rossillon **troba**
> paissan Guillem senes gran compaingnia, et **ausis** lo e **trais**
> li lo cor del cors
> 3.7

>> And when one day came, Raimon of Castel Roussillon found
>> Guilhem eating without much company, and killed him and
>> drew his heart out of his body.

Troba, in the vicarious present, does not possess relief, as do the
dramatic preterits that surround it— **venc**, **ausis**, and **trais**. But
dramatic relief does find expression in a historical present elsewhere:

> E si s'**abelli** d'en Bernart e de soas chansos, e s'**enamora** de
> lui et el de la dompna, si qu'el **fetz** sas chansos e sos vers
> d'ella
> 5.6

>> And she was pleased by Sir Bernart and by his songs, and fell
>> in love with him and he with the lady, so that he made his
>> songs about her.

S'enamora, a historical present, expresses the dramatic event that
was prepared for by preterit **s'abelli** and that led to preterit **fetz** as
its consequence.

READING 25

La Chanson de la Croisade albigeoise

*The Cathars were a religious sect, Christian to its members but heretical
in the eyes of the church. They were widespread throughout the Midi but
centered at Albi. The Cathars believed in two forces, one good and the
other evil. Since the evil force controlled the world, the world was inherently evil; hence the Catholic sacrament of marriage, for example, represented for the Cathars an untenable compromise to which they preferred
a life of unrestricted worldly activity followed by voluntary accession to a
kind of sainthood, called "perfection," which was usually undertaken
late in life.*

*Pope Innocent III became concerned by the tolerance shown for the
Cathars by Count Raymond VI of Toulouse. When a papal legate, Pierre
de Castelnau, was murdered near Saint-Gilles in 1208, Innocent summoned a French nobleman, Simon de Montfort, to lead a crusade against
the heretics. Never before had the church called for a crusade against be-
lievers who regarded themselves as Christians.*

*The crusade lasted through a first phase from 1209 to 1229, culmi-
nating in the Treaty of Paris, and was prolonged intermittently until
1249. Although the terms of the treaty did not call explicitly for conces-
sion of the county of Toulouse to the king of France, their ramifications
eventually produced that result. The Albigensian Crusade has come to be
regarded by many scholars and Occitan regionalists as the cause of the
end of courtly civilization as the troubadours knew it. (For reservations
about this view, see ch. 32.)*

The events of the crusade were chronicled in an Occitan narrative poem called La Chanson de la Croisade albigeoise. *The first part, comprising some 3,000 lines, was composed by Guilhem de Tudela, a Spanish cleric who approved of the crusade; the second, longer part (about 7,000 lines) was written by an anonymous poet who sympathized with the cause of Toulouse, though he declared his own orthodox Catholic faith. The anonymous poet achieved effects of vivid immediacy that have persuaded many readers that he must have been an eyewitness to the events he describes.*

The following passage from the second part concerns the protracted siege of Toulouse by the French army, which began in September 1217. In June 1218 the Toulousains made a sortie to attack the "Cat," a large and threatening French siege machine. They made contact with the enemy at once and inflicted heavy losses.

> En Ramons Yzarns crida, "Dem lor als taverners!
> Cavaler, a las armas! Menbre·us lo castiers!"
> Dels brans e de las lansas e dels cairels grossiers
> recomensa la guerra e·l trebalhs e·l chapliers.
> Pero ilh de la vila lor son tant sobrancers
> que dedins en las cledas foro contr'engalers
> e firen lor abaton los cristals e·ls ormers.
> Mas a cels de la fora venc aitals desturbiers
> qu'ilh no podon sufrir los perilhs turmenters,
> e laichen las gueridas; mas desobre·ls destriers   10
> recomensa·l martiris ab aitals glaziers
> que pes e punhs e braces hi volan a cartiers,
> e de sanc ab cervelas es vermelhs lo terriers.
> E per l'aiga·ls combaton sirvent e nautoniers.
> E for'a Montoliu es lo chaples pleniers;   15
> qu'en Bartas esperona tro·l bocal dels porters.
> Ab tant venc vas lo comte cridan us escuders,
> "Senher coms de Montfort, trop paretz tahiners;
> huei prendretz gran dampnatge, car etz tant sentorers!
> Que·ls homes de Tholoza an mortz los cavalers   20
> e las vostras mainadas e·ls milhors soldadiers,
> e lai es mortz Wilelmes e Thomas e Garniers,
> e·n Simonetz del Caire, e·i es nafratz Gauters.
> E·n Peire de Vezis e n'Aymes e·n Rayners
> contraston la baralhas e defendo·ls targiers.   25
> E si gaires nos dura la mortz ni l'encombriers
> ja mais d'aquesta terra no seretz heretiers!"
> E·l coms trembl'e sospira e devenc trist e ners,
> e ditz al sacrifizi, "Jhesu Crist dreiturers,
> huei me datz mort en terra o que sia sobrers!"   30
> E enapres el manda diire als mainaders
> ez als baros de Fransa ez als sieus logadiers
> que tuit vengau essems e·ls arabitz corsers;

ab aitant ne repairan   ben seissanta milhers.
E·l coms devant les autres   venc abrivatz primers
e·n Sicartz de Montaut   e·l sieus gonfanoners   35
e·n Joans de Brezi   e·l Folcautz e·n Riquers,
ez apres, las grans preichas   de totz los bordoners.
E lo critz e las trumpas   e·l corns e·l senharers,
lo glazis de la frondas   e·l chaples dels peiriers
sembla neus o auratges,   troneire o tempiers,   40
si qu'en trembla la vila   e l'aiga e·l graviers.
E a lor de Toloza   venc tals espaventers
que motz en abateron   e·ls fossatz vianders.
Mas en petida d'ora   es faitz lo recobriers,   45
car ilh saihiron fora   entre·ls ortz e·ls vergers
e perprendon la plassa,   sirvens e dardacers.
De sagetas menudas   e de cairels dobliers
e de peiras redondas   e de grans colps marvers
d'entrambas las partidas   es aitals lo flamers   50
que sembla vens o ploja   o perilhs rabiners.
Mas de l'amban senestre   dessarra us arquers
e feric Gui lo comte   sus e·l cap dels destriers
que dedins la cervela   ·s lo cairels meitadiers.
E cant le cavals vira,   us autre balestiers   55
ab arc de torn garnit   lui tirec costalers
e feric si en Gui   e·ls giros senestriers
que dedins la carn nuda   l'es remazutz l'acers,
que del sanc es vermelhs   lo costatz e·l braguers.
E·l coms venc a so fraire,   que lh'era plazentiers,   60
e dechen a la terra   e ditz motz aversers:
"Bels fraire," dit lo coms,   "mi e mos companhers
ha Dieus gitatz en ira   et ampara·ls roters;
que per aquesta plaga·m   farai ospitalers!"
Mentr'en Guis se razona   e deve clamaders,   65
ac dins una peireira   que fe us carpenters;
qu'es de Sent Cerni traita   la peireir'e·l solers,
e tiravan la donas,   e tozas e molhers.
E venc tot dreit la peira   lai on era mestiers
e feric si lo comte   sobre l'elm, qu'es d'acers,   70
que·lhs olhs e las cervelas   e·ls caichals estremiers
e·l front e las maichelas   li partic a cartiers;
e·l coms cazec en terra   mortz e sagnens e niers.
Cela part esperonan   Gaucelis e n'Aimers
ez an cubert lo comte,   coitos e scïenters,   75
ab una capa blaua;   e crec l'espaventers.
Ladoncs auziratz planher   tant baros cavalers,
e planher sotz los elmes   e dire·ls reproers.
En auta votz escridan,   "Dieus! Non est dreiturers
car tu la mort del comte   ni·l dampnatge sofers;   80

ben es fols qui t'ampara   ni es tos domengers,
que·l coms, qu'era benignes   e ben aventurers,
es mortz ab una peira,   cum si fos aversers.
E mas los teus mezeiches   deglazïas e fers,
ja mais en esta terra   nos non aurem mesters!"
Ab tant portan lo comte   al clergues legendiers;   85
e·l cardenals e l'abas   e·l'evesques Forquers
lo receubron ab ira,   ab crotz e essesiers.
E lains en Toloza   intrec us messatgers
que·ls comtec las noelas;   es es tals alegriers
que per tota la vila   corron ves los mostiers   90
ez alumnan los ciris   per totz los candelers;
ez escridan, "La joya!   Car es Deus merceners
car paratges alumpna   es er oimais sobrers.
E·l coms, qu'era malignes   e homicidïers,
es mortz ses penedensa,   car era glazïers."   95
Mas li corn e las trompas   e·l gaug cominalers
e·ls repics e las mautas   e·ls sonetz dels clochiers
e las tabors e·ls tempes   e·ls grailes menuders
fan retendir la vila   e los pazimenters.
Ladoncs se leva·l setis,   per trastotz los semdiers,   100
ques era d'outra l'aiga   e tenia·ls graviers.
Mas empero laichero   los avers e·ls saumers
e los traps e las tendas   e·ls arnes e·ls diners;
e·ls homes de la vila   n'agro motz prezoners.
Mas de lains perdero   tal que·i era mestiers,   105
n'Aimeriguet lo jove,   cortes e plazentiers,
don fo grans lo dampnatges   e·l mals e·l desturbiers
    a totz cels de la vila.

Meter: Lines of twelve syllables with caesura (6 + 6), in rhyming laisses. For eye
    rhymes ending in an artificial -s instead of true rhymes, see the note on de-
    clension below. The rhyme root in this laisse is the suffix -ier, -er, which is
    ambiguous concerning the position of the vowel, open or closed; there are
    scattered rhymes in close ẹ (nẹrs 28, niẹrs 73) and in open ę (molhęrs 68,
    sofęrs 80, fęrs 84). The final line of the laisse is a half line that does not
    rhyme, and is repeated as the first half line of the following laisse.

Note on Declension

The passage includes conspicuous departures from normal case usage. In
    ten percent of the lines an artificial final -s, which may be purely ortho-
    graphic, has been added to maintain the rhyme in -ers:

    sobrancers 5, engalers 6, glazïers 11, nautoniers 14, dreiturers 29,
    milhers 34, dardacers 47, destriers 53, solers 67, acers 70, mesters 85,
    menuders 99

Some of these artificial consonants have spread to other elements of the noun phrase:

aitals glazïers 11, **sirvens e dardacers** 47, **dels destriers** 53

In vv. 98–99, scribal confusion has generalized the final **-s:**

e·ls repics 98 for **e·l repics; e·ls sonetz** 98 for **e·l sonetz; e·ls tempes** 99 for **e·l tempes; e·ls grailes menuders** 99 for **e·l graile menuder**

Less frequently, oblique forms have replaced nominative forms independently of any influence from rhyme, in anticipation of the general disappearance of the nominative:

pes e punhs e braces 12; **·ls homes** 20; **·ls homes** 105

In other cases declensional **-s** has dropped from an article or other introductory element in the noun phrase, leaving the noun itself normally marked:

la baralhas 25, **la frondas** 40, **tant baros cavalers** 77, **al clergues legendiers** 86

Such declension of the heavy element in the noun phrase (a noun or adjective but not an article) has parallels among the charters (Grafström, *Graphie* 78.5c: **el casals, al meus, al endevenidors,** etc.). It appears to have been an intermediate stage in the evolution of the system.

Despite all these exceptions, some of which are striking, the declensional system continues to function normally in some 94 percent of the marked forms in the passage (counting nouns, adjectives, articles, and pronouns).

Major editions: Meyer, *Albigeoise,* vv. 8383–8491; Martin-Chabot, laisse 205, vv. 57–165; Gougaud 418–25.

Manuscript: Paris, Bibliothèque Nationale fonds français 25425 (anc. La Vallière 91), fols. 104v–106v. Brunel, *Bibliographie,* no. 200.

Rejected readings in the manuscript: (6) contra engalers. (8) Mas aicels. (15) fora a. (18) talieners. (28) trembla e. (34) seissanta] .lx. (54) cervela es *(caesura marked in manuscript by a point between the two words; elision across the caesura).* (55) Aysi moric le comte de Montfort *in margin.* (56) garait lintrec de costals, *em. Martin-Chabot.* (67) peira el sorbers, *em. Meyer,* Albigeois; *Martin-Chabot.* (86) potan. (88) e ab ess. (94) car] e ar, *em. Meyer,* Albigeois. (97) tropas.

Notes

(1) **Dem lor**] That is, **Dem [lo] lor** 'Let us give it to them.'

(2) **castïers**] Three syllables (CASTĪGĀRE, -ĀRĬUS). The plan was to unseat the French knights by striking at their unprotected legs.

(5) **sobrancers**] For **sobrancer,** nom. pl., with final **-s** for the eye rhyme. See note on declension.

(11) **glazïers**] Three syllables (GLĂDĬUM, -ĀRĬUS). Cf. **glazïers** 96, **deglazïas** 84.

(16) Introductory **que** seems to have the force of a semicolon. En Bartas brings news of the attack to Montoliu, where a squire relays it to Simon de Montfort.

(18) **tahiners**] Cf. *S-W* 8: 9.

(19) **sentorers**] Because Simon was attending Mass (**sacrifizi** 29).

(20) **·ls homes**] Object case in subject function.

(25) **la baralhas**] For **las baralhas**; declension on the noun; see note on declension.

(27) **heretiers**] 'Inheritor,' used rhetorically as a synonym for 'lord'; Simon could never become the literal heir of the county of Toulouse.

(28) **trist e ners**] Nom. sg.; normal **tristz** may have been reduced by simplification of the final consonant cluster (cf. **bocs** 22.33 note).

(30) Simon's prayer will be answered, but not in the way he wants. Compare the prayer of the parents of Saint Alexis, in the OFr. *Vie de Saint Alexis*, for a son according to God's will; they do have a son, but he abandons them in order to dedicate himself to the service of God.

(33) **vengau**] Unusual form of elision: **ven-ga-on** > **vengau**; cf. **aun** for **an** (**aver** 3rd pl.).

(34) **seissanta milhers**] Epic hyperbole.

(35) **les**] *Sic*. Cf. **le** for **lo** (ch. 11).

(40) **la frondas**] Cf. **la baralhas** 25.

(44) **abateron**] The implicit subject refers to the French.

(47) **sirvens e dardacers**] Predicate nominative; **ilh** 46 is the subject of both **salhiron** and **perprendon**.

(53) **dels destriers**] The **-s** of **destriers** is an eye rhyme that has spread to the **-s** of **dels** (see note on declension above). Clearly a single warhorse. Note that the horse is treated as part of the warrior (an inalienable possession).

(66) **us carpenters**] Like Christ.

(67) Introductory **que** seems to have the force of a semicolon, as in v. 16.

(77) **auziratz**] Epic language. **tant baros cavalers**] For **tans**; declension on heavy elements (noun and adjective).

(83) **aversers**] Cf. **aversers** 61.

(86) **al clergues legendiers**] Declension on heavy elements.

(87) **Forquers**] Folquet de Marselha, a troubadour who became a monk, then bishop of Toulouse and leader of the crusade.

(93) **La**] Intense deictic use, exclamatory 'What!'

(96) The people of Toulouse suppose that Simon interrupted his participation in Mass and so died impenitent.

(101) **per trastotz los semdiers**] The siege extended through all the pathways around the city; now it is lifted through all the pathways.

CHAPTER 26

Subjunctive Mood

✦ Review forms of the present and past subjunctive (chs. 2 and 7).

The present and past subjunctive express a syntactic mood that contrasts with the indicative, the mood of straightforward, factual statement. As the term itself suggests (CL SUBJUNCTĪVUS 'binding together, connecting'), it typically occurs in a subordinate clause, where the subjunctive expresses doubt, uncertainty, or subjectivity. In an independent clause the subjunctive expresses a wish (the "optative subjunctive"), in contrast to the indicative mood, which observes a fact. In the texts included in this book, the ratio of subjunctives in subordinate clauses to those in the main clause is about four to one.

SUBJUNCTIVE IN SUBORDINATE CLAUSES

A subordinate clause in the subjunctive may be introduced by a verb, a relative pronoun, a conjunction, or an interrogative. While the use of the subjunctive in some contexts is regular, in others it is expressive rather than obligatory.

Usually the subject of a subordinate clause in the subjunctive is different from the subject of the independent clause. When the two subjects are identical, the subordinate may take an infinitive:

> may **vuelh pelar** mon prat c'autre·l mi **tonda**   19.28
>
> I prefer to harvest my meadow than that another should clip it.

When the subject of a subordinate is the same as the independent (**vuelh**, 1st sg.), the subordinate usually takes the infinitive (**pelar**); when the subordinate subject differs from the independent, it

257

takes the subjunctive (**tonda**). But the subordinate may take the
subjunctive even if the subjects are the same:

> eu no·m **puesc** sofrir
> qu'eu no·us **fasa** lausar a tota gen 23.6–7
>
>> I cannot keep
>> from making everyone praise you.

Introduced by a Verb

A verb expressing will or desire, such as **voler** 'to want,' **dezirar** 'to
desire,' or **pregar** 'to pray,' may introduce the subjunctive:

> Amors a usatje d'egua
> que tot jorn **vol** c'om la **sega**
> e que **pueg** de legu'en lega. 14.49–51
>
>> Love has the custom of a mare
>> that wants a man to follow it all day
>> and to mount from league to league.

> sel q'ieu plus **desir** que m'**aia** 6.10
>
>> the one I most desire to have me

> Toz mos amics **prec** . . .
> Que·i **vengan** tut e m'**onren** fort 10.37–38
>
>> All my friends I pray . . .
>> to come [where I am], all [of them], and honor me well.

So may a verb expressing a belief, whether it is positive, interrogative, or negative:

> be **cre·m vensa** 28.36
>
>> I really think he will conquer me.

> **Cujatz** que ieu non **conosca**
> d'amors s'es orba o losca? 14.55–56
>
>> Do you think that I don't know
>> if love is blind or one-eyed?

> no **cuid** aprob   altre dols li **demor**. 11.42
>
>> I do not believe that in comparison any other grief remained
>> for him.

However, positive belief unqualified by doubt takes the indicative:

> **cre** q'a malvatz port
> **venra** 22.46–47
>
>> I believe he will come
>> to a bad port.

A verb expressing a command, advice, or other attempt to influence another person, such as **dire** 'to tell, instruct, command,'
lauzar 'to advise,' **prezicar** 'to preach,' takes the subjunctive:

el manda **diire** als mainadiers

. . . .

que tuit **vengau** essems   25.31–33

He sent to tell the troops

. . . .

to come all together.

lauzatz me doncx que tostemps lo·y **sofieyra?**   19.35

Do you advise me then to put up with it always?

van **prezican** . . .

qu'en Dieu servir **metam** cor et aver.   26.47–48

They go about preaching . . .

that we should put our heart and wealth in serving God.

A verb of inherently negative meaning, such as **temer** 'to fear,'
sofrir 'to keep from,' or **laisar** 'to cease,' may introduce the subjunctive:

Mas yeu que **tem** de l'ira que·m **cofonda**   19.21

But as for me, who fear that sadness will overwhelm me . . .

Such a verb may introduce a pleonastic negation in the subordinate (a negative term lacking negative meaning, merely a projec-
tion of the negativity in the verb):

eu no·m puesc **sofrir**

qu'eu **no·us fasa** lausar a tota gen   23.6–7

I cannot keep

from making everyone praise you.

ni·m **lais** . . .

q'ieu **non tracte**   22.27–28

Nor do I stop

scheming.

Impersonal verbs of judgment—such as **caler** 'to concern,' **convenir** 'to be fitting,' **estar** 'to be suitable,' **tanher** 'to be fitting,' and
expressions such as **aver ops** 'to be necessary'—take the subjunctive. This usage may seem paradoxical, since impersonal expression might be thought to efface doubt or uncertainty, but the force
of the speaker's subjective judgment overrides the impersonality of
expression (Jensen, *Syntax* 285):

anz **cove**

c'om las **prec** e lor **clam** merce.   17.30–31

Rather men

should woo [women] and beg their mercy.

When introduced by a verb, the subjunctive usually occurs in a
noun clause introduced by **que** and functioning as direct object.
The **que** may be omitted:

e **vuoil sia** totz temps saubut   7.3

And I want it to be known forever . . .

Instead of the verb alone, the independent clause more generally may express the meaning that introduces the subjunctive in
the subordinate:

a lieis no **ven a plazer**
qu'il m'**am**   18.35–36

It does not please her
to love me.

ni **ai cor** que m'en **estraia**.   6.8

Nor do I have any intention to cease.

Introduced by a Relative Pronoun

A relative pronoun may introduce the subjunctive if its antecedent
is nonexistent:

e jois et amors
non an **que·ls manteingna**
ni **qui** ja·ls **reveingna**.   21.23–25

And joy and love
have no one to maintain them
or to bring them back.

or virtual:

de be **que·n digua** no·i men.   2.19

He does not lie in any good thing that he may say.

eu non lau rei
qi non **guarde** lei.   24.7–8 var.

I do not praise a king
who would not obey the law.[1]

A particular type of indefinite antecedent is the indefinite relative:

qui qu'en **sia** lauzaire   2.18

whoever may praise her

de **cui que veia** jauzion   18.6

of anyone I see rejoicing

que qu'om vos **dia**   4.19

whatever they tell you

---

[1] In **guarde** the **-e** is a sporadic marker of the subjunctive; cf. chapter 2. Mss.
CIK read **guarde**, but mss. *D**bMRT* read **garda**, indicative: 'a king who does not
obey.'

wherever I may be

The subjunctive may occur if the antecedent is modified by a comparative or superlative adjective expressing subjectivity:

Mielhers es . . .
e **genser qu'**e·l mon se **mire**.   2.20–21

> She is better . . .
> and nobler than [any other woman] who may be seen in the
> world.

But the subjunctive does not occur if the comparative or superlative is asserted as fact:

pel meillor rei **que** anc **portet** escut   21.45

> for the best king who ever bore a shield

Subjective effect may also be felt in quasi-superlative adjectives such as **primier** 'first,' **tot** 'all':

Religïons fon li **premieir'**enpresza
de gent **que** trieu ni bruida non **volgues**   26.25–26

> The first religious order was founded
> by people who did not want strife or noise.

mas que entres rizen
tota arma **que** lai **volgues** entrar   27.19–20

> But let every soul enter smiling
> that wants to enter there.

The "consecutive relative" **que**, which resembles both a relative pronoun and a conjunction, takes the subjunctive:[2]

Qu'om no pot lo jorn mal traire
qu'aja de lieys sovinensa   2.15–16

> One cannot suffer on the day
> that one has memory of her.

car nuilla cortz non es ja ben complia
que l'uns en **plor** e que l'autre en **ria**   27.21–22

> For no court is ever quite perfect
> if one man weeps and if the other laughs.

ni ai cor **que** m'en **estraia**.   6.8

> Nor have I any intention to cease.

On the "conditional **qui**," which sometimes introduces the subjunctive, see chapter 27.

---

[2] Smith and Bergin 209; Jensen, *Syntax*, par. 453–55; on ModOc, see Wheeler in Harris and Vincent 274–75.

Introduced by a Conjunction

Certain conjunctions imply doubt, uncertainty, or subjectivity, on the part of the speaker, about the subordinate proposition, and so take the subjunctive.

ab sol que 'provided that':

> ab sol que **venguem** Dieu del tort 12.35
>> provided that we avenge God for the wrong

ans que 'before':

> anz c'ab mi **plaidei** 22.48
>> before he'll talk to me

avan que 'before':

> avan
> qu'el **sia** lai defor vengutz 30.46–47
>> before
>> he had come outside the place

ja 'even though':

> ja **siatz** vos donzela bel'e blonda 19.18
>> even though you are a pretty maiden and blond

per so que 'in order to':

> Non levet sos oilz ni sa cara
> per so que sai ni lai **gardes** 30.54–55
>> He did not raise his eyes or his face
>> to look to either side.

per tal que 'in order to':

> fatz chansons per tal que **fass**'ausir
> vostre bon prez 23.5–6
>> I make songs to make
>> your good name heard.

que 'so that':

> l'autre cove que blanda,
> que lur destreg no **cresca** ni s'**espanda** 19.11–12
>> The other should pardon,
>> lest their torment grow or expand.

que 'if':

> nuilla cortz non es ja ben complia
> que l'uns en **plor** e que l'autre en **ria** 27.21–22
>> No court is ever quite perfect
>> if one man weeps and if the other laughs.

que . . . o que 'either . . . or':

ferai vos una bella partia:
q'en **tornes** lai don moc lo premier dia,
ho que·m **sias** de mos tortz perdonans   27.37–39

> I shall offer you an attractive choice:
> either I return to where I started on the first day,
> or you pardon me for my wrongs.

si non 'unless':

Si non, con els, **mangem** la bona fresza   26.9

> Unless, like them, we eat good shelled beans

si que 'so that':

si qu'el **prenda** lo paire e·ls enfans
e·ls **meta** lay   27.47–48

> so that he will take the father and the children
> and put them there

tan (. . .) **que** 'until,' 'so much . . . that,' 'so many . . . that,'
'so . . . that':

Enquer me lais Dieus viure tan
c'**aia** mas mans soz so mantel!   8.23–24

> God let me live until
> I can get my hands beneath her cloak again!

tant cre que·m destreingna
lo dols que m'**esteingna**   21.10–11

> I believe that grief torments me
> so much that it will kill me.[3]

non aucizeron d'omes tanz
qe n'**aian** estort
lo valen d'un ort   24.36–38

> They did not kill so many men
> that they got from it
> the price of a garden.

Dieus no fes tan bon gramavi
. . .
que fol no **fasa**·l pus savi   14.45–47

> God has not created a teacher so good
> . . .
> that [Love] can't make a fool of the wisest.

---

[3] In logical word order: "cre que lo dols me destreingna tant que m'esteingna."
Destreingna is a subjunctive introduced by the verb of (hyperbolic) belief **cre**.

tro que 'until':

> tro qu'eu **sacha** ben de la fi   8.11
>> until I know for sure about our pact

zero (implicit **que**) A concessive subordinate clause may have no explicit introduction in the main clause (cf. **que** 'if,' **que . . . o que** 'either . . . or'):

> E no·us demandara tregua
> **siatz** dejus o dinnatz.   14.53–54
>> And [love] won't ask you for a truce
>> whether you are fasting or have feasted.

Exceptions to these patterns occur, however, in which the subordinate verb is felt to be objective:

> qui nos soste   tan quan per terr'**annam**
> e qui nos pais   que no **murem** de fam,
> per cui salv esmes   per pur tan que·ll **clamam**.   11.4–6
>> who sustains us as long as we walk on earth
>> and who nourishes us so that we do not die of hunger,
>> by whom we are saved if only we call out to him.

The forms **annam**, **murem**, and **clamam** are all indicative.

Introduced by an Interrogative

Interrogative adverbs and adjectives may be used as conjunctions introducing an indirect question in the subjunctive.

cal 'which', adj.:

> no sap vas cal part **fuia**   14.17
>> He does not know which way to flee.

com 'how', adv.:

> van prezican com **poscam** Deu aver   26.8
>> They go about preaching how we can have God.

on 'where', adv.:

> Qu'om no sap
>
> . . . . . .
>
> ni on tant fins joys s'**esclaire**   2.8–11
>> No one knows
>>
>> . . . . . .
>>
>> or where such pure joy shines.

Past versus Present Subjunctive in Subordinate Clauses

The past subjunctive occurs in the same contexts as the present but contrasts with the present in one of three ways.

1. A main verb in a past or conditional tense may cast the sub-ordinate into the past subjunctive regardless of its reference in time:

> qu'enaissi·m fadet mos pairis
> q'ieu **ames** e non **fos** amatz.   15.48–49
>
>> that my godfather fated me
>> to love but not to be loved.

Jaufre is still cursed, and expects to remain so.

> auvent la gent   fazi'en so sermo,
> **creessen** Deu   qui sostenc passio   11.23–24
>
>> In the hearing of the people he would make his sermon,
>> that they should believe in God who endured Crucifixion.

Boeci intended for them to begin believing and to continue believing.

2. A subordinate verb in the past subjunctive may refer to a time before that of the main verb:

> Non farei ja, qu'eu non vueill **puscaz** dir
> qu'eu anc ves vos **agues** cor de faillir   23.13–14
>
>> I will never do it, for I don't want you to be able to say
>> that I ever had an intention to be false to you.

> Lo coms Jaufres cui es Bersilianda
> **volgra fos** primiers natz   20.33–34
>
>> I wish Count Geoffrey, to whom Brocéliande belongs,
>> had been the first born.

3. The subordinate may be in the past subjunctive because it expresses greater doubt, uncertainty, or subjectivity than the present subjunctive would have expressed:

> E ferai vos una bella partia:
> q'en **tornes** lai don moc lo premier dia,
> ho que·m **sias** de mos tortz perdonans   27.37–39
>
>> So I shall offer you an attractive choice:
>> either I return to where I started on the first day,
>> or you pardon me for my wrongs.

It is more doubtful that Peire Cardenal could return to his mother's womb (past subjunctive **tornes**) than that God should forgive him (present subjunctive **sias**). This type of past subjunctive in a subordinate clause is analogous to the same tense in the main clause (see below) and to the second conditional tense in its relation to the first conditional (see ch. 27).

On the past subjunctive in hypothetical sentences, see chapter 27.

In main clauses the subjunctive expresses a wish:

> Enquer me **lais** Dieus viure tan
> c'aia mas mans soz so mantel!   8.23–24
>
>> God let me live until
>> I can get my hands beneath her cloak again!

A wish can come very close to a command:

> Cavaler, a las armas!   **Menbre**·us lo castïers!   25.2
>
>> Knights, to arms! Remember the plan!

or a curse:

> totz **sia** mauditz lo pairis   15.51
>
>> a curse on the godfather

A wish may express acceptance:

> mas tot **sia** cum a Dieu platz.   15.21
>
>> but let all be as it pleases God.

The independent subjunctive may be introduced by **que**, as though it were in a subordinate clause:

> Que l'**aus** amar a presenssa   6.21
>
>> Let her dare to love him openly.

Constructions with and without introductory **que** may blend together:

> s'anc li fi tort, q'il m'o **perdon**,
> et il **prec** en Jezu del tron   10.22–23
>
>> If ever I wronged him, let him pardon me
>> and pray to Sir Jesus of heaven.

The independent subjunctive may also be introduced by **si**:

> "la vostra parelhayria,
> senher," so dis la vilaina,
> "lay on se tanh si s'**estia**. . . . "   13.24–26
>
>> "As for your companionship,
>> sir," said the peasant girl,
>> "let it stay where it belongs. . . . "

See also chapter 8 on imperatives, which use the subjunctive form for the second person singular of some verbs (**diguas**), the first person plural of **-ar** verbs (**parlem**), the second person plural of non-**ar** verbs (**sapchatz, siatz**), and negative imperatives of all verbs.

The past subjunctive in a main clause expresses a very wishful wish, one unlikely to be fulfilled and therefore all the more intense. It may often be translated with an intercalated 'I wish.'

> Tant es sos pretz verais e fis
> qe lai e·l renc dels Sarrazis
> **fos** ieu per lieis chaitius clamatz. 15.12–14
>
>> Her merit is so true and fine
>> that there in the kingdom of the Saracens
>> [I wish] I were called, for her sake, a captive.

It too may be introduced by **que**:

> E que **jagues** ab vos un ser
> e qe·us **des** un bais amoros! 7.19–20
>
>> [I wish] I could lie with you one evening
>> and give you a loving kiss!

or by **car**:

> Ai, car me **fos** lai pelleris 15.33
>
>> Ah! [I wish] I were a pilgrim there.

A wish may serve as an oath or guarantee:

> Mensongers en **fos** eu e faus! 16.26
>
>> [I wish] I were a liar and false!

READING 26

Peire Cardenal,
Ab votz d'angel, lengu'esperta, non blesza

*In this **sirventes** Peire Cardenal satirizes the Dominican order and the Inquisition. He probably wrote it in 1229 or soon after (Lavaud 163). The form and rhyme sounds of the song are probably modeled on those of a **canso** by Peirol that has been dated before 1205.[4]*

1
Ab votz d'angel, lengu'esperta, non blesza *Avec la voix d'un ange, langue expery*
non balbutier
a moz suptils, plans plus c'obra d'Engles, *plus plat que l'oeuvre anglais*
ben asetatz, ben dig, e ses represza, *bien placés, bien dit, sans repetition*

---

[4] P-C 366,20 ed. Aston, no. 20; on the date, see Lavaud 46, and Aston 13–14, 179–80.

meills escoutatz, ses tossir, que apres,
ab planz, sanglotz, mostron la via
de Jhesu Crist que quecx deuria
tener, com el la volc per nos tener;
van prezican com poscam Deu aver . . .

2
. . . Si non, con els, mangem la bona fresza
e·ll mortairol si batut c'om begues,
ab gras sabrier de galina pagesza
e d'autra part, jove jusvert ab bles,
e vin qui meiller non podia,
don plus leu Franssës s'enebria.
S'ap bel viure ni manjar ni jazer
conquer on Dieu, be·l podon conquerrer . . .   15

3
. . . Aissi com els que bevon la servesa
e manjo·l pan per Dieu de pur regres,
e·l bro del gras bueu lur fai gran feresza
et onchura d'oli non volon ges
ni peis fresc, gras, de pescaria   20
ni broet ni salsa que fria.
Per qu'eu conseil qi·n Dieu ha son esper
c'ap lurs conduitz passe, qui·n pot aver.

4
Religïons fon li premieir'enpresza   25
de gent que trieu ni bruida non volgues,
mas Jacopi apres manjar n'an quesza,
ans desputon del vi, cals meillers es.
Et an de plaitz cort establia,
et es Vaudès qui·ls ne desvia;   30
e los sicretz d'ome volon saber,
per tal que meills si puoscon far temer.

5
Esperitals non es la lur paubreza;
gardan lo lor, prenon so que mieu es.
Per mols gonels testutz de lan'englesa   35
laisson selis, car trop aspres lur es.
Ni parton ges lur daparraria
aissi com Saint Martin fazia;
mai almornas, de c'on sol sostener
la paubra gen, volon totas aver.   40

6

Ab prims vestirs amples, ab capa tesza,
d'un camelin d'estiu, d'envern espes,
ab fortz caussars solatz a la francesza
cant fai grant freg, de fin cor marceilhes,
  ben ferm lïatz per maïstria
  (car mals lïars es grans follia),
van prezican ab lur soutil saber,
qu'en Dieu servir metam cor et aver.

7

S'ieu fos maritz, molt agra gran fereza
c'om desbrgiatz lonc ma moiller segues;
qu'ellas et els an faudas d'un'amplesza,
e fuec ab grais fort leumen s'es enpres.
  De Beguinas re no·us diria;
  tals es turgua que frutefia,
tals miracles fan, so sai hieu per ver;
de sains paires saint podon esser l'er.

Meter:

a	b	a	b	c	c	d	d
10'	10	10'	10	8'	8'	10	10

Sirv. 7 u 8. **-ẹza, -ẹs, -ia, -ẹr.**
Frank 382:65.

P-C 335,1. Major editions: Lavaud, no. 28; Riquer, no. 318.
Four manuscripts: *I* fol. 172v; *K* fol. 157v–158; *T* fol. 92v–93; *f* fol. 17v. Base *I*.
Attributions: Uniform.
Stanza order

IK	1	4	5	3	2	6	7
T	1	4	5	6	3	2	7
f	1	5	6	3	2	7	4

I have ordered the stanzas as Lavaud did, following his argument (160–61) that stanza 1 is the beginning in all mss. and 7 the end in *IKT;* that the unfinished sentence at the end of stanza 1 must be completed with 2, and likewise that 3 must follow 2; and that these observations leave stanzas 4, 5(. . .)6 in that order in *IKT*, with 4 out of place only in *f.* (Lavaud's report on the stanza order in the mss. contains several inaccuracies.)

Rejected readings in the base manuscript: (4) abres *IK*, apres *Tf.* (6) que *T*, qu *f*, cui *IK*. (16) conquerron *IK*, conquer hom *Tf.* (20) onchira *IK*, onchura *f*, unchura *T.* (23) qui·n *Tf*, qi *IK.* (25) fou *IK*, fon *T*, fan *f.* (27) n'an queza *f*, non aquesta *IK*, noz queza *T.* (28) an *IK*, ans *Tf.* (32) car tener *IK*, far temer *Tf.* (34) predon *IK*, prenon *Tf.* (36) sels *IK*, selis *f*, sellis *T.* (37) porton *IK*, parton *Tf.* (41) vestus *IK*, vestirs *Tf;* teszia *IK*, teza *f;* tezas *T.* (43) fort caussar solat *IK*, prim causar solatz *f*, primrs causas solatz *T.* (48) metan *IKf*, metam *T.* (49) marritz *IK*, maritz *f*, martz *T;* agra gran *Tf*, agran *IK;* fareza *IK*, fereza *Tf.* (50)

lont *IK*, lonc *T*, loncs *f.* (51) fauda *IK*, faudas *Tf.* (54) turqua *IK*, turgua *f*, tugas *T*; frutefia *KTf*, frutesza *I*.

Selected variants: (34) mieu *IKT*, mieus *f.* (52) fuec *IK*, fuoc *Tf.*

Notes

(13) **podia**] Ellipsis for **podia eser**.

(14) Cf. the slur against the French as **taverners**, 25.1.

(17) **Aissi com**] Ironic.

(23) The poet advises the faithful to eat at the table of the abstemious, not with hypocritical Dominicans.

(27) **Jacopi**] Name for the Dominican order, from their establishment in Paris in 1218 in the hospice of pilgrims to Saint James of Compostela; cf. the Tour Saint-Jacques. **n'an**] **Ne** negates **aver**.

(29) **de plaitz cort**] The Inquisition.

(30) **Vaudes**] Waldensian, a follower of the heretic Waldo of Lyon (d. 1176).

(37) **dapraria**] Metathesis for **draparia**.

(38) **com saint Martin fazia**] Saint Martin of Tours (fourth century) divided his cloak and shared it with a beggar.

(49) **feresza**] The same word also rhymes at v. 19.

(51) **ellas et els**] Oblique for nominative, as also in **fuec** 52.

(53) A beguine is a member "of certain lay sisterhoods which began in the Low Countries in the 12th century, who devoted themselves to a religious life, but did not bind themselves by strict vows, and might leave their societies for marriage" (*OED*).

CHAPTER 27

Conditional Mood

→ Review the forms of the first and second conditional tenses (chs. 4 and 7).

The first and second conditional tenses express hypothetical actions—that is, actions whose truth is subject to an explicit or implicit condition. The usage of the two conditional tenses may be illustrated, for the sake of clarity, in artificial sentences:

Si sabía, cantaría

> If I knew how, I would sing.

Si saubés, cantéra

> If I had known how, I would have sung.

That is, the conditional tenses are so called because they express actions subject to conditions (**cantaría**, 'I would sing'; **cantéra**, 'I would have sung'). They do not express the condition itself (**si sabía** 'If I knew how,' in the imperfect; **si saubés** 'If I had known,' in the past subjunctive).

CONDITIONAL EXPRESSING HYPOTHESES

A hypothetical sentence includes two parts, a subordinate clause expressing the condition (typically an *if* clause: **Si sabía**) and the independent clause expressing the result (**cantaría**). The condition is most commonly introduced by **si** 'if' but may be introduced by other conditional conjunctions, such as **ab sol que** 'provided that,' or by the "conditional **qui**" meaning 'if someone.' Whatever the means of introducing the condition, the tenses expressing the condition and the result usually fall into one of three patterns:

271

If (present), then (future)

If (imperfect), then (first conditional)

If (past subjunctive), then (second conditional)

These are not, however, the only possible sequences, since the result clause may also take the present, the imperative, or other tenses.

Likely Hypotheses: *If* Clauses in the Present

If clauses in the present most often have the result in the future:

Si Folcos d'Angieus no·l **socor**
e·l reis de cui ieu tenc m'onor,
faran li mal tut li plusor
felon Gascon et Angevi. 10.13–16

> If Foulque of Angers doesn't help him,
> and the king from whom I hold my fief,
> many men will do him harm,
> treacherous Gascons and Angevins.

Such a hypothesis is presented as likely to come true.
The future result may alternate with a future perfect:

Si ben non **es** savis ni pros,
cant ieu serai partiz de vos
vias l'**auran tornat** en jos,
car lo veiran jov'e mesqui. 10.17–20

> If he is not very wise and worthy
> when I shall have left you,
> soon they will have overturned him,
> for they will see [that he is] young and weak.

An *if* clause in the present may also take a result clause in the present (often with future implication):

S'ap bel viure ni manjar ni jazer
conquer on Dieu, be·l **podon** conquerrer 26.15–16

> If by living well and eating and lying around
> a man conquers God, they may well conquer him.

The result clause may take the imperative, which has intrinsic futurity:

Pero si·eus **ditz** d'aut pueg que sia landa,
vos o **crezatz** 19.13–14

> But if she tells you that a high hill is a plain,
> you believe it.

In the following passage a present perfect in the *if* clause takes a subjunctive expressing a wish in the result:

s'ieu **ay falhit** per l'ira c'ay avuda,
no·m **tenga** dan 19.51–52

If I have failed because of the anger I had,
don't let it harm me.

Neutral Hypotheses: *If* Clauses in the Imperfect

If clauses in the imperfect regularly take the first conditional in the result. No exceptions to this rule occur in this book, and very few in the language (Jensen, *Syntax* 276).

> **Poiriam** far acordansa
> amdos, toza plazenteira,
> si n'**eratz** per mi celada? 28.61–63
>
> > Could we reach an agreement
> > together, charming girl,
> > if I concealed your part in it?

Such hypotheses are presented neutrally, as neither likely nor unlikely.

Such regularity may have been reinforced by the frequent rhyme between the two verbs (**Si sabía**, **cantaría**), produced by the identical tense marker **-ía** in the imperfect of non-**ar** verbs and in the first conditional of all verbs:

> Doussa res, s'esser **podia**
> que ja mais alba ni dia
> no fos, grans merces **seria** 4.10–12
>
> > Sweet creature, if it could be
> > that never there were dawn or day,
> > a great mercy it would be.

Although this hypothesis is an objectively unlikely one, the lover entertains it as though it were plausible.

Unlikely Hypotheses: *If* Clauses in the Past Subjunctive

If clauses in the past subjunctive usually take the second conditional in the result clause:

> Amics, s'ie·us **trobes** avinen,
> humil e franc e de bona merce,
> be·us **amera** 23.1–3
>
> > Friend, if I had found you charming,
> > humble, open, and compassionate,
> > I would have loved you indeed.

> q'el s'en **tengra** per ereubut
> **sol q**'a lui **fezes** cosseillier. 7.11–12
>
> > For he would feel ecstatic
> > if only I served as his pillow.

Such a hypothesis is seen as unlikely or impossible.

The hypothesis may express a future possibility, as seen from the past, which went unrealized:

> Reis dels cortes e dels pros emperaire
> **foratz**, seingner, si **acses** mais vescut   21.15–16
>
>> You would have been king of the courtly and emperor of the noble,
>> lord, if you had lived longer.

> qu'eu no·ls **feira** si non **fos** natz enans   27.40
>
>> For I would not have committed them [my sins], if I had not been born first.

An *if* clause in the past subjunctive may also take a first conditional in the result, less remote from possibility:

> ja res no·m **seri**'afanz
> **sol** midonz **vengues** a plazer   16.44–45
>
>> Nothing would be a hardship for me
>> if only I could please my lady.

Or a present, not remote at all:

> S'eu en **volgues** dire lo ver,
> eu **sai** ben de cui mou l'enganz   16.22–23
>
>> If I wanted to tell the truth,
>> I know well from whom the deception comes.

Or an imperative:

> s'anc **fos** druda,
>   del patz **pessatz**   19.53–54
>
>> If ever you have been a sweetheart [i.e., in love],
>>   think about this peace.

Implicit Conditions

A hypothesis may be stated summarily, with only implicit expression of the condition. Such sentences closely resemble use of the conditional tenses, first or second, standing alone (see below), where the condition is not felt at all.

The first conditional, with an implicit condition in the imperfect:

> Toza, ses vos no·m **poiria**
> res dar d'aquest mal guirensa   28.25–26
>
>> Girl, without you nothing could
>> give me a cure of this illness.

The condition is implicit in **ses vos**, since it implies 'unless you (gave me a cure),' perhaps **si vos non me la davatz**.

The second conditional, with an implicit condition in the past subjunctive:

ens Archimbautz, aisi com sol,
venc totz derrers, e per son vol
non **fora** dimergues ni festa. 30.13–15

> Sir Archimbaut, as he usually did,
> came last of all, and according to his wish,
> it would not have been Sunday or a feast day.

The condition is implicit in **per son vol**, perhaps **si son vol agues**.

Complex Structures

Occasional coordinate structures of complex conditions demonstrate the freedom and expressivity of OOc syntax. For example, a dual condition in the imperfect (implying a first conditional result) and the past subjunctive (implying a second conditional result) leads to a result in the future:

> si ja ren no·n **sabi**'aver
> mas chascun jorn m'en **vengues** maus,
> toz temps n'**aurai** bon cor sivaus 16.10–12

> Even if I could never manage to get any of it,
> [bad enough]
> but every day sorrow would come to me,
> [even worse]
> I'll always have a good heart, at least.
> [yet I remain stubbornly hopeful]

In the following sentence, a dual condition in the present (implying a future result) and the imperfect (implying a first conditional) does lead to a first conditional:

> S'ieu **ai** sa mal et en enfern l'**avia**,
> segon ma fe, tortz e pecchatz **seria** 27.41–42

> If I have harm here and had it in Hell,
> by my faith, it would be a wrong and a sin.

Peire Cardenal feels that he does in fact suffer in this life and entertains the hypothesis that he may continue to do so in the next, a neutral hypothesis; if it came true, he would consider his suffering a shame.

Conditional qui

A construction called the "conditional **qui**" involves the use of the relative pronoun with no antecedent. The construction means 'if someone' and may introduce a hypothetical sentence with the usual patterns of tenses.

The following likely hypothesis has the condition in the present tense and the result in the present, with future implications:

Qui per sen de femna **renha**
dretz **es** que mals li·n avenha   14.67–68

> If someone lives according to a woman's wit
> it is right that harm should befall him.

This neutral hypothesis has the condition in the imperfect and
the result in the first conditional:

qui d'aicest cujar no·m **cresia**
eu non **creiria** lui fort be   30.26–27

> If someone did not agree with me about this opinion,
> I would not agree with him very well.

This unlikely hypothesis has the condition in the past subjunctive and the result in the second conditional:

Ni o **feyra** qui m'**aucizes**   9.55

> Nor would I have [revealed that I could speak] even if some-
> one had killed me.

CONDITIONAL STANDING ALONE

First Conditional

When employed independently of larger structures, the first conditional of **voler** or **dever** serves to mitigate ('make mild') an asser-
tion that would have been too strong in the present tense:

Ben **volria** mon cavallier
tener un ser e mos bratz nut   7.9–10

> I would like [not **volh** 'I want'] very much to hold
> my knight one evening naked in my arms.

Lavar de ser e de mati
nos **deuriam** segon razo   12.10–11

> We should [not **devem** 'we must'] wash ourselves
> evening and morning according to reason.

The first conditional also expresses a future seen from the past:

quan me dissez . . .
que calc'ora **pori**'endevenir
que n'**auria** enquera jausimen.   23.29–31

> when you told me . . .
> that at any time it could happen
> that I would again have joy

Second Conditional

The second conditional also mitigates verbs referring to the present, most frequently verbs such as **voler** and **dever**:

Lo coms Jaufres cui es Bersilianda
   volgra fos primiers natz   20.33–34

    I wish [in the present time, now; but not **volh** 'I want'] Count
      Geoffrey, to whom Brocéliande belongs,
      had been the first born.

Be·m **degra** de chantar tener   29.1

    I should indeed [but not **dei** 'I must'] cease to sing.

The difference between the first and second conditionals in such
usage is one of degree: the second conditional represents actions
even more hypothetical, even further removed from indicative
fact, than the first conditional.

The second conditional also expresses "actions that could have
taken place in the past but did not" (Smith and Bergin 212). Such
usage may be considered a remoter version of the future seen from
the past; it can often be translated with an English expression such
as 'would have done,' 'could have done':

Melhor cosselh **dera** na Berenguieira
   que vos no mi donatz.   19.39–40

    Lady Berenguieira would have given better counsel
      than you give me.

Ladoncs **auziratz** planher   tant baros cavalers   25.77

    Then you could have heard so many knight-barons lament.

READING 27

Peire Cardenal, *Un sirventes novel voill comensar*

*Lavaud (225) dates this poem around 1232–33 on the grounds that Peire
Cardenal has children, according to v. 47, whereas in 1229 he was not
married (reading 26, v. 29). Note, however, that reading 26 is dated 1229
at the earliest, but it may have been written later; and that Peire Cardenal
has children in the present poem only according to an emendation of v.
47—an emendation that seems necessary, it is true, to make sense and
syntax of the passage. Lavaud's conclusion is advisedly guarded: "Il a
donc pu se marier vers 1230 et le présent sirventès date, en ce cas, de 1232
au plus tôt."*

1
Un sirventes novel voill comensar
que retrarai al jorn del jutgamen
a sel que·m fes e·m formet de nïen.
S'il mi cuja de ren ochaisonar
e s'il mi vol metr'en la diablia,   5
hieu li dirai, "Seingner, merce, non sia,

que·l mal siegle tormentei totz mos ans;
e gardas mi, si·us platz, dels tormentans."

2
Tota sa cort farai miravillar
cant auziran lo mieu plaideiamen,   10
qu'eu dic qu'el fai vès los sieus faillimen
si los cuja delir ni enfernar;
car qui pert so que gazaingnar poiria
per bon dreg ha de viutat carestia,
que deu esser dous e multiplicans   15
de retener sas armas trespassans.

3
Vostra porta non degratz ja vedar,
que Saint Peire hi pren gran aunimen,
que n'es portiers; mas que entres rizen
tota arma que lai volgues entrar,   20
car nuilla cortz non es ja ben complia
que l'uns en plor e que l'autre en ria;
e si tot es sobeiras reis poissans,
si no·ns obres, er vos en faitz demans.

4
Los diables degratz dezeretar   25
et agras mais d'armas e plus soven,
e·l deseretz plagra a tota gen;
e vos mezeis pogratz vos perdonar.
(Tot per mon grat trastotz los destruiria,
pus tug saben c'absolver s'en poiria.)   30
Bel seingner Dieus, sias dezeritans
dels enemics enveios e pezans!

5
Heu non mi voill de vos dezesperar,
ans ai en vos mon bon esperamen
que me vaillatz a mon trespassemen;   35
per que deves m'arm'e mon cors salvar.
E ferai vos una bella partia:
q'en tornes lai don moc lo premier dia,
ho que·m sias de mos tortz perdonans—
qu'eu no·ls feira si non fos natz enans.   40

6
S'ieu ai sa mal et en enfern l'avia,
segon ma fe, tortz e pecchatz seria;
qu'eu vos puosc ben esser recastenans
que per un ben ai de mal mil aitans.

7   *Je vous prie*

Per merce·us prec, domna Sainta Maria,
c'ap vostre fill nos siatz bona guia *soyez bonne guide* [45]
si qu'el prenda lo paire e·ls enfans *afin qu'il prenne*
e·ls meta lay on estai Sans Johans.
là où est

Meter:

   a   b   b   a   c   c   d   d
   10   10   10   10   10' 10' 10   10
   Sirv. 5 u 8, 2–4.
   -ar, -ẹn, -ia, -ans.
   Frank 577:110 bis (corrected from 382:23; see Frank, Errata, 2.228).

P-C 335,67. Major editions: Lavaud, no. 36; Riquer, no. 319.

Music: For transcription, see pages 576–78; from *R* fol. 69. Editions: Fernández de la Cuesta and Lafont 586–87; van der Werf and Bond 233*.

Six manuscripts: *C* fol. 284v–285; *I* fol. 169; *K* fol. 154–v; *R* fol. 69v–70; *T* fol. 105; *f* fol. 17v–18. Base *I*.

Attributions: Uniform.

Stanza order

   CIKRT   1   2   3   4   5   6   7
   f   1   2   4   3   —   6   7

Lavaud (223–24) adopts the order of stanzas 4–3 in *f* on the grounds, first, that the third person verbs **destruiria** 29 and **poiria** 30 prove that in stanza 4 the speaker talks of God in the third person (which requires the forms **degra** 25, **agra** 26, and **el mezeis pogra** 28; see variants) and, second, that it seems unlikely that he should do so after having addressed God in the second person in stanza 3. It seems far simpler, however, to recognize vv. 29–30 as an aside to the audience, which leaves the address to God in the second person in the rest of stanza 4, as in 3, and makes understandable the stanza order given in all the mss. except *f*.

Rejected readings in the base manuscript: (8) del *IK*, dels *CRT*, los *f*. (10) pladeramen *IK*, plaideyamen *CRTf*. (12) cuja·n *IK*, cuja *CRf*, cujas *T*. (19) rizens *IK*, rizen *CRTf*. (24) obres es vos en *IK*, obretz er vos en *R*, ubres er vos en *f*, huebre er voz en *T*, obre sera li·n *C*. (27) deservitor *IK*, dezeretz *CT*, dezeret *Rf*. (29) lus *IK*, los *CRTf*. (30) pur *IK*, pus *CR*, pos *Tf*. (35–36) *Thus T, inverted in IKCR*. (35) e que·m *IKCR*, qe me *T*. (36) arma e *ICKR*, arma *T*. (40) fiera *IK*, feira *C*, fera *RT*; fotz *IK*, fos *CRT*. (41) et emfern poria *IK*, et en enferm poiria *T*, et en yfern ardia *CR*, ez en ufern l'avia *f*. (47) e que pregatz los paires e·ls enfans *IK*, si qu'el prenda lo paire e·ls enfans *f*, si que prendatz los paires e·ls enfans *C*, e que prendatz los pairos e·ls efanz *R*, = *39 in T*. (48) e metes los *IK*, e·ls meta lay *f*, e·ls metatz lay *C*, e que·ns metatz lai on es *R*, = *40 in T*.

Selected variants: (16) sas *IKC*, las *RTf*. (17) degratz *IKR*, degra *C*, degra·ns *T*, degran *f*. (18) saint Peire *IK*, sayns Peires *C*, san .p. *RTf*. (25) degratz *IKR*, degras *T*, degra *Cf*. (26) agras *IKT*, agratz *R*, agra *Cf*. (28) vos mezeis pogratz vos *IK*, e vos meteus pogras zo *T*, elh mezeus pogra s'o *C*, el mezeis pogra s'en *Rf*. (30) saben *IK*, sabẽ *CT*, sabem *R*.

(7) 'I tormented the wicked world all my years' (as a satirist), 'so protect me, please, from the torturers' (devils in Hell).

(13) Conditional **qui**.

(23) **es**] = **etz** (second person plural).

(24) **obres**] = **obretz**.

(26) **agras**] = **agrátz**. 'And you would get more souls, and [get them] more often.'

(31) **sias**] = **siátz**. Syntax: **eser** + verb: **sias dezeritans** 31, **esser recaste-nans** 43.

(36) **deves**] = **devetz**.

(39) **sias**] = **siátz**.

(40) **feira si non fos**] Unlikely or impossible hypothesis.

(47) **lo paire e·ls enfans**] See headnote.

(48) **Sans Johans**] Cf. 21.14 note.

CHAPTER 28

Case System

→ Review the forms and history of stable and shifting declension (chs. 9, 22, 23).

BACKGROUND

During the nineteenth century, philologists steeped in the classical tradition took it as self-evident that the case system of OOc, like the one in Old French, must have worked accurately without exception, as case systems did in Latin and Greek. Accordingly, editors tended to correct the manuscript whenever it departed from their conception of the case system. More recently, scholars less imbued in classicism, and more alert to the variety and flexibility of natural language, have considered their predecessors' assumption over-confident and have produced editions more respectful of manuscript departures from Latinate declension.

The editorial policy governing the preparation of texts for this book has attempted to steer between two extremes, neither insisting on a perfection of case usage that may never have been known nor ignoring the possibility that the manuscripts failed to transmit the case usage of the poets. This possibility is particularly germane in the case of early poets and late manuscripts, or manuscripts written in Italy (where the vernacular had lost the case system entirely), during a time when Occitan was in the process of evolution in regard to declension.

CASE USAGE

The analysis of word order in chapter 24 provides the point of departure for our discussion of case usage. Clustered around the

281

verb, the subject and the complement take the nominative and the oblique case, respectively. That is, the nominative case applies to the subject of the sentence, either a noun or a phrase. The oblique case applies to direct and indirect objects (either noun or phrase), to objects of prepositions, and to genitive, dative, and adverbial modifying phrases. Some complements, however, are linked to the subject (predicate nominative, predicate adjective), and so take the nominative. The noun of address normally takes the nominative.

In historical terms, the declensional system of Classical Latin, with its five cases, simplified in Vulgar Latin and then OOc to the two cases that survived (see ch. 22). The distinctive endings of the CL genitive, dative, accusative, and ablative cases melded as the result of the loss of the final vowel (see ch. 13), producing a single form undifferentiated for syntactic function:

> CL gen. DĬŬRNĪ, dat. DĬŬRNŌ, acc. DĬŬRNUM, abl. DĬŬRNŌ >
> OOc **jǫrn**

Therefore, all the functions formerly carried out by these cases came to be expressed by the single oblique form. Nominative forms, because of their phonological shape, tended to remain distinct from the oblique:

> CL DĬŬRNUS > OOc **jǫrns**

and so formed the alternative to it. The vocative case (for nouns of address), identical in form to the nominative in most CL types, was assimilated to the nominative in OOc.

Nominative Case

The nominative is used for the subject of the sentence:

> **Us cavaliers** si jazia   4.1
>> A knight was lying . . .

> pres lo **malautia** en la nau   1.4
>> Sickness took him in the ship.

and for a noun in apposition to the subject:

> Marcebrus, **filhs** Marcebruna,
> fon engenratz en tal luna   14.61–62
>> Marcabru, son of Marcabruna,
>> was engendered under such a moon . . .

The subject of an implicit verb is normally in the nominative, whether the subject is in the main clause:

> serca fol sa folatura,
> **cortes** cortez'aventura,
> e·l **vilas** ab la vilayna   13.79–81

A fool seeks his folly,
a courtly man [seeks] a courtly adventure,
and the peasant [seeks an adventure] with the peasant girl.

or in a subordinate clause introduced by **que**:

> chans ni flors d'albespis
> no·m platz plus que l'**iverns gelatz**. 15.6–7
>
> Neither song nor hawthorn flower
> pleases me more than frozen winter [pleases me].

Com may function as a conjunction introducing a nominative subject of an understood verb:

> el, com **hom iratz e gelos**, enqueri lo fait 3.6
>
> He, as a wrathful and jealous man [would have done],
> investigated the situation.

or

> He, like a wrathful and jealous man . . .

Com may also, however, function as a preposition introducing an object in the oblique, even though the oblique object may correspond to a logical subject of an understood verb:

> Si non, con **els**, mangem la bona fresza 26.9
>
> Unless, like them, we eat good shelled beans

or, logically, 'Unless, as they [do], . . . ' In a comparison, **de** 'than' may also introduce an object in the oblique that corresponds to the logical subject of an understood verb:

> punh pus süau de **mosca** 14.59
>
> It [love] stings more softly than a fly.

Logically, 'than a fly stings.'

Linking verbs—such as **eser** 'to be,' **anar** 'to go,' **(de)venir** 'to become,' **se faire** 'to pretend to be' (lit., 'to make oneself'), **remaner** 'to remain,' and **semblar** 'to seem'—permit a predicate nominative or a predicate adjective:

> Jaufres Rudels de Blaia si fo mout **gentils hom** 1.1
>
> Jaufre Rudel of Blaye was a very noble man.

> Vau de talan **embroncs e clis** 15.5
>
> I go bent and bowed with desire.

> E venc **bels hom et adreichs** 5.3
>
> He became a handsome man and clever.

> tal se fay **cavalgayre**
> c'atretal deuria fayre 13.40–41
>
> Such a one [that is, some people] pretends to be a horseman
> who ought to do the same . . .

En Barnartz si remas de sai **tristz e dolentz**   5.14

    Sir Bernart remained over here sad and grieving.

c'aqel jornz me sembla **nadaus**[1]   16.46

    That day seems like Christmas to me.

As do reflexive verbs:

No·y a cosselh mas que·s grata
tro que s'es **vieus** escorjatz.   14.41–42

    There's no solution but to scratch himself
    until he has skinned himself alive.

Verbs or expressions meaning 'to be called' take a nominative complement:

fos ieu per lieis **chaitius** clamatz   15.14

    [I wish] I were called, for her sake, a captive.

"Reis Joves" avias nom agut   21.17

    You had gained the name "Young King."

Nouns of address are normally in the nominative:

Amics Bernarz del Ventadorn,
com vos podez del chan soffrir . . . ?   17.1–2

    Friend Bernart de Ventadorn,
    how can you keep yourself from song . . . ?

Dieus senher, al tieu lavador
l'arma del comte met en paus   12.69–70

    Lord God, in your washing place
    put the soul of the count to rest.

Cavaler, a las armas!   25.2

    Knights, to arms!

But not necessarily, as we see in oblique forms used for nouns of address such as **trachor** 'traitor,' singular, or **barons** 'lords' (Appel, *Provenzalische* 5.248 and 3.295).

Oblique Case

The direct object takes the oblique:

Fes Marcebrus **lo vers e·l so**.   12.2

    Marcabru made the measure and the melody.

---

[1] But **semblar** may also take a direct object:

    Diabol semblet de la testa   30.16

        He looked like a devil with his head.

Los diables degratz dezeretar 27.25

> You ought to disinherit the devils.

So does a noun in apposition to the direct object:

feric Gui **lo comte** 25.53

> He wounded Guy, the count.

And an adjective modifying the direct object:

Ver ditz qui m'apella **lechai**
ni desiron d'amor de loing 15.43–44

> He speaks the truth who calls me covetous
> and desirous of love from afar.

Ben volria mon cavallier
tener un ser e mos bratz **nut** 7.9–10

> I would like very much to hold
> my knight one evening naked in my arms.

This last citation shows that declension could communicate meaning independently of word order, since **nut** modifies **cavallier** and not **mos bratz**, as word order might suggest.

Just as the subject of an infinitive in Latin takes the accusative, so in OOc it takes the oblique:

Qu'ieu vey **lo jorn**
venir apres l'alba 4.8–9

> For I see the day
> coming after the dawn.

auzez esbaudir
lo rosignolet nuoit e jorn 17.3–4

> You hear the nightingale
> rejoicing night and day.

The oblique may continue the function of the Latin genitive, usually with a proper noun immediately following the thing possessed:

De part **Boeci**   lor manda tal raizó 11.55

> On Boethius's behalf he told them this message.

qe·l met'en loc **San Joan**. 21.14

> May He put him in the place of Saint John.

But occasionally with common nouns:

q'el vol la terra **mos enfans** 22.42

> that he wants my children's land

qe·l jutgamen crei
mon seignor, **lo rei**. 22.51–52

For I accept the decision
of my lord, the king.

In the last citation the verb **crei** intervenes between the thing possessed and the possessor.

The oblique may also continue the Latin dative:

> Pero **Boeci**   anc no venc e pesat   11.67
>> But it never came into Boethius's mind.

> **Dieu** lau, fors sui de cadena   17.12
>> Praise to God, I am free from the chain.

The object of a preposition takes the oblique:

> Estat ai en **greu cossirier**
> per **un cavallier** q'ai agut   7.1–2
>> I have been in heavy grief
>> for a knight that I have had.

> Lavar de **ser** e de **mati**
> nos deuriam segon **razo**   12.10–11
>> We should wash ourselves
>> evening and morning according to reason.

Adverbial phrases may be expressed in the oblique without a preposition in OOc, although English translation may require one. Frequent are phrases of time with nouns:

> esta sobre l'arbr'entrenan
> **la nuoit** ab la ploi'ez al gel   8.15–16
>> . . . that remains on the tree
>> at night, in the rain and the frost.

> **L'autrier** trobei la bergeira   28.1
>> The other day I found the shepherdess

And phrases of manner with adjectives:

> Alberguem lo **tot plan e gen**   9.15
>> Let's put him up, simply and nicely.

> E venc **tot dreit** la peira   25.69
>> And the stone came straight.

The oblique is used occasionally for an absolute construction—that is, one not connected syntactically to its context, like the ablative absolute in CL:

> **auvent la gent**   fazi'en so sermo   11.23
>> In the hearing of the people [lit., the people hearing] he would make his sermon.

fe que·m devetz, no·m toquetz d'esta pauza.   31.21

    Faith you owe me, don't touch me at this time.

Or for an exclamation (an infrequent use of the CL accusative):

    Seingner, **merce**, non sia   27.6

      Lord, mercy, let it not be.

Evolution in Case Usage

While case usage followed the five-case system regularly in Classical Latin, by the time of Modern Occitan all distinction in case had disappeared. In reading 32, a song recorded in 1973, only historically oblique forms occur. These include forms that serve as the subject of a verb, both singular:

    M'ajudèsse **lo vent**   e **son bufar** de farga   32.1

      Let the wind help me and its breath from a forge.

and plural

    un òme disliurat   del pes de sas cadenas
    qu'an fargat **los reis fòls**   e **los barons sagnós**
    e **los mong'engorits**   del rebat del brasàs   32.13–15

      a man freed of the weight of his chains
      which the mad kings forged, and the bloody barons,
      and the monks reddened by the glare of the fire

During the focal period of this book, the twelfth through the early fourteenth centuries, case usage in OOc was in the process of evolution. The five CL cases had been reduced to two, but those two showed occasional signs of simplifying to one. Exceptions to two-case usage, which remained predominant, may be categorized into the following six types.

    1. Proper nouns observe normal declension rather erratically. They occasionally show the oblique for a noun of address:

    Monet, tu m'iras al mati   9.67

      Monet, you will go for me in the morning.

A proper noun in the oblique also occurs occasionally as the subject of a sentence:

    Saint Peire hi pren gran aunimen   27.18

      Saint Peter takes great shame by that.

(There is a variant reading **Sayns Peires**.)

    The *Leys d'amors* recognized that proper nouns are "indifferent" to case: "Regularmen li propri nom cant al nominatiu el vocatiu singulars son indifferen, coma: **Guilhems o Guilhem m'a ensenhat**" (Anglade, *Las leys* 3.100).

Rarely the nominative form of a proper noun expresses an oblique function:

> n'ai razon tant novell'e tant granda
> del joven rei q'a fenit sa demanda
> **son frair Richartz**　　　　　　　　　　20.3–5

> I have a subject so unusual and so great,
> about the Young King, who has dropped his claim
> on his brother Richard.

Brunel observes such usage in the charters from the earliest times (*Plus anciennes chartes* 1.xiii; cf. 20.5 note).

2. If one word begins in **s-**, another word preceding it may drop an expected ending **-s**.

> que·l **sol** s'espan　　　　　　　　　　　8.17

> when the sun spreads

> quant cela·m mostra **bel** semblanz　　　16.37

> since she shows me friendly looks

According to the *Leys d'amors*, final **-s** in this context was not pronounced, though it should have been written (Anglade, *Les leys* 3.95); for examples of the same phenomenon in vernacular charters, see Grafström (*Graphie*, par. 78.5b, p. 238).

3. Among nouns of the shifting declension, either etymological form—the nominative or the oblique—may generalize to both cases.

> qe totz lo mons vos avi'elegut
> pel meillor rei que anc portet escut
> e·l plus ardit e·l meillor **torneiaire**.　21.44–46

> The whole world had chosen you
> for the best king who ever bore a shield
> and the bravest one and the best tourney goer.

Since **torneiaire**, etymologically nominative (from **torneiar** + **-ador**, nom. **-aire**), is the object of **pel** and is modified by the oblique **meillor**, it has evidently become an accepted oblique form.

4. Declension occurs sporadically on the heavy element of the noun phrase—that is, the noun—while other elements are undeclined. This appears to have been an intermediate stage in the evolution of the system. In the following examples, the adjective or article preceding a noun should, historically, have had a final **-s**. This is true for masculine nominative singular:

> que·**l gran dezirs** m'auciria　　　　　　4.39

> My great desire would kill me.

feminine nominative singular:

> donc venc Boeci　**ta gran dolors** al cor　11.41

> Then such great grief came to Boethius's heart . . .

masculine oblique plural:

> E fez de leis mains vers ab bons sons, ab **paubre motz**.   1.3
>
> And he made about her many songs with good melodies, [but] with poor words.

and feminine oblique plural:

> contraston **la baralhas**   25.25
>
> They resist the attacks.

Such declension of heavy elements in the noun phrase has parallels among the charters: **el casals, al meus, al endevenidors**, etc. (Grafström, *Graphie*, par. 78.5c, pp. 238–39).

5. Rarely, manuscripts of compositions from the thirteenth century include oblique forms in nominative functions that cannot be shown to be scribal errors unless on the basis of declension alone. Instances such as these may be regarded as evidence of the expansion of the oblique case to take over the nominative function:

> Aissi com els que bevon la servesa
> e manjo·l pan per Dieu de pur regres,
> e·l **bro** del gras bueu lur fai gran feresza   26.17–19
>
> Just like those who drink beer
> and eat bread of pure bran for [love of] God,
> And the broth of the fat ox gives them great repulsion.

Here we have possible confusion over whether to take **bro** as a direct object parallel to **pan** and analogous to **servesa**, or to understand it correctly as the subject of **fai**.

> Poiriam far acordansa
> **amdos**, toza plazenteira   28.61–62
>
> Could we reach an agreement
> together [both of us], charming girl?

6. More frequently, the scribes of troubadour manuscripts generalized oblique forms. Thus in a scribal rubric in ms. *R*:

> Aisi comensa **so** de Marcebru, que fo lo **premier trobador** que fos.   12.0
>
> Here begins a song of Marcabru, who was the first troubadour who ever was.

The case system would have suggested nominative **sos** and **premiers trobaire**. Since it is not modified by a nominative form but by oblique **premier**, we should not say that **trobador** functions here as a nominative (as we say that in **pel . . . meillor torneiaire**, historically nominative **torneiaire** functions as an oblique; see type 4 above); rather, the language has evolved so as to employ (formerly) oblique **so, premier**, and **trobador** in a system without case.

On declension in reading 25, where it is heavily influenced by considerations of rhyme, see the note there.

When we have indication that the scribe introduced oblique forms where the troubadour had used the nominative (or the opposite), the editor is obliged to emend. The policy for emendation followed in this book has been to recognize the validity of departures from historical declension of the types listed above, but in other circumstances to emend. In particular, it has been assumed that common nouns followed the two-case system in twelfth-century poetic texts, as they did, with almost perfect regularity, in legal documents.[2] This policy runs the risk that declension in the charters may have been intrinsically Latinate because of the Latinate quality of legal discourse, hence more consistent with Latin declension than was true in lyric song and other forms of fiction. In the absence of any more satisfactory standard, however, this policy has been adopted here.

Thus when the fourteenth-century scribe of ms. *C*, from southwestern France, omitted final **-s** on nouns and adjectives in twelfth-century compositions, it has been restored:

e·l **focs** [foc *C*] fo·m **bos** [bo *C*]   9.22

> and I liked the fire [lit., 'the fire was good to me'].

Que·l **jorns** [jorn *C*] ve e la **nueytz** [nueyt *C*] vai   4.5

> For the day comes and the night goes.

Ms. *R*, French, early fourteenth century, shows the same tendency to delete final **-s**:

pauc m'o pres si·l **vens** [ven *R*] m'erissa   13.13

> I care little if the wind blows my hair.

Contrariwise, the fourteenth-century Italian scribe of ms. *N* inserted final **-s** where it was incorrect:

per la fueilla **vert** [verz *N*] e·l ramel   8.18

> through the green foliage and the branches

Ms. *I*, Italian, end of the thirteenth century, either adds or deletes final **-s** in the manner of one to whom declension for case makes no sense:

---

[2] "Mis à part les noms de personne, les règles de la déclinaison à deux cas pour chaque nombre sont presque toujours observées [dans la langue des chartes du XIIᵉ siècle]. L'emploi du cas régime pour le cas sujet se remarque seulement de façon, sinon constante, du moins fréquente, indice certain de la perte de la différenciation des deux cas, dans les pièces du Comminges à la fin du XIIe siècle" (Brunel, *Plus anciennes chartes* 1.xiv). Grafström (*Graphie* 241) finds an isolated early example in a charter of 1128.

elm e gonfanon
e **perpon** [perponz *I*] e pan
e jois et amors
non an que·ls manteingna   21.21–24

> helmets and gonfalons,
> doublets and lappets
> and joy and love
> have no one to maintain them.

ab **fortz caussars solatz** a la francesza
    [fort caussar solat *I*]
cant fai grant freg, de fin cor marceilhes,
    ben ferm **lïatz** per maïstria   26.43–45

> with strong shoes soled in the French style
> when it is very cold, of fine Marseille leather,
> quite strongly sewn with skill

In this last passage, the editorial correction of singular **fort caussar solat** in the manuscript is assured not only by the plural agreement of **lïatz** but by the likelihood of reference to shoes in a pair.

NEUTER GENDER

The neuter gender of CL survives into OOc in the form of adjectives
that modify a neuter demonstrative pronoun (**o**, **so**, **aco**; see ch.
10) or a substantivized neuter adjective (**tot**):

prenon **so** que **mieu** es   26.34

> They take what is mine.

quar **tot** quan sol donar lauzor
es al pus del tot **oblidat**   29.22–23

> Everything that used to give praise
> has been forgotten as much as possible.

or that modify a clause or an idea:

vuoil sia totz temps **saubut**
cum eu l'ai amat a sobrier   7.3–4

> I want it to be known forever
> how excessively I have loved him.

La una·m pres sotz so mantelh,
et a mi fon mout **bon e belh**   9.19–20

> The one took me under her cloak
> and [that] was just fine with me.

Although the survival of the neuter is not generally recognized
in nouns, uninflected **cor** 'heart,' from CL neuter cŏʀ, occurs as
subject and is indistinguishable from a neuter nominative:

que·l **cor** del cors reman sai   4.31

> For the heart in my body remains here.

(See also 8.9, 19.7, 19.53.) **Cor** is usually masculine, of course; in 3.8 it is the antecedent of masculine **el**.

NUMBER

A coordinate subject of two singular nouns usually takes singular agreement in the verb:

si cum **clau** mars e Durensa   2.10

> as the sea and the Durance enclose

tant **es** sotils mos geins e m'artz   22.3

> So subtle are my wit and my art.

But occasionally we find a plural verb:

Cela part **esperonan**   Gaucelis e n'Aimers   25.74

> Gaucelin and Sir Aimer spurred in that direction.

READING 28

Guiraut Riquier, *L'autrier trobei la bergeira*

Guiraut Riquier of Narbonne was active from 1254 until 1292. He left more than one hundred compositions in various genres, including a collection of fifteen epistles in which he describes his life as a courtier in Narbonne and at the Castilian court of Alfonso X, el Sabio.

*Guiraut imitated Marcabru (ch. 13) in a series of six **pastorelas** in which the first-person protagonist encounters the same shepherdess over a period of twenty-two years, according to the dates provided in the rubrics (which purport to have been copied from the poet's original manuscript). This selection is the fourth **pastorela**, and is dated 1267.*

Rubric in ms. C:

La quarta pastorella d'en Guiraut Riquier, l'an .mcc.lx.vij.

1
L'autrier trobei la bergeira
que d'autras vetz ai trobada
gardan anhels, e sezia,
e fon de plazen maneira;
pero mout fon cambiada,
quar un effant pauc tenia
en sa fauda que durmia,
e filava cum membrada.
E cugey que·m fos privada
per tres vetz que vist m'avia   10

[Handwritten marginal annotations in French:]
pour
gardant des agneaux
elle était / une manière agréable
mais / était changée
petit enfant
qui dormait sur ses jupes
Et elle filait comme une femme prude
je croyais qu'elle se souviendrait de moi
les trois fois qu'elle m'avait vu

tro vi que no·m conoyssia,
que·m dis, "Lai laissatz l'estrada?"

2
"Toza," fi·m yeu, "tant m'agrada
la vostra plazen paria
qu'er m'es ops vostra valensa." [15]
Elha·m dis, "Senher, ta fada
no suy quo·us pessatz que sia,
quar en als ai m'entendensa."
"Toza, faitz hi gran falhensa,
tant a que·us am ses falcia." [20]
"Senher, tro en aquest dia
no·us vi, segon ma parvensa."
"Toza, falh vos connoyssensa?"
"Senher, non, qi m'entendia."

3
"Toza, ses vos no·m poiria [25]
res dar d'aquest mal guirensa,
tant a que m'etz abellida."
"Senher, aital me dizia
en Guirautz Riqiers ab tensa,
mas anc no·n fuy escarnida." [30]
"Toza, ·n Guirautz no·us oblida;
ni·us pren de mi sovinensa?"
"Senher, mai que vos m'agensa
elh e sa vista grazida!"
"Toza, ben trop l'es gandida." [35]
"Senher, si ven, be cre·m vensa."

4
"Toza, mos gaugz se comensa,
quar selh per qui etz auzida
chantan suy hieu, ses duptansa."
"Senher, non etz, ni crezensa [40]
no n'auria e ma vida,
ni neys no n'avetz semblansa."
"Toza, Belhs Deportz m'enansa
que·us es tres vetz aütz guida."
"Senher, res non es la crida; [45]
trop vos cujatz dar d'onransa."
"Toz,' avetz de mi membransa?"
"Senher, oc, mais non complida."

5
"Toza, ye·us ai enbrugida
e tenc m'o a gran pezansa; [50]
no·us pessetz pus vos enqueira."

"Senher, be·m tenc per fromida
qu'eras ai preza venjansa
de l'autra vista derreira."
"Toza, ab qui etz parieira
en l'efant? Es d'alegransa?"
"Senher, ab selh qu'esperansa
n'ai de mais, que·m pres en gleira."
"Toza, quo·us giec en ribeira?"
"Senher, quar es ma uzansa."

6

"Poiriam far acordansa
amdos, toza plazenteira,
si n'eratz per mi celada?"
"Senher, non d'autr'amistansa
que·ns fem a la vetz primeira,
pus tro aissi·m suy gardada."
"Toza, be·us ai assajada,
e truep vos de sen enteira."
"Senher, s'ieu ne fos leugeira,
mal m'agratz vos assenada."
"Toza, vau far ma jornada."
"Senher, mete·us en carreira!"

Meter:

```
a    b    c    a    b    c    c    b    b    c    c    b
7'   7'   7'   7'   7'   7'   7'   7'   7'   7'   7'   7'
```

Past. 6 s 12.

Coblas capcaudadas, that is, stanzas in which the final rhyme of one
becomes the initial rhyme of the next. This feature is part of a larger
pattern: five rhyme sounds provide all the rhymes in the song, and
succeed one another in the same order in each position (*a, b,* or *c*).

a = **-eira**, **-ada**, **-ia**, **-ẹnsa**, **-ida**, **-ansa**.
b = **-ada**, **-ia**, **-ẹnsa**, **-ida**, **-ansa**, **-eira**.
c = **-ia**, **-ẹnsa**, **-ida**, **-ansa**, **-eira**, **-ada**.
Frank 773:1.

P-C 248,50. Major editions: Pfaff, no. 60; Audiau, no. 12; Riquer, no. 350;
Paden, *Medieval Pastourelle,* no. 137.
One manuscript: *C* fol. 309r.
Rejected readings in the manuscript: (15) ops] *Om. C, supplied by Rochegude.*
(55) Toz'ab *C.*

Notes

(14) **plazen paria**] Cf. **parelh paria** 13.19; **plazen paria** 13.19 var. in ms.
C.

(24) **qi m'entendia**] Conditional **qui** (see ch. 27), here tantamount to a
second person.

(34) **grazida**] Semantically equivalent to a present active participle: 'pleasing.'

(43) **Belhs Deportz**] "Good Conduct," the **senhal**, or secret name, used by Guiraut Riquier to designate an unidentified lady in many of his songs.

(51) **enqueira**] OOc **enquerre** from LL ĩnquaerĕre, which represents a recomposition of CL ĩnquīrĕre on the basis of the root quaerĕre. See chapter 11.

(72) **mete·us**] In the plural imperative (regularly **metetz**), before reflexive **vos**, the **-tz** may disappear (Appel, *Provenzalische* xxiii).

CHAPTER 29

Demonstratives

→ Recall that demonstratives include pronouns, certain adjectives, and the definite article.

Review the synchronic morphology of demonstrative suffixes in chapter 10 and the historical morphology of demonstrative prefixes and roots in chapter 23.

PERSONAL PRONOUN el
AND DEFINITE ARTICLE lo

The OOc personal pronoun and definite article derive from the same source, CL ĬLLUM 'that one.' When ĬLLUM was stressed as a normal word, *íllum*, it produced **ęl** 'he.' But ĬLLUM could also be treated as part of the following word in Vulgar Latin; when it was, the first syllable fell and the second syllable produced **lo** 'the.'

The common origin of the personal pronoun and the definite article is reflected in their similar functions in OOc. The definite article points with some particularizing force to its noun and hence can at times be translated as a possessive adjective. The article helps to identify the case and number of the noun it modifies (**lo jorns** nom. sg.; **los jorns** obl. pl.). Analogously, the personal pronoun points to its verb and helps to identify its subject (**el part** 3rd sg.; **ieu part** 1st sg.). However, the weakness of the article is shown by enclisis (**al**, **del**) and proclisis (**l'us**, **l'arma**). Similarly, the personal pronoun is frequently omitted.

Finally, **el** and **lo** overlap in the forms for the personal pronoun in the oblique case. Distinct forms of **el** are used as objects of prepositions (called disjunctive position because not joined to a verb, or tonic position because stressed): **ad el** 'to him' 1.5; **con els** 'like them' 26.9; **d'ella** 'about her' 3.4. But forms of **lo** are used for the personal pronoun as direct objects of verbs (called atonic, or unstressed position):

> pres **lo** malautia
>
> > Sickness took him.

1.4

> los destruiria
>
> > He would destroy them.

27.29

> Estan cum **ella**, lo reis Enrics d'Engletera si **la** tols per moiller e si **la** trais de Normandia e si **la** menet en Angleterra
>
> > While he [Bernart] was with her, King Henry of England took her as his wife, and took her away from Normandy and took her to England.

5.13

> c'om **las** prec
>
> > A man should beg them.

17.31

No such overlap occurs in the nominative, where the personal pronoun shows only forms from **el**. These optional subject pronouns, which occur infrequently, may be regarded as stressed forms; unstressed subject pronouns do not occur, because they are implicit in the morphology of the verb.

PERSONAL PRONOUN li

The indirect object, singular, is usually expressed by **li**, both masculine and feminine:

> eu non **li** donei m'amor
>
> > I did not give him my love.

7.6

> Soven baizan **li** dizia
>
> > Often kissing [her], he was saying to her . . .

4.3

Reduced forms of **li** include proclitic **l'**, **lh'** and enclitic **·l**, **·lh** (spelled **·il**, **·ll**, **·ill**).

The origin of dative **li** is CL ĬLLĪ, dative, by the same unstressed development that produced **lo** from CL ĬLLUM.

PERSONAL PRONOUNS lui, lei, lor

In the oblique singular, masculine **lui** and feminine **lẹi** (variant spellings **leis**, **liei**, **lieis**, **lies**) function as objects of prepositions, as do **el** and **ella**. In some instances there seems to be greater emphasis on **lui**, **lei** than on **el**, **ella**, but no such contrast is consistently palpable:

el fetz sas chansos e sos vers **d'ella**, de l'amor qu'el avia **ad
ella** e de la valor **de leis**. 5.6

> He made his songs about her, about the love that he had for
> her and about her merit.

com el, ms. variants **ab el**, **ab lui** 5.14

> with him

Lui and **lei** also function as objects of verbs, as do **lo** and **la**, either
as direct objects:

eu non creiria **lui** fort be 30.27

> I would not agree with him [perhaps emphatic: 'certainly not
> him!'] very well.

Hieu amie **lies** de bon cor 31.8

> I loved her sincerely.

or as indirect objects:

lui tirec costalers 25.56

> He shot at him from the side.

lei no n'es danz 16.16

> There is no harm [to love] [**amor**, fem.].

OOc **lui** should be pronounced with stress on the **u**, **lúi**, as in
Italian *lui* (except that in OOc the stressed vowel has shifted to [y]).
Its origin, like that of Italian and French *lui* (in which the stress
shifted from OFr. *lúi* to Modern Fr. *luí*), is VL *ɪʟʟúɪ, representing a
reconstruction of CL dative ɪʟʟī on the analogy of dative cúī 'to
whom' (nom. qoī 'who'). Feminine **lẹi** represents VL *ɪʟʟéɪ, from
*ɪʟʟáeɪ, a reconstruction of CL feminine dative ɪʟʟī by analogy with
the dative in -ae of the feminine declension (ᴛᴇʀʀᴀᴇ).

The plural of **lui** and **lei** is **lor**, masculine or feminine:

eu **lor** redra   Roma per traazo 11.57

> He will surrender Rome to them [the Greeks] by treachery.

Aujatz ieu que **lur** respozi 9.7

> Hear what I answered them [two women].

Lor can also serve as the object of a preposition, as do **els**, **ellas**:

De las dompnas mi desesper;
ja mais en **lor** no·m fiarai 18.17–18

> I despair of the ladies;
> never again will I trust them.

Lor is also the possessive adjective and pronoun 'their.'

The source of **lọr** is CL ɪ̆ʟʟōʀᴜᴍ, genitive plural masculine, 'of
them, their.'

Like **lui** and **lei**, **celui** and **celęi** function as objects of prepositions, possibly with greater emphasis than **cel**, **cella**:

> et eu irai m'en a **scellui**
> on tut peccador troban fi   10.27–28
>
>> I shall go away to him
>> in whom all sinners find peace.

They also serve as objects of verbs, either direct:

> ieu d'amar no·m puosc tener
> **celei** don ja pro non aurai   18.11–12
> [**celei** = the adored lady; var. **cellui** masc.]
>
>> I cannot keep from loving
>> her, from whom I shall never get favor.

or indirect:

> a vos canta, **seluy** guinha,
> a vos parla, l'autre cinha   14.20–21
>
>> To you it sings, at him it peeps,
>> to you it speaks, to the other it makes the sign of the cross.

Celui can function as a nominative singular:

> Lo vers es fins e naturaus,
> e bos **celui** qui ben l'enten   16.50–51
>
>> My verse is true and natural,
>> and good [is] he who understands it well.

NEAR PRONOUNS AND
ADJECTIVES est, cest, aicest

Est means 'this':

> Ja mais d'amor non gauzirai
> si no·m gau d'**est**'amor de loing   15.8–9
>
>> Never shall I enjoy love
>> if I do not enjoy this love from afar.

But **est** may be only slightly stronger in meaning than the definite article:

> Quar li mellor de tot **est** mon
> vos van servir   Appel, *Provenzalische* 61.20–21
>
>> For the best in all this world [or 'in all the world']
>> are going to serve you.

Cest may be completed by a relative pronoun:

> **sest** mal c'an fach perdona lor   Appel, *Provenzalische* 104.63
>
>> Forgive them this wrong they have done.

Or by adjectives:

> En **cest** sonet coind' e leri
> fauc motz e capuig e doli[1]

> > In this little song, pretty and gay,
> > I make words and plane and smooth them.

But **cest** may overlap with **est**:

> Iratz e gauzens m'en partrai
> qan veirai **cest**'amor de loing   15.15–16

> > Saddened and rejoicing will I depart
> > when I see this love from afar.

Compare **est'amor de loing** 15.8–9, cited above.

Aquest has strong intensive value:

> (God has made two washing places, one in the Holy Land,
> the other in Spain:)
> e d'**aquest** de say vos conort   12.9

> > And I exhort you about this one here.

FAR PRONOUNS AND ADJECTIVES cel, aicel

Cel serves as antecedent to a relative:

> Mout mi plai car sai que val mais
> **sel** q'ieu plus desir que m'aia   6.9–10

> > I am very pleased, for I know he is worth most,
> > the one that I most desire to have me.

Aquel has strong intensive value:

> Ja Deus no·m don **aqel** poder
> qe d'amor no·m prenda talanz   16.8–9

> > May God never give me such power
> > that desire for love would not strike me.

NEUTER PRONOUNS o, so, aiso, lo

The neuter pronoun in its three degrees of force serves to link elements of the sentence. In its weak form, the root **o**, it is the formal object of a verb, expressing a purely syntactic relation. It usually refers to a clause, less frequently to a phrase.[2] In translation this pronoun may often be omitted as redundant. **O** refers to a preceding clause:

---

[1] Arnaut Daniel, "En cest sonet coind' e leri," in Hill and Bergin, item 68.1–2.

[2] A clause, by definition, includes a verb; a phrase, by definition, does not.

> s'anc li fi tort, q'il m'**o** perdon   10.22
>> If ever I wronged him, let him pardon me (for it).

or to a following clause:

> qu'us non **o** preza   si·s trada son parent   11.8
>> For not a one cares (about it) if he betrays his kinsman.

or to a preceding phrase:

> el li dis süavet, "Hai las!"
> Pero ges non **o** dis tam bas . . .   30.71–72
>> He said to her softly, "Alas!"
>> But he surely did not say it so low
>> that . . .

So tends to express stronger demonstrative force than **o**, but it requires some kind of completion. Usually it cannot be omitted in translation. Frequently **so** is the antecedent to a relative, as in the expression **so que** 'that which, what':

> E quant el auzi **so qu**'ella dis   3.11
>> And when he heard what she said . . .

So is frequently used as the formal object of a verb of speech, referring to a direct quotation:

> **So** dis n'Agnes e n'Ermessen:
> "Trobat avem qu'anam queren!"   9.13–14
>> This [is what] Lady Agnes and Lady Ermessen said:
>> "We have found what we have been looking for!"

Aiso/aco has independent force:

> Guillems vai son libre queren,
> e per **aiso** demora tan
> qu'en Archimbaut ne prend'avan   30.44–46
>> Guilhem went to seek his book,
>> and to do so he delayed until
>> Sir Archimbaut took some.

Aco in the nominative singular:

> **Aqo** non es amors   16.19
>> That [unworthy thing] is not love.

In the oblique singular, with intensifying force:

> mas ieu per **tot aquo**
> no·m mogui ges.   9.53–54
>> But for all of that [or 'for all they could do']
>> I didn't move at all.

One may also recognize a neuter usage of the pronoun **lo**, analogous to **o**, **so**, **aiso**:

Mout ai estat cuendes e gais,
mas nostre seigner no·l vol mais.

I have been very pleasant and joyful,
but our Lord wants it no more [for me to be so].

SUMMARY OF THE PERSONAL PRONOUN

The forms of the personal pronoun outlined here in regard to syntax, in chapter 23 in regard to prefixes and roots, and in chapter 10 in regard to suffixes, may be summarized in table 29.1.

TABLE 29.1. *Personal Pronouns in OOc*

	Masculine		Feminine	
	Sg.	Pl.	Sg.	Pl.
Subject				
Atonic (= person marker)				
	(in verb)	(in verb)	(in verb)	(in verb)
Tonic personal pronoun				
	ęl	**il**	**ęla**	**ęlas**
Emphatic (= introductory pronoun)				
	celúi	—	**celéi**	—
Direct object of verb or object of preposition				
Atonic personal pronoun				
	lo	**los**	**la**	**las**
Tonic personal pronoun				
	ęl	**ęls**	**ęla**	**ęlas**
	lúi	**lǫr**	**léi**	**lǫr**
Emphatic (= introductory pronoun)				
	celúi	—	**celéi**	—
Indirect object of verb				
Atonic personal pronoun				
	li	—	**li**	—
Tonic personal pronoun				
	lúi	**lǫr**	**léi**	**lǫr**
Emphatic (= introductory pronoun)				
	celúi	—	**celéi**	—

Pronouns maintained a wider inventory of forms than did nouns, including three degrees of emphasis and two categories of oblique forms (one for the direct object or object of preposition, another for the indirect object).

Guiraut Riquier, *Be·m degra de chantar tener*

*This song was written in 1292, according to the rubric, where it is identi-
fied as a **vers**.*

    Rubric of ms. C:

    Lo .xxvij. vers d'en Giraut Riquier, l'an .M.CC.LXXXXIJ.

1
Be·m degra de chantar tener,   *Bien j'aurais dû me tenir de chanter*
quar a chan coven alegriers   *car le chant convient à la joi*
e mi destrenh tant cossiriers   *et mon tourment tant m'inquiète*
que·m fa de totas partz doler,   *qu'il me fait souffrir de toutes côtés*
remembran mon greu temps passat,   *en me souvenant de mon passé lourd*
esgardan lo prezent forsat,   *regardant le present restreint*
e cossiran l'avenidor,   *et craignant l'avenir*
que per totz ai razon que plor.   *que pour tout j'ai raison de pleurer*

2
Per que no·m deu aver sabor   *pour cette raison mon chant ne doit*
mos chans, qu'es ses alegretat,   *avoir saveur pour moi, puisqu'il est*
mas Dieus m'a tal saber donat   *tant de sagesse Dieu m'a donne*
qu'en chantan retrac ma folhor,   *qu'en chantant je raconte ma folie*
mo sen, mon gauch, mon desplazer,
e mon dan e mon pro, per ver;   *douleur, suffisance, par vérité*
qu'a penas dic ren ben estiers,   *à peine je dis quelque chose de bien*
mas trop suy vengutz als derriers.   *mais je suis venu trop tard.*

3
Qu'er non es grazitz lunhs mestiers,   *nul metier n'est loué*
menhs en cort que de belh saber   *mieux en court que la belle sagesse*
de trobar; qu'auzir e vezer   *de trouver (des chansons) puisque*
hi vol hom mais captenhs leugiers   *veut l'homme entendre et voir la frivolité*
e critz mesclatz ab dezonor;   *et des cris melangés avec le déshonneur*
quar tot quan sol donar lauzor   *tout ce qui devrait donner louanges*
es al pus del tot oblidat,   *est oublié autant que possible*
que·l mons es quays totz en barat.   *le monde est presque tromperie*

4
Per erguelh e per malvestat   *mechanceté*
de christians ditz, luenh d'amor   *pour ainsi dire, loin*
e dels mans de nostre senhor   *et des commandements*
em del sieu sant loc discipat   *du lieu saint sont chassés*
ab massa d'autres encombriers;   *beaucoup tourments*
don par qu'elh nos es aversiers   *il paraît qu'il est hostile envers nous*
per desadordenat voler   *pour notre volonté des ordonné*
e per outracujat poder.   *et par pouvoir excessif*

5

Lo greu perilh devem temer *nou devrions craindre*
de dobla mort, qu'es prezentiers, *près*
que·ns sentam Sarrazis sobriers *supérieurs* 35
e Dieus que·ns giet a non-chaler; *nous jette en indifférence*
et entre nos qu'em azirat *nous haissons?*
tost serem del tot aterrat, *nous serons tous atterrés*
e no·s cossiran la part lor, *et ne considèrent pas*
segon que·m par, nostre rector. *nos chess, selon ce qui* 40
me parait

6

Selh que crezem en unitat,
poder, savïeza, bontat,
done a sas obras lugor *créatures/lumière*
don sian mundat peccador. *par laquelle sois purifiés*

7

Dona, maires de caritat,   45
acapta nos per pïetat
de ton filh, nostre redemptor,
gracia, perdon, et amor.

Meter:

a	b	b	a	c	c	d	d
8	8	8	8	8	8	8	8

Sirv. 5 s 8, 2–4.
Coblas capcaudadas.
a = **-er**, **-or**, **-iers**, **-at**, **-er**.
b = **-iers**, **-at**, **-er**, **-or**, **-iers**.
c = **-at**, **-er**, **-or**, **-iers**, **-at**.
d = **-or**, **-iers**, **-at**, **-er**, **-or**.
Frank 577:214.

P-C 248,17. Major editions: Pfaff, no. 53; Hamlin, Ricketts, and Hathaway, no. 70.

One manuscript: *C* fol. 307v–306r (folios 307 and 306 are transposed).

Rejected readings in the manuscript: (39) cossiram *C, em. Hamlin, Ricketts, and Hathaway 238.* (43) as / sas *(line break).*

Notes

(15) **estiers**] Otherwise than with God's help (v. 11). Without God's help he says almost nothing well, neither his folly nor his wit, etc., since he has come too late.

(16) **trop . . . als derriers**] 'Too late'; lit., 'too much among the last'; apparently **a** means 'among' here, by extension from the frequent meaning 'to (a person as destination).' Hamlin, Ricketts, and Hathaway (237) translate the passage as 'Pendant les dernières années (de notre époque).'

(33–36) **Temer . . . que sentam . . . que giet**] Subjunctive after **temęr**.

(34) **dobla mort**] Death of the body by the Saracen peril (v. 35) and death of the soul abandoned by God (v. 36).

(42) The Trinity, to which the faithful attribute unity as well as power, wisdom, and goodness.

PART 5

Lexicon; Research Tools

CHAPTER 30

Sources of the Lexicon

The lexicon of OOc derives primarily from Latin in its various forms: Classical Latin, the formal language of the republic and the empire, either written or spoken; Vulgar Latin, the language in informal usage by either cultivated or illiterate speakers; Late Latin, from the second to the sixth centuries A.D.; Church Latin, specific to ecclesiastical discourse; and Medieval Latin, from the sixth century onward (see ch. 11).

But OOc also shows significant influence from the substratum of languages spoken in the Occitan area before the Roman conquest of Gaul. The conquest began when Rome sent aid to the Greek colony of Marseille in 125 B.C., continued with the foundation of Narbonne in 118 B.C., and culminated in Caesar's Gallic Wars, in 58–51 B.C. OOc was also influenced by a superstratum of Germanic languages entering the area with the Germanic migrations that marked the end of the Roman Empire, in the fifth and sixth centuries. Other sources, such as Hebrew, Greek, Arabic, Armenian, Persian, Old French, and onomatopoetic word formation, contributed fewer items to the vocabulary. Occitan also generated a significant number of words from within itself.

SUBSTRATUM

The most archaic sources of OOc vocabulary can be traced to little-known languages that were spoken in the region as early as the second millennium B.C. Aquitanian was one such language, which apparently resisted Celtic in the southwest of modern France, from the Garonne to the Pyrenees; another, called Ligurian, may have survived for a time in the southeast and the Alps. Place-names that are neither Latin nor Celtic may be attributed to these or other early languages. It is relatively easy to ascertain that a name is not

Latin, since we have abundant sources of information about that language; with greater effort we may eliminate the possibility that a root is Celtic, if it occurs in names from areas that the Celts never entered as well as others that they did.

Many rivers in France retain Pre-Celtic names, including the **Durensa** 'Durance,' in Provence, from the river name **dora*; the **Rozer** 'Rhône,' from a root **rod* 'to flow' or 'wetness,' combined with a Celtic suffix; and the **Viana** 'Vienne,' from the river name **vig*. The town of **Basatz** (modern Bazas) preserves the name of an Aquitanian people, the Vasates, which is compounded of Aquitanian *basa* 'town' and a Celtic suffix *-ates* 'inhabitants of a town.' Most Pre-Celtic roots are of uncertain meaning, as in **Bordels** 'Bordeaux,' **Narbona** 'Narbonne,' and **Toloza** 'Toulouse.'

The Phoenicians, a seafaring Semitic people, built the cities of Tyre and Sidon in present-day Lebanon. They explored the coastline of the western Mediterranean before the Greeks. The Phoenicians may have left traces of their language in a handful of place-names, including **Castel Rosilhon**, from Semitic *rus, ros* 'head, chief, capital,' with the Pre-Celtic suffix **kin*, of uncertain meaning. Early forays by Greek navigators would leave names of the Pyrenees mountain range and of cities such as Marseille and Nice.

The Celts were a largely nonliterate Indo-European tribe that occupied central France, parts of Spain, the Alps, and probably Britain at least as early as the sixth century B.C. Later the Celts would be conquered by Rome and then dispersed by the Germanic migrations into the marginal areas (the "Celtic fringe") of Scotland, Wales, Cornwall, Ireland, and Brittany. We know the Celtic language of Gaul, called Gaulish, from mentions by ancient historians, from scattered ancient inscriptions, and from comparative study of later Celtic languages. Gaulish seems to have yielded readily to Latin in the speech of cities but to have endured longer in the countryside, where it left traces in place-names and in the vocabulary of farming. It became extinct by about A.D. 500.

Celtic roots that are detectible in the OOc lexicon include the names of tribes such as the *Arverni* (**Alvernhe**), the *Andicavi* (**Angieus**), the *Cenomani* (**Maines**), the *Pictavi* (**Peitau, Peiteus**), and the *Turones* (**Tours**). Celtic personal names, presumably designating a man's property, underlie the place-names **Vensa** and **Ventadorn**. Descriptive place-names of Celtic origin include **Braiman** 'man from Brabant,' perhaps from Celtic **bracu* 'mud' and **bani* 'region'; **Canda**, the city of Candes, at the confluence of the Loire and Vienne Rivers, from Celtic *cóndate* 'confluence of rivers,' influenced by CL CANDĬDUS 'gleaming white'; and **Niort**, from Celtic *novio-* 'new' and *-ó-ritum* 'ford.' Common nouns from Celtic include the names of such features of country life as **balai** 'rod, switch,' **cambisa** 'field,' **landa** 'plain,' **lauzeta** 'lark,' and **pesa** 'piece of meat or bread,' beside more general terms such as **drut** 'lover,' **lais** 'plaintive melody,' and adjectives such as **com** 'sway-backed,' **galhart** 'outrageous,' **truan** 'wretched, treacherous.'

LATIN

The reader who has noticed that the substratum seems to have contributed to the development of OOc primarily nouns, with a few adjectives, will anticipate that Latin provided the preponderance of verbs and other parts of speech. Indeed, Latin is the source of two-thirds of the OOc lexicon, as well as the phonology, morphology, and syntax of the language.

Classical Latin provided the bulk of words for ordinary experience, such as the verbs **amar, anar, aver, cantar, dever, eser, faire, metre, poder, venir, voler**; nouns denoting *woman* and *man* (**femna, ome**); family members (**filh, filha, fraire, maire, paire, seror**); parts of the body (**cor, cors, man, pe, testa**); *day* and *night* (**jorn, noch**); *earth* and *sea* (**mar, terra**). CL provided the range of parts of speech, including pronouns (**ieu, tu, el, ella, qui, que**), adjectives (**bon, caut, dous, dur, fort, gran**), adverbs (**non, oc, tost**), conjunctions (**que, si**), prepositions (**a, ab, contra, de, entre, josta, sor, vas**), and interjections (**ai!**).

CL provided the stock for words in OOc that may seem characteristically medieval, such as **castel** 'castle,' **cort** 'court,' **rei** 'king,' **sirven** 'servant,' and **vila** 'town.' CL also provided words in areas marked by contributions from other sources, such as rural words (notable for Celtic elements), including **aiga** 'water,' **albespin** 'hawthorn,' **araire** 'plow,' **arbre** 'tree,' **peis** 'fish,' **sebisa** 'hedge'; military words (frequently Germanic) such as **comte** 'count,' **duc** 'duke,' **sageta** 'arrow,' **senhor** 'lord'; and religious words (frequently from Church Latin), such as **crotz** 'cross,' **fe** 'faith,' **saint** 'saint,' **sermon** 'sermon.' The CL stock included a number of words Latin had borrowed from Greek, such as CAMĔRAM 'arched ceiling' (**cambra**), HŌRAM 'hour' (**ora**), PLATĔAM 'street' (**plasa**), SPĂTHAM 'sword' (**espaza**).

CL was the source of 90 percent of the bound morphemes (prefixes and suffixes) in this book, including all the most productive ones, such as initial **a-**(AD), final **-a** (-AM) and **-ier** (-ARIUM), infinitive **-ar** (-ĀRE) and **-ir** (-ĪRE). It also was the origin of personal names such as **Flọri**, a hero of romance, and **Marsili**, the villain in epic, and of place-names such as **Blaia** (BALABIUS, a man's name), **Capestanh** (CAPUT STAGNĪ 'the end of the pond'), **Compeingna** (COMPĔNDĬA 'shortcut'), **Guiana** (AQUĪTĀNĬA, with lenition of [k] and T, then aphaeresis), and **Proẹnsa** (PROVĬNCĬA).

Vulgar Latin made distinctive contributions of numerous free morphemes. The informal language was affected by Greek (χολαφοσ > VL cŏlăphum > **cǫlp** 'blow') and Celtic (*medā*- 'balance' > VL *medantāre > **mazantar** 'to weigh, to shake'). VL also felt the early effects of Germanic. Gothic *ga-hlaiba* 'one who shares bread, fellow soldier' (from *hlaiba*; cf. E. 'loaf') produced a calque, or part-for-part translation: VL cum-pane, companiōnem, OOc **companhon** 'companion.' Germanic **gart* 'yard' became VL *gardīnus, OOc **jardiṇ**.

VL produced new words in certain types, frequently by compounding.

Demonstratives reinforced with ĕccĕ: VL *ĕccĕ hŏc > **so**; VL ĕccĕ hāc > **sai**; VL ĕccĕ ĭllum > **cęl**; VL ĕccĕ ĭstum > **cęst**. Reinforced with atque: VL *atque hŏc > **acǫ**; VL *ăccu ĭstum > **aquęst**.

Adverbs: VL ad ĭd ĭpsum (tĕmpus) > **adęs**, influenced in the vowel by another new adverb, **apręs** < LL ad prĕssum; VL *ad sătis > **asatz**; VL *ad trans > **atras**; VL *dum intĕrim > **demęntre**.

Relative pronouns: VL *dē ŭnde > **dǫn**.

Prepositions: VL *dē ĭnănte > **denan**.

Verbs: VL *comĭnĭtĭāre > **comensar**; VL *fŏrtĭāre > **forsar**.

Adjectives: VL *ămōrōsum > **amorǫs**.

Diminutives: VL aucĕllum (diminutive of CL avem) > **auzęl**; VL *pūllĭcĕllam (diminutive of CL puellam) > **piusęla**.

Nouns: CL amīc-ĭtĭam, with substitution of suffix, became VL *amīc-ĭtātem, whence **amistat**.

A bound morpheme apparently due to Vulgar Latin is -ācum, which gives **-ai** in **lecai**, **verai**. But VL is not the distinctive source of any personal names or place-names in this book.

Church Latin was the source of a limited number of free morphemes, names of persons, and place-names. Most of these words reflect specific ecclesiastical concerns. They refer to officers of the church (**cardenal** 'cardinal,' **evęsque** 'bishop,' **papa** 'pope'); the liturgy (**męsa** 'Mass,' **ofręnda** 'offertory,' **sacrifici** 'consecration of the host'); sacred history (**miracle** 'miracle,' **pasiǫṇ** 'passion, Crucifixion,' **redemciǫṇ** 'redemption,' **redemptǫr** 'redeemer'); deviltry (**diable** 'devil,' **ęrętge** 'heretical,' **maligne** 'wicked'); or more general religious concepts (**clęrgue** 'cleric,' **glęira** 'church,' **religïǫṇ** 'religious order'). But other words from ChL expressed concerns of Occitan society in general, such as **damnatge** 'loss,' **martiri** 'slaughter,' **meravęlha** 'wonder' (as in **meravelhas aver** 'to be amazed'). ChL parabŏlāre gave **parlar** 'to speak,' and ChL

RĔMĔMŎRĀRĪ gave **remembrar** 'to remember.' The adjective **esperital** had both an ecclesiastical and an erotic meaning, 'spiritual' (poverty, as in the monastic rule) and 'spirited, full of spirit, lively' (said of a woman's eyes). Many of these words from ChL show a limited application of normal sound changes, since the OOc terms felt the continuing influence of ChL forms.

Personal names from ChL included biblical ones like **Crist** (ChL CHRĬSTUS, from Greek *khristos*, 'anointed,' translating Hebrew *masiah*, 'anointed,' whence 'messiah') and **Jhesu** (ChL JĒSUS, a Hebrew name). Some became baptismal names, such as **Maria** (ChL MARIA < Hebrew *Miriam*, influenced by CL MARĬUS) and **Peire** (ChL PĔTRUS, from the Hebrew for 'rock'). Place-names applied to localities in the Occitan region included **Montoliu**, the name of one of the gates of Toulouse (ChL MONTEM OLIVĀRUM 'Mount of Olives'), and the names of the towns **Saint Circ** (ChL CYRĬCUS) and **Saint Marsel** (ChL MARCĔLLUS, from CL MARCUS + diminutive ĔLLUM).

Some of these words came into ChL from the Greek of the early church. Thus ĂBBĀTEM > **abat** 'abbot,' ĔLĔĔMŎSŸNAM > **almorn** 'alms,' ANGĔLUM > **angel**, MŎNĂCHUM > **monge** 'monk,' MŎNĂSTĔRĬUM > **mostier** 'church,' PSALMUM > **salm**. From Hebrew came ChL SATANAS, SATAN > **satan**. ChL BLĂSPHĒMĀRE 'to blaspheme' blended with CL AESTĬMĀRE 'to value' and produced VL *BLĂSTĔMĀRE, whence **blasmar** 'to blame.' The rhetorical term **trobar** 'to compose,' whence **trobador**, may derive from *trópos* 'figurative usage of a word,' whence ChL *TRŎPĀRE 'to compose a trope' (an element of the liturgy).

Late Latin made a significant contribution in free morphemes, added a small number of bound ones, and provided a few personal names. The absorption of vocabulary from other source languages continued, as Hebrew, through LL, gave **mana** 'manna, food provided miraculously to the Israelites'; Greek gave **cara** 'face,' **gelos** 'jealous,' **pestre** 'priest'; Celtic gave **braca** 'britches, trousers,' **camin** 'road,' **cerveza** 'beer,' **cleda** 'shelter made of wattle,' **gona** 'tunic,' **lega** 'league,' **vezoch** 'billhook.' Some of these words from LL may have reflected developments in social practice (**cavalgar, cavalier, vilan**) or technology (**acier** 'steel,' **clocca** 'bell,' **peiriera** 'catapult'). Most of them, however, did not: **bas** 'low,' **cat** 'cat,' **cavec** 'owl,' **ensems** 'together,' **gros** 'great,' **mot** 'word,' **uzar** 'to use.' Late Latin proper nouns include **Martin** and **Sarrazin** (from Byzantine Greek).

Medieval Latin contributed only a small number of words to OOc, such as **ancian** 'ancient,' **capelan** 'chaplain,' **cortes** 'courtly,' **vescomte** 'viscount.' **Jacopin** 'Jacobin monk, member of the Dominican order,' from ML JACŌBUS, came from the first Dominican convent, founded in 1229 in Paris on the rue Saint-Jacques.

The Germanic migrations of the fifth and sixth centuries A.D. may have been set in motion when Attila and his Huns charged out of the Asian steppes in 395. We have earlier evidence of a Germanic language in the form of Gothic, the language of the Goths, a tribe settled in Dacia (modern Romania). Gothic was employed by Archbishop Wulfila, who died in A.D. 383, to translate parts of the Bible (see Bennett). At this time, Rome had already adopted a policy of settling Germanic tribes within the empire. We have mentioned the calque on Gothic *gahlaiba* in VL companiōnem, OOc **companhon**. Specifically Gothic etyma are posited for **cauzir** 'to choose' (*kausjan*), **gai** 'merry' (**gāheis*), and **guidar** 'to guide' (**wīdan*). Other Germanic roots were adopted into Romance languages so generally that we infer they must have been borrowed into VL before the migrations: thus Frankish **werra*, OOc **guerra** 'war'; Germ. **wisa*, OOc **guiza** 'kind, type'; and Germ. **blank*, OOc **blanc** 'white.' Germanic verbs with the infinitive ending *-ōn* commonly took **-ar** in OOc, as did Germ. **haribergōn*, from the elements *haribergo* 'army-shelter,' OOc **albergar** 'to find lodging'; and Germ. **wardōn*, OOc **gardar** 'to look.' Germanic infinitives in *-jan* commonly took **-ir**, as did **warnjan*, OOc **garnir** 'to equip.'

When the migrations began, the Visigoths, or West Goths, moved into southwestern Gaul, where they gained the cities of Toulouse, Bordeaux, and Poitiers in A.D. 419. It was the Visigoths who defeated Attila the Hun in 451 at the battle of the Catalaunian Plain, the name of which, from the name of a Celtic tribe, is the origin of the French place-name Châlons(-sur-Marne). The Ostrogoths, or East Goths, moved into Italy, where their leader Odoacer deposed the boy emperor Romulus Augustulus in 476, an event sometimes considered the symbolic end of the Roman Empire. In turn, another Ostrogoth, Theodoric, killed Odoacer, established rule with his capital at Ravenna, and gained possession of the territory of Provence, before dying in 526. Theodoric is depicted as **Teiric** in the OOc *Boeci* (reading 11).

Within a decade after the death of Theodoric, another tribe, the Franks, had extended their control from the region of modern Holland and Belgium to include all of Gaul. Their original leader, Clovis (died 511), founded the Merovingian dynasty of Francia. The Franks accepted Christianity, intermarried freely with the Gallo-Roman population, and adopted Latin as their language of religion and administration.

The Germanic element in the OOc lexicon is most striking in personal names, including about half of those in this book. Germanic roots that occur frequently are *rīc* 'powerful,' as a suffix in **Aimeric**, **Enric**, **Teiric**, and as a prefix in **Richart**, **Riquer**; *hard* 'strong,' in **Amblart**, **Bernart**, **Girart**, **Launart**, **Renart**, **Richart**, **Sicart**; *waldan* 'to lead,' in **Arnaut** (*Arn-wald* 'Eagle-leader'), **Folcaut** (*Folc-wald* 'Folk-leader'; cf. Michel Foucault), **Giraut** (*Gerwald* 'Lance-leader'); and *hari* 'army' in **Garnier** (*Warin-hari* 'Shelter-army'), **Gauter** (*Waldo-hari* 'Lead-army'), **Rayner** (*Raginhari* 'Counsel-army'), **Riquer** (*Rīc-hari* 'Powerful-army'). The militaristic and aristocratic qualities in the meanings of these roots reflect the ethos of the Germanic peoples who used them, and may explain in part how the names became popular, as they must have done, among non-Germanic peoples who adopted them.

OOc had a number of place-names from Germanic sources denoting localities elsewhere, such as **Englaterra** (Old E. *Engle* 'people of Anglia' + CL TĚRRA) and **Coberlanda**, in England (Old E. *Cumbraland*, from Welsh *Cymry* 'the Welsh' + Germ. *land*); **Irlanda**, with its first element from Irish (*Eriu* 'Ireland') and its Germanic second element; **Fransa** ('Land of the Franks') and French places such as **Brezi**, **Garlanda**, and **Normandia**. But there were also Occitan place-names of Germanic origin, such as **Dalon** and **Mirmanda**, both from Germanic personal names.

The adjective **franc** 'noble' etymologically described the Frank. Frankish or general Germanic sources provided OOc military terms such as **albęrc** 'hauberk, shirt of chain mail' (**halsberg* 'neck-protection'), **baron** 'great lord' (*baro*), **bran** 'sword' (**brand*; cf. Marlon Brando), **dart** 'lance' (*daroth*), **elm** 'helmet' (**helm*), **estendart** 'banner' (**standhard*), **gaita** 'watchman' (**wahta*), **targa** 'shield' (**targa*), **tręga** 'truce' (**treuwa*). Germanic elements in the vocabulary of the household include **bro** 'broth' (**brod*) and **raustir** 'to roast' (**raustjan*). Value-laden terms include **aunir** 'to dishonor' (**haunjan*), **felǫn** 'criminal' (**fillo* 'knacker, horse slaughterer'), **murtrir** 'to kill' (**murθrjan*), and **orgǫlh** 'pride' (**ŭrgōlī*). More general concerns are expressed in **bǫsc** 'wood' (Germ. **bosk*; cf. E. *bosky*), **fręsc** 'fresh' (**frisk*), **gaire** adv. 'long' (**waigaro*, Fr. *guère*), **gazanhar** 'to win' (**waiðanjan*), **gratar** 'to scratch' (**krattōn*). The adverb **trǫp** 'too much' comes from Frankish *thorp* 'village,' later 'herd' (cf. OOc **tropęl** 'band,' Fr. *troupeau* and *trop*).

Among bound morphemes, Germanic sources account for the prefix **mes-**, as in **mescreire** 'to distrust' (**missi-*; cf. E. *misuse*, etc.); the suffixes **-art**, which spread from personal names to words such as **galhart** 'outrageous' (Ctc. **galia* 'strength' + Germ. *hard*); and **-enc**, as in **sebenc** 'bastard' (CL SAEPEM 'hedge' + Germ. *-inc*: 'one born under the hedge').

Greek elements that entered OOc, but presumably not by way of Church Latin, included words from commerce, such as **bọrsa** 'purse' (βυρσα), **baratar** 'to traffic' (πραττειν), and **tapi** '(pilgrim's) cloak' (Byzantine ταπιτιον). Judgmental terms include **ávol** 'bad (reputation), disagreeable (reason),' from αβουλοσ 'thoughtless,' with influence of CL Hăbĭlem to explain the lack of **-a** in the feminine (**avol**, not ***avola**), and **bagasa** 'slut' from late *βακχασσα, classical βακχασ 'bacchante' (compare It. *bagascia*, Sp. *bagasa*, OFr. *baiasse*, and E. *baggage* as insulting terms for a woman). More complimentary is the suffix **-ẹsa**, as in **comtesa**, **duchesa**, from Greek -ισσα, VL *-ĭssam. The suffix **-eiar** 'to deal in (secular affairs),' from Greek -ιζειν, VL -ĭdĭāre, occurs in **barreiar** 'to plunder' (VL *barra 'crossbar'), **carreiar** 'to transport by wagon' (CL carrum), **domneiar** 'to court ladies, to womanize' (CL dŏmĭnăm), **guerreiar** 'to make war' (Germ. *werra), **pastorjar** 'to pasture' (CL pastōrem), **plaideiar** 'to plead' (**plait**, **plag** < CL placĭtum), **torneiar** 'to participate in a tourney' (CL tŏrnāre, with substitution of the suffix **-eiar**).

Old French provided a number of words in OOc, several recognizable by the characteristic French monophthongization of Classical Latin au to French [o], since the normal sound changes of OOc left CL au unaffected. Some of these words may derive from the affective language of monasticism, such as **joi** 'joy' (OFr. *joi* < CL gaudĭum sg.), **jọia** 'joy' (OFr. *joie* < CL gaudĭa pl.); compare the normal OOc development of the vowel in the synonym **gauch**.[1] **Sanglọt** 'sigh,' another monastic term, shows the French treatment of the nasalized vowel (OFr. *sanglot* < CL sĭngŭltum, VL *sĭnglŭtum, influenced by glŭttīre 'to swallow').[2] The language of luxury commerce provided **ormier** 'golden ornament' (OFr. *or mier* 'pure gold' < CL aurum mĕrum) and **sembeliṇ** 'sable' (OFr. *sembelin*, *sebelin* < Middle High German *zobelîn* < Russian *sobol*,' because the fur was imported from Siberia by way of Germany to France).

---

[1] gaudium "désigne l'exultation de l'âme< dans la possession, la présence ou l'évocation du Bien; et, plus particulièrement chez les Chrétiens, dans la communion avec Dieu" (Guiraud 419–20). On gaudium denoting religious joy in the Vulgate, see Gay-Crosier 52. On gaudium in monastic observance of Lent, see Saint Benedict's *Rule*, ch. 49.6–7; on joyful experience in monastic tradition, see Miquel 113–14, 142–43, 151, 194–95, 250–51. The Benedictine abbeys at Fleury (Saint-Benoît-sur-Loire) and Saint-Martial (Limoges) produced all the extant Occitan literary manuscripts dating from before the thirteenth century (Avalle, *Letteratura* 19–41).

[2] "Il y a dans le monachisme, au moyen âge, toute une littérature de *suspiria*" (Leclercq 61).

Epic poetry brought **poisan** 'powerful' (OFr. *poisant* in the chansons de geste) and names of heroes such as **Corberan**, **Gormont**, and **Insebart**. **Verai** 'true' is believed to have come from OFr. *verai*.[3] The order of Beguines, **Beguinas**, was so called after the sobriquet of its founder, Lambert *le Bègue*, or 'the stammerer' (OFr. *bègue* < Dutch **beggen* 'to chatter, to talk excessively'). OOc received French names for a French city such as **Montfọrt**, and for a French person such as a **Picart** 'man from Picardy,' while Occitanizing the name of the city **Monsaurel** by restoring the characteristic diphthong.

Some words from eastern Mediterranean languages entered OOc as a result of the crusades (from the first, A.D. 1095–99, to the seventh, A.D. 1270). Arabic provided **drogoman** 'interpreter' (*tarğumān*). From Armenian came **tafur** 'vagabond' (*thaphur*), applied to pillagers who followed the crusading armies. From Persian came **tabọr** 'drum' (*tabīr*, with substitution of suffix), which Europeans first heard on crusade during preliminaries of battle. Other words from such languages entered OOc by other routes, however. **Mesquiṇ** 'weak' came from Arabic by way of Spain. The colloquial speech of the Jewish population in Provence, which combined Hebrew words with Occitan, was the source of **trefaṇ** 'faithless, deceptive,' from Hebrew *ṭerēfā* 'forbidden meat.'

Welsh contributed the name of **Tristan**, who died of love in Celtic romance, and Italian brought the **Lombart**, or Lombard.

Onomatopoetic elements include *buff-* in **bufar** 'to puff, to blow on,' *ŭf-* in **ufana** 'show, outward appearance,' *flik-* and *flok-* in **de flic en floc** 'with snip and snap (she cut my hair),' *garg-* in **garganta** 'throat' (cf. E. *to gargle*), *tokk-* in **tocar** 'to touch,' *vi-*, *viol-* in **viola** 'a stringed instrument.'

WORD FORMATION WITHIN OLD OCCITAN

The reader will find in the Glossary an inventory of prefixes, infixes, and suffixes occurring in the texts included in this book. It includes 66 suffixes, 12 prefixes, and a single infix (feminine **i**, as in **ilh** 'she'). Evidently suffixation is the most powerful type of word formation, analogous to the morphological changes in verbs, nouns, and demonstratives that also occur at the end of the word. This preference for the end of the word relates to the position of accent, which tends to fall on the final syllable in words ending in a consonant and on the penult of words ending in a vowel (**cantár**, **cánta**; see ch. 1).

---

[3] Or perhaps directly from VL vērācum (Jensen, "Dilemma").

Suffixes

Among the suffixes listed, 46 create nouns, 20 create adjectives, 4 create verbs, and 4 create adverbs.[4] For example, the feminine-noun suffix **-a**, from CL -ᴀᴍ, is etymological in **filha** (CL ꜰīʟĭᴀᴍ) and many other words but has been extended analogically to identify female persons, in **bergiera** 'shepherdess' (LL ʙᴇ̆ʀʙĭᴄᴀ̄ʀĭᴜᴍ 'shepherd'), **druda** 'sweetheart' (Ctc. **druto-* 'strong,' OOc **drut** 'lover'), and so on. The feminine suffix has been added to masculine nouns or adjectives like **camin** 'road,' to produce **camina**, with the same meaning, and appears in abstractions like **corsa** 'haste' (CL ᴄŭʀsᴜᴍ 'running, zeal'). It has also been added to verb roots in words called "deverbals," like **aizina** 'opportunity,' from **aizinar** 'to try one's hand at'; **barata** 'bargain,' from **baratar** 'to barter'; and **crida** 'rumor,' from **cridar** 'to shout.' Another type of deverbal is the zero suffix in verb roots used directly as nouns, such as **aizin** (1) 'dwelling,' **barat** 'fraud,' **crit** 'cry, shout.'[5] Another feminine marker, **-ęsa**, was added to masculine nouns denoting rank (**comtesa**, **duchesa**).

Other noun suffixes designate abstractions, actions, agents, collective meanings, or results.[6] There are augmentatives (**-ás** [1]), depreciatives (**-astrǫn**), and diminutives (**-ęc**; **-ęl** and **-ęla**; **-ęt** and **-ęta**; **-ǫn** [1]). Some noun suffixes do not appreciably change the meaning of the root, as in **bǫrsa** or **borsin**, both meaning 'purse' (see also **-an** [2], **-isa**).

Suffixes forming adjectives from nouns include **-al**, **-art**, **-ęnc**, **-il**, **-uc**; **-ęs** means 'pertaining to' (the noun root), as in **cortęs** 'courtly'; **-ǫs** designates quality or abundance, as in **orgolhǫs** 'proud,' from **orgǫlh** 'pride.' Adjectives may also be formed from verb roots by adding **-ǫn** (2). Suffixes forming adjectives from adjectives tend to affect meaning slightly if at all, as in **vęr** and **verai** 'true,' or **cert** and **certan** 'certain, sure' (**-ai**, **-an** [2]). "Synthetic comparatives," as they are called, are expressed in a single word (**belazǫr** 'more beautiful,' from **bęl** 'beautiful'; **gensǫr** 'more noble,' from **gęn** 'noble'), in contrast to "analytic comparatives," consisting of two words (**plus leu** 'more easily').

Suffixes creating verbs are few but powerful, including three in the **-ar** conjugation (**-ar** [2], **-alhar**, **-eiar**), plus **-ir**. This means that only infinitives in **-ar** and **-ir** were created during OOc; the infinitive types in **-ęr** (**avęr**), **-́er** (**éser**), and **-́re** (**pérdre**) were not pro-

---

[4] The total number is larger than 66 because several suffixes create more than one type of word.

[5] "Aizin (1)" refers to the first of the two entries under **aizin** in the Glossary. Similarly "**-ás** (1)," below, refers to the first entry under **-ás** in the Prefixes, Infixes, and Suffixes listing.

[6] Abstractions: **-ada**, **-amęn** (1), **-anda**, **-aria**, **-atge**, **-atura**, **-edat**, **-ęza**, **-ia**, **-ier**, **-imęn**, **-ǫr**, **-tat**, **-ura**. Actions: **-amęn**, **-an**, **-ansa**, **-elada**, **-ęnsa**. Agents: **-adǫr** masc. and **-airitz** fem., **-an** (1), **-idǫr**, **-ier**, **itǫr**. Collective meanings: **-anda**, **-atge**, **-atura**, **-ęna**. Results: **-amęn** (1), **-ida**, **-imęn**.

ductive. The **-ar** type alone accounts for 72 infinitives in the Glossary of this book, and the **-ir** type adds 24 more. These infinitives were created in OOc from roots going back to Germanic (**abrandar, aunir**) and to Celtic (**abrivar**) as well as to Latin (**abelir, abenar**).

Suffixes creating adverbs include **-amẹn** (2), from LL expressions like APERTĀ MENTĔ, lit., 'with an open mind' (ablative of manner), hence **apertamen** 'openly.' "Adverbial **s**" was etymological in words like CL MĂGIS, MĬNUS, PLŪS and their reflexes in OOc, **mais, mens, plus,** but extended analogically to **alhọns** (CL ĂLĬŬNDE), **anz** (2), (CL ĂNTE), **doncs** (CL DŬNQUE), and so on.

Prefixes

Prefixes may intensify the meaning of the root (**tras-** in **trastot** 'all,' **de-** in **definar** 'to die') or negate it (**des-**, as in **descobrir** 'to reveal'). Others modify the root with a more particular meaning, as do **tras-** 'over' in **traspasar** 'to pass over, to die'; **re-** 'again' in **recomensar** 'to begin again'; **per-** 'thoroughly' in **perprendre** 'to capture.' But a prefix may have little effect on the meaning of a root, as in **desliurar** 'to set free' versus **liurar** 'to deliver'; **departir** or **partir** 'to depart'; and **esgardar** or **gardar** 'to look at.'

Prefixes form nouns, verbs, adjectives, adverbs, and prepositions.[7]

It appears that suffixes are particularly apt to form nouns (with 46 in the Glossary, against 4 for verbs), while prefixes are apt to create verbs (with 11 in the Glossary, against 4 for nouns). This distribution counterbalances the greater articulation of verbal morphology at the end of the word (set marker, tense marker, person marker), leaving the beginning free for a prefix, while nouns, with their less elaborate declension at the end of the word (two cases, two numbers, but in most nouns a single variable—final **s** or zero), allow a greater variety of suffixes.

SUMMARY OF SOURCES OF THE LEXICON

Table 30.1 shows the etymological sources of the OOc lexicon as represented in the Glossary of this book, according to types of morpheme: place-names, bound morphemes (prefixes, infixes, suffixes), free morphemes (ordinary words), and personal names. Percentage figures read down, not across; in the "Places" column we see that the 81 words in the sample include 29% from the substratum, 36% from Latin, and so on. For distribution of the total sample into substratum, Latin, etc., see the "Total" column. Since there

---

[7] Nouns: **des-, en-** (2), **tras-, re-**; verbs: **a-** (2), **bis-, de-, des-, en-** (1), **en-** (2), **es-** (1), **mes-, per-, re-, tras-**; adjectives: **a-** (2), **des-, en-** (2), **tras-**; adverbs: **a-** (2), **de-, en-** (2); prepositions: **en-** (2).

can be many reasons for uncertainty in the assignment of an etymon to a word, the percentages in the table should not be taken as precise; nevertheless, they are significant enough to suggest some observations.

TABLE 30.1. *Sources of the OOc Lexicon by Morpheme Types*

	Places	Bound	Free	Person	Total
Substratum	29%	1%	1%	0%	2%
Latin	36%	91%	69%	27%	67%
Superstratum	18%	4%	5%	48%	7%
Other	6%	3%	2%	6%	2%
OOc	11%	3%	24%	19%	22%
Number	81	78	1,724	81	1,964

The table shows that place-names are the most conservative sector of the OOc lexicon, since nearly a third of them preserve traces of the substratum, chiefly Celtic place-names that were accepted by successive waves of later inhabitants. The bound morphemes in this book are almost all from Latin, as are the preponderance of free morphemes; there is no doubt, then, that OOc is primarily Latinate in its word stock (67% of the total sample), and the near totality of bound morphemes from Latin shows that the productive elements of word formation were almost exclusively so. Personal names are the most innovative sector of the lexicon; although they preserve an important element of names from Latin (with none, in this book, from the substratum), they show a strong preference for Germanic types, which implies that Germanic names enjoyed high prestige.

Considering all the sources of words in each category, we see that place-names retain a relatively even distribution, representing the substratum, Latin, the Germanic superstratum, and names generated from within OOc. Bound morphemes are relatively restricted in derivation from Latin alone. Free morphemes draw significantly on generation within OOc, as do personal names.

All in all, two-thirds (67%) of the words in this sample lexicon of OOc come from Latin; two-ninths (22%) come from within OOc; and the remaining one-ninth (11%) come from other sources, including the substratum and the superstratum.

READING 30

Flamenca

---

[8] See *Grundriss* 1972–, 4.2, 120, with reference to vv. 1723–37.

The outstanding example of narrative romance (**novas**) in Old Occitan, Flamenca *seems to have been composed near the end of the thirteenth century, when the sole manuscript was compiled. The author may have been* en Bernardet, *whose patron, the lord of Alga, proved less generous than the poet would have liked.*[8]

In the passage given here, the lover, Guilhem de Nevers, disguised as a priest, succeeds at last in whispering his first word to the heroine, Flamenca. Her two-syllable response and their subsequent exchange, always in units of two syllables, are closely modeled on a passage from a **canso** by the twelfth-century troubadour Peire Rogier, "Ges non puesc en bon vers fallir" (P-C 356,4, ed. Nicholson, no. 6), stanza 6.

The subject of the first sentence is Guilhem, the lover. He is accompanied by his servant Vidal, by his chaplain, and by the innkeeper, his host. Flamenca, whom Guilhem loves and who will in due time love him passionately in return, is married to Archimbaut, a jealous husband.

Al serven ques ac nom Vidal
fes aportar aiga e sal
per aiga benezeita far,
e quan n'ac pres al mas lavar
fon reveillatz le capellas.   5
De l'aiga·l donet a las mas
et an lur prima comensada,
e quant agron tersa cantada
e lur clas ricamen sonat
aisi con fo acostumat,   10
tota li gens venc a la messa.
Apres la preissa plus espessa
ens Archimbautz, aisi com sol,
venc totz derrers, e per son vol
non fora dimergues ni festa.   15
Diabol semblet de la testa,
de cels ques hom irissatz peiñ;
ges non a tort si noqua·s feiñ
Flamenca per s'amor joiosa,
quar mout pot esser angoissosa   20
domna qu'aital diabol ve;
empero apres lui s'en ve
et entra s'en en son estug.
Guillems o hac ben vist, so·m cug,
car en re mais non atendia;   25
qui d'aicest cujar no·m cresia
eu non creiria lui fort be,
si m'en plevia neis sa fe.
Guillems saup mout ben sa fasenda,
l'ofizi saup ben e l'uffrenda   30
de cor, e la cominio.
Le capellas non fes sermo

ni mandet festa la semana.
Guillems hac vos clara e sana
e canta ben apertamen 35
a l'Agnus Dei, et el pren
pas enaisi con far devia,
et a son oste, que sezia
e·l cor, desempre n'a donat.
L'ostes non ho a ges celat, 40
si ben s'era laïns e·l cor,
quar als borzes en dona for,
e·l pas pel monasteir s'esten.
Guillems vai son libre queren,
e per aiso demora tan 45
qu'en Archimbaut ne prend'avan
qu'el sia lai defor vengutz
on estai sos jois escundutz.
Per nulla ren non vol baisar
n'Archimbaut, neis sa pas donar; 50
ab tan s'en eis, e Dieus l'ajut!
Car hanc mais per tan esperdut
no·s tenc per ren con el fai ara.
Non levet sos oilz ni sa cara
per so que sai ni lai gardes. 55
Vaus Flamenca s'en vai ades,
e cuja ben certanamen
ab sidons aia parlamen
e·l pusca dir sivals u mot,
mas sobr'Amor o laissa tot 60
e dis, "S'Amors hui non m'aduz
de mon desir a qualque luz,
ja mais en leis no·m fisarai;
mas, si Dieu plaz, be·i avenrai.
Amors non fail ges a la cocha, 65
mas a mi par que trop i locha
pel gran desir qu'e·l cor m'afflama."
Et aitals es totz homs ques ama.
Guillems davan sidonz estet;
quan il lo sauteri baiset, 70
el li dis süavet, "Hai las!"
Pero ges non o dis tam bas
ques il fort be non o ausis.
Guillems s'en vai humils e clis,
e cuj'aver mout enansat; 75
s'el agues ara derochat
en un tornei cent cavalliers
e gasainatz cinc cènts destriers
non aia joia tan perfecha,

car res e·l mon tan non delecha *fait rejouir* 80
tot fin aman con cel jois fa
que ven de lai on son cor ha. *qui vient de là où il a son coeur*
Le capellans no·s bistenset, *n'hésitait pas*
apres la messa comenset
so mieijorn, aisi con solia. *sexte, comme il le faisait toujours* 85
Guillems lo sauteri tenia
e fes parer los salms i vis, *fait semblant qu'il regardait les psaumes*
mais avan que d'el si partis *qu'il le quitta,*
a·l fueil plus de cent ves baisat, *il baisait la page plus de cent fois,*
e cel mot, "Ai las!" recordat. *se ne s'est souvenu* 90
En Archimbautz s'en eis dese *alla tout de suite*
e mena·n sa moiller ab se,
que ges non la vol oblidar. *il ne voulait pas du tout l'oublier*
Aitant com la poc endreissar *Autant qu'il pouvait la suivre*
Guillems ab oils de cor l'endreisa. *vêtement* 95
Lo vestir plega e l'adreissa, *plia et mis en ordre (à sa place)*
lo calici e la patena *le calice et la patène (plat)*
met en luc salv, e pois ne mena *l'a mis dans son lieu sûr, e puis il*
son hoste e son capella. *Son hôte et son chapelain* *amena (en dehors)*

Meter: Octosyllabic couplets.

Major edition: Gschwind, vv. 3879–3977.

Manuscript: Carcassonne, Bibliothèque Municipale 34 (anc. 2703), fols. 68v–70. "Ecrit au 13e s. en Provence" (Brunel, *Bibliographie,* no. 78).

Rejected readings in the manuscript: (7) comensada] cantada; cf. v. 8. (9) clas] clars. (13) ens] ems. (24) so·m] son. (27) ben *(rhymes with* fe *28).* (49) non] *om.* (50) neisa pas. (54) leves. (71) hui; cf. Ai v. 90. (77) cent] .C. (78) cinc cents] .V.C. (80) delecha] deleiga. (83) bitenset. (89) cent] .C.

Selected variant: (79) aia] agra Gschwind.

Notes

(2) **aiga e sal**] On the tradition of mixing salt with holy water, see *Dictionnaire d'archéologie chrétienne et de liturgie* 4: 1687.

(4) **al mas lavar**] The definite article introduces the infinitive **lavar** ('for hand-washing'), not fem. **mas**. Cf. Gschwind 150.

(32–33) The chaplain abbreviated the service, as Guilhem no doubt desired.

(34–37) Guilhem de Nevers is a skillful impostor as a priest. For the figure of the amorous priest, cf. "hende Nicolas" in Chaucer's Miller's Tale.

(36) **Agnus Dei**] Liturgical formula, an invocation to Christ as the sacrificial lamb of God. During the Mass the formula is first stated twice as "Agnus Dei, qui tollis peccata mundi, miserere nobis" 'Lamb of God, who take away the sins of the world, have pity on us'; then a third time, as "Agnus Dei, dona nobis pacem" 'Lamb of God, give us peace' (*Dictionnaire d'archéologie chrétienne et de liturgie* 1: 965–69).

(37) **pas**] The *pax*, or 'Peace,' an instrument in liturgy; a small tablet that was passed through the congregation during the communion service, as each worshiper kissed it. After Archimbaut and Flamenca enter their private box (**estug** 23), Guilhem performs the offertory (**ufrenda** 30) and communion (**cominio** 31), and sings the **Agnus Dei**, ending "Give us peace"; he then passes the **pas** from the altar, where he is officiating, into the choir (**cor** 39), where his host, the innkeeper, receives it and passes it on to the townsfolk (**borzes** 42). Apparently worshipers offered a kiss of peace as they passed the tablet (see v. 49). The use of such a liturgical instrument is thought to have begun in the thirteenth century and to have spread from England; see "Pace, strumento di," in *Enciclopedia cattolica* 9: 499.

(44) Guilhem fetches the psalter, which Flamenca will kiss (70).

(46) **Archimbaut**] Object form in subject function (cf. ch. 28), unnecessarily corrected by Gschwind to **Archimbautz**.

(79) **aia**] Dependent on **cuj'** 75: 'Guilhem thought that he had made great progress; [he thought] that he would not have such perfect joy even if he had just unhorsed a hundred knights.'

Exercise

Analyze the sound changes involved in the following etymologies:

1. Pre-Celtic **rod* + Ctc. *-ano* > CL Rʜŏᴅᴀ̆ɴᴜᴍ > **Rǫzer**, Fr. *Rhône*
2. Ctc. *Arverni* + CL -ɪ̆ᴀ > CL Aʟᴠᴇ̆ʀɴɪ̆ᴀ > **Alvę̌rnhe**, Fr. *Auvergne*
3. Ctc. **bracu* 'mud' + **bani* 'region' > **Braiman** 'man from Brabant'
4. CL (from Gk.) sᴘᴀ̆ᴛʜᴀᴍ > **espaza** 'sword'
5. CL Aǫᴜɪ̄ᴛᴀ̄ɴɪ̆ᴀ > **Guiana** 'Aquitaine (Guyenne)'
6. ChL ᴇᴘɪ̆sᴄŏᴘᴜᴍ > **evę̌sque** 'bishop'
7. ChL ᴘᴀ̄ᴘᴀᴍ > **papa** 'pope'
8. ChL ᴍɪ̄ʀᴀ̆ᴄŭʟᴜᴍ > **miracle** 'miracle'; cf. VL **ᴍɪ̄ʀᴀ̆ᴄᴜʟᴜᴍ 'mirror' > **miralh**
9. Germ. *Theud-rīc* 'People-powerful' > **Teiric** 'Theodoric the Great'
10. Germ. **wahta* > **gaita** 'watchman'

CHAPTER 31

Research Tools

To help the reader of this book become an active contributor to scholarship in OOc, we shall review in this chapter some basic tools for research in the field.

BIBLIOGRAPHIES OF TEXTS

For the texts of OOc lyric poetry, the standard reference is P-C, Pillet and Carsten's *Bibliographie der Troubadours* (1933). This work offers an alphabetical listing of troubadours, with an alphabetical listing (by incipit, or first line) of the works attributed to each one. Under the incipit, P-C lists manuscripts containing the poem, with the folio on which it begins; notes divergent attributions of the text; identifies its genre; records editions in which it may be found; and adds references to critical discussions.[1] While P-C remains essential for the editor of troubadour poetry (even though occasionally the abbreviations employed seem opaque), it no longer serves the literary reader, since many of its references to editions and discussions are superannuated.[2]

To bring these references up-to-date, one may consult the listing of editions by individual poem in Frank (1953–57; 2: 89–192) and the listing by author in Chambers (*Proper Names*, 1971; 18–33). About one-third of the known troubadours are updated again in the rich anthology by Riquer (1975). Taylor (1977), a second edition of which has been announced, includes about eighty troubadours by name, with a wide-ranging selection of related materials; see also Taylor's essay "Bibliography" (Akehurst and Davis 467–74). One may also work backward from the most recent volumes in the annual bibliographies (see below).

[1] Still useful is the concise description of troubadour manuscripts by Jeanroy (*Bibliographie sommaire*).

[2] For troubadour studies before the nineteenth century, see Vincenti.

For OOc lyric verse of the late Middle Ages, Zufferey has extended the format of P-C in his *Bibliographie des poètes provençaux des XIVe et XVe siècles* (1981).

For a bird's-eye view of the manuscript sources of the whole literature, consult Brunel (*Bibliographie*, 1935), which includes all the extant literary manuscripts copied to the end of the fifteenth century, while excluding archival materials such as administrative, commercial, and legal documents. Brunel (xiv) counts 376 manuscripts in all, which, if they could be placed side by side, would fill about ten yards of shelf space. He counts 3 manuscripts compiled during the eleventh century, 5 from the twelfth, 72 from the thirteenth, 164 from the fourteenth, 83 from the fifteenth, and the rest from the sixteenth century through the eighteenth. For lyric poetry Brunel simply lists the 95 chansonniers, with reference to P-C for individual compositions. In the "Table méthodique des oeuvres" (116–26), Brunel indicates with an asterisk well over one hundred works that had been published incompletely or not at all as of 1935, chiefly works of religious, moral, or didactic literature, especially in prose. A more recent listing of editions of nonlyric poetry has been provided by Frank (2: 193–214). Taylor includes a section on nonlyric works. One should also consult the *Dictionnaire des lettres françaises: Le Moyen Âge* (1992).

DICTIONARIES

A one-volume dictionary sold at a price that students can afford, and the first reference for any lexical question in OOc, is the *PD*, Levy's *Petit dictionnaire provençal-français* (1909), often reprinted. Levy provides brief definitions in French and the grammatical category of each word (such as *v.* 'verbe' or *s.m.* 'substantif masculin'). The mere listing of forms is helpful because Levy employs a quasi-phonetic orthography that suggests how each word is accented and pronounced. (The Glossary of this book follows Levy's example; see the headnote for an explanation of his principles.) In the *PD*, Levy occasionally contradicts his conclusions in earlier volumes of the more thorough *S-W* (see below). The number of entries in the *PD* is on the order of twenty thousand, compared with about two thousand in the Glossary of this book. An occasionally useful reverse index of the *PD*, which allows the scholar to find a rhyme, for example, by spelling a word backward, has been published by Harris (1981).[3]

---

[3] Harris (x) specifies that his *Index inverse* contains 23,684 words, although it excludes certain types of forms in the *PD*.

Behind the compact *PD* stand the massed volumes of two research dictionaries. The work of a true pioneer in the field, François-Just-Marie Raynouard (1761–1836), was published posthumously, in 1838–44—his *Lexique roman: ou, Dictionnaire de la langue des troubadours*. Writing before the birth of the idea of the Romance languages as we know it, Raynouard argued that OOc was the ancestor of French, Italian, and Spanish—a role we grant to Vulgar Latin. Raynouard's format integrates his diachronic theory, since he groups words together according to families; but the alphabetical index in volume 6 makes it easy to find any word. Volume 1 contains a philological treatise and an edition of narrative and lyric texts. The *Lexique* proper occupies volumes 2–5 and contains, with the appendix of addenda in volume 6, on the order of twenty thousand words. The essential difference between *PD* and *LR* lies in the citations Raynouard provides for every word, with reference to their sources; there are tables of authors and works cited at the end of volume 5. He also gives variant forms, provides French translations of the citations, and refers to related words in the other Romance languages.

Emil Levy (1855–1917) launched a supplement to the *LR* half a century after its publication: the *Provenzalisches Supplement-Wörterbuch, Berichtigungen und Ergänzungen zu Raynouards Lexique Roman (1894–1924)*.[4] Levy lived to finish seven volumes; the eighth and final one was completed by his colleague Carl Appel. As the title states, Levy intended only to supplement Raynouard's dictionary, not to replace it; when he had neither corrections nor additions for a word, he said nothing, leaving the reader to infer that Raynouard's treatment stood unaltered. The *S-W* may be estimated to contain twenty thousand words, very much the same range as both *LR* and *PD*; there is no convenient way to estimate how many of these entries correct those in Raynouard or add new ones. When Levy does enter a word, he gives reference to Raynouard's treatment, if any; offers extensive citations, with notation of details such as variant readings and manuscript sources; and, where necessary, discusses other scholars' opinions. When Levy is uncertain of a word's meaning, he says so. He identifies his citations with abbreviations that are tabulated at the beginning or end of various volumes. For an invaluable bibliographical guide to the *S-W*, consult Baldinger, *Complément* (1983).

The *Französisches Etymologisches Wörterbuch (FEW)* was founded by Walther von Wartburg (1888–1971) and has continued to appear, edited by a team of linguists, since his death. Volume 1 was published in 1928; as of this writing (1993), volumes 22, 23,

---

[4] Ezra Pound wrote in his Canto 20 that he visited Levy in Freiburg to discuss troubadour lexicography (Paden, "Pound's Use").

and 25 are coming out in fascicles. The *FEW* is an authoritative compilation of etymological data on French and Occitan, but it is not easy to use. Each article lists the reflexes of a given etymon in Old French, Old Occitan, and a luxuriant profusion of dialects, grouping the reflexes according to form and meaning, and adding remarks on the history of the word family. The original alphabetical listing of etyma, including words in Latin, Celtic, and Germanic, ran from volume 1 to volume 14. The presentation of Germanic etyma was then revised and expanded in volumes 15–17; volume 18 contains etyma from English, volume 19 those from Arabic, volume 20 those from other languages, volumes 21–23 those from unknown or uncertain origins. With volume 24 began the systematic revision of volume 1, first continuing in German as the language of the *FEW*, then shifting to French. The scholar seeking the etymon of a given word therefore confronts several possible places to look among the volumes, twenty-five and growing. To add to the difficulty, the word indexes in the individual volumes, while often helpful, are not always complete; and once the researcher finds the right article, he or she must decipher a dense, if not impenetrable, florescence of abbreviations.[5] Despite these challenges, however, the *FEW* remains the first and frequently the last obligatory consultation for an etymon in OOc. The one-volume *Dictionnaire étymologique de la langue française*, compiled by Oscar Bloch and Walther von Wartburg (1968), may be used as a key to the *FEW*, providing that the OOc word in question has a cognate in French, as many do. It is hoped that the Glossary of the present book, by its systematic references to the *FEW* for all the etyma found there, will facilitate access to this monument of linguistic scholarship.

Kurt Baldinger has simultaneously launched two projects, the *Dictionnaire onomasiologique de l'ancien occitan (DAO)* and the *Dictionnaire onomasiologique de l'ancien gascon (DAG)*, both appearing in fascicles since 1975. They are organized on the principle of onomasiology, the study of the expression of ideas in language (Gk. ονομα 'name'). Instead of an alphabetical order of words, they follow an order of concepts proceeding from Universe, to Mankind, to Relations between Mankind and the Universe. The *DAO*, which supplements the vocabularies of *LR* and *S-W* with the *FEW* and glossaries from more recent editions, has published, as of 1994, six fascicles containing articles from "1 univers, 2 monde . . . " to "999 caille-lait" (rennet). A supplement in five fascicles gives words found in neither *LR* or *S-W*. The *DAO* gives all recorded spellings, with their dates but without contexts. The *DAG* includes words attested in the Gascon region of southwestern France, with contexts and sources.

[5] There is no general index for the first fourteen volumes, nor for the first twenty-four (not yet, at least). Abbreviations of place-names and publications were listed in the *Beiheft* (2nd ed., 1950) and the *Supplement* (1957).

Helmut Stimm and Wolf-Dieter Stempel have launched *Diction-naire de l'occitan médiéval* (1996–), which offers clear taxonomy of meanings; selected citations; extensive references to sources, including lyric poetry, other literature, and documents; remarks on etymology; and references to other dictionaries listing the term.

For proper names we have two dictionaries: Chambers (*Proper Names, 1971*) on proper names in general and Wiacek (1968) on geographical and ethnic names. For items in Wiacek's narrower area, the scholar should consult both works.

LITERARY STUDIES

For concise introductory treatments of troubadour poetry, see Di Girolamo (1989), Marrou (1971), Mölk (1982), and Riquer (1975, 1: 9–102). The standard older treatment, still invaluable for its expertise in the troubadours and its wealth of historical information, although dated by its positivism and its condescending attitude, is Jeanroy (*Poésie lyrique*, 1934). Taylor (1977) has a section on literary history and criticism. For a guide to research on troubadour song, see Switten (1995), supplemented by Aubrey's study (1996). The *Handbook of the Troubadours* (ed. Akehurst and Davis, 1995) includes essays by various hands on all the major aspects of the subject.

Chambers, *Old Provençal Versification* (1985), provides an introduction and an overview. For tabulation of the metrical form of all known troubadour poems, see Frank; for an explanation of Frank's methods, see the note on meter that accompanies the reading in chapter 2.

ANTHOLOGIES

The fullest selection in English is Hill and Bergin (1973), with 181 texts and a glossary but no translations. Fuller yet is Riquer, with 371 texts, Spanish translations, and an extensive introduction, but no glossary. Hamlin, Ricketts, and Hathaway (1985) contains 61 texts, a concise introduction, helpful notes to the texts, and a glossary.

Two classics in the field are Bartsch (1904) and Appel, *Provenzalische* (1930). In addition to the texts, Bartsch remains valuable for its glossary (written in French); Appel offers a mine for morphology, and has an excellent glossary (in German). Both Bartsch and Appel provide a broad representation of the literature, including not only the lyric poetry of troubadours. Appel adds narrative poetry, didactic poetry, and prose, while Bartsch offers a selection of fourteenth-century texts.

The Modern Language Association publishes the *MLA Interna-tional Bibliography of Books and Articles on the Modern Languages and Literatures*, including sections on Occitan literature and language; there is an elaborate subject index. As the title indicates, the *MLA Bibliography* does not include book reviews, unlike the other annual bibliographies described below. The entire bibliography since 1963 is now computerized, published on CD-ROM, and frequently updated, which enables the scholar to search for specific subjects, such as a troubadour, a genre, or a scholar, with speed and efficiency. Coverage of books has never been as thorough as coverage of articles.

Britain's Modern Humanities Research Association publishes the *Year's Work in Modern Language Studies*, with a section "Occitan Studies," divided since 1979 into subsections on literature and language; the one on language, formerly sporadic, appeared annually from 1991 through 1994. The *YWMLS* is written in prose, with useful descriptive and evaluative remarks. There are indexes of subjects and names.

The *Romanische Bibliographie* (1961–) grew out of the bibliographical supplements to the *Zeitschrift für romanische Philologie* (1875–1960). There are separate sections listing items on Occitan linguistics and literature.

Tenso, the bulletin of the Société Guilhem IX, has included detailed enumerative bibliographies of Occitan studies since 1984, with a separate linguistic bibliography since 1987. Both are indexed.

These four annual bibliographies provide four distinct perspectives on the field: American, British, German, and the most specialized. For 1993, the most recent year available for all four publications as of this writing, the numbers of items included are shown in table 31.1.

TABLE 31.1 *Focus of Four Annual Bibliographies*

	Literature	Language	Year Published
MLA Bibliography	35	107	1994
Year's Work	104	289	1994
Romanische Bibliographie	123	69	1995
Tenso	145	305	1994–95

Each scholar will learn to rely on one or another of these research instruments, depending on factors such as accessibility, informativeness, coverage, and speed of publication. All four provide valuable service.

The Société Guilhem IX is the American organization for Occitan studies. It publishes *Tenso* (see above), with articles, reviews, bibliographies, and notices of events of interest, and sponsors sessions at scholarly meetings.

The European society for Occitan studies is the Association Internationale d'Etudes Occitanes, which has published, since 1985, a series of occasional *Bulletins de l'Association Internationale d'Etudes Occitanes*, addressing what needs to be done in general (no. 1; 1985) and especially in sociolinguistics (nos. 2–3; 1988); reviewing research in progress (no. 4; 1989); listing additions to the bibliography by Taylor (nos. 5–6; 1990); and discussing research tools, chiefly in Occitan linguistics and modern literature (nos. 7–8; 1990).

GENERAL REFERENCE

For earlier works in Occitan linguistics, see Klingebiel (*Bibliographie*, 1986). For a recent synthesis of historical research on the social background of the troubadours, see Paterson (1993).

Extending beyond the immediate area of Occitan, some recent and invaluable resources are the following.

The *Dictionnaire des lettres françaises: Le Moyen Âge* contains articles with bibliography on individual troubadours, Occitan works and genres, as well as French and Latin texts.

Medieval France: An Encyclopedia is intended as "an introduction to the political, economic, social, religious, intellectual, literary, and artistic history of France from the early 5th century to the late 15th" (vii).

The *Grundriss der romanischen Literaturen des Mittelalters* (1968–93) proposed to review and systematize knowledge of all the medieval Romance literatures. It appeared in fascicles; each volume comprises two parts, the first historical, the second documentary. Most important for Occitan is volume 2: *Les genres lyriques*, ed. Erich Köhler (1979–90). Other Occitan matters are treated in volumes 1: *Généralités*, ed. Maurice Delbouille (1972); 3: *Les épopées romanes*, ed. Rita Lejeune (1981–); 4: *Le roman jusqu'à la fin du XIIIe siècle*, ed. Jean Frappier and Reinhold R. Grimm (1978–84); 5: *Les formes narratives brèves*, ed. Wolf-Dieter Lange (1985–); 6: *La littérature didactique, allégorique et satirique*, ed. Hans Robert Jauss (1968–70); and 11: *La littérature historiographique des origines à 1500*, ed. Hans Ulrich Gumbrecht et al. (1986–93).

The *Lexikon des Mittelalters* (1980–) is appearing in fascicles. As of 1996 we have seven complete volumes and parts of the eighth, running from A- to Theoria. The *Lexikon* is strong on history, art history, church history, and law.

The *Dictionary of the Middle Ages* (1982–89) is especially valuable on historical matters.

The *Enciclopedia dantesca* (1970–78) embraces Dante's world, which included much of importance to Occitan study.

The *International Medieval Bibliography* appears in two numbers annually, with about five thousand items listed in each recent issue. The broad historical perspective includes sections ranging alphabetically from Archaeology, Architecture, Archives, Art History . . . to Daily Life, Demography . . . to Social History, Technology, Theology, and Women's Studies. There are indexes of authors and subjects.

READING 31

Raimon de Cornet, *A San Marsel d'Albeges, prop de Salas*

*Raimon de Cornet was the only prolific poet among the successors of the troubadours, known as the School of Toulouse, who wrote in Occitan during the fourteenth and fifteenth centuries. A priest and friar, Raimon was active around 1324–40. He left more than forty Occitan lyrics, two Latin poems, and other works, including verse letters, an **ensenhamen**, or didactic treatise, a grammar, and several texts on computation.*

In this selection Raimon narrates a comic episode in the first person, drawing humorous effect from his identity as a priest. The effect recalls the fabliau of Guilhem IX (reading 9) and has parallels with the fourteenth-century Spanish Libro de buen amor *by Juan Ruiz, archpriest of Hita, as well as with Chaucer's Miller's Tale.*

Rubric in ms. T^a:
Frayre Ramon de Cornet, Truffa.

1
A San Marsel d'Albeges, prop de Salas,
estie logatz ab un senhor de pestre
don fi mon dan d'una trop bela garsa
que·m fetz esquern, qu'ieu volgra que fos arsa
ez ieu pendutz, qu'en degra trop miels estre,   5
car no·m gardiey d'aytals fazendas malas;
e dir vos ay tot l'esquern per far rire.

2
Hieu amie lies de bon cor, per ver dire,
ez ela mi, segon que fe semlansa,
si que tot jorn nos bayzem d'amor fina;   10
mas pueus d'un jorn, quan li venc en ayzina,

pres del mieu cors trop sobriera venjansa,
no say per que, mas, segon mon albire,
car sol me vi bayzar un'autra toza.

3

Apres d'un jorn, ab cara fort joyoza,   15
s'en venc a mi dins un loc cecretari,
en mon ostal, qu'ieu pres de lies tenia;
ieu, que la vi, diey a mon clergue via,
car cugie far l'orde de San Macari;
mas ela dihs, "Un pauc suy vergonjoza;   20
fe que·m devetz, no·m toquetz d'esta pauza."

4

Hyeu fuy dolens, a for trop d'avol cauza,
que, lies bayzan e tocan sas popetas,
dormigui tan tro qu'en fon ora bassa;
e dir vos ay que·m fetz la vils bagassa.
De flic en floc, ab unas tozoyretas   25
tot lo mieu cap tondet—vejatz gran bauza!
Pueus anet s'en ab mos pels en sa borsa.

5

Ressidiey me, pueus cugie de gran corsa
far lo mestier, mas lies no vi ne prezi,
ni de mos pels no conoygui la fauta;   30
mas per gran dol me diey sus en la gauta,
e lauzi·n Dieu car lo cotel no·m mezi,
que trop per luy fora mes en encorsa.
Er vos diray cum me pres de ma testa.

6

Pueus l'endema fon de San Miquel festa   35
e cugie dir a las gens granda messa,
mas quan me fuy revestitz ab ma capa
rizeron tug e dishero que·l papa
degra donar perdos a preveyressa,
car m'ac tondut; pueus feyro lor enquesta   40
quals o poc far, que tan gen me saub tondre.

7

"Pro fa qui·n va e dos tans qui n'escapa,"
so·m cogitie quan vi la traydoressa
e l'autra gen que·m menero tempesta,   45
qu'ab pauc de dol no·m cugie viu rebondre.

Meter:

   a   b   c   c   b   a   d
  10' 10' 10' 10' 10' 10' 10'

Sirv. 6 s 7, 1–4.
Coblas capcaudadas.
a = **-alas, -ire, -ǫza, -auza, -ǫrsa, -ęsta.**
b = **-ęstre, -ansa, -ari, -ętas, -ęzi, -ęssa.**
c = **-arsa, -ina, -ia, -assa, -auta, -apa.**
d = **-ire, -ǫza, -auza, -ǫrsa, -ęsta, -ǫndre.**
Frank 810a: note.

Zufferey, *Bibliographie* 558,8. Major edition: Noulet and Chabaneau, no. 51.
Two manuscripts: *T^a*, fol. 43v; *Z* fol. 123–v. Base *T^a*.
Stanza order: Uniform.
Rejected reading in the base manuscript: (46) no *T^a*, no·m *Z*.
Variants in *Z:* (0) En Ramon de Cornet. (2) estey logat. (5) pendut. (8) ami. (10) baysam. (15) apres un. (21) esta. (22) dolens] temens; fort. (25) vil. (33) Deus; car] can. (38) revestit.

Notes

(1) Saint-Marcel (commune in the canton of Cordes, arrondissement of Gaillac, Tarn), about 12 miles north of Albi (hence in the Albigeois) and about 3 miles west of the village of Salles.

(2) **estię**] The first person singular preterit ending **-ię** recurs in **amię** 8; **cugię** 19, 29, 37, 46; **cogitię** 44. It is regarded as a reduction of **-ięi**, the diphthongized form of normal **-ęi**, by Noulet and Chabaneau (170), who compare the orthographic variation **lęis/lięis/lięs**. **un senhor de pestre**] Cf. Chaucer's Monk, "A manly man, to been an abbot able" (General Prologue to the *Canterbury Tales*, v. 167).

(10) **amor fina**] Closer to the modern image of courtly love is **fin'amors** in Bernart de Ventadorn (16.4).

(19) **far l'orde de san Macari**] To make love. Pun on CL CARŌ, ACC. CARNEM, OOc **carn**, ModOc *car, charn*, by which **Macari** = **ma carn, ma car** 'my flesh.' Saint Macaire, fourth century; feast, 15 January; Latin MACAREUM (L & S).

(24) **dormiguí**] Compare **conoyguí** 31. Beginning in the fourteenth century, preterit 1st sg. **partí** and the remaining forms in the preterit were reconstructed using 3rd sg. **partíc** as the root (Lafont in Holtus, Metzeltin, and Schmitt 11). Such forms were criticized in the *Leys d'amors*, no doubt because of their novelty at the time (Gatien-Arnoult 2: 384–86; Anglade, *Las leys* 3: 160–61).

(27) Shaving the head was a sign of ignominy or derision; in law it was a punishment like whipping, blinding, or cutting off a foot or a hand. At the end of World War II, French women who had collaborated with the occupying Germans had their heads shaved. Cf. also the story of Samson and Delilah.

(30) **prézi**] Preterit, 1st sg.; cf. **mézi** 33, **láuzi** 33. Reconstruction of OOc pret., 1st sg. **pris**, using 3rd sg. **pres** as the root, with the ending -yod from 1st sg. **cantéi, vendéi**. Similar reconstruction of OOc 1st sg. **mis**

on the root 3rd sg. **mes**. In OOc **lauzar** was weak (1st sg. **lauzéi**), but in **láuzi** it has been treated as strong, like **prézi**, **mézi**.

(33–34) The narrator thanks God for not putting a knife in his hands, because in his grief he could have wounded or killed himself, and so could have been damned as a suicide. It is a commonplace of romance that the lover who cannot see his lady wishes to kill himself, as in Marie de France, "Lanval": "C'est merveille k'il ne s'ocit!" (Rychner, v. 346).

(36) **de San Miquel**] The archangel Michael, chief of the heavenly host, often depicted with a sword. His feast occurs on 29 September.

(37) **e**] Introduces the main verb and is therefore omitted from English translation; that is, **cugié** is the main verb and is not coordinate with **fon** 36.

(40) **preveyressa**] 'Concubine of a priest.' There may be an ironic effect in the suffix, by contrast with its respectful usage in **comtesa**, **duchesa**, and so on.

CHAPTER 32

Epilogue: Modern Occitan

ORTHOGRAPHY AND DIALECTS

Most twentieth-century transcriptions of Modern Occitan employ an orthography formulated by Louis Alibert in 1935 and promoted by the Institut des Etudes Occitanes, in Toulouse. We shall see an instance of this orthography in the reading that accompanies this chapter.

The Alibert orthography presents ModOc in a manner resembling the orthography of the troubadours. It does not attempt to represent the phonetic realization of ModOc in its various dialects but rather to mediate among those dialects by providing a representation of the language that can be employed by speakers of all of them. Since the common ground shared by the dialects is the historical form of the language from which they have developed, the Alibert orthography presents a conservative view. It is thus analogous to the orthography of Modern English or French, both of which retain features several hundred years old: the English orthography *knight* represents the Chaucerian pronunciation [knɪht] instead of modern [najt]; French *aimer* represents eleventh- or twelfth-century [ajmer], not modern [ęmę].

Unlike French or English, however, ModOc lacks a spoken standard. In fact, there are five or more dialects with numerous subdialects (Bec, *Langue occitane* 37–55). Dialects of the northern group palatalize initial **ka-** and **ga-**, as in Old French: **chanta** 'he sings' is pronounced [tʃanto]; **jalina** 'hen' is pronounced [dʒalino]. These dialects include Limousin to the west, around Limoges, Auvergnat in the center, and Alpine Provençal east of the Rhône. The dialects of the southern group, which preserve initial **ka-** and **ga-**, as in Spanish and Italian (**canta** 'he sings,' **gal** 'chicken'), include Languedocien around Toulouse and Provençal east of the Rhône, along the coast. Even this image of five dialect areas fails, however,

336

to represent adequately the diversity of ModOc, since these dialects lack clear geographical borders.

> Les zones dialectales, pour réelles qu'elles soient, s'inter
> pénètrent à leurs frontières et l'on passe, la plupart du
> temps, insensiblement d'une zone à l'autre. . . . En pous
> sant les choses à l'extrême, on pourrait donc dire, comme
> certains dialectologues, que les dialectes n'existent pas: il
> n'y a que des aires indépendantes et, par voie de con
> séquence, autant de dialectes que de villages. (Bec, *Langue*
> *occitane* 34–35)

The dialects were already distinct in the medieval language,[1] but
for the reader of troubadour texts, which combine traits of the dialects into the medieval koine (see Preface), the most striking contrast between OOc and ModOc is the evolution from one to many
forms of the language, from the koine into a condition of extreme
dialectal diversity. The Alibert orthography attempts to bestride
this evolution.

EXTERNAL HISTORY

The dialectalization of ModOc has resulted from the decentering
and effacement of the koine in competition with French. Although
this competition has left a series of palpable traces, its inner dynamism, the cause that has propelled it forward, remains difficult to
grasp. The two most dramatic moments in this competition between languages occurred in the sixteenth and the nineteenth centuries: one was adverse for Occitan, the Edict of Villers-Cotterêts
(1539), and the other was favorable, the foundation of the Félibrige
(1854). Both were bound up in conflicting forces.

By the Edict of Villers-Cotterêts, François I declared that all legal documents in the kingdom must be composed in French.[2] "The
main purpose of the act . . . was the reform of the judicial system.
The use of French in legal documents was aimed at avoiding retrials by eradicating from judgments all 'ambiguity, uncertainty or
reason to demand an interpretation'" (Knecht 358). The intention
was principally to suppress Latin, but Occitan became an inciden

---

[1] "The people of Montaillou [in the Pyrenees] were very much aware of a local
dialect spoken by about a thousand people at the most" in the fourteenth century (Le Roy Ladurie 286).

[2] For the text of the edict, see Isambert et al. (12: 600–40). Clause 111 prescribes
the use of French in legal documents: "Et pour ce que telles choses [doubts
about the meaning of legislation] sont souvent advenues sur l'intelligence des
mots latins contenus esdits arrests, nous voulons d'oresnavant que tous
arrests . . . soient prononcés, enregistrés et délivrés aux parties en langage
maternel françois et non autrement" (12: 622–23).

tal victim in the south, where it had been employed in an administrative koine since the beginning of the twelfth century. In fact, however, French had already begun to blend with Occitan in legal documents as early as the fourteenth century and became progressively more widespread, depending on the region, during the fifteenth (Bec, *Langue occitane* 75, 80–81). Furthermore, the edict was only sporadically enforced. Although French supplanted Occitan within a decade after the edict in Provence, Latin continued to be used into the early seventeenth century in the region of Nantes (Knecht 359); Gascon continued in legal usage to the end of the century (King Henry IV wrote in Gascon), and Catalan continued in legal usage in Roussillon until 1738.[3] Evidence that French entered southern literary culture before the edict comes from the Consistòri del Gai Saber in Toulouse, founded in 1323 with the express purpose of maintaining the Occitan literary standard—but which transformed itself, in 1513, into the Collège de rhétorique et de poésie françaises (Brun 204). In 1554 the Collège de rhétorique awarded one of its annual prizes, a silver eglantine, to Pierre de Ronsard, for his recently published *Amours* (Nolhac 297–98).

Although the edict has been mistaken for the real cause of a decline in Occitan, for all these reasons it must be considered symbolic. The real cause of the penetration of French into Occitan territory, and of the edict as well, must have been the complex, powerful, and diffuse cultural drive of the Renaissance, with its privileging of pan-European cultural ideals, and the contemporary evolution of the nation-state.[4] The edict may thus be seen as a juridical version of the impulse to enhance the vernacular that animated Du Bellay ten years later in his *Défense et illustration de la langue française* (1549). The monarchy of François I was receptive to Renaissance values, in part because of its earlier evolution from less powerful feudal origins.

In this broad framework we may see the larger significance of the Albigensian Crusade, too often cited as an explanation, sufficient in itself, of the decline from the troubadours of Old Occitan to the lesser poets of Middle Occitan.[5] The crusade accomplished both less than this and more: less because it invaded only Languedoc, not Provence, the Limousin, or Auvergne, and because the invasion of 1209–29 can scarcely have led to the demise of the troubadour era if that age continued until the end of the thirteenth

---

[3] The revolution was hostile to dialects on the grounds that they hindered national unity, but Occitan was nevertheless employed at times for revolutionary propaganda (Bec, *Langue occitane* 84–85).

[4] "C'est l'esprit de la Renaissance qui pénètre jusqu'aux conseils de la Couronne" (Brun 91).

[5] We are cautioned against such exaggeration by Marrou (173) and by A. Lewis (67). See Paden, "Troubadours."

century, or even until the mid-fourteenth (Bec, *Langue occitane* 89); but more because the eventual result of the provisions of the Treaty of Paris (1229) was to bring Languedoc into the secure possession of the king of France. The crusade was one of many moves, lacking in concert or intention, that contributed to the centralization of French culture today.

Within Occitania a first rebirth was evidenced in the work of poets such as the Gascon Protestant Pey de Garros (died 1581), the Provençal Bellaud de la Bellaudière (died 1588), and Pierre Goudouli of Toulouse (died 1649). A second Occitan renaissance occurred in the nineteenth century with the foundation of the Félibrige, or association of *félibres* 'nurselings,' seven poets of Provence who set out to reform Provençal spelling, renew the language, and revive the culture. The greatest of these poets, Frédéric Mistral, triumphed with the publication of his romantic epic *Mirèio* ('Mireille') in 1859, and shared the Nobel Prize in literature in 1904.[6] Another was Théodore Aubanel, whose collection of love poems, *La mióugrano entre-duberto* ('The Split Pomegranate'), appeared in 1860. The orthography proposed by the Félibrige, based on the local dialect of Maillane, Mistral's birthplace near Arles in the department of Bouches-du-Rhône, never gained a wide following west of the Rhône. It is largely supplanted today by the Alibert orthography, based on the Languedocien of the Toulouse region. For a linguist and a proponent of the Alibert orthography such as Pierre Bec, himself a Gascon poet, the Félibrige marked a decisive step in the restoration of the language: "Avant elle, c'était l'anarchie la plus totale; avant elle surtout, *on ne croyait pas* à une survie possible de l'occitan et, encore moins, à ses possibilités littéraires" (Bec, *Langue occitane* 106; his italics). For Bec, the Félibrige readied the Occitan movement, once strengthened by a superior orthographic system, for a future renaissance.

INTERNAL HISTORY

The two centuries of Middle Occitan, from about 1350 to 1550, saw the development of features that remain characteristic of the language (Bec, *Langue occitane* 90–91).

In phonology, unstressed final **a** closed to **o**: **porta** is pronounced [pórto]. Close **o** and pretonic **o** closed to [u]: **onor** is pronounced [unúr]; **Tolosa**, [tulúzo]. In the OOc ending **-ía**, the accent shifted and the two syllables became one, with the result either [-jó] or [-jé]. Hence OOc **avía** 'he had' came to be pronounced [abyó] or [avjé].

---

[6] The Nobel Prize recognized Mistral's accomplishments in both poetry and philology. On his dictionary of ModOc, *Lou tresor dóu Felibrige*, see below.

In morphology, declension in two cases disappeared entirely. Analogical feminine adjectives such as **granda** and **forta** replaced etymological **gran** and **fort**. Enclitic pronouns were restored to syllabic value (OOc **l'om que·m vei** 'the man who sees me' became **l'ome que me vei**). In the present tense, the first and second persons singular took on an analogical unstressed vowel where they lacked one: OOc 1st sg. **cant** became **cante**, **canti**, or **canto**; 2nd sg. **partz** became **partes**. Strong preterit forms took on weak endings: OOc **ac** 'he had' became **aguét**, like **cantét**. The preterit tense marker, zero in OOc, was replaced, except in the third person singular, with an **r** generalized from the third person plural, and preterit person markers were normalized, so that the conjugation changed as follows:

	OOc	Middle Oc
1st sg.	**cantéi**	**cantéri**
2nd sg.	**cantést**	**cantéres**
3rd sg.	**cantét**	**cantét**
1st pl.	**cantém**	**cantérem**
2nd pl.	**cantétz**	**cantéretz**
3rd pl.	**cantéron**	**cantéron**

POPULATION

It is not easy to know how many people speak Occitan. The French census does not register linguistic competence; the last governmental report on the linguistic situation, issued in 1864, noted that in some departments in the Pyrenees as many as 90 percent of the people knew no French—that is, they were monolingual in Occitan. In 1921 Joseph Anglade estimated that 12 to 14 million people in France spoke or understood the language (*Grammaire* 5). Nine years later, Jules Ronjat hazarded that 10 million French people spoke Occitan, including perhaps 9 million for whom it was their usual language (26). An assessment made in 1974 showed a total of 7 to 8 million speakers of Occitan in France, including 6 million bilinguals who understood and spoke the language but used it only occasionally, and 1 to 2 million bilinguals who usually spoke it, but not outside their towns or families. The same survey found an additional 120,000 bilingual speakers of Alpine Provençal in Italy, 60,000 of whom used that dialect daily, and in Spain an additional 5,000 speakers of a Gascon dialect (Kloss and McConell 5: 232, 335, 454). According to this report, then, all these speakers of Occitan in France and Italy were bilingual—which means that there must be no monolingual speakers of Occitan left, with the possible exception of the Gascon speakers in Spain. In 1976 *Le monde de l'éducation* reported that Occitan was still spoken regularly by at least 2 million *occitanophones*, one-sixth of the total number of those who spoke it at all (cited in Quemada 142). Another source, in 1978, estimated a total of 3 to 5 million speakers—regular, usual, or occasional—in France (Kloss and McConnell 5: 232).

In 1981 Georg Kremnitz reported that there were few if any monolingual speakers left (1, 11–15, 59–63). Occitan was still spoken by perhaps 1 or 2 million people regularly, and occasionally by another 1 or 2 million. Speakers tended to be older (over 60), and male rather than female. Occitan was spoken in villages but scarcely heard at all in cities. Occitan was rarely learned as a first language, which was French throughout France; there was a notable tendency to learn Occitan between the ages of eight or nine and thirteen or older.

The *New York Times* reported, just a little more than a decade later, that "in a region of 15 million people across the southern tier of France, only three million are believed to speak at least some Occitan" (Simons).

These estimates suggest a rapid decline in the total number of speakers of the language. Anecdotal information, even less reliable, confirms the impression. It is not uncommon to meet young *Méridionaux* who say that their grandparents spoke only Occitan, their parents spoke Occitan at home but French at work, and they themselves speak only French, with lingering childhood memories of Occitan, if that. Some of these people have set to learning Occitan as a foreign language. The development of the European Union, together with the perceived threats of global English and the Americanization of Europe, has inspired a contrary movement of regional loyalty as a defense against rapid social and cultural change.

PROSPECT

Dalmatian, a Romance language of the Adriatic coast southeast of Venice, died in 1898 with the death of its last native speaker. The centennial of that event, in 1998, bodes ill for Occitan, in the opinion of many speakers of the language.[7] A documentary videotape called *La batalha de la lenga* reports a deep pessimism. One retired gentleman depicted in the video says to the camera, as he tends a herd of sheep in the countryside of Languedoc:

> E ben, vertadièrament, . . . lo patés, ieu ai lo socit que finisca que se pèrda. Nautres lo parlam, mas los joves lo par-

---

[7] Wheeler is gloomier yet: "It is hard to be optimistic about the survival of Occitan as a living language into the twenty-first century" (277).

lan pas pus. Lo parlan . . . , lo comprenon, mas lo parlan pas gaire.

> Well, in truth, our dialect, I am afraid that it will finally be lost. We speak it, but young people speak it no more. They speak it . . . , they understand it, but they don't speak it much.

Or an Occitan poet, Yves Rouquette:

> Si on arrive (je n'en suis pas là) à la sérénité, c'est parce qu'on est parfaitement désespéré . . . et que pour être parfaitement désespéré il faut beaucoup avoir aimé et aimer encore le monde. . . . Je suis totalement désespéré, je n'ai aucun espoir sur la langue d'oc. . . . Je crois que je suis un homme comme tous les autres; ma langue vaut rien, les autres non plus; elle va mourir, les autres mourront. La seule chose qui mourra pas, c'est . . . notre trace. (Bickerton and Davies, transcript 13, 32–33)

Although it is true that increasing numbers of *Méridionaux* are learning the language in Occitan schools called **calendretas** ('fledgling skylarks'), a survey has shown that even in such schools, "the proportion of teachers predicting the language's demise is roughly equivalent to the number of those who wish to see Occitan raised to co-functionality with French."[8] Even today, "transmission of the Occitan dialects through the family is waning—moribund, if not already defunct" (Klingebiel, rev. 488).

If Occitan does live on, it will live no doubt among bilinguals, as it already does, who will preserve it as a language of emotional expression. "Es una lenga de la vida, de l'afectivitat" (Bickerton and Davies, transcript 30): 'It is a language of life, of emotion. . . .' Pierre Bec pleads, "Une France humainement élargie ne serait-elle pas assez riche pour avoir plusieurs cultures?" (*Langue occitane* 125).

Whatever its destiny, Occitan has had, and always will have had, the history of a major European language and culture.

RESEARCH TOOLS

For characterization of ModOc, see Bec, *Langue occitane* (1967). A more detailed linguistic sketch is provided by Wheeler. Fernández González, in his *Gramática histórica* (1985), presents OOc and ModOc together in a diachronic perspective. The standard historical treatment of ModOc is Ronjat (1930–41). An outstanding sociolinguistic study is Kremnitz (1981).

[8] Cichon 330, quoted by Klingebiel, rev. 489. On the **calendretas**, see Bickerton and Davies, transcript 18.

The standard dictionary of ModOc is Mistral's *Lou tresor dóu Felibrige* (1879–87). Mistral attempted to include all the modern dialects of Occitan, with frequent citations, formal variants, etymologies, paradigms, place-names, personal names, proverbs, and background information on customs, institutions, traditions, and history. A major source of the *Tresor*, and still valuable, is Honnorat (1846–47), with more than 100,000 words. Another complement to Mistral is Coupier (1995), rich in Modern Occitan synonyms.

On the literature of Modern Occitan, see Lafont and Anatole (1970).

READING 32

Martí, *Cridarai*

Born in 1940, Martí has become a leader of the Occitan resistance movement, a singer whose performances have taken on the character of political action meetings. In the song "Cridarai" he rallies his listeners to the defense of Occitania. The historical allusions in the song evoke the Chanson de la Croisade albigeoise. *As a regionalist anthem it may also be compared with the less politicized song by Peire Vidal, "Ab l'alen tir vas me l'aire" (ch. 2).*

M'ajudèsse lo vent   e son bufar de farga,
de sas èrsas iretjas   m'ajudèsse la mar;
    cridarai!
Tot al lòng del camin   ieu sonarai las pèiras,
los bartàs, los valats,   los arbres mai los bòscs.   5
    Cridarai
tant qu'aurai una votz   e quicòm dins mon pitre,
    cridarai
a me·n faire petar   la carn de la garganta,
e me·n faire gisclar   la sang dins un crit baug: 10

cridarai, cridarai,   cridarai, cridarai,
com'un òme tancat   per agaitar l'asuèlh,
un òme disliurat   del pes de sas cadenas
qu'an fargat los reis fòls   e los barons sagnós
e los mong engorits,   del rebat del brasas,   15
ont cremèron vivents   mos fraires del passat
qu'avián cantat l'amor   e l'amistat umana,
e manjat lo pan blanc   pastat de libertat.

Cridarai, cridarai,   cridarai, cridarai!

Transcription from the record, in the International Phonetic Alphabet
(the symbol ' denotes stress on the following syllable):

[maʒy'dɛse lu βɛn e su by'fa de 'fargo
de sus 'ɛrsos i'rɛdʒos maʒy'dɛse la mar

    kriða're
tut al lun dal ka'mi jɛw suna're las 'pejros
lus 'bartas lus βa'lats lus 'arbres maj lus bɔs   5
    kriða're
tan kaw're yna βɔts e ki'kɔm din mun 'pitre
    kriða're
a men 'fajre pe'ta la kar de la gar'ganto
a men 'fajre dʒis'kla la san dinz yn crit bɔ   10

kriða're kriða're kriða're kriða're
kom yn 'ome tan'ta pɛr aga'tʃa la'zyl
yn 'ome dezliw'rat dal pes de sus ka'ðenos
kan far'ga lus rejs fɔls e lus ba'run sa'ŋus
e lus munʒɛngu'rits dal re'ba de 'brasus   15
un kra'maro βi'βen mus 'frajres dal pa'sat
ka'vjan kan'tat la'mɔr e lamis'tat y'mano
e man'ʒa lu pã blã pas'tat de liber'tat

kriða're kriða're kriða're kriða're]

Meter: Twelve-syllable line with caesura (6 + 6), as in other songs of Martí, and in
the *Chanson de la Croisade albigeoise* (see ch. 25), which Martí evokes by
mention of the burning of heretics and troubadours. Assonances on a delimit
the three strophes: couplets ending in feminine (**á–a**), then masculine (**á**),
occur in verses 1–2, 9–10, and 17–18. The word refrain of three syllables
(the title of the song, "Cridarai!") has no direct analogue in the *Chanson*.
However, its quadruple repetition at the end produces a concluding full line
reminiscent, perhaps, of the half line in the *Chanson*, which ends each laisse
and is repeated at the beginning of the next.

Major editions: Pécout 82–83. Recording: *Martí: Lo pais que vol viure,* 33 rpm
(Paris: Chant du monde, [1973]). Orthography from Pécout, text from
recording.

Variants (sigla: *J* = jacket of recording; *P* = Pécout; *R* = recording): (11) cridarai]
Once JP, four times R. (12) coma *JP,* com' *R.* (14) sagnós *PR,* sagnoses *J.* (15)
monges enrogits *JP,* mong'engorits *R.* (19) cridarai] *Twice P, four times JR.*

Notes

(1) **ajudèsse**] Past subjunctive, 3rd sg., OOc **ajudés**. ModOc has generalized the final unstressed vowel, originally a support vowel to make the
2nd sg. person marker **-s** perceptible:

	OOc	ModOc
1st sg.	ajudés	ajudésse
2nd sg.	ajudésses	ajudésses
3rd sg.	ajudés	ajudésse

(2) **iretjas**] Mistral **eirège, irètge**, from OOc **erętge** 'hérétique, Cathare'; the meaning 'hérétique' is now archaic, having been replaced by 'obstiné, capricieux,' or as Pécout translates the line, 'hargneux' (E. 'surly, morose').

(14) **los reis fòls**] Perhaps a reference to Philip Augustus (1180–1223) and Louis VIII (1223–1226), kings during the crusade but both lucidly sane, in derogatory association with Charles VI (1380–1422), who was afflicted by madness. **los barons sagnós**] Such as Simon de Montfort (see ch. 25).

(15) **los monges**] Such as Folquet de Marselha, at first a troubadour, then a monk, then elected bishop of Toulouse, and in that capacity one of the spiritual leaders of the crusade.

(17) **avián**] Since OOc **-ía**, the stress has shifted, and the two syllables have become one.

APPENDIXES

Morphological Tables

I. VERBS

	-ar	non-**ar**	irregular	
	cantár	**partír**	**avér**	**éser**
	'to sing'	'to leave'	'to have'	'to be'

A. Present Set

Present Indicative

1st sg.	cant	part	ai	sọi
2nd sg.	cántas	partz	as	ẹst
3rd sg.	cánta	part	a	ẹs
1st pl.	cantám	partẹ́m	avẹ́m	ẹm
2nd pl.	cantátz	partẹ́tz	avẹ́tz	ẹtz
3rd pl.	cántan, -on	párton	an	sọṇ

Present Subjunctive

1st sg.	cant	párta	ája	sía
2nd sg.	cantz	pártas	ájas	sías
3rd sg.	cant	párta	ája	sía
1st pl.	cantẹ́m	partám	ajám	siám
2nd pl.	cantẹ́tz	partátz	ajátz	siátz
3rd pl.	cánton	pártan	ájan, -on	sían, -on

Imperfect

1st sg.	cantáva	partía	avía	ẹ́ra
2nd sg.	cantávas	partías	avías	ẹ́ras
3rd sg.	cantáva	partía	avía	ẹ́ra
1st pl.	cantavám	partiám	aviám	erám
2nd pl.	cantavátz	partiátz	aviátz	erátz
3rd pl.	cantávan, -on	partían, -on	avían, -on	ẹ́ran, -on

349

B. Future Set

Future

1st sg.	cantarái	part(i)rái	aurái	serái
2nd sg.	cantarás	part(i)rás	aurás	serás
3rd sg.	cantará	part(i)rá	aurá	será
1st pl.	cantarẹ́m	part(i)rẹ́m	aurẹ́m	serẹ́m
2nd pl.	cantarẹ́tz	part(i)rẹ́tz	aurẹ́tz	serẹ́tz
3rd pl.	cantarán	part(i)rán	aurán	serán

First Conditional

1st sg.	cantaría	part(i)ría	auría	sería
2nd sg.	cantarías	part(i)rías	aurías	serías
3rd sg.	cantaría	part(i)ría	auría	sería
1st pl.	cantariám	part(i)riám	auriám	seriám
2nd pl.	cantariátz	part(i)riátz	auriátz	seriátz
3rd pl.	cantarían	part(i)rían	aurían, -on	serían

C. Past Set

Preterit

1st sg.	cantẹ́i	partí	aic, aguí	fui
2nd sg.	cantẹ́st	partíst	aguíst	fust
3rd sg.	cantẹ́t	partí, -ít, -íc	ac	fọn
1st pl.	cantẹ́m	partím	aguẹ́m	fọm
2nd pl.	cantẹ́tz	partítz	aguẹ́tz	fọtz
3rd pl.	cantẹ́ron	partíron	ágron	fọ́ron

Past Subjunctive

1st sg.	cantẹ́s	partís	aguẹ́s	fọs
2nd sg.	cantẹ́sses	partísses	aguẹ́sses	fọ́sses
3rd sg.	cantẹ́s	partís	aguẹ́s	fọs
1st pl.	cantessẹ́m	partissẹ́m	aguessẹ́m	fossẹ́m
2nd pl.	cantessẹ́tz	partissẹ́tz	aguessẹ́tz	fossẹ́tz
3rd pl.	cantẹ́sson	partísson	aguẹ́sson	fọ́sson

Second Conditional

1st sg.	cantẹ́ra	partíra	ágra	fọ́ra
2nd sg.	cantẹ́ras	partíras	ágras	fọ́ras
3rd sg.	cantẹ́ra	partíra	ágra	fọ́ra
1st pl.	canterám	partirám	agrám	forám
2nd pl.	canterátz	partirátz	agrátz	forátz
3rd pl.	cantẹ́ran	partíran	ágran	fọ́ran

D. Participles

Present Participle

cantán	partẹ́n	(avẹ́n)	(essẹ́n)

Past Participle

cantát, -áda	partít, -ída	avút, agút	estát

II. NOUNS

A. Stable

	Masc.	Fem. -a	Fem. non-a
	'day'	'lady'	'share'
Nom. sg.	jǫrns	dǫmna	partz
Obl. sg.	jǫrn	dǫmna	part
Nom. pl.	jǫrn	dǫmnas	partz
Obl. pl.	jǫrns	dǫmnas	partz

B. Invariable

	Masc.	Fem.
	'body, self'	'voice'
Nom. sg.	cǫrs	vǫtz
Obl. sg.	cǫrs	vǫtz
Nom. pl.	cǫrs	vǫtz
Obl. pl.	cǫrs	vǫtz

C. Shifting

	Masc. -á-	Masc. -ʾe	Masc. -ǫ́n	Masc. -ǫ́r
	'abbot'	'man'	'baron'	'lord'
Nom. sg.	ábas	ǫm	bar	sénher
Obl. sg.	abát	ǫ́me	barǫ́n	senhǫ́r
Nom. pl.	abát	ǫ́me	barǫ́n	senhǫ́r
Obl. pl.	abátz	ǫ́mes	barǫ́ns	senhǫ́rs

	Masc. -adǫ́r	Fem. -ę́r	Fem. -ǫ́r
	'lover'	'woman'	'sister'
Nom. sg.	amáire	mǫ́lher	sǫr
Obl. sg.	amadǫ́r	molhę́r	serǫ́r
Nom. pl.	amadǫ́r	molhę́rs	serǫ́rs
Obl. pl.	amadǫ́rs	molhę́rs	serǫ́rs

III. DEMONSTRATIVES

	Weak	Introductory	Strong

A. Linking ('it, that,' etc.)

	Weak	Introductory	Strong
Neuter	ǫ	sǫ	aisǫ́, acǫ́

B. Near Range ('this,' etc.)

Masculine

	Weak	Introductory	Strong
Nom. sg.	ęst	cęst	aicę́st, aquę́st
Obl. sg.	ęst	cęst	aicę́st, aquę́st
Nom. pl.	ist	cist	aicist, aquist
Obl. pl.	ęstz	cęstz	aicę́stz, aquę́stz

Feminine

	Weak	Introductory	Strong
Nom. sg.	ę́sta	cę́sta	aicę́sta, aquę́sta
Obl. sg.	ę́sta	cę́sta	aicę́sta, aquę́sta
Nom. pl.	ę́stas	cę́stas	aicę́stas, aquę́stas
Obl. pl.	ę́stas	cę́stas	aicę́stas, aquę́stas

C. Far Range

	Weak Personal Pronoun 'he, she'	Weak Definite Article 'the'	Introductory 'that'	Strong 'that!'
Masculine				
Nom. sg.	ęl	lo	cęl	aicęl, aquęl
Obl. sg.	ęl	lo	cęl	aicęl, aquęl
Nom. pl.	il	li	cil	aicíl, aquíl
Obl. pl.	ęls	los	cęls	aicęls, aquęls
Feminine				
Nom. sg.	ęla	la	cęla	aicęla, aquęla
Obl. sg.	ęla	la	cęla	aicęla, aquęla
Nom. pl.	ęlas	las	cęlas	aicęlas, aquęlas
Obl. pl.	ęlas	las	cęlas	aicęlas, aquęlas

Glossary

The glossary lists all the occurrences of every word in the texts. Occasional variant readings that add information of interest are also glossed.

The head form of each entry is normalized according to the principles adopted by Levy in the *Provenzalisches Supplement-Wörterbuch* and the *Petit dictionnaire provençal-français*, for the sake of convenience in consulting these standard references and because such principles provide a quasi-phonetic transcription. The vowels **e** and **o** are distinguished as open (**ę**, **ǫ**) or closed (**ẹ**, **ọ**) when they occur in stressed position. (No such distinction is made for the ending **-ier**, **-er** from Classical Latin -ārĭŭm, however, in view of the uncertainty of the vowel position.) Open **ę** and **ǫ** are not diphthongized. The voiceless sibilant is indicated by **s** (**pesar** 'to think,' Fr. *penser*), the voiced sibilant by **z** (**pezar** 'to displease,' Fr. *peser*). Palatal **l** and **n** are written **lh**, **nh** (**melhor**, **senhor**). **Ca-** is preferred to **cha-** (**cantar**), and **ga-** to **gua-** (**gardar**). "N-mobile" is written **ṇ**. Final **-t** in **-nt** is dropped (**frǫn**).

In the body of the entry, meanings are listed first; there follows a listing of forms categorized according to grammatical functions.

Etymological information is provided within square brackets at the end of each entry. The etymon is given first, with reference to the relevant article in the *Französisches etymologisches Wörterbuch* (*FEW*). Substantive etyma from CL are given in the accusative because the accusative is an attested CL form, even though the effective source of the Romance oblique is a Vulgar Latin oblique combining the CL accusative with the less influential genitive, dative, and ablative. Verbal etyma are given in the infinitive. VL etyma are generally given in CL orthography for consistency. To assist the student in recognizing Latin etyma as well as the Occitan term, derivatives or cognates (which may vary widely in meaning) are listed in Italian, Spanish, and French, occasionally in German, and in English.

a (1) *Vb. trans.* 2.24, 8.6, 11.11, 11.14, 11.17, 12.4, 12.13, 12.26, 12.30 var., 12.39, 13.28, 14.27, 14.41, 14.44, 14.49, 15.19, 16.20, 16.42, 17.20, 17.38, 17.45, 18.13, 18.13, 18.28, 19.3, 19.34, 20.4, 21.64, 28.20, 28.27, 29.11, 30.18, 30.39, 30.40, 30.89, *pres. 3rd sg. of* **aver**, *which see.*

a (2) *prep.* to *(a person as indirect object)* 1.5, 3.6, 3.7, 5.9, 7.12, 9.20, 11.41, 12.40, 13.17, 14.20, 14.21, 15.21, 15.24, 18.4, 18.30, 18.35, 18.38, 20.26, 21.13, 22.29, 23.17, 25.1, 25.8, 25.31, 25.32, 25.32, 25.43, 25.109, 27.3, 27.27, 29.43, 30.38, 30.42, 30.66, 31.18, 31.37, 31.40; to *(a destination)* 1.4, 1.5, 3.7, 3.11, 3.11, 9.21, 11.69, 12.15, 12.17, 12.24, 12.33, 12.54, 13.38, 13.38, 13.72 var., 22.46, 24.29, 25.2, 25.61, 30.11, 30.62; to *(a person as destination)* 1.5, 5.10, 5.14, 9.69, 10.27, 25.60, 25.86, 31.16;
  among 29.16; as *(function)* 11.47, 24.4, 24.4; at *(a place)* 12.51, 13.75, 25.15, 31.1; at *(a time)* 10.37, 11.60, 13.56, 23.48, 24.41, 25.29, 27.35, 30.36; by *(agent in causative construction)* 1.2, 3.7, 23.7, 30.1; by *(spatial)* 9.24, 12.47; for *(a person)* 5.6; for *(a purpose)* 30.6; from *(experience)* 13.59; in *(circumstance)* 30.65; in *(a place)* 4.13, 12.69, 21.14 var., 21.40; in *(a time)* 9.67; into 18.43 var.; on *(an occasion)* 27.2, 28.65; with *(an instrument)* 23.42, 23.42, 26.2; with *(manner)* 1.7.
  In compound prepositions **d'aqui a** as far as 21.69; **pus a** after 14.9; **tro a** down to 9.48; **tro c'a** as far as 2.9, 21.56 var.
  Introducing adverbial phrases **a cartiers** in pieces 25.12, 25.72; **a comt'et a garanda** by count and by measure 20.10; **a dreg** with reason 19.58; **a for** as though 31.22; **a la francesza** in the French style 26.43; **a leu** easily 19.52; **a lonhs** far away 19.4; **a lur volontat** according to their desire 9.44; **a ma vida** for my life 7.16; **a mon talen** just as I wished 9.58; **a obs** to the advantage 11.66; **a pauc . . . no** almost 19.7; **a penas** scarcely 29.15; **a presen** openly 6.22; **a presenssa** openly 6.21; **a randa** all at once 19.9, entirely 20.9; **a sa deviza** as he wants 14.11; **a saupuda** openly 19.59; **a sobrier** excessively 7.4; **a tapi** in a pilgrim's cloak 9.2; **al latz** in his trap 14.48; **al lòng del** along 32.4; **al meyns** at least 4.13; **al mieu plazer** to please me 17.23; **al pus del tot** as much as possible 29.23.
  Introducing inf. 3.7, 5.2 (= **per** 5.2 var., **de** 5.2 var.), 9.25, 11.62, 11.64, 11.80, 16.45, 18.35, 21.43, 32.9; *with def. art.* 12.27, 13.55, 30.4 (see note).
  In verbal constructions **convenir a** to be suitable to 29.2; **dire de no a** to say no to, to refuse to do 12.65; **getar a** to toss into, to consider with 29.36; **se rendre a** to join 5.15; **se tener a deport** to amuse oneself 22.38; **tener a** *(with noun)* to consider (as) 23.33, 24.6, 28.50; **voler ben a** to love 3.5.
  Forms: **a** *passim;* **ad** 1.5, 5.6, 12.54; **az** 18.30. **al** = **a** + **lo** *def. art.* 1.5, 3.11, 5.14, 4.13, 4.13, 9.48, 9.67, 11.41, 11.60, 12.15, 12.24, 12.27, 12.33, 12.47, 12.65, 12.69, 13.38, 13.55, 13.59, 14.9, 14.48, 17.23, 18.4, 21.14 var., 21.40, 21.56 var., 25.29, 27.2, 29.23, 30.1, 30.4, 32.4; **al** = **a** + **los** *def. art.* 25.86; **au** = **a** + **lo** 9.24 var.; **als** = **a** + **los** *def. art.* 1.2, 9.24, 25.1, 25.31, 25.32, 25.32, 29.16, 30.42.
  [CL ăᴅ *FEW* 24: 129; It. *a*, Sp. *a*, Fr. *à*]
a- (3) *prep.* = **ab** *in combined forms* **al** 8.16, **als** 23.28; *see* **ab**.
ab *prep.* with, by means of 2.1, 6.16, 11.49, 12.42, 13.48 var., 13.73, 15.28, 16.47, 22.37, 23.28, 24.15, 25.76, 25.83, 26.15, 26.47, 30.95, 31.26, **als** (= **ab** + **los**) 23.28; with, having 1.3, 1.3, 16.41, 24.23, 25.56, 25.88, 26.1, 26.41, 26.41, 26.43, 31.15; with, in partnership with 13.60, 14.37, 14.38, 28.55, 28.57; with, in relation to 18.33, 27.46; with, in the company of 2.14, 4.2, 4.14, 5.14 var. (= **com** 5.14), 7.19, 10.36, 13.81, 20.31, 21.27, 21.38, 30.58, 30.92; with, in the home of 31.2; with, including

8.28, 25.11; with, together with *(foods)* 26.11; with *(ingredient)* 26.12; with *(manner)* 25.88, 26.5; with, provided there is 13.62; with, taking along 31.28;

according to 14.67 var. (= **per** 14.67); among 29.29; and 12.67, 25.13; from *(fuel)* 26.52; in *(circumstance)* 21.1, 21.1; in *(clothing)* 31.38; in *(weather)* 8.1, **ab la . . . ez al** (= **ab** + **lo**) 8.16; of *(food)* 26.24; on *(food)* 6.1, 6.1; to *(interlocutor)* 22.48; to *(music)* 21.33;

ab aitant with that, then 25.34; **ab pauc** for little (reason) 19.27; **ab pauc (. . .) no** almost 9.41, 9.63, 31.46; **ab so que** provided that 7.23; **ab sol que** provided that 12.35; **ab tant** with that, then 25.17, 25.86, 30.51; **ab tensa** insistently 28.29; **s'acordar ab** to be attuned to, to be harmonious with 22.22; **mesclat ab** mixed with 29.21; **se tener ab** to persevere 17.16.

Forms: **ab** *passim;* **a-** 8.16, 23.28 (**al** 8.16 = **ab** + **lo**, **als** 23.28 = **ab** + **los**); **am** 10.36; **ap** 12.42, 13.60, 19.27, 21.38, 26.15, 26.24, 27.46.

[CL ăpŭd 'near' *FEW* 25, part 2: 62; OFr. *o(d)* 'with']

abát *nom. sg.* **ábas** *n. masc.* abbot: *nom. sg.* **abas** 25.87. [ChL (from Greek) *acc.* ăbbātem, *nom.* abbas *FEW* 24: 15; It. *abbate*, Sp. *abad*, Fr. *abbé*, G. *Abt*, E. *abbot*]

abatre *vb. trans.* to knock down, to fell: *pres. 3rd pl.* **abaton** 25.7; *pret. 3rd pl.* **abateron** 25.44. [LL ăbăttŭĕre *FEW* 24: 22; It. *abbattere*, Sp. *abatir*, Fr. *abattre*, E. *to abate*]

abelir *vb. trans.* to please, to charm; **m'etz abellida** you *(fem.)* pleased me 28.27; *refl. with* **de** to take a liking to 5.4, 5.6, 7.13: *pret. 3rd sg.* **abelli** 5.4, 5.6, **abellic** 5.4 var., 5.6 var.; *pp., fem., nom. sg.* **abellida** 7.13, 28.27. [**a-** + **bel** + **-ir**]

abenar *vb. trans.* to compensate for: *pres. 3rd sg.* **abena** 17.19. [**a-** + **ben** + **-ar** (2)]

abrandar *vb. trans.* to burn: *pres. 3rd sg.* **abranda** 19.7, 20.29. [**a-** + **brand-** (Germ. *brand FEW* 1: 499) + **-ar** (2)]

abres *see* **aprendre**.

abric *n. masc.* shelter: *obl. sg.* 13.75. [**abrigar** 'to shelter' (CL aprīcāre 'to warm' *FEW* 25: 58; Sp. *abrigar*)]

abril *n. masc.* April: *obl. sg.* **abril** 22.27. [CL aprīlem *FEW* 25: 60; It. *aprile*, Sp. *abril*, Fr. *avril*, E. *April*]

abrivar *vb. trans.* to hasten; *pp., masc., nom. sg.* **abrivatz** in haste, quickly 25.35. [**a-** + **briu** 'haste' (Ctc. **brivos FEW* 1: 542; It. *brio*, Sp. *brio*) + **-ar** (2)]

absolver *vb. trans.* to absolve, to pardon: *inf.* **absolver** 27.30. [CL absŏlvĕre *FEW* 24: 55; It. *ascioglere*, Sp. *absolver*, Fr. *absoudre*, E. *to absolve*]

ac *pret. 3rd sg. of* **aver**, *which see*.

acaptar *vb. trans.* to grant: *imper. 2nd sg.* **acapta** 29.46. [VL *ăccăptāre *FEW* 24: 66; It. *accattare* 'to beg,' Fr. *acheter*]

acer *see* **acier**.

acho *see* **aco**.

acier *n. masc.* steel: *nom. sg.* **acers** 25.58; **acers** *used as obl. sg.* 25.70. [LL ăcĭārĭum *FEW* 24: 105; It. *acciaio*, Sp. *acero*, Fr. *acier*]

aco *dem. pron., neuter* that: *nom. sg.* **aqo** 16.19; *obl. sg.* **acho** 8.6, **aquo** 9.53. [VL *atque hŏc *FEW* 4: 443 *ăccu hŏc]

acoatar *vb. refl.* to attach oneself (to, **ab**) by the **coa** 'tail' *(phallic)*, to entail oneself, to tie oneself by the tail: *pres. 3rd sg.* **acoata** 14.38. [**a-** + **coa** + **-at** + **-ar** (2); cf. Adams 515 note 1; the phallic reference is clear in citations from Ogier and from Montaigne in *LR* 3: 419; cf. MFr. *acouer* 'to overtake (an animal) from behind' *FEW* 2: 524]

acolhir *vb. trans.* to receive 14.27, to accept 10.35, to welcome 5.11: *pres. 1st sg.* **acueill** 10.35; *pret. 3rd sg.* **acuilli** 5.11, **acuillic** 5.11 var., **acuillit** 5.11 var.; *pp., fem., obl. sg.* **aculhid'** 14.27; *substantivized inf., masc., obl. sg.* **acuillir** hospitality 21.29. [**a-** + **colhir**]

acordansa *n. fem.* agreement: *obl. sg.* **acordansa** 28.61. [**acordar** + **-ansa**]

acordar *vb. refl.* to be in harmony with, to be attuned to: *pres. 1st sg.* **acort** 22.22. [LL ᴀᴄᴄʜᴏʀᴅᴀ̄ʀᴇ *FEW* 1: 13; It. *accordare,* Sp. *acordar,* Fr. *accorder,* E. *to accord*]

acostumar *vb. intrans.* to be accustomed; *pp., neuter, nom. sg.* **acostumat** usual, customary 30.10. [**a-** + **costuma** + **-ar** (2)]

acses *see* **aver.**

acu- *see* **acolhir.**

ad *see* **a** (2).

adastrar *vb. trans.* to endow: *pret. 3rd sg.* **adastrec** 13.44. [**ad-** + **astre** 'star' (CL ᴀsᴛʀᴜᴍ *FEW* 1: 165) + **-ar** (2)]

adenan *adv.* forward; **se traire adenan** to advance 8.10. [**a-** + **denan**]

adęs *adv.* always 17.21, 23.37; still 17.42; at once 30.56. [VL ᴀᴅ ĭᴅ ĭᴘsᴜᴍ (ᴛĕᴍᴘᴜs) *FEW* 24: 141; *influenced by* **apręs** (2); It. *adesso*]

adomesgar *vb. trans.* to tame: *pres. 3rd sg.* **adomesg'** 13.58. [**a-** + **domesge** 'of the house' (CL ᴅŏᴍĕsᴛĭᴄᴜᴍ *FEW* 3: 123) + **-ar** (2)]

adǫnc *adv.* then 8.5. [**a-** + **donc**]

adǫncs *adv.* then 15.26. [**adonc** + **-s**]

adręch *adj.* clever: *masc., nom. sg.* **adreichs** 5.3; *obl. sg.* **adreig** 6.27. [**a-** + **drech** (2)]

adreisar *vb. trans.* to put away: *pres. 3rd sg.* **adreissa** 30.96. [**a-** + **dreissar** (VL *ᴅī̄ʀĕᴄᴛĭᴀʀᴇ *FEW* 2: 83; It. *drizzare,* Fr. *dresser,* E. *to dress*]

aduire *vb. trans.* to lead: *pres. 3rd sg.* **aduz** 30.61. [CL ᴀᴅᴅᴜ̄ᴄĕʀᴇ *FEW* 24: 137; It. *addurre,* Sp. *aducir,* E. *to adduce*]

afaire *n. masc.* conduct 13.29: *obl. sg.* **afayre** 13.29. [VL ᴀ̆ᴅ + ꜰᴀ̆ᴄĕʀᴇ *FEW* 3: 349; Fr. *affaire,* E. *affair*]

afan *n. masc.* grief 11.72, 23.36, 24.28; hardship 16.44; effort 22.2: *nom. sg.* **afanz** 16.44, **affanz** 24.28; *obl. sg.* **afán** 11.72, **afan** 23.36; *obl. pl.* **affans** 22.2. [**afanar** 'to suffer' (VL *ᴀ̆ꜰᴀ̆ɴɴᴀ̄ʀᴇ *FEW* 24: 240; It. *affannarsi,* Sp. *afanar*)]

afayre *see* **afaire.**

affans, affanz *see* **afan.**

afizar *vb. trans.* to assure: *pres. 1st sg.* **afi** 12.12; *imper. 2nd pl.* **afiatz** 19.66. [**a-** + **fizar**]

aflamar *vb. intrans.* to burn: *pres. 3rd sg.* **afflama** 30.67. [**a-** + **flamar** (CL ꜰʟᴀ̆ᴍᴍᴀ̄ʀᴇ *FEW* 3: 601; It. *fiammare,* Fr. *flammer,* E. *to flame*)]

ag *pret. 3rd sg.* of **aver,** *which see.*

agaitar *vb. trans.* to survey: *inf.* **agaitar** 32.12. [**a-** + **gaita** + **-ar** (2)]

agarar *vb. trans.* to look: *pres. part., undeclined* **anar . . . agaran** 21.55. [**a-** + **garar**]

agensar *vb. trans.* to please: *pres. 3rd sg.* **agensa** 2.3, 28.33. [**a-** + **gensar**]

aglan *n. fem.* acorn: *obl. sg.* **aglan** 21.75. [CL ɢʟᴀɴᴅᴇᴍ *fem. FEW* 4: 148; It. *ghianda fem.,* Fr. *gland masc.; by agglutination* **una glan** > **un'aglan**]

agnus (Latin) *n. masc.* lamb; **Agnus Dei** 'Lamb of God' (liturgical formula): *vocative sg.* **agnus** 30.36 (see note).

agr', **agra** *see* **aver.**

agradar *vb. trans.* to please: *pres. 3rd sg.* **agrada** 13.52, 28.13; *substantivized inf., masc., obl. sg.* **agradar** pleasing 16.29. [**a-** + **grat** + **-ar** (2)]

agran, agras, agratz, agro, agron, aguda, aguem, agues, aguessetz, agui *see* **aver.**

agurs *see* **aür.**

agut *see* **aver.**

ai (1) *see* **aver.**

ai (2) *interj.* Ah! Oh! *Forms:* **ai** 15.33, 18.5, 18.29; **ay** 4.6, 4.15, 4.24, 4.33, 4.42; **ai las** alas! 4.23, 18.9, 30.90, **hai las** 30.71. [CL ᴀɪ]

aia, aiam, aian *see* **aver.**

aicęst *dem. adj.* this: *masc., obl. sg.* **aicest** 30.26. [CL ᴇ̆ᴄᴄᴇ̆ ɪ̆sᴛᴜᴍ, VL *ᴀᴄᴄᴜ(ᴍ) ɪ̆sᴛᴜᴍ *FEW* 4: 821]

aiga *n. fem.* water 30.2, 30.3, 30.6; river 25.14, 25.42, 25.102: *nom. sg.* **aiga** 25.42; *obl. sg.* **aiga** 25.14, 25.102, 30.2, 30.3, 30.6. [CL ᴀ̆ǫ̆ᴜ̆ᴀᴍ *FEW* 25: 67, which notes that the OOc form in **ai-** has not been explained; It. *acqua*, Sp. *agua*, Fr. *eau*; cf. E. *aquatic*]

aillors *see* **alhors.**

aire (1) *n. masc.* air, breeze: *obl. sg.* **aire** 2.1. [CL ᴀ̄ᴇ̆ʀᴇᴍ *FEW* 24: 226; It. *aria*, Sp. *aire*, Fr. *air*, E. *air*]

aire (2) *n. masc.* family, origin: *obl. sg.* **ayre** 13.36. [CL ᴀ̆ɢʀᴜᴍ 'field' *FEW* 24: 257, 25, pt. 2: 166]

aïs *adj.* hateful, full of hatred: *neuter, nom. sg.* 15.47 (see note), 15.50. [**aïr** 'to hate' (Frankish **hatjan FEW* 16: 178, Fr. *haïr*) + **-is**]

aisi (1) *adv.* here 5.17, 12.0; now 12.39, 28.66. *Forms:* **aisi** 12.0, **aissi** 5.17, 28.66, **aysi** 12.39. [CL ᴇ̆ᴄᴄᴇ̆ ʜɪ̄ᴄ, VL *ᴀᴄᴄᴜ(ᴍ) ʜɪ̄ᴄ *FEW* 4: 425; Sp. *aquí*; cf. Fr. *ici*]

aisi (2) *adv.* thus, so; **aisi . . . a mon talen** just as I wished 9.57; **aisi com** as 8.12, 26.38, 30.10, 30.13, 30.85, just like 26.17; **aisi (. . .) com** just as 18.19, 18.47. *Forms:* **aisi** 21.54 var.; **aissi** 8.12, 10.41, 17.3, 17.44, 18.19, 18.47, 20.9, 26.17, 26.38; **aysi** 19.9, 19.16, 25.55 var.; **ayssi** 9.57. [LL ᴀᴄ sɪ̄ᴄ *FEW* 11: 577; Sp. *así*, Fr. *ainsi*; cf. It. *cosí*]

aisi (3) 8.5, *see* **aizinar.**

aisǫ *dem. pron. neuter* this, that 22.37; **d'aiso** in this way 18.49; **per aiso** for that purpose 30.45, for this reason 15.20. *Forms:* **aiso** 30.45; **aisso** 15.20, 18.49, 22.37. [CL ᴇ̆ᴄᴄᴇ̆ ʜǒᴄ, VL *ᴀ̆ᴄᴄᴇ̆ ʜǒᴄ *FEW* 4: 443, 5.555; cf. **aco, so, o**]

aissi (1) here 5.17, 28.66, *see* **aisi** (1).

aissi (2) thus 8.12, 10.41, 17.3, 17.44, 18.19, 18.47, 20.9, 26.17, 26.38, *see* **aisi** (2).

aisso *see* **aiso.**

aital *adj.* such (*introduces subordinate clause beginning with* **que** 14.8, 25.8, 25.11, 25.50; *refers to preceding context* 12.54, 13.18, 13.60, 16.19, 19.25, 24.23, 30.21, 31.6); such as this 9.9, 13.21; the same 30.68; *indef. pron. neuter* the same thing 28.28.

　　Forms: masc., nom. sg. **aitals** 25.8, 25.50, 30.68; *obl. sg.* **aital** 9.9, 24.23, 30.21, **aytal** 12.54, 13.21, **aitals** *used as obl. sg.* 25.11; *fem., nom. sg.* **aitaus** 16.19, **aytal** *used as nom.* 13.18; *obl. sg.* **aital** 13.60, 19.25, **aytal** 14.8; *obl. pl.* **aytals** 31.6; *neuter, obl. sg.* **aital** 28.28. [**aisi** (2) + **tal** *FEW* 13, part 1: 57]

aitan (1) *n. masc.* the same amount, as much; **mil aitans** a thousand times more 27.44: *obl. pl.* **aitans** 27.44. [**aitan** (2)]

aitan (2) *adv.* so, so very 10.9; **aitan can** as much as 23.40; **aitan com** as much as 9.61, as long as 30.94; **ab aitan** with that, then 25.34; **d'aitan** this much 24.22. *Forms:* **aitan** 9.61, 10.9, 23.40, 24.22; **aitant** 25.34, 30.94. [**aicel** (CL ECCILLE, VL *ACCU ILLE *FEW* 4: 555) + **tan** (2) *FEW* 13, part 1: 94]

aitans *see* **aitan** (1).

aitant *see* **aitan** (2).

aitaus *see* **aital**.

aitre *see* **autre**.

aiuda *see* **ajuda**.

aiudar *see* **ajudar**.

aiziṇ (1) *n. masc.* dwelling: *obl. sg.* **aizi** 10.40. [**aizinar**]

aiziṇ (2) *adj.* agreeable: *masc., obl. pl.* **aizis** 15.40. [**aizinar**]

aizina *n. fem.* opportunity: *obl. sg.* **ayzina** 31.11. [**aizinar** + **-a**]

aizinar *vb. refl.* to enjoy (*with* **de**): *pres. subj. 3rd sg.* **aisi** 8.5. [**aitz** (CL ĀDJĂCĒNTEM 'neighboring' *FEW* 24: 155; cf. E. *ease*) + **-in** + **-ar** (2)]

aizis *see* **aizin** (2).

aja *see* **aver**.

ajuda *n. fem.* help: *obl. sg.* **aiuda** 19.49. [**ajudar**]

ajudar *vb. trans.* to help: *pres. subj. 3rd sg.* **ajut** 30.51; *past subj. 3rd sg.* **ajudèsse** 32.1, 32.2; *inf.* **aiudar** 12.70. [CL ĀDJŪTĀRE *FEW* 24: 164; It. *aiutare*, Sp. *ayudar*, Fr. *aider*, E. *to aid*]

al (1) *passim* = **a** + **lo**: *see* **a** (2), **lo** (2) *def. art.*

al (2) 8.16 = **ab** + **lo**, *see* **ab**.

ala *n. fem.* wing: *obl. pl.* **alas** 18.2. [CL ĀLAM *FEW* 24: 286; It. *ala*, Sp. *ala*, Fr. *aile*; cf. E. *aileron*]

alba *n. fem.* dawn: *nom. sg.* **alba** 4.11; *obl. sg.* **alba** 4.9, 4.18, 4.27, 4.36, 4.45. [CL ALBAM (LŪCEM) 'white (light)' *FEW* 24: 309; It. *alba*, Sp. *alba*, Fr. *aube*]

albegarai *see* **albergar**.

albẹrc (1) *n. masc.* inn 1.4; lodging 3.7, 15.23 (= **ostal** 15.23 var.); dwelling 12.18, 15.23; *obl. sg.* **alberc** 1.4, 3.7, 12.18, 15.23. [**albergar**; It. *albergo*, Sp. *albergo*, Fr. *auberge*]

albẹrc (2) *n. masc.* hauberk, shirt of chain mail: *nom. pl.* **auberc** 21.19; *obl. pl.* **aubercs** 22.36. [Frankish **halsberg* *FEW* 16: 134; It. *usbergo*, Fr. *haubert*, E. *hauberk*]

albergar *vb. intrans.* to lodge, to find lodging 15.24; *trans.* to lodge, to give lodging to 9.15: *fut. 1st sg.* **albegarai** 15.24, **albergarai** 15.24 var., **albergerai** 15.24 var., **herbergerai** 15.24 *(French form in French mss.)*; *imper. 1st pl.* **alberguem** 9.15. [Germ. **haribergōn* *FEW* 16: 158 + **-ar** (2)]

albespiṇ *n. masc.* hawthorn bush: *obl. sg.* **albespi** 8.14; *obl. pl.* **albespis** 15.6. [CL ĂLBAM SPĪNAM, VL **ĂLBĬSPĪNAM, *ĂLBĬSPĪNUM* *FEW* 1: 60; Fr. *aubépine, aubépin*]

albire *n. masc.* opinion: *obl. sg.* **albire** 31.13. [CL ARBĬTRĬUM *FEW* 25: 87; Sp. *albedrío* 'free will,' Fr. *arbitre*; cf. E. *arbiter*]

alegr' *see* **alegrar**.

alegransa *n. fem.* joy; **d'alegransa** illegitimate (child) 28.56. [**alegrar** + **-ansa**]

alegrar *vb. trans.* to delight 23.35; *refl.* to rejoice 23.37 var.: *pres. 3rd sg.* **alegr'** 23.35; *inf.* **alegrar** 23.37 var. [**alegre** (CL ălăcrem, VL *alĕcrem FEW 24: 289; It. *allegro*, Sp. *alegre*, Fr. *allègre*, E. *allegro*) + **-ar** (2)]

alegreṭ *adj.* cheerful: *fem., nom. sg.* **alegreta** 13.14. [**alegre** + **-et**]

alegretat *n. fem.* happiness: *obl. sg.* **alegretat** 29.10. [**alegre** + **-tat**; cf. CL ălăcrĭtātem]

alegrier *n. masc.* rejoicing: *nom. sg.* **alegriers** 25.90, 29.2. [**alegre** + **-ier**]

alęn *n. masc.* breath: *obl. sg.* **alen** 2.1. [**alenar** 'to breathe' (CL ănhēlāre, LL ălēnāre FEW 24: 580; It. *alenare*)]

alhǫns *adv.* elsewhere 19.4. [CL ălĭŭnde FEW 24: 324 + **-s**]

alhǫrs *adv.* elsewhere: **aillors** 19.4 var. [CL ălĭōrsum FEW 24: 321; Fr. *ailleurs*]

almǫrna *n. fem.* alms, charitable gift: *obl. pl.* **almornas** 26.39. [ChL (from Gk.) ĕlĕĕmŏsўnam FEW 3: 212; It. *limósina*, Sp. *limosna*, Fr. *aumône*, E. *alms*]

als (1) *pron.* something else: *obl. sg.* **als** 28.18. [**al** (CL ălĭud, ălĭd, VL *ale FEW 24: 324) + **-s**]

als (2) 1.2, 9.24, 25.1, 25.31, 25.32, 25.32, 25.86, 29.16, 30.42 = **a** + **los**, *see* **a** (2), **lo** (2) *def. art.*

als (3) 23.28 = **ab** + **los**, *see* **ab** and **lo** (2).

alt- *see* **aut-**, *except that for* **altretal**, **altrestal** *see* **atretal** (2).

alumnar *vb. intrans.* to burn bright, to thrive 25.94; *trans.* to light (candle) 25.92: *pres. 3rd sg.* **alumpna** 25.94, *3rd pl.* **alumnan** 25.92. [CL ĭllūmĭnāre, VL *allūmĭnāre FEW 24: 340; It. *alluminare*; Sp. *iluminar*, *alumbrar*; Fr. *illuminer*, *allumer*; E. *to illuminate*]

am (1) 6.22, 16.43, 17.9, 18.36, 28.20, *see* **amar**.

am (2) 10.36, *see* **ab**.

ama *see* **amar**.

amadǫr *n. masc.* lover: *nom. pl.* **amador** 18.13. [CL amātōrem FEW 24: 396; It. *amatore*, Sp. *amador*]

aman *n. masc.* lover: *obl. sg.* **aman** 30.81; *obl. pl.* **amanz** 16.30. [CL amantem FEW 24: 387; Sp. *amante*, Fr. *amant*]

amar *vb. trans.* to love: *pres. 1st sg.* **am** 16.43, 17.9, 18.36 var., 28.20, *3rd sg.* **ama** 16.21, 17.46, 30.68, **am'** 6.22, *3rd pl.* **amon** 12.63, 16.24; *pres. subj. 3rd sg.* **am** 18.36; *imperf. 1st sg.* **amava** 17.39, *3rd sg.* **amava** 3.4; *fut. 1st sg.* **amarai** 23.10; *pret. 1st sg.* **amie** 31.8, **ami** 31.8 var. *3rd sg.* **amet** 5.16, 11.29, 14.65; *past subj. 1st sg.* **ames** 15.49; *2nd cond. 1st sg.* **amera** 23.3; *pp., masc., nom. sg.* **amatz** 14.66, 15.49, 15.52, 19.16, 20.16; *obl. sg.* **amat** 7.4; *inf.* **amar** 6.7, 6.21, 10.33, 18.11, 23.26. [CL amāre FEW 24: 388; It. *amare*, Sp. *amar*, Fr. *aimer*]

amban *n. masc.* parapet: *obl. sg.* **amban** 25.52. [Ctc. *ande-banno- 'roof' FEW 24: 546; Fr. *auvent* 'roof']

ambedǫs *num.* both: *masc., nom. pl.* **ambedui** 10.26; *obl. pl. (used as nom. pl.)* **amdos** 28.62; *fem., obl. pl.* **ambedos** 9.57. [CL ămbōs dŭōs FEW 24: 410; It. *ambedue*, Sp. *ambos á dos*; cf. **entrams**]

amenar *vb. trans.* to drive: *pres. 3rd sg.* **amena** 17.43. [**a-** + **menar**]

amera, ames, amet *see* **amar**.

ami (1) 31.8 var., *see* **amar**.

ami' (2) 19.1, **amia** *see* **amiga**.

amic *n. masc.* friend, close male acquaintance 10.37, 11.45, 12.41, 17.1, 19.57; lover 4.14, 4.21, 6.3, 6.33, 7.17, 19.10, 23.1, 23.38: *nom. sg.*

amics 6.3, 12.41, **amicx** 4.14; *obl. sg.* **amic** 4.21, 19.10, **amig** 11.45; *obl. pl.* **amics** 10.37; *vocative sg.* **amics** 6.33, 7.17, 17.1, 19.57, 23.1, 23.38, **amic** 19.57 var. [CL ămīcum *FEW* 24: 450; It. *amico*, Sp. *amigo*, Fr. *ami*; cf. E. *amical*]

amie *see* **amar**.

amig *see* **amic**.

amiga *n. fem.* friend, close female acquaintance 19.1; beloved 4.21: *obl. sg.* **amia** 4.21; *vocative sg.* **ami'** 19.1. [CL amīcam *FEW* 24: 450; It. *a-mica*, Sp. *amiga*, Fr. *amie*, E. *Amy*]

amistansa *n. fem.* friendship: *obl. sg.* **amistansa** 28.64. [**amistat** + **-ansa**]

amistat *n. fem.* friendship: *obl. sg.* **amistat** 13.62, 19.37, 32.17. [VL *amīcĭtātem *FEW* 24: 440; Sp. *amistad*, Fr. *amitié*]

amon (1) 12.63, 16.24, *see* **amar**.

amon (2) *adv.* uphill, high: **amon** 18.56. [**a-** + **mon** 'mountain' (CL mŏntem *FEW* 6, part 2: 91; It. *monte*, Sp. *monte*, Fr. *mont*, E. *mount*)]

amor *n. fem.* love; desire 9.41; the force of love *(personified)* 14.8, 14.13, 14.19, 14.25, 14.31, 14.37, 14.43, 14.49, 14.56, 16.17, 21.23, 30.60, 30.61, 30.65; love for an individual 5.6, 7.6, 7.15, 9.71, 13.52, 19.68, 23.33, 30.19; a love affair 5.7, 8.13; divine love (human love of God) 15.23, 29.26, (God's love of humans) 29.48.

amar per amor to love sincerely 3.4; **amor de lonh** love from afar, love for a faraway beloved 15.4, 15.9, 15.16, 15.23 var., 15.30, 15.37, 15.39, 15.44, 15.46; **fin'amor** 16.4, **amor fina** 31.10, true love.

Forms: nom. sg. **amors** 5.7, 14.8, 14.13, 14.25, 14.31 var., 14.43, 14.49, 14.63, 16.4, 16.17, 16.18, 16.19 var., 16.30, 18.25, 21.23, 30.61, 30.65, **amor** 8.13, 13.52, 14.31, 16.19, 19.68; *obl. sg.* **amor** 3.4, 5.6, 7.6, 7.15, 8.29, 9.71, 14.19 var., 14.37 var., 14.56 var., 15.4, 15.8, 15.9, 15.16, 15.23, 15.23 var., 15.30, 15.37, 15.39, 15.44, 15.46, 16.6, 16.9, 16.15, 17.7, 17.16, 17.44, 17.48 var., 18.10, 18.60, 19.68, 23.33, 29.26, 29.48, 30.19, 30.60, 31.10, 32.17, **amors** *(obl. sg. in ms. R)* 14.19, 14.37, 14.56, 15.44 var.; *obl. pl.* **amors** 9.41.

[CL amōrem *masc. FEW* 24: 469; It. *amore masc.*, Sp. *amor masc.*, OFr. *amour fem.*, Fr. *amour masc. except in poetic usage*]

amoros *adj.* loving (erotic) 7.20; who is in love 19.53: *masc., obl. sg.* **amoros** 7.20, 19.53. [VL *ămōrōsum *FEW* 24: 476; It. *amoroso*, Sp. *amoroso*, Fr. *amoureux*, E. *amorous*]

amors *see* **amor**.

amparar *vb. trans.* to protect 25.63, to defend 25.81: *pres. 3rd sg.* **ampara** 25.63, 25.81. [CL antĕpărāre *FEW* 7: 631; Sp. *amparar*]

ample *adj.* ample, full: *masc., obl. pl.* **amples** 26.41. [CL amplum *FEW* 24: 488; It. *ampio*, Sp. *ancho*, Fr. *ample*, E. *ample*]

ampleza *n. fem.* breadth, fullness: *obl. sg.* **amplesza** 26.51. [**ample** + **-eza**]

an (1) *n. masc.* year: *obl. sg.* **an** 21.41, 29.0; *obl. pl.* **ans** 22.26, 27.7, **anz** 17.22. [CL ănnum *FEW* 24: 627; It. *anno*, Sp. *año*, Fr. *an*; cf. E. *annual*]

an (2) *vb. intrans.* 21.54, *see* **anar**.

an (3) *vb. trans.* 17.48, 21.24, 25.20, 25.75, 26.27, 26.29, 26.51, 30.7, 32.14, *see* **aver**.

anar *vb. intrans.* to go 8.13, 9.67, 12.15, 12.33, 13.8, 14.13, 18.4; to proceed 11.69; to walk, to live 11.4, 15.36; to go away 4.5, 28.71; to go about *(habitual action)* 15.5; to go around, to circulate *(gossip)* 8.27.

anar a la mort to die 12.17; en anar to walk away 31.43; s'en anar to go away 5.10, 9.2, 10.5, 10.27, 18.39, 18.58, 30.74, 31.28, to go (vaus toward) 30.56, to flee 3.11, to disappear 21.27.

Auxiliary anar *with pres. part.* to go about 8.29, 21.12, 26.8, 26.47; *auxiliary* anar *with pres. part.* = *past of the simple verb* (*cf.* soler) anava ditan I had written 11.78, an sercan he sought 21.54, vai queren he sought 30.44, anam queren we have been seeking 9.14.

Forms: pres. 1st sg. vau 13.8, 15.5, 18.39, 18.58, 28.71, vauc 21.12, *2nd sg.* ves 24.29, *3rd sg.* va 8.13, 31.43, vai 4.5, 15.36, 18.4, 30.44, 30.56, 30.74, vay 14.13, *1st pl.* anam 9.14, 12.17, annam 11.4, *3rd pl.* van 8.27, 8.29, 26.8, 26.47; *pres. subj. 3rd sg.* an 21.54; *imperf. 1st sg.* anava 11.78; *fut. 1st sg.* irai 10.5, 10.27, irei 10.5 var., *2nd sg.* iras 9.67, *3rd pl.* iran 12.33, 21.27; *pret. 1st sg.* aniey 9.2, *3rd sg.* anet 3.11, 5.10, 31.28; *inf.* anar 12.15, annár 11.69.
[CL ămbŭlāre, īre, vadĕre; VL *ămbĭtāre *FEW* 24: 400, LL andāre; It. *andare, gire;* Sp. *andar, ir;* Fr. *aller, ir(ai), (je) vais*]

anc *adv.* ever 10.22, 12.29, 19.53, 21.4, 21.45, 23.14, 24.32; *with neg.* anc . . . non never 6.7, 9.8, 9.29, 11.67, 12.7, 14.31, 14.65, 18.41, 24.33, 28.30; anc mais . . . no never 30.52; non . . . anc mais never even 18.26; anc sol no not even 9.29. *Forms:* anc *passim,* hanc 30.52. [Pre-Roman Indo-European *anque *FEW* 24: 631; It. *anche*]

ancar *adv.* still 8.19; again 8.23, 23.31. *Forms:* ancar 8.19 var.; enquer 8.19, 8.23; enquera 23.31. [anc + ar (er, era)]

ancian *adj.* ancient, old: *fem., nom. sg.* ansiayna 13.84. [ML ăntĭānum *FEW* 24: 640; It. *anziano,* Sp. *anciano,* Fr. *ancien,* E. *ancient*]

anel *n. masc.* ring: *obl. sg.* anel 8.22. [CL anĕllum *FEW* 24: 557; It. *anello,* Sp. *anillo,* Fr. *anneau*]

anet *see* anar.

ángel *n. masc.* angel: *obl. sg.* angel 26.1. [ChL (from Gk.) angĕlum *FEW* 24: 563; It. *angelo,* Sp. *anjel,* Fr. *ange,* E. *angel*]

angoisos *adj.* frightened: *fem., nom. sg.* angoissosa 30.20. [angoisa (CL angŭstĭam 'confinement' *FEW* 24: 573; It. *angoscia,* Sp. *congoja,* Fr. *angoisse,* E. *anguish*) + -os]

angut *see* aver.

anhel *n. masc.* lamb: *obl. pl.* anhels 28.3. (CL agnĕllum *FEW* 24: 265; It. *agnello,* Fr. *agneau*]

aniey, annár, annam *see* anar.

ans (1) 22.26, 27.7, *see* an (1).

ans (2) 9.59, 12.17, 12.24, 14.24, 14.33, 19.45, 26.28, 27.34, *see* anz (2).

ansiayna *see* ancian.

ant *see* aver.

antre *see* entre.

anz (1) 17.22, *see* an (1).

anz (2) *adv.* rather, instead; first 12.17, 12.24; anz . . . que *adv.* rather . . . than 17.28; *conj.* before 5.7, 14.24, 22.48; en anz en dies in earlier days 11.20. *Forms:* anz 5.7, 11.27, 17.26, 17.28, 17.30, 20.28, 22.2, 22.48; ans 9.59, 12.17, 12.24, 14.24, 14.33, 19.45, 26.28, 27.34; anzs 11.20. [CL ănte + -s *FEW* 24: 639; It. *anzi,* Sp. *antes*]

aondar *vb. trans.* to help 18.32, to affect 19.19: *pres. 3rd sg.* aonda 19.19; *pres. subj. 3rd sg.* aon 18.32. [CL ăbŭndāre *FEW* 24: 60; It. *abbondare,* Sp. *abundar,* Fr. *abonder,* E. *to abound*]

aǫra *adv.* now: **aora** 11.21. [CL ʜᴀ̄(ᴄ) ʜᴏ̄ʀᴀ̄ *FEW* 4: 477; Sp. *ahora*]

ap *see* **ab.**

apaisar *vb. trans.* to nourish 6.2; *refl.* to nourish oneself 6.1: *pres. 1st sg.* **apais** 6.1, *3rd sg.* **apaia** 6.2. [**a-** + **paisar**]

apelar *vb. trans.* to call: *pres. 3rd sg.* **apella** 15.43, *2nd pl.* **apelatz** 19.42; *imperf. 3rd pl.* **apellaven** 11.39; *pp., masc., nom. sg.* **apellatz** 20.22 var. [CL ᴀ̆ᴘᴘᴇ̆ʟʟᴀ̄ʀᴇ *FEW* 25: 32; It. *appellare*, Sp. *apelar*, Fr. *appeler*, E. *to appeal*]

apercębre *vb. refl.* to notice *with* **en** (2): *pret. 3rd sg.* **aperceup** 5.8; *past subj. 3rd sg.* **apercebes** 5.7, **aperceubes** 5.7 var., *3rd pl.* **aperceubessen** 5.7 var.; *pp., masc., nom. sg.* **aperceubutz** 5.8 var. [**a-** + **percebre** (CL ᴘᴇ̆ʀᴄʏ̆ᴘᴇ̆ʀᴇ *FEW* 8: 219; Sp. *percibir*, Fr. *percevoir*, E. *to perceive*)]

apertamęn *adv.* openly; **cantar ben apertamen** to sing with full throat 30.35. [**apert** (CL ᴀ̆ᴘᴇ̆ʀᴛᴜᴍ, pp. of ᴀᴘᴇʀɪ̄ʀᴇ 'to open' *FEW* 25: 5; It. *aperto*, Sp. *abierto*) + **-amen** (2)]

apezar *vb. trans.* to be heavy (to), to weigh upon: *pres. part., undeclined* **apesant** (*with* **estar**) 12.73. [**a-** + **pezar**]

aplanar *vb. trans.* to smooth: *pres. 3rd sg.* **aplana** 14.57. [**a-** + **planar** (LL ᴘʟᴀ̆ɴᴀ̄ʀᴇ *FEW* 9: 14; It. *pianare*, Fr. *planer*, E. *to plane*)]

aportar *vb. trans.* to bring: *pret. 3rd pl.* **aportero** 9.45; *imper. 2nd pl.* **aportatz** 9.33; *inf.* **aportar** 30.2. [CL ᴀ̆ᴘᴘᴏ̆ʀᴛᴀ̄ʀᴇ *FEW* 25: 48; It. *apportare*, Sp. *aportar*, Fr. *apporter*]

apręndre *vb. trans.* to learn: *pp., masc., obl. pl.* **apres** 26.4, **abres** 26.4 var. [CL ᴀ̆ᴘᴘʀᴇ̆ʜᴇ̆ɴᴅᴇ̆ʀᴇ, ᴀ̆ᴘᴘʀᴇ̆ɴᴅᴇ̆ʀᴇ *FEW* 25: 51; It. *apprendere*, Sp. *aprender*, Fr. *apprendre*, E. *to apprehend*]

apręs (1) 26.4, *see* **aprendre.**

apręs (2) *adv.* afterward 25.38; *prep.* after 4.9, 4.18, 4.27, 4.36, 4.45, 26.27, 30.12, 30.22, 30.84, 31.15 var.; **apres de** after 31.15. [LL ᴀᴅ ᴘʀᴇ̆ssᴜᴍ *FEW* 24: 178; It. *appresso*, Fr. *après*]

aprob *see* **aprop.**

aprochar *vb. intrans.* to come near, to approach: *pp., masc., nom. sg.* **aprochatz** (*with* **eser**) 10.32. [LL ᴀ̆ᴘᴘʀᴏ̆ᴘʏ̄ᴀʀᴇ *FEW* 25: 55; It. *approcciare*, Fr. *approcher*, E. *to approach*]

aprǫp *adv.* in comparison 11.42; *prep.* in the eyes of 11.35; after 4.18 var. (= **apres** 4.18), 4.27 var. (= **apres** 4.27). *Forms:* **aprop** 4.18 var., 4.27 var.; **aprob** 11.35, 11.42. [**a-** + **prop**]

aqel, aqelas, aqels, aqil *see* **aquel.**

aqo *see* **aco.**

aquęl *dem. pron.* that one (*with* **que** who), (*masc. pl.*) those (who) 21.58, (*fem. pl.*) women (who) 16.24; **aquel . . . que** such . . . that 16.8, the . . . when 16.46; *dem. adj.* that 5.9, 5.15, 9.52, 12.21; that very, the same 1.7.

> *Forms: masc., nom. sg.* **aquel** 12.21, **aqel** 16.46; *obl. sg.* **aquel** 1.7, **aqel** 16.8; *nom. pl.* **aqil** 21.58; *obl. pl.* **aqels** 21.54 var.; *fem., obl. sg.* **aquella** 5.9, 5.15, 9.52; *obl. pl.* **aqelas** 16.24.

> [CL ᴇ̆ᴄᴄᴇ̆, ᴇ̆ᴄᴄᴜ (*influenced by* ᴀᴛǫᴜᴇ) + ɪ̆ʟʟᴜᴍ, VL *ᴀ̆ᴄᴄᴜ ɪ̆ʟʟᴜᴍ *FEW* 4: 555]

aquęst *dem. adj.* this; **aquest de sai** this one here 12.9: *masc., nom. sg.* **aquest** 9.31; *obl. sg.* **aquest** 12.9, 12.60, 14.2, 18.30, 28.21, 28.26; *fem., obl. sg.* **aquesta** 25.27, 25.64; *obl. pl.* **aquestas** 5.17. [VL *ᴀ̆ᴄᴄᴜ ɪ̆sᴛᴜᴍ *FEW* 4: 821] aqui *adv.* here; **d'aqui a** as far as 21.69. [CL ĕ̆ccĕ̆ hīc, VL *accu(m) hīc *FEW* 4: 425]

aquo *see* aco.

ar *adv. referring to the time of the verb: with verb referring to present or imminent future time* now 7.5, 10.5, 10.26, 10.31, 13.52, 14.26, 19.3, 19.5, 19.37, 23.3, 25.94 var., 28.15, 28.53, 29.17, 31.35; *with verb referring to past time* then 23.28 var., 30.53, just then 30.76.

Forms: **ar** 10.31, 13.52, 19.37, 25.94 var.; **ara** 7.5, 10.26, 30.53, 30.76; **aras** 23.28 var.; **er** 14.26, 19.5, 28.15, 29.17, 31.35; **era** 10.5, 23.3; **eras** 19.3, 28.53.

[CL hā hōrā, ĕ̄a hōrā, *FEW* 4: 477; *optional* -s]

arabit *adj.* Arabian (horse): *masc., obl. pl.* **arabitz** 25.33. [CL arabem + -it]

araire *n. masc.* plow: *obl. sg.* **arayre** 13.38. [CL ă̆ră̆trum *FEW* 25: 84; It. *arato*, Sp. *arado*]

arandar *vb. trans.* to chase around: *pres. 3rd sg.* **aranda** 20.28. [a- + randon 'haste' (Frankish *rand* 'running' *FEW* 16.661) + -ar (2)]

aras *see* ar.

arayre *see* araire.

arbre *n. masc.* tree: *obl. sg.* **arbre** 8.15 var., **arbr'** 8.15; *obl. pl.* **arbres** 32.5. [CL ă̆rbŏrem *FEW* 25: 88; It. *albero*, Sp. *árbol*, Fr. *arbre*; cf. E. *arbor*]

arc *n. masc.* bow; **arc de torn garnit** bow or crossbow equipped with a windlass 25.56. [CL ă̆rcum *FEW* 25: 134; It. *arco*, Sp. *arco*, Fr. *arc*, E. *arc*]

ardia *see* ardre.

ardimẹn *n. masc.* courage: *obl. sg.* **ardimen** 9.42. [ardit + -imen]

ardit *adj.* bold, brave: *obl. sg.* **ardit** 21.36, 21.46; *obl. pl.* **arditz** 12.50. [Frankish *hardjan* + -it *FEW* 16: 155; Fr. *hardi*, E. *hardy*]

ardre *vb. intrans.* to burn 27.41 var.; *trans.* 14.15, 31.4; *refl.* 24.27: *pres. 2nd sg.* **arz** 24.27, *3rd sg.* **art** 14.15; *imperf. 1st sg.* **ardia** 27.41 var.; *pp., fem., nom. sg.* **arsa** 31.4. [CL ă̆rdēre *FEW* 25: 146; It. *ardere*, Sp. *arder*; cf. E. *ardent*]

arẹna *n. fem.* sand: *obl. sg.* **arena** 17.33. [CL ă̆rēnam *FEW* 25: 174; It. *arena*, Sp. *arena*, Fr. *arène*, E. *arena*]

arma *n. fem.* soul: *obl. sg.* **arma** 12.70, 24.26, 27.20, **arm'** 27.36; *obl. pl.* **armas** 27.16, 27.26. [CL ă̆nĭmam *FEW* 24: 586; It. *anima*, Sp. *alma*, Fr. *âme*; cf. E. *to animate*]

armas *n. fem. pl.* arms, weapons: *obl. pl.* **armas** 3.2, 25.2. [CL ă̆rma *neuter pl. FEW* 25: 242; It. *arme*, Sp. *armas*, Fr. *armes*, E. *arms*]

arnẹs *n. masc.* harness *(metaphor for male sexual organs)* 9.64; equipment 25.104; adornment 24.40, 24.43: *nom. sg.* **arnes** 9.64; *obl. sg.* **arnei** 24.40, 24.43; *obl. pl.* **arnes** 25.104. [Old Norse *hernest FEW 16: 205; It. *arnese*, Sp. *arnés*, Fr. *harnais*, E. *harness*]

arquier *n. masc.* archer: *nom. sg.* **arquers** 25.52. [arc + -ier]

arsa *see* ardre.

art (1) *n. fem.* art, skill: *nom. sg.* **artz** 22.3, 24.25. [CL ă̆rtem *FEW* 25: 348; It. *arte*, Sp. *arte*, Fr. *art*, E. *art*]

art (2) 14.15, *see* ardre.

artetal *see* atretal (2).

artz *see* art (1).

arz *see* ardre.

asajar *vb. trans.* to test, to try: *pp., fem., obl. sg.* **assajada** 28.67; *inf.* **assa-**

jar 12.51. [a- (2) + CL ĔxĂGĬUM *FEW* 3: 257 + -ar (2); It. *assaggiare*, Sp. *asayar*, E. *to assay*; cf. Fr. *essayer*]

asatz *adv.* quite 23.25, many 15:19. *Forms:* **asatz** 23.25, **assatz** 15.19. [VL *AD SĂTIS *FEW* 24: 184; It. *assai*, Fr. *assez*]

asenar *vb. trans.* to make sensible: *pp., fem., obl. sg.* **assenada** 28.70. [a- + sen (1) + -ar (2)]

asetar *vb. trans.* to place, to seat: *pp., masc., obl. pl.* **asetatz** 26.3. [VL *ASSĔDĬTĀRE *FEW* 11: 406; It. *assettare*]

asetgar *vb. trans.* to besiege: *pres. 3rd sg.* **asetg'** 20.28. [VL *ASSĔDĬCĀRE (?) *FEW* 11: 412; cf. **seti**]

asiramen *see* **aziramen.**

aspramẹn *adv.* harshly, roughly: **aspramen** 14.30. [aspre + -amen (2)]

aspre *adj.* harsh, rough: *masc., nom. sg.* **aspres** 26.36. [CL ĂSPĔRUM *FEW* 1: 156; It. *aspro*, Sp. *aspero*, Fr. *âpre*]

assa 13.72 var., 19.59 var. = **a sa**, *see* **son** (4).

assajada, assajar, *see* **asajar.**

assas 29.43 var. = **a sas**, *see* **son** (4).

assatz *see* **asatz.**

assenada *see* **asenar.**

asuèlh *see* **azolh.**

atẹndre *vb. trans.* to await, to hope for 16.52, 16.54, 23.39; (*with* **en**) to think of 30.25; *refl.* to be attentive to (*with* **a**) 16.14; *pres. 1st sg.* **aten** 16.14, 23.39, *3rd sg.* **aten** 16.52, 16.54; *imperf. 3rd sg.* **atendia** 30.25. [CL ĂTTĔNDĔRE *FEW* 1: 168; It. *attendere*, Sp. *atender*, Fr. *attendre*, E. *to attend*]

aterrar *vb. trans.* to bring low: *pp., masc., nom. pl.* **aterrat** 29.38. [a- + terra + -ar (2)]

atraire *vb. trans.* to bring: *pres. subj. 3rd sg.* **atraia** 6.12; *pret. 3rd sg.* **atrais** 6.11; *inf.* **atrayre** 13.37 var. [CL ĂTTRĂHĔRE *FEW* 1: 169; It. *attrarre*, Sp. *atraer*, Fr. *attraire*, E. *to attract*]

atras *adv.* back 12.44. [VL *AD TRANS *REW, FEW* 13, part 2: 198; Sp. *atrás*]

atrayre *see* **atraire.**

atretal (1) *adj.* same: *fem., nom. pl.* **atretals** 18.24. [LL ĂLTĔRUM TĀLEM *FEW* 13, part 1: 57]

atretal (2) *adv.* the same. *Forms:* **atretal** 13.41, **artetal** 13.41 var., **atrestal** 13.41 var., **altretal** 13.41 var., **altrestal** 13.41 var. [atretal (1)]

aturar *vb. refl.* to dwell, to remain: *pres. 3rd sg.* **atura** 13.89 var. [CL ŎBTŪRĀRE 'to plug,' VL *ĂTTŪRĀRE *FEW* 7: 293; It. *turare*, Sp. *aturar*]

au *see* **a** (2).

auberc, aubercs *see* **alberc** (2).

aucel *see* **auzel.**

aucire *vb. trans.* to kill: *pres. subj. 3rd pl.* **aucizo** 9.72; *1st cond. 3rd sg.* **auciria** 4.39; *pret. 3rd sg.* **ausis** 3.7, *3rd pl.* **aucizeron** 24.36; *past subj. 3rd sg.* **aucizes** 9.55. [CL ŎCCĪDĔRE, VL *AUCĪDĔRE *FEW* 7: 299; It. *uccidere*, OFr. *ocire*]

aüda *see* **aver.**

audir, aug, aujatz, aujaz, *see* **auzir.**

aun *see* **aver.**

aunimẹn *n. masc.* shame: *obl. sg.* **aunimen** 27.18. [aunir 'to dishonor' (Frankish *haunjan FEW* 16: 183 + -ir, Fr. *honnir*) + -imen]

aür *n. masc.* augury: *obl. pl.* **agurs** 12.45. [CL AUGŬRĬUM 'omen,' VL *AGŬRĬUM *FEW* 1: 175; Sp. *agüero*, Fr. *(bon)heur*, E. *augury*]

aura, aurai, auran *see* **aver.**

aürar *vb. trans.* to prophesy: *pres. 3rd sg.* **aüra** 13.88. [CL AUGŬRĀRE *FEW* 1: 174, VL *ĀGŬRĀRE *REW*; Sp. *agorar*]

auratge *n. masc.* windstorm: *nom. sg.* **auratges** 25.41. [**aura** (CL [from Gk.] AURAM *FEW* 1: 177) + **-atge**; Fr. *orage*]

aurem, aures, auret, auretz, aurez, auria, auriaz, aurie, auríen, *see* **aver.**

aus *see* **auzar.**

ausir, ausis 30.73, *see* **auzir.**

ausis 3.7, *see* **aucire.**

aut *adj.* high: *masc., obl. sg.* **aut** 12.18, 19.13; *fem., obl. sg.* **auta** 25.79. [CL ALTUM *FEW* 24: 375; It. *alto*, Sp. *alto*, Fr. *haut*; cf. E. *altitude*]

autre (1) *pron.* another (person) 11.10, 13.63, 13.86, 13.90, 14.21, 14.66, 19.11, 19.28, 19.59, 19.62, 20.11, 20.32, 24.27, 24.28, 25.35, 27.22: *masc., nom. sg.* **autre** 19.11, 19.28, 27.22, **aitre** 11.10 (see note); *obl. sg.* **autre** 13.63, 13.90, 14.21, 20.32, **autrui** 20.11; *genitive sg. with def. art.* **l'autrui** 24.27, 24.28; *obl. pl.* **autres** 25.35; *fem., obl. sg.* **autra** 13.86, 14.66, 19.59, 19.62. [**autre** (2); **autrui** influenced by **lui**]

autre (2) *adj.* other 3.10, 5.7, 11.42, 11.61, 13.46, 14.39, 15.45, 17.13, 17.18, 19.37, 22.24, 23.33, 25.55, 26.12, 28.2, 28.54, 28.64, 29.29, 31.14, 31.45: *masc., nom. sg.* **autre** 15.45, 17.18, 25.55, **altre** 11.42; *obl. sg.* **autre** 3.10; *nom. pl.* **autr'** 17.13; *obl. pl.* **autres** 29.29; *fem., nom. sg.* **autra** 5.7, 14.39; *obl. sg.* **autra** 13.46, 22.24, 26.12, 28.54, 31.14, 31.45, **autr'** 19.37, 23.33, 28.64; *obl. pl.* **autras** 28.2, **altras** 11.61. [CL ALTĔRUM *FEW* 24: 355; It. *altro*, Sp. *otro*, Fr. *autre*; cf. E. *altruism*]

autrejar *vb. trans.* to give 7.15; to assure, to tell 22.47: *pres. 1st sg.* **autrei** 7.15, 22.47. [VL *AUCTŌRĪZĀRE *FEW* 1: 172; Fr. *octroyer*]

autres *see* **autre** (1), (2).

autrier *n. masc. in adverbial expression* **l'autrier** the other day 13.1, 28.1. [**autre** + **ier** 'yesterday' (CL HĔRI *FEW* 4: 414; It. *ieri*, Sp. *ayer*, Fr. *hier*)]

autrui *see* **autre** (1).

aütz *see* **aver.**

auvent *see* **auzir.**

auzar *vb. trans.* to dare: *pres. 1st sg.* **aus** 8.10; *pres. subj. 3rd sg.* **aus** 6.21. [LL AUSĀRE *FEW* 1: 184; It. *osare*, Sp. *osar*, Fr. *oser*]

auzęl *n. masc.* bird: *nom. pl.* **aucel** 8.2; *obl. pl.* **auzels** 15.2. [VL AUCĔLLUM *FEW* 1: 171; It. *uccello*, Fr. *oiseau*]

auzir *vb. trans.* to hear: *pres. 1st sg.* **aug** 2.4, 2.7, 4.7, 4.16, 4.25, 4.34, 4.43, *2nd pl.* **auzez** 17.3; *fut. 2nd pl.* **auziretz** 9.61, **auzirez** 5.17, *3rd pl.* **auziran** 27.10; *pret. 3rd sg.* **auzi** 1.2, 3.9, 3.11; *past subj. 3rd sg.* **ausis** 30.73; *2nd cond. 2nd pl.* **auziratz** 25.77; *imper. 2nd pl.* **aujatz** 9.7, 12.3, 14.55 var., **aujaz** 17.5; *pres. part., fem., obl. sg.* **auvent** 11.23; *pp., fem., nom. sg.* **auzida** renowned 28.38; *inf. (active sense)* **auzir** 17.9, 29.19, **audir** 21.62 var., *(passive sense)* **ausir** 23.5; *substantivized inf., masc., obl. sg.* **auzir** the power of hearing 1.6, 3.9. [CL AUDĪRE *FEW* 1: 173; It. *udire*, Sp. *oir*; cf. E. *audio*]

avan *adv.* first; *conj.* **avan que** before 30.46, 30.88. [LL ĂBĂNTE *FEW* 24: 11; It. *avanti*, Sp. *avante*, Fr. *avant*]

ave *see* **avenir.**

avem *see* **aver.**

avenenz *see* **avinen.**

avenha *see* **avenir.**

avenidọr *n. masc.* future: *obl. sg.* **avenidor** 29.7. [**avenir** + **-idor**]

avenir *vb. intrans.* to succeed 30.64; *impersonal* to befall 14.68, 18.57: *pres. 3rd sg.* **ave** 18.57 var.; *pres. subj. 3rd sg.* **avenha** 14.68; *fut. 1st sg.* **avenrai** 30.64. [CL ādvĕnīre *FEW* 24: 193; It. *avvenire,* Sp. *avenir,* Fr. *avenir* n.]

aventura *n. fem.* adventure, good fortune 13.80; **mal'aventura** bad luck 14.71: *nom. sg.* **aventura** 14.71; *obl. sg.* **aventura** 13.80. [CL ādvĕntūra neuter pl. 'things that will come about,' VL *adventūra 'adventure' *FEW* 24: 197; It. *avventura,* Sp. *aventura,* Fr. *aventure,* E. *adventure*]

aventurier *adj.* enterprising: *masc., nom. sg.* **aventurers** 25.82. [**aventura** + **-ier**]

avẹr *vb. trans.* to have 4.41, 5.5, 5.6, 8.25, 8.30, 9.38, 11.28, 12.13, 13.28, 14.49, 15.32, 16.12, 16.20, 17.20, 18.28, 18.31, 18.34, 20.3, 21.24, 23.15, 23.31, 26.27, 26.51, 27.14, 27.34, 27.44, 28.58, 29.8, 29.9, 30.34, 30.79, 32.7; to possess *(feudal)* 20.20, 22.16, *(erotic)* 6.10, 7.2; to own wealth, to be wealthy 16.24, 24.12; *substantivized inf., sg.* **aver** wealth 24.40, 24.43, 26.48, *pl.* **avers** possessions 25.103; to feel (an emotion) 1.7, 10.39, 13.10, 18.27, 19.51, 21.73, 23.29, 26.49; to serve as, to be 28.44; *inchoative* to begin to have, to get, to receive 2.23, 2.27, 8.24, 11.25, 12.18, 13.54, 16.10, 16.13, 16.14, 17.45, 18.12, 22.35, 23.23, 23.24, 23.32, 23.39, 23.40, 25.105, 26.24, 26.40, 27.26, 30.58; to make (a friend) 11.45; to win over 26.8, to receive (news) 18.57; *durative* to keep 12.25 var. (= **te** 12.25), to dedicate 16.6.

3rd sg. of **aver,** *impersonal, with* **i** *(Fr.* il y a) there is, there are 9.29, 12.26, 14.41, 15.19; *3rd sg. of* **aver** *without* **i** *in the same sense* 3.3, 12.39, 25.66; **tant a que** it has been so long since 28.20, 28.27.

aver cor to intend 6.8, 15.38, 23.14; **aver (lo, son) cor** . . . one's heart is . . . 17.36, to love *(with adverb of place referring to lady)* 30.82; **aver crezensa a** to believe 6.29, 28.41; **aver dan** to suffer 21.64, 21.79; **aver (m') entendensa en** to have (my) mind on 28.18; **aver (son) esper en** to hope in 26.23; **aver in jutamen** to have power of (last) judgment over 11.17; **aver mal** to suffer 27.41, 27.41; **aver membransa** to remember 28.47; **aver meravillas** to be amazed 18.7; **aver mestier** to serve 25.85; **aver nom** to be called 3.3, 21.17, 30.1, to be renowned 11.38; **aver ops a X** to be necessary to X, for X to need 24.9; **aver semblansa** to resemble 28.42; **aver sovinensa** to remember 2.16; **aver talan** to wish 7.21, 8.6, 19.37, 20.2; **aver tort** to be wrong 30.18; **aver valor aprob** to be esteemed by 11.34.

Used with inf. in separable future forms: **dir** . . . **ay** 31.7, 31.25.

Used with pp. in compound tenses: present of **aver** (= *Fr.* passé composé) 2.13, 2.24, 3.10, 5.16, 6.25, 7.1, 7.2, 7.4, 7.7, 9.14, 10.29, 10.33, 10.39, 11.11, 11.14, 11.77, 12.4, 12.30 var., 13.50, 13.51, 14.27, 14.44, 16.36, 16.42, 17.38, 17.40, 17.48, 18.13, 18.13, 18.46, 18.54, 19.3, 19.34, 19.51, 19.51, 19.55, 19.63, 20.4, 21.3, 22.10, 23.42, 25.20, 25.63, 25.75, 26.29, 28.2, 28.49, 28.53, 28.67, 29.11, 30.7, 30.39, 30.40, 30.89, 32.14; *pres. subj. of* **aver** 24.37; *imperf. of* **aver** 1.6, 21.17, 21.44, 21.58, 23.16, 28.10, 32.17; *fut. of* **aver** 10.19, 24.20; *pret. of* **aver** 3.8, 9.43, 30.4, 30.8, 30.24, 31.41; *past subj. of* **aver** 1.6, 7.23, 9.56, 21.16, 30.76; *2nd cond. of* **aver** 19.57, 28.70; *inf. of* **aver** 30.75.

Forms: Pres. 1st sg. **ai** 2.13, 2.27, 4.41, 5.16, 6.8, 6.25, 7.1, 7.2, 7.4, 7.7, 8.25, 10.29, 10.33, 10.39, 15.32, 15.38, 16.6, 16.13, 16.14, 16.36, 17.36, 17.40, 18.7, 18.34, 18.54, 19.55, 20.2, 20.3, 21.3, 23.23, 23.24,

23.32, 23.39, 23.42, 27.34, 27.41, 27.44, 28.2, 28.18, 28.49, 28.53, 28.58, 28.67, 29.8, **ay** 13.10, 19.37, 19.51, 19.51, 19.63, 31.7, 31.25; *3rd sg.* **a** 2.24, 8.6, 11.11, 11.14, 11.17, 12.4, 12.13, 12.26, 12.30 var., 12.39, 13.28, 14.27, 14.41, 14.44, 14.49, 15.19, 16.20, 16.42, 17.20, 17.38, 17.45, 18.13, 18.13, 18.28, 19.3, 19.34, 20.4, 21.64, 28.20, 28.27, 29.11, 30.18, 30.39, 30.40, 30.89, **ha** 26.23, 27.14, 25.63, 30.82; *1st pl.* **avem** 8.30, 9.14; *2nd pl.* **avetz** 13.50, 13.51, 18.57, 28.42, 28.47, **avez** 3.10; *3rd pl.* **an** 17.48, 21.24, 25.20, 25.75, 26.27, 26.29, 26.51, 30.7, 32.14, **ant** 11.77, 18.46, 22.10, **aun** 21.24 var.

   Pres. subj. 1st sg. **aia** 8.24; *3rd sg.* **aia** 2.23, 6.10, 6.29, 24.12, 30.58, 30.79, **aja** 2.16; *1st pl.* **aiam** 12.25 var.; *3rd pl.* **aian** 24.37.

   Imperf. 3rd sg. **avia** 1.6, 3.3, 3.3, 5.5, 5.6, 11.38, 23.16, 27.41, 28.10, **avi'** 21.44; *2nd pl.* **avias** 21.17; *3rd pl.* **avion** 21.58, **avián** 32.17.

   Fut. 1st sg. **aurai** 16.12, 18.12, 23.40, 32.7; *3rd sg.* **aura** 18.31, 20.20, 24.9, 24.20; *1st pl.* **aurem** 12.18, 25.85; *2nd pl.* **auretz** 13.54 var., 18.57, **aurez** 13.54, 18.57 var., **aures** 18.57 var., **auret** 13.54 (see note); *3rd pl.* **auran** 10.19, 21.73.

   1st cond. 1st sg. **auria** 7.21, 23.31, 28.41, **aurie** 23.31 var.; *2nd pl.* **auriaz** 23.15; *3rd pl.* **auríen** 11.25.

   Pret. 1st sg. **agui** 18.41; *3rd sg.* **ac** 1.7, 3.8, 9.29, 9.38, 11.34, 25.66, 30.1, 30.4, 31.41, **hac** 30.24, 30.34, **ag** 11.28; *1st pl.* **aguem** 9.43; *3rd pl.* **agron** 30.8, **agro** 25.105.

   Past subj. 1st sg. **agues** 9.56, 23.14, 23.29; *3rd sg.* **agues** 1.6, 30.76; *2nd pl.* **aguessetz** 7.23, 21.16 var., **acses** 21.16, **avessez** 7.23 var.

   2nd cond. 1st sg. **agra** 26.49, **agr'** 19.57; *3rd sg.* **agra** 27.26 var.; *2nd pl.* **agratz** 27.26 var., 28.70, **agras** 27.26; *3rd pl.* **agran** 26.49 var.

   Pp. (with **eser***), masc., nom. sg.* **aütz** 28.44; *(with* **aver***) masc., obl. sg.* **agut** 7.2, 10.39 var., 21.17, **avut** 10.39, 21.17 var., **angut** 21.17 var.; *fem., obl. sg.* **aguda** 19.51 var., **avuda** 19.51, **aüda** 19.51 var.

   Inf. **aver** 11.45, 16.10, 16.24, 18.27, 21.79, 22.16, 22.35, 26.8, 26.24, 26.40, 29.9, 30.75; *substantivized, masc., obl. sg.* **aver** 24.40, 24.43, 26.48; *obl. pl.* **avers** 25.103.

   [CL ʜᴀ̆ʙᴇʀᴇ *FEW* 4: 363; It. *avere,* Sp. *haber,* Fr. *avoir*]

aversier (1) *n. masc.* devil: *nom. sg.* **aversers** 25.83. [**aversier** (2)]

aversier (2) *adj.* impious 25.61, hostile 29.30: *masc., nom. sg.* **aversiers** 29.30; *obl. pl.* **aversers** 25.61. [CL ᴀ̆ᴅᴠᴇ̆ʀsᴀʀɪ̆ᴜᴍ *FEW* 24: 198; It. *avversario,* Sp. *adversario,* Fr. *adversaire,* E. *adversary*]

avessez, avetz, avez *see* **aver.**

avi (1) *n. masc.* grandfather, ancestor, lineage: *obl. sg.* **avi** 14.43. [CL ᴀ̆ᴠᴜᴍ 'grandfather' *FEW* 1: 189 (It. *avo*) + **-i**; cf. CL ᴀ̆ᴠɪ̆ᴀᴍ 'grandmother']

avi' (2) 21.44, **avia, avián, avias** *see* **aver.**

avinẹn *adj.* attractive, charming: *masc., nom. sg.* **avinenz** 3.2; *obl. sg.* **avinen** 2.26, 23.1, **avinent** 16.41 var. (= **covenen** 16.41); *vocative* **avinens** 7.17, **avenenz** 7.17 var. [pres. part. of **avenir**]

avinẹnsa *n. fem.* praise: *obl. sg.* **avinenssa** 6.24. [**avinen** + **-ensa**]

avinent, avinenz *see* **avinen.**

avion *see* **aver.**

ávol *adj.* bad (reputation) 12.59, disagreeable (reason) 31.22: *masc., obl. sg.* **avol** 12.59; *fem., obl. sg.* **avol** 31.22. [Gk. *áboulos* 'thoughtless' *FEW* 24: 46; influence of CL ʜᴀ̆ʙɪ̆ʟᴇᴍ may explain the lack of **-a** in the feminine (**avol**, not ***avola**); Sp. *ávol*]

avuda, avut, ay *see* **aver.**

ayre *see* **aire** (2).
aysi (1) 12.39, *see* **aisi** (1).
aysi (2) 19.9, 19.16, 25.55 var., *see* **aisi** (2).
ayssi *see* **aisi** (2).
aytal, aytals *see* **aital.**
ayzina *see* **aizina.**
az *see* **a** (2).
aziramęn *n. masc.* anger: *obl. sg.* **asiramen** 23.8. [**azirar** + **-amen** (1)]
azirar *vb. trans.* to hate; *refl.* to become angry 29.37: *pp., masc., nom. pl.*
  azirat 29.37. [VL *ADĪRĀRE *FEW* 24:142; It. *adirare,* Sp. *airar*]
azǫlh *n. masc.* horizon: *obl. sg.* **asuèlh** 32.12. [**azolhar** 'to look at' (VL
  *ADŎCŪLĀRE *FEW* 7: 314, 7: 321); It. *adocchiare,* Sp. *aojar*]

badar *vb. intrans.* to gape, to stand in astonishment: *pres. 3rd sg.* **bad'**
  13.89; *imper. 2nd sg.* **bada** 13.55, 13.55. [LL BĂTĀRE *FEW* 1: 287; It.
  badare, Fr. *bayer,* E. *to bay*]
bagasa *n. fem.* slut: *nom. sg.* **bagassa** 31.25. [LGr. **bakchassa* from CGr.
  bakchās 'bacchante' Keller; cf. **bacassa *FEW* 1: 196; It. *bagascia,* Sp.
  bagasa, OFr. *baiasse*]
bailia *n. fem.* power, authority: *obl. sg.* **baylia** 13.27. [**baile** 'bailiff' (CL
  BAJŬLUM *FEW* 1: 207; It. *bailo,* Sp. *baile*) + **-ia**]
bais *n. masc.* kiss: *obl. sg.* **bais** 7.20. [CL BĂSĬUM *FEW* 1: 272; It. *bacio,* Sp.
  beso]
baizar *vb. trans.* to kiss: *pres. 1st pl.* **baysam** 31.10 var.; *pret. 3rd sg.* **baiset**
  30.70, *1st pl.* **bayzem** 31.10; *pres. part., masc., obl. sg. (or undeclined)*
  baizan 4.3, **bayzan** 31.23; *pp., masc., obl. sg.* **baisat** 30.89; *inf.* **baisar**
  30.49, **bayzar** 31.14. [CL BĂSĬĀRE *FEW* 1: 269; It. *baciare,* Sp. *besar,* Fr.
  baiser]
balai *n. masc.* rod, switch: *obl. pl.* **balais** 6.15. [Ctc. **banatlo,* **balatno*
  FEW 1: 232; Fr. *balai*]
balaiar *vb. trans.* to beat: *pres. 3rd sg.* **balaia** 6.16. [**balai** + **-ar** (2)]
balais *see* **balai.**
balansar *vb. intrans.* to hesitate: *pres. 3rd sg.* **balansa** 14.5. [**balansa** 'uncertainty' (VL *BILANCĬAM *FEW* 1: 363; It. *bilancia,* Sp. *balanza,* Fr. *balance,* E. *balance*) + **-ar** (2)]
balcǫn *n. masc.* balcony: *obl. sg.* **balcon** 3.11. [Frankish *balko *FEW* 1: 215
  + **-on** (1); It. *balcone,* Sp. *balcón,* Fr. *balcon,* E. *balcony*]
balestier *n. masc.* crossbowman: *nom. sg.* **balestiers** 25.55. [**balesta**
  'crossbow' (CL BALLĬSTAM *FEW* 1: 222; It. *balestra,* Sp. *ballesta*) + **-ier**]
baralha *n. fem.* attack, offensive: *obl. pl.* **baralhas** 25.25 (see note).
  [**baralhar** 'to quarrel' (CL VĀRĀRE 'to measure the breadth of a river by
  indirect means' + **-alhar** *FEW* 14: 174–75); Sp. *baraja* 'quarrel']
barat *n. masc.* fraud: *obl. sg.* **barat** 29.24. [**baratar** (Gk. *práttein *FEW* 9:
  330 + **-ar** [2])]
barata *n. fem.* bargain: *obl. sg.* **barata** 14.37. [**baratar** (Gk. *práttein
  FEW 9: 330 + **-ar** [2]) + **-a**; It. *baratta,* OFr. *barate,* E. *barter*]
barǫn *n. masc.* baron, great lord: *obl. pl.* **baros** 25.32, 25.77; *(used as nom.
  pl.)* **barons** 32.14. [Germ. *baro *FEW* 1: 254 + **-on** (1); It. *barone,* Sp.
  barón, Fr. *baron,* E. *baron*]
barręi *n. masc.* violence: *obl. sg.* **barrei** 24.15. [**barreiar** 'to plunder' (VL
  *BARRA 'crossbar' *FEW* 1: 257 + **-eiar**)]

bartás *n. masc.* thicket: *obl. pl.* **bartàs** 32.5. [**barta** 'bush' (Ctc. **barros FEW* 1: 262) + **-as** (2)]

bas (1) *adj.* low 12.18; late 31.24: *masc., obl. sg.* **bas** 12.18; *fem., obl. sg.* **bassa** 31.24. [LL ʙᴀ̆ssᴜᴍ *FEW* 1: 275; It. *basso*, Fr. *bas*, E. *base*]

bas (2) *adv.* low 30.72. [**bas** (1)]

batre *vb. trans.* to beat: *pres. subj. 3rd sg.* **bata** 14.39; *pp., masc., obl. sg.* **batut** well beaten 26.10. [CL ʙᴀ̆ᴛᴛᴜ̆ᴇʀᴇ *FEW* 1: 296; It. *battere*, Sp. *batir*, Fr. *battre*]

bauc *adj.* mad, crazy: *masc., obl. sg.* **baug** 32.10. [Germ. **bald*, VL ʙᴀʟᴅɪᴜs *FEW* 15: 32–33; cf. E. *bold*]

bauza *n. fem.* trick: *obl. sg.* **bauza** 31.27. [**bauzar** 'to deceive' (Germ. **bauson FEW* 15.83) + **-ar** (2) + **-a**]

baylia *see* **bailia**.

baysam, bayzan, bayzar, bayzem *see* baizar.

be (1) 2.19, 3.5, 18.31, 23.42, *see* **ben** (1).

be (2) 6.6, 13.47, 15.22, 15.25, 19.50, 19.55, 19.63, 23.3, 26.16, 28.36, 28.52, 28.67, 29.1, 30.27, 30.64, 30.73, *see* **ben** (2).

bé (3) 11.49, *see* **ben** (2).

begues, begut *see* **beure**.

bẹl *adj.* beautiful (woman) 2.27, 3.5, 13.85, 16.41, 19.1, 19.18, 19.31 var. (= **bo** 19.31), 19.49, 19.65, 31.3, (woman's eyes) 15.35, 16.47, 18.43 var., (cloth) 21.20; handsome (man) 5.3, 7.17, 18.48, 25.62; friendly (face, manner) 16.37, 21.7; gracious (conversation, skill, comportment) 15.28, 21.30, 28.43, 29.18; attractive (choice) 27.37; agreeable (prospect) 21.42; pleasant (terrain) 22.33 var.; *see also Proper Names:* **Belhs Deportz**.

    eser bel a to please (**bel** *neuter*) 2.7, 8.7, 9.20, (**bels** *masc.*) 15.2; **bel senher Dieus** fair lord God 27.31; **bel viure** living well 26.15.

    Forms: masc., nom. sg. **bels** 5.3, 15.2, 18.48, **belhs** 28.43; *obl. sg.* **bel** 19.31 var., 21.20, 21.30, 21.42, 26.15, **belh** 2.27, 29.18; *vocative sg.* **bels** 7.17, 25.62, **bel** (*before* **s-**) 27.31; *obl. pl.* **bels** 15.28, 15.35, 16.47, 18.43 var., 22.33 var., **bel** (*before* **s-**) 16.37; *fem., nom. sg.* **bella** 3.5, **bel'** 19.18, **bell'** 16.41; *obl. sg.* **bela** 31.3, **bella** 21.7, 27.37; *vocative sg.* **bela** 13.85, 19.49, 19.65, **bel'** 19.1; *neuter, nom. sg.* **bel** 2.7, 8.7, **belh** 9.20. [CL ʙᴇ̆ʟʟᴜᴍ *FEW* 1: 321; It. *bello*, Sp. *bello*, Fr. *beau*]

belazọr *comparative adj.* more beautiful: *fem., nom. sg.* **belayre** 13.33. [**bel** + **-azor**]

belh, belhs, bell', bella, bels *see* **bel**.

beltat *n. fem.* beauty: *nom. sg.* **beutatz** 12.32; *obl. sg.* **beutat** 13.45. [**bel** + **-tat**]

beluga *n. fem.* spark: *nom. sg.* **beluia** 14.13. [Gk. *pomphólyx* 'bubble,' ML ꜰᴀᴍꜰᴀʟᴜ̄ᴄᴀᴍ 'foam,' **ʙɪsʟᴜ̄ᴄᴀᴍ* 'spark' *FEW* 9: 146–50; Fr. *berlue* 'poor vision']

bẹṇ (1) *n. masc.* good (*collective*) 1.2 var., 2.19, 18.31, 19.15, 23.42; good thing 15.31, 17.18, 17.20, 27.44; **voler ben (a)** to love, **voler ben major (a)** to love (someone) better 3.5: *nom. sg.* **bes** 17.18, 19.15; *obl. sg.* **ben** 1.2 var. (= **bon** 1.2), 15.31, 17.20, 27.44, **be** 2.19, 3.5, 18.31, 23.42. [**ben** (2)]

bẹṇ (2) *adv.* well *passim*; for sure 8.11, 16.23; fully 25.34; indeed 3.10, 15.29, 19.67, 23.3, 29.1, 30.24; just 18.24, 18.49, 18.54; quite 6.6, 19.32, 25.82, 26.45, 28.52; really 27.21; surely 6.18, 9.16, 13.23, 13.47, 13.59,

15.22, 16.33, 19.63, 25.81, 27.43, 28.35, 28.36; truly 19.55; very 10.17; very much 7.9.

ben certanamen most certainly 30.57; **ben . . . vengut** welcome 21.30; **canta ben apertamen** he sings with full throat 30.35; **esta ben** it is well 8.5; **fort be** very well 30.27, 30.73; **molt ben** very well 16.36; **si ben** although 15.25, 30.41, even though 23.18.

Forms: **ben** 2.4, 2.7, 3.10, 5.3, 6.18, 7.9, 8.5, 8.11, 9.16, 10.17, 13.23, 13.59, 15.29, 16.23, 16.33, 16.36, 16.51, 18.24, 18.49, 18.54, 19.32, 19.67, 21.30, 23.17, 23.18, 23.34, 25.34, 25.81, 25.82, 26.3, 26.3, 26.45, 27.21, 27.43, 28.35, 29.15, 30.24, 30.29, 30.30, 30.35, 30.41, 30.57; **be** 6.6, 13.47, 15.22, 15.25, 19.50, 19.55, 19.63, 23.3, 26.16, 28.36, 28.52, 28.67, 29.1, 30.27, 30.64, 30.73; **bé** 11.49.

[CL bĕne *FEW* 1: 323; It. *bene,* Sp. *bien,* Fr. *bien*]

bendich *n. masc.* pleasing expression, eloquence: *obl. sg.* **bendig** 5.10. [CL bĕnĕdĭctum *FEW* 1: 324; It. *benedetto,* Fr. *benêt* 'fool'; cf. **benezech**]

benestan *adj.* seemly, honorable: *masc., nom. pl.* **benestan** 21.28. [**ben** (2) + **estan,** *pres. part. of* **estar**]

benezęch *adj.* blessed, holy (water): *fem., obl. sg.* **benezeita** 30.3. [CL bĕnĕdĭctum *FEW* 1: 324; cf. **bendich**]

benigne *adj.* benevolent: *masc., nom. sg.* **benignes** 25.82. [CL bĕnĭgnum *FEW* 1: 325; It. *benigno,* Sp. *benigno,* Fr. *bénin,* E. *benign*]

bergiera *n. fem.* shepherdess: *obl. sg.* **bergeira** 28.1. [LL bĕrbĭcārĭum, VL *vĕrvēcārĭum *FEW* 14: 336 + **-a**; Fr. *bergère*]

bes *see* **ben** (1).

besan *see* **bezan.**

bęstia *n. fem. collective* livestock: *obl. sg.* **bestia** 13.20. [CL bēstĭam, borrowed as though *bĕstĭam *FEW* 1: 342; It. *bestia,* Sp. *bestia,* Fr. *bête,* E. *beast*]

bęure *vb. trans.* to drink: *pres. 3rd pl.* **bevon** 26.17; *past. subj. 3rd sg.* **begues** 26.10; *pp., undeclined* **begut** 9.43. [CL bĭbĕre *FEW* 1: 350; It. *bere,* Sp. *beber,* Fr. *boire*; cf. E. *bibulous*]

beutat, beutatz *see* **beltat.**

bevon *see* **beure.**

bezan *n. masc.* penny: *obl. sg.* **besan** 21.74. [CL bўzăntĭum *FEW* 1: 669, from a coin struck at Byzantium; It. *besante,* Sp. *besante,* Fr. *besant,* E. *bezant*]

bistensar *vb. refl.* to hesitate: *pret. 3rd sg.* **bistenset** 30.83, **bitenset** 30.83 var. [**bis-** + **tensar** 'to dispute' (VL *tĕntĭāre *FEW* 13, part 1: 228)]

blanc *adj.* white: *masc., obl. sg.* **blanc** 32.18. [Germ. *blank *FEW* 15: 145; It. *bianco,* Sp. *blanco,* Fr. *blanc,* E. *blank*]

blandir *vb. trans.* to show kindness toward, to flatter 20.27; to pardon 19.11: *pres. subj. 3 sg.* **blanda** 19.11, 20.27. [CL blandīre *FEW* 1: 394; It. *blandire,* Sp. *blandir,* E. *to blandish*]

blasmar *vb. trans.* to criticize: *pres. 3 sg.* **blasma** 17.34, *3rd pl.* **blasmen** 16.15; *pp., masc., nom. sg.* **blasmatz** 23.48. [VL *blăstĕmāre *FEW* 1: 403 = ChL blăsphēmāre + CL aestĭmāre; It. *biasimare,* Sp. *lastimar,* Fr. *blâmer,* E. *to blame*]

blau *adj.* blue: *fem., obl. sg.* **blaua** 25.76. [Frankish *blāo *FEW* 1: 398; Fr. *bleu,* E. *blue*]

blęs *adj.* stammering: *fem., obl. sg.* **blesza** 26.1. [CL blaesum *FEW* 1:392; OFr. *blois*]

blęt *n. masc.* beet: *obl. pl.* **bles** 26.12. [CL BLĬTUM *FEW* 1: 410; Sp. *bledo*, Fr. *blette, bette*]

blǫn *adj.* blond: *fem., nom. sg.* **blonda** 19.18. [Germ. **blunda- FEW* 15: 171; It. *biondo*, Sp. *blondo*, Fr. *blond*, E. *blond*]

blǫs *adj.* lacking: *masc., nom. sg.* **blos** 11.31. [OHG *blōz FEW* 15: 170; OFr. *blos*]

bo *see* **bon** (1), (2).

bǫca *n. fem.* mouth: *obl. sg.* **boca** 12.25, **boch'** 16.7. [CL BŬCCAM 'cheek' *FEW* 1: 586; It. *bocca*, Sp. *boca*, Fr. *bouche*]

bocal *n. masc.* entryway: *obl. sg.* **bocal** 25.16. [**boca** + **-al**; Fr. *boucau* 'entryway of a port']

bocaraṇ *n. masc.* an article of clothing made of linen cloth dyed dark red (cf. *LR* 3: 232): *nom. pl.* **bocaran** 21.20. [*Bokhara (Buhārā FEW* 19: 36, city of the Uzbeks, in central Asia, from which fine linen was imported) + **-an** (2); It. *bucherame*, Sp. *bocarán*, Fr. *bougran*, E. *buckram*]

boch' *see* **boca**.

bocs *see* **bosc**.

bǫṇ (1) *n. masc.* good (things) 1.2: *obl. sg.* **bon** 1.2, **bo** 11.58. [**bon** (2)]

bǫṇ (2) *adj.* good *passim;* **de bon cor** sincerely 2.28, 23.10, 31.8; **eser bon e bel a** to please 8.7, 9.20.

    Forms: masc., nom. sg. **bos** 9.22, 9.27, 9.39, 16.51, 24.9; *obl. sg.* **bon** 2.28, 3.10, 5.14, 6.17, 8.7, 8.26, 9.20, 14.45, 16.12, 16.14, 16.36, 21.78, 23.6, 23.10, 27.14, 27.34, 31.8, **bo** 11.28, 11.32, 19.31; *vocative sg.* **bos** 7.17; *obl. pl.* **bons** 1.3, **bos** 22.33 var.; *fem., nom. sg.* **bona** 27.46; *obl. sg.* **bona** 23.2, 26.9; *obl. pl.* **bonas** 5.12.

    [CL BŎNUM *FEW* 1: 435; It. *buono*, Sp. *bueno*, Fr. *bon*]

bontat *n. fem.* goodness: *obl. sg.* **bontat** 29.42. [CL BŎNĬTĀTEM *FEW* 1: 433; It. *bontà*, Sp. *bondad*, Fr. *bonté*, E. *bounty*]

bordonier *n. masc.* pilgrim, crusader: *obl. pl.* **bordoners** 25.38. [**bordon** 'pilgrim's staff' (CL BŬRDŌNEM 'mule' *FEW* 1: 633; It. *bordone* 'joist,' Sp. *bordón*) + **-ier**]

borgęs *n. masc.* burgher: *obl. pl.* **borzes** 30.42. [**borc** (Germ. **burg- FEW* 15: 21; It. *borgo*, Sp. *burgo*) + **-es** (2); Fr. *bourgeois*]

bǫrsa *n. fem.* purse: *obl. sg.* **borsa** 31.28. [Gk. *byrsa FEW* 1: 667, LL BŬRSAM B-W; It. *borsa*, Sp. *bolsa*, Fr. *bourse*, E. *purse*]

borsiṇ *n. masc.* purse, bag: *obl. sg.* **borssi** 9.68. [**borsa** + **-in**]

borzes *see* **borges**.

bos *see* **bon** (2).

bǫsc *n. masc.* wood, forest: *nom. pl.* **bosc** 8.2; *obl. pl.* **bòscs** 32.5, **bocs** 22.33. [Germ. **bosk FEW* 1: 447; It. *bosco*, Fr. *bois*; cf. E. *bosky*]

bǫu *n. masc.* ox: *obl. sg.* **bueu** 26.19. [CL BŎVEM *FEW* 1: 447; It. *bove*, Sp. *buey*, Fr. *boeuf*, E. *beef*]

braces *see* **bratz**.

braguier *n. masc.* (pair of) trousers: *nom. sg.* **braguers** 25.59. [**braia** 'breeches' (CL [from Ctc.] BRĀCA *FEW* 1: 482; It. *braca*, Sp. *braga*, Fr. *braie*) + **-ier**]

bran *n. masc.* sword: *nom. pl.* **bran** 21.19; *obl. pl.* **brans** 22.36, 25.3. [Germ. **brand FEW* 15: 251; It. *brando*, E. *(Marlon) Brando*]

branca *n. fem.* branch: *obl. sg.* **branca** 8.14. [LL BRANCA 'paw' *FEW* 1: 496; It. *branca*, Sp. *branca*, Fr. *branche*, E. *branch*]

brans *see* **bran**.

brasàs *see* **brazás.**

bratz *n. masc.* arm: **braces** *used as nom. pl.* 25.12; *obl. pl.* **bratz** 1.5, 7.10, **braz** 1.6. [CL BRĂCHĬUM *FEW* 1: 488; It. *braccio*, Sp. *brazo*, Fr. *bras*; cf. E. *to embrace*]

brau *adj.* rude, harsh, cruel: *masc., nom. sg.* **braus** 3.3. [CL BĂRBĂRUM, VL *BRÁBARUM *FEW* 1: 248; It. *bravo*, Sp. *bravo*, Fr. *brave*, E. *brave*]

braz *see* **bratz.**

brazás *n. masc.* fire: *obl. sg.* **brasàs** 32.15. [**braza** (Germ. **brasa FEW* 1: 504; It. *bragia*, Sp. *brasa*, Fr. *braise*) + **-ás** (1)]

brẹc *adj.* notched, chipped: *fem., nom. sg.* **brecha** 14.26. [Germ. *brecha* n. *FEW* 1: 508; It. *breccia*, Sp. *brecha*, Fr. *brèche*]

brẹu (1) *n. masc.* letter: *obl. sg.* **breu** 11.52; *obl. pl.* **breus** 11.65. [**breu** (2)]

brẹu (2) *adj.* short; **en breu** soon 15.39: *masc., obl. sg.* **breu** 8.28, 15.39. [CL BRĔVEM 'short,' LL 'document' *FEW* 1: 520; It. *breve*, Sp. *breve*, Fr. *bref*, E. *brief*]

breumẹns *adv.* soon; **breumens** 4.38. [**breu** (2) + **-men** + **-s**]

breus *see* **breu** (1).

brizar *vb. intrans.* to shatter: *pres. 3rd sg.* **briza** 14.7. [VL BRĪSĀRE *FEW* 1: 531; Fr. *briser*]

brọ *n. masc.* broth: *obl. sg. (used as nom. sg.)* **bro** 26.19. [Germ. **brod FEW* 15: 291; It. *brodo*, E. *broth*]

broẹt *n. masc.* soup: *obl. sg.* **broet** 26.22. [**bro** + **-et**]

bruida *n. fem.* noise: *obl. sg.* **bruida** 26.26. [**brugir** 'to make noise' *FEW* 10: 546 (VL *BRŪGĔRE B-W + **-ir**) + **-ida**; cf. Fr. *bruit*]

bueu *see* **bou.**

bufar *vb. trans.* to blow on: *pres. 3rd sg.* **bufa** 12.47 var.; *substantivized inf., masc.* **bufar** breath 32.1. [Onomatopoetic *buff-, puff- FEW* 1: 594; It. *buffare*, Sp. *bufar*, Fr. *bouffer*, E. *to puff*]

c' (1) *rel. pron., see* **que** (1).

c' (2) *conj., see* **que** (3).

cabal *adj.* superior, distinguished: *nom. sg.* **cabaus** 16.5. [**cap** + **-al** *FEW* 2: 342]

cadegut *see* **cazer.**

cadẹna *n. fem.* chain 11.73, fig. enslavement *(of love)* 17.12, *(political)* 32.13: *obl. sg.* **cadena** 17.12; *obl. pl.* **cadenas** 32.13, **kadenas** 11.73, **kdenas** 11.73 var. [CL CATĒNAM *FEW* 2: 502; It. *catena*, Sp. *cadena*, Fr. *chaîne*, G. *Kette*, E. *chain*; cf. E. *concatenation*]

caichals *see* **caisal.**

cairẹl *n. masc.* bolt, a short, heavy shaft with a blunt head intended to be shot from a crossbow: *nom. sg.* **cairels** 25.54; *obl. pl.* **cairels** 22.35, 25.3, 25.48. [VL *QUADRĔLLUM *FEW* 2: 1406; It. *quadrello*, Sp. *cuadrillo*, Fr. *carreau*, E. *quarrel*; cf. E. *quadrant*]

caisal *n. masc.* molar (tooth): *obl. pl.* **caichals** 25.71. [**cais** 'jaw' (VL *CAPSĔUM *FEW* 2: 317) + **-al**]

caitiu *adj.* miserable, wretched: *nom. sg.* **caitius** 18.40, **chaitius** 15.14, *obl. sg.* **caitiu** 18.30. [CL CAPTĪVUM 'prisoner,' VL *CACTĪVUM *FEW* 2: 332; It. *cattivo*, Sp. *cautivo*, Fr. *chétif*, E. *caitiff, captive*]

cal (1) *interrogative pron., in indirect question* who 31.42; *interrogative adj., in direct question* which? 12.32, 24.17, *in indirect question* which 14.17, 26.28: *masc., nom. sg.* **cals** 26.28, **quals** 31.42; *fem., nom. sg.* **cals**

12.32, **qals** 24.17; *obl. sg.* **cal** 14.17. [CL QUĀLEM *FEW* 2: 1413; It. *quale,*
Sp. *cual,* Fr. *quel;* cf. E. *quality*]

cal (2) 14.39, 20.1, 22.49, *see* **caler.**

calar *vb. refl.* to be silent, to fall silent: *pres. 2nd pl.* **calatz** 19.38. [CL (from
Gk.) CALĀRE 'to lower' *FEW* 2: 60; It. *calare,* Sp. *calar,* Fr. *caler*]

calc' *see* **calque.**

calęr *vb. impersonal* to concern, to interest: *pres. 3rd sg.* **cal** 14.39, 20.1,
22.49. [CL CALĒRE 'to be hot, to be ardent' *FEW* 2: 84; It. *calere;* cf. E.
nonchalant]

calfar *vb. trans.* to warm: *pret. 1st sg.* **calfei** 9.23. [CL CALEFACĔRE, VL
*CALFARE *FEW* 2: 80; Fr. *chauffer;* cf. E. *chauffeur*]

calici *n. masc.* chalice: *obl. sg.* **calici** 30.97. [CL CALĬCEM *FEW* 2: 95; Fr. *calice,* E. *chalice*]

calmisa *n. fem.* pasture: *obl. sg.* **calmissa** 13.8 var. [**calm** (LL CALMA 'un-
cultivated land' *FEW* 2: 101, OFr. *chaume*) + **-isa**]

calque *indef. adj.* some, any: *masc., obl. sg.* **qualque** 23.15, 23.46; *fem.,
obl. sg.* **calc'** 23.30, **qualque** 30.62. [**cal** (1) + **que** (1) *FEW* 2: 1412; It.
qualche, Sp. *cualque,* Fr. *quelque*]

cals *see* **cal** (1).

cambiairitz *adj. fem.* changeable, fickle: *obl. sg.* **camjairitz** 19.42. [**cambiar** + **-airitz**]

cambiar *vb. trans.* to change 28.5, to exchange 13.70: *pp., fem., nom. sg.*
cambiada 28.5; *inf.* **camjar** 14.70. [CL CAMBĬĀRE 'to exchange' *FEW* 2:
120; It. *cambiare,* Fr. *changer,* E. *to change*]

cambisa *n. fem.* field: *obl. sg.* **chambissa** 13.8 var. [**cambon** (Ctc. **cambos
FEW* 2: 127) + **-isa**]

cambra *n. fem.* bedroom, chamber: *nom. sing.* **cambra** 15.41. [CL (from
Gk.) CAMĔRAM 'arched ceiling' *FEW* 2: 135; It. *camera,* Sp. *cámara,* Fr.
chambre, G. *Kammer,* E. *chamber, camera*]

camelin̦ *n. masc.* camel's hair (cloth): *obl. sg.* **camelin** 26.42. [CL
CAMĒLĪNUM 'of a camel'; cf. CAMĒLUM *FEW* 2: 129; OFr. *chamelin*]

camin̦ *n. masc.* road: *obl. sg.* **camin** 12.48, 32.4; *obl. pl.* **camis** 15.19. [LL
(from Ctc.) CAMMĪNUM *FEW* 2: 147; It. *cammino,* Sp. *camino,* Fr.
chemin]

camina *n. fem.* road: *obl. sg.* **chamina** 13.8 var. [**camin** + **-a**]

camiza *n. fem.* shirt: *obl. sg.* **camiza** 13.6, **chamisa** 13.8 var. [LL (from
Ctc.?) CAMĬSĬAM *FEW* 2: 142; It. *camicia,* Sp. *camisa,* Fr. *chemise,* E.
chemise]

camjairitz *see* **cambiairitz.**

camjar *see* **cambiar.**

campanha *n. fem.* field: *obl. sg.* **campaingna** 21.66 var., **canpaingna**
21.66 var. [CL CAMPĀNĬAM 'province of Italy,' LL CAMPANIA *FEW* 2: 153; It.
campagna, Sp. *campaña,* Fr. *Champagne,* E. *champagne*]

can (1) *n. masc.* a song 8.4, 14.35, 15.2, 15.6, 16.2, 16.3, 21.1, 29.2, 29.10;
singing 17.2, 21.34; power to sing 11.77: *nom. sg.* **chans** 14.35, 15.2,
15.6, 29.10, **chantz** 16.2, **chanz** 16.3; *obl. sg.* **chan** 8.4, 17.2, 21.1,
21.34, 29.2, **cánt** 11.77. [CL CANTUM *FEW* 2: 237; It. *canto,* Sp. *canto,* Fr.
chant, E. *chant;* cf. E. *canticle*]

can (2) *rel. pron.* what amount; *adv.* how 4.23, 18.10; **aitan can** as much as
23.40; **mas can** just 9.30; **tot** (. . .) **can** all that 2.3, 2.26, 10.33, 12.28,
12.29, 15.36, 29.22.

Forms: **can** 23.40; **cant** 10.33, 12.28, 12.29, 15.36; **qant** 18.10; **quan** 2.26, 4.23, 9.30, 29.22; **quant** 2.3.
[CL QUANTUM *FEW* 2: 1420; It. *quanto,* Sp. *cuanto*; cf. E. *quantity*]

can (3)*conj.* when 2.4, 2.7, 2.28, 3.7, 3.8, 3.9, 3.10, 3.11, 5.8, 7.8, 9.37, 9.43, 10.18, 11.11, 11.40, 13.44, 14.29, 15.3, 15.16, 15.22, 15.27, 17.3, 17.37, 18.1, 18.15, 19.67, 21.72, 21.73, 23.24, 23.29, 25.55, 26.44, 27.10, 30.4, 30.8, 30.70, 31.11, 31.38, 31.44; provided that, if 13.63; even if 16.10 var.; since 16.37, 23.3, 31.33 var. (= **car** 31.33); **lan can** when 15.1; **tan can** as long as 11.4.

Forms: **can** 13.44, 13.63, 14.29, 19.67, 23.24, 31.33; **cant** 10.18, 23.3, 25.55, 26.44, 27.10; **qan** 15.1, 15.16, 15.22, 17.37, 18.1, 18.15, 21.72; **qand** 7.8, 15.3, 15.27; **qant** 17.3; **quan** 2.4, 2.7, 2.28, 9.43, 11.4, 11.40, 16.10, 21.73, 23.29, 30.4, 30.70, 31.11, 31.38, 31.44; **quant** 3.7, 3.8, 3.9, 3.10, 3.11, 5.8, 9.37, 11.11, 16.37, 30.8.
[CL QUANDŌ *FEW* 2: 1417; It. *quando,* Sp. *cuando,* Fr. *quand*]

candelier *n. masc.* candle stand: *obl. pl.* **candelers** 25.92. [CL CANDE-LABRUM, VL *CANDELĀRĬUM *FEW* 2: 181; It. *candelaio,* Sp. *candelero,* Fr. *chandelier,* E. *chandelier*]

candius *conj.* as long as; **quandius que** as long as 11.1. [CL QUAMDĬŪ *FEW* 2: 1415 + **-s**]

canin *adj.* canine, of dogs, vile: *masc., obl. sg.* **canin** 12.37 var. [CL CANĪNUM *FEW* 2: 191; It. *canino,* Sp. *canino,* E. *canine*]

canpaingna *see* **campanha.**

canson *n. fem.* song: *nom. pl.* **chansos** 5.11; *obl. pl.* **chansons** 23.5, **chan-sos** 3.4, 5.6, 5.6, 5.12, 5.17. [CL CANTĬŌNEM *FEW* 2: 235; It. *canzone,* Sp. *canzón,* Fr. *chanson*]

cant *see* **can** (1), (2), (3).

cantador *adj. masc.* full of song: *nom. sg.* **chantaire** 2.25. [**cantar** + **-ador**]

cantar *vb. intrans.* to sing 3.4, 5.3, 8.3, 14.20, 17.6, 30.35; *trans.* 30.7 var., 30.8, 32.17.

Forms: pres. *3rd sg.* **canta** 14.20, 30.35, **chanta** 17.6, *3rd pl.* **chan-ton** 8.3; *imperf. 3rd sg.* **cantava** 3.4; *gerund* **chantan** in song, because of singing 28.39; **en chantan** as I sing 29.12; *pp., masc., undeclined* **cantat** 32.17; *fem., obl. sg.* **cantada** 30.7 var., 30.8; *inf.* **cantar** 5.4, **chantar** 5.3, 10.1, 18.59, 29.1; *substantivized inf., masc.* singing, *nom. sg.* **chantars** 16.1, 16.5, *obl. sg.* **cantar** 5.4, **chantar** 10.1, 18.59, 29.1.
[CL CANTĀRE *FEW* 2: 224; It. *cantare,* Sp. *cantar,* Fr. *chanter,* E. *to chant*]

cap *n. masc.* head: *obl. sg.* **cap** 9.47, 25.53, 31.27. [CL CAPUT, VL *CAPUM *FEW* 2: 345; It. *capo,* Sp. *cabo,* Fr. *chef,* E. *chief*; cf. E. *capital*]

capa *n. fem.* hood 26.41; cape 13.5, 25.76; cope 31.38: *obl. sg.* **capa** 25.76, 26.41, 31.38, **cap'** 13.5. [LL CAPPAM 'hood' *FEW* 2: 277; It. *cappa,* Sp. *capa,* Fr. *chape,* E. *cape*]

capdel *n. masc.* guide: *nom. sg.* **capdels** 21.18. [LL CAPITĔLLUM 'small head' *FEW* 2: 259; It. *capitello,* Sp. *caudillo,* Gascon *capdet* > Fr. *cadet,* E. *cadet*]

capdelar *vb. trans.* to advise: *pres. 2nd pl.* **capdelatz** 19.24. [**capdel** + **-ar** (2)]

capdels *see* **capdel.**

capelan *n. masc.* chaplain: *nom. sg.* **capellans** 30.83, **capellas** 30.5,

30.32; *obl. sg.* **capella** 30.99. [ML căpĕllānum *FEW* 2: 287; It. *cappellano*, Sp. *capellan*, Fr. *chapelain*, E. *chaplain*]

caple *n. masc.* combat 25.15, carnage 25.40: *nom. sg.* **chaples** 25.15, 25.40. [**caplar** 'to strike' Adams 545 (VL *cappāre 'to castrate, to cut' *FEW* 2: 280)]

caplier *n. masc.* slaughter: *nom. sg.* **chapliers** 25.4. [**caple** + **-ier**]

capǫn *n. masc.* capon, castrated rooster: *obl. pl.* **capos** 9.25. [CL cāpōnem, VL *cappōnem *FEW* 2: 268; It. *cappone*, Sp. *capón*, Fr. *chapon*, E. *capon*]

captal *n. masc.* captain, leader: *obl. pl.* **chaptaus** 12.61. [CL capitālem *FEW* 2: 254; It. *capitale*, Sp. *caudal*, Fr. *capital*, E. *capital*]

captenęr *vb. trans.* to defend: *inf.* **captener** 18.19. [**cap** + **tener**]

captęnh *n. masc.* behavior: *obl. pl.* **captenhs** 29.20. [**captener** Adams 543]

car (1) *adj.* dear; **car tener** to hold dear, to respect, to fear 26.32 var. [CL cārum *FEW* 2: 443; It. *caro*, Sp. *caro*, Fr. *cher*; cf. E. *to cherish*]

car (2) *conj.* *(stronger sense)* because, since 7.6, 7.13, 11.3, 15.32, 17.39, 18.11, 19.5 var., 19.42, 20.3, 20.9, 25.19, 25.80, 25.94, 25.96, 26.36, 28.60, 31.6, 31.33, 31.41; **car sol** just because 31.14; *(weaker sense)* for 6.9, 10.20, 11.26, 13.18, 15.18, 15.45, 16.14, 17.19, 17.47, 18.24, 18.51, 18.56, 19.11, 20.35, 21.3, 21.12, 21.44 var. (= **qe** 21.44), 25.46, 25.93, 26.46, 27.13, 27.21, 28.6, 28.18, 28.38, 29.2, 29.22, 30.20, 30.25, 30.42, 30.52, 30.80, 31.19.

Introducing subjunctive that, would that, I wish that 15.33; *introducing indicative* that 16.28, 18.7; so that, to 17.44.

Forms: **car** *passim*; **quar** 11.3, 11.26, 19.5 var., 28.6, 28.18, 28.38, 28.60, 29.2, 29.22, 30.20, 30.42.

[CL quārē *FEW* 2: 1421; Fr. *car*]

cara *n. fem.* face: *obl. sg.* **cara** 30.54, 31.15. [LL (from Gk.) caram *FEW* 2: 350; Sp. *cara*, Fr. *chère*, E. *cheer*]

carantęna *n. fem.* penance: *obl. sg.* **carantena** 17.40. [**caranta** 'forty' (CL quadrāgĭntā, VL *quaranta *FEW* 2: 1391) + **-ena**; It. *quarantina*, Sp. *cuarentena*, Fr. *quarantaine*, E. *quarantine*]

carbǫn *n. masc.* coal, ember: *obl. sg.* **carbo** 9.24 var., **carbon** 9.24 var.; *obl. pl.* **carbos** 9.24. [CL carbōnem *FEW* 2: 359; It. *carbone*, Sp. *carbon*, Fr. *charbon*, E. *carbon*]

carbonada *n. fem.* grilled meat: *obl. sg.* **charbonada** 24.27. [(**carn**) **carbonada**, pp., fem. of **carbonar** 'to grill' (**carbon** + **-ar** {2})]

cárcer *n. fem.* prison: *obl. sg.* **charcer** 11.71. [CL carcĕrem *FEW* 2: 364; It. *carcere*, Sp. *cárcel*, OFr. *chartre*; cf. E. *to incarcerate*]

cardenal *n. masc.* cardinal: *nom. sg.* **cardenals** 25.87. [ChL cardĭnālem *FEW* 2: 366; It. *cardinale*, Sp. *cardenal*, Fr. *cardinal*, E. *cardinal*]

carestia *n. fem.* lack, want: *obl. sg.* **carestia** 27.14. [CL carĭstĭam 'family banquet'; cf. *REW* 1694a, *FEW* 2: 373; It. *carestia*, Sp. *carestía*, OFr. *cherestie*]

caritat *n. fem.* charity, love: *obl. sg.* **caritat** 29.45. [CL carĭtātem *FEW* 2: 376; It. *carità*, Sp. *caridad*, Fr. *charité*, E. *charity*]

carn *n. fem.* flesh: *obl. sg.* **carn** 25.58, 32.9. [CL carnem *FEW* 2: 390; It. *carne*, Sp. *carne*, Fr. *chair*; cf. E. *carnal*]

carpentier *n. masc.* carpenter: *nom. sg.* **carpenters** 25.66. [CL carpentārĭum 'cartwright' *FEW* 2: 399; It. *carpentiere*, Sp. *carpintero*, Fr. *charpentier*, E. *carpenter*]

carrẹi *n. masc.* wagon train; booty 24.23 (see note): *obl. sg.* **charrei** 24.23. [**carreiar** 'to transport by wagon' (**car** 'wagon' [CL (from Gk.) CARRUM *FEW* 2: 436} + **-eiar**)]

carriera *n. fem.* road, path: *obl. sg.* **carreira** 28.72. [VL (VIAM) *CARRĀRĬAM 'road for wagons' *FEW* 2: 414; It. *carriera,* Sp. *carrera,* Fr. *carrière,* E. *career*]

cartier *n. masc.* quarter, piece, smithereen: *obl. pl.* **cartiers** 25.12, 25.72. [CL QUARTĀRĬUM 'of a fourth part'; cf. QUARTUM *FEW* 2: 1424; Fr. *quartier,* E. *quarter*]

cas *n. masc.* punishable deed: *obl. sg.* **cas** 12.54. [CL CĀSUM *FEW* 2: 481; It. *caso,* Sp. *caso,* Fr. *cas,* E. *case*]

cascuṇ *pron.* each one 8.3, 12.13; *adj.* each 16.11: *masc. nom. sg.* **cascus** 12.13, **chascus** 8.3; *obl. sg.* **chascun** 16.11. [LL (from Gk.) CATA influenced by CL QUĪSQUE *FEW* 2: 483; It. *ciascuno,* Sp. *cada uno,* Fr. *chacun*]

castẹl *n. masc.* castle: *obl. sg.* **castel** 5.1, 5.2; *obl. pl.* **chastels** 20.29. *See also Proper Names.* [CL CASTĚLLUM *FEW* 2: 470; It. *castello,* Sp. *castillo,* Fr. *château,* E. *castle*]

castïar *vb. trans.* to chastise: *pres. 3rd sg.* **chastia** 11.49. [CL CASTĪGĀRE *FEW* 2: 472; It. *castigare,* Sp. *castigar,* Fr. *châtier,* E. *to chasten, to castigate*]

castïazǫn *n. fem.* chastisement: *obl. sg.* **quastiazo** 11.22. [CL CASTĪGĀTĬŌNEM; cf. CASTĪGĀRE *FEW* 2: 472; E. *castigation*]

castïer *n. masc.* counsel, plan: *nom. sg.* **castiers** used as *obl. sg.* 25.2. [**castiar** + **-ier** *FEW* 2: 471]

cat *n. masc.* cat: *nom. sg.* **catz** 9.50, **chatz** 14.30, **cat** 9.50 var.; *obl. sg.* **cat** 9.33, 9.45, 9.72, **gat** 9.50 var. [LL CATTUM *FEW* 2: 520; It. *gatto,* Sp. *gato,* Fr. *chat,* E. *cat*]

catre *num.* four: **quatre** 9.62. [CL QUATTŬOR *FEW* 2: 1440; It. *quattro,* Sp. *cuatro,* Fr. *quatre;* cf. E. *quatuor*]

catz *see* **cat.**

causa (1) *n. fem.* 11.38, *see* **cauza.**

causa (2) *n. fem.* stocking: *obl. pl.* **causas** 13.7. [CL CALCĔUM, VL CALCĔAM *FEW* 2: 72; It. *calza,* Sp. *calza,* Fr. *chausse*]

causar *n. masc.* shoe; *obl. sg.* **caussar** 26.43 var., **causar** 26.43 var.; *obl. pl.* **caussars** 26.43, **causas** 26.43 var. [**causa** (2) + **-ar** (1)]

causas (1) *n. fem.* 13.7, *see* **causa** (2).

causas (2) *n. masc.* 26.43 var., *see* **causar.**

causir, causirai, causit *see* **cauzir.**

caussar *see* **causar.**

caut *adj.* hot: *masc., nom. sg.* **cautz** 9.27. [CL CALĬDUM, CALDUM *FEW* 2: 90; It. *caldo,* Sp. *caldo,* Fr. *chaud*]

cauza *n. fem.* reason 11.38, 31.22; creature 13.15; deed, action 13.77: *obl. sg.* **causa** 11.38, **cauza** 13.77, 31.22; *vocative sg.* **cauza** 13.15. [CL CAUSAM *FEW* 2: 542; It. *cosa,* Sp. *cosa,* Fr. *chose,* E. *cause*]

cauzir *vb. trans.* to discern 15.8, 23.21; to choose 6.25: *fut. 1st sg.* **chausirai** 15.8 var.; *pp., masc., obl. sg.* **chausit** 6.25; *inf.* **chausir** 23.21. [Gothic *kausjan FEW* 16: 302 (cf. E. *to choose*) + **-ir**; Fr. *choisir*]

caval *n. masc.* horse: *nom. sg.* **cavals** 25.55; *obl. pl* **cavals** 22.36. [CL CABALLUM *FEW* 2: 11; It. *cavallo,* Sp. *caballo,* Fr. *cheval;* cf. E. *chivalry*]

cavalaria *n. fem.* deeds of arms 10.34 (see note): *obl. sg.* **cavalaria** 10.34. [**caval** + **-aria**] cavaler *see* cavalier.

cavalgadọr *n. masc.* horseman, rider: *nom. sg.* cavalgayre 13.40. [caval-
gar + -ador]

cavalgar *vb. intrans.* to ride a horse: *pres. part., masc., obl. sg.* cavalgan
21.6. [LL CABALLICĀRE *FEW* 2: 7; It. *cavalcare,* Sp. *cabalgar,* Fr.
chevaucher]

cavalgayre *see* cavalgador.

cavalier *n. masc.* knight: *nom. sg.* cavaliers 4.1, cavalliers 3.1, 13.30 var.,
cavayers 13.30, cavalier 13.30 var.; *obl. sg.* cavalier 23.19, cavallier
6.19, 7.2, 7.9; *obl. pl.* cavalliers 30.77, cavalers 25.20, 25.77; *vocative
pl.* cavaler 25.2. [LL CABALLĀRĬUM *FEW* 2.5; It. *caballaio,* Sp. *caballero,*
Fr. *chevalier*]

cavals *see* caval.

cavayers *see* cavalier.

cavẹc *n. masc.* owl: *nom. sg.* cavecs 13.88. [LL CAVANNUM 'owl' *FEW* 2: 550
(Fr. *chouan* 'Breton royalist'; cf. Fr. *chouette* 'pretty') + -ec]

cays, quays *see* cazer.

cazẹr *vb. intrans.* to fall: *pret. 3rd sg.* cazec 25.73; *pp., masc., nom. sg.*
cazutz 18.53, quays 29.24, *obl. sg.* cadegut 11.72; *inf.* cazer 3.11, 18.3.
[CL CADĔRE, LL CADĒRE *FEW* 2: 29; It. *cadere,* Sp. *caer,* Fr. *choir*; cf. E.
cadence]

ce *see* que (1).

cecretari *see* secretari.

cẹl (1) *n. masc.* Heaven: *obl. sg.* cél 11.74. [CL CAELUM *FEW* 2: 35; It. *cielo,*
Sp. *cielo,* Fr. *ciel*]

cẹl (2) *n. masc.* apprehension, fear: *nom. sg.* cels 24.19. [celar]

cẹl (3) *dem. pron.* that one, the one, he, she.

  Forms: Masc., nom. sg. cel 16.33, 23.27, sel 6.10, 14.18, selh 28.38,
29.41, celui 16.51, cil 23.21; *obl. sg.* cel 6.11, 17.33, sel 27.3, selh
28.57, cellui 18.12 var., sellui 23.24, scellui 10.27, seluy 14.20; *nom.
pl.* cil 11.70, sil 12.52; *obl. pl.* cels 20.31, 21.76, 25.8, 25.109, 30.17, sels
12.33, 12.56, celz 22.29.

  Fem., nom. sg. cela 16.37, sela 13.22, cil 18.27; *obl. sg.* celei 18.12,
celi 18.12 var., celleis 18.12 var.

  [VL ĔCCĔ ĬLLUM *FEW* 4: 552; Fr. *celui*]

cẹl (4) *dem. adj.* that: *masc., nom. sg.* cel 30.81; *obl. sg.* cel 30.90; *fem., obl.
sg.* cela 25.74. [cel (3)]

celar *vb. trans.* to conceal, to hide: *fut. 1st sg.* selaray 19.29; *pp., fem.,
nom. sg.* celada 28.63; *neuter, obl. sg.* celat 30.40. [CL CĒLĀRE *FEW* 2:
573; It. *celare,* Sp. *celar,* Fr. *celer*; cf. E. *to conceal*]

celei *see* cel (3).

celestial *adj.* heavenly: *masc., nom. sg.* celestials 12.5. [celeste (CL CAE-
LESTEM *FEW* 2: 34) + -al; It. *celestiale,* Sp. *celestial,* E. *celestial*]

celi *see* cel (3).

celitz *n. masc.* hairshirt (worn as penance): *obl. sg.* selis 26.36, sellis
26.36 var. [CL CĬLĬCĬUM *FEW* 2: 671; It. *cilicio,* Sp. *cilicio,* Fr. *cilice*]

celleis, cellui *see* cel (3).

cels (1) 24.19, *see* cel (2).

cels (2) 20.31, 21.76, 25.8, 25.109, 30.17, celui, celz, *see* cel (3).

cẹn *num.* hundred: *modifies masc. noun* cent 30.77, cents 30.78; *modifies
fem. noun* cen 9.51, 9.62, 19.34, cent 30.89; *substantivized* cen 2.6,

16.49. [CL cĕntum *FEW* 2: 590; It. *cento,* Sp. *ciento,* Fr. *cent*; cf. E. *century*]

cenchar *vb. trans.* to gird, to bind: *pres. 3rd sg.* **sincha** 14.21 var. [**cencha** (CL cĭnctum *FEW* 2: 681) + **-ar** (2)]

cẹra *n. fem.* wax: *obl. sg.* **cera** 14.32. [CL cēram *FEW* 2: 597; It. *cera,* Sp. *cera,* Fr. *cire*]

cercar *vb. trans.* to search for: *pres. 3rd sg.* **serca** 13.79; *pres. part.* (*used with* **anar**) **sercan** 21.54; *pp., invariable* **cercat** 23.42 var. [LL cĭrcāre *FEW* 2: 698; It. *cercare,* Sp. *cercar,* Fr. *chercher*; cf. E. *circle*]

certanamẹn *adv.* certainly: **certanamen** 30.57. [**certan** (**cert** [CL cĕrtum *FEW* 2: 612] + **-an** (2)) + **-amen** (2)]

cervẹla *n. fem.* brain: *obl. sg.* **cervela** 25.54; *obl. pl.* **cervelas** 25.13, 25.71. [CL cĕrĕbĕllum *FEW* 2: 603; It. *cervello,* Fr. *cerveau*; cf. E. *cerebral*]

cervẹza *n. fem.* beer: *obl. sg.* **servesa** 26.17. [LL (from Ctc.) cervēsĭam *FEW* 2: 613; Sp. *cerveza,* Fr. *cervoise*]

cẹst *dem. adj.* this: *fem., obl. sg.* **cest'** 15.16, 15.37. [VL ĕccĕ ĭstum *FEW* 4: 820]

cha- *see* **ca-**; **chantz, chanz,** *see* **can** (1).

cho *see* **so** (3).

christians *see* **cristiaṇ**.

cigna *see* **senhar**.

cil *see* **cel** (3).

cinc *num.* five: **cinc** 30.78. [CL quīnque, VL cīnque *FEW* 2: 1481; It. *cinque,* Sp. *cinco,* Fr. *cinq*]

cinha *see* **senhar**.

ciri *n. masc.* candle: *obl. pl.* **ciris** 25: 92. [CL cērĕum *FEW* 2: 605; It. *cero,* Sp. *cirio,* Fr. *cierge*]

clam *see* **clamar**.

clamadier *n. masc.* one who complains, plaintiff: *nom. sg.* **clamaders** 25.65. [**clamat** (*pp. of* **clamar**) + **-ier**]

clamar *vb. trans.* to call 15.14; to invoke 11.6; to beg 10.28, 17.31: *pres. 1st pl.* **clamam** 11.6, *3rd pl.* **clamon** 10.28 var.; *pres. subj. 3rd sg.* **clam** 17.31; *pp., masc., nom. sg.* **clamatz** 15.14. [CL clāmāre *FEW* 2: 730; It. *chiamare,* Sp. *llamar,* E. *to claim*]

clar *adj.* bright 11.60, clear 30.34: *masc., obl. sg.* **al di clar** at dawn 11.60; *fem., obl. sg.* **clara** 30.34. [CL clārum *FEW* 2: 744; It. *chiaro,* Sp. *claro,* Fr. *clair,* E. *clear*]

clas *n. masc.* peal, ringing of bells: *obl. sg.* **clas** 30.9. [CL classĭcum 'trumpet call,' VL *classum *FEW* 2: 746; It. *chiasso,* Fr. *glas*]

claure *vb. trans.* to enclose: *pres. 3rd sg.* **clau** 2.10; *pp., masc., obl. pl.* **claus** 12.25. [CL claudĕre *FEW* 2: 750; It. *chiudere,* Fr. *clore,* E. *to close*]

clẹda *n. fem.* shelter made of wattle (woven twigs and branches), used as a siege machine: *obl. pl.* **clẹdas** 25.6. [LL (from Ctc.) clētam 'wattle' *FEW* 2: 778; Fr. *claie*]

clẹrgue *n. masc.* cleric, member of the clergy 25.86; clerk, ecclesiastical assistant 31.18: *obl. sg.* **clergue** 31.18; *obl. pl.* **clergues** 25.86. [ChL clērĭcum *FEW* 2: 775; It. *chierico,* Sp. *clérigo,* Fr. *clerc,* E. *cleric, clerk*]

cliṇ *adj.* bowed, bent over: *masc., nom. sg.* **clis** 15.5, 30.74. [**clinar** 'to bow' (LL clīnāre *FEW* 2: 783; It. *chinare*; cf. E. *incline*)]

cloquier *n. masc.* bell tower: *obl. pl.* **clochiers** 25.98. [**clọcca** 'bell' (LL clŏccam *FEW* 2: 792; Fr. *cloche,* E. *clock*) + **-ier**]

co *see* **com** (2), (5).

cǫa *n. fem.* tail: *obl. sg.* **coa** 9.49, 14.36. [CL CAUDAM *FEW* 2: 532; It. *coda*, Sp. *cola*, Fr. *queue*, E. *queue, coda*]

cobrir *vb. trans.* to cover: *pp., masc., obl. sg.* **cubert** 25.75. [CL COOPĔRĪRE *FEW* 2: 1149; It. *coprire*, Sp. *cubrir*, Fr. *couvrir*, E. *to cover*]

coc *see* **coire**.

cǫcha *n. fem.* haste; press of battle; pressing need 30.65: *obl. sg.* **cocha** 30.65. [**cochar**]

cocha-dinar *n. masc.* one who dines in haste: *nom. pl.* **coita-disnar** 12.47 var. [**cochar** + **dinar**]

cochar *vb. trans.* to torment; to hasten; *pp.* troubled, desirous, in haste: *pp., masc., nom. sg.* **cochatz** 19.2, 19.32, **cochat** *used as nom. sg.* 13.64; *nom. pl.* **coytat** 12.47. [CL COGĔRE 'to drive'; *pp.* COACTUM, from which VL *COCTĀRE *FEW* 2: 831]

cochǫs *adj.* hurried, hasty: *masc., nom. pl.* **coitos** 25.75. [**cocha** + **-os**]

cofon, cofonda *see* **confondre**.

cogastrǫn *n. masc.* scullion, kitchen boy: *obl. sg.* **coguastro** 9.29. [**cǫc** 'cook' (CL CŎQUUM, LL CŎCUM *FEW* 2: 1170) + **-astron**]

cogitar *vb. refl.* to think, to reflect: *pret. 1st sg.* **cogitie** 31.44. [CL CŌGĬTĀRE *FEW* 2: 841; It. *cogitare*, E. *to cogitate*; cf. **cuidar** (1)]

coguastro *see* **cogastron**.

coignatz *see* **conhat**.

cǫinde *adj.* pleasant, charming: *masc., nom. sg.* **cuendes** 10.29; *fem., nom. sg.* **coinda** 16.41 var., **coind'** 16.41. [CL CŎGNĬTUM *FEW* 2: 843; OFr. *cointe*, E. *quaint*; cf. E. *cognition*]

coindęt *adj.* charming, attractive, pretty: *fem., nom. sg.* **coindeta** 6.4 var., **coindet'** 6.4. [**coinde** + **-et**]

cǫire *vb. trans.* to cook 5.2, to sear 9.53: *pret. 3rd sg.* **coc** 9.53; *inf.* **coszer** 5.2. [CL CŎQUĔRE, LL CŎCĔRE *FEW* 2: 1167; It. *cuocere*, Sp. *cocer*, Fr. *cuire*, E. *to cook*]

coita-disnar *see* **cocha-dinar**.

coitos *see* **cochos**.

col *see* **colhir**.

colgar *vb. intrans.* to set (*of the sun*): *pres. part., masc., obl. sg.* **colgan** 21.56. [CL CŎLLŎCĀRE *FEW* 2: 910; It. *collocare*, Sp. *colgar*, Fr. *coucher*, E. *to couch*]

colhir *vb. trans.* to receive; **colhir en mal**, to take amiss 11.50; to gain, to acquire 12.59; to pick, to gather 6.15: *pres. 3rd sg.* **col** 11.50, **cuoill** 6.15, **cuelh** 12.59. [CL COLLĬGĔRE *FEW* 2: 903; It. *cogliere*, Sp. *coger*, Fr. *cueillir*; cf. E. *to collect*]

cǫlp *n. masc.* blow: *obl. sg.* **colp** 21.75; *obl. pl.* **colps** 25.49. [VL (from Gk.) CŎLĂPHUM, CŎLPUM *FEW* 2: 876; It. *colpo*, Fr. *coup*]

coltęl *n. masc.* knife: *obl. sg.* **coultel** 8.30, **cotel** 31.33. [CL CŬLTĔLLUM *FEW* 2: 1501; It. *coltello*, Sp. *cuchillo*, Fr. *couteau*; cf. E. *cutlery*]

cǫm (1) *adj.* curved, swaybacked (*horse*): *masc., nom. pl.* **com** 12.48. [Ctc. *cŭmbos *FEW* 2: 1526; Sp. *combo*]

cǫm (2) *adv.,* in direct question how? 17.2, why? 19.38, 28.59; *in indirect question* how 7.4, 8.27, 12.4, 12.66, 14.19, 14.63, 18.29, 19.50, 22.28, 22.35, 23.27, 26.8, 31.35; (a way) how 19.31.

    Forms: **com** 8.27, 12.4, 12.66, 14.19, 14.63, 17.2, 19.31, 26.8; **co** 19.38, 19.50, 23.27; **quo** 28.59; **cum** 7.4, 18.29, 22.28, 22.35, 31.35.

[CL QUŌMŎDO, LL QUOMO, QUOMODO ET *FEW* 2: 1544; It. *come*, Sp. *como*, Fr. *comme*]

cǫm (3) *prep.* with. *Forms:* **com** 5.14 (= **ab** 5.14 var.); **con** 3.1, 3.1; **cum** 5.13. [CL QUŌMŎDO *FEW* 2: 1542; It. *con*, Sp. *con* represent CL CŬM]

cǫm (4) *prep.* like *with obl.* [cf. **com** (5)] 19.59, 26.9, 28.8, 32.12; **aisi com** just like 26.17. *Forms:* **com** 19.59, 26.17, 32.12; **con** 26.9; **cum** 28.8; **coma** 32.12 var. [**com** (2)]

cǫm (5) *conj.* as 15.21, 26.7; when 13.33; like *with nom.* [cf. **com** (4)] 3.6, 14.13, 18.54: (*adj.*) . . . **com** as (*adj.*) . . . as 14.35; **com si** as though 25.83; **aisi** (. . .) **com** just as 8.12, 18.19, 18.47, 26.38 (see note), 30.10, 30.13, 30.85; **aitan com** as long as 30.94, as much as 9.61; **enaissi com** just as, like 8.14, 30.37; **si com** just as 2.10, 14.69; **tal** . . . **com** such . . . as 4.21: **tan** . . . **com** as . . . as 2.9, 28.17, 30.53, 30.81, as much as 15.46.

　　　Forms: **com** 3.6, 4.13, 4.35, 8.12, 8.14, 13.33, 14.69, 26.7, 26.38, 30.13, 30.94; **co** 18.54; **quo** 28.17; **con** 30.10, 30.37, 30.53, 30.81, 30.85; **cum** 2.9, 2.10, 4.21, 9.61, 15.21, 15.46, 18.19, 18.47, 25.83.

　　　[**com** (2)]

coma *see* **com** (4).

comanda *n. fem.* command, control: *obl. sg.* **comanda** 19.4, 20.35. [**comandar** + **-a**]

comandar *vb. trans.* to commend, to recommend 21.13; to command 20.5: *pres. 1st sg.* **coman** 21.13, *3rd sg.* **comanda** 20.5. [VL COMMANDĀRE *FEW* 2: 951; It. *comandare*, Sp. *comandar*, Fr. *commander*, E. *to command*]

combatre *vb. trans.* to fight against: *pres. 3rd pl.* **combaton** 25.14. [LL COMBATTUĔRE *FEW* 2: 937, VL *COMBATTĔRE B-W; It. *combattere*, Sp. *combatir*, Fr. *combattre*, E. *to combat*]

comensa, comensada *see* **comensar**.

comensansa *n. fem.* beginning, origin, purpose: *obl. sg.* **comensansa** 14.2. [**comensar** + **-ansa**]

comensar *vb. intrans.* to begin 2.17, 3.11 var., 12.0; *trans.* to begin 22.20, 27.1, 30.7, 30.84; *refl.* to begin 28.37: *pres. 3rd sg.* **comensa** 2.17, 12.0, 28.37; *pret. 1st sg.* **comenssiei** 22.20, *3rd sg.* **comenset** 30.84, **comenzet** 3.11 var.; *pp., fem., obl. sg.* **comensada** 30.7; *inf.* **comensar** 27.1. [VL *COMĬNĬTĬĀRE *FEW* 2: 944; It. *cominciare*, Sp. *comenzar*, Fr. *commencer*, E. *to commence*]

cominal *adj.* common, shared among (*with dat.*) 12.43; common, vulgar 16.18: *masc., nom. sg.* **cominaus** 12.43; *fem., nom. sg.* **cominaus** 16.18, **comunals** 16.18 var., **comunaus** 16.18 var. [CL COMMŪNĀLEM; cf. COMMŪNEM *FEW* 2: 963; Sp. *comunal*, Fr. *communal*, E. *communal*]

cominalier *adj.* communal, shared by the community: *masc., nom. sg.* **cominalers** 25.97. [**cominal** + **-ier**]

cominaus *see* **cominal**.

cominiǫn *n. fem.* communion: *obl. sg.* **cominio** 30.31. [CL COMMŪNĬŌNEM; Sp. *comunión*, Fr. *communion*, E. *communion*]

comjat *n. masc.* order to depart: *obl. sg.* **comjat** 5.9. [CL COMMĔĀTUM *FEW* 2: 947; It. *commiato*, *congedo*, Fr. *congé*]

compaignon *see* **companhon**.

compaingnia *see* **companhia**.

compaingnon *see* **companhon**.

companhatge *n. masc.* company, relationship: *obl. sg.* **companatje** 13.61. [**companhon** + **-atge**]

companhers *see* **companhier.**

companhia *n. fem.* company, the act of accompanying 13.17; *(collective)* companions 3.7: *obl. sg.* **companhia** 13.17, **compaingnia** 3.7. [**companhon** + **-ia**; It. *compagnia*, Sp. *compañía*, Fr. *compagnie*, E. *company*]

companhier *n. masc.* companion: *obl. pl.* **companhers** 25.62. [**companhon** + **-ier**]

companhon *n. masc.* companion: *obl. sg.* **companhon** 12.20, **compaignon** 10.21, **compaingnon** 21.35. [VL COMPANĬŌNEM *FEW* 2: 968; compound of CL CŬM 'with' + PĀNEM 'bread'; calque on Gothic *gahlaiba* 'fellow soldier with whom one shares bread' (*ga-* + *hlaiba* = E. *loaf*); It. *compagno*, Sp. *compaño*, Fr. *compagnon*, E. *companion*]

complir *vb. trans.* to complete; *pp.* complete, perfect: *pp., fem., nom. sg.* **complia** 27.21; *obl. sg.* **complida** 28.48. [CL COMPLĒRE *FEW* 2: 981 + **-ir**; It. *compiere*, Sp. *cumplir*, Fr. *accomplir*, E. *to accomplish*]

comtar *vb. trans.* to tell: *pret. 3rd sg.* **comtec** 25.90, **contet** 5.16. [CL COMPŬTĀRE *FEW* 2: 995; It. *contare*, Sp. *contar*, Fr. *compter*, E. *to count*]

comte (1) *n. masc.* count: *nom. sg.* **coms** 5.14, 20.33, 22.9, 25.28, 25.35, 25.60, 25.62, 25.73, 25.82, 25.95, **cóms** 11.34, **coms palatz** (*see* **palatz**) 20.22, **cons** 24.14, **comte** 25.55 var.; *obl. sg.* **comte** 5.14, 12.70, 25.17, 25.53, 25.70, 25.75, 25.80, 25.86; *vocative sg.* **coms** 25.18; *nom. pl.* **comte** 22.7. [CL CŎMĬTEM 'companion' *FEW* 2: 941; It. *conte*, Sp. *conde*, Fr. *comte*, E. *count*]

comte (2) *n. masc.* count, accounting: *obl. sg.* **comt'** 20.10, **comte** 20.10 var. [LL COMPŬTUM *FEW* 2: 996; It. *conto*, Sp. *cuento*, Fr. *compte*, E. *count*]

comtec *see* **comtar.**

comtesa *n. fem.* countess: *nom. sg.* **comtessa** 1.6; *obl. sg.* **comtessa** 1.2, 1.5. [**comte** (1) + **-esa**]

comunals, comunaus *see* **cominal.**

con *see* **com** (3), (4), (5).

conceilh *see* **conselhar.**

conduch *n. masc.* feast, food: *obl. pl.* **conduitz** 26.24. [CL CONDŬCTUM 'lodging' *FEW* 2: 1026; It. *condotto*, Sp. *conducho*]

conduire *vb. trans.* to conduct: *pp., masc., nom. sg.* **condug** 1.4. [CL CONDŪCĔRE *FEW* 2: 1026; Sp. *conducir*, Fr. *conduire*; cf. E. *to conduct*]

conduitz *see* **conduch.**

confinar *vb. intrans.* to border: *imperf. 3rd sg.* **confinava** 3.1. [**confin** 'border' (CL CONFĪNEM *FEW* 2: 1035) + **-ar** (2)]

confondre *vb. trans.* to confound, to overwhelm: *pres. 3rd sg.* **cofon** 18.22; *pres. subj. 3rd sg.* **cofonda** 19.21. [CL CONFŬNDĔRE *FEW* 2: 1046; It. *confondere*, Sp. *confundir*, Fr. *confondre*, E. *to confound*]

conhat *n. masc.* brother-in-law: *nom. sg.* **coignatz** 20.32. [CL COGNĀTUM 'kinsman,' LL 'brother-in-law' *FEW* 2: 843; It. *cognato*, Sp. *cuñado*; cf. E. *cognate*]

conoisensa *n. fem.* understanding 2.24, wisdom 6.28, memory 28.23: *nom. sg.* **conoissenssa** 6.28, **connoyssensa** 28.23; *obl. sg.* **conoissensa** 2.24. [**conoiser** + **-ensa**]

conoiser *vb. trans.* to know, to recognize 6.20, 13.59, 14.55, 28.11; to realize 18.26 var. (*synonym of* **saubi** 18.26), 31.31; to distinguish, to tell apart 13.23: *pres. 1st sg.* **conosc** 13.23, 13.59, *3rd sg.* **conois** 6.20; *pres. subj. 1st sg.* **conosca** 14.55; *imperf. 3rd sg.* **conoyssia** 28.11; *pret. 1st sg.* **conuc** 18.26 var., **conoygui** 31.31; *pres. part.* **conoissen** discerning 6.27. [CL cognōscĕre, VL *conōscĕre FEW 2: 848; It. *conoscere,* Sp. *conocer,* Fr. *connaître;* cf. E. *cognoscente*]

conǫrt *n. masc.* solace, comfort: *obl. sg.* **conort** 22.21. [**conortar**]

conortar *vb. trans.* to exhort 12.9, to advise 24.22; *refl.* to comfort oneself 22.37: *pres. 1st sg.* **conort** 12.9, 22.37, 24.22. [VL *conhŏrtāri FEW 2: 1051; Sp. *conhortar;* cf. E. *to exhort*]

conosc, conosca, conoygui, conoyssia *see* **conoiser.**

conquerǫr *vb. trans.* to conquer, to win: *pres. 3rd sg.* **conquer** 26.16, *3rd pl.* **conquerron** 26.16 var.; *fut. 3rd sg.* **conquerra** 20.18, *3rd pl.* **conquerran** 22.31; *pret. 3rd sg.* **conquis** 20.13; *inf.* **conquerrer** 26.16. [VL conquaerĕre FEW 2: 1058; Sp. *conquerir,* Fr. *conquérir,* E. *to conquer*]

cons *see* **comte** (1).

consęlh *n. masc.* counsel, advice 19.1, 19.39, 20.25; solution 14.41; plan, secret 9.17 var.: *obl. sg.* **conseil** 20.25, **conseill** 9.17 var., **cosselh** 14.41, 19.1, 19.39. [CL consĭlĭum FEW 2: 1072; It. *consiglio,* Sp. *consejo,* Fr. *conseil,* E. *counsel*]

conselhar *vb. trans.* to counsel, to advise: *pres. 1st sg.* **conseil** 26.23, *2nd pl.* **cosselhatz** 19.6, **cosselhat** 19.6 var.; *pres. subj. 3rd sg.* **conceilh** 12.71 var. [CL consĭlĭārī, cf. FEW 2: 1069; It. *consigliare,* Sp. *consejar,* Fr. *conseiller,* E. *to counsel*]

conselhier *n. masc.* adviser; pillow 7.12: *obl. sg.* **cosseillier** 7.12. [CL consĭlĭārĭum 'adviser' FEW 2: 1071; It. *consigliere,* Sp. *consejero,* Fr. *conseiller,* E. *counselor*]

conseil, conseill *see* **conselh.**

consir *n. masc.* worry, care: *obl. sg.* **consir** 23.29. [**consirar**]

consirar *vb. intrans.* to reflect 2.28; *trans.* to consider 29.7, 29.39: *pres. 1st sg.* **cossire** 2.28, *1st pl.* **cossiram** 29.39 ms., *3rd pl.* **cossiran** 29.39; *pres. part., masc., obl. sg.* **cossiran** 29.7. [CL consīdĕrāre FEW 2: 1068; It. *considerare,* Sp. *considerar,* Fr. *considérer,* E. *to consider*]

consirier *n. masc.* worry, distress, grief: *nom. sg.* **cossiriers** 29.3; *obl. sg.* **cossirier** 7.1. [**consir** + **-ier**]

contęn *n. masc.* debate, dispute: *obl. sg.* **conten** 2.20. [**contendre** 'to contend' (CL contendĕre FEW 2: 1103; It. *contendere,* Sp. *contender,* E. *to contend*)]

contensǫn *n. fem.* battle: *obl. sg.* **contenço** 11.56, **contenco** 11.56 ms. [CL contentĭōnem FEW 2: 1103; It. *contenzione,* Sp. *contención,* Fr. *contention,* E. *contention*]

contet *see* **comtar.**

cǫntra *prep.* against 19.17; in the direction of 18.2; in opposition, in combat 25.6: **contr'amon** *adv.* upward, high 18.56. *Forms:* **contra** 18.2; **contr'** 18.56, 19.17, 25.6. [CL contrā FEW 2: 1116; It. *contra,* Sp. *contra,* Fr. *contre;* cf. E. *contrary*]

contrafǫrt *n. masc.* adversary: *obl. sg.* **contrafort** 12.27, 12.53. [**contra** + **fort** (1)]

contrastar *vb. trans.* to resist: *pres. 3rd pl.* **contraston** 25.25. [VL contrastāre FEW 2: 1123; It. *contrastare,* Sp. *contrastar,* Fr. *contraster,* E. *to contrast*]

conuc *see* **conoiser.**

convenir *vb. intrans.* to befit 29.2; *trans.* to promise 19.50; *impersonal* to please 23.26; to be fitting, *(with agent as subject in E.)* should 17.30, 19.11: *pres. 3rd sg.* **conve** 23.26, **cove** 17.30, 19.11, **coven** 29.2; *pres. part.* **covenen** fitting, suitable, pretty 16.41, **covinen** 16.41 var.; *pp., fem., nom. sg.* **covenguda** 19.50. [CL CONVENĪRE *FEW* 2: 1128; It. *convenire*, Sp. *convenir*, Fr. *convenir*, E. *to convene*]

convertir *vb. intrans.* to convert, to change one's religion, to change one's love; *inf.* **convertir** 23.38. [CL CONVERTĔRE *FEW* 2: 1134 + **-ir**; It. *convertire*, Sp. *convertir*, Fr. *convertir*, E. *to convert*]

cọr (1) *n. masc.* heart, the anatomical organ 3.7, 3.8; heart, the organ of love 4.31, 7.15, 16.2, 16.3, 18.8, 18.16, 19.7, 19.31 var., 19.53, 23.12, 23.43, 30.67; love 30.95; heart, spirit, thought 2.13, 8.9, 11.41, 13.57, 13.87, 16.7, 16.12, 16.14, 17.36, 18.4, 18.13, 21.29, 23.32, 26.48, 30.82; intention 6.8, 15.38, 23.14.

 de bon cor from the heart, sincerely 2.28, 23.10, 31.8; **de cor** from the heart, sincerely 14.65; **saber de cor** to know by heart, by rote 30.31.

 Forms: nom. sg. **cor** 4.31, 8.9, 19.7, 19.53, **cors** 8.9 var., 18.8, 19.53 var.; *obl. sg.* **cor** 2.13, 3.7, 3.8, 6.8, 11.41, 13.57, 13.87, 15.38, 16.2, 16.3, 16.7, 16.12, 16.14, 17.36, 18.4, 18.13, 18.16, 19.31 var., 21.29, 23.12, 23.14, 23.32, 23.43, 26.48, 30.67, 30.82, 30.95.

 [CL CŏR *FEW* 2: 1176; It. *cuore*, Fr. *coeur*; cf. E. *cordial*]

cọr (2) *n. masc.* choir, the part of a church reserved for singers: *obl. sg.* **cor** 30.39, 30.41. [CL CHŏRUM 'group of singers' *FEW* 2: 652; It. *coro*, Sp. *coro*, Fr. *choeur*, E. *choir*]

cọr (3) *n. masc.* leather: *obl. sg.* **cor** 26.44. [CL CŏRĬUM *FEW* 2: 1187; It. *cuoio*, Sp. *cuero*, Fr. *cuir*]

cọra *interrogative adv., in direct question* **cora** when? 7.18, *in indirect question* **coras** when 15.17. [CL QUĀ HŌRĀ *FEW* 4: 478 (+ **-s**)]

coral *adj.* of the heart, sincere: *masc., nom. sg.* **coraus** 12.41; *fem., nom. sg.* **coraus** 16.4. [**cor** (1) + **-al**]

coras *see* **cora**.

coratge *n. masc.* heart, thought; **de coratje** sincere 13.62. [**cor** (1) + **-atge**; It. *coraggio*, Sp. *coraje*, Fr. *courage*, E. *courage*]

coraus *see* **coral**.

coret *see* **corre**.

corn *n. masc.* horn 25.97, blowing of horns 25.39: *nom. sg. or pl.* **corns** 25.39; *nom. pl.* **corn** 25.97. [CL CŏRNU *FEW* 2: 1202; It. *corno*, Sp. *cuerno*, Fr. *cor*; cf. E. *cornea*]

corna-viṇ *compound n. masc.* wine guzzler, one who drinks wine from the bottle as though blowing a horn: *nom. pl.* **corno-vi** 12.46, **corna-vi** 12.46 var. [*pres. 3rd sg. or pl.* of **cornar** 'to sound a horn' (**corn** + **-ar** [2]) + **viṇ**]

corns *see* **corn**.

coronar *vb. trans.* to crown: *pp., masc., nom. sg.* **coronatz** 20.11. [CL CŏRŌNĀRE, cf. CŏRŌNAM *FEW* 2: 1210; It. *coronare*, Sp. *coronar*, Fr. *couronner*, E. *to crown*]

corps *see* **cors** (1).

cọrre *vb. intrans.* to run: *pres. 1st pl.* **correm** 12.24, *3rd pl.* **corron** 25.91; *pret. 3rd sg.* **coret** 3.11. [CL CŭRRĔRE *FEW* 2: 1573; It. *córrere*, Sp. *correr*, Fr. *courir*; cf. E. *current*]

corręi *n. masc.* belt 9.63; strap, unit of small value 22.32: *nom. sg.* **corretz** 9.63; *obl. sg.* **correi** 22.32. [CL CORRĬGĬAM *FEW* 2: 1225; It. *correggia,* Sp. *correa,* Fr. *courroie*]

correm *see* **corre.**

corręn *adv.* quickly: **corren** 9.34. [*pres. part. of* **corre**]

corretz *see* **correi.**

corron *see* **corre.**

cǫrs (1) *n. masc., invariable* dead body, corpse 3.7; the body at the time of salvation 27.36; (living) body 4.31, 16.41; person 2.27, 11.28; **·l mieu cors** myself, me 31.12; **so . . . cors** herself 19.31: **cors** *passim,* **corps** 11.28. [CL CŎRPUS *FEW* 2: 1218; It. *corpo,* Sp. *cuerpo,* Fr. *corps,* E. *corps, corpse, corpus*]

cors (2) 18.8, *see* **cor** (1).

cǫrsa *n. fem.* haste; **de gran corsa** in haste 31.29. [CL CŬRSUM 'running, zeal' *FEW* 2: 1581 (It. *corso,* Sp. *coso,* Fr. *cours,* E. *course*) + **-a**]

corsier *n. masc.* warhorse, charger: *obl. pl.* **corsers** 25.33. [**cǫrs** 'haste' (CL CŬRSUM *FEW* 2: 1581) + **-ier**]

cǫrt *n. fem.* court, residence of a lord 5.12, 29.18; collective body of persons in attendance on a lord 27.9; meeting of persons in attendance on a lord 27.21; judicial assembly 26.29: *nom. sg.* **cortz** 27.21; *obl. sg.* **cort** 5.12, 26.29, 27.9, 29.18. [CL COHŎRTEM 'farmyard, retinue of an official' *FEW* 2: 852, LL CŬRTEM B-W; It. *corte,* Sp. *corte,* Fr. *court,* E. *court*]

cortęs *adj.* courtly, polite (*person*) 5.3, 13.32, 17.15, 20.35, 21.15, 25.107, *substantivized n. masc.* courtly man 13.80; sophisticated, elegant (*adventure, amusement*) 13.80, 15.28 var.: *masc., nom. sg.* **cortes** 5.3, 13.80, 17.15, 20.35; *obl. sg.* **cortes** 15.28 var., 25.107, **corteis** 15.28 var.; *obl. pl.* **cortes** 15.28 var., 21.15; *fem., nom. sg.* **corteza** 13.32; *obl. sg.* **cortez'** 13.80. [**cort** + **-es** (2), or ML CŬRTENSEM Niermeyer and van de Kieft 293; It. *cortese,* Fr. *courtois,* E. *courteous*]

cortesia *see* **cortezia.**

cortez', corteza *see* **cortes.**

cortezia *n. fem.* courtesy, the virtues of the courtly person: *obl. sg.* **cortesia** 3.2. [**cortes** + **-ia**]

cortz *see* **cort.**

cosdumna *see* **costuma.**

coss- *see* **cons-.**

costal *n. masc.* flank, side: *obl. pl.* **costals** 25.56 var. [**costa** 'side' (CL COSTAM 'rib' *FEW* 2: 1252) + **-al**]

costaliers *adv.* from the side: **costalers** 25.56. [**costal** + **-ier** + **-s**]

costat *n. masc.* rib, side: *nom. sg.* **costatz** 25.59. [CL COSTĀTUM *FEW* 2: 1252; It. *costato,* Sp. *costado,* Fr. *côté*]

costuma *n. fem.* custom, behavior: *obl. sg.* **cosdumna** 11.79. [CL CONSUĒTŪDĬNEM *FEW* 2: 1092; It. *costume,* Sp. *costumbre,* Fr. *coutume,* E. *custom*]

coszer *see* **coire.**

cotel, coultel *see* **coltel.**

cove, covenen, covenguda, covinen *see* **convenir.**

coytat *see* **cochar.**

coziṇ *n. masc.* cousin: *obl. sg.* **cozi** 10.12. [CL CONSŎBRĪNUM, VL *co(ɴ)sɪɴuᴍ *FEW* 2: 1075; It. *cugino,* Sp. *sobrino,* Fr. *cousin,* E. *cousin*]

cre *see* **creire.**

creator *n. masc.* creator: *obl. sg.* **creator** 12.46. [CL CREATŌREM *FEW* 2: 1297; It. *creatore,* Sp. *creador,* Fr. *créateur,* E. *creator*]

creatura *n. fem.* creature: *nom. sg.* **criatura** 13.71. [LL CREATŪRAM *FEW* 2: 1298; It. *creatura,* Sp. *criatura,* Fr. *créature,* E. *creature*]

crec *see* **creiser.**

creire *vb. trans.* to believe *passim;* to believe in 11.24, 11.46; to profess 29.41: *pres. 1st sg.* **crei** 22.23, 22.51, 24.30, 24.41, **cre** 4.20, 21.10, 22.46, 28.36, *1st pl.* **crezem** 29.41, *3rd pl.* **crezon** 12.45; *pres. subj. 3rd sg.* **creza** 6.14; *imperf. 3rd sg.* **cresia** 30.26, *2nd pl.* **creziatz** 19.36 var.; *1st cond. 1st sg.* **creiria** 30.27, *2nd pl.* **creriaz** 19.36 var.; *pret. 3rd sg.* **credet** 11.46; *past subj. 3rd pl.* **creessen** 11.24; *imper. 2nd pl.* **crezatz** 4.38, 19.14; *pres. part.* **crezen** believing, believer 6.30; *pp., fem., nom. sg.* **crezuda** 19.65. [CL CRĒDĔRE *FEW* 2: 1308; It. *credere,* Sp. *creer,* Fr. *croire;* cf. E. *creed*]

creiser *vb. intrans.* to grow, to increase: *pres. subj. 3rd sg.* **cresca** 19.12; *pret. 3rd sg.* **crec** 25.76. [CL CRĒSCĔRE *FEW* 2: 1328; It. *crescere,* Sp. *crecer,* Fr. *croître;* cf. E. *to increase*]

cremar *vb. trans.* to burn: *pret. 3rd pl.* **cremèron** 32.16. [CL CRĔMĀRE *FEW* 2: 1311; Fr. *cramer*]

creriaz *see* **creire.**

cresca *see* **creiser.**

cresia, creza, crezatz, crezem, crezen *see* **creire.**

crezensa *n. fem.* belief, credulity 28.40; trust 6.29: *obl. sg.* **crezensa** 28.40, **crezenssa** 6.29. [VL *CREDĔNTĬAM *FEW* 2: 1308; It. *credenza,* Sp. *creencia,* Fr. *croyance,* E. *credence*]

creziatz, crezon, crezuda *see* **creire.**

cria *see* **cridar.**

criatura *see* **creatura.**

crida *n. fem.* rumor: *nom. sg.* **crida** 28.45. [**cridar** + **-a**]

cridar *vb. trans.* to shout 25.1, 25.17, 32.3, 32.6, 32.8, 32.11, 32.11, 32.11, 32.11, 32.19, 32.19, 32.19, 32.19; to proclaim by shouting 4.7, 4.16, 4.25, 4.34, 4.43: *pres. 3rd sg.* **crida** 25.1, **cria** 4.7, 4.16, 4.25, 4.34, 4.43; *fut. 1st sg.* **cridarai** 32.3, 32.6, 32.8, 32.11, 32.11, 32.11, 32.11, 32.19, 32.19, 32.19, 32.19; *pres. part., masc., undeclined* **cridan** 25.17. [CL QUĪRĪTĀRE, VL *CRĪTĀRE *FEW* 2: 1488; It. *gridare,* Sp. *gritar,* Fr. *crier,* E. *to cry*]

cristal *n. masc.* crystal ornament: *obl. pl.* **cristals** 25.7. [CL CRŸSTĂLLUM *FEW* 2: 1386; It. *cristallo,* Sp. *cristal,* Fr. *cristal,* E. *crystal*]

cristian *n. masc.* Christian (person): *obl. pl.* **christians** 29.26. [CL CHRISTĬĀNĪ *FEW* 2: 655; It. *cristiano,* Sp. *cristiano,* Fr. *chrétien,* E. *Christian*]

crit *n. masc.* cry, shout 29.21, 32.10; outcry 25.39: *nom. sg.* **critz** 25.39; *obl. sg.* **crit** 32.10; *obl. pl.* **critz** 29.21. [**cridar**]

croset *see* **crozar.**

crotz *n. fem., invariable* cross: *obl. pl.* **crotz** 25.88. [CL CRŬCEM *FEW* 2: 1381; It. *croce,* Sp. *cruz,* Fr. *croix,* G. *Kreuz,* E. *cross*]

crozar *vb. refl.* to take the cross: *pret. 3rd sg.* **croset** 1.4. [**crotz** + **-ar** (2)]

crup-en-cami *n. masc., compound* squat-in-a-road, loiterer: *nom. pl.* **crup-en-cami** 12.48 var. [**cropir** 'to squat' (Germ. **kruppa *FEW* 16: 419 + **-ir**) + **en camin**]

cubert *see* **cobrir.**

cuelh *see* **colhir.**

cuendes *see* **coinde.**

cug, cugey, cugie *see* **cuidar** (1).

cui *see* **qui** (1), (2).

cuidar (1) *vb. trans.* to believe *passim*; to think 14.55, 19.43, 31.29; to hope 23.37, 28.46, 31.19; to intend 27.4, 27.12, 31.37; *in pret.* to try 11.68, 31.46: *pres. 1st sg.* **cuid** 11.33, 11.42, **cug** 19.24, 19.44, 23.37, 30.24, *3rd sg.* **cuja** 27.4, 27.12, 30.57, **cuj'** 13.27, 30.75, *2nd pl.* **cujatz** 14.55, 19.43, 28.46, **cujas** 27.12 var.; *imperf. 1st sg.* **cujava** 18.9; *1st cond. 2nd pl.* **cujariatz** 19.36 var.; *pret. 1st sg.* **cugey** 28.9, **cugie** 31.19, 31.29, 31.37, 31.46, *3rd sg.* **cuidet** 11.68; *2nd cond. 2nd pl.* **cujaratz** 19.36. [CL cogĭtāre *FEW* 2: 841; Sp. *cuidar,* OFr. *cuidier,* E. *to cogitate*; cf. **cogitar**]

cuidar (2) *n. masc.* belief: *obl. sg.* **cujar** 30.26. [**cuidar** (1)]

cujaratz, cujariatz, cujas, cujatz, cujava *see* **cuidar** (1).

cum (1) 7.4, 18.29, 22.28, 22.35, 31.35, *see* **com** (2).

cum (2) 5.13, *see* **com** (3).

cum (3) 28.8, *see* **com** (4).

cum (4) 2.9, 2.10, 4.21, 9.61, 15.21, 15.46, 18.19, 18.47, 25.83, *see* **com** (5).

cuoill *see* **colhir.**

d' = de *before vowel* 1.2, 2.26, 3.2, 3.3, 3.4, 3.8, 3.10, 4.21, 5.2, 5.6, 5.6, 5.9, 5.11, 5.12, 5.12, 5.13, 8.6, 8.19, 8.25, 8.29, 9.3, 9.4, 9.69, 9.70, 10.11, 10.13, 11.38, 11.79, 12.7, 12.9, 12.18, 12.26, 12.31, 12.67, 13.45, 13.68, 14.2, 14.8, 14.19, 14.49, 14.56, 14.66, 15.2, 15.4, 15.6, 15.8, 15.9, 15.44, 15.46, 16.6, 16.9, 16.24, 17.27, 17.37, 17.44, 18.10, 18.11, 18.49, 18.60, 19.7, 19.10, 19.13, 19.19, 19.25, 19.37, 19.53, 19.65, 19.65, 19.65, 20.1, 20.11, 21.8, 21.69, 21.75, 22.13, 22.32, 22.49, 23.36, 24.22, 24.36, 24.38, 25.27, 25.45, 25.50, 25.70, 25.102, 26.1, 26.2, 26.12, 26.20, 26.31, 26.42, 26.42, 26.42, 26.51, 27.26, 28.2, 28.26, 28.46, 28.56, 28.64, 29.0, 29.26, 29.29, 30.26, 30.88, 31.1, 31.3, 31.6, 31.10, 31.11, 31.15, 31.21, 31.22. *For meanings, see* **de.**

dal = de + lo 16.2, 16.3, *see* **de** *and* **lo** (2).

damnatge *n. masc.* loss: *nom. sg.* **dampnatges** 25.108; *obl. sg.* **dampnatge** 25.19, 25.80. [**damnar** (ChL dāmnāre *FEW* 3: 10; It. *dannare,* Sp. *dañar,* Fr. *damner,* E. *to damn*) + **-atge**; Sp. *domaje,* Fr. *dommage,* E. *damage*]

dan *n. masc.* loss 29.14; grief 22.28; harm 16.16, 24.20; **aver dan** to suffer 21.64, 21.79; **faire son dan** to be harmed 31.3; **tener dan a** to harm, to be held against 19.52: *nom. sg.* **danz** 16.16, 24.20, **dans** 22.28; *obl. sg.* **dan** 19.52, 21.64, 21.79, 29.14, 31.3. [CL dāmnum *FEW* 3: 11; It. *danno,* Sp. *daño,* Fr. *dam*]

dapraria *see* **draparia.**

dar *vb. trans.* to give *passim*; to grant 25.30; **dar sus a** to strike 3.11, 31.32: *fut. 3rd sg.* **dara** 14.53 var.; *pret. 1st sg.* **diey** 31.18, 31.32, *3rd sg.* **det** 19.5, *3rd pl.* **deron** 9.25; *2nd cond. 3rd sg.* **dera** 19.39; *past subj. 1st sg.* **des** 7.20; *imper. 1st pl.* **dem** 25.1, *2nd pl.* **datz** 25.30; *pp., masc., obl. sg.* **dat** 3.10; *inf.* **dar** 3.7, 3.11, 5.9, 20.25, 22.43, 28.26, 28.46. [CL dăre *FEW* 3: 14; It. *dare,* Sp. *dar*]

dardasier *n. masc.* lancer, soldier armed with a lance: **dardacers** *used as nom. pl.* 25.47. [**dart** + **-asier** *FEW* 15, part 2: 56]

dart *n. masc.* lance: *obl. pl.* **dartz** 22.35. [Frankish *daroth FEW* 3: 16; It.
dardo, Sp. *dardo*, Fr. *dard*, E. *dart*]

dat, datz *see* **dar**.

davan *prep.* before: **davan** 30.69, **devant** 25.35. [**de** + **avan**; It. *davante*]

de *prep. Possessive: subjective genitive (e.g., 'his death' implies 'he died')* 1.7,
1.7, 3.3, 3.8, 5.2, 5.6, 5.10, 5.11, 5.16, 7.22, 8.1, 8.4, 8.14, 8.20, 9.3, 9.4,
9.69, 9.70, 10.11, 11.53, 11.79, 12.0, 12.31, 12.33, 12.42, 12.58, 12.65,
12.70, 13.4, 14.2, 14.6, 14.35, 14.49, 14.67, 15.2, 15.6, 15.13, 16.6,
16.30, 19.10, 19.53, 21.75, 21.78, 22.13, 22.32, 24.38, 25.16, 25.40,
25.53, 25.80, 25.98, 26.1, 26.2, 26.6, 26.31, 26.56, 29.0, 29.26, 29.27,
29.47, 30.95, 31.19, 31.36, 32.9, 32.13, 32.15; *objective genitive (e.g., 'his
memory' implies 'I remember him')* 2.16, 10.25, 10.25, 18.6, 18.41,
21.18, 28.26, 28.32, 28.47, 29.45.

Spatial: of, from *(in personal names)* 1.1, 3.1, 3.3, 3.4, 3.6, 3.7, 3.8,
5.1, 5.4, 5.5, 5.14, 5.16, 5.16, 10.11, 10.13, 16.53, 17.1, 24.14, 25.23,
25.24, 25.36, 25.37; of *(denoting possession of a place)* 1.1, 1.2, 5.10,
5.13, 10.10, 11.34, 11.37, 11.74, 20.12, 20.17, 20.20, 20.21, 20.23, 20.24,
25.18, 25.27; from *(place of origin or beginning)* 1.2, 2.2, 2.3, 2.9, 3.1,
5.1, 5.1, 5.9, 12.56, 20.31, 25.5, 25.8, 25.20, 25.32, 25.43, 25.67, 25.105,
25.106, 25.109; from *(vantage point)* 25.52; in *(region)* 3.5, 31.1; on
(throne) 10.23; *introducing place-name* 3.1, 3.3, 3.6, 5.1, 5.15; **d'outra**
across 25.102; **de . . . d'aqui a** from . . . as far as 21.68–69; **de lai** from
there 8.7, 15.3, 30.82; **de lai . . . denan** before that 21.48; **de lonh** from
afar 15.2, 15.4, 15.9, 15.16, 15.23, 15.25, 15.30, 15.32, 15.37, 15.39,
15.44, 15.46; **de sai** over here 5.14, 12.8, 12.9; **de sus** on high 12.18;
lonh de far from 29.26, 29.27; **pres de** near, near to 15.25, 31.17;
probet de near, near to 12.6, 12.37, 12.38; **prop de** near, near to 31.1.

Temporal: in 12.10, 12.10, 26.42, 26.42; of *(time period)* 13.42; since
18.42; **apres de** after 31.15; **d'esta pauza** for a while 31.21; **d'un jorn**
(on) one day 31.11; **de mantenen** at once 6.35; **en petida d'ora** soon
25.45.

Other meanings: about 1.3, 2.19, 3.4, 3.4, 5.6, 5.6, 5.6, 5.12, 5.16,
8.11, 8.25, 8.27, 8.29, 9.36, 11.78, 12.9, 14.19, 16.34, 17.24, 18.10,
18.17, 19.25, 19.43, 19.54, 20.4, 20.8, 20.18, 20.23, 20.25, 21.15, 21.15,
23.19, 24.22, 26.28, 26.53, 31.35; because of 1.7, 13.10, 17.35, 18.8,
30.16, 31.22; by *(agent with passive)* 14.18, 14.66, 19.65, 26.26, 32.15;
by *(cause)* 13.64, 18.49; for *(purpose)* 11.56, 12.47, 26.29; for *(reason)*
3.2, 3.2, 3.2, 11.38; for *(use)* 5.2; from *(cause)* 11.5, 31.46; from *(point
of departure)* 12.72, 16.2, 16.3, 24.24, 29.28; from *(separation)* 4.21,
4.32, 5.8, 5.13, 8.26, 10.10, 10.18, 12.20, 13.16, 14.32, 17.44, 18.37,
18.60, 18.60, 19.4, 21.57, 30.62, 30.88, 32.13; from *(source)* 2.27, 10.14,
11.48, 14.43, 16.23, 16.24, 17.35, 18.46, 18.57, 20.11, 21.4, 23.32, 26.21,
27.3, 32.1; from . . . to **de . . . en** 14.51, 31.26, **de . . . tro** 9.47, 21.56; in
respect to 11.30, 20.1, 22.49, 30.26; inside 4.31; instead of 12.18, 27.14;
of *(descriptive)* 5.2, 5.10, 11.2, 11.33, 11.39, 13.29, 14.8, 19.37, 21.7,
21.8, 23.2, 25.3, 26.51, 27.2, 28.4, 28.64, 28.68, 29.18, 29.34, 31.2,
31.31, 32.16; of *(goal)* 16.9; of *(ingredients)* 26.11, 26.18, 26.19, 26.20,
32.18; of *(instrument)* 21.34, 21.34, 25.3, 25.40; of *(material)* 13.7,
25.70, 26.35, 26.42, 26.44, *(metaphorical material)* 11.45, 22.18; with
(descriptive) 12.26, 13.85, 13.87, 15.5; with *(equipment)* 25.56; with
(manner) 18.2, 31.10; with *(means)* 19.7, 26.39, 32.2.

Quantity: 25.38, 25.48, 25.48, 25.49, 25.49; **aitan de** as much 27.44; **mais de** more 16.13, 27.26, most 23.36, 23.36; **massa de** many 29.29; **pauc de** little 13.68, 19.19; **tant de** so much, so many 17.27, 22.5, 24.36; **trop de** too much 28.46.

Syntactic functions: introducing adj. 2.26, 11.58; *introducing inf.* 1.4, 5.2 var., 6.7, 7.24, 10.1, 12.13, 18.11, 18.59, 19.29, 21.67, 22.1, 23.14, 23.26, 27.16, 27.33, 29.1, 29.19; *introducing n.* 13.70; *introducing logical subject* 12.67, 14.56, 19.13, 19.21, 23.27; *introducing quotation* 12.65; *partitive* 21.37, 28.2, 30.6, 30.17.

After comparative: 9.51, 11.36, 14.59, 19.34, 30.89.

Expressions with nouns: **d'alegransa** illegitimate (child) 28.56; **d'autra part** on the other hand 26.12; **d'entrambas las partidas** on both sides 25.50; **de bon cor** sincerely 2.28, 23.10, 31.8; **de cor** sincerely 14.65; **de cor** by heart 30.31; **de coratge** sincere 13.62; **de gran corsa** in haste 31.29; **de part** on behalf of 11.55; **de totas partz** on every side 29.4; **esperansa de** hope for 28.58; **jausimen de** enjoyment of 15.46; **partz de** share in 24.18, 24.18; **sonh de** care for 8.25; **venjansa de** vengeance for 28.54, vengeance on 31.12.

With verbs: **s'abelir de** to become fond of 5.4, 5.4, 5.4, 5.6, 5.6, 7.14; **adastrar de** to endow with 13.45; **s'aisir de** to enjoy 8.6; **s'aprochar de** to approach 10.32; **s'enamorar de** to fall in love with 1.2, 5.6, 5.6, 5.12, 5.12; **eser dezeritans de** to disinherit 27.32; **faire son dan de** to be harmed by 31.3; **faire X de Y** to make X of Y, to make Y into X 11.51, 22.33; **faire X Y de Z** to make X into Y from Z 16.42; **gardar de** to protect from 27.8; **se gardar de** to keep from 31.6; **jausir de** to enjoy 15.8, 15.9, 23.38, 23.46; **manjar de** to eat of 3.10; **se membrar de** to remember 8.19; **ocaisonar de** to accuse of 27.4; **perdonar de** to pardon (for) 27.39; **se remembrar de** to remember 15.4; **reptar de** to accuse of 11.64; **sofrir de** to keep from 17.2; **se sovenir de** to remember 17.37; **venjar de** to avenge for 12.35; **viure de** to live on 20.10.

With adjectives: **al long de** along 32.4; **desiron de** desirous of 15.44; **las de** weary of 12.62; **massissa de** full of 13.3, 13.3; **vermelh de** red with 25.13, 25.59.

With adverbs: **al pus del tot** as much as possible 29.23; **de tot** (*with neg.*) at all 11.31; **del tot** completely 29.38; **dinz dal** from within 16.2; **fors de** out of, free from 17.12.

With prepositions: **sal de** except 12.7.

Forms: **de** *before consonants, passim;* **d'** *before vowels, see listing under* **d'***; see also listings under* **dal, del, dels, di** (3).

[CL DĒ *FEW* 3: 21; It. *di*, Sp. *de*, Fr. *de*]

dęca *n. fem.* flaw: *obl. sg.* **decha** 14.27. [**decaer** (*variant form of* **decazer**) + **-a**]

decazęr *vb. intrans.* to decline: *inf.* **decazer** 16.17 var., **dechader** 16.17, **deschaer** 16.17 var. [LL DĒCĂDĔRE *FEW* 2: 30, VL *DĒCĂDĔRE B-W; Fr. *déchoir;* cf. E. *decadent*]

decepciǫn *n. fem.* deceptiveness: *obl. sg.* **decepcio** 11.52. [LL DĒCĔPTĬŌNEM *FEW* 3: 24; Sp. *decepción,* Fr. *déception,* E. *deception*]

decha *see* **deca.**

dechader *see* **decazer.**

dechen *see* **descendre.**

dedins *adv.* inside; *prep.* within 25.54, 25.58; **dedins en** within 25.6. [**de-** + **dins**; cf. Fr. *dedans*]

defendre *vb. trans.* to defend: *pres. 3rd pl.* **defendo** 25.25. [CL ᴅᴇ̄ꜰᴇ̆ɴᴅᴇ̆ʀᴇ *FEW* 3: 28; It. *difendere*, Sp. *defender*, Fr. *défendre*, E. *to defend*]

definar *vb. intrans.* to die: *pret. 3rd sg.* **definet** 5.15. [**de-** + CL ꜰɪ̄ɴɪ̄ʀᴇ *FEW* 3: 557 + **-ar** (2); OFr. *définer*]

defor *adv.* outside: **defor** 30.47. [CL ᴅᴇ̄ꜰᴏ̆ʀɪs *FEW* 3: 705; It. *difuori*, Fr. *dehors*]

deglaziär *vb. trans.* to cut to pieces: *pres. 2nd sg.* **deglazias** 25.84. [**de-** + **glazi** 'sword' + **-ar** (2)]

degr', degra, degran, degras, degratz *see* **dever**.

degrunar *vb. intrans.* to fall from the husk: *pres. 3rd sg.* **degruna** 14.63. [**de-** + **grun** *PD* (CL ɢʀᴜ̄ᴍᴀᴍ 'husk, shell' *FEW* 4: 283) + **-ar** (2)]

dei (1) 22.16, *see* **dever**.

Dei (2) 30.36 (Latin), *see Proper Names:* **Deus**.

dejuṇ *adj.* fasting, on an empty stomach: *masc., nom. sg.* **dejus** 14.54. [**dejunar** (VL *ᴅɪ̆sᴊᴇ̄ᴊᴜ̄ɴᴀ̄ʀᴇ *FEW* 3: 95; Fr. *déjeuner*)]

del = **de** + **lo** 1.7, 2.27, 3.3, 3.5, 3.6, 3.7, 3.7, 4.31, 5.1, 5.2, 7.22, 8.1, 8.4, 9.47, 10.10, 10.23, 11.45, 12.35, 12.37, 12.38, 12.42, 12.47, 12.56, 12.70, 12.72, 12.72, 13.10, 14.18, 14.32, 16.53, 17.1, 17.2, 17.35, 19.29, 19.43, 19.54, 20.4, 21.56, 21.78, 24.24, 25.23, 25.53, 25.59, 25.80, 26.19, 26.28, 27.2, 27.8, 29.23, 29.28, 29.38, 31.12, 32.4, 32.13, 32.15, 32.15, 32.16, *see* **de** *and* **lo** (2).

delechar *vb. trans.* to delight: *pres. 3rd sg.* **delecha** 30.80. [CL ᴅᴇ̄ʟᴇ̆ᴄᴛᴀ̄ʀᴇ *FEW* 3: 32; It. *dilettare*, Sp. *deleitar*, E. *to delight*]

delir *vb. trans.* to destroy: *inf.* **delir** 27.12. [CL ᴅᴇ̄ʟᴇ̄ʀᴇ *FEW* 3: 32]

della 5.6 var., 5.6 var., 5.16 var. = **de la**.

dellai 21.48 var. = **de lai**.

dellamor 5.6 var. = **de l'amor**.

dellas 24.18 var. = **de las**.

delleis 1.3 var., 1.4 var., 3.4 var., 5.6 var. = **de leis**.

dellui 5.6 var., 5.12 var. = **de lui**.

dels = **de** + **los** 15.13, 20.8, 20.18, 20.23, 21.15, 21.15, 24.18, 25.3, 25.3, 25.16, 25.40, 25.53, 25.98, 27.8, 27.32, 29.27, *see* **de** *and* **los** (2).

dem *see* **dar**.

deman (1) *n. masc.* complaint: *nom. sg.* **demans** 27.24. [**demandar**]

deman (2) 2.6, 8.12, *see* **demandar**.

demanda *n. fem.* claim: *obl. sg.* **demanda** 20.4. [**demandar** + **-a**]

demandar *vb. trans.* to ask (for): *pres. 1st sg.* **deman** 2.6, 8.12, *3rd sg.* **demanda** 19.2, 19.5, 20.26; *fut. 3rd sg.* **demandara** 14.53; *2nd cond. 3rd sg.* **demandera** 14.53 var.; *inf.* **demandar** 14.53 var. [CL ᴅᴇ̄ᴍᴀ̄ɴᴅᴀ̄ʀᴇ *FEW* 3: 36; It. *domandare*, Sp. *demandar*, Fr. *demander*, E. *to demand*]

demans *see* **deman** (1).

demenar *vb. trans.* to express: *pres. 3rd sg.* **demena** 17.5. [**de-** + **menar**]

demẹntre que *conj.* while 12.14. [VL *ᴅᴜᴍ ɪɴᴛᴇ̆ʀɪᴍ *FEW* 3: 178; It. *(do)mentre*, Sp. *mientras*]

demorar *vb. intrans.* to remain 11.42, to delay 30.45: *pres. 3rd sg.* **demora** 30.45; *pres. subj. 3rd sg.* **demor** 11.42. [CL ᴅᴇ̄ᴍᴏ̆ʀᴀ̄ʀɪ̄ *FEW* 3: 39; It. *dimorare*, Sp. *demorar*, Fr. *demeurer*, E. *to demur*]

denan *adv.* before 21.48. [VL *ᴅᴇ̄ ɪ̆ɴᴀ̆ɴᴛᴇ *FEW* 4: 616; It. *dinanzi*, Sp. *delante*]

denier *n. masc.* penny, *pl.* money: *obl. pl.* **diners** 25.104. [CL ᴅᴇ̄ɴᴀ̄ʀɪ̆ᴜᴍ *FEW* 3: 40; It. *denaro*, Sp. *dinero*, Fr. *denier*, E. *d.* (abbreviation for 'pence')]

departir *vb. intrans.* to depart: *substantivized inf., masc., nom. sg.* **departirs** departure 10.9. [**de-** + **partir** *FEW* 7: 684; cf. CL dĭspĕrtīre, dĭspărtīre; It. *spartire*, Sp. *despartir*, Fr. *départir*, E. *to depart*]

deport *n. masc.* pleasure, delight 10.39, 10.41, 12.63; **tener a deport** to consider an amusement 24.6; **se tener a deport** to keep oneself amused 22.38. *See also* **Belhs Deportz** *in Proper Names.* [**deportar** 'to amuse' (LL dēpŏrtāre 'to amuse' *FEW* 9: 221; It. *diportarsi*, Sp. *deportarse*; cf. E. *to disport oneself, sport*)]

dera *see* **dar.**

dereire *adv.* behind: **derreire** 9.45. [LL dē rĕtrō *FEW* 3: 49; It. *dietro*, Fr. *derrière*]

derier *adj.* last, most recent 28.54; last, at the end of the line 29.16, 30.14; final 19.45: *masc., nom. sg.* **derrers** 30.14; *obl. pl.* **derriers** 29.16; *fem., nom. sg.* **derieira** 19.45; *obl. sg.* **derreira** 28.54. [**dereire** + **-ier**]

derocar *vb. trans.* to destroy 20.29; to overturn, to unhorse 30.76: *pres. 3rd sg.* **derroca** 20.29 ms., **derroc'** 20.29; *pp., undeclined* **derochat** 30.76. [**de-** + **roca** (LL rocca *FEW* 10: 440; It. *rocca*, Sp. *roca*, Fr. *roche*, E. *rock*) + **-ar** (2)]

deron *see* **dar.**

derreira *see* **derier.**

derreire *see* **dereire.**

derrers, derriers *see* **derier.**

derroc', derroca *see* **derocar.**

des *see* **dar.**

desadordenat *see* **dezadordenat.**

desavinen *see* **dezavinen.**

desbraiat *adj.* wearing no trousers: *masc., nom. sg.* **desbraiatz** 26.50. [**des-** + **braia** 'breeches' (LL [from Ctc.] braca *FEW* 1: 482; It. *braca*, Sp. *braga*, Fr. *braie*) + **-at**]

descaptener *vb. trans.* to cease defending: *fut. 1st sg.* **descaptenrai** 18.20. [**des-** + **captener**]

descendre *vb. intrans.* to dismount: *pres. 3rd sg.* **dechen** 25.61. [CL dĕscĕndĕre *FEW* 3: 52; It. *scendere*, Sp. *descender*, Fr. *descendre*, E. *to descend*]

deschaer *see* **decazer.**

descobrir *vb. trans.* to reveal: *pres. subj. (in negative imper.) 2nd pl.* **descobratz** 19.56. [**des-** + **cobrir**]

desconvenir *vb. intrans.* to be improper: *pres. 3rd sg.* **descove** 23.18. [**des-** + **convenir**]

dese *adv.* at once: **dese** 30.91, **desse** 18.7. [shortened form of **desempre**]

desempre *adv.* at once: **desempre** 30.39. [**de-** + CL sĕmper *FEW* 11: 442]

desenar *vb. intrans.* to go mad: *pres. 3rd sg.* **desena** 17.46. [**des-** + **sen** (1) + **-ar** (2)]

deseretz *see* **dezeret.**

deserrar *vb. trans.* to release (a bow), to shoot: *pres. 3rd sg.* **dessarra** 25.52. [**des-** + **serrar**]

deservitor *n. masc.* one who serves badly: *obl. sg.* **deservitor** (*used as nom. sg.*) 27.27 var. [**des-** + **servir** + **-idor**]

desesper *see* **dezesperar.**

desir (1) 30.62, 30.67, *see* **dezir.**

desir (2) 6.10, **desiran**, *see* **dezirar.**

desirier *see* **dezirier.**

desiron *see* **deziron.**

desliurar *vb. trans.* to set free: *pp., masc., obl. sg.* **disliurat** 32.13. [des- + liurar 'to deliver' (CL LĪBĔRĀRE *FEW* 5: 303; Fr. *livrer*)]

desnaturat *adj.* degenerate: *masc., nom. pl.* **desnaturat** 12.64. [des- + natura + -at]

desǫbre *prep.* on, seated on: **desobre** 25.10. [de- + sobre]

desǫtz *adv.* below: **desotz** 5.17. [de- + sotz]

despiuselatge *n. masc.* deflowering: *obl. sg.* **despieuselatje** 13.69. [des- + piusela (VL *PŪLLICĔLLAM *FEW* 9: 526; It. *pulcella*, Fr. *pucelle*) + -atge]

desplazẹr *n. masc.* displeasure: *obl. sg.* **desplazer** 29.13. [des- + plazer]

despolhar *vb. trans. and refl.* to undress: *pret. 1st sg.* **despulley** 9.44. [CL DĒSPŎLĬĀRE, DĬSPŎLĬĀRE *FEW* 12: 204; It. *spogliare*, Sp. *despojar*, Fr. *dépouiller*, E. *to despoil*]

desputar *vb. intrans.* to dispute: *pres. 3rd pl.* **desputon** 26.28. [CL DĬSPŪTĀRE *FEW* 3: 98; It. *disputare*, Sp. *disputar*, Fr. *disputer*, E. *to dispute*]

dessarra *see* **deserrar.**

desse *see* **dese.**

destǫlre *vb. trans.* to turn aside: *pp., masc., nom. sg.* **destoutz** 13.16. [des- + tolre]

destrẹch *n. masc.* torment: *nom. sg.* **destreg** 19.12. [CL DĬSTRĬCTUM *FEW* 3: 100; Fr. *détroit*, E. *Detroit*]

destrẹnher *vb. trans.* to torment 21.10, 29.3; to restrain, to temper 19.47: *pres. 3rd sg.* **destrenh** 19.47, 29.3; *pres. subj. 3rd sg.* **destreingna** 21.10. [CL DĬSTRĬNGĔRE *FEW* 3: 101]

destric *n. masc.* pain, harm: *obl. sg.* **destric** 23.36. [destrigar (des- + trigar 'to delay' [LL TRĪCĀRE *FEW* 13: 259])]

destrier *n. masc.* warhorse, charger: **destriers** *used as obl. sg.* 25.53; *obl. pl.* **destriers** 25.10, 30.78. [destra 'right hand,' because the charger was led on the right hand (CL DĔXTRAM *FEW* 3: 62; It. *destra*, Sp. *diestra*) + -ier]

destruire *vb. trans.* to destroy: *pres. 3rd sg.* **destrui** 18.22; *1st cond. 3rd sg.* **destruiria** 27.29. [CL DĒSTRŬĔRE *FEW* 3: 56; It. *struggere*, Sp. *destruir*, Fr. *détruire*, E. *to destroy*]

desturbier *n. masc.* disarray, confusion: *nom. sg.* **desturbiers** 25.8, 25.108. [destorbar (CL DĬSTŬRBĀRE *FEW* 3: 102; It. *sturbare*, Sp. *estorbar*) + -ier]

desviar *vb. trans.* to deter: *pres. 3rd sg.* **desvia** 26.30. [des- + via (1) + -ar (2)]

det *see* **dar.**

Deu God *see Proper Names.*

deu, deuri', deuria, deuriam *see* **dever.**

Deus (1) God *see Proper Names.*

deus (2) 21.47, *see* **devas.**

devant *see* **davan.**

devas *prep.* toward, in *(direction)* 20.30, 22.17; since 21.47. *Forms:* **devas** 20.30, 22.17; **deus** 21.47. [de- + vas (2)]

deve *see* **devenir.**

devedar *vb. trans.* to forbid: *pres. 3rd sg.* **deveda** 18.52. [de- + vedar]

devem see **dever.**

devenir vb. intrans. to become 25.28; **devenir clamaders** to complain 25.65: pres. 3rd sg. **deve** 25.65; pret. 3rd sg. **devenc** 25.28. [CL DĒVĔNĪRE FEW 3: 60; It. divenire, Sp. devenir, Fr. devenir]

devęr vb. trans. to owe 31.21; auxiliary to be destined to 21.79; to deserve to 31.5; to be supposed to 30.37; to be able to 29.9; must 6.18, 22.16, 27.36, 29.33; ought 13.41, 18.27, 27.17 var., 27.25, 29.1; should 12.11, 12.15, 18.27, 18.51, 21.59, 26.6, 27.15, 27.17, 27.25, 31.40.
> Forms: Pres. 1st sg. **dei** 22.16; 3rd sg. **deu** 6.18, 18.51, 27.15, 29.9; 1st pl. **devem** 21.79, 29.33; 2nd pl. **devetz** 31.21, **deves** 27.36; 3rd pl. **devon** 21.59.
> Imperf. 3rd sg. **devia** 30.37.
> 1st cond. 3rd sg. **deuria** 13.41, 26.6, **deuri'** 12.15; 1st pl. **deuriam** 12.11.
> 2nd cond. 1st sg. **degra** 29.1, 31.5; 3rd sg. **degra** 18.27, 27.17 var., 27.25, 31.40, **degr'** 18.27; 2nd pl. **degratz** 27.17, 27.25, **degras** 27.25 var.; 3rd pl. **degran** 27.17 var.
> [CL DĒBĒRE FEW 3: 21; It. dovere, Sp. deber, Fr. devoir]

devįn adj. able to foresee the future: masc., nom. sg. **devis** 15.20. [CL DĪVĪNUM FEW 3: 109; It. divino, Sp. adivino, Fr. devin, E. divine]

deviza n. fem. wish, desire: obl. sg. **deviza** 14.11. [**devizar** 'to explain' (VL *DĪVĪSĀRE, *DĒVĪSĀRE FEW 3: 110; It. divisare 'to propose,' E. to devise)]

devon see **dever.**

dezadordenat adj. disordered: masc., obl. sg. **desadordenat** 29.31. [**des-** + **ad-** + **ordenar** (CL ŌRDĬNĀRE FEW 7: 399; It. ordinare, Fr. ordonner)]

dezavinęn adj. improper: neuter, nom. sg. **desavinen** 17.29. [**des-** + **avinen**]

dezeręt n. masc. disinheritance: nom. sg. **deseretz** 27.27. [**dezeretar**]

dezeretar vb. trans. to disinherit: pres. part., masc., nom. sg. **dezeritans** 27.31; inf. **dezeretar** 27.25. [**des-** + **eretar** (LL HĒRĒDĬTĀRE FEW 4: 410; Sp. heredar, Fr. hériter, E. to inherit)]

dezesperar vb. intrans. to abandon hope: pres. 1st sg. **desesper** 18.17; inf. **dezesperar** 27.33. [**des-** + **esperar**]

dezir n. masc. desire: nom. sg. **dezirs** 4.39; obl. sg. **desir** 30.62, 30.67. [**dezirar**]

dezirar vb. trans. to desire: pres. 1st sg. **dezir** 16.38, **desir** 6.10; pres. part., masc., obl. sg. **desiran** 15.44 var. [CL DĒSĪDĔRĀRE FEW 3: 53; It. desiderare, Fr. désirer, E. to desire]

dezirier n. masc. desire: obl. sg. **desirier** 18.8, 18.16. [**dezir** + **-ier**]

dezirǫn adj. desirous, yearning: masc., obl. sg. **desiron** 15.44, 18.30; fem., nom. sg. **desironda** 19.29. [**dezirar** + **-on** (2)]

dezonǫr n. fem. dishonor: obl. sg. **dezonor** 29.21. [**des-** + **onor**]

di (1) n. masc. day: obl. sg. **di** 11.60; obl. pl. **dies** 11.20. [CL DĬEM FEW 3: 72; It. dì; cf. **dia** (1)]

di (2) 12.3, 16.54, vb. trans., see **dire.**

di (3) 17.35 prep. = **de.**

dia (1) n. masc. or fem. day: masc., nom. sg. **dias** 16.49, **dia** 16.49 var., obl. sg. **dia** 1.7 (see note), 3.7 (see note), 11.60 var., 27.38, 28.21; fem., nom. sg. **dia** 3.7 var., obl. sg. **dia** 11.79; no evidence for gender, nom. sg. **dia** 4.11. [CL DĬEM fem., VL *DIAM FEW 3: 72; Sp. día masc.; cf. **di** (1)]

dia (2) vb. trans. 4.19 pres. subj. 3rd sg. of **dire,** which see.

diable *n. masc.* devil: *obl. sg.* **diable** 14.38, **diabol** 30.16, 30.21; *obl. pl.* **diables** 27.25. [ChL ᴅɪ̆ᴀ̆ʙᴏ̆ʟᴜᴍ *FEW* 3: 65; It. *diavolo*, Sp. *diablo*, Fr. *diable*, Germ. *Teufel*, E. *devil*]

diablia *n. fem.* Hell: *obl. sg.* **diablia** 27.5. [**diable** + **-ia**]

diabol *see* **diable**.

dias *see* **dia** (1).

diatz, dic *see* **dire**.

dies *see* **di** (1).

Dieu, Dieus God *see Proper Names*.

diey *see* **dar**.

dig (1) *n. masc.* 23.32, *see* **dit** (1).

dig (2) *vb. trans.* 11.43, 19.3, 26.3, *see* **dire**.

dig', diga, digua, diguas, *see* **dire**.

digz *see* **dit** (1).

dihs, diire, *see* **dire**.

diluns *n. masc.* Monday: *obl. sg.* **diluns** 22.25. [LL ᴅɪ̄ᴇᴍ ʟᴜ̄ɴɪs 'day of the moon' *FEW* 5: 454; It. *lunedì*, Sp. *lunes*, Fr. *lundi*]

dimartz *n. masc.* Tuesday: *obl. sg.* **dimartz** 22.25. [LL ᴅɪ̄ᴇᴍ ᴍᴀ̆ʀᴛɪs 'day of Mars' *FEW* 5: 453; It. *martedì*, Sp. *martes*, Fr. *mardi*]

dimęngue *n. masc.* Sunday: *nom. sg.* **dimergues** 30.15. [LL ᴅɪ̄ᴇᴍ ᴅᴏ̆ᴍɪ̆ɴɪ̆ᴄᴜᴍ 'Lord's day' *FEW* 3: 129; It. *domenica*, Sp. *domingo*, Fr. *dimanche*]

dinar *vb. intrans.* to dine: *pret. 1st sg.* **dirney** 9.26; *substantivized inf., masc., obl. sg.* **dinnar** dinner, meal 12.47. [VL *ᴅɪ̆sᴊᴇ̄ᴊᴜ̄ɴᴀ̄ʀᴇ 'to break fast,' *ᴅɪ̆sᴊᴜ̄ɴᴀ̄ʀᴇ *FEW* 3: 95; Fr. *dîner, déjeuner*, E. *to dine*]

dinat *adj.* who has eaten, on a full stomach: *masc., nom. sg.* **dinnatz** 14.54. [**dinar**]

diners *see* **denier**.

dinnar *see* **dinar**.

dinnatz *see* **dinat**.

dins *adv.* inside 19.7, 25.66; *prep.* within, in 31.16, 32.7; in, with 32.10; **dinz de** from within 16.2. [LL ᴅᴇ̆ ɪ̄ɴᴛᴜs *FEW* 3: 31]

dire *vb. trans.* to say, to tell, to speak; **dire de no** to say no 12.65.

 Forms: Pres. 1st sg. **di** 12.3, **dic** 16.27, 17.24, 19.55, 23.44, 27.11, 29.15, **dig** 11.43; *3rd sg.* **di** 16.54, **ditz** 13.39, 15.43, 19.13, 19.58, 25.29, 25.61, **diz** 23.21, 23.27; *3rd pl.* **dizon** 12.65, **dison** 23.18.

 Pres. subj. 1st sg. **diga** 20.2 ms., **dig'** 20.2; *3rd sg.* **digua** 2.19, **dia** 4.19; *2nd pl.* **diatz** 19.46.

 Imperf. 3rd sg. **dizia** 4.3, 28.28.

 Fut. 1st sg. **dirai** 18.36, 27.6, **diray** 14.19, 31.35, **dir . . . ay** 31.7, 31.25; *3rd pl.* **diran** 22.44, **dirant** 6.24.

 1st cond. 1st sg. **diria** 26.53.

 Pret. 1st sg. **dis** 9.9; *3rd sg.* **dis** 3.8, 3.10, 3.11, 9.13, 11.14, 13.11, 13.25, 13.53, 13.67, 13.84, 28.12, 28.16, 30.61, 30.71, 30.72, **dihs** 31.20, **dit** 25.62; *2nd pl.* **dissez** 23.29; *3rd pl.* **dishero** 31.39.

 Imper. 2nd sg. **diguas** 9.71.

 Pp., neuter, nom. sg. **dit** 3.6, **dig** 19.3, 26.3.

 Inf. **dire** 1.2, 2.7, 14.1, 16.22, 25.78, 31.8, **dir** 2.22, 9.35, 17.10, 23.13, 30.59, 31.37, **diire** 25.31.

 [CL ᴅɪ̄ᴄᴇ̆ʀᴇ *FEW* 3: 70; It. *dire*, Sp. *decir*, Fr. *dire*; cf. E. *to dictate*]

dirney *see* **dinar**.

dis *see* dire.

discipat *see* disipar.

dishero *see* dire.

disipar *vb. trans.* to drive, to disperse: *pp., masc., nom. pl.* discipat 29.28. [CL dĭssĭpāre *FEW* 3: 99; It. *dissipare,* Sp. *disipar,* Fr. *dissiper,* E. *to dissipate*]

disliurat *see* desliurar.

dison, dissez *see* dire.

dit (1) *n. masc.* word: *obl. sg.* dig 23.32; *obl. pl.* ditz 15.28 var., digz 15.28. [substantivized pp. of dire]

dit (2) *vb. trans.* 3.6, 25.62, *see* dire.

dit (3) *adj.* so-called: *masc., obl. pl.* ditz 29.26. [pp. of dire]

ditar *vb. intrans.* to write, to compose: *pres. part., undeclined* ditan 11.78. [CL dĭctāre *FEW* 3: 71; It. *dettare,* Fr. *dicter,* G. *dichten,* E. *to dictate*]

ditz (1) *vb. trans.* 13.39, 15.43, 19.13, 19.58, 25.29, 25.61, *see* dire.

ditz (2) *n. masc.* 15.28 var., *see* dit (1).

ditz (3) *dj.* 29.26, *see* dit (3).

diz, dizia, dizon *see* dire.

dobla *see* doble.

doblar *vb. trans.* to double, to increase twofold: *pp., fem., nom. sg.* doblada 13.47. [doble + -ar (2)]

doble *adj.* double; dobla mort double death (of the body and the soul) 29.34: *fem., obl. sg.* dobla 29.34. [CL dŭplum *FEW* 3: 187; It. *doppio,* Sp. *doble,* Fr. *double,* E. *double*]

doblier *adj.* double, thicker or sturdier than usual: *masc., obl. pl.* dobliers 25.48. [doble + -ier]

doctor *n. masc.* doctor, teacher: *obl. sg.* doctor 11.39. [CL dŏctōrem *FEW* 3: 112; It. *dottore,* Sp. *doctor,* Fr. *docteur,* E. *doctor*]

dol *n. masc.* grief; worry 13.10: *nom. sg.* dols 11.42, 12.21, 21.11, 24.20; *obl. sg.* dol 13.10, 21.1, 21.73, 31.32, 31.46. [LL dŏlum 'pain' *FEW* 3: 121; It. *duolo,* Sp. *duelo,* Fr. *deuil*; cf. E. *doleful*]

dolchor *see* dousor.

doler *vb. intrans.* to grieve; *pres. part.* grieving, sad: *pres. part., masc., nom. sg.* dolens 31.22, dolentz 5.14, dolenz 10.2; *obl. sg.* dolen 17.36; *inf.* doler 17.17, 29.4. [CL dŏlēre *FEW* 3: 118; It. *dolere,* Sp. *doler*]

dolor *n. fem.* grief: *nom. sg.* dolors 4.20, 11.41; *obl. sg.* dolor 1.7, 5.15, 9.59, 17.20. [CL dŏlōrem *FEW* 3: 119; It. *dolore,* Sp. *dolor,* Fr. *douleur*]

dols *see* dol.

dolza *see* dous.

domengier *n. masc.* vassal: *nom. sg.* domengers 25.81. [domenge 'property,' 'own' *adj.* (CL dŏmĭnĭcum *FEW* 3: 129) + -ier]

dŏmĭnus (Latin) *n. masc.* lord: *vocative sg.* domine 11.75; *gen. sg.* Domini 12.1.

domna *n. fem.* lady; ma dompna my lady *(title)* 3.3, 18.50: *nom. sg.* domna 3.5, 3.8, 19.3, 30.21, dompna 5.9, 6.17, 6.22, 18.50, 23.19; *obl. sg.* domna 3.3, 3.4, dompna 3.3, 5.6; *vocative sg.* domna 27.45, dona 29.45; *nom. pl.* domnas 17.30, donas 25.68; *obl. pl.* domnas 17.24, dompnas 18.17. [CL dŏmĭnam *FEW* 3: 126, dŏmnam *Oxf.*; It. *donna,* Sp. *dueña,* Fr. *dame,* E. *dame*; cf. na]

domnei *n. masc.* flirtation, courting ladies: *obl. sg.* dompnei 22.40. [domneiar (domna + -eiar)]

dọn (1) *n. masc.* lord, *(as predicate nominative)* a lordly man: *nom. sg.*
donz 11.28; sir *(title of respectful address): vocative sg.* **don** 13.22,
13.64, 13.78, 13.88. [CL DŎMĬNUM, LL DOMNUM *FEW* 3: 131; It. *don*, Sp.
dueño, Fr. *don*, E. *don* (as at Oxford); cf. **en** (1)]

dọn (2) *n. masc.* gift 8.21, largesse 21.32: *nom. sg.* **dons** 21.32; *obl. sg.* **don**
8.21. [CL DŎNUM *FEW* 3: 138; It. *dono*, Sp. *don*, Fr. *don*]

dọn (3) *vb. trans.* 15.38, 16.8, 22.12 *pres. subj. 3rd sg.* of **donar,** *which see.*

dọn (4) *rel. pron.* = **de que** *(see also* **de, que** [1]); about that, about which
10.2; because of whom 25.108; by which 29.44; from whom 18.12,
23.24, from which 8.7, 23.43, 24.30, from where 27.38; of which 8.6; of
whom 11.43; on which 26.14; so that 24.29, 29.30; where 12.23, 31.3;
which is why 7.7, 23.6; **don sa** whose 21.51.

    Forms: **don** *passim,* **dont** 8.6, **dunt** 11.43.

    [VL *DĒ ŬNDE *FEW* 14: 32; It. *donde*, Sp. *donde*, Fr. *dont*]

dona *see* **domna.**

donar *vb. trans.* to give *passim*; to grant 29.43: *pres. 3rd sg.* **dona** 30.42,
2nd pl. **donatz** 19.40; *pres. subj. 3rd sg.* **don** 15.38, 16.8, 22.12, **done**
29.43; *pret. 1st sg.* **donei** 7.6, *3rd sg.* **donet** 8.21, 30.6; *pp., masc., obl. sg.*
donat 29.11, *undeclined (fem. object)* **donat** 2.24, 30.39; *inf.* **donar**
29.22, 30.50, 31.40, *substantivized* largesse 21.29, 22.40. [CL DŌNĀRE
FEW 3: 137; It. *donare*, Sp. *donar*, Fr. *donner*, E. *to donate*]

donas *see* **domna.**

donat, donatz *see* **donar.**

dọnc *adv.* then: **donc** 11.41. [LL DŬNC *FEW* 3: 179; It. *dunque*, Fr. *donc*]

dọncs *adv.* then: **doncx** 19.35, **doncs** 19.61. [**donc** + **-s**]

done, donei, donet *see* **donar.**

dons *see* **don** (2).

dont *see* **don** (4).

donz *see* **don** (1).

donzẹla *n. fem.* maiden: *nom. sg.* **donzela** 19.18; *vocative sg.* **donzela**
19.33 ms., **donzel'** 19.33. [CL DŎMĬNĬCĔLLAM, VL *DŎMNĬCĔLLAM *FEW* 3:
133; It. *donzella*, Sp. *doncella*, Fr. *demoiselle*]

doptansa *n. fem.* doubt; **ses duptansa** without doubt, surely 14.1, 28.39:
obl. sg. **duptansa** 14.1, 28.39. [**doptar** + **-ansa**]

doptar *vb. trans.* to fear: *pres. 1st sg.* **dopti** 18.23 ms., **dopt'** 18.23. [CL
DŬBĬTĀRE *FEW* 3: 170; Sp. *dudar*, Fr. *douter*, E. *to doubt*]

dormir *vb. intrans.* to sleep: *pres. 3rd sg.* **dorm** 8.9; *imperf. 3rd sg.* **durmia**
28.7; *pret. 1st sg.* **dormigui** 31.24; *pres. part.* **en durmen** while sleeping
23.40; *substantivized inf., masc., obl. sg.* **dormir** sleeping 17.8, 20.17.
[CL DŎRMĪRE *FEW* 3: 143; It. *dormire*, Sp. *dormir*, Fr. *dormir*; cf. E. *dor-
mitory*]

dọs *num.* two: *masc., obl. pl.* **dos** 15.32, 16.30, 17.22, 31.43. [CL DŬO, LL
DŬOS *FEW* 3: 181; It. *due*, Sp. *dos*, Fr. *deux*]

dosa *see* **dous.**

dossayna *see* **dousan.**

dossor *see* **dousor.**

dọus *adj.* sweet, delightful 2.8, 14.35, 15.2, 23.23; sweet *(in address to a
woman)* 4.4, 4.10, 4.19, 4.28, 4.37, *(said of a woman)* 16.39; kind, merciful 27.15: *masc., nom. sg.* **dous** 27.15, **doutz** 15.2; *obl. sg.* **dous** 2.8,
douz 23.23; *fem., nom. sg.* **dosa** 14.35, **dolza** 16.39; *vocative sg.* **doussa**
4.4, 4.10, 4.19, 4.28, 4.37. [CL DŬLCEM *FEW* 3: 177; It. *dolce*, Sp. *dulce*,
Fr. *doux*]

dousaṇ *adj.* sweet, delightful: *fem., obl. sg.* **dossayna** 13.77. [**dous** + **-an** (2)]

dousǫr *n. fem.* sweetness, mildness (of spring) 8.1; warmth (of the sun) 18.4; mercy 12.4: *obl. sg.* **doussor** 18.4, **dolchor** 8.1, **dossor** 12.4. [**dous** + **-or**; Sp. *dulzor*, Fr. *douceur*; cf. CL DŬLCŌREM]

doussa *see* **dous.**

doussor *see* **dousor.**

doutz, douz *see* **dous.**

draparia *n. fem.* garment: *obl. sg.* **dapr̆aria** 26.37. [**drap** (LL [from Ctc.] DRAPPUS 'cloth' *FEW* 3: 156; It. *drappo*, Sp. *trapo*, Fr. *drap*) + **-aria**]

dręch (1) *n. masc.* right, what is right, justice; rightful claim 18.34; **a dręch** rightly, justly 19.58; **per bon dręch** by rights, deservedly 27.14: *obl. sg.* **dreich** 22.50, **dreg** 12.54, 19.58, 27.14, **dreitz** 18.34. [CL DĪRĒCTUM *FEW* 3: 90; It. *diritto*, Sp. *derecho*, Fr. *droit*; cf. E. *adroit*]

dręch (2) *adj.* straight, straightforward, righteous 14.25; right, just, fair 14.68: *fem., nom. sg.* **dreita** 14.23, **drecha** 14.25; *neuter, nom. sg.* **dretz** 14.68. [**dręch** (1)]

dręch (3) *adv.* straight: **dreit** 25.69, **dreg** 9.69. [**dręch** (1)]

drechura *n. fem.* rights, what is right, righteousness: *obl. sg.* **drechura** 13.78. [**dręch** (2) + **-ura**]

drechurier *adj.* righteous, just: *masc., nom. sg.* **dreiturers** 25.79; *vocative sg.* **dreiturers** 25.29. [**drechura** + **-ier**]

dreg (1) *n. masc.* 12.54, 19.58, 27.14, **dreich** *see* **dręch** (1).

dreg (2) *adv.* 9.69, **dreit** *see* **dręch** (3).

dreita *see* **dręch** (2).

dreiturers *see* **drechurier.**

dreitz *see* **dręch** (1).

dretz *see* **dręch** (2).

drogoman *n. masc.* interpreter: *obl. pl.* **drogomanz** 24.4, **drugomanz** 24.4 var. [Arabic *tarğumān FEW* 19: 182, Byzantine Gk. *dragoumanos*; It. *dragomanno*, Fr. *drogman*, E. *dragoman* 'interpreter']

druda *n. fem.* sweetheart, mistress, woman in love: *nom. sg.* **druda** 19.53. [**drut** + **-a**]

drudaria *n. fem.* love, loving: *obl. sg.* **drudari'** 8.22. [**drut** + **-aria**]

drut *n. masc.* lover: *nom. sg.* **drutz** 15.27. [Ctc. **druto-* 'strong' *FEW* 3: 164; It. *drudo*, Fr. *dru*]

duc *n. masc.* duke: *nom. sg.* **ducs** 20.21. [CL DŬCEM *FEW* 3: 197; It. *duce*, Fr. *duc*, E. *duke*]

ducat *n. masc.* duchy, domain ruled by a duke: *nom. sg.* **duchatz** 20.36. [CL DŬCĀTUM *FEW* 3: 196; It. *ducato*, Sp. *ducado*, Fr. *duché*, E. *duchy*]

duchęsa *n. fem.* duchess: *obl. sg.* **duchesa** 5.10. [**duc** + **-esa**]

dunt *see* **don** (4).

duptansa *see* **doptansa.**

dur *adj.* hard: *masc., obl. sg.* **dur** 23.43. [CL DŪRUM *FEW* 3: 194; It. *duro*, Sp. *duro*, Fr. *dur*]

durar *vb. intrans.* to last: *pres. 3rd sg.* **dura** 16.49, 25.26; *pret. 3rd sg.* **duret** 5.7. [CL DŪRĀRE *FEW* 3: 189; It. *durare*, Sp. *durar*, Fr. *durer*; cf. E. *to endure*]

durmen, durmia *see* **dormir.**

e (1) *prep.* in, on. *Forms:* **e** followed by **m-** 7.10, 7.18, 10.40, 11.50, 13.82, 18.53, 28.41; **e·l** 2.21, 8.18, 9.68, 11.60, 12.48, 12.49 var., 15.13, 18.54,

20.25, 23.23, 25.53, 25.67, 27.7, 30.39, 30.41, 30.67, 30.80; **e la** 13.31; **e·ls** 25.33, 25.44, 25.57; **e** *followed by other nonnasal consonants* 11.27, 11.33, 11.44, 11.54, 11.59, 11.67, 11.71, 11.73, 11.75, 11.76, 18.43 var. *For meanings, see* **en** (3).

e (2) *conj.* and. *Introducing sentence (continuity of narrative, no change of grammatical subject)* 1.2, 1.3, 1.4, 1.7, 3.7, 3.8, 3.10, 5.3, 5.5, 5.9, 5.13, 5.15, 14.53, 22.25, 23.37, 23.44, 24.9, 25.31, 26.29, 30.68; *(continuity of narrative with change of subject)* 1.5, 1.6, 1.7, 2.26, 3.3, 3.4, 3.5, 3.6, 3.9, 3.11, 5.4, 5.6, 5.8, 5.9, 5.10, 5.11, 5.16, 5.17, 12.17, 12.60, 16.33, 17.32, 21.19, 21.64, 22.9, 23.46, 25.15, 25.26, 25.28, 25.35, 25.39, 25.43, 25.55, 25.60, 25.69, 25.84, 25.89, 25.95, 28.9. Now *(the narrative focuses)* 5.5; even 25.14; and so *(conclusion)* 1.6, 5.10; so 2.22, 5.11, 6.17, 11.16, 27.37; but 3.11; *(introducing subjunctive expressing wish or command)* 7.19, 20.31; *(address in direct question)* 24.17.

    Introducing main verb 31.37.

    Adding coordinate sentence 1.5, 1.6, 3.6, 3.11, 4.5, 5.11, 5.12, 8.2, 9.20, 9.22, 9.23, 9.26, 9.27, 9.27, 9.29, 9.65, 10.8, 10.27, 11.63, 12.32, 12.52, 12.71, 14.8, 14.17, 14.60, 15.3, 15.20, 15.24, 16.52, 18.26, 19.19, 21.58, 22.43, 23.27, 23.45, 24.7, 24.28, 25.13, 25.47, 25.63, 25.68, 25.73, 25.76, 25.105, 26.19, 26.20, 26.30, 26.52, 27.22, 27.27, 27.28, 29.37, 29.39, 30.36, 31.7, 31.25. And yet, but *(opposition)* 11.50, 18.10, 23.5, 30.14; and so *(conclusion)* 9.50, 30.43; so 12.44, 18.28, 23.34, 27.8, 27.23; so that 2.18, 9.17, 14.12; but 29.3; *(introducing subjunctive expressing wish or command)* 7.19, 20.35, 21.60, 30.51; *expressing emotion* 16.25.

    Adding verb phrase 1.1, 1.4, 1.4, 1.4, 1.6, 2.6, 3.4, 3.4, 3.6, 3.6, 3.7, 3.7, 3.7, 3.7, 3.7, 3.11, 3.11, 3.11, 5.3, 5.3, 5.4, 5.6, 5.8, 5.10, 5.11, 5.13, 5.14, 5.14, 6.2, 6.5, 6.11, 6.13, 7.3, 7.20, 8.21, 9.32, 9.47, 9.50, 9.71, 10.23, 10.35, 10.36, 11.34, 11.53, 11.54, 11.68, 12.9, 13.4, 13.34, 13.47, 14.7, 14.27, 14.59, 16.6, 16.13, 16.14, 16.28, 16.35, 16.54, 17.31, 17.35, 17.38, 17.41, 18.13, 18.14, 18.15, 18.37, 18.38, 18.39, 18.52, 18.54, 18.55, 18.60, 19.15, 20.2, 20.15, 20.29, 21.2, 21.18, 22.5, 22.38, 23.47, 23.48, 24.12, 25.7, 25.25, 25.53, 25.57, 25.61, 25.61, 25.65, 25.70, 25.75, 25.90, 25.92, 25.93, 25.94, 25.102, 26.18, 26.31, 27.26, 27.48. So 25.10, 28.3, 28.4, 28.8, 28.68, 30.4, 30.7, 30.8, 30.23, 30.35, 30.45, 30.57, 30.61, 30.75, 30.87, 30.92, 30.98, 30.99, 31.33, 31.39; but *(opposition)* 28.50; so *(result)* 12.53.

    Adding noun phrase 5.6, 5.12, 10.14, 13.81, 16.51, 21.28, 21.35, 21.65, 21.65, 21.68, 31.5, 31.9.

    Adding element within phrase 1.6, 2.10, 2.17, 2.21, 2.24, 2.25, 3.1, 3.3, 3.6, 3.7, 3.9, 5.3, 5.3, 5.3, 5.5, 5.5, 5.6, 5.6, 5.6, 5.8, 5.9, 5.10, 5.10, 5.11, 5.14, 6.1, 6.2, 6.4, 6.25, 6.26, 6.27, 6.27, 6.28, 6.34, 7.8, 7.15, 7.17, 8.7, 8.16, 8.22, 8.30, 9.4, 9.13, 9.15, 9.20, 9.28, 9.34, 9.42, 9.43, 9.46, 9.60, 9.62, 9.62, 9.64, 9.70, 10.12, 10.16, 10.20, 10.24, 10.25, 10.29, 10.34, 10.38, 10.39, 10.40, 10.40, 11.5, 11.17, 11.28, 12.2, 12.10, 12.14, 12.19, 12.29, 12.31, 12.45, 12.50, 12.56, 12.58, 12.68, 13.3, 13.5, 13.6, 13.7, 13.12, 13.14, 13.36, 13.37, 13.38, 13.49, 13.56, 13.57, 14.15, 14.26, 14.51, 14.57, 15.5, 15.12, 15.15, 15.19, 15.34, 15.37, 15.41, 15.49, 16.20, 16.26, 16.29, 16.38, 16.39, 16.39, 16.41, 16.50, 17.4, 17.8, 17.45, 18.3, 18.16, 18.22, 18.23, 18.37, 18.59, 18.60, 19.5, 19.15, 19.18, 20.3, 20.10, 20.28, 20.29, 20.32, 20.36, 21.1, 21.3, 21.5, 21.6, 21.8, 21.15, 21.18, 21.23, 21.32, 21.34, 21.36, 21.59, 21.61, 21.62, 21.63, 21.71, 22.3, 22.9,

22.35, 22.36, 22.36, 22.39, 22.40, 23.8, 23.35, 23.36, 23.37, 23.42, 23.42, 24.1, 24.2, 24.5, 24.18, 25.14, 25.28, 25.32, 25.32, 25.38, 25.40, 25.46, 25.47, 25.59, 25.62, 25.74, 25.75, 25.82, 25.84, 25.88, 25.95, 25.100, 25.107, 26.3, 26.10, 26.12, 26.13, 26.48, 26.51, 27.3, 27.5, 27.15, 27.26, 27.32, 27.36, 27.41, 27.42, 27.47, 25.7, 28.34, 29.7, 29.19, 29.21, 29.25, 29.27, 29.32, 29.36, 29.48, 30.2, 30.9, 30.30, 30.31, 30.34, 30.38, 30.59, 30.74, 30.78, 30.90, 30.96, 30.97, 31.23, 31.43, 31.45, 32.1, 32.7, 32.10, 32.17, 32.18. *Expressing emotion* 2.20.

 Series of two **e** . . . **e** 5.4, 5.10, 5.13, 13.65, 14.7, 17.13, 17.48, 20.29, 21.3–4, 21.32, 21.46, 23.2, 23.4, 24.31–32, 25.3, 25.4, 25.12, 25.21, 25.42, 25.68, 25.73, 25.78, 25.108, 32.14–15, both . . . and 29.14; *series of three* 3.2, 3.5, 16.7, 16.54, 18.13–14, 21.19–20, 24.1–2, 25.24, 25.28–29, 25.39, 25.48–49, 25.87; *series of four* 3.3, 10.41–42, 24.19–20, 25.22–23, 25.71–72; *series of five* 21.21–23, 21.29–31, 24.9–13, 25.103–04; *series of six* 25.36–38; *series of eight* 25.97–99.

 Forms: **e** *passim; see also listings under* **es** (2), **et**, **ez**.

 [CL ᴇᴛ *FEW* 3: 248; It. *e(d)*, Sp. *y*, Fr. *et*; cf. E. *et cetera*]

ẹc *interj.* behold: **ec** 11.44, 11.72. [CL ᴇ̆ᴄᴄᴇ, VL ᴇ̆ᴄᴄᴜᴍ *FEW* 3: 202; It. *ecco*]

efant, efanz, effant *see* **enfan**.

ẹga *n. fem.* mare: *obl. sg.* **egua** 14.49. [CL ᴇ̆ǫᴜᴀᴍ *FEW* 3: 233; Sp. *yegua*; cf. E. *equine*]

egal *adj.* equal, mutual: *fem., nom. sg.* **egaus** 16.32. [CL ᴀᴇǫᴜᴀ̄ʟᴇᴍ *FEW* 1: 44; It. *uguale*, Sp. *igual*, Fr. *égal*, E. *equal*]

egalier *adj.* equal: *masc.*, **engalers** *used as nom. pl.* 25.6. [**egal** + **-ier**]

egua *see* **ega**.

eis (1) *see* **eisir**.

ẹis (2) *adv.* even 11.18, same 11.15: **eps** 11.15, 11.18. [CL ɪ̆ᴘsᴜᴍ *FEW* 4: 808; It. *esso*, Sp. *eso*]

eisamẹn *adv.* all the same: **epsamen** 11.15. [**eis** (2) + **-amen** (2)]

eisart *n. masc.* cleared field, assart: *obl. pl.* **issartz** 22.33. [LL ᴇ̆xsᴀ̄ʀᴛᴜᴍ *FEW* 3: 319; Fr. *essart*, E. *assart*]

eisẹmple *n. masc.* example: *obl. sg.* **essemple** 11.32. [CL ᴇxᴇ̆ᴍᴘʟᴜᴍ *FEW* 3: 291; It. *esempio*, Sp. *ejemplo*, Fr. *exemple*, E. *example*]

eisilh *n. masc.* exile: *obl. sg.* **eisil** 10.5, **issill** 18.40. [CL ᴇ̆xɪ̆ʟɪ̆ᴜᴍ *FEW* 3: 295; It. *esilio*, Sp. *exilio*, Fr. *exil*, E. *exile*]

eisir *vb. intrans.* to go out, to exit: *pres. 3rd sg.* **eis** 30.51, 30.91; *pp., masc., nom. sg.* **issitz** 19.4 var., **yssitz** 19.4, *obl. sg. (used as nom. sg.)* **yssit** 19.4 ms. [CL ᴇ̆xɪ̄ʀᴇ *FEW* 3: 297; It. *uscire*, Sp. *exir*; cf. E. *exit*]

ẹl (1) *personal pron., 3rd sg. and pl.* he, she, it, they; him, her, it, them; **el mezeis** he himself 6.16, 27.28 var.; **lies** her (home) 31.17.

 Forms bearing normal stress (CL ɪ̆ʟʟᴇ > OOc **él**, etc.):

 Masc., nom. sg. **el** 1.2, 1.4, 1.6, 1.6, 3.6, 3.8, 3.11, 3.11, 5.6, 5.6, 5.6, 5.9, 5.10, 5.15, 6.6, 6.16, 7.11, 11.36, 11.65, 11.70, 12.14, 20.28, 22.42, 24.20, 25.31, 26.7, 27.11, 27.47, 30.36, 30.47, 30.53, 30.71, 30.76; **elh** 27.28 var., 28.34, 29.30; **eu** 11.49, 11.57; **il** 10.22, 10.23, 12.14 var., 27.4, 27.5. *Obl. sg.* **el** 1.5, 5.14, 9.17, 30.88; **lui** 1.7, 5.4, 5.6, 5.8, 5.12, 5.14 var., 5.16, 6.7, 6.31, 6.32, 10.36 var. (= **li** 10.36, **pregar** *takes either direct or indirect object*), 11.25, 11.48, 11.51, 19.65 var., 30.22, 30.27, **a lui** 7.12; **luy** 31.34. *Dat. sg.* **lui** 25.56. *Nom. pl.* **ilh** 25.5, 25.9, 25.46; **els** 26.51. *Obl. pl.* **els** 26.9, 26.17. *Dat. pl.* **lor** 11.55, 11.57, 20.15, 20.15, 24.39, 25.1, 25.5, 25.7, **a lor** 25.43; **lur** 26.19, 26.36.

Fem., nom. sg. **ela** 3.10, 19.34, 19.41, 19.47, 19.58, 31.9, 31.20; **ella** 1.5, 1.6, 1.7, 1.7, 1.7, 3.9, 3.11, 3.11, 5.11, 5.12, 18.39; **elha** 28.16; **el'** 8.12; **il** 18.36, 19.34 var. (= **ela** 19.34), 30.70, 30.73; **ill** 6.20; **ylh** 2.23. *Obl. sg.* **ela** 19.65; **ella** 3.4, 5.6, 5.6, 5.12, 5.12, 5.13; **liey** 2.17; **leis** 1.3, 1.4, 3.4, 5.6, 30.63; **lieis** 15.14, 15.24, 15.25, 18.22, 18.31, 18.35, 18.37; **lieys** 2.14, 2.16, 13.8, 18.12 var.; **lies** 31.8, 31.17, 31.23, 31.30. *Dat. sg.* **lei** 16.16. *Nom. pl.* **ellas** 17.27, 26.51. *Obl. pl.* **lor** 17.47, 18.18. *Dat. pl.* **lor** 9.71, 17.28, 17.31; **lur** 9.7, 9.9.

Unstressed forms (CL ĭLLUM > OOc **lo**, etc., *by attraction to stress in the following word*):

Masc., obl. sg. **lo** 1.4, 1.5, 1.7, 3.7, 3.7, 3.7, 3.7, 5.11, 6.11, 9.15, 10.20, 11.27, 11.49, 11.64, 11.71, 18.36, 18.50, 19.2, 19.35, 19.56, 19.66, 20.26, 21.13, 22.16, 24.22, 25.88. *Dat. sg.* **li** 3.7, 5.4, 6.5, 6.29, 7.6, 9.35, 10.8, 10.15, 10.22, 10.36 (= **lui** 10.36 var.), 11.42, 11.70, 14.68, 24.16, 25.72, 27.6. *Obl. pl.* **los** 27.12, 27.29, 27.48 var.; **lus** 27.29 ms. (= **los** 27.29).

Fem., obl. sg. **la** 5.13, 5.13, 5.13, 11.14, 13.27, 14.50, 15.17, 16.34, 17.41, 17.42, 18.28, 18.29, 19.60, 19.68, 22.43, 25.68, 26.7, 30.93, 30.94, 31.18. *Dat. sg.* **li** 3.8, 3.11, 4.3, 5.11, 15.22, 18.4, 18.38, 18.52, 30.71, 31.11. *Obl. pl.* **las** 17.31, 17.34, 18.19, 18.20, 18.23, 18.23.

Clitic forms:

Proclitic, masc., obl. sg. **l'** 3.8, 5.11, 6.14, 6.21, 7.4, 9.49, 10.13, 10.19, 11.39, 14.39, 16.51, 16.53, 16.54, 16.54, 19.2, 20.2, 27.41, 30.51, 30.96. *Dat. sg.* **lh'** 25.60; **l'** 1.6, 3.5, 4.14, 6.12, 6.13, 6.14, 7.15, 12.41, 25.58, 28.35.

Proclitic, fem., obl. sg. **l'** 1.6, 3.4, 11.14, 17.39, 18.36, 19.42, 19.55, 19.63, 21.54, 30.6, 30.95. *Dat. sg.* **l'** 11.73, 19.30.

Enclitic, masc., obl. sg. **·l** 19.28, 20.2, 21.2, 21.14, 26.16; **·ll** 11.9. *Dat. sg.* **·il** 6.30, 18.32, 22.14, 22.43; **·ll** 11.6; **·ill** 24.9; **·l** 11.37, 11.47, 11.54, 11.69, 14.36, 14.39, 23.20. *Obl. pl.* **·ls** 20.28, 21.24, 21.25, 25.14, 26.30, 27.40, 27.48; **·lz** 11.59. **·ls** *used as dat.* 25.90.

Enclitic, fem., obl. sg. **·l** 14.48. *Dat. sg.* **·l** 12.36, 30.59; **·ill** 16.35, 16.35.

Enclitic, neuter, obl. sg. **·l** 10.30, 20.5.

[CL ĭLLUM *FEW* 4: 554; It. *egli*, Sp. *él*, Fr. *il*]

e·l (2) *prep.* in the, *see* **e** (1).

ela *see* **el** (1).

elegir *vb. trans.* to choose: *pp., masc., obl. sg.* **elegut** 21.44. [CL ēLĬGĔRE *FEW* 3: 214; It. *eleggere*, Sp. *elegir*, Fr. *élire*]

ellai 5.15 var. = **e lai**.

ellas *see* **el** (1).

ęlm *n. masc.* helmet: *obl. sg.* **elm** 25.70; *nom. pl.* **elm** 21.21; *obl. pl.* **elms** 22.36, **elmes** 25.78. [Frankish **helm FEW* 16: 193; It. *elmo*, Sp. *yelmo*, Fr. *heaume*, E. *helmet*]

els (1) *personal pron., see* **el** (1).

e·ls (2) *prep.* in the, *see* **e** (1).

em (1) *vb. intrans.* 29.28, 29.37, *pres. 1st pl. of* **eser**, *which see.*

em (2) *pron.* 5.7 = **en** (2).

embrǫnc *adj.* bent, leaning forward: *masc., nom. sg.* **embroncs** 15.5. [**en**-(2) + **bronc** 'jutting out' (VL *BRŬNCUM *FEW* 3: 565; It. *bronco*, Sp. *bronco*)]

embrugir *vb. trans.* to make famous: *pp., fem., obl. sg.* **enbrugida** 28.49. [en- (2) + **brugir** 'to make noise' *FEW* 10: 546 (VL *ʙʀūɢɛ̆ʀᴇ B-W + -ir)]

emendamẹn *n. masc.* amends, penance: *obl. sg.* **emendament** 11.12. [**emendar** (CL ᴇ̄ᴍᴇ̆ɴᴅᴀ̄ʀᴇ *FEW* 3: 219) + **-amen** (1)]

emfern *see* **enfern**.

emperadọr *n. masc.* emperor: *nom. sg.* **emperaire** 21.15; *obl. sg.* **emperador** 11.35, 11.44, 12.31. [CL ᴉ̆ᴍᴘᴇ̆ʀᴀ̄ᴛōʀᴇᴍ *FEW* 4: 585; It. *imperatore*, Sp. *emperador*, Fr. *empereur*, E. *emperor*]

empẹri *n. masc.* empire: *obl. sg.* **emperi** 11.37. [CL ᴉ̆ᴍᴘᴇ̆ʀᴉ̆ᴜᴍ *FEW* 4: 587; It. *impero*, Sp. *imperio*, Fr. *empire*, E. *empire*]

emperọ *adv.* nevertheless: 25.103, 30.22. [en- (2) + **pero**]

emportar *vb. trans.* to take away: *pres. subj. 3rd sg.* **enport** 24.42. [en- (1) + **portar**]

emprẹndre *vb. intrans.* to happen 9.57; *trans.* to found 26.25; *refl.* to be undertaken, to begin 14.9; to spread 21.52, to catch (fire) 26.52: *pres. subj. 3rd sg.* **enpreingna** 21.52; *pp., masc., nom. sg.* **enpres** 26.52, *obl. sg.* **empres** 9.57; *fem., nom. sg.* **enpresza** 26.25, **empriza** 14.9. [en- (2) + **prendre**]

ems *see* **en** (1).

ẹn (1) *n. masc.* sir *(title in respectful address or reference): nom. sg.* **en** 3.8, 5.14, 5.15, 5.16, 22.44, 25.1, 25.16, 25.65, 28.29, 30.46, 30.91, **ens** 30.13, **ems** 30.13 ms., **·n** 22.12, 25.23, 25.24, 25.24, 25.36, 25.37, 25.37, 25.37, 28.31, **n'** 5.16, 5.16, 20.7, 22.11, 22.11, 25.24, 25.74; *obl. sg.* **en** 3.3, 3.8, 5.6, 5.11, 9.3, 9.4, 9.69, 9.70, 10.23, 25.57, 29.0, **·n** 5.9, 20.26, **n'** 19.57 var., 25.107, 30.50. [CL ᴅᴏᴍᴉ̆ɴᴜᴍ, *vocative* ᴅᴏᴍᴉ̆ɴᴇ *FEW* 3: 131; cf. **don** (1)]

ẹn (2) *pron.* equivalent in meaning to **de** + object pron.; *may often be omitted in translation* from (it, *etc.*) 15.31, 16.14, 16.16, 16.54, 22.19, 23.31, 24.37, 25.105, 26.30, 27.38, 31.24; of (it, *etc.*) 2.18, 11.31, 11.31, 11.32, 13.28, 14.60, 16.10, 16.20, 18.27, 18.28, 19.57, 25.44, 27.19, 28.42; about (it, *etc.*) 1.2, 2.4, 2.6, 2.7, 2.19, 6.13, 6.24, 9.35, 11.23, 16.22, 16.26, 16.27, 18.10, 18.21, 19.8, 19.22, 19.32, 19.63, 21.12, 23.5, 27.22, 27.22, 27.24, 28.41, 28.69, 30.28; concerning (it, *etc.*) 28.63; because of (it, *etc.*) 8.21 var., 9.65, 11.16, 13.52 var., 13.76, 13.90, 13.92, 14.68, 15.32, 16.11, 16.12, 18.5, 23.36, 23.47, 23.48 var., 25.42, 27.12 var., 32.9, 32.10; for (it, *etc.*) 2.23, 8.30, 11.12, 11.13, 13.54, 15.38, 22.15, 23.25, 31.5; by *(agent)* 28.30; away 9.21, 30.92, 30.98, 31.43; some *(partitive)* 14.11, 26.24, 30.4, 30.39, 30.42, 30.46; **no·n auretz de me** you won't get any (news) from me 18.57.

With a num. 6.25, 25.34; *with* **aitan can** 23.40; *with* **mais** 28.58; *with* **autre** 19.59, 19.62; *redundant usage referring to a phrase beginning in* **de** 1.7, 19.65, 20.3, 23.32, *to a clause beginning in* **que** 7.21, *to a clause beginning in* **car** 28.33.

In refl. constructions **s'en abellir** 7.13; **s'en absolver** 27.30; **s'en anar** 3.11, 5.10, 9.2, 10.5, 10.27, 14.72, 18.39, 18.58, 21.27, 30.56, 30.74, 31.28; **s'en apercebre** 5.7, 5.8; **s'en destrenher** 19.47; **s'en entrar** 30.23; **s'en estordre** 22.6; **s'en estraire** 6.8; **s'en issir** 30.51; **s'en metre** 22.4; **s'en partir** 5.10, 15.15; **s'en penar** 11.26; **s'en perdonar** 27.28 var.; **s'en repentir** 11.11; **s'en salvar** 11.68; **s'en tenir** 7.11; **s'en venir** 30.22, 31.16; *with impersonal verb* **s'en sovenir** 23.3.

Forms: **en** *passim*; **ne** 23.48, 25.34, 26.30, 28.69, 30.46, 30.98; **n'**, **·n**

1.2, 1.7, 2.4, 2.6, 2.7, 2.19, 2.23, 6.24, 6.25, 7.21, 8.21 var., 8.30, 9.35, 11.12, 11.13, 11.16, 11.31, 13.28, 13.52 var., 13.54, 13.76, 13.90, 13.92, 14.60, 14.68, 15.20, 15.31, 15.32, 15.38, 16.10, 16.12, 16.13, 16.14, 16.16, 16.20, 16.54, 18.28, 18.57, 19.32, 19.57, 19.59, 19.62, 19.65, 20.3, 23.5, 23.31, 23.32, 23.40, 23.47, 24.37, 25.105, 26.24, 27.12 var., 27.19, 27.24 var., 28.30, 28.41, 28.42, 28.58, 28.63, 30.4, 30.39, 30.92, 31.33, 31.43, 31.43, 32.9, 32.10; **em** 5.7.
[CL ĭɴᴅᴇ *FEW* 4: 636; It. *ne*, Fr. *en*]

ęn (3) *prep.* in 1.4, 1.7, 2.17, 3.3, 5.12, 6.19, 6.32, 7.1, 7.7, 7.8, 7.22, 8.3, 10.4, 10.4, 10.6, 10.6, 10.7, 10.11, 10.24, 10.24, 11.17, 11.18, 12.45, 12.45, 12.49, 12.55, 12.70, 13.21, 13.27, 13.51, 14.14, 14.62, 15.1, 15.40, 16.40, 17.14, 17.33, 18.45, 18.48, 19.31, 20.15, 20.35, 21.14, 21.43, 22.18, 22.19, 22.34, 23.47, 25.6, 25.79, 25.85, 26.23, 27.5, 27.34, 27.41, 28.7, 28.56, 28.58, 29.18, 30.63, 30.77, 30.98, 31.17, 31.28, 31.34; **on** 1.7, 3.11, 8.18, 25.30, 28.18, 28.59, 31.32; **into** 9.1, 10.5, 11.72, 18.40, 18.43, 18.44, 25.89; **at** 13.89; **to** 1.4, 1.4, 5.13, 16.6, 17.11, 25.73, 30.25.

Expressions: **de flic en floc** with snip and snap 31.26; **de l'or'en sai** ever since 18.42; **de leg'en lega** from one league to the next 14.51; **en anz en dies** in earlier days 11.20; **en breu** soon 15.39; **gitar en ira** to visit wrath upon 25.63; **s'entendre en** to understand 5.10, 5.10, 5.10, 6.17, 17.7; **s'en entrar en** to enter 30.23; **se fizar en** to trust 18.18; **se metre en carriera** to take one's road 28.72; **se metre en enans** to get a head start 22.4; **tornar en jos** to overturn 10.19; **tro en** until 28.21; **venir** *impersonal* **en aizina a** to get the chance 31.11.

With pres. part. 2.5, 11.68, 23.40, 25.45, 29.12, 29.24, 29.41; *with inf.* 16.29, 16.29, 26.48.

Forms: **en** *passim*; **in** 11.17; **·n** 26.23; **e** *see listing under* **e** (1).
[CL ĭɴ *FEW* 4: 614; It. *in*, Sp. *en*, Fr. *en*]

enaisi *adv.* thus: **enaissi** 1.6; **enaisi com** just as 30.37, just like 8.13; **enaisi . . . que** so that 15.48; **aisi com . . . enaisi** just as . . . so 19.20. [**en-** (2) + **aisi**]

enamorar *vb. refl.* to fall in love with: *pres. 3rd sg.* **enamora** 5.6; *pret. 3rd sg.* **enamoret** 1.2, 5.6 var., 5.12. [**en-** (2) + **amor** + **-ar** (2)]

enans (1) *n. masc.* advantage, head start: *obl. sg.* **enans** 22.4. [**enans** (2)]

enans (2) *adv.* first: 22.20, 27.40; **enans que** *conj.* before: **ennanz que** 23.22. [LL ĭɴᴀɴᴛᴇ *FEW* 4.616 + **-s**]

enansar *vb. intrans.* to make progress 30.75; *trans.* to bring forward, to advance 28.43: *pres. 3rd sg.* **enansa** 28.43; *pp., undeclined* **enansat** 30.75. [**enans** (2) + **-ar** (2)]

enapręs *adv.* then, after that: **enapres** 25.31. [**en-** (2) + **apres** (2)]

enbrugida *see* embrugir.

encensier *n. masc.* censer, container in which liturgical incense is burned: *obl. pl.* **essesiers** 25.88. [**encens** (CL ĭɴᴄᴇ̆ɴsᴜᴍ *FEW* 4: 621; It. *incenso*, Sp. *encienso*, Fr. *encens*, E. *incense*) + **-ier**]

encombrier *n. masc.* torment, woe: *nom. sg.* **encombriers** 25.26; *obl. pl.* **encombriers** 29.29. [**encombre** (**en-** [2] + Ctc. **cŏmbŏrŏs* 'abatis, a defense of felled trees' *FEW* 2: 938) + **-ier**; It. *ingombrare*, Sp. *escombrar*, Fr. *encombrer*, E. *to encumber*]

encontrada *n. fem.* region: *obl. sg.* **encontrada** 3.1, 3.3, 5.9. [**encontra** 'against' (LL ĭɴᴄŏɴᴛʀᴀ *FEW* 2: 1116; It. *incontro*, Sp. *encontra*, Fr. *encontre*, E. *encounter* n.) + **-ada**]

encorsa *n. fem.* seizure (by the devil), damnation: *obl. sg.* **encorsa** 31.34. [**encorsar** 'to seize' (CL ĭncŭrsāre 'to attack'; cf. OFr. *ancorse* 'attack' *FEW* 2: 1578)]

endeman̦ *n. masc.* the following day: *obl. sg.* **endeman** 8.17, **endema** 11.60, 31.36. [**en-** (2) + **deman** 'tomorrow' (LL dē māne 'from early, morning' *FEW* 3: 37; It. *domani*, Fr. *demain*); Fr. *lendemain*]

endeutar *vb. intrans.* to incur debt: *pp., masc., nom. sg.* **endeutatz** 14.12. [**en-** (2) + **deuta** (VL dēbĭta *FEW* 3: 22; Sp. *deuda*, E. *debt*) + **-ar** (2)]

endevenir *vb. intrans.* to happen 23.30; *trans.* to happen to, to befall 18.55: *pres. 3rd sg.* **esdeve** 18.55; *inf.* **endevenir** 23.30. [**en-** (2) *or* **es-** (1) + **devenir**]

endreisar *vb. trans.* to follow: *pres. 3rd sg.* **endreisa** 30.95; *inf.* **endreissar** 30.94. [**en-** (2) + **dreisar** (VL *dīrēctĭāre *FEW* 3: 86; It. *drizzare*, Sp. *derezar*, Fr. *dresser*, E. *to dress*)]

enebriar *vb. refl.* to get drunk: *pres. 3rd sg.* **enebria** 26.14. [CL ĭnēbrĭāre; cf. ēbrium *FEW* 3: 20; It. *inebbriare*, Fr. *enivrer*, E. *to inebriate*]

enemic *n. masc.* enemy: *obl. pl.* **enemics** 27.32. [CL ĭnĭmīcum *FEW* 4: 694; It. *nemico*, Sp. *enemigo*, Fr. *ennemi*, E. *enemy*]

enfan *n. masc.* child: *obl. sg.* **efant** 11.79, 28.56, **effant** 28.6; *obl. pl.* **enfans** 22.42, 27.47, **enfanz** 24.26, **efanz** 27.47 var. [CL ĭnfantem *FEW* 4: 662; It. *infante*, Sp. *infante* 'prince,' Fr. *enfant*, E. *infant*]

enf̧ern *n. masc.* Hell: *obl. sg.* **enfern** 27.41, **emfern** 27.41 var., **enferm** 27.41 var., **yfern** 27.41 var., **ufern** 27.41 var. [CL ĭnfĕrnum *FEW* 4: 667; It. *inferno*, Sp. *infierno*, Fr. *enfer*; cf. E. *infernal*]

enfernal *adj.* infernal, in Hell: *masc., nom. sg.* **ifernaus** 12.23. [CL ĭnfĕrnālem; cf. ĭnfĕrnum *FEW* 4: 667; Fr. *infernal*, E. *infernal*]

enfernar *vb. trans.* to damn to Hell; *inf.* **enfernar** 27.12. [**enfern** + **-ar** (2)]

engalers *see* **egalier.**

engan *n. masc.* deceit, deception, trick: *nom. sg.* **enganz** 16.23; *obl. sg.* **engan** 24.31. [**enganar**]

enganar *vb. trans.* to deceive: *pres. 3rd sg.* **enjaina** 13.63. [VL *ĭngănnāre *FEW* 4: 683; It. *ingannare*, Sp. *engañar*]

engenhos *adj.* deceptive: *masc., nom. sg.* **enginhos** 9.31. [CL ĭngĕnĭōsum *FEW* 4: 688; It. *ingegnoso*, Sp. *ingenioso*, Fr. *ingénieux*, E. *ingenious*]

engenrar *vb. trans.* to engender, to beget: *pret. 3rd sg.* **engenret** 13.31; *pp., masc., nom. sg.* **engenratz** 14.62. [CL ĭngĕnĕrāre *FEW* 4: 685; Fr. *engendrer*, E. *to engender*]

enginhos *see* **engenhos.**

engļes *adj.* English, made in England: *fem., obl. sg.* **englesa** 26.35. *See also Proper Names.* [**Engla(terra)** + **-es** (2)]

engorits *see* **enrogir.**

enic *adj.* hostile: *masc., obl. sg.* **enic** 23.12. [**enemic**]

eniv̧ers *prep.* toward: **enivers** 11.12. [**en** (2) + **i** (2) + **vers** (1)]

enjaina *see* **enganar.**

ennanz *see* **enans** (2).

enoiar *vb. trans.* to annoy: *pp., fem., nom. sg.* **enoiada** 13.52 var. [LL ĭnŏdĭāre *FEW* 4: 704; It. *annoiare*, Sp. *enojar*, Fr. *ennuyer*, E. *to annoy*]

enoj̧os *adj.* awful: *masc., obl. sg.* **enuj̧os** 9.37. [**enoi** 'worry' (**enoiar**) + **-os**]

enport *see* **emportar.**

enpreingna, enpres, enpresza *see* **emprendre.**

enqerra *see* **enquerre.**

enquer, enquera *see* ancar.

enquęrre *vb. trans.* to ask (for, about) *passim*; to investigate 3.6: *pres. 2nd pl.* enqueres 19.25; *pres. subj. 1st sg.* enqueira 28.51, *3rd sg.* enquieyra 19.43; *fut. 3rd sg.* enqerra 14.53 var.; *pret. 3rd sg.* enqueri 3.6. [CL ĭnquīrĕre, LL ĭnquaerĕre *FEW* 4: 708; It. *inchiedere*, Sp. *inquirir*, Fr. *enquérir*, E. *to inquire*]

enquęsta *n. fem.* enquiry, investigation: *obl. sg.* enquesta 31.41. [CL ĭnquīrĕre *FEW* 4: 706, LL *ĭnquaesītam B-W; It. *inchiesta*, Fr. *enquête*, E. *inquest*]

enquieyra *see* enquerre.

enrogir *vb. trans.* to make red: *pp., masc., obl. pl. (used as nom. pl.)* enrogits 32.15 var., engorits 32.15. [en- (2) + roge 'red' (CL rŭbĕum *FEW* 10: 536; Sp. *rubio*, Fr. *rouge*) + -ir]

ens *see* en (1).

ensęms *adv.* together: essems 25.33. [LL ĭnsĭmul, VL *ĭnsĕmul *FEW* 4: 716 (It. *insieme*, Fr. *ensemble*) + -s]

ensenhadǫr *n. masc.* teacher: *obl. sg.* enseingnador 17.35. [ensenhar + -ador]

ensenhar *vb. trans.* to teach: *pres. 3rd sg.* ensenha 14.69; *pp., masc., nom. sg.* enseingnatz educated 5.3. [VL *ĭnsĭgnāre *FEW* 4: 714; It. *insegnare*, Sp. *enseñar*, Fr. *enseigner*]

enteira *see* entier.

enten *see* entendre.

entendęnsa *n. fem.* attention 28.18, affection 6.18: *obl. sg.* entendensa 28.18, entendenssa 6.18. [entendre + -ensa]

entęndre *vb. trans.* to understand 16.51, 16.53, 28.24; to devote 16.6; *refl.* s'entendre en to be well versed in, direct one's thoughts toward 5.10, 6.17, 17.7: *pres. 3rd sg.* enten 6.17, 16.6, 16.51, 16.53, 17.7; *imperf. 3rd sg.* entendia 5.10, 28.24. [CL ĭntĕndĕre *FEW* 4: 744; It. *intendere*, Sp. *entender*, Fr. *entendre*, E. *to intend*]

entier *adj.* perfect; de sen enteira thoroughly sensible 28.68: *fem., obl. sg.* enteira 28.68. [CL ĭntĕgrum *FEW* 4: 735; It. *intero*, Sp. *entero*, Fr. *entier*, E. *entire*]

entra *see* entrar.

entrams *num.* both: *fem., obl. pl.* entrambas 25.50. [entre + ams (CL ămbōs *FEW* 1: 85; It. *ambi*, Sp. *ambos*, Fr. *ambe* n. 'combination of two'; cf. E. *ambidextrous*, ambedos)]

entrar *vb. intrans.* to enter: *pres. 3rd sg.* entra 30.23; *pret. 3rd sg.* intrec 25.89; *past subj. 3rd sg.* entres 27.19; *inf.* entrar 27.20. [CL ĭntrāre *FEW* 4: 777; It. *entrare*, Sp. *entrar*, Fr. *entrer*, E. *to enter*]

entratge *n. masc.* entrance fee: *obl. sg.* intraje 13.68. [entrar + -atge]

ęntre *prep.* between, among *passim*; in *(arms)* 1.5: entre 1.6, 2.12, 11.32, 17.47, 25.46, 29.37, antre 1.5. [CL ĭnter *FEW* 4: 748; Sp. *entre*, Fr. *entre*; cf. E. *to interact*]

entrenan *in expression* estar entrenan to resist, to remain standing: 8.15 (see note). [entre + enan (LL ĭnante *FEW* 4: 616)]

entres *see* entrar.

entro *adv.* until; entro que *conj.* until 9.56. [CL (ĭn)ter hŏc *FEW* 4: 749]

enujos *see* enojos.

enveada, envei *see* enveiar.

envęia *n. fem.* envy 11.27, 18.5; malice 11.51: *nom. sg.* enveia 18.5; *obl. sg.*

eveia 11.27, **evea** 11.51. [CL ĭnvĭdĭam *FEW* 4: 800; It. *invidia*, Sp. *en-vidia*, Fr. *envie*, E. *envy*]

enveiar *vb. trans.* to envy: *pres. 1st sg.* **envei** 24.39; *pp., fem., nom. sg.* **enveada** 13.52 var. [**enveia** + **-ar** (2)]

enveiọs *adj.* envious: *masc., obl. pl.* **enveios** 27.32. [CL ĭnvĭdĭŏsum; cf. *FEW* 4: 800; It. *invidioso*, Sp. *envidioso*, Fr. *envieux*, E. *envious*]

envern *see* **ivern.**

eps, epsamen *see* **eis-.**

ẹr (1) *n. masc.* heir: *nom. pl.* **er** 26.56. [CL hērēdem, VL *hērem *FEW* 4: 413; Fr. *hoir*, E. *heir*]

er (2) *vb. intrans.* 9.18, 12.23, 12.29, 12.41, 14.12, 14.35, 15.27, 17.15, 19.45, 19.67, 20.16, 20.17, 25.94, 27.24, *see* **eser.**

er (3) *adv.* 14.26, 19.5, 28.15, 29.17, 31.35, *see* **ar.**

era (1) *vb. intrans.* 1.6, 3.3, 3.5, 3.6, 5.2, 5.10, 11.36, 21.43, 25.60, 25.69, 25.82, 25.95, 25.96, 25.102, 25.106, 30.41, *see* **eser.**

era (2) *adv.* 10.5, 23.3, *see* **ar.**

eras (1) *vb. intrans.* 21.18, *see* **eser.**

eras (2) *adv.* 19.3, 28.53, *see* **ar.**

eratz, eravas *see* **eser.**

erẹbre *vb. trans.* to fill with rapture: *pp., masc., obl. sg.* **ereubut** 7.11, **errebut** 7.11 var., **erebut** 7.11 var. [CL ērĭpĕre]

erẹtge *adj.* heretical *(OOc)*, capricious *(ModOc)* 32.2: *fem., obl. pl.* **iretjas** 32.2. [ChL haerĕtĭcum *FEW* 4: 375; It. *eretico*, Sp. *hereje*, Fr. *hérétique*, E. *heretical*]

eretier *n. masc.* inheritor, owner by inheritance: *nom. sg.* **heretiers** 25.27. [**eretar** (CL hĕrēdĭtāre *FEW* 4: 411; Sp. *heredar*, Fr. *hériter*, E. *to in-herit*) + **-ier**]

erguelh *see* **orgolh.**

erisar *vb. trans.* to dishevel 13.13; *pp.* shaggy 30.17: *pres. 3rd sg.* **erissa** 13.13; *pp., masc., obl. pl.* **irissatz** 30.17. [VL *ērīcĭāre 'to stand up' (of hair); cf. CL ērīcĭum 'hedgehog' *FEW* 3: 238; It. *arricciare*, Sp. *rizar*, Fr. *hérisser*]

errebut *see* **erebre.**

errọr *n. fem.* bewilderment: *obl. sg.* **error** 7.7. [CL ērrōrem *FEW* 3: 241; It. *errore*, Sp. *error*, Fr. *erreur*, E. *error*]

es (1) *vb. intrans., see* **eser.**

es (2) *conj.* 25.90, 25.94, *see* **e** (2).

esbaudir *vb. intrans.* to rejoice: *inf.* **esbaudir** 17.3. [**es-** (1) + Frankish *bald* 'cheerful' *FEW* 15: 32 + **-ir**]

escaldar *vb. trans.* to heat: *imperf. 3rd sg.* **esquaudava** 5.2. [**es-** (1) + **calt** 'warm' (CL calĭdum, caldum *FEW* 2: 90; It. *caldo*, Sp. *caldo*, Fr. *chaud*) + **-ar** (2)]

escapar *vb. intrans.* to escape: *pres. 3rd sg.* **escapa** 31.43. [VL *excappāre *FEW* 3: 270; It. *scappare*, Sp. *escapar*, Fr. *échapper*, E. *to escape*]

escarn *n. masc.* trick: *obl. sg.* **esquern** 31.4, 31.7. [**escarnir**]

escarnir *vb. trans.* to put to shame: *pp., fem., nom. sg.* **escarnida** 28.30. [Frankish *skĭrnjan *FEW* 3: 271 + **-ir**; It. *schernire*, Sp. *escarnir*, E. *to scorn*]

escarsedat *n. fem.* stinginess: *nom. sg.* **eschasetatz** 12.19. [**escars** 'greedy' (VL *excarpsum 'narrow' *FEW* 3: 271; It. *scarso*, Sp. *escaso*, Fr. *échars* 'light' {breeze}, E. *scarce*) + **-edat**] escazẹr *vb. impers.* to fall to: *pres. 3rd sg.* **eschai** 15.31. [VL *EXCADĔRE, *EXCADĒRE *FEW* 3: 262; It. *scadere,* Fr. *échoir* 'to befall']

escercar *vb. trans.* to seek: *pres. 2nd pl.* **essercatz** 19.30. [**es-** (1) + **cercar**]

eschasetatz *see* **escarsedat.**

escïen *n. masc.* knowledge; **mon escïen** in my opinion 17.32. [CL SCĬĔNTEM *FEW* 11: 305, *pres. part. of* SCĪRE 'to know']

esclairar *vb. trans.* to transform (from dark to bright) 21.60; *refl.* to brighten up 13.34, to shine 2.11: *pres. 1st sg.* **esclaire** 13.34; *pres. subj. 3rd sg.* **esclaire** 2.11, 21.60. [VL *EXCLĀRĬĀRE *FEW* 3: 276; Fr. *éclairer*]

escoisẹndre *vb. trans.* to scratch: *pres. 3rd sg.* **escoyssen** 9.50. [**es-** (1) + **coisendre** 'to tear' (CL CONSCĬNDĔRE *FEW* 2: 1060)]

escọndre *vb. trans.* to hide: *pres. 1st sg.* **escon** 18.60; *pp., masc., nom. sg.* **escundutz** 30.48. [CL ABSCŎNDĔRE, VL *EXCŎNDĔRE *FEW* 24: 51; It. *ascondere,* Sp. *escondir,* E. *to abscond*]

escorjar *vb. trans.* to flay: *pret. 3rd pl.* **escorgeron** 9.47; *pp., masc., nom. sg.* **escorjatz** 14.42. [LL *EXCŎRTĬCĀRE *FEW* 3: 282; It. *scorticare,* Sp. *escorchar,* Fr. *écorcher*]

escotar *vb. trans.* to listen (to): *pres. 1st sg.* **escout** 2.5; *imper. 2nd pl.* **escotatz** 14.4, 14.10, 14.16, 14.22, 14.28, 14.34, 14.40, 14.46, 14.52, 14.58, 14.64, 14.70; *pp., masc., obl. pl.* **escoutatz** 26.4. [CL AUSCŬLTĀRE, VL *EXCŬLTĀRE *FEW* 1: 185; It. *ascoltare,* Sp. *escuchar,* Fr. *écouter*]

escoyssen *see* **escoisendre.**

escridar *vb. trans.* to cry: *pres. 3rd pl.* **escridan** 25.79, 25.93. [**es-** (1) + **cridar**]

escriure *vb. trans.* to write: *pp., masc., obl. sg.* **escrit** 5.16; *fem., obl. pl.* **escriptas** 5.17; *inf.* **escriure** 11.53. [CL SCRĪBĔRE *FEW* 11: 335; It. *scrivere,* Sp. *escribir,* Fr. *écrire;* cf. E. *script*]

escudier *n. masc.* squire: *nom. sg.* **escuders** 25.17; *obl. sg.* **escudier** 3.7. [**escut** + **-ier**]

escundutz *see* **escondre.**

escut *n. masc.* shield: *obl. sg.* **escut** 21.45; *nom. pl.* **escut** 21.22 var. [CL SCŪTUM *FEW* 11: 357; It. *scudo,* Sp. *escudo,* Fr. *écu;* cf. E. *scutcheon*]

esdeve *see* **endevenir.**

esduire *vb. trans.* to remove, to withdraw: *pres. subj. 3rd sg.* **esduy'** (= **esduya**) 19.31. [**es-** + **duire** (CL DŪCĔRE 'to lead' *FEW* 3: 171; It. *condurre,* Sp. *ducir,* Fr. *conduire;* cf. E. *to conduct*)]

ẹser *vb. intrans.* to be *passim;* to exist 12.28; to be true, to happen 14.48 (**si tant es que** if so much is true that, if it really happens that); to be considered as, treated as 26.30; to go 19.4; **eser a** to belong to 20.33; **eser de = eser om de,** to be a man of (?) 10.25; **X es ops a Y** Y needs X 28.15.

  With *pres. part.,* **eser** *in the present subjunctive is equivalent to the optative subjunctive of the verb* 27.31, 27.39.

  With *pp.,* **eser** *in the present tense expresses either* (1) *the present result of a past action or event* 7.5, 7.13, 10.1, 10.32, 13.52 var., 14.18, 14.42, 15.3, 18.25, 18.53, 25.23, 29.16, 29.28 (**eser** *in the present subjunctive* 21.30), *or* (2) *a present state, if the pp. functions as an adj.* 7.8, 12.64, 19.32, 27.21, 29.37, *or* (3) *a present passive* 14.9, 14.60, 19.65, 20.6, 26.52, 28.38, 29.17, 29.23 (**eser** *in the present subjunctive* 7.3, 15.51, 29.44), *or* (4) *a past event (as in the Modern Fr.* passé composé*)* 13.16, 17.14, 19.58, 22.4, 22.34, 25.22, 25.58, 25.83, 25.96, 28.27, 28.35,

28.44, 28.66 (**eser** *in the present subjunctive* 30.47); *or* (5) *if the present tense functions vicariously for a past, a past passive* 25.45, 25.67.

With pp., **eser** *in the preterit expresses* (1) *a past active* (**fo morta** 3.11, **morz fo** 11.43, **fuy yssitz** 19.4, **fos nada** 13.44), *or* (2) *a past state* 28.5, 30.10, *or* (3) *a past passive* 1.4, 1.5, 3.6, 9.57, 14.62, 14.66, 19.50, 20.24, 26.25, 28.30, 30.5, *or* (4) *a pluperfect active* (**s'en fo aperceubutz** 5.8, **me fuy revestitz** 31.38). **Eser** *in the past subjunctive expresses a wish* 15.14; *expresses result of a verb in the preterit* 15.49, 15.52; *expresses result of a wish in the past subjunctive* 15.35; *expresses result of a wish in the 2nd conditional* 20.34, 31.4; *expresses a condition contrary to fact* 17.22; *after* **si non** 'unless, if not' 27.40. **Eser** *in the 2nd conditional expresses hypothetical result* (1) *of a condition contrary to fact in the past subjunctive* 17.25, *or* (2) *of a negated condition in the preterit* 31.34.

Forms: Pres. 1st sg. **soi** 10.32, 13.14, 13.52 var., 19.8, 19.55, **soy** 13.16, **sui** 2.25, 6.4, 6.5, 7.5, 7.8, 7.13, 10.2, 15.3, 15.20, 15.25, 17.12, 18.53, 22.4, 22.17, 22.34, 22.43, **suy** 4.29, 28.17, 28.39, 28.66, 29.16, 31.20; *2nd sg.* **est** 25.79; *3rd sg.* **es** 2.3, 2.7, 2.20, 6.3, 6.28, 8.7, 8.12, 9.16, 9.31, 10.1, 10.9, 10.17, 11.13, 12.14, 12.16, 12.21, 12.28, 12.66, 14.8, 14.9, 14.18, 14.26, 14.42, 14.43, 14.48, 14.56, 14.60, 14.68, 15.2, 15.12, 15.32, 15.47, 15.50, 16.4, 16.5, 16.16, 16.18, 16.19, 16.30, 16.32, 16.33, 16.35, 16.50, 16.52, 17.29, 17.32, 18.25, 19.20, 19.58, 20.6, 20.33, 20.35, 22.3, 22.41, 23.25, 23.27, 24.28, 25.13, 25.15, 25.22, 25.23, 25.45, 25.50, 25.54, 25.58, 25.59, 25.67, 25.70, 25.81, 25.81, 25.83, 25.90, 25.93, 25.96, 26.28, 26.30, 26.33, 26.34, 26.36, 26.46, 26.52, 26.54, 27.19, 27.21, 28.15, 28.44, 28.45, 28.56, 28.60, 29.10, 29.17, 29.23, 29.24, 29.30, 29.34, 30.68, **·s** 25.54; *1st pl.* **em** 29.28, 29.37, **esmes** 11.6; *2nd pl.* **etz** 25.19, 28.27, 28.38, 28.40, 28.55, **es** 13.33, 17.14, 19.32, 19.65, 27.23, 28.35; *pres. 3rd pl.* **son** 11.18, 12.64, 15.1, 15.18, 16.25, 18.24, 25.5, **sunt** 11.21.

Pres. subj. 1st sg. **sia** 2.25 var., 4.29, 13.22, 25.30, 28.17; *3rd sg.* **sia** 2.18, 4.20, 6.6, 7.3, 15.21, 15.51, 19.13, 19.44, 20.8, 27.6, 30.47; *2nd pl.* **siatz** 14.24, 14.54, 19.18, 19.33, 21.30 var., 27.46, **sias** 14.54 var., 21.30, 27.31, 27.39, **siais** 21.30 var.; *3rd pl.* **sian** 29.44.

Imperf. 3rd sg. **era** 1.6, 3.3, 3.5, 3.6, 5.2, 5.10, 11.36, 21.43, 25.60, 25.69, 25.82, 25.95, 25.96, 25.102, 25.106, 30.41; *2nd pl.* **eratz** 28.63, **eras** 21.18, **eravas** 21.18 var.

Fut. 1st sg. **serai** 10.3, 10.18, 23.47, 23.48, **er** 15.27; *3rd sg.* **sera** 12.32, 12.43, 14.23, 20.21, 24.17, 27.24 var., **er** 9.18, 12.23, 12.29, 12.41, 14.12, 14.35, 17.15, 19.45, 19.67, 20.16, 20.17, 25.94, 27.24; *1st pl.* **serem** 29.38; *2nd pl.* **seretz** 19.16, 23.48 var., 25.27, **serez** 23.47; *3rd pl.* **seran** 24.21.

1st cond. 3rd sg. **seria** 4.12, 13.47, 16.40, 16.44 ms., 27.42, **seri'** 16.44, **saria** 13.52 var.

Pret. 1st sg. **fui** 10.25, 18.42, **fuy** 19.4, 28.30, 31.22, 31.38; *3rd sg.* **fo** 1.1, 1.1, 1.4, 1.5, 3.1, 3.2, 3.8, 3.11, 5.1, 5.2, 5.2, 5.8 var., 5.16, 9.22, 11.28, 11.30, 11.31, 11.34, 11.43, 11.58, 11.63, 12.0, 12.7, 12.29, 13.30, 14.31, 14.66, 25.108, 30.10, **fon** 3.6, 9.20, 9.27, 9.27, 9.39, 9.57, 13.4, 13.32, 14.62, 19.50, 20.14, 26.25, 28.4, 28.5, 30.5, 31.24, 31.36; *2nd pl.* **foz** 13.44 var., **fos** 13.44, 19.53; *3rd pl.* **foro** 25.6, **foren** 11.20, 11.21, 11.63.

Past subj. 1st sg. **fos** 15.14, 15.33, 15.49, 15.52, 16.26, 19.27, 26.49, 27.40, 28.69, **fotz** 27.40 ms. (back spelling); 3rd sg. **fos** 4.12, 11.33, 12.0, 15.35, 17.22, 20.34, 20.35, 25.83, 28.9, 28.69, 31.4; 2nd pl. **fossetz** 13.35.

2nd cond. 1st sg. **fora** 31.34; 3rd sg. **fora** 30.15, **for'** 20.35 var.; 2nd pl. **foratz** 21.16; 3rd pl. **foron** 17.25.

Inf. **esser** 4.10, 14.25, 26.56, 27.15, 27.43, 30.20, **estre** 31.5. [CL ĔSSE, VL ĔSSĔRE FEW 3: 246; It. essere, Sp. ser, Fr. être]

esgardar vb. trans. to look at 16.48, to consider 29.6, to take heed of 13.83: pres. 3rd sg. **esgarda** 16.48, 3rd pl. **esgardo** 13.83; pres. part. undeclined **esgardan** 29.6. [**es-** (1) + **gardar**]

esmerar vb. trans. to refine: pp., fem., obl. sg. **esmerada** 13.45. [LL EXMĔRĀRE FEW 6: 40; Sp. esmerar]

esmes see **eser**.

espandre vb. trans. to spread 20.2; refl. to spread 19.12, to shine (of the sun) 8.17: pres. 3rd sg. **espan** 8.17; pres. subj. 1st sg. **espanda** 20.2, 3rd sg. **espanda** 19.12. [CL EXPANDĔRE FEW 3: 303; It. spandere, Sp. espandir, E. to expand]

espaventar vb. refl. to be afraid: pres. 1st sg. **espaven** 9.40. [CL *EXPAVĔNTĀRE FEW 3: 305; It. spaventare, Sp. espaventar, Fr. épouvanter]

espaventier n. masc. fear, panic: nom. sg. **espaventers** 25.43, 25.76. [**espaventar** + **-ier**]

espaza n. fem. sword: obl. sg. **espaza** 3.11. [CL (from Gk.) SPĂTHAM FEW 12: 143; It. spada, Sp. espada, Fr. épée; cf. E. spatula]

espelir vb. trans. to tell; refl. to spread abroad 8.28: pres. 3rd sg. **espel** 8.28. [Frankish *spellōn FEW 17: 177; Fr. épeler, E. to spell]

espęr n. masc. hope: obl. sg. **esper** 16.36, 26.23. [**esperar**]

esperamęn n. masc. hope: obl. sg. **esperamen** 27.34. [**esperar** + **-amen** (1)]

esperansa n. fem. hope: obl. sg. **esperansa** 28.57. [**esperar** + **-ansa**]

esperar vb. trans. to wait for: pres. 3rd sg. **espera** 13.90, 13.92 var., 1st pl. **esperam** 11.3. [CL SPĒRĀRE FEW 12: 167; It. sperare, Sp. esperar, Fr. espérer; cf. E. despair]

espęrdre vb. trans. to be troubled; pp., masc., obl. sg. **esperdut** distraught 30.52. [**es-** (1) + **perdre**]

esperital adj. spiritual (poverty, as in the monastic rule) 26.33; spirited, full of spirit, lively (eyes of a woman) 16.47: masc., obl. pl. **esperitaus** 16.47; fem., nom. sg. **esperitals** 26.33. [ChL SPIRITĀLEM, SPIRITŬĀLEM FEW 12: 190; It. spirituale, Sp. espiritual, Fr. spirituel, E. spiritual]

esperonar vb. intrans. to spur, to ride in haste: pres. 3rd sg. **esperona** 25.16, 3rd pl. **esperonan** 25.74. [**esperon** 'spur' (Frankish *sporo FEW 17: 185; It. sprone, E. spur + **-on** [1]) + **-ar** (2)]

espęrt adj. skilled: fem., obl. sg. **esperta** 26.1 [CL ĔXPĔRTUM FEW 3: 310; It. esperto, Sp. experto, Fr. expert, E. expert]

espęs adj. thick (of clothing) 26.42; dense (of a crowd) 30.12; abundant, strong (of wine) 9.28, (of pepper) 9.28 var.: masc., nom. sg. **espes** 9.28, 9.28 var.; obl. pl. **espes** 26.42; fem., obl. sg. **espessa** 30.12. [CL SPĬSSUM FEW 12: 200; It. spesso, Sp. espeso, Fr. épais]

esquaudava see **escaldar**.

esquern see **escarn**.

esse- *see* ese-.
essemple *see* eisemple.
essems *see* ensems.
essercatz *see* escercar.
essesiers *see* encensier.
essi 5.10 var. = e si.
est (1) *vb. intrans.* 25.79, *see* eser.
ęst (2) *demonstrative adj.* this: *fem., obl. sg.* esta 25.85, 31.21, est' 15.9. [CL
    ĭstum *FEW* 4: 821; Sp. *este*]
esta *see* estar.
establir *vb. trans.* to found: *pp., fem., obl. sg.* establia 26.29. [CL stăbĭlīre
    FEW 12: 221; It. *stabilire*, Sp. *establecer*, Fr. *établir*, E. *to establish*]
estar *vb. intrans.* to be *(in a place)* 4.13, 5.12, 5.14, 8.15, 21.76, 27.48,
    30.48; to be *(in a situation)* 5.13, 7.1, 7.7, 11.76, 31.2; to live 21.32; to be
    (with predicate adj. or n.) 10.29, 11.1, 11.73, 12.14 var., 13.76, 21.59; to
    stand 30.69 (sál en estánt he jumps to his feet 11.68); *refl.* to stay
    13.26; *impersonal* to be suitable, to befit 8.5, 23.17.
        Forms: Pres. 3rd sg. esta 8.5, 8.15, 23.17, estai 4.13, 27.48, 30.48;
    1st pl. estam 11.1, 12.14 var.; *3rd pl.* estan 21.76, están 11.73, estánt
    11.76.
        Pres. subj. 3rd sg. estia 13.26.
        Fut. 2nd pl. estaretz 13.76.
        Pret. 1st sg. estie 31.2, estey 31.2 var.; *3rd sg.* estet 5.12, 5.14, 30.69.
        Pres. part. estan 5.13, estánt 11.68.
        Pp., undeclined estat *(with masc. subject)* 10.29; *(with fem. subject)*
    7.1, 7.7.
        Inf. estar 21.32, 21.59.
        [CL stāre 'to stand' *FEW* 12: 242; It. *stare*, Sp. *estar*; cf. E. *stable*
    adj.]
esteingna *see* estenher.
estęla *n. fem.* star; estela guauzinaus morning star, the planet Venus
    12.34: *nom. sg.* estela 12.34. [CL stēllam, VL *stēlam *FEW* 12: 254; It.
    stella, Sp. *estrella*, Fr. *étoile*; cf. E. *stellar*]
estendart *n. masc.* banner: *nom. sg.* estendartz 24.9. [Frankish *stand-
    hard* 'immovable' *FEW* 17: 219; It. *stendardo*, Sp. *estandarte*, Fr. *éten-
    dard*, E. *standard*]
estęndre *vb. refl.* to continue on its way: *pres. 3rd sg.* esten 30.43. [CL
    extĕndĕre *FEW* 3: 327; It. *stendere*, Sp. *extender*, Fr. *étendre*, E. *to ex-
    tend*]
estęnher *vb. trans.* to kill: *pres. subj. 3rd sg.* esteingna 21.11. [CL
    ĕxstĭngŭĕre, LL *ĕstĭngĕre *FEW* 3: 321; F. *éteindre*, E. *to extinguish*]
estet, estey, estia, estie *see* estar.
estiers *adv.* otherwise: estiers 29.15. [CL ĕxtĕrĭus *FEW* 3: 328]
estíu *n. masc.* summer: *obl. sg.* estiu 26.42. [CL aestīvum adj. *FEW* 1: 46;
    Sp. *estío*; cf. E. *estival*]
estọrser *vb. trans.* to squeeze out 24.37; *refl.* to escape 22.6: *pp., masc.,
    obl. sg.* estort 22.6, 24.37. [CL extŏrquĕre, ĕxtŏrquĕre *FEW* 13, part 2:
    99; It. *storcere*, Sp. *estorcer*; cf. E. *to extort*]
estra *see* estraire.
estrada *n. fem.* road: *obl. sg.* estrada 28.12. [CL (viam) strātam 'paved
    road' *FEW* 12: 291; It. *strada*, Sp. *estrada*, G. *Strasse*, E. *street*]

estrai, estraia *see* **estraire.**

estraing *see* **estranh.**

estraire *vb. trans.* to take back 19.5; *refl. with* **de** + *verb* to cease 6.7, 6.8, *with* **de** + *noun* to renounce 21.57: *pres. 3rd sg.* **estrai** 19.5 var., **estra** 19.5; *pres. subj. 1st sg.* **estraia** 6.8; *pret. 1st sg.* **estrais** 6.7; *inf.* **estraire** 21.57. [CL EXTRAHĔRE *FEW* 3: 331; Fr. *extraire,* E. *to extract*]

estranh *adj.* foreign: *masc., obl. sg.* **estraing** 8.25 var. [CL EXTRĀNĔUM *FEW* 3: 332; It. *strano,* Sp. *extraño,* Fr. *étrange,* E. *strange*]

estranhar *vb. refl.* to withdraw affection from (*with* **de**): *pret. 3rd sg.* **estranjet** 5.8. [**estranh** + **-ar** (2)]

estre *see* **eser.**

estremier *adj.* farthest, back (molar): *masc., obl. pl.* **estremiers** 25.71. [**estrẹm** (CL EXTRĒMUM *FEW* 3: 335; It. *stremo,* E. *extreme*) + **-ier**]

estug *n. masc.* box, private seating: *obl. sg.* **estug** 30.23. [**estujar** 'to keep in a box' (VL *STŬDĬĀRE *FEW* 12: 310); Fr. *étui*]

et *conj.* and, *etc.* 1.2, 1.5, 1.6, 1.7, 3.3, 3.3, 3.6, 3.7, 3.9, 3.11, 5.3, 5.3, 5.6, 5.10, 5.10, 5.10, 5.11, 5.12, 5.12, 5.15, 5.16, 6.1, 6.27, 9.20, 9.23, 9.26, 9.28, 9.29, 9.47, 10.16, 10.23, 10.24, 10.27, 10.34, 10.40, 11.17, 12.45, 12.71, 13.37, 13.38, 14.8, 16.6, 16.29, 17.32, 18.26, 18.28, 18.54, 20.10, 20.29, 21.1, 21.19, 21.23, 21.32, 22.36, 22.43, 25.63, 26.20, 26.29, 26.30, 26.48, 26.51, 27.26, 27.41, 29.37, 29.48, 30.7, 30.23, 30.36, 30.38, *see* **e** (2).

etz *see* **eser.**

ęu (1) *personal pron., 1st sg.* I; **eu meseisa** I myself *(fem.)* 23.44.

    Forms: Masc., nom. sg. **eu** 8.11, 8.12, 8.25, 8.27, 10.27, 10.39, 11.43, 11.75, 11.78, 15.30, 15.47, 16.22, 16.23, 16.26, 16.28, 16.38, 17.11, 17.24, 22.34, 22.43, 24.7, 26.23, 27.11, 27.40, 27.43, 30.27; **heu** 27.33; **ieu** 2.2, 2.5, 2.22, 2.25, 4.4, 4.7, 4.8, 4.16, 4.17, 4.22, 4.25, 4.26, 4.28, 4.29, 4.34, 4.35, 4.37, 4.40, 4.43, 4.44, 5.16, 5.16, 9.7, 9.23, 9.26, 9.37, 9.53, 10.14, 10.18, 12.66, 13.9, 13.15, 13.43, 13.49 var., 13.74, 14.55, 15.14, 15.38, 15.49, 15.50, 15.52, 18.11, 18.26, 18.34, 18.36 var., 18.50, 19.51, 22.23, 22.28, 26.49, 27.41, 31.4, 31.5, 31.17, 31.18, 32.4; **yeu** 19.21, 28.13; **hieu** 26.55, 27.6, 28.39, 31.8; **hyeu** 31.22; *with enclitic* **ie·** 19.1.

    Fem., nom. sg. **eu** 6.5, 7.4, 7.6, 7.15, 7.24, 23.6, 23.7, 23.13, 23.14, 23.17, 23.32, 23.38, 23.44; **ieu** 6.4, 6.10, 6.25, 6.31, 6.35, 7.5, 19.41, 19.44, 19.57, 23.12, 23.16, 23.22, 23.28, 28.69; *with enclitic* **ie·** 6.14, 23.1, 23.4, 23.12.

    See also **me, nos.**

    [CL ĔGŎ *FEW* 3: 207; It. *io,* Sp. *yo,* Fr. *je,* E. *ego*]

ęu (2) *personal pron. masc., nom., 3rd sg.* 11.49, 11.57. *See* **el** (1).

·eus 19.13, 19.27 = **·us,** *atonic form of* **vos,** *which see.*

evea, eveia *see* **enveia.**

evẹsque *n. masc.* bishop: *nom. sg.* **evesques** 25.87. [ChL EPĬSCŎPUM *FEW* 3.231; It. *vescovo,* Sp. *obispo,* Fr. *évêque,* E. *bishop*]

ez *conj.* and, *etc.: before vowel* 8.16, 9.50 var., 23.8, 23.42, 23.42, 24.2, 24.7, 24.9, 24.12, 25.32, 25.32, 25.38, 25.75, 25.92, 25.93, 27.41 var., 31.5, 31.9; *before consonant* 23.36 var., *see* **e** (2).

fa *see* **faire.**

fach (1) *n. masc.* deed 14.57, 21.28; deeds, work 12.65, 24.32; situation

3.6: *obl. sg.* **fait** 3.6, **faich** 24.32, **fag** 12.65; *nom. pl.* **faig** 21.28; *obl. pl.* **faitz** 24.32 var., **fatz** 14.57. [*pp. of* **faire;** CL Fǎctum *FEW* 3: 362; It. *fatto,* Sp. *hecho,* Fr. *fait,* E. *fact*]

fach (2) *vb. trans.* 17.40, 24.20 var., *pp. of* **faire,** *which see.*

fada (1) *n. fem.* fairy: *nom. sg.* **fada** 13.43. [CL Fātam *FEW* 3: 433; It. *fata,* Sp. *hada,* Fr. *fée;* cf. E. *fay, fairy*]

fada (2) *adj.* 28.16, *see* **fat** (2).

fadar *vb. trans.* to destine: *pret. 3rd sg.* **fadet** 15.48, 15.52. [**fada** (1) + **-ar** (2); Sp. *hadar*]

fag (1) 12.65, *see* **fach** (1).

fag (2) 24.20 var., **fagz** 24.20 var., *see* **faire.**

fai *see* **faire.**

faich (1) 24.32, *see* **fach** (1).

faich (2) 18.54, *see* **faire.**

faig *see* **fach** (1).

fail, faillensa, faillimen, faillir, *see* falh-

faire *vb. trans.* to do *passim*; to make 8.20, 11.12, 11.23, 11.51, 12.4, 13.61, 14.3, 14.45, 15.36, 17.23, 17.40, 17.41, 19.29, 20.1, 22.33, 25.45, 25.66, 27.3, 27.24, 28.65, 30.3, 30.32, 31.41; to write 11.52; to compose (songs) 1.3, 3.4, 5.6, 5.12, 5.17, 10.2, 12.2, 22.1, 23.5; to cause 9.66, 17.19, 24.20, 26.19; to give 9.51; to offer 27.37; to serve as 7.12; *in speech tag* to say 13.22; *vicarious verb representing repetition of another verb in context* 7.14, 13.41, 14.30, 30.37, 30.53, 30.81.

Causative with inf. to cause to, to make *(verb)* 1.5, 1.7, 2.14, 3.6, 3.7, 3.7, 3.7, 5.8, 5.9, 9.35, 11.52, 11.53, 11.59, 11.59, 11.71, 16.42, 17.17, 18.49, 23.5, 23.7, 25.100, 26.32, 27.9, 29.4, 30.2, 30.87, 31.7, 32.9, 32.10; *causative with pres. part.* to make *(verb)* 6.30.

Refl. to pretend to be 13.40, to be granted 19.10, to become 25.64; *in speech tag* to say 13.9, 13.14, 13.43, 13.74, 28.13.

Impersonal to remain, to be left 4.23 (see note); *impersonal* **fai** there is 13.82; *impersonal of weather* **fai freg** it is cold 26.44.

eser a faire to need to be changed 21.43; **faire acordansa** to reach an agreement 28.61; **faire carantena** to undergo penance 17.40; **faire com** to act like 18.54; **faire companhia** to keep company 13.17; **faire conort a** to soothe 22.21; **faire costuma de** to follow the custom of 11.79; **faire dan de** to be harmed by 31.3; **faire escarn** to play a trick 31.4; **faire falhensa** to make a mistake 28.19; **faire falhimen ves** to commit wrong toward 6.31, 23.16, 27.11; **faire mal** to cause pain 9.66, 17.19, to hurt 10.8, 10.15, 23.8; **faire onor a** to honor 5.4, 17.27; **faire pecat** to commit sin 23.47; **faire pebrada** to prepare (food) with a pepper sauce 3.7; **faire que** to act like 19.61, 20.9; **faire sacrament** to swear an oath 11.10; **faire semblansa** to seem 31.9, **faire semblansa de** to act like, to resemble 14.6; **faire torment** to commit torture 11.19.

Forms: Pres. 1st sg. **fauc** 2.26, 22.2, **fatz** 23.5, **faz** 11.79; *3rd sg.* **fai** 4.23, 11.10, 11.12, 11.15, 16.48, 16.54, 17.19, 18.49, 18.52, 20.9, 20.28, 22.21, 26.19, 26.44, 27.11, 30.53, **fay** 13.22, 13.40, 13.82, 14.6, 14.30, 19.10, **fa** 2.14, 29.4, 30.81, 31.43; *2nd pl.* **faitz** 23.8, 28.19; *3rd pl.* **fan** 12.36, 14.3, 25.100, 26.55, **fant** 22.29.

Pres. subj. 1st sg. **fasa** 23.7, **fassa** 6.31, **fass'** 23.5; *3rd sg.* **fasa** 14.47, **fassa** 22.33.

Imperf. 3rd sg. **fazia** 3.4, 5.4, 11.23 var., 26.38, **fazi'** 11.23; *2nd pl.* **faziatz** 13.66 var.

Fut. 1st sg. **farai** 4.4, 10.2, 25.64, 27.9, **faray** 19.67, **ferai** 27.37, **farei** 23.13; *3rd sg.* **fara** 9.35, 17.17, 19.61; *2nd pl.* **farez** 23.47; *3rd pl.* **faran** 10.8, 10.15, 11.19.

1st cond. 2nd pl. **fariatz** 13.66.

Pret. 1st sg. **fi** 10.22, 13.9, 13.15, 13.43, 13.74, 28.13, 31.3, **fis** 7.14 var.; *3rd sg.* **fetz** 5.6, 5.8, 5.9, 5.12, 5.17, 7.14, 15.36, 31.4, 31.25, **fez** 1.3, 1.7, 3.6, 3.7, 3.7, 5.4, 11.52, 11.53, 11.59, 11.59, 11.71, **fes** 3.7, 9.66, 12.2, 14.45, 27.3, 30.2, 30.32, 30.87, **fe** 25.66, 31.9, **fei** 24.32, 24.44; *1st pl.* **fezem** 8.20, **fem** 28.65; *3rd pl.* **feyron** 9.51, **feyro** 31.41.

Past subj. 1st sg. **fezes** 7.12, 17.41, 19.36.

2nd cond. 1st sg. **feira** 27.40, **feyra** 9.55, **fera** 27.40 var.; *3rd pl.* **feron** 17.27.

Pp., masc., nom. sg. **faitz** 25.45, 27.24, **faiz** 17.23; *obl. sg.* **fait** 11.11, 16.42, 23.16, 24.20, **faich** 18.54, **fat** 12.4; *obl. pl.* **faitz** 24.20 var., **fatz** 12.4 var., 24.20 var., **fach** 24.20 var., **fagz** 24.20 var., **fag** 24.20 var.; *fem., obl. sg. undeclined* **fach** 17.40; *neuter, nom. sg.* **fait** 1.5.

Inf. **faire** 2.22, 11.52, 21.32, 21.43, 32.9, 32.10, **fayre** 13.41, **far** 3.7, 6.30, 7.24, 11.51, 13.17, 13.61, 13.77, 19.29, 20.1, 21.9, 22.1, 22.50, 26.32, 28.61, 28.71, 30.3, 30.37, 31.7, 31.19, 31.30, 31.42.

[CL FACĔRE, LL FARE *FEW* 3: 353; It. *fare*, Sp. *hacer*, Fr. *faire*; cf. E. *affair*]

fais *n. masc.* burden: *obl. sg.* **fais** 10.31, **fays** 12.58. [CL FĂSCEM *FEW* 3: 430; It. *fascio*, Sp. *fajo, haz*, Fr. *faix*; cf. E. *fascicle*]

faison *n. fem.* form, appearance: *obl. sg.* **faiso** 21.7. [CL FĂCTĬŌNEM *FEW* 3: 360; Fr. *façon*, E. *fashion*]

fait (1) 3.6, *n. masc.*, see **fach** (1).

fait (2) 1.5, 11.11, 16.42, 23.16, 24.20, *pp., masc., obl. sg.* of **faire**, which see.

faititz *adj.* shapely: *fem., vocative sg.* **faytissa** 13.9. [CL FĂCTĪCĬUM 'artificial' *FEW* 3: 359; It. *feticcio*, Sp. *hechizo*; Fr. *factice, fétiche*; E. *factitious, fetish*]

faitz (1) 24.32 var., *n. masc.*, see **fach** (1).

faitz (2) 23.8, 28.19, *pres. 2nd pl.* of **faire**, which see.

faitz (3) 24.20 var., 25.45, 27.24, *pp., masc., nom. sg. or obl. pl.* of **faire**, which see.

faiz 17.23, *pp., masc., nom. sg.* of **faire**, which see.

falcia see **falsia**.

falda *n. fem.* lap 28.7; *pl.* skirts 26.51; *obl. sg.* **fauda** 28.7, *obl. pl.* **faudas** 26.51. [Gothic **falda FEW* 15, part 2: 99; It. *falda*, Sp. *falda*]

falh see **falhir**.

falhensa *n. fem.* disloyalty 6.32, mistake 28.19: *obl. sg.* **falhensa** 28.19, **faillensa** 6.32. [**falhir** + **-ensa**]

falhimen *n. masc.* disloyalty: *obl. sg.* **faillimen** 6.31, 23.16, 27.11. [**falhir** + **-imen**]

falhir *vb. intrans. and trans.* to fail, to become deficient 12.62, 14.7, 28.23; to be false 19.11, 23.14; to desert 11.70, 30.65; to commit an offense 19.51: *pres. 3rd sg.* **falh** 14.7, 19.11, 28.23, **fail** 30.65; *pret. 3rd pl.* **faliren** 11.70; *pp., masc., obl. sg.* **falhit** 19.51, *obl. pl.* **falhitz** 12.62; *inf.* **faillir** 23.14. [CL FĂLLĔRE 'to deceive' *FEW* 3: 390 + **-ir**; It. *fallire*, Sp. *fallecer*, Fr. *faillir*]

fals *adj.* false *(oath)* 11.10; faithless *(person)* 17.37; untruthful, lying 16.26: *masc., nom. sg.* **faus** 16.26; *obl. sg.* **fals** 11.10; *fem., obl. sg.* **falsa** 17.37. [CL FĂLSUM *FEW* 3: 394; It. *falso,* Sp. *falso,* Fr. *faux,* E. *false*]

falsia *n. fem.* infidelity: *obl. sg.* **falcia** 28.20. [**fals** + **-ia**]

falta *n. fem.* loss: *obl. sg.* **fauta** 31.31. [VL *FĂLLĬTAM *FEW* 3: 390; Sp. *falta,* Fr. *faute,* E. *fault*]

fam *n. fem.* hunger: *obl. sg.* **fam** 11.5. [CL FĂMEM *FEW* 3: 407; It. *fame,* Sp. *hambre,* Fr. *faim;* E. *to famish*]

fan, fant, far, fara, farai, faran, faray, farei, farez *see* **faire.**

farga *n. fem.* forge, smithy: *obl. sg.* **farga** 32.1. [CL FĂBRĬCAM *FEW* 3: 343; It. *fabbrica,* Sp. *forja, fragua,* Fr. *forge,* E. *forge*]

fargar *vb. trans.* to forge: *pp., fem., obl. pl. undeclined* **fargat** 32.14. [CL FĂBRĬCĀRE *FEW* 3: 344; It. *fabbricare,* Sp. *fraguar,* Fr. *forger,* E. *to forge*]

fariatz, fasa *see* **faire.**

fasenda *see* **fazenda.**

fass', fassa *see* **faire.**

fat (1) 12.4, *pp., masc., obl. sg. of* **faire,** *which see.*

fat (2) *adj.* silly, foolish: *fem., nom. sg.* **fada** 28.16. [CL FĀTŬUM *FEW* 3: 438; Fr. *fat,* E. *fatuous*]

fatz (1) 14.57, *see* **fach** (1).

fatz (2) 12.4 var., 23.5, 24.20 var., *see* **faire.**

fauc *see* **faire.**

fauda, faudas *see* **falda.**

faus *see* **fals.**

fauta *see* **falta.**

fay, fayre *see* **faire.**

fays *see* **fais.**

faytissa *see* **faititz.**

faz *see* **faire.**

fazẹnda *n. fem.* occupation 30.29; matter, affair 31.6: *obl. sg.* **fasenda** 30.29; *obl. pl.* **fazendas** 31.6. [CL FĂCĬĔNDA 'things to be done' *FEW* 3: 355; It. *faccenda,* Sp. *hacienda* 'farm']

fazi', fazia, faziatz *see* **faire.**

fẹ (1) *n. fem.* faith, good faith 30.28; *in entreaties* **fe que·m devetz** by the faith you owe me 31.21; **per fe** with trust 23.10; **segon ma fe** by my faith 27.42: *obl. sg.* **fe** 23.10, 27.42, 30.28, 31.21. [CL FĬDEM *FEW* 3: 504; It. *fede,* Sp. *fe,* Fr. *foi,* E. *faith*]

fe (2) 25.66, 31.9, *pret. 1st sg. of* **faire,** *which see.*

fei *see* **faire.**

fein *see* **fenher.**

feira *see* **faire.**

fel *see* **felon** (2).

fello (1) *n. masc.* 11.51, see **felon** (1).

fello (2) *adj.* 9.46, 11.20, **fellon,** *see* **felon** (2).

felnia *n. fem.* plot 11.62, treachery 11.64: *obl. sg.* **felni'** 11.62, 11.64. [**felon** (2) + **-ia**]

felọn (1) *n. masc.* criminal: *obl. sg.* **fello** 11.51. [**felon** (2)]

felọn (2) *adj.* cruel (heart) 13.57, 23.12; wicked 11.20, 12.38; nasty 9.46, 23.4 var.; treacherous 10.16; *masc., obl. sg.* **felo** 12.38, **felon** 23.12, **fello** 9.46, **fellon** 23.4 var., **fel** 13.57; *nom. pl.* **felon** 10.16, **fello** 11.20. [Frankish *fillo* 'knacker' *FEW* 3: 524 + **-on** (1); ML FĔLLŌNEM, It. *fellone,* Fr. *félon,* E. *felon*]

felpidǫr *n. masc.* one who wears plush, dandy (?); *or* one who manufactures plush, tailor (?): *nom. pl.* **felpidor** 12.49 var. (see note). [**felpa* (ML FALŬPPA, VL **FÉLEPPA FEW* 3: 400; It. *felpa,* ModOc *féupo*) + *-idor;* cf. **folpidor**]

fem *see* **faire.**

fęmna *n. fem.* (mere) woman (*derogatory, in contrast to* **domna**): *obl. sg.* **femna** 14.67, 18.49. [CL FĒMĬNAM *FEW* 3: 451; It. *femmina,* Sp. *hembra,* Fr. *femme;* cf. E. *feminine*]

fęnher *vb. trans.* to pretend; *refl.* to pretend to be 30.18: *pres. 3rd sg.* **fein** 30.18. [CL FĬNGĔRE *FEW* 3: 556; It. *fingere,* Sp. *fingir, heñir,* Fr. *feindre;* cf. E. *fiction*]

fenir *vb. trans.* to cease 21.1; to drop (a claim) 20.4: *pres. 1st sg.* **fenis** 21.1; *pp., fem., obl. sg. undeclined* **fenit** 20.4. [CL FĪNĪRE, VL **FENĪRE FEW* 3: 559; It. *finire,* Sp. *fenecer,* Fr. *finir,* E. *to finish*]

fęr (1) *n. masc.* iron: *obl. sg.* **fer** 9.8. [CL FĔRRUM *FEW* 3: 476; It. *ferro,* Sp. *hierro,* Fr. *fer*]

fęr (2) *adj.* savage, ferocious: *masc., nom. sg.* **fers** 3.3 var.; *obl. pl.* **fers** 9.38; *fem., obl. sg.* **fera** 12.49. [CL FĔRUM *FEW* 3: 481; It. *fiero,* Sp. *fiero,* OFr. *fiers* masc., nom. sg., Fr. *fier,* E. *fierce*]

fera (1) 27.40 var., *see* **faire.**

fera (2) 24.10, *see* **ferir.**

fera (3) 12.49, *see* **fer** (2).

ferai *see* **faire.**

feręza *n. fem.* displeasure: *obl. sg.* **feresza** 26.19, 26.49, **fereza** 26.49 var., **faresza** 26.49 var. [**fer** (2) + **-eza**]

ferir *vb. trans.* to strike (with a sword): *pres. 2nd sg.* **fers** 25.84; *pres. subj. 1st sg.* **fiera** 27.40 var., **fieyra** 19.37, *3rd sg.* **fera** 24.10; *pret. 3rd sg.* **feric** 25.53, 25.57, 25.70; *pres. part., masc., nom. pl.* **firen** 25.7. [CL FĔRĪRE *FEW* 3: 466; It. *ferire,* Sp. *herir,* Fr. *férir*]

fęrm *adv.* strongly 26.45. [**ferm** *adj.* (CL FĬRMUM *FEW* 3: 576; It. *fermo,* Sp. *firme,* Fr. *ferme,* E. *firm*)]

fermar *vb. trans.* to fix, to sustain: *pret. 3rd sg.* **fermet** 15.37 var. [CL FĬRMĀRE *FEW* 3: 574; It. *firmare* 'to sign,' Sp. *firmar,* Fr. *fermer* 'to close'; cf. E. *to affirm*]

feron *see* **faire.**

fers (1) 3.3 var., 9.38, *see* **fer** (2).

fers (2) 25.84, *see* **ferir.**

fes *see* **faire.**

fęsta *n. fem.* ecclesiastical feast, festival: *nom. sg.* **festa** 30.15, 31.36; *obl. sg.* **festa** 30.33. [CL FĔSTAM *FEW* 3: 484; It. *festa,* Sp. *fiesta,* Fr. *fête,* E. *feast*]

festuga *n. fem.* straw: *obl. sg.* **festuia** 14.15. [CL FĔSTŪCAM *FEW* 3: 485; It. *festuca*]

fetz, feyra, feyro, feyron, fez, fezem, fezes, *see* **faire.**

fi (1) 8.11, 8.20, 10.28, 10.32, 19.57, *see* **fin** (1).

fi (2) 10.22, 13.9, 13.15, 13.43, 13.74, 28.13, 31.3, *pret. 1st sg. of* **faire,** *which see.*

fiarai, fiav' *see* **fizar.**

fïel *adj.* faithful: *masc., obl. sg.* **fiel** 11.45. [CL FĪDĒLEM *FEW* 3: 502; It. *fedele,* Sp. *fiel,* Fr. *fidèle;* cf. E. *fidelity*]

fiera, fieyra *see* **ferir.**

figura *n. fem.* face: *obl. sg.* **figura** 13.85. [CL fīgūram *FEW* 3: 513; It. *figura*, Sp. *figura*, Fr. *figure*, E. *figure*]

fil *see* **filh**.

filar *vb. trans.* to spin (wool into thread): *imperf. 3rd sg.* **filava** 28.8. [LL fīlāre *FEW* 3: 533; It. *filare*, Sp. *hilar*, Fr. *filer*, E. *to file*]

filh *n. masc.* son: *nom. sg.* **filhs** 14.61, **fils** 5.2, 5.16, 14.61 var., **fills** 14.61 var.; **filh** 14.61 var.; *obl. sg.* **filh** 29.47, **fill** 27.46, **fil** 10.7. [CL fīlĭum *FEW* 3:522; It. *figlio*, Sp. *hijo*, Fr. *fils*; cf. E. *filial*]

filha *n. fem.* daughter: *nom. sg.* **filha** 13.4. [CL fīlĭam 3: 517; It. *figlia*, Sp. *hija*, Fr. *fille*]

filhs, **fill**, **fills**, **fils** *see* **filh**.

fin (1) *n. fem.* end 8.20, 10.32, 11.40, 19.57; pact 8.11; peace 10.28: *nom. sg.* **fis** 11.40; *obl. sg.* **fi** 8.11, 8.20, 10.28, 10.32, 19.57. [CL fīnem n. 'end, zenith, culminating point' *FEW* 3: 567; It. *fine*, Sp. *fin*, Fr. *fin*; cf. E. *final*]

fin (2) *adj.* true, sincere (*modifying* love 16.4, 31.10; joy of love 2.11; lover 4.14, 16.30, 16.39, 30.81; love poem 16.50; amorous conversation 15.26); fine (*modifying* leather 26.44, reputation 15.12): *masc., nom. sg.* **fins** 2.11, 16.50, **fis** 4.14, 15.12, 15.26; *obl. sg.* **fin** 26.44, 30.81; *obl. pl.* **fins** 16.30; *fem., nom. sg.* **fina** 16.39 ms., **fin'** 16.4, 16.39; *obl. sg.* **fina** 31.10. [**fin** (1) as adj.; It. *fino*, Sp. *fino*, Fr. *fin*, E. *fine*]

finamen *adv.* truly, sincerely: **finamen** 17.39. [**fin** (2) + **-amen** (2)]

fins *see* **fin** (2).

firen *see* **ferir**.

fis (1) 11.40, *n. fem., see* **fin** (1).

fis (2) 7.14 var., *pret. 1st sg. of* **faire**, *which see.*

fis (3) 4.14, 15.12, 15.26, *adj., see* **fin** (2).

fisar *vb. trans.* to sting; *pres. 3rd sg.* **fissa** 13.10. [VL *fīxāre *FEW* 3: 586; It. *fissare*, Sp. *fijar*, Fr. *fixer*, E. *to fix*]

fisarai *see* **fizar**.

fissa *see* **fisar**.

fizar *vb. refl.* to trust: *imperf. 1st sg.* **fiav'** 11.75; *fut. 1st sg.* **fisarai** 30.63, **fiarai** 18.18, **fierai** 18.18 var. [CL fīdĕre, VL *fīdāre *FEW* 3: 501; It. *fidare*, Sp. *fiar*, Fr. *fier*; cf. E. *to confide*]

flac *adj.* flabby: *masc., nom. sg.* **flacs** 22.44. [CL flăccum 'floppy' (ears) *FEW* 3: 593; It. *fiacco* 'weary,' Sp. *flaco* 'lean,' Fr. *flache* 'flawed' (wood); cf. E. *flaccid*]

flairar *n. masc.* sense of smell: *obl. sg.* **flairar** 1.6. [CL frāgrāre, LL flāgrāre 'to smell strongly' *FEW* 3: 747; Fr. *flairer* 'to smell out'; cf. E. *fragrant*]

flamier *n. masc.* blaze: *nom. sg.* **flamers** 25.50. [**flama** (CL flammam *FEW* 3:601; It. *fiamma*, Sp. *flama*, Fr. *flame*, E. *flame*) + **-ier**]

flazar *n. masc.* power to draw breath: *obl. sg.* **flazar** 1.6 var. [LL flātāre 'to blow' *FEW* 3: 610; It. *fiatare*]

flic *n. masc.* snip (*sound of scissors*): *obl. sg.* **flic** 31.26. [Onomatopoetic *flik- FEW* 3: 621]

floc *n. masc.* snap (*sound of scissors*): *obl. sg.* **floc** 31.26. [Onomatopoetic *flok- FEW* 3: 627]

flor *n. fem.* flower: *nom. sg.* **flors** 15.6; *obl. sg.* **flor** 17.6. [CL flōrem *FEW* 3: 636; It. *fiore*, Sp. *flor*, Fr. *fleur*, E. *flower*]

fo *see* **eser**.

fǫc *n. masc.* fire: *nom. sg.* **focs** 9.22, **fuec** 26.52, **fuoc** 26.52 var.; *obl. sg.* **foc** 14.18. [CL fŏcum *FEW* 3: 658; It. *fuoco*, Sp. *fuego*, Fr. *feu*]

foillo *see* **folhar.**

foizǫn *n. fem.* abundance, plenty: *obl. sg.* **foiso** 11.26. [CL fŭsĭōnem *FEW* 3: 914; Fr. *foison*]

fǫl (1) *n. masc.* fool: *nom. sg.* **fols** 13.79 var., 16.33, 18.54, **fol** *before* **s-** 13.79; *obl. sg.* **fol** 14.47, 19.59, **folh** 13.79 var.; *obl. pl.* **fols** 24.1; *vocative sg.* **fol** 13.55. [CL fŏllem 'bag, ball,' *by extension* 'windbag, empty-headed person' *FEW* 3: 694; It. *folle*, Fr. *fou*, E. *fool*]

fǫl (2) *adj.* foolish: *masc., nom. sg.* **fols** 16.49 var., 17.32, 23.25, 25.81; *obl. sg.* **fol** 23.4 var.; *obl. pl.* **fòls** 32.14; *fem., nom. sg.* **fola** 16.16. [LL fŏllum *adj. FEW* 3: 694; cf. **fol** (1)]

folatge *n. masc.* folly: *obl. sg.* **folatje** 13.64. [**fol** (1) + **-atge**]

folatura *n. fem.* folly: *obl. sg.* **folatura** 13.79. [**fol** (1) + **-atura**]

foledat *n. fem.* folly: *nom. sg.* **foudaz** 17.43; *obl. sg.* **folledat** 11.2. [**fol** (1) + **-edat**]

fǫlh (1) *n. masc.* leaf; page 30.89: *obl. sg.* **fueil** 30.89. [CL fŏlĭum *FEW* 3: 685; It. *foglio*, E. *folio*]

folh (2) *see* **fol** (1).

fǫlha *n. fem.* leaf; *collective* leaves 8.18; *nom. sg.* **fueilla** 8.18. [CL fŏlĭa *neuter pl. FEW* 3: 685; It. *foglia*, Sp. *hoja*, Fr. *feuille*]

folhar *vb. intrans.* to bear leaves, to leaf out: *pres. 3rd pl.* **foillo** 8.2. [**folh** (1) + **-ar** (2)]

folhia *n. fem.* folly: *obl. sg.* **follia** 11.2, 17.11, 26.46, **foillia** 13.23 var., **fulia** 13.23. [**fol** (1) + **-ia**]

folhǫr *n. fem.* folly: *obl. sg.* **folhor** 29.12, **follor** 17.14. [**fol** (1) + **-or**]

folledat *see* **foledat.**

follia *see* **folhia.**

follor *see* **folhor.**

folpidǫr *n. masc.* ragbag, place for discarded refuse (?): *obl. sg. in expression* **inz e·l folpidor** 12.49 var. (see note). [VL *foleppa, *var. of* faluppa (?) *FEW* 3: 397 + **-idor**; cf. **felpidor**]

fols (1) 13.79 var., 16.33, 18.54, 24.1, *n. masc., see* **fol** (1).

fols (2) 16.49 var., 17.32, 23.25, 25.81, *adj., see* **fol** (2).

fòls (3) 32.14, *adj., see* **fol** (2).

fǫn (1) *n. fem.* fountain: *obl. sg.* **fon** 18.48. [CL fŏntem *FEW* 3: 696; It. *fonte*, Sp. *fuente*, E. *fount, font*]

fon (2) *vb. intrans. passim, pret. 3rd sg. of* **eser,** *which see.*

fon (3) *vb. intrans.* 18.8, *pres. 3rd sg. of* **fondre,** *which see.*

fǫndre *vb. intrans.* to melt: *pres. 3rd sg.* **fon** 18.8. [CL fŭndĕre *FEW* 3: 866; It. *fondere*, Sp. *fundir*, Fr. *fondre*, E. *to found*; cf. E. *foundry*]

fǫr (1) *n. masc.* manner; **a for . . . de** for 31.22. [CL fŏrum 'marketplace' *FEW* 3: 738; It. *foro* 'square,' Sp. *fuero* 'law,' Fr. *fur* in expression *au fur et à mesure* 'gradually,' E. *forum*]

for' (2) *vb. intrans.* 20.35 var., *2nd cond. 1st sg. of* **eser,** *which see.*

fǫr (3) *adv.* 30.42, **for'** 25.15, *see* **fors** (1).

fora (1) 30.15, 31.34, *vb. intrans., 2nd cond., 1st or 3rd sg. of* **eser,** *which see.*

fora (2) 25.8, 25.46, *adv., see* **fors** (1).

foratz, foren *see* **eser.**

forfach *n. masc.* crime: *obl. pl.* **forfaizc** 11.15. [**fors** (1) + **fach** (1)]

formar *vb. trans.* to create: *pret. 3rd sg.* **formet** 15.37, 27.3. [CL FŏRMĀRE *FEW* 3: 717; It. *formare*, Sp. *formar*, Fr. *former*, E. *to form*]

fǫrn *n. masc.* oven: *obl. sg.* **forn** 5.2. [CL FŭRNUM *FEW* 3: 909; It. *forno*, Sp. *horno*, Fr. *four*; cf. E. *furnace*]

fornęl *n. masc.* hearth: *obl. sg.* **fornelh** 9.21. [**forn** + **-el**]

fornier *n. masc.* baker: *nom. sg.* **forniers** 5.2. [CL FŭRNĀRĬUM *FEW* 3: 902; It. *fornaio*, Sp. *hornero*, OFr. *fournier*]

foro, foron *see* **eser.**

fǫrs (1) *adv.* outside. *Forms:* **fors** 19.4; **for** 30.42; **for'** 25.15; **fora** 25.8, 25.46. [CL FŏRĪS, FŏRĀS *FEW* 3: 705; It. *fuori*, Sp. *fuera*, Fr. *hors*]

fǫrs (2) *prep.* except 6.14; **fors de** out of, free from 17.12; *conj.* **fors que** except that 19.20 var. [**fors** (1)]

forsar *vb. trans.* to compel, to have power over 20.6, 22.8; *pres. 3rd pl.* **forssan** 22.8; *pp., masc., nom. sg.* **forsatz** 20.6; *pp. as adj., masc., obl. sg.* **forsat** constrained, cramped 29.6. [VL *FŏRTĬĀRE *FEW* 3: 731; It. *forzare*, Sp. *forzar*, Fr. *forcer*, E. *to force*]

fǫrt (1) *adj.* strong: *masc., nom. sg.* **fortz** 9.28, 22.17; *obl. sg.* **fort** 12.53, 26.43 var.; *obl. pl.* **fortz** 26.43. [CL FŏRTEM *FEW* 3: 735; It. *forte*, Sp. *fuerte*, Fr. *fort*, E. *fort* n. 'stronghold, fortified place']

fǫrt (2) *adv.* well 10.38; greatly 5.11, 19.8; warmly 5.11; closely 3.6; very 31.15; **fort be** very well 30.27, 30.73; **per fort** necessarily 22.30 var., 26.52. [**fort** (1)]

fos *see* **eser.**

fosat *n. masc.* trench: *obl. pl.* **fossatz** 25.44. [LL FŏSSĀTUM *FEW* 3: 741; Fr. *fossé*]

fossetz *see* **eser.**

fǫtre *vb. trans.* to fuck, to have sexual intercourse with: *pres. subj. 3rd sg.* **fota** 14.51 var.; *pret. 1st sg.* **fotey** 9.61; *pp., undeclined* **fotut** 9.56. [CL FŭTŬĔRE, VL *FŭTTĔRE *FEW* 3: 928; It. *fottere*, Sp. *hoder, joder*, Fr. *foutre*]

fotz *see* **eser.**

foudaz *see* **foledat.**

fraire *n. masc.* brother *passim*; friar 31.0: *nom. sg.* **frairs** 20.5 var.; *obl. sg.* **fraire** 20.5 var., 25.60, **frair** 20.5, 20.27, **frayre** 31.0; *obl. pl.* **fraires** 32.16; *vocative sg.* **fraire** 25.62. [CL FRĀTREM *FEW* 3: 767; It. *fra, fratello*, Sp. *fraile* 'friar,' Fr. *frère*; cf. E. *fraternity*]

fraitz *see* **franher.**

franc *adj.* noble 2.12, 16.39; open 23.2: *masc., obl. sg.* **franc** 23.2; *fem., nom. sg.* **francha** 16.39 ms., **franch'** 16.39; *obl. sg.* **franca** 2.12. [Frankish *frank* *FEW* 15: 163; It. *franco*, Sp. *franco*, Fr. *franc*, E. *frank*]

francamęn *adv.* heartily: **francamen** 9.5. [**franc** + **-amen** (2)]

francęs *adj.* French; **a la francesza** in the French style 26.43: *fem., obl. sg.* **francesza** 26.43. *See also Proper Names.* [**Fransa** + **-es** (2)]

franch', francha *see* **franc.**

franher *vb. trans.* to break: *pres. 3rd sg.* **franh** 14.7; *pp., masc., obl. pl.* **fraitz** 12.62. [CL FRĂNGĔRE *FEW* 3: 756; It. *frangere*, Fr. *fraindre*; cf. E. *fragile*]

fręg *n. masc.* cold: *nom. sg.* **freg** 13.13; *obl. sg.* **freg** 26.44. [CL FRĪGĬDUM, VL *FRĬGĬDUM (influenced by RĬGĬDUM 'stiff') *FEW* 3: 801; It. *freddo*, Sp. *frío*, Fr. *froid*, E. *frigid*]

fręsc *adj.* fresh: *masc., obl. sg.* **fresc** 26.21. [Germ. *frisk *FEW* 15: 179; It. *fresco*, Fr. *frais*]

frẹza *n. fem.* shelled bean: *obl. sg.* **fresza** 26.9. [CL (FĂBAM) FRĒSAM *FEW* 3: 779]

frire *vb. intrans.* to fry: *pres. subj. 3rd sg.* **fria** 26.22. [CL FRĪGĔRE *FEW* 3: 795; It. *friggere,* Sp. *freír,* Fr. *frire,* E. *to fry*]

fromir *vb. trans.* to accomplish; *pp., fem., obl. sg.* **fromida** satisfied 28.52. [Germ. **frŭmjan FEW* 15, part 2: 185 + **-ir**]

frǫn *n. masc.* forehead: *obl. sg.* **front** 25.72. [CL FRŎNTEM *FEW* 3: 822; It. *fronte,* Sp. *frente,* Fr. *front,* E. *front*]

frǫnda *n. fem.* catapult: *obl. pl.* **frondas** 25.40. [CL FŬNDĂM 'sling,' FŬNDŬLA *Oxf.,* VL **FLŬNDA FEW* 3: 862; OFr. *flondre;* It. *fionda,* Sp. *honda,* Fr. *fronde*]

front *see* **fron.**

frutefiar *vb. intrans.* to bear fruit: *pres. 3rd sg.* **frutefia** 26.54. [CL FRŬCTĬFĬCĀRE *FEW* 3: 823; It. *fruttificare,* Sp. *fructificar,* Fr. *fructifier,* E. *to fructify*]

fuec *see* **foc.**

fueil *see* **folh** (1).

fueilla *see* **folha.**

fui *see* **eser.**

fuire *vb. intrans.* to flee: *pres. subj. 3rd sg.* **fuia** 14.17. [CL FŬGĔRE, LL FŬGĪRE *FEW* 3: 839, VL **FŪGĪRE B-W;* It. *fuggire,* Sp. *huir,* Fr. *fuir;* cf. E. *fugitive*]

fulia *see* **folhia.**

fust *n. masc.* wood 9.8, 14.15; (pilgrim's) staff 15.34: *nom. sg.* **fustz** 15.34; *obl. sg.* **fust** 9.8, 14.15. [CL FŪSTEM 'stick, club' *FEW* 3: 919; It. *fusto* 'stalk, shaft,' Fr. *fût*]

fuy *see* **eser.**

gabar *vb. intrans.* to boast: *pres. part., masc., nom. pl.* **anar . . . gaban** 8.29. [Old Norse *gabb FEW* 16: 3 + **-ar** (2); It. *gabbare,* Fr. *gaber,* E. *to gab*]

gai *adj.* joyous, lively, merry: *masc., nom. sg.* **gais** 6.3, 10.29, **guays** 2.25; *obl. sg.* **guay** 12.26 var.; *fem., nom. sg.* **gaia** 6.4; *obl. sg.* **gaia** 5.5. [Gothic **gāheis FEW* 16: 9; It. *gaio,* Fr. *gai,* E. *gay*]

gaigre *see* **gaire.**

gaire *adv.* long 25.26; **non . . . gaire** scarcely 11.13, hardly 16.1: **gaires** 16.1, 25.26; **gaigre** 11.13. [Germ. **waigaro FEW* 17: 470; It. *guari,* Fr. *guère*]

gais *see* **gai.**

gaita *n. fem.* watchman: *nom. sg.* **gaita** 4.7, 4.43, **guaita** 4.16, 4.25, 4.34. [Germ. **wahta FEW* 17: 456; OFr. *gaite*]

galhart *adj.* outrageous: *masc., nom. sg.* **gaillartz** 22.41. [Ctc. **galia* 'strength' *FEW* 4: 31 + **-art**; It. *gagliardo,* Sp. *gallardo,* Fr. *gaillard,* E. *galliard*]

galina *n. fem.* hen: *obl. sg.* **galina** 26.11. [CL GĂLLĪNAM *FEW* 4: 40; It. *gallina,* Sp. *gallina*]

ganda *n. fem* avoidance, delay: *obl. sg.* **ganda** 20.1. [**gandir** + **-a**]

gandir *vb. intrans.* to escape (from = *indirect object*): *pp., fem., nom. sg.* **gandida** 28.35. [Gothic **wandjan FEW* 17: 503]

gara *see* **garar.**

garanda *n. fem.* measure: *obl. sg.* **garanda** 20.10. [Germ. **warōn* 'to heed' *FEW* 17: 535 + **-anda**]

garandar *vb. trans.* to grant: *pres. 3rd sg.* **guaranda** 19.10. [**garanda** + **-ar** (2)]

garar *vb. trans.* to look at 13.91 var.; to watch over, to care for 12.52: *pres. 3rd sg.* **gara** 13.91 var.; *fut. 3rd pl.* **guararan** 12.52. [Germ. **warōn FEW* 17: 533; Fr. *gare* 'look out!']

garda *n. fem.* protection: *obl. sg.* **garda** 10.11. [**gardar** + **-a**]

gardar *vb. intrans.* to look 30.55; *trans.* to look at 13.33; to watch over 28.3; to protect 12.71, 27.8; to guard 3.6, 5.8; to keep 26.43; to obey 24.8; to observe 22.25; *refl.* to protect oneself 28.66; *refl. with* **de** *or* **en** to watch out for, to be careful of 15.72, 31.6.

    Forms: pres. 1st sg. **gart** 13.33, 22.25, *3rd sg.* **garda** 24.8, *2nd pl.* **gardatz** 14.72, *3rd pl.* **gardan** 26.34; *pres. subj. 3rd sg.* **gart** 12.71, **guarde** 24.8 var.; *pret. 1st sg.* **gardiey** 31.6; *past subj. 3rd sg.* **gardes** 30.55; *imper. 2nd pl.* **gardas** 27.8; *pres. part., fem., obl. sg.* **gardan** 28.3; *pp., fem., nom. sg.* **gardada** 28.66; *inf.* **gardar** 3.6, 5.8.

    [Germ. **wardōn FEW* 17: 510 + **-ar** (2); It. *guardare,* Sp. *guardar,* Fr. *garder,* E. *to guard*]

garganta *n. fem.* throat: *obl. sg.* **garganta** 32.9. [Onomatopoetic *garg-FEW* 4: 56 + **-anta**; Sp. *garganta*]

garnir *vb. trans.* to equip: *pp., masc., obl. sg.* **garnit** 25.56, *nom. pl.* **guarnit** 11.56; *substantivized inf., masc., obl. pl* **garnirs** equipment 21.32. [Germ. **warnjan FEW* 17: 533 + **-ir**; It. *guarnire,* Sp. *guarnecer,* Fr. *garnir,* E. *to garnish*]

garsa *n. fem.* girl: *obl. sg.* **garsa** 31.3. [**garson** + **-a**]

garsoṇ *n. masc.* rascal 12.44, dupe 22.43: *nom. sg.* **gartz** 22.43; *obl. pl.* **garsos** 12.44. [Frankish **wrakkjo FEW* 17: 619 + **-on** (1)]

gart *see* **gardar**.

gartz *see* **garson**.

gasainatz *see* **gazanhar**.

gastar *vb. trans.* to damage: *pp., masc., nom. sg.* **gastatz** 14.18. [CL VASTĀRE influenced by Germ. **wōstjan FEW* 14: 206; It. *guastare,* Sp. *gastar,* Fr. *gâter,* E. *to waste*]

gat *see* **cat**.

gatge *n. masc.* payment, wage: *obl. sg.* **gatje** 13.65. [Frankish **waddi,* LL WADIUM *FEW* 17: 446; It. *gaggio,* Fr. *gage,* E. *wage*]

gau *see* **jauzir**.

gauch *n. masc.* joy: *nom. sg.* **gaug** 25.97, **gaugz** 28.37; *obl. sg.* **gauch** 29.13, **gaug** 21.3. [CL GAUDĬUM *FEW* 4: 82; It. *gaudio,* Sp. *gozo;* cf. **joi**, **joia**]

gauta *n. fem.* cheek: *obl. sg.* **gauta** 31.32. [VL **GAUTA FEW* 4: 10; Fr. *joue*]

gauzens *see* **jauzir**.

gauzimens *see* **jauzimen**.

gauzinal *adj.* of morning, of cockcrow; **estela gauzinal** morning star, the planet Venus 12.34: *fem., nom. sg.* **guauzinaus** 12.34. [CL GĂLLĬCĪNĬUM 'cockcrow' *Oxf.* + **-al**; cf. ML GALLICIANALE *FEW* 4: 36]

gauzirai *see* **jauzir**.

gazaingnar *see* **gazanhar**.

gazanh *n. masc.* winning, gain: *nom. sg.* **gazanhs** 12.23, **gazanh** 12.23 ms., **gazains** 12.23 var. [**gazanhar**]

gazanhar *vb. trans.* to win: *pp., masc., obl. pl.* **gasainatz** 30.78; *inf.* **gazaingnar** 27.13. [Frankish **waiðanjan FEW* 17: 467 + **-ar** (2); It. *guadagnare,* Sp. *ganar,* Fr. *gagner,* E. *to gain*] gazanhs *see* **gazanh.**

geins *see* **gęnh.**

gęl *n. masc.* frost: *obl. sg.* **gel** 8.16. [CL gĕlum *FEW* 4: 90; It. *gelo*, Sp. *hielo*, Fr. *gel*; cf. E. *jelly*]

gelar *vb. intrans.* to freeze: *pp., masc., nom. sg.* **gelatz** 15.7. [CL gĕlāre *FEW* 4: 89; It. *gelare*, Sp. *helar*, Fr. *geler*]

gelǫs *adj.* jealous: *nom. sg.* **gelos** 3.6. [LL (influenced by Gk.) zĕlōsum *FEW* 14: 660; It. *geloso*, Sp. *celoso*, Fr. *jaloux*, E. *jealous, zealous*]

gęn (1) *n. fem.* people: *nom. sg.* **gens** 5.7, 13.84, 30.11, **genz** 16.16; *obl. sg.* **gen** 2.12, 23.7, 26.40, 27.27, 31.45, **gent** 11.23, 26.26; *obl. pl.* **gens** 31.37. [CL gĕntem *FEW* 4: 108; It. *gente*, Sp. *gente*, Fr. *gens*; cf. E. *gentle*]

gęn (2) *adj.* noble 6.25, 21.29; becoming 16.35, 23.17; pretty 19.31 var.: *masc., nom. sg.* **gens** 19.31 var.; *obl. sg.* **gen** 6.25, **gent** 21.29; *neuter, nom. sg.* **gen** 16.35, 23.17. [CL gĕnĭtum 'born,' pp. of gĭgnĕre, gĕnĕre *FEW* 4: 105]

gęn (3) *adv.* well 21.5, 21.6, 21.31, 23.21, 23.26, 31.42; nicely 9.15. [**gen** (2)]

generaciǫn *n. fem.* birth: *obl. sg.* **generacion** 5.2. [CL gĕnĕrătĭōnem *FEW* 4: 98; It. *generazione*, Sp. *generación*, Fr. *génération*, E. *generation*]

gęnh *n. masc.* wit 15.28 var., 22.3; conduct 13.36: *nom. sg.* **geins** 22.3; *obl. sg.* **genh** 13.36, **ginh** 15.28 var. [CL ĭngĕnĭum *FEW* 4: 688; It. *ingegno*, Fr. *engin*, E. *engine*]

gęns (1) *n. fem.* 5.7, 13.84, 30.11, 31.37, *see* **gen** (1).

gęns (2) *adj.* 19.31 var., *see* **gen** (2).

gęns (3) *adv.* **non** . . . **gens** not at all *passim*; **ni** . . . **gens** and not at all 26.37. *Forms:* **gens** 11.48; **ges** 9.39, 9.54, 13.68, 16.17, 17.25, 19.20, 22.1, 23.28, 26.20, 26.37, 30.18, 30.40, 30.65, 30.72, 30.93; **gez** 23.21; **gies** 13.91 var.; **jes** 18.28, 18.57, 19.9, 19.20 var. [CL gĕnus *FEW* 4: 116, or gĕntĭum Walsh 89–99]

gensar *vb. intrans.* to become noble: *pres. 3rd sg.* **genssa** 6.26. [**gensor** + **-ar** (2)]

gensǫr *comparative of* **gen** (2) *adj.* more noble: *masc., obl. sg.* **genzor** 11.38; *fem., nom. sg.* **genser** 2.21; *obl. sg.* **gensor** 15.10. [**gen** (2) + **-sor**]

genssa *see* **gensar.**

gent (1) 11.23, 26.26, *n. fem., see* **gen** (1).

gent (2) 21.29, *adj., see* **gen** (2).

gentil *adj.* noble: *masc., nom. sg.* **gentils** 1.1, 3.3; *obl. sg.* **gentil** 13.29; *fem., nom. sg.* **gentils** 13.43 var., **gentil** 3.5, 13.43; *obl. sg.* **gentil** 5.5. [CL gĕntīlem *FEW* 4: 111; It. *gentile*, Sp. *gentil*, Fr. *gentil*, E. *gentle, genteel*]

genz *see* **gen** (1).

genzor *see* **gensor.**

gequir *vb. trans.* to give up, to drop 19.61; to leave 28.59; *refl.* to cease 18.59 var.: *pres. 1st sg.* **giec** 18.59 var., *3rd sg.* **giec** 19.61, 28.59. [Germ. **jehhjan FEW* 16: 283 + **-ir**]

gerra *see* **guerra.**

gerrei *see* **guerreiar.**

ges *see* **gens** (3).

geu (French) *n. masc.* play (= OOc **joc**): *obl. sg.* **geu** 15.28 var. [CL jŏcum *FEW* 5: 45; Fr. *jeu*]

gez *see* **gens** (3).

giec *see* **gequir.**

gies *see* **gens** (3).

giet *see* **gitar.**
ginh *see* **genh.**
giroṇ *n. masc., pl.* side: *obl. pl.* **giros** 25.57. [Frankish **gêro FEW* 16:32; It. *gherone,* Fr. *giron*]
gisclar *vb. intrans.* to spurt: *inf.* **gisclar** 32.10. [VL *cīscŭlāre *FEW* 2: 714; Fr. *gicler*]
gitar *vb. trans.* to throw; **gitar a non-caler** to become indifferent toward 29.36; **gitar en ira** to visit wrath upon 25.63: *pres. subj. 3rd sg.* **giet** 29.36; *pp., masc., obl. pl.* **gitatz** 25.63; *inf.* **gitar** 11.71. [CL jăctāre, jĕctāre *FEW* 5: 22; It. *gettare,* Sp. *jitar,* Fr. *jeter*; cf. E. *jet*]
glavi *see* **glazi.**
glazi *n. masc.* sword 14.44; slaughter 25.40: *nom. sg.* **glazis** 25.40; *obl. sg.* **glavi** 14.44. [CL glădĭum *FEW* 4: 145; Fr. *glaive,* E. *glaive*]
glazïer (1) *n. masc.* carnage, slaughter: **glazïers** *used as obl. sg.* 25.11. [**glazi** + **-ier**]
glazïer (2) *adj.* bloodthirsty: *masc., nom. sg.* **glazïers** 25.96 [**glazi** + **-ier**]
glazis *see* **glazi.**
glęira *n. fem.* church: *obl. sg.* **gleira** 28.58. [ChL ĕcclēsiam, VL *eclęsia *FEW* 3: 203; It. *chiesa,* Sp. *iglesia,* Fr. *église*; cf. E. *ecclesiastical*]
gonęl *n. masc.* robe: *obl. pl.* **gonels** 26.35. [**gona** (LL {from Ctc.} gŭnna *FEW* 4: 326; It. *gonna*) + **-el**]
gonęla *n. fem.* cloak: *obl. sg.* **gonela** 13.5. [**gona** (LL {from Ctc.} gŭnna *FEW* 4: 326) + **-ela**; It. *gonnella,* Fr. *gonnelle*]
gonels *see* **gonel.**
gonfanoṇ *n. masc.* gonfalon, battle standard used to rally troops: *nom. pl.* **gonfanon** 21.21. [Frankish **gundfano FEW* 16: 103 + **-on** (1); It. *gonfalone,* Sp. *gonfalón,* Fr. *gonfalon,* E. *gonfalon*]
gonfanonier *n. masc.* standard-bearer: *nom. sg.* **gonfanoners** 25.36. [**gonfanon** + **-ier**]
gracia *n. fem.* (divine) grace: *obl. sg.* **gracia** 29.48. [CL grătĭam *FEW* 4: 246; It. *grazia,* Sp. *gracia,* Fr. *grâce,* E. *grace*]
graile *n. masc.* bugle: **grailes** *used as nom. pl.* 25.99. [CL grăcĭlem 'slender' *FEW* 4: 203; Fr. *grêle,* E. *grail*]
grais *n. masc.* grease: *obl. sg.* **grais** 26.52. [VL *crassia *FEW* 2: 1277 influenced by **gras, gros**; It. *grascia,* Sp. *grasa,* Fr. *graisse,* E. *grease*]
gramavi *n. masc.* grammar teacher: *obl. sg.* **gramavi** 14.45. [CL grămmātĭcum *FEW* 4: 217; It. *grammatico,* Sp. *gramático,* Fr. *grammairien,* E. *grammarian*]
gran *adj.* great *passim*; high (Mass) 31.37; **se metre en grans** to get in trouble 22.34.

> *Forms: Masc., nom. sg.* **grans** 25.108, **gran** *used as nom. sg.* 4.39 (see note), 9.65 (see note); *obl. sg.* **gran** 6.12, 7.21, 8.21, 10.6, 11.34, 13.10, 17.20, 21.31, 23.24, 25.19, 27.18, 30.67, 31.32, **grant** 11.16, 11.74, 26.44; *obl. pl.* **grans** 9.38, 22.34, 25.49.
> *Fem., nom. sg.* **grans** 4.12, 18.5, 26.46, **gran** 11.41 (see note); *obl. sg.* **gran** 1.7, 3.7, 5.4, 5.10, 7.7, 10.6, 11.2, 17.26, 26.19, 26.49, 28.19, 28.50, 31.27, 31.29, **grán** 11.52, **grant** 11.51, **granda** 20.3, 31.37; *nom. pl.* **grans** 25.38; *obl. pl.* **grans** 21.9, **granz** 11.73.
> [CL grăndem *FEW* 4: 223; It. *grande,* Sp. *grande,* Fr. *grand,* E. *grand*]

gras *adj.* fat: *masc., obl. sg.* **gras** 26.11, 26.19, 26.21; *obl. pl.* **gras** 12.26. [CL crăssum 'thick' influenced by grŏssum 'fat' *FEW* 2: 1285; It. *grasso,* Sp. *graso,* Fr. *gras,* E. *crass*]

grat *n. masc.* thanks 2.23; **tot per mon grat** just to please me, for all of me 27.29; *obl. sg.* **grat** 2.23, 27.29. [CL GRĂTUM adj. 'pleasing' *FEW* 4: 253; It. *grato*, Sp. *grado*, Fr. *gré*; cf. E. *grateful*]

gratar *vb. trans.* to scratch: *pres. 3rd sg.* **grata** 14.41. [Germ. **krattōn FEW* 16: 377 + **-ar** (2); It. *grattare*, Fr. *gratter*, E. *to grate*]

gravier *n. masc.* riverbank: *nom. sg.* **graviers** 25.42; *obl. pl.* **graviers** 25.102. [**grava** 'sand' (Pre-Latin **grava FEW* 4: 259) + **-ier**; Fr. *gravier*]

grazir *vb. trans.* to esteem, to praise; *pp., masc., nom. sg.* **grazitz** praised 29.17; *fem., nom. sg.* **grazida** pleasant 28.34. [**grat** + **-ir**; It. *gradire*]

grei *see* **greu** (1).

greu (1) *n. masc.* care, vexation: *nom. pl.* **grei** 22.8. [**greu** (2)]

greu (2) *adj.* heavy 7.1; grievous 9.60, 10.9, 17.26 var., 23.24 var.; unpleasant 29.5; dire 29.33: *masc., nom. sg.* **grieus** 10.9; *obl. sg.* **greu** 7.1, 9.60, 23.24 var., 29.5, 29.33; *fem., obl. sg.* **greu** 17.26 var. [CL GRĂVEM *FEW* 4: 265, VL GRĔVEM (influenced by CL LĔVEM 'light'; see Löfstedt 114); It. *greve*, Fr. *grief* adj., E. *grief* n.]

greu (3) *adv.* with difficulty 14.60; scarcely 17.15, 17.20. [**greu** (2)]

grieus *see* **greu** (2)

gris *n. masc.* gray fur: *obl. sg.* **gris** 10.42. [Frankish **grīs FEW* 16: 83; It. *grigio*, Sp. *gris*, Fr. *gris*]

grondir *vb. intrans.* to scold: *pres. subj. 1st sg.* **gronda** 19.17. [CL GRŬNDĪRE 'to grunt' *FEW* 4: 292; It. *grugnire*, Sp. *gruñir*, Fr. *gronder* 'to scold']

gros *adj.* great: *masc., obl. pl.* **gros** 9.24. [LL GRŌSSUM *FEW* 4: 280; It. *grosso*, Sp. *grueso*, Fr. *gros*, E. *gross*]

grosier *adj.* heavy, massive: *masc., obl. pl.* **grossiers** 25.3. [**gros** + **-ier**]

guaita *see* **gaita**.

guaranda *see* **garandar**.

guararan *see* **garar**.

guarde *see* **gardar**.

guarnit *see* **garnir**.

guauzinaus *see* **gauzinal**.

guay, guays *see* **gai**.

guera *see* **guerra**.

guerida *n. fem.* shelter: *obl. pl.* **gueridas** 25.10. [*pp., fem. of* **guerir** 'to save' (Frankish **warjan FEW* 17: 527; It. *guarire*, Sp. *guarecer*, Fr. *guérir*)]

guerpir *vb. trans.* to give up: *pres. 1st sg.* **guerpisc** 10.41; *pp., masc., obl. sg.* **guerpit** 10.33. [Frankish **werpjan* 'to throw' *FEW* 17: 566; OFr. *guerpir* 'to give up,' Fr. *déguerpir* 'to take to one's heels']

guerra *n. fem.* war 10.7, 22.18, 22.22, 22.39, 24.18; battle 25.4; conflict between two lovers 8.20: *nom. sg.* **guerra** 25.4; *obl. sg.* **guerra** 10.7, **gerra** 22.18, 22.22, 22.39, **guera** 8.20; *obl. pl.* **guerras** 24.18. [Frankish **werra FEW* 17: 567; It. *guerra*, Sp. *guerra*, Fr. *guerre*, E. *war*]

guerreiar *vb. intrans.* to make war 22.15: *pres. subj. 3rd sg.* **gerrei** 22.15; *pres. part., masc., obl. sg.* **guerreian** skilled in war 21.50. [**guerra** + **-eiar**]

guida *n. fem.* guide: *nom. sg.* **guia** 27.46, **guida** 28.44. [**guidar** + **-a**; It. *guida*, Sp. *guía*, Fr. *guide*, E. *guide*]

guidar *vb. trans.* to guide: *fut. 1st sg.* **guizarai** 15.8 var. [Gothic **wīdan FEW* 17: 604 + **-ar** (2); It. *guidare*, Sp. *guiar*, Fr. *guider*, E. *to guide*]

guinhar *vb. trans.* to peep at, to ogle: *pres. 3rd sg.* **guinha** 14.20, **gigna** 14.20 var. [Frankish **wingjan FEW* 17: 593 + **-ar** (2); It. *ghignare*, Sp. *guiñar*, Fr. *guigner*]

guinhọn *n. masc.* whisker: *obl. pl.* **guinhos** 9.38. [Frankish **wingjan* 'to wink'? FEW 17: 590 + **-on** (1)]

guirẹnsa *n. fem.* cure: *obl. sg.* **guirensa** 28.26. [**guerir** 'to save' (see **guerida**) + **-ensa**]

guiza *n. fem.* kind: *obl. sg.* **guiza** 14.8. [Germ. **wīsa* FEW 17: 596; It. *guisa*, Sp. *guisa*, Fr. *guise*, E. *guise*]

guizarai *see* **guidar**.

ha, hac *see* **aver**.

hai *see* **ai** (2).

hanc *see* **anc**.

hay (Spanish) *impersonal 3rd sg. of* haber 'there is' 18.57 var. [CL HABET + Sp. *y* FEW 4: 364; cf. **i** (2), Fr. *il y a*]

herberger (French) *vb. trans.* to lodge: *fut. 1st sg.* **herbergerai** 15.24. [Cf. OOc **albergar**]

heretiers *see* **eretier**.

heu *see* **eu** (1).

hi *see* **i** (1).

hieu *see* **eu** (1).

ho (1) 30.40, *pron., neuter sg., see* **o** (1).

ho (2) 27.39, *conj., see* **o** (3).

hom, home, homes *see* **ome**.

homicidïers *see* **omicidïer**.

homs *see* **ome**.

honor, honors *see* **onor**.

hostal *see* **ostal**.

hoste *see* **oste**.

huebre *see* **obrir**.

huei *see* **oi**.

huelhs *see* **olh**.

hueymais, hueymay *see* **oimais**.

hui *see* **oi**.

humayna *see* **uman**.

humil, humils *see* **umil**.

huoill, huoills, huoils *see* **olh**.

hyeu *see* **eu** (1).

i (1) *personal pron.* = **a** + *personal pron. 3rd sg.:* to her 19.56, 19.66, to it 16.14, to them 11.22; with her 19.64; among them 11.26; in it 16.4, 30.87; from her 19.35; *weak meaning* in regard to that *may be omitted in translation* 2.19, 9.8, 16.31, 22.25, 23.15, 28.19, 30.64, 30.66.
　　　Forms: **i** 2.19, 11.22, 11.26, 16.4, 16.14, 16.31, 19.64, 22.25, 23.15, 30.64, 30.66, 30.87; **hi** 28.19; **y** 9.8, 19.35, 19.56, 19.66.
　　　[**i** (2)]

i (2) *adv.* there 11.63, 12.30, 13.83, 20.16, 21.76, 25.12, 25.23, 25.106, 27.18, 29.20; to that place 10.38; *with impersonal* **aver** there is, there are: *pres.* **i a** 12.26, 14.41, 15.19; *pret.* **i ac** 9.29.
　　　Forms: **i** 10.38, 11.63, 12.30, 20.16, 21.76, 25.23, 25.106; **hi** 15.19, 25.12, 27.18, 29.20; **y** 9.29, 12.26, 13.83, 14.41.
　　　[CL HīC 'here' influenced by īBī 'there' FEW 4: 425; Fr. *y*]

ie· *personal pron. 1st sg. with enclitic forms:* **ie·l** 6.14, **ie·us** 19.1, 23.1, 23.4, 23.12. *See* **eu** (1).

ieu *see* **eu** (1).

ifernaus *see* **enfernal**.

il (1) *personal pron., 3rd person, masc., nom. sg.* 10.22, 10.23, 12.14 var., 27.4, 27.5, *see* **el** (1).

il (2) *personal pron., 3rd person, fem., nom. sg.* 18.36, 19.34 var. (= **ela** 19.34), 30.70, 30.73. *See* **el** (1).

·il (3) *personal pron., 3rd person, enclitic, masc., dat. sg.* 6.30, 18.32, 22.14, 22.43. *See* **el** (1).

ilh *personal pron., 3rd person, masc., nom. pl.* 25.5, 25.9, 25.46. *See* **el** (1).

ill (1) *personal pron., 3rd person, fem., nom. sg.* 6.20. *See* **el** (1).

·ill (2) *personal pron., 3rd person, enclitic, fem., dat. sg.* 16.35, 16.35. *See* **el** (1).

in (1) 11.17, *see* **en** (3).

in (2) (Latin) *prep.* in 12.1.

intraje *see* **entratge**.

intrec *see* **entrar**.

inz *adv.* within; **inz en** *prep.* in 12.49 var. [CL ĭNTŬS *FEW* 4: 784; OFr. *enz*]

ira *n. fem.* anger 19.7, 19.51; (divine) wrath 25.63; grief 19.19, 19.21, 21.60, 25.88: *obl. sg.* **ira** 19.7, 19.19, 19.21, 19.51, 21.60, 25.63, 25.88. [CL ĪRAM *FEW* 4: 812; It. *ira*, OFr. *ire*, E. *ire*]

irai *see* **anar**.

iraiser *vb. refl.* to become angry: *pp., fem., nom. sg.* **yrascuda** 19.58. [CL ĪRĂSCĔRE *FEW* 4: 812]

iran, iras *see* **anar**.

irat *adj.* angry 19.53; given to anger, wrathful 3.6; sad 2.14, 12.62 var., 15.15, 21.59; grieved, wronged 19.8: *masc., nom. sg.* **iratz** 3.6, 15.15, 19.8; *obl. sg.* **irat** 19.53; *nom. pl.* **irat** 21.59; *obl. pl.* **iratz** 2.14, 12.62 var. [CL ĪRĀTUM *FEW* 4: 812; It. *irato*]

irei *see* **anar**.

iretjas *see* **eretge**.

irissatz *see* **erisar**.

·is *see* **se** (1).

issartz *see* **eisart**.

issill *see* **eisilh**.

issitz *see* **eisir**.

ivẹrn *n. masc.* winter: *nom. sg.* **iverns** 15.7; *obl. sg.* **envern** 26.42. [CL HĪBĔRNUM (TĔMPUS) adj. 'of winter' *FEW* 4: 421; It. *inverno*, Sp. *invierno*, Fr. *hiver*; cf. E. *to hibernate*]

ja (1) *adv.* now 19.30; already 19.34 var., 19.57; ever 16.44, 19.47, 21.25, 23.11, 23.19, 27.21; **ja mais** (. . .) **non** never 3.10, 4.11, 15.8, 18.36, 21.60, 22.11, 23.9, 25.27, 25.85, 30.63, never again 18.18; **ja . . . mais . . . non** no more 20.27; **ja** (. . .) **non** never 9.17, 11.19, 16.8, 16.10, 17.10, 17.17, 18.12, 18.31, 20.17, 22.13, 22.30, 23.13, 27.17; **ja pois . . . non** never again 6.23. [CL JĂM *FEW* 5: 27; It. *già*, Sp. *ya*, Fr. *(dé)jà*]

ja (2) *conj.* even though 19.18. [**ja** (1)]

jagues *see* **jazer**.

jardiṇ *n. masc.* garden: *nom. sg.* **jardis** 15.41. [VL *GARDĪNUS (Germ. *gart* *FEW* 16: 21 + **-in**); It. *giardino*, Sp. *jardin*, Fr. *jardin*, E. *garden*]

jausen *see* **jauzir**.

jausimen *see* **jauzimen**.

jausir, jauzen *see* **jauzir.**

jauzimen *n. masc.* joy: *nom. sg.* **gauzimens** 15.46; *obl. sg.* **jauzimen** 16.13, **jausimen** 23.31. [jauzir + -imen]

jauzion *adj.* joyful: *masc., obl. sg.* **jauzion** 18.6; *fem., nom. sg.* **jauzionda** 19.27. [CL GAUDIBŬNDUM]

jauzir *vb. trans.* to enjoy *with direct object* 15.28, *with* **de** 15.8; to make happy 23.45; *refl.* to enjoy *with* **de** 15.9, 23.37: *pres. 1st sg.* **gau** 15.9; *fut. 1st sg.* **gauzirai** 15.8, 15.28; *pres. part., masc., nom. sg.* **gauzens** rejoicing 15.15; *obl. sg.* **jausen** rejoicing 23.32, **jauzen** 2.13; *inf.* **jausir** 23.37, 23.45. [CL GAUDĒRE *FEW* 4: 79; It. *godere,* Sp. *gozar,* Fr. *jouir*]

jazer *vb. intrans.* to lie: *imperf. 3rd sg.* **jazia** 4.1; *past subj. 1st sg.* **jagues** 7.19; *pres. part., masc., obl. sg.* **jazen** 2.13 var.; *substantivized inf.* **jazer** 26.15. [CL JACĒRE *FEW* 5: 4; It. *giacere,* Sp. *yacer,* Fr. *gésir* as in *ci-gît* 'here lies'; cf. E. *adjacent*]

jes *see* **gens** (3).

joc *n. masc.* game, play: *nom. sg.* **jocs** 15.22 var. *See also* **geu** (French). [CL JŎCUM *FEW* 5: 45; It. *giuoco,* Sp. *juego,* Fr. *jeu,* E. *joke*]

joi *n. masc.* joy; **joi e (ni) deport** joy or pleasure 10.39, 10.41, 12.63; **joi d'amor** joy of love 16.6: *nom. sg.* **jois** 6.2, 15.22, 15.45, 17.21, 19.19, 21.23, 21.60, 23.34, 30.48, 30.81, **joys** 2.11, 2.17, 19.19; *obl. sg.* **joi** 6.1, 6.12, 10.25, 10.39, 10.41, 12.63, 13.3, 13.34, 16.6, 16.52, 16.54, 17.5, 17.48, 18.2, 18.60, 21.57, 23.39, 23.46, **joy** 15.28 var. [OFr. *joi* (CL GAUDĬUM *FEW* 4: 82); cf. **gauch, joia**]

joia *n. fem.* joy: *obl. sg.* **joia** 30.79, **joya** 25.93. [OFr. *joie* (CL GAUDĬA pl. *FEW* 4: 82; It. *gioia,* Sp. *joya* 'jewel,' E. *joy*); cf. **gauch, joi**]

joios *adj.* joyful: *fem., obl. sg.* **joiosa** 30.19, **joyoza** 31.15. [joi + -os]

jois *see* **joi.**

jorn *n. masc.* day *passim*; daylight 4.8, 4.17, 4.26, 4.35, 4.44; **tot jorn** all day 14.50, 31.10: *nom. sg.* **jorns** 4.5, **jornz** 16.46; *obl. sg.* **jorn** 2.15, 4.8, 4.17, 4.26, 4.35, 4.44, 14.50, 16.11, 17.4, 17.41 var., 27.2, 31.10, 31.11, 31.15; *nom. pl.* **jorn** 15.1; *obl. pl.* **jorns** 13.42. [CL DĬŬRNUM 'daily' *FEW* 3: 105; It. *giorno,* Fr. *jour*; cf. E. *journal*]

jornada *n. fem.* day's work: *obl. sg.* **jornada** 28.71. [jorn + -ada]

jorns, jornz *see* **jorn.**

jos *adv.* down 3.11; **tornar en jos** to overturn 10.19. [CL DĒŌRSUM, VL JOSU *FEW* 3: 44; It. *giuso*]

josta *prep.* beside: **just'** 13.1. [CL JŬXTA *FEW* 5: 97; It. *giusta*]

joven (1) *n. masc.* young age 11.7; *abstract* youthfulness 6.1, 6.2, *(quasi-allegorical)* 14.7; *collective* young people 12.20, 12.59, 21.18: *nom. sg.* **jovens** 6.2, 12.59, 14.7; *obl. sg.* **joven** 6.1, 12.20, 21.18, **jovent** 11.7. [CL JŬVĔNTUM *FEW* 5: 96; OFr. *jovent*]

joven (2) *adj.* young *passim*; fresh 26.12: *masc., nom. sg.* **joves** 21.17; *obl. sg.* **joven** 20.4, **jove** 25.107, 26.12, **jov'** 10.20; *nom. pl.* **jove** 11.1, 11.7; *fem., nom. sg.* **joves** 3.5, 5.10; *obl. sg.* **joven** 5.5. [CL JŬVĔNEM *FEW* 5: 95; It. *giovane,* Sp. *joven,* Fr. *jeune*]

jovens, jovent *see* **joven** (1).

joves *see* **joven** (2).

joy *see* **joi.**

joya *see* **joia.**

joyoza *see* **joios.**

joys *see* **joi.**

just' *see* **josta**.

jusvẹrt *n. masc.* verjuice, a sour juice of green or unripe fruit: *obl. sg.*
    jusvert 26.12. [**jus** (CL jūs) + **vert**]

jutjamẹn *n. masc.* (last) judgment 23.48, 27.2; power of judgment, authority 11.17; decision 22.51: *obl. sg.* **jutjamen** 11.17, 23.48, **jutgamen** 22.51, 27.2. [**jutjar** + **-amen** (1)]

jutjar *vb. trans.* to decide: *inf.* **jutjar** 11.61. [CL jūdĭcāre *FEW* 5: 58; It. *giudicare*, Sp. *juzgar*, Fr. *juger*, E. *to judge*]

kadenas *see* **cadena**.
ki *see* **qui** (1).

l', ·l (1) *personal pron., 3rd person, proclitic or enclitic, masc. or fem., sg.* 1.6, 1.6, 3.4, 3.5, 3.8, 4.14, 5.11, 6.12, 6.13, 6.14, 6.14, 6.21, 7.4, 7.15, 9.49, 10.13, 10.19, 10.30, 11.14, 11.37, 11.39, 11.47, 11.54, 11.69, 11.73, 12.36, 12.41, 14.36, 14.39, 14.39, 14.48, 16.51, 16.53, 16.54, 16.54, 17.39, 18.36, 19.2, 19.28, 19.30, 19.42, 19.55, 19.63, 20.2, 20.2, 20.5, 21.2, 21.14, 21.54, 23.20, 25.58, 26.16, 27.41, 28.35, 30.6, 30.51, 30.59, 30.95, 30.96, *see* **el** (1).

l', ·l (2) *def. art., proclitic or enclitic, masc. or fem.* 1.6, 1.6, 2.1, 2.1, 2.21, 2.23, 3.1, 3.9, 4.5, 4.9, 4.18, 4.27, 4.31, 4.36, 4.39, 4.45, 5.5, 5.6, 5.7, 5.7, 5.11, 5.14, 5.15, 8.14, 8.15, 8.17, 8.17, 8.18, 8.30, 8.30, 9.22, 9.27, 9.27, 9.37, 9.42, 9.45, 9.50, 9.60, 9.68, 9.72, 10.12, 10.14, 11.10, 11.10, 11.17, 11.36, 11.37, 11.44, 11.60, 11.69, 12.2, 12.25, 12.28, 12.32, 12.34, 12.46, 12.58, 12.58, 12.70, 13.1, 13.13, 13.28, 13.38, 13.63, 13.63, 13.75, 13.81, 14.21, 14.47, 15.7, 15.23, 15.26, 15.30, 15.38, 15.39, 15.41, 16.7, 16.7, 16.20, 16.23, 16.30, 16.32, 16.52, 16.54, 17.8, 17.33, 18.2, 18.34, 18.42, 18.54, 18.54, 19.11, 19.11, 19.15, 19.21, 19.23, 19.41, 19.51, 20.13, 20.31, 20.32, 20.36, 21.4, 21.46, 21.46, 21.56, 21.65, 21.75, 22.9, 22.18, 22.51, 23.23, 23.48, 24.14, 24.19, 24.19, 24.20, 24.20, 24.27, 24.28, 24.31, 24.31, 24.32, 24.35, 25.4, 25.4, 25.11, 25.14, 25.16, 25.26, 25.28, 25.35, 25.36, 25.39, 25.39, 25.40, 25.42, 25.42, 25.52, 25.53, 25.58, 25.59, 25.60, 25.67, 25.70, 25.72, 25.73, 25.76, 25.80, 25.82, 25.87, 25.87, 25.87, 25.95, 25.97, 25.101, 25.102, 25.108, 25.108, 26.18, 26.19, 26.56, 27.7, 27.22, 27.22, 27.27, 28.1, 28.12, 28.54, 28.56, 29.0, 29.7, 29.24, 30.6, 30.30, 30.30, 30.36, 30.39, 30.40, 30.41, 30.43, 30.67, 30.80, 30.89, 31.7, 31.19, 31.36, 31.39, 31.45, 32.12, 32.17, 32.17, *see* **lo** (2).

la (1) *personal pron., 3rd person, fem., obl. sg.* 5.13, 5.13, 5.13, 11.14, 13.27, 14.50, 15.17, 16.34, 17.41, 17.42, 18.28, 18.29, 19.60, 19.68, 22.43, 25.68, 26.7, 30.93, 30.94, 31.18, *see* **el** (1).

la (2) *def. art. fem., sg.* 1.2, 1.4, 1.5, 1.6, 1.6, 1.7, 1.7, 1.7, 2.12, 3.3, 3.4, 3.5, 3.6, 3.7, 3.8, 3.11, 4.2, 4.5, 5.6, 5.6, 5.8, 5.9, 5.10, 5.16, 6.33, 8.1, 8.11, 8.13, 8.14, 8.16, 8.16, 8.18, 8.30, 9.3, 9.19, 9.49, 9.59, 9.69, 10.12, 10.32, 10.37, 11.23, 11.36, 11.40, 11.54, 11.65, 12.17, 12.25, 12.42, 13.8, 13.11, 13.16, 13.24, 13.25, 13.31, 13.38 var., 13.39, 13.42, 13.53, 13.56, 13.67, 13.75, 13.77, 13.79 var., 13.81, 13.84, 13.89, 13.90, 13.91 var., 13.92 var., 14.2, 14.13, 14.14, 14.15, 14.32, 14.33, 14.36, 14.69, 15.41, 16.7, 17.6, 17.11, 17.14, 18.1, 18.4, 18.48, 20.20, 20.21, 21.60, 21.77, 22.42, 24.41, 25.4, 25.5, 25.25, 25.26, 25.42, 25.47, 25.54, 25.58, 25.61, 25.67, 25.69, 25.80, 25.91, 25.93, 25.100, 25.105, 25.109, 26.5, 26.9, 26.17, 26.33, 26.40, 26.43, 27.5, 28.1, 28.14, 28.45, 28.65, 29.39, 30.11, 30.12, 30.16,

30.31, 30.33, 30.65, 30.84, 30.97, 31.25, 31.31, 31.32, 31.44, 32.2, 32.9, 32.9, 32.10, *see* **lo** (2).

la (3) *adv.* 25.8, *see* **lai**.

ladoncs *adv.* then: **ladoncs** 25.77, 25.101. [**lai** + **doncs**]

lai *adv.* there 2.3, 5.15, 11.62, 11.63 (= **i** 11.63), 12.22, 12.36, 15.3, 15.13, 15.33, 20.26, 20.31, 21.26, 25.22, 27.20, 28.12; then 21.48.

    de lai *referring to beloved woman* over there 19.65 var. = **d'ela** by her 19.65; **de lai don** from the place from which 8.7; **de la fora** from the outside 25.8; **de lai ni denan** or before that time 21.48; **de lai on** from the place where 30.82; **lai defor . . . on** outside the place where 30.47; **lai** (. . .) **don** to the place where 12.22, to the place (time, state) from which 27.38; **lai on** where 11.61, 13.26, 25.69, 27.48; **sai e lai** here and there 12.36 var.; **sai ni lai** to either side 30.55.

    Forms: **lai** *passim;* **lay** 12.36, 13.26, 27.48; **la** 25.8.

    [CL ĬLLĀC influenced by HĪC *FEW* 4: 549; It. *là*, Sp. *allá*, Fr. *là*]

laichen, laichero *see* **laisar**.

laina *see* **lana**.

laïns *adv.* within, inside; **laïns en** in 30.41, into 25.89; **de laïns** on the inside 25.106. [**lai** + **inz**]

lais (1) *n. masc.* lay, complaint, plaintive melody: *obl. sg.* **lais** 23.37. [Ctc. **laid FEW* 20: 11; It. *lai*, Fr. *lai*, E. *lay*]

lais (2) *vb. trans.* 8.23, 10.12, 18.59, 22.27, 23.22, *see* **laisar**.

laisar *vb. trans.* to let, to allow 8.23, 11.69, 18.32, 18.43, 23.46; to leave, to depart from 25.10, 28.12; to give up 9.32, 26.36; to abandon 11.16; to leave behind 2.13, 10.7, 18.15, 25.103, to leave up to (*with* **sobre**) 30.60; to leave, to bequeath 10.12, 11.32, 22.14; *refl.* to let oneself, to accept 3.11, 18.3, 23.22; to cease (*with* **de**) 18.59, (*with* **que** and pleonastic **non**) 22.27.

    Forms: Pres. 1st sg. **lais** 10.12, 18.59, 22.27, 23.22; *3rd sg.* **laissa** 9.32, 18.3, 30.60, **laisa** 11.16; *2nd pl.* **laissatz** 23.46, 28.12; *3rd pl.* **laisson** 26.36, **laichen** 25.10.

    Pres. subj. 3rd sg. **lais** 8.23, **laisse** 18.32.

    Fut. 1st sg. **laissarai** 10.7 var., 22.14, **laisserai** 10.7.

    Pret. 3rd sg. **laisset** 3.11, 18.43, **laiset** 11.32, 11.69, 18.15; *3rd pl.* **laichero** 25.103.

    Pp., masc., obl. sg. **layssat** 2.13.

    [CL LĂXĀRE *FEW* 5: 227; It. *lasciare*, Sp. *dejar*, Fr. *laisser*, E. *to lease*]

lana *n. fem.* wool: *obl. sg.* **laina** 13.7, **lan'** 26.35. [CL LĀNAM *FEW* 5: 149; It. *lana*, Sp. *lana*, Fr. *laine*]

lancan *adv.* in the time when, when: *lanqan* 15.1. [= **l'an can** 'in the year when' (VL ILLUM ANNUM QUANDO *FEW* 24: 624)]

landa *n. fem.* plain: *nom. sg.* **landa** 19.13. [Ctc. **landa FEW* 5: 159; It. *landa*, Fr. *lande*, E. *lawn*]

lansa *n. fem.* lance: *obl. pl.* **lansas** 25.3. [CL (perhaps from Ctc.) LANCĔAM *FEW* 5: 153; It. *lancia*, Sp. *lanza*, Fr. *lance*, E. *lance*]

larc *adj.* generous: *masc., obl. sg.* **larc** 6.27, 21.5. [CL LĂRGUM *FEW* 5: 188; It. *largo*, Sp. *largo*, Fr. *large*, E. *large*]

las (1) *personal pron., 3rd person, fem., obl. pl.* 17.31, 17.34, 18.19, 18.20, 18.23, 18.23, *see* **el** (1).

las (2) *def. art. fem., pl.* 5.6 var., 5.11, 11.61, 11.77, 17.47, 18.2 var., 18.17, 24.18, 25.2, 25.3, 25.6, 25.10, 25.21, 25.38, 25.39, 25.40, 25.50, 25.71,

25.72, 25.90, 25.97, 25.98, 25.99, 25.104, 27.16 var., 30.6, 31.37, 32.4, see **lo** (2).

las (3) *adj.* weary 12.62; **ai las** alas! 4.23, 18.9, 30.71, 30.90: *masc., obl. pl.* **las** 12.62. [CL ᴌᴀ̆ssuᴍ *FEW* 5: 196; It. *lasso,* Sp. *laso,* Fr. *las,* E. *lassitude, alas!*]

latiṇ *n. masc.* Latin *(contrasted with vernacular)* 10.24; language 8.3; words 8.25, 9.9: *obl. sg.* **latin** 10.24; **lati** 8.3, 8.25, 9.9. [CL ᴌᴀ̆ᴛīɴuᴍ *FEW* 5: 199; It. *latino,* Sp. *latino, latín, ladino,* Fr. *latin,* E. *Latin*]

latz (1) *n. masc.* trap, snare: *obl. sg.* **latz** 14.48. [CL ᴌᴀǫuᴇus *FEW* 5: 180; It. *laccio,* Sp. *lazo,* Fr. *lacs,* E. *lace*]

latz (2) *n. masc.* direction: *obl. pl.* **latz** 20.30. [CL ᴌᴀ̆ᴛus *FEW* 5: 205; It. *lato,* Sp. *lado,* Fr. *lé* 'breadth']

lau (1) *n. masc.* 17.12, *see* **laus.**

lau (2) *vb. trans.* 24.7, *see* **lauzar.**

laus *n. masc.* praise: *obl. sg.* **laus** 12.59, **lau** 17.12. [CL ᴌᴀuᴅᴇᴍ *FEW* 5: 210; It. *lode,* Sp. *loa;* cf. E. *laudatory*]

lausar *see* **lauzar.**

lausor, lausors *see* **lauzor.**

lauza, lauzada *see* **lauzar.**

lauzadǫr *n. masc.* one who praises; **eser lauzaire** to praise 2.18: *nom. sg.* **lauzaire** 2.18. [CL ᴌᴀuᴅᴀ̆ᴛōʀᴇᴍ acc., ᴌᴀuᴅᴀ̆ᴛoʀ nom. *FEW* 5: 207; It. *lodatore,* Fr. *loueur*]

lauzar *vb. trans.* to praise 1.6, 13.50, 23.7, 24.7; to thank 31.33; to advise 16.35, 19.22, 19.35: *pres. 1st sg.* **lau** 24.7, *3rd sg.* **lauza** 16.35, *2nd pl.* **lauzatz** 19.22, 19.35; *pret. 1st sg.* **lauzi** 31.33, *3rd sg.* **lauzet** 1.6; *pp., fem., obl. sg.* **lauzada** 13.50; *inf.* **lausar** 23.7. [CL ᴌᴀuᴅᴀ̄ʀᴇ *FEW* 5: 207; It. *lodare,* Sp. *loar,* Fr. *louer*]

lauzẹta *n. fem.* lark: *obl. sg.* **lauzeta** 18.1. [**alauza** (Ctc. *alauda FEW* 1: 58) + **-eta**; by aphaeresis **l'alauzeta** > **la lauzeta**; cf. 18.1 note; Fr. *alouette*]

lauzi *see* **lauzar.**

lauzǫr *n. fem.* praise 5.10, 29.22; fame 21.51; *nom. sg.* **lausors** 21.51; *obl. sg.* **lauzor** 29.22, **lausor** 5.10. [**laus** + **-or**]

lavadǫr *n. masc.* washing place: *obl. sg.* **lavador** 12.6, 12.15, 12.24, 12.33, 12.42, 12.51, 12.60, 12.69. [CL ᴌᴀ̆ᴠᴀ̆ᴛōʀĭuᴍ *FEW* 5: 216; It. *lavatoio,* Sp. *lavadero,* Fr. *lavoir,* E. *lavatory*]

lavar *vb. trans.* to wash: *inf.* **lavar** 12.10, 12.13, *substantivized* **al . . . lavar** for washing 30.4. [CL ᴌᴀ̆ᴠᴀ̄ʀᴇ *FEW* 5: 219; It. *lavare,* Sp. *lavar,* Fr. *laver,* E. *to lave*]

lay *see* **lai.**

layssat *see* **laisar.**

le *def. art., masc., nom. sg., see* **lo** (2).

lecai *adj.* covetous: *masc., obl. sg.* **lechai** 15.43. [**lec** 'greedy' (**lecar**) + **-ai**]

lecar *vb. trans.* to lick: *pres. 3rd sg.* **lecha** 14.29. [Frankish *lekkōn FEW* 16: 462; It. *leccare,* Fr. *lécher,* E. *to lick*]

lechai *see* **lecai.**

lẹga *n. fem.* league, a measure of distance *(Modern Fr.* lieue kilométrique = *4 kilometers):* *obl. sg.* **lega** 14.51, **legu'** 14.51. [LL (from Ctc.) ᴌᴇuᴄᴀ *FEW* 5: 262; It. *lega,* Sp. *legua,* Fr. *lieue,* E. *league*]

legendier *adj.* who reads religious services: *masc., obl. pl.* **legendiers** 25.86. [**legenda** (CL ᴌᴇ̆ɢᴇ̆ɴᴅᴀ 'things to be read' *FEW* 5: 244) + **-ier**]

legu' *see* **lega.**

lẹi (1) *n. fem.* law, code of conduct 22.24; a law, a legislative proposal 11.61; law, the body of laws in effect 24.8: *obl. sg.* **lei** 22.24, 24.8; *obl. pl.* **leis** 11.61. [CL LĒGEM *FEW* 5: 293; It. *legge*, Sp. *ley*, Fr. *loi*; cf. E. *legal*]

lei (2) *personal pron., fem.* 16.16, *see* **el** (1).

leial *adj.* loyal: *fem., nom. sg.* **leiaus** 16.39. [CL LĒGĀLEM *FEW* 5: 241; It. *leale*, Sp. *leal*, Fr. *loyal*, E. *loyal*]

leis (1) 11.61, *see* **lei** (1).

leis (2) *personal pron., fem., obl. sg.* 1.3, 1.4, 3.4, 5.6, 30.63, *see* **el** (1).

lẹit *n. masc.* bed: *obl. sg.* **leit** 1.5, **lieig** 7.8. [CL LĔCTUM *FEW* 5: 239; It. *letto*, Sp. *lecho*, Fr. *lit*]

lẹn *adv.* slowly: **len** 16.48. [CL LĔNTUM *FEW* 5: 254; It. *lento*, Sp. *lento*, Fr. *lent*]

lẹnga *n. fem.* tongue: *obl. sg.* **lengu'** 26.1. [CL LĬNGŬAM *FEW* 5: 364; It. *lingua*, Sp. *lengua*, Fr. *langue*; cf. E. *linguist*]

lẹra *n. fem.* lyre, stringed instrument: *obl. sg.* **lera** 14.35. [CL LȲRAM *FEW* 5: 483; It. *lira*, Sp. *lira*, Fr. *lyre*, E. *lyre*]

les *def. art. masc., obl. pl.* 25.35, *see* **lo** (2).

lẹtra *n. fem.* letter, Scripture: *nom. sg.* **letra** 14.69. [CL LĬTTĔRAM *FEW* 5: 379; It. *lettera*, Sp. *letra*, Fr. *lettre*, E. *letter*]

lẹu *adv.* easily: **leu** 26.14; **a leu** easily 19.52. [CL LĔVEM *FEW* 5: 290; It. *lieve*, Sp. *leve*]

leugier *adj.* frivolous: *masc., obl. pl.* **leugiers** 29.20; *fem., nom. sg.* **leugeira** 28.69; *obl. sg.* **leugeyra** 19.42. [VL *LĔVĬĀRĬUM *FEW* 5: 289; It. *leggiero*, Sp. *ligero*, Fr. *léger*]

leumẹn *adv.* easily: 26.52. [**leu** + **-men**]

levar *vb. trans.* to raise 30.54; to exalt 13.51; *refl.* to be raised (*of a siege*), to be ended 25.101: *pres. 3rd sg.* **leva** 25.101; *pret. 3rd sg.* **levet** 30.54; *past subj. 3rd sg.* **leves** 30.54 ms.; *pp., fem., obl. sg.* **levada** 13.51. [CL LĔVĀRE *FEW* 5: 284; It. *levare*, Sp. *llevar*, Fr. *lever*; cf. E. *levy*]

lezọr *n. fem.* opportunity: *obl. sg.* **lezor** 12.13. [**lezer** 'permission' (CL LĬCĒRE *FEW* 5: 310) + **-or**]

lh' (1) *personal pron., proclitic, masc., dat. sg.* 25.60, *see* **el** (1).

·lh (2) *def. art., enclitic, fem., nom. sg.* 16.32 var., *see* **lo** (2).

·lhs *def. art., enclitic, masc., obl. pl.* 25.71, *see* **lo** (2).

li (1) *personal pron., 3rd person unstressed dat., masc. or fem.* 3.7, 3.8, 3.11, 4.3, 5.4, 5.11, 6.5, 6.29, 7.6, 9.35, 10.8, 10.15, 10.22, 10.36, 11.42, 11.70, 14.68, 15.22, 18.4, 18.38, 18.52, 24.16, 25.72, 27.6, 30.71, 31.11, *see* **el** (1).

li (2) *def. art. masc., nom. pl., or fem., nom. sg.* 4.7, 4.16, 4.25, 4.34, 4.43, 6.23, 6.23, 6.34, 6.34, 8.2, 8.2, 10.15, 11.18, 12.22, 12.64, 14.3, 15.1, 18.46, 21.70, 25.97, 26.25, 30.11, *see* **lo** (2).

li (3) *adv.* there 15.22. [CL ILLĪC *FEW* 4: 599; It. *lì*, Sp. *allí*]

lïar *vb. trans.* to sew: *pp., masc., obl. pl.* **lïatz** 26.45; *substantivized inf., masc., nom. sg.* **lïars** sewing (of shoes) 26.46. [CL LĪGĀRE *FEW* 5: 330; It. *legare*, Sp. *liar*, Fr. *lier*]

libertat *n. fem.* liberty: *obl. sg.* **libertat** 32.18. [CL LĪBĔRTĀTEM *FEW* 5: 305; It. *libertà*, Sp. *libertad*, Fr. *liberté*, E. *liberty*]

libre *n. masc.* book: *obl. sg.* **libre** 30.44. [CL LĪBRUM *FEW* 5: 298; It. *libro*, Sp. *libro*, Fr. *livre*; cf. E. *library*]

licẹncia *n. fem.* permission: *obl. sg.* **licencia** 11.19. [CL LĬCĔNTĬAM *FEW* 5: 311; It. *licenza*, Sp. *licencia*, Fr. *license*, E. *license*]

lieig *see* leit.

lieis, lies, liey, lieys *see* el (1).

ligna *see* linhar.

linha *n. fem.* straight line: *nom. sg.* linha 14.23. [CL LĪNĔAM *FEW* 5: 354; Sp. *liña*, Fr. *ligne*, E. *line*]

linhar *vb. trans.* to put in a line: *pres. 3rd sg.* ligna 14.20 var. [linha + -ar (2)]

linhatge *n. masc.* lineage, family: *obl. sg.* linhatje 12.37. [linha + -atge]

liuranda *n. fem.* food, victuals: *obl. sg.* liuranda 20.11. [liurar 'to deliver' (CL LĪBĔRĀRE *FEW* 5: 303; Fr. *livrer*) + -anda]

liurazon *n. fem.* allowance, supply: *obl. sg.* liurazon 20.10. [CL LĪBĔRĀTĬŌNEM 'release' *FEW* 5: 303; Fr. *livraison*]

·ll (1) *personal pron., unstressed, enclitic* 11.6, 11.9, *see* el (1).

ll', ·ll (2) *def. art., proclitic or enclitic* 17.13, 26.10, *see* lo (2).

lo (1) *personal pron., 3rd person, masc., obl. sg.* 1.4, 1.5, 1.7, 3.7, 3.7, 3.7, 3.7, 5.11, 6.11, 9.15, 10.20, 11.27, 11.49, 11.64, 11.71, 18.36, 18.50, 19.2, 19.35, 19.56, 19.66, 20.26, 21.13, 22.16, 24.22, 25.88, *see* el (1).

lo (2) *def. art.* the; *deictic nuance* this 25.1; *possessive nuance* my 2.1, 4.31, 7.22, 9.47, 9.48, 10.37, 16.2, 16.3, your 23.32, 25.2, his 14.48, 18.2 var. (= sas 18.2), 27.16 var. (= sas 27.16), 25.59; *exclamatory* what! 25.93.

Introducing inf. al mas lavar for washing hands 30.4, al murir when he dies 12.27, al partir when you depart 13.55; *with proper name* ·l Folcautz 25.37; *with possessive adj.* lo mieu 27.10, 31.27, al mieu 17.23, del mieu 31.12, ·l sieus 25.36, lo seus 5.4, del sieu 2.27, ·l son 10.12, al son 1.5, lo nostre 9.33, 11.46, la soa 3.3, la nostr' 8.13, la vostra 13.24, 28.14, la lur 26.33, la . . . lor 29.39, las mias 11.77, las soas 5.6 var. (= soas 5.6); *with possessive pron.* lo mieus 23.43, los teus 25.84, los sieus 27.11, lo vostre 23.35, lo lor 26.34.

Expressions tut li plusor many men 10.15, tug . . . li pluzor everyone 12.22; l'us . . . l'autre the one . . . the other 11.10, 13.63, 19.11, 27.22.

Forms: Masc., nom. sg. lo 5.4, 5.4, 5.8, 5.13, 5.16, 6.3, 9.28 var., 10.9, 11.58, 11.62, 11.64, 11.71, 12.0, 12.5, 12.23, 12.72, 13.88, 15.51, 16.2, 16.40, 16.50, 17.21, 17.23, 18.8, 18.48, 19.15, 20.33, 21.11, 21.44, 21.53, 22.2, 22.9, 23.43, 24.19, 25.13, 25.15, 25.39, 25.40, 25.45, 25.50, 25.54, 25.59, 25.62, 25.108, 29.0, 32.1; le 24.16, 25.55, 25.55 var., 30.5, 30.32, 30.83; *proclitic* l' 11.69, 13.63, 15.7, 16.23, 19.11, 19.11, 24.28, 25.26, 25.58, 25.76, 25.87, 25.87, 27.22, 27.22, 30.40, 31.36; *enclitic* ·l 4.5, 4.31, 4.39, 5.5, 5.7, 5.14, 8.17, 9.22, 9.27, 9.27, 9.50, 10.14, 11.10, 11.10, 11.36, 12.28, 13.13, 13.81, 14.47, 15.26, 15.41, 18.34, 18.54, 19.15, 20.31, 20.36, 21.65, 22.9, 22.18, 24.14, 24.19, 24.20, 24.20, 24.35, 25.4, 25.4, 25.11, 25.28, 25.35, 25.36, 25.37, 25.39, 25.39, 25.40, 25.42, 25.59, 25.60, 25.73, 25.82, 25.87, 25.95, 25.97, 25.101, 25.108, 25.108, 26.19, 27.27, 29.24, 31.39; ·ls *used as nom. sg.* 25.98, 25.98, 25.99, 25.99.

Obl. sg. lo 1.2, 2.15, 3.6, 3.7, 3.8, 3.9, 4.8, 4.17, 4.26, 4.35, 4.44, 5.2, 5.2, 8.4, 9.33, 9.50, 10.31, 11.16, 11.28, 11.35, 11.46, 11.53, 11.74, 11.74, 12.2, 12.55, 14.15, 15.29, 16.20, 16.22, 17.4, 17.5, 17.8, 17.21, 17.24, 17.36, 18.14, 19.7, 20.12, 21.47, 21.76, 22.32, 22.45, 22.52, 23.32, 23.32, 23.35, 24.38, 25.2, 25.17, 25.53, 25.70, 25.75, 25.86, 25.107, 26.34, 27.10, 27.38, 27.47, 29.6, 29.33, 30.70, 30.86, 30.96, 30.97, 31.27,

31.30, 31.33, 32.18; *proclitic* **l'** 1.6, 2.1, 2.1, 3.9, 5.15, 11.37, 11.44, 11.60, 12.58, 13.1, 13.38, 13.63, 13.75, 14.21, 15.23, 20.32, 24.31, 25.52, 25.70, 28.1, 28.56, 29.0, 29.7, 30.30, 30.36, 31.7, 31.19, 32.12; *enclitic* **·l** 1.6, 2.21, 2.23, 8.14, 8.15, 8.17, 8.18, 8.30, 9.37, 9.42, 9.45, 9.60, 9.68, 9.72, 10.12, 11.17, 12.2, 12.25, 12.58, 15.38, 16.7, 16.7, 16.20, 16.52, 16.54, 17.8, 18.2, 18.54, 20.13, 21.4, 21.46, 21.46, 21.56, 21.75, 22.51, 23.23, 23.48, 24.31, 24.32, 25.16, 25.53, 25.67, 25.72, 25.80, 26.18, 27.7, 30.39, 30.41, 30.67, 30.80, 30.89; **·ll** 26.10. **al** (= **a** [2] + **lo**) 1.5, 3.11, 4.13, 4.13, 5.14, 9.48, 9.67, 11.41, 11.60, 12.15, 12.24, 12.27, 12.33, 12.47, 12.65, 12.69, 12.72 var., 13.38, 13.55, 13.59, 14.9, 14.48, 17.23, 18.4, 21.14 var., 21.40, 21.56 var., 25.29, 27.2, 29.23, 30.1, 30.4, 32.4. **al** (= **ab** + **lo**) 8.16. **dal** 16.2, 16.3. **del** 1.7, 2.27, 3.3, 3.5, 3.6, 3.7, 3.7, 4.31, 5.1, 5.2, 7.22, 8.1, 8.4, 9.47, 10.10, 10.23, 11.45, 12.35, 12.37, 12.38, 12.42, 12.47, 12.56, 12.70, 12.72, 12.72, 13.10, 14.18, 14.32, 16.53, 17.1, 17.2, 17.35, 19.29, 19.43, 20.4, 21.56, 21.78, 24.24, 25.23, 25.59, 25.80, 26.19, 26.28, 27.2, 27.8, 29.23, 29.28, 29.38, 31.12, 32.4, 32.13, 32.15, 32.15, 32.16; **dels** *used as obl. sg.* 25.53.

Nom. pl. **li** 6.23, 6.23, 6.34, 6.34, 8.2, 8.2, 10.15, 11.18, 12.22, 12.64, 14.3, 15.1, 18.46, 21.70, 25.97; **los** *used as nom. pl.* 32.14, 32.14, 32.15; *proclitic* **l'** 26.56; **ll'** 17.13; *enclitic* **·l** 5.11, 12.46; **·ls** *used as nom. pl.* 25.20, 25.98, 25.98, 25.99, 25.99, 25.105.

Obl. pl. **los** 6.15, 9.38, 9.38, 11.15, 11.65, 11.66, 12.44, 12.50, 12.52, 12.57, 21.37, 25.7, 25.9, 25.20, 25.38, 25.78, 25.84, 25.91, 25.92, 25.92, 25.100, 25.101, 25.103, 25.104, 26.31, 27.11, 27.25, 30.87, 32.5, 32.5, 32.5, 32.5; **lo** *before* **s-** 13.42; **les** 25.35; *enclitic* **·lhs** 25.71; **·ls** 2.14, 12.25 var., 12.50, 12.61, 16.7, 19.15 var., 23.28, 25.7, 25.10, 25.21, 25.25, 25.33, 25.44, 25.46, 25.46, 25.57, 25.63, 25.71, 25.78, 25.102, 25.103, 25.104, 25.104, 27.47. **als** (= **a** [2] + **los**) 1.2, 9.24, 25.1, 25.31, 25.32, 25.32, 29.16, 30.42; **al** *used as obl. pl.* 25.86. **als** (= **ab** + **los**) 23.28. **dels** 15.13, 20.8, 20.18, 20.23, 21.15, 21.15, 24.18, 25.3, 25.3, 25.16, 25.40, 25.53, 25.98, 27.8, 27.32, 29.27.

Fem., nom. sg. **la** 1.6, 3.5, 3.8, 4.5, 5.9, 8.13, 9.19, 11.40, 13.11, 13.24, 13.25, 13.39, 13.53, 13.67, 13.84, 14.69, 15.41, 25.4, 25.26, 25.42, 25.67, 25.69, 26.33, 28.14, 28.45, 31.25, 32.2; **li** 4.7, 4.16, 4.25, 4.34, 4.43, 26.25, 30.11; *proclitic* **l'** 5.7, 16.30, 25.42; *enclitic* **·lh** 16.32 var.; **·l** 12.32, 16.32, 24.19, 30.43.

Obl. sg. **la** 1.2, 1.4, 1.5, 1.6, 1.7, 1.7, 1.7, 2.12, 3.3, 3.4, 3.6, 3.7, 3.11, 4.2, 5.6, 5.6, 5.8, 5.10, 5.16, 6.33, 8.1, 8.11, 8.14, 8.16, 8.16, 8.18, 8.30, 9.3, 9.49, 9.59, 9.69, 10.12, 10.32, 10.37, 11.23, 11.36, 11.54, 11.65, 12.17, 12.25, 12.42, 13.8, 13.16, 13.31, 13.38 var., 13.42, 13.56, 13.75, 13.77, 13.79 var., 13.81, 13.89, 13.90, 13.91 var., 13.92 var., 14.2, 14.13, 14.14, 14.15, 14.32, 14.33, 14.36, 16.7, 17.6, 17.11, 17.14, 18.1, 18.4, 18.48, 20.20, 20.21, 21.60, 21.77, 22.42, 24.41, 25.5, 25.25, 25.47, 25.54, 25.58, 25.61, 25.80, 25.91, 25.93, 25.100, 25.105, 25.109, 26.5, 26.9, 26.17, 26.40, 26.43, 27.5, 28.1, 28.65, 29.39, 30.11, 30.12, 30.16, 30.31, 30.33, 30.65, 30.84, 30.97, 31.31, 31.32, 31.44, 32.9, 32.9, 32.10; *proclitic* **l'** 3.1, 4.9, 4.18, 4.27, 4.36, 4.45, 5.6, 12.34, 12.70, 13.28, 15.30, 15.39, 17.33, 18.42, 19.21, 19.23, 19.41, 19.51, 24.27, 25.14, 25.102, 28.12, 28.54, 30.6, 30.30, 31.45, 32.17, 32.17. **del** 19.54 (see note).

Nom. pl. **las** 5.11, 17.47, 25.39, 25.97, 25.98, 25.99.

Obl. pl. **las** 5.6 var., 11.61, 11.77, 18.2 var., 18.17, 24.18, 25.2, 25.3,

25.6, 25.10, 25.21, 25.38, 25.50, 25.71, 25.72, 25.90, 25.104, 27.16 var.,
30.6, 31.37, 32.4; **la** *used as obl. pl.* 25.25, 25.40.
[CL ĭLLUM *FEW* 4: 554; It. *lo*, Sp. *lo*, Fr. *le*]

lọc *n. masc.* place; **en luoc de** as 7.22 (see note): *obl. sg.* **loc** 13.21, 21.14,
29.28, 31.16, **luec** 4.13 (see note), 15.40 var., **luoc** 7.22, 15.40 var., **luc**
30.98; *obl. pl.* **locs** 13.82, 15.40. [CL LŏCUM *FEW* 5: 395; It. *luogo*, Fr.
lieu; cf. E. *local*]

lochar *vb. intrans.* to delay: *pres. 3rd sg.* **locha** 30.66. [CL LŭCTĀRĪ *FEW* 5:
439; It. *lottare*, Sp. *luchar*, Fr. *lutter*; cf. E. *reluctant*]

locs *see* **loc**.

logadier *n. masc.* mercenary, salaried foot soldier: *obl. pl.* **logadiers**
25.32. [**logat** (pp. of **logar** vb. trans. 'to pay') + **-ier**]

logar *vb. intrans.* to lodge, to put up: *pp., masc., nom. sg.* **logatz** 31.2. [CL
LŏCĀRE *FEW* 5: 389; Fr. *louer*]

loignor *see* **lonhor**.

loindas *see* **lonhdan**.

loing *see* **lonh**.

loingnes *see* **lonhar**.

lọnc (1) *adj.* long *(in time)* 5.7, 5.12, 15.1, 15.40 var., 17.40, 23.20; **tot al**
lòng de all along 32.4: *masc., obl. sg.* **lonc** 5.7, 5.12, 23.20, **lòng** 32.4;
nom. pl. **lonc** 15.1; *obl. pl.* **loncs** 15.40 var.; *fem., obl. sg.* **longa** 17.40.
[CL LŏNGUM *FEW* 5: 406; It. *lungo*, Fr. *long*, E. *long*]

lọnc (2) *prep.* beside. *Forms:* **lonc** 13.75, 26.50; **lont** 26.50 var., **loncs**
26.50 var. [**lonc** (1) with optional **-s**; *FEW* 5: 407]

loncs (1) 15.40 var., *see* **lonc** (1).

loncs (2) 26.50 var., *see* **lonc** (2)

lòng, longa *see* **lonc** (1).

lọnh, lọnh *adv.* far. *Forms:* **loing** 10.40, 15.2, 15.4, 15.9, 15.11, 15.16,
15.18, 15.23, 15.25, 15.30, 15.32, 15.37, 15.39, 15.44, 15.46, 19.4 var.,
luenh 29.26. [CL LŏNGĒ *FEW* 5: 405; It. *lungi*, Fr. *loin*]

lonhar *vb. refl.* to go far from: *past subj. 3rd sg.* **loingnes** 5.9. [**long** + **-ar**
(2)]

lonhdaṇ *adj.* from far away: *masc., nom. sg.* **loindas** 15.27. [VL
*LŏNGĪTĀNUM *FEW* 5: 406; It. *lontano*, Fr. *lointain*]

lonhọr *comp. adj.* longer: *fem., obl. sg.* **loignor** 17.41, 20.1. [CL LŏNGĬŌREM
FEW 5: 406]

lont *see* **lonc** (2).

lọr (1) *personal pron., 3rd person, dat. pl., masc. or fem., or obl. pl.* 9.71,
11.55, 11.57, 17.28, 17.31, 17.47, 18.18, 20.15, 20.15, 24.39, 25.1, 25.5,
25.7, 25.43, *see* **el** (1). [**lor** (2)]

lọr (2) *possessive adj., normally invariable* their; *possessive adj. with def.*
art. **la . . . lor** 29.39, **la lur** 26.33; *possessive pron. with def. art.* **lo lor**
26.34.
    Forms: masc., nom. sg. **lur** 19.12; *obl. sg.* **lor** 8.3, 8.25, 11.77, 26.34,
lur 9.21, 26.47, 30.9; *obl. pl.* **lor** 20.29, 22.10, **lurs** 26.24; *fem., nom. sg.*
lor 5.7, **lur** 26.33; *obl. sg.* **lor** 17.34, 29.39, 31.41, **lur** 9.44, 26.37, 30.7.
    [CL ĭLLŌRUM gen. pl. 'of them' *FEW* 4: 551; It. *loro*, Fr. *leur*]

los (1) *personal pron., 3rd person, unstressed, masc., obl. pl.* 27.12, 27.29,
27.48 var., *see* **el** (1). [CL ĭLLŌS, Sp. *los*, Fr. *les*]

los (2) *def. art. masc., obl. pl.* 6.15, 9.38, 9.38, 11.15, 11.65, 11.66, 12.44,
12.50, 12.52, 12.57, 21.37, 25.7, 25.9, 25.20, 25.38, 25.78, 25.84, 25.91,

25.92, 25.92, 25.100, 25.101, 25.103, 25.104, 26.31, 27.11, 27.25, 30.87, 32.5, 32.5, 32.5, 32.5, 32.14, 32.14, 32.15, *see* **lo** (2). [**los** (1)]

losc *adj.* one-eyed: *fem., nom. sg.* **losca** 14.56. [CL LŪSCUM *FEW* 5: 474; It. *losco*, Sp. *lusco*, Fr. *louche*]

·ls (1) *personal pron., enclitic, masc., obl. pl.* 20.28, 21.24, 21.25, 25.14, 25.90, 26.30, 27.40, 27.48, *see* **el** (1). [**los** (1)]

·ls (2) *def. art., enclitic, masc., obl. pl.* 2.14, 12.25 var., 12.50, 12.61, 16.7, 19.15 var., 23.28, 25.7, 25.10, 25.20, 25.21, 25.25, 25.33, 25.44, 25.46, 25.46, 25.57, 25.63, 25.71, 25.78, 25.98, 25.98, 25.99, 25.99, 25.102, 25.103, 25.104, 25.104, 25.105, 27.47, *see* **lo** (2). [**los** (1)]

luc, luec *see* **loc.**

luenh *see* **lonh.**

lugor *n. fem.* light: *obl. sg.* **lugor** 29.43. [LL LŪCŌREM *FEW* 5: 437; Fr. *lueur*]

lui *personal pron.* 3rd person, *dat. or obl., masc.* 1.7, 5.4, 5.6, 5.8, 5.12, 5.14 var., 5.16, 6.7, 6.31, 6.32, 7.12, 10.36 var., 11.25, 11.48, 11.51, 19.65 var., 25.56, 30.22, 30.27, *see* **el** (1). [CL ĬLLĪ dat. + CŬĬ 'to whom' dat. *FEW* 4: 554]

luna *n. fem.* moon, time: *obl. sg.* **luna** 14.62. [CL LŪNAM *FEW* 5: 451; It. *luna*, Sp. *luna*, Fr. *lune*; cf. E. *lunatic*]

lunhs *see* **nul.**

luoc *see* **loc.**

lur (1) *personal pron., 3rd person, masc. or fem., dat. pl.* 9.7, 9.9, 26.19, 26.36, *see* **el** (1). [**lor** (2)]

lur (2) *possessive adj.* 9.21, 9.44, 19.12, 26.33, 26.37, 26.47, 30.7, 30.9, *see* **lor** (2).

lurs *possessive adj., see* **lor** (2).

lus *personal pron., see* el (1). [**los** (1)]

lutz *n. fem.* light: *obl. sg.* **luz** 30.62. [CL LŪCEM *FEW* 5: 479; It. *luce*, Sp. *luz*]

luxurios *adj.* lecherous: *nom. pl.* **luxurios** 12.46. [CL LŬXŬRĬŌSUM *FEW* 5: 481; It. *lussurioso*, Sp. *lujurioso*, Fr. *luxurieux*, E. *luxurious*]

luy *personal pron., see* **el** (1). [**lui**]

luz *see* **lutz.**

·lz *personal pron., enclitic, see* **el** (1). [**los** (1)]

m' (1) *personal pron., see* **me.**

m' (2) *possessive adj. fem.* 7.6, 7.15, 9.71, 10.14, 22.3, 27.36, 28.18, *see* **mon** (2).

ma *see* **mon** (2).

mai (1) *n. masc.* the month of May: *obl. sg.* **mai** 15.1. [CL MĂĬUM *FEW* 6, part 1: 64; It. *maggio*, Sp. *mayo*, Fr. *mai*, E. *May*]

mai (2) *adv.* 18.26, 26.39, 28.33, 32.5, *see* **mais.**

maichelas *see* **maisela.**

mainada *n. fem.* troop of men owing military service to a lord: *obl. pl.* **mainadas** 25.21. [VL *MĂNSĬŌNĀTAM *FEW* 6, part 1: 249; It. *masnada*, Sp. *mesnada*, OFr. *maisniee*]

mainadier *n. masc.* leader or member of a **mainada**: *obl. pl.* **mainaders** 25.31. [**mainada** + **-ier**]

maint *adj.* many a: *masc., obl. sg.* **maint** 21.35, **maing** 23.23; *obl. pl.* **mains** 1.3, **mans** 13.82; *fem., obl. sg.* **manta** 14.3; *obl. pl.* **maintas** 6.15, **mantas** 5.12. [Germ. *manigiθδ *FEW* 16: 514, OFr. *maint*]

maion *see* **maizon.**

maire *n. fem.* mother: *obl. sg.* **maire** 21.4, **mayre** 13.31; *vocative sg.* **maires** 29.45. [CL MĂTREM *FEW* 6, part 1: 477; It. *madre*, Sp. *madre*, Fr. *mère*; cf. E. *maternal*]

mais *adv.* but 9.53, 10.26, 10.30, 11.26 var., 11.38, 12.19, 13.40, 13.68, 13.78, 14.26, 15.17, 15.21, 15.31, 15.47, 15.50, 16.11, 16.16, 16.48, 17.21, 19.20, 19.21, 19.44, 19.56, 19.58, 19.67, 22.30, 22.45, 23.21, 25.8, 25.10, 25.45, 25.52, 25.97, 25.103, 25.106, 26.27, 26.39, 27.19, 28.30, 28.48, 30.60, 30.64, 30.66, 30.88, 31.11, 31.13, 31.20, 31.30, 31.32, 31.38; anything but 6.24; rather 21.26; more 6.9, 9.59, 17.9, 17.18, 23.48, 24.11, 24.12, 28.33, 28.58, 29.20; longer 21.16; again 17.11, 19.64; since 19.5 var., 20.15 var., 25.84, 29.11, 29.16; and 32.5; **mais de** more 16.13, 27.26, more than 9.51, 19.34, most 23.36.

In negative contexts except 17.39, 23.35, 23.40; **mais que** except that, but 9.9; **mais can** except for 9.30; **mais car** except that 18.56; **plus . . . mais** more . . . than 24.44.

With negatives **mais** (. . .) **non** never 4.32, no longer 10.3, 20.16, 23.34; **non . . . mais** no . . . but 14.41, nothing but 18.16, only 13.28, 16.20, never 17.25, no longer 10.30, 22.50; **anc mais . . . non** never 30.52, **non . . . anc mai** never even 18.26; **ja** (. . .) **mais** (. . .) **non** never 3.10, 4.11, 15.8, 18.18, 18.36, 20.27, 21.60, 22.11, 23.9, 25.27, 25.85; **per totz temps mais** for evermore 21.2; **re mais** (. . .) **non** nothing else 16.43, 30.25; **voler mais** to prefer 9.59, 19.28, 29.20.

Forms: **mais** 3.10, 4.11, 4.32, 6.9, 9.59, 10.3, 10.26, 10.30, 15.8, 16.13, 16.20, 16.43, 16.48, 17.9, 17.11, 17.18, 17.21, 17.25, 17.39, 18.18, 18.36, 20.16, 20.27, 21.2, 21.16, 21.60, 22.11, 23.9, 23.34, 23.36, 24.11, 24.12, 24.30, 25.27, 25.85, 27.26, 28.48, 28.58, 29.20, 30.25, 30.52, 30.88; **mai** 18.26, 26.39, 28.33, 32.5; **mas** 6.24, 9.9, 9.30, 9.53, 10.30, 11.26, 11.38, 12.19, 13.78, 14.26, 14.41, 15.17, 15.21, 15.31, 15.47, 15.50, 16.11, 16.16, 18.16, 18.56, 19.5 var., 19.20, 19.21, 19.44, 19.58, 20.15 var., 21.26, 22.30, 22.45, 23.21, 23.35, 23.40, 24.44, 25.8, 25.10, 25.45, 25.52, 25.84, 25.97, 25.103, 25.106, 26.27, 27.19, 28.30, 29.11, 29.16, 30.60, 30.64, 30.66, 31.11, 31.13, 31.20, 31.30, 31.32, 31.38; **may** 19.28, 19.34, 19.56; **mays** 9.51, 13.28, 13.40, 13.68, 19.64, 19.67; **mos** 23.48.

[CL MĂGIS *FEW* 6, part 1: 31; It. *mai*, Sp. *más*, Fr. *mais*]

maisęla *n. fem.* jaw: *obl. pl.* **maichelas** 25.72. [CL MAXĬLLAM, VL *MAXĔLLAM *FEW* 6, part 1: 560; It. *mascella*, Sp. *mejilla*, OFr. *maissele*]

maïstria *n. fem.* skill: *obl. sg.* **maïstria** 26.45. [**maïstre** 'master' (CL MĂGĬSTRUM *FEW* 6, part 1: 42) + **-ia**]

maizǫn *n. fem.* house: *obl. sg.* **maison** 1.7 var., **mason** 1.7 var., **maion** 1.7. [CL MĂNSĬŌNEM *FEW* 6, part 1: 248; Sp. *mesón* 'inn,' Fr. *maison*, E. *mansion*]

majǫr *comparative adj.* greater: *masc., obl. sg.* **major** 3.5. [CL MAĬŌREM *FEW* 6, part 1: 59; It. *maggiore*, Sp. *mayor*, Fr. *majeur*, E. *major*]

mal (1) *n. masc.* harm 10.8, 10.15, 14.68, 16.11, 17.19, 19.15, 27.44, 25.108; hurt 9.66, 23.8, 23.42, 28.26; nasty gossip 6.13; **aver mal** to have harm, to suffer 15.32, 27.41; **colre en mal** to take amiss 11.50; **mal traire** to suffer 2.15; **saiar a mal** to test by hurting 23.42.

Forms: nom. sg. **mals** 14.68, 19.15, 25.108, **maus** 16.11; *obl. sg.* **mal** 2.15, 6.13, 9.66, 10.8, 10.15, 11.50, 17.19, 23.8, 23.42, 27.41, 27.44, 28.26; *obl. pl.* **mals** 15.32. [**mal** (2)]

mal (2) *adj.* bad 11.21, 14.71, 31.6; wicked 3.3, 14.43, 17.35, 27.7; mean 9.46, 23.4; poor, unskilled 26.46; **mala merce** ill favor, unfriendly reception 18.53.

    Forms: masc., nom. sg. **mals** 3.3, 26.46; *obl. sg.* **mal** 9.46, 14.43, 17.35, 23.4, 27.7; *nom. pl.* **mal** 11.21; *fem., nom. sg.* **mal'** 14.71; *obl. sg.* **mala** 18.53; *obl. pl.* **malas** 31.6.

    [CL ᴍᴀ̆ʟᴜᴍ *FEW* 6, part 1: 127; It. *malo,* Sp. *malo,* Fr. *mal;* cf. E. *malevolent*]

mal (3) *adv.* badly, unwisely 11.7, 19.24; bad 18.29; wickedly 19.34 var.; scarcely 20.12, 28.70. [**mal** (2)]

malamęn *adv.* badly; **menar malament** to mistreat, to abuse 11.9. [**mal** (2) + **-amen** (2)]

malas *see* **mal** (2).

malastruc *adj.* ill-starred, unlucky: *masc., obl. sg.* **malastruc** 21.41. [**mal** (3) + **astre** 'star' (CL ᴀꜱᴛʀᴜᴍ *FEW* 1: 165) + **-uc**; Fr. *malotru*]

malautia *n. fem.* sickness: *nom. sg.* **malautia** 1.4. [**malaut** (CL ᴍᴀ̆ʟᴇ̆ ʜᴀ̆ʙɪ̆ᴛᴜᴍ *FEW* 6, part 1: 92) + **-ia**]

malavęch *n. masc.* discomfort: *nom. sg.* **malaveg** 9.65. [CL ᴍᴀ̆ʟᴇ̆ꜰɪ̆cɪ̆ᴜᴍ *FEW* 6, part 1: 86]

maldire *vb. trans.* to curse: *pp., masc., nom. sg.* **mauditz** 15.51. [**mal** (3) + **dire**)]

maligne *adj.* wicked, malignant; *masc., nom. sg.* **malignes** 25.95. [ChL ᴍᴀ̆ʟɪ̆ɢɴᴜᴍ *FEW* 6, part 1: 108; It. *maligno,* Sp. *maligno,* Fr. *malin;* cf. E. *malignant*]

mals (1) *n. masc.* 14.68, 15.32, 19.15, 25.108, *see* **mal** (1).

mals (2) *adj.* 3.3, 26.46, *see* **mal** (2).

maltalan *n. masc.* ill will: *obl. pl.* **maltalans** 22.10. [**mal** (2) + **talen**]

maltraire *n. masc.* suffering: *obl. sg.* **maltraire** 21.1. [**mal** (1) + **traire**]

malvatz (1) *n. masc.* bad man 14.6; fool 20.8, 20.9: *obl. sg.* **malvatz** 14.6, 20.9; *obl. pl.* **malvatz** 20.8. [**malvatz** (2)]

malvatz (2) *adj.* bad: *masc., obl. sg.* **malvatz** 22.46. [VL ᴍᴀ̆ʟɪ̆ꜰᴀ̄ᴛɪ̆ᴜᴍ *FEW* 6, part 1: 101; It. *malvagio,* Sp. *malvado,* Fr. *mauvais*]

malvestat *n. fem.* wickedness: *obl. sg.* **malvestat** 29.25. [**malvatz** (2) + **-tat**]

man (1) *n. masc.* command: *obl. pl.* **mans** 29.27. [**mandar**]

maṇ (2) *n. fem.* hand: *obl. pl.* **mans** 8.24, **mas** 30.4, 30.6. [CL ᴍᴀ̆ɴᴜᴍ *FEW* 6, part 1: 295; It. *mano,* Sp. *mano,* Fr. *main;* cf. E. *manual*]

man (3) *vb. trans.* 23.44, *see* **mandar**.

mana *n. fem.* manna, a substance miraculously provided as food for the Israelites (Exod. 16.31): *obl. sg.* **mana** 13.92 var., **mayna** 13.90. [LL (from Hebrew) ᴍᴀɴɴᴀ *FEW* 6, part 1: 233; It. *manna,* Sp. *maná,* Fr. *manne,* E. *manna*]

mandamęn *n. masc.* power, control: *obl. sg.* **mandamen** 11.18. [**mandar** + **-amen** (1)]

mandar *vb. trans.* to send 11.55, 19.15, 23.44; to govern 20.7; to declare 30.33; **mandar dire** to send to tell, to command 25.31: *pres. 1st sg.* **man** 23.44, *3rd sg.* **manda** 11.55, 19.15, 20.7, 25.31; *pret. 3rd sg.* **mandet** 30.33. [CL ᴍᴀ̆ɴᴅᴀ̄ʀᴇ *FEW* 6, part 1: 152; It. *mandare,* Sp. *mandar,* Fr. *mander;* cf. E. *mandate*]

mandet *see* **mandar**.

maneira *see* maniera.

mangem *see* manjar.

manier *adj.* tame: *fem., nom. sg.* manieyra 19.44. [LL MĂNŬĀRĬUM 'operated by hand' *FEW* 6, part 1: 281]

maniera *n. fem.* manner: *obl. sg.* maneira 28.4. [manier + -a; It. *maniera*, Sp. *manera*, Fr. *manière*, E. *manner*]

manieyra *see* manier.

manjar (1) *n. masc.* food 3.10; meal 26.27: *obl. sg.* manjar 3.10, 26.27. [manjar (2)]

manjar (2) *vb. trans.* to eat *passim*; to destroy 14.19: *pres. 3rd sg.* minha 14.19 (see note), *3rd pl.* manjo 26.18; *pres. subj. 1st pl.* mangem 26.9; *fut. 1st sg.* manjarai 3.10; *pp., masc., obl. sg.* manjat 3.8, 9.43, 32.18; *inf.* manjar 3.7, 9.25, 21.33, 26.15. [CL MĂNDŪCĀRE 'to chew' *FEW* 6, part 1: 176; It. *mangiare*, Sp. *manjar* n. 'food,' Fr. *manger*]

mans (1) *n. masc.* 29.27, *see* man (1).

mans (2) *n. fem.* 8.24, *see* man (2).

mans (3) *adj.* 13.82, *see* maint.

manta, mantas *see* maint.

manteingna *see* mantener.

mantel *n. masc.* cloak: *obl. sg.* mantel 8.24, mantelh 9.19. [LL MĂNTŬM *FEW* 6, part 1: 277 + -el; It. *mantello*, Sp. *manteo*, Fr. *manteau*, E. *mantel*]

mantenen *adv.* at once 1.6; de mantenen urgently 6.35. *Forms:* mantenent 1.6, mantenen 6.35. [mantener; cf. Fr. *maintenant*]

mantenensa *n. fem.* support, help: *obl. sg.* mantenensa 6.36. [mantener + -ensa]

mantenent *see* mantenen.

mantener *vb. trans.* to maintain, to support 21.24; to help, to take sides with 19.63: *pres. subj. 3rd sg.* manteingna 21.24; *pp., fem., obl. sg.* mantenguda 19.63. [CL MĂNŬTĔNĒRE 'to hold in hand' *FEW* 6, part 1: 299; It. *mantenere*, Sp. *mantener*, Fr. *maintenir*, E. *to maintain*]

mar *n. fem.* sea: *nom. sg.* mars 2.10, mar 32.2; *obl. sg.* mar 1.4, 11.56, 11.65, 12.7. [CL MĂRE *FEW* 6, part 1: 319; It. *mare*, Sp. *mar*, Fr. *mer*; cf. E. *marine*]

marce *see* merce.

marceilhes *see* marselhes.

marchaandas *see* mercadanda.

marit *n. masc.* husband: *nom. sg.* maritz 26.49; *obl. sg.* marit 7.22. [CL MĂRĪTUM *FEW* 6, part 1: 355; It. *marito*, Sp. *marido*, Fr. *mari*; cf. E. *marital*]

marques *n. masc.* marquis: *obl. sg.* marques 12.55, 20.12. [marca 'march, border region' (Germ. *marka FEW* 16: 523) + -es (2)]

marrababelio 9.11 (see note).

marrit *adj.* grief-stricken 18.58: *masc., nom. sg.* marritz 18.58, 26.49 var. [pp. of marrir 'to grieve' (Frankish *marrjan FEW* 16: 535 + -ir)]

mars *see* mar.

marselhes *adj.* from Marseille: *masc., obl. sg.* marceilhes 26.44. [Marselha + -es (2)]

martiri *n. masc.* slaughter: *nom. sg.* martiris 25.11. [ChL MĂRTȲRĬUM *FEW* 6, part 1: 418]

martz *n. masc.* the month of March: *obl. sg.* **martz** 22.27. [CL MĂRTĬUM *FEW* 6, part 1: 393; It. *marzo*, Sp. *marzo*, Fr. *mars*, E. *March*]

marvier *adj.* rapid: *masc., obl. pl.* **marvers** 25.49. [**marvir** 'to prepare' (Gothic *manwjan FEW* 16: 515 + **-ir**) + **-ier**]

mas (1) *n. fem.* 30.4, 30.6, *see* **man** (2).

mas (2) *possessive pron.* 8.24, 9.41, *see* **mon** (2).

mas (3) *adv., see* **mais**.

masa *n. fem.* quantity; **masa de** many 29.29: *obl. sg.* **massa** 29.29. [CL (from Gk.) MĂSSAM *FEW* 6, part 1: 452; It. *massa*, Sp. *masa*, Fr. *masse*, E. *mass*]

masis *adj.* brimful: *fem., obl. sg.* **massissa** 13.3. [**masa** + **-is**]

matiṇ *n. masc.* morning: *obl. sg.* **mati** 8.19, 9.67, 12.10. [CL MĂTŪTĪNUM *FEW* 6, part 1: 541; It. *mattino*, Sp. *matines*, Fr. *matin*; cf. E. *matinee*]

mauditz *see* **maldire**.

maus *see* **mal** (1).

mauta *n. fem.* peal, ringing of bells: *nom. pl.* **mautas** 25.98. [VL *MŎVĬTAM 'movement' *FEW* 6, part 3: 171; It. *smotta*, Sp. *muebda*, Fr. *meute* 'pack of hounds']

may *see* **mais**.

mayna *see* **mana**.

mayre *see* **maire**.

mays *see* **mais**.

mazan *n. masc.* sound (of music) 21.33; tumult (of war) 24.18: *obl. sg.* **mazan** 21.33; *obl. pl* **mazanz** 24.18. [**mazantar** 'to weigh, to shake' (VL *MEDANTĀRE *FEW* 6, part 1: 570, Ctc. *medā- 'balance' + **-an** {1} + **-ar** {2})]

mę *personal pron., 1st person, obl. sg.* me.

    Forms: Masc. **me mezeis** myself 4.22, 18.14; *refl.* **me** 2.1, 4.22, 9.23, 9.26, 13.16, 15.3, 18.45, 22.34, 31.29, 31.32, 31.38, **mi** 18.17, 18.59, 21.57, 27.33; *proclitic* **m'** 9.2, 13.13, 13.34, 13.48, 15.15, 16.14, 22.20, 22.22; *enclitic* **·m** 4.32, 9.54, 11.75, 15.9, 18.18, 18.37, 18.47, 19.23, 22.1, 22.4, 22.27, 22.37, 22.38, 25.64, 28.52, 21.6;

    direct object **me** 9.5, 9.23, 9.47, 9.53, 13.16, 15.3, 18.45, 22.34, 31.14, 31.29, 31.38, 31.42, 32.9, 32.10, **mi** 18.14, 18.17, 18.59, 21.57, 25.62, 27.4, 27.5, 27.8, 27.33, 29.3, 31.9; *proclitic* **m'** 2.3, 4.30, 4.39, 8.10, 9.21, 9.40, 9.55, 10.1, 10.38, 13.34, 15.15, 15.43, 16.14, 16.42, 16.48, 17.38, 18.36, 18.38, 18.46, 18.60, 19.7, 19.34, 21.11, 22.4, 22.6, 22.15, 22.19, 22.22, 28.10, 28.13, 28.43, 31.41, 32.1, 32.2; *enclitic* **·m** 4.32, 8.26, 9.19, 9.44, 9.54, 10.36, 11.75, 13.48, 15.48, 15.52, 16.9, 18.11, 18.18, 18.22, 18.22, 18.37, 18.39, 18.47, 18.59, 19.21, 19.23, 19.24, 21.10, 22.1, 22.8, 22.27, 22.37, 22.38, 25.64, 27.3, 27.3, 28.11, 28.58, 29.1, 29.4, 30.63, 31.6, 31.46;

    indirect object **me** 5.16, 8.19, 8.23, 9.25, 9.26, 9.51, 9.66, 15.31, 16.28, 16.46, 16.49, 19.2, 19.35, 19.50, 25.30, 27.35, 31.32, 31.35, **mi** 9.39, 15.38, 15.42, 17.37, 18.44, 19.40; *proclitic* **m'** 2.7, 2.24, 8.7, 9.65, 9.67, 10.9, 10.22, 13.33, 15.2, 15.47, 15.50, 16.11, 18.5, 18.13, 18.13, 18.21, 18.55, 19.3, 19.5, 19.22, 19.34 var., 21.60, 22.10, 28.15, 28.16, 28.27, 29.11, 30.28, 30.61, 30.67; *enclitic* **·m** 8.21, 9.22, 15.4, 15.7, 15.9, 15.22, 15.45, 16.1, 16.8, 16.37, 16.44, 17.10, 18.8, 18.15, 18.15, 18.33, 18.43, 19.5, 19.5, 19.6, 19.52, 19.58, 20.1, 20.26, 22.12, 22.21, 22.29, 22.49, 27.39, 28.9, 28.12, 28.25, 29.9, 29.40, 30.26, 31.4, 31.25, 31.33, 31.44, 31.45;

ethical dat. **me** 15.33; *proclitic* **m'** 2.5, 13.9, 13.15, 13.43, 13.74, 15.32, 22.20, 28.50; *enclitic* **·m** 9.63, 15.25, 28.13, 30.24; *in expression* **m'en anar**, *enclitic* **m'** 9.2, 10.5, 10.27, 18.39, 18.58;

object of prep. **me** 4.22, 18.57, **mi** 9.20, 18.41, 19.66, 22.18, 22.48, 28.32, 28.47, 28.63, 30.66, 31.16; *proclitic* **m'** 9.45;

disjunctive **mi** 13.49 var. *(obl. absolute)* 25.62, 31.9.

Fem. refl. **me** 23.41, 23.45; *proclitic* **m'** 6.1, 6.8, 7.13; *enclitic* **·m** 23.6, 23.22, 23.37, 23.38, 23.45;

direct object **me** 23.41; *proclitic* **m'** 6.1, 6.2, 6.7, 6.8, 6.10, 7.13, 13.13, 13.50, 13.51, 23.25, 23.35, 28.24, 28.33, 28.70; *enclitic* **·m** 23.6, 23.22, 23.34, 23.35, 23.37, 23.38, 23.45, 23.46, 28.36, 28.52, 28.66, 31.21;

indirect object **me** 6.6, 23.26, 23.29, 28.28, **mi** 6.9, 19.28, 23.8; *proclitic* **m'** 3.10, 6.11, 6.29, 7.23, 13.13, 13.52, 19.25, 23.3, 23.36; *enclitic* **·m** 13.66, 23.11, 31.21;

ethical dat. **me** 23.45, **mi** 19.26;

object of prep. **me** 23.27, **mi** 23.4, 23.17.

[CL MĒ *FEW* 6, part 1: 566; It. *mi*, Sp. *me*, Fr. *moi, me*]

medicinal *n. masc.* remedy: *nom. sg.* **medicinals** 12.16. [CL MĔDĬCĪNĀLEM *FEW* 6, part 1: 603]

mędre *vb. trans.* to reap, to harvest: *pret. 3rd. sing.* **mes** 11.26. [CL MĔTĔRE *FEW* 6, part 2: 59; It *mietere*]

mei *see* **mon** (2).

meijǫrn *n. masc.* sext, liturgical service held daily at the sixth hour of the day, at or before noon: *obl. sg.* **mieijorn** 30.85. [**mei** 'half' (CL MĔDĬUM *FEW* 6, part 1: 627) + **jorn**]

meiller, meillers, meillor, meillors *see* **melhor**.

meills *see* **melhs**.

meillur' *see* **melhorar**.

meillz *see* **melhs**.

meitadier *adj.* penetrating by half its length, halfway in: *masc., nom. sg.* **meitadiers** 25.54. [**meitat** 'half' (CL MĔDĬĔTĀTEM *FEW* 6, part 1: 612) + **-ier**]

męl *n. masc.* honey: *obl. sg.* **mel** 14.32. [CL MĔL *FEW* 6, part 1: 652; It. *miele*, Sp. *miel*, Fr. *miel*; cf. E. *mellifluous*]

meler *see* **melhor**.

melhǫr *(nom.* **mę́lher)** *comparative adj.* better 2.20, 15.10, 16.52, 19.39, 26.13, 26.28; **lo melhor** best 21.4, 21.37, 21.45, 21.46, 25.21, most highly regarded 11.36.

Forms: masc., nom. sg. **meiller** 16.52, 26.13, **meler** 11.36, **meillers** 26.28; *obl. sg.* **melhor** 19.39, **meillor** 21.4, 21.45, 21.46; *obl. pl.* **meillors** 21.37, **milhors** 25.21; *fem., nom. sg.* **mielhers** 2.20, *obl. sg.* **meillor** 15.10.

[CL MĔLĬŌREM *FEW* 6, part 1: 675; It. *migliore*, Sp. *mejor*, Fr. *meilleur*]

melhorar *vb. intrans.* to become better: *pres. 3rd sg.* **meillur'** 6.26, **meillura** 6.26 ms. [CL MĔLĬŌRĀRE *FEW* 6, part 1: 676; It. *megliorare*, Sp. *medrar*; cf. E. *to ameliorate*]

męlhs *adv.* better 17.7, 24.10, 26.4, 26.32; more 13.76; **trop melhs** very well 31.5. *Forms:* **meills** 26.4, 26.32, **meillz** 24.10, **mels** 13.76, **miels** 31.5, **miellz** 17.7. [CL MĔLĬUS *FEW* 6, part 1: 675; It. *meglio*, Fr. *mieux*]

meliana *n. fem.* noon: *obl. sg.* **meliayna** 13.56. [CL (HŌRAM) MĚRĪDĬĀNAM FEW 6, part 2: 33]

mels *see* **melhs.**

membra, membrada *see* **membrar.**

membransa *n. fem.* recollection, memory: *obl. sg.* **membransa** 28.47. [**membrar** + **-ansa**]

membrar *vb. trans., impersonal* to remember, *e.g.,* **me membra** I remember 8.19: *pres. 3rd sg.* **membra** 11.3, **menbra** 8.19; *pres. subj. 3rd sg.* **menbre** 25.2; *pp., fem., obl. sg.* **membrada** sensible 28.8. [CL MĔMŎRĀRE FEW 6, part 1: 697; cf. E. *to remember*]

men *see* **mentir.**

menar *vb. trans.* to take, to lead 5.13, 9.21; to carry out 11.62; to spend 11.7; to raise 31.45; **en menar** to lead away 30.92, 30.98; **menar malament** to mistreat 11.9: *pres. 3rd sg.* **mena** 11.9, 30.92, 30.98, *1st pl.* **menam** 11.7; *pret. 3rd sg.* **menet** 5.13, *3rd pl.* **meneron** 9.21, **menero** 31.45; *inf.* **menár** 11.62. [CL MĬNĀRĪ, LL MĬNĀRE FEW 6, part 2: 111; It. *menare,* Fr. *mener*]

menbra, menbre *see* **membrar.**

menero, meneron, menet *see* **menar.**

mẹns *adv.* less; **al mens** at least 4.13. *Forms:* **menz** 24.13, **menhs** 29.18, **meyns** 4.13. [CL MĬNUS FEW 6, part 2: 129; It. *meno,* Sp. *menos,* Fr. *moins*]

mensongier *adj.* lying, not telling the truth: *masc., nom. sg.* **mensongers** 16.26. [**mensonga** 'lie' (VL *MĔNTĬŌNĬAM FEW 6, part 1: 739) + **-ier**]

ment *see* **mentir.**

mentaure *vb. trans.* to mention: *pret. 1st sg.* **mentaugui** 9.8. [CL MĔNTE HĂBĒRE 'to have in mind' FEW 6, part 1: 732; OFr. *mentevoir*]

mentir *vb. intrans.* to lie, to tell a falsehood 2.19, 16.28, 19.34 var., 20.15; *refl.* to break one's word, to act in bad faith 9.36: *pres. 1st sg.* **men** 16.28, *3rd sg.* **men** 2.19, 9.36, **ment** 20.15; *pp., undeclined* **mentit** 19.34 var. [CL MĔNTĪRĪ FEW 6, part 1: 748; It. *mentire,* Sp. *mentir,* Fr. *mentir*]

mẹntre *conj.* while: **mentr'** 25.65. [VL DŬM ĬNTĔRĬM 'during' FEW 3: 178; It. *mentre,* Sp. *mientras*]

menudas *see* **menut.**

menudier *adj.* slender: *masc., obl. pl.* **menuders** used as *nom. pl.* 25.99. [**menut** + **-ier**]

menut *adj.* slender: *fem., obl. pl.* **menudas** 25.48. [CL MĬNŪTUM FEW 6, part 2: 138; It. *minuto,* Sp. *menudo,* Fr. *menu,* E. *minute*]

menz *see* **mens.**

meravẹlha *n. fem.* wonder; **meravelhas aver** to be amazed 18.7: *obl. pl.* **meravillas** 18.7. [ChL MĪRĂBĬLĬA FEW 6, part 2: 146; It. *meraviglia,* Sp. *ṃaravilla,* Fr. *merveille,* E. *marvel*]

meravelhar *vb. intrans.* to be amazed: *inf.* **miravillar** 27.9. [**meravelha** + **-ar** (2)]

mercadan *n. masc.* merchant: *obl. pl.* **merchadanz** used as *nom. pl.* 16.25 var. [**mercat** 'market' (CL MĔRCĀTUM FEW 6, part 2: 13) + **-an** (1)]

mercadanda *n. fem.* female merchant: *nom. pl.* **marchaandas** 16.25. [**mercadan** + **-a**]

mercadier *adj.* like a merchant: *fem., nom. pl.* **mercadeiras** 16.25 var. [**mercat** 'market' (CL MĔRCĀTUM FEW 6, part 2: 13) + **-ier**]

mercẹ *n. fem.* mercy, kindness 4.12, 10.21, 10.28 var., 17.31, 18.25 var., 18.34, 27.45; power to forgive or to be kind 11.76; thanks 13.12; **bona**

merce warm welcome, compassion 23.2; **mala merce** ill favor, unfriendly reception 18.53; *as exclamation* **merce** (have) mercy, (take) pity 27.6: *nom. sg.* **merces** 4.12, 18.25 var., 18.34; *obl. sg.* **merce** 10.21, 10.28 var., 13.12, 17.31, 18.53, 23.2, 27.6, 27.45, **marce** 11.76. [CL MĚRCĒDEM 'wage' *FEW* 6, part 2: 17; It. *mercè*, Sp. *merced*, Fr. *merci*, E. *mercy*]

mercenier *adj.* merciful: *masc., nom. sg.* **merceners** 25.93. [CL MĚRCĚNĀRĬUM 'working for pay' *FEW* 6, part 2: 15, influenced in meaning by **merce**]

merces *see* **merce**.

merchadanz *see* **mercadan**.

merir *vb. trans.* to repay for: *pres. subj. 3rd sg.* **meyra** 19.41. [CL MĚRĒRE *FEW* 6, part 2: 29; Sp. *merecer*, OFr. *merir*]

męs (1) *n. masc.* messenger: *obl. pl.* **mes** 11.59. [CL MĬSSUM, pp. of MĬTTĚRE 'to send' *FEW* 6, part 2: 184]

męs (2) *n. masc.* month: *obl. pl.* **mes** 22.26. [CL MĒNSEM *FEW* 6, part 1: 715; It. *mese*, Sp. *mes*, Fr. *mois*]

mes (3) *vb. trans.* 11.26, *see* **medre**.

mes (4) *vb. trans.* 1.4, 16.36, 22.4, 22.34, 31.34, *see* **metre**.

męsa *n. fem.* Mass: *obl. sg.* **messa** 30.11, 30.84, 31.37. [ChL MĬSSAM *FEW* 6, part 2: 173; It. *messa*, Sp. *misa*, Fr. *messe*, E. *Mass*]

mesatgier *n. masc.* messenger: *nom. sg.* **messatgers** 25.89; *obl. sg.* **mesager** 8.8. [**mesatge** 'message' (**mes** {1} + **-atge**) + **-ier**]

mesclar *vb. trans.* to mix 29.21; *refl.* to become involved with (*with* **i** [1]) 19.64, to mix with (*with* **en**) 14.14: *pres. 3rd sg.* **mescla** 14.14, *2nd pl.* **mesclatz** 19.64; *pp., masc., obl. pl.* **mesclatz** 29.21. [VL MĬSCŬLĀRE *FEW* 6, part 2: 165; It. *mischiare*, Sp. *mezclar*, Fr. *mêler*]

mescreire *vb. trans.* to distrust: *pres. 1st sg.* **mescre** 18.23. [**mes-** + **creire**]

mesdren *see* **metre**.

meseisa *see* **mezeis**.

mesquiṇ *adj.* weak; *masc., obl. sg.* **mesqui** 10.20. [Arabic *miskīn FEW* 19: 127; It. *meschino*, Sp. *mezquino*, Fr. *mesquin*]

messa *see* **mesa**.

messatgers *see* **mesatgier**.

mestier *n. masc.* trade, profession, craft 29.17; deed *(erotic)* 31.30; **aver mestier** to serve 25.85; **eser mestiers** to be needed 25.69, 25.106: *nom. sg.* **mestiers** 25.69, 25.106, 29.17; *obl. sg.* **mestier** 31.30, **mesters** *used as obl. sg.* 25.85. [CL MĬNĬSTĚRĬUM, MĬSTĚRĬUM *FEW* 6, part 2: 120; It. *mestiere*, Sp. *menester*, Fr. *métier*, E. *ministry*]

mestitz *adj.* half-breed: *fem., obl. sg.* **mestissa** 13.2. [LL MĬXTĪCĬUM *FEW* 6, part 2: 195; It. *mestizzo*, Sp. *mestizo*, Fr. *métis*, E. *mestizo*]

met, meta, metam, metan, metatz, mete, metes *see* **metre**.

meteus *see* **mezeis**.

mętre *vb. trans.* to put 11.27, 11.59, 12.70, 21.14, 26.48, 27.5, 27.48, 30.98, 31.34; to give 31.33; to direct 16.36; *refl. with* **en** to gain 22.4, to get in 22.34, to set to 1.4, to take to 28.72; **metre castiazon** to chastise 11.22. *Forms: pres. 3rd sg.* **met** 30.98; *pres. subj. 3rd sg.* **meta** 21.14 ms., 27.48, **met'** 21.14, *1st pl.* **metam** 26.48, *2nd pl.* **metatz** 27.48 var., *3rd pl.* **metan** 26.48 var.; *pret. 3rd sg.* **mes** 1.4, **mezi** 31.33, *3rd pl.* **mesdren** 11.27; *imper. 2nd sg.* **met** 12.70, *2nd pl.* **metes** 27.48 var., **mete·us** 28.72 (see note); *pp., masc., nom. sg.* **mes** 22.4, 22.34, 31.34, *obl. sg.* **mes** 16.36; *inf.* **metre** 11.22, 11.59 ms., **metr'** 11.59, 27.5.

[CL mǐttĕre 'to send' *FEW* 6, part 2: 192; It. *mettere,* Sp. *meter,* Fr. *mettre;* cf. E. *to transmit*]

męu (1) *tonic possessive pron., 1st sg.* mine; *with def. art.: masc., nom. sg.*
mieus 23.43. [**meu** (2)]

męu (2) *tonic possessive adj., 1st sg.* my, mine; *in noun phrase with def. art.*
11.77, 17.23, 27.10, 31.12, 31.27; *as predicate adj.* 18.42, 26.34: *masc.,*
nom. sg. **mieus** 18.42, 26.34 var.; *obl. sg.* **mieu** 17.23, 27.10, 31.12,
31.27; *fem., obl. pl.* **mias** 11.77; *neuter, nom. sg.* **mieu** 26.34. [CL mĕum
FEW 6, part 2: 65; It. *mio,* Sp. *mío,* Fr. *mien*]

meyns *see* **mens.**

meyra *see* **merir.**

mezęis *adj. intensifies reference of a pron.; modifies personal pron.* myself
18.14, 23.44, yourself 27.28 var.; *modifies personal pron. used in context*
with reflexive pron. yourself 27.28, himself 6.16, 27.28 var.; *modifies*
reflexive pron. myself 4.22, himself 18.14 var., herself 18.14 var.;
modifies possessive pron. **los teus mezeiches** your own men 25.84.
       Forms: masc., nom. sg. **mezeis** 6.16, **mezeus** 27.28 var., **meteus**
27.28 var.; *obl. sg.* **meteus** 18.14, **mezeus** 18.14 var., **mezeys** 4.22;
nom. pl. **mezeis** 27.28; *obl. pl.* **mezeiches** 25.84; *fem., nom. sg.*
meseisa 23.44, **meteisia** 23.44 var., **mezeussa** 23.44 var.; *obl. sg.*
meteissa 18.14 var.
       [VL mĕt ĭpsum *FEW* 4: 808]

mezi *see* **metre.**

mezura *n. fem.* moderation: *obl. sg.* **mezura** 13.83. [CL mēnsūram *FEW* 6,
part 1: 722; It. *misura,* Sp. *mesura,* Fr. *mesure,* E. *measure*]

mi *see* **me.**

mia *see* **miga.**

mias *see* **meu** (2).

midǫnz *n. fem.* milady: *obl. sg.* **midonz** 16.45, 18.33. [etymology uncertain; perhaps from ethical dat. mihi and fem. domus 'home, family,
beloved' (see Paden, "Etymology"); not from dominus 'lord,' since
midonz is fem. (cf. *FEW* 3: 130); see also **sidonz**]

mieijorn *see* **meijorn.**

mielhers *see* **melhor.**

miellz, miels *see* **melhs.**

mieu (1) *possessive pron.* 17.23, *see* **meu** (1).

mieu (2) *possessive adj.* 26.34, 27.10, 31.12, 31.27, *see* **meu** (2).

mieus (1) *possessive pron.* 23.43, *see* **meu** (1).

mieus (2) *possessive adj.* 18.42, 26.34 var., *see* **meu** (2).

miga *adv. with* non (not) at all. *Forms:* **miga** 11.58, **mia** 4.30, **miia** 11.11,
11.14. [CL mīcam 'crumb' *FEW* 6, part 2: 76; It. *mica,* Sp. *miga,* Fr. *mie*]

miia *see* **miga.**

mil *num.* thousand; **mil aitans** a thousand times as much 27.44. [CL
mīlle *FEW* 6, part 2: 91; It. *mille,* Sp. *mil,* Fr. *mille*]

milhers *see* **milier.**

milhors *see* **melhor.**

milier *n. masc.* thousand: *obl. pl.* **milhers** *used as nom. pl.* 25.34. [**mil** +
-ier]

minha *see* **manjar** (2).

miracle *n. masc.* miracle: *obl. pl.* **miracles** 26.55. [ChL mīrăcŭlum *FEW* 6,
part 2: 148; It. *miracolo,* Sp. *milagro,* Fr. *miracle,* E. *miracle;* cf. **miralh**]

miralh *n. masc.* mirror: *obl. sg.* **miraill** 18.44; *vocative sg.* **miraills** 18.45.
[VL *mīrăcŭlum 'mirror' *FEW* 6, part 2: 155; cf. **miracle**]
miranda *n. fem.* watchtower: *obl. sg.* **miranda** 20.20. [CL mīrăndum
'amazing' *FEW* 6, part 2: 152]
mirar *vb. trans.* to look at, to see; *refl.* to be seen 2.21, to look at oneself
18.45: *pres. subj. 3rd sg.* **mire** 2.21; *pret. 1st sg.* **miriei** 18.45. [CL mīrārī
FEW 6, part 2: 155; It. *mirare,* Sp. *mirar,* Fr. *mirer*; cf. E. *to admire*]
miravillar *see* **meravelhar.**
mo *see* **mon** (2).
moc, mogui *see* **mover.**
mọl *adj.* soft: *masc., obl. pl.* **mols** 26.35. [CL mŏllem *FEW* 6, part 2: 57; It.
molle, Sp. *muelle,* Fr. *mou*; cf. E. *to mollify*]
molhẹr (*nom. sg.* **mọlher**) *n. fem.* wife: *nom. sg.* **moiller** 3.3; *obl. sg.*
molher 9.69, **moiller** 3.6, 5.5, 5.13, 26.50, 30.92, **moillier** 5.8, **moler**
9.3, **muiller** 3.7; *nom. pl.* **molhers** 25.68. [CL mŭlĭĕrem, VL mulíẹrem
FEW 6, part 2: 200; It. *moglie,* Sp. *mujer,* OFr. *muiler*]
mols *see* **mol.**
mọlt (1) *n. masc., in expression* **molt de** much: *obl. sg.* **molt** 16.13. [**molt**
(2)]
mọlt (2) *adj. sg.* much, *pl.* many: *masc., obl. pl.* **motz** 25.44, 25.105. [CL
mŭltum *FEW* 6, part 2: 210; It. *molto,* Sp. *mucho*]
mọlt (3) *adv.* very 1.1, 3.2, 3.3, 5.11, 9.20, 10.29, 14.43, 16.36, 17.36, 26.49,
30.20, 30.29; greatly 5.4, 6.9, 11.36, 18.44, 23.18, 28.5, 30.75. *Forms:*
molt 3.2, 3.3, 11.36, 16.36, 17.36, 26.49, **mout** 1.1, 5.11, 6.9, 9.20,
10.29, 18.44, 23.18, 28.5, 30.20, 30.29, 30.75, **mot** 14.43, **mont** 5.4 (see
note). [**molt** (2)]
mọn (1) *n. masc.* world; **tot lo mon** everyone 21.44: *nom. sg.* **mons** 21.44,
29.24, **monz** 24.16; *obl. sg.* **mon** 2.21, 3.5, 18.14, 21.44 var., 21.52,
21.76, 30.80. [CL mŭndum *FEW* 6, part 2: 220; It. *mondo,* Sp. *mundo,* Fr.
monde]
mọn (2) *atonic possessive adj., 1st sg.* my; **ma dompna** milady 3.3, 18.50.
Forms: Masc., nom. sg. **mos** 6.3, 9.63, 9.64, 15.34, 15.34, 15.48,
16.5, 22.3, 22.41, 28.37, 29.10, **mon** *used as nom. sg.* 8.9; *obl. sg.* **mon**
2.13, 7.9, 7.15, 7.16, 7.18, 8.26, 9.58, 10.7, 10.21, 10.40, 13.36, 13.36,
13.69, 16.36, 17.32, 18.13, 19.28, 21.1, 21.3, 22.52, 27.29, 27.34, 27.35,
27.36, 29.5, 29.13, 29.13, 29.14, 29.14, 30.62, 31.3, 31.13, 31.17, 31.18,
32.7, **mo** 9.68, 29.13; *nom. pl.* **mei** 11.80; *obl. pl.* **mos** 7.10, 7.16, 10.37,
18.43 var., 22.42, 25.62, 27.7, 27.39, 31.28, 31.31, 32.16.
Fem., nom. sg. **ma** 18.50, 28.60, **m'** 22.3; *obl. sg.* **ma** 3.3, 4.28, 7.16,
13.12, 21.3, 26.50, 27.42, 28.22, 28.41, 28.71, 29.12, 31.35, 31.38, **m'**
7.6, 7.15, 9.71, 10.14, 27.36, 28.18; *obl. pl.* **mas** 8.24, 9.41.
[CL mĕum *FEW* 6, part 2: 65; OIt. *mo,* Sp. *mi,* Fr. *mon*]
monasteir *see* **mostier.**
mondar *vb. trans.* to cleanse: *pp., masc., nom. pl.* **mundat** 29.44. [CL
mŭndāre *FEW* 6, part 2: 216; It. *mondare,* Sp. *mondar,* Fr. *monder*]
mong' *see* **monge.**
mọnga *n. fem.* nun: *obl. sg.* **monga** 1.7 var., **morga** 1.7. [ChL mŏnăcham]
mọnge *n. masc.* monk: *nom. pl.* **mong'** 32.15; *obl. pl.* **monges** *used as*
nom. pl. 32.15 var. [ChL (from Gk.) mŏnăchum, mŏnĭcum *FEW* 6, part 2:
69; It. *monaco,* Sp. *monge,* Fr. *moine,* G. *Mönch,* E. *monk*]
mons *see* **mon** (1).

mont *see* **molt** (3).

monz *see* **mon** (1).

morai *see* **morir.**

mọrdre *vb. trans.* to bite: *inf.* **mordre** 14.29. [CL mŏrdēre, VL *mŏrdĕre *FEW* 6, part 2: 129; It. *mórdere,* Sp. *mordér,* Fr. *mordre;* cf. E. *mordant*]

morga *see* **monga.**

morir *vb. intrans.* to die 1.6, 3.11, 4.38, 5.14, 11.5, 11.43, 18.32, 19.23, 23.22, 23.45, 23.46, 25.22, 25.55 var., 25.73, 25.96; *with* **ab** to be killed by 25.83; **aver mort** *trans.* to have killed 14.44, 17.38, 18.38, 18.46, 25.20; *pp.,* as good as dead 19.55, **per mort** near death 1.4 (cf. **mort** [1]); *substantivized inf., masc., obl. sg.* **murir** death 12.27.

Forms: *pres. 1st pl.* **murem** 11.5; *fut. 1st sg.* **morai** 23.45; *1st cond. 1st sg.* **morria** 4.38; *pret. 3rd sg.* **mori** 1.6, 5.14, **moric** 25.55 var.; *pp., masc., nom. sg.* **mortz** 19.55 var., 25.22, 25.73, 25.83, 25.96, **morz** 11.43, **mort** *before* **s-** 19.55; *obl. sg.* **mort** 1.4, 17.38, 18.38, 18.46; *obl. pl.* **mortz** 14.44, 25.20; *fem., nom. sg.* **morta** 3.11; *inf.* **morir** 18.32, 23.22, 23.46, **murir** 12.27, 19.23.

[CL mŏrī, LL mŏrīre *FEW* 6, part 2: 137; It. *morire,* Sp. *morir,* Fr. *mourir;* cf. E. *moribund*]

mọrt (1) *n. masc.* dead man 11.17; **per mort** as a dead man 1.4, 18.38: *obl. sg.* **mort** 11.17, 18.38. [pp. of **morir**]

mọrt (2) *n. fem.* death 1.7, 12.17, 21.77, 24.13, 24.41, 25.30, 25.80; time of imminent death 10.37; slaughter 25.26; **dobla mort** death of the body and of the soul 29.34: *nom. sg.* **mortz** 25.26; *obl. sg.* **mort** 1.7, 10.37, 12.17, 21.77, 24.13, 24.41, 25.30, 25.80, 29.34. [CL mŏrtem *FEW* 6, part 2: 143; It. *morte,* Sp. *muerte,* Fr. *mort;* cf. E. *mortal*]

mortairọl *n. masc.* a kind of thick gravy: *obl. sg.* **mortairol** 26.10. [ChL mŏrtārĭŏlum *FEW* 6, part 2: 148; Sp. *morteruelo*]

mortz (1) *n. fem.* 25.26, *see* **mort** (2).

mortz (2) *pp.* 14.44, 19.55 var., 25.20, 25.22, 25.73, 25.83, 25.96, *see* **morir.**

morz *see* **morir.**

mos (1) *possessive adj., see* **mon** (2).

mos (2) *adv.* 23.48, *see* **mais.**

mọsca *n. fem.* fly (winged insect): *obl. sg.* **mosca** 14.59. [CL mŭscam *FEW* 6, part 2: 257; It. *mosca,* Sp. *mosca,* Fr. *mouche;* cf. E. *mosquito*]

mostier *n. masc.* church: *obl. sg.* **monasteir** 30.43; *obl. pl.* **mostiers** 25.91. [ChL (from Gk.) mŏnăstērĭum *FEW* 6, part 2: 73; It. *monastero,* Sp. *monasterio,* Fr. *moutier,* E. *monastery*]

mostrar *vb. trans.* to show 16.37, 23.12, 26.5; to begin with 21.42: *pres. 3rd sg.* **mostra** 16.37, *3rd pl.* **mostron** 26.5; *imperf. 1st sg.* **mostrava** 23.12; *pret. 3rd sg.* **mostret** 21.42. [CL mŏnstrāre, VL mōstrāre *FEW* 6, part 2: 99; It. *mostrare,* Sp. *mostrar,* Fr. *montrer;* cf. E. *to demonstrate*]

mọt (1) *n. masc.* word 2.6, 25.61, 26.2, 30.59; the word **ai las!** 30.90; *pl.* words, lyrics of a song 1.3, 14.3: *obl. sg.* **mot** 2.6, 30.59, 30.90; *nom. pl.* **mot** 14.3; *obl. pl.* **motz** 1.3, 25.61, **moz** 26.2. [LL mŭttum *FEW* 6, part 2: 305; It. *motto,* Sp. *mote,* Fr. *mot,* E. *motto*]

mot (2) *adv.* 14.43, *see* **molt** (3).

motz (1) *n. masc.* 1.3, 25.61, *see* **mot** (1).

motz (2) *adj.* 25.44, 25.105, *see* **molt** (2).

mou *see* **mover.**

mout *see* **molt** (3).

movẹr *vb. intrans. with* **de** to come from 16.2, 16.3, 16.23, 27.38, to be prompted by 17.35; *trans.* to move, to beat (wings) 18.1; *refl.* to move, to budge, to stir 9.54: *pres. 3rd sg.* **mou** 16.2, 16.23, 17.35; *pret. 1st sg.* **moc** 27.38, **mogui** 9.54; *inf.* **mover** 16.3, 18.1. [CL MŏVĒRE *FEW* 6, part 2: 168; It. *muovere,* Sp. *mover,* Fr. *mouvoir,* E. *to move*]

moz *see* **mot** (1).

mudar *vb. intrans.* to change: *pres. 3rd sg.* **muda** 19.52. [CL MŪTĀRE *FEW* 6, part 2: 291; It. *mutare,* Sp. *mudar,* Fr. *muer*]

muiller *see* **molher.**

multiplican *adj.* generous: *masc., nom. sg.* **multiplicans** 27.15. [pres. part. of CL MŭLTĭPLĭCĀRE 'to multiply' *FEW* 6, part 2: 205]

mundat *see* **mondar.**

murem, murir *see* **morir.**

murtrier *n. masc.* murderer: *obl. pl.* **murtriers** 24.5 var. [**murtrir** + **-ier**]

murtrir *vb. trans.* to kill; *substantivized inf., masc., obl. sg.* **murtrir** murder 24.5, **mordrir** 24.5 var. [Frankish **murθrjan FEW* 16: 584 + **-ir**; cf. Fr. *meurtrir,* E. *to murder*]

musas *see* **muza** (1).

mut *adj.* mute, incapable of speech 9.16; speechless, silent 21.59: *masc., nom. sg.* **mutz** 9.16; *nom. pl.* **mut** 21.59. [CL MŪTUM *FEW* 6, part 2: 313; It. *muto,* Sp. *mudo,* Fr. *muet,* E. *mute*]

muz' *see* **muza** (2).

muza (1) *n. fem.* muse, poem 11.77: *obl. pl.* **musas** 11.77. [CL MŪSAM 'muse, poem' *FEW* 6, part 2: 246; It. *musa,* Sp. *musa,* Fr. *muse,* E. *muse*]

muza (2) *n. fem.* waiting in vain: *obl. sg.* **muz'** 13.56. [**muzar** 'to waste time, to stand with one's nose in the air or mouth open' (**mus** 'face' [LL MŪSUM 'muzzle' *FEW* 6, part 2: 282]) + **-ar** (2)]

n', ·n (1) *n. masc.* sir 5.9, 5.16, 5.16, 19.57 var., 20.7, 20.26, 22.11, 22.11, 22.12, 25.23, 25.24, 25.24, 25.24, 25.36, 25.37, 25.37, 25.37, 25.74, 25.107, 28.31, 30.50, *see* **en** (1).

n' (2) *n. fem.* 9.13, 9.13, 9.49, 20.25, *see* **na.**

n', ·n (3) *pron.* = **de** + *object pron.* 1.2, 1.7, 2.4, 2.6, 2.7, 2.19, 2.23, 6.24, 6.25, 7.21, 8.21 var., 8.30, 9.35, 11.12, 11.13, 11.16, 11.31, 13.28, 13.52 var., 13.54, 13.76, 13.90, 13.92, 14.60, 14.68, 15.20, 15.31, 15.32, 15.38, 16.10, 16.12, 16.13, 16.14, 16.16, 16.20, 16.54, 18.28, 18.57, 19.32, 19.57, 19.59, 19.62, 19.65, 20.3, 23.5, 23.31, 23.32, 23.40, 23.47, 24.37, 25.105, 26.24, 27.12 var., 27.19, 27.24 var., 28.30, 28.41, 28.42, 28.58, 28.63, 30.4, 30.39, 30.92, 31.33, 31.43, 31.43, 32.9, 32.10, *see* **en** (2).

n' (4) *adv.* 26.27, *see* **non.**

·n (5) *prep.* 26.23, *see* **en** (3).

na *title introducing woman's name* lady: *nom. sg.* **na** 19.39, **n'** 9.13, 9.13, 9.49; *obl. sg.* **n'** 20.25. [Enclitic form from CL DŏMĭNAM *FEW* 3: 126; cf. **domna**]

nada *see* **naiser.**

nadal *n. fem.* Christmas: *nom. sg.* **nadaus** 16.46. [CL (DĭEM) NĀTĀLEM 'day of birth (of Christ)'; It. *natale,* Fr. *Noël,* E. *Noel*]

nafrar *vb. trans.* to wound: *pp., masc., nom. sg.* **nafratz** 25.23. [ONorse **nafra* 'to pierce' *FEW* 16: 595 + **-ar** (2); cf. Fr. *navrer*]

naiser *vb. intrans.* to be born: *pres. 3rd sg.* **nays** 2.17; *past subj. 3rd sg.* **nasqes** 21.4; *pp., masc., nom. sg.* **natz** 20.34, 27.40; *fem., nom. sg.* **nada** 13.44. [CL NĀSCĪ, NĂSCĔRE *FEW* 7: 22; It. *nascere,* Sp. *nacer,* Fr. *naître;* cf. E. *nascent*]

natura *n. fem.* nature, inborn character: *obl. sg.* **natura** 13.72. [CL NĀTŪRAM *FEW* 7: 48; It. *natura,* Fr. *nature,* E. *nature*]

natural *adj.* natural, since birth 16.33; expressive of inborn character, sincere, authentic 16.50: *masc., nom. sg.* **naturaus** 16.33, 16.50. [CL NĂTŪRĀLEM *FEW* 7: 52; It. *naturale,* Sp. *natural,* Fr. *naturel,* E. *natural*]

natz *see* **naiser.**

nau *n. fem.* ship: *obl. sg.* **nau** 1.4. [CL NĂVEM *FEW* 7: 68; It. *nave,* Sp. *nave,* Fr. *nef,* E. *nave*]

nautonier *n. masc.* boatman, sailor: *obl. pl.* **nautoniers** *used as nom. pl.* 25.14. [VL *NAUTŌNEM *FEW* 7: 57 + **-ier**; Fr. *nautonier*]

nays *see* **naiser.**

ne (1) *pron.* = **de** + *object pron.* 23.48, 25.34, 26.30, 28.69, 30.46, 30.98, *see* **en** (2).

ne (2) *conj.* 16.43, 16.44, 21.53, 21.54 var., 31.30, *see* **ni.**

neciera *n. fem.* lack: *obl. sg.* **nessieyra** 19.36. [CL NĔCĔSSĀRĬA 'necessary things' *FEW* 7: 78; Fr. *nécessaire*]

nęgre *adj.* black 21.46 var.; black and blue, discolored by bruises 25.73; somber 25.28: *masc., nom. sg.* **ners** 25.28, **niers** 25.73; *obl. sg.* **negre** 21.46 var. [CL NĬGRUM; *FEW* 7: 135 suggests that OOc **ner, nier** represent normal development, while **negre** reflects a new contact with ML; It. *nero,* Sp. *negro,* Fr. *noir,* E. *Negro*]

negun *adj. with* **non** not . . . any: *fem., obl. sg.* **negun'** 22.24. [CL NĔC ŪNUM *FEW* 7: 82; Sp. *ninguno*]

neien *see* **nïen.**

nęis *adv.* even 2.28, 21.70; *in negative context* not even 28.42, or 30.50; **si** . . . **neis** even if 30.28. *Forms:* **neis** 2.28, 21.70, 30.28, 30.50, **neys** 28.42. [VL NĔC ĪPSUM *FEW* 7: 73; OFr. *neis*]

ners *see* **negre.**

nessieyra *see* **neciera.**

nęu *n. fem.* snow: *nom. sg.* **neus** 25.41. [CL NĬVEM *FEW* 7: 157; It. *neve,* Sp. *nieve*]

neys *see* **neis.**

ni *conj.* or *in contexts marked by negation or uncertainty* (cf. **o** [3]).

    In negative context 2.11, 4.11, 6.23, 8.8, 8.9, 9.8, 10.4, 10.17, 12.63, 13.87, 15.6, 15.10, 16.43, 18.34, 18.34, 19.10, 19.12, 19.20, 20.18, 20.19, 20.19, 20.19, 20.20, 20.21, 20.22, 20.23, 20.23, 20.24, 21.25, 21.48, 21.50, 21.51, 21.54, 21.75, 21.76, 22.11, 22.12, 22.23, 22.25, 22.26, 22.26, 22.26, 22.27, 22.50, 23.10, 23.39, 24.33, 24.34, 24.34, 24.35, 24.35, 24.40, 24.43, 26.21, 26.22, 26.22, 26.26, 30.15, 30.33, 30.54, 30.55, 31.30.

    With **non** *in the same clause (in translation the negation can be expressed in either the conjunction or the adverb)* **ni** (. . .) **non** and not, nor 6.30, 17.10, 18.35, 23.28, 23.39, 24.39, **non** . . . **ni** neither . . . nor 20.7, (*zero* [*an implicit "neither"*]) . . . **ni** . . . **non** . . . **ni** neither . . . nor . . . nor 22.7–8; **non** . . . **ni** . . . **ni** not . . . either . . . or 15.11, 19.60.

    In context of another negative clause, force of negation continues in **ni** and not 6.8, 8.10, 9.55, 11.48, 14.66, 22.27, 23.10, 26.37, 28.32; *force of negation not perceptible in* **ni** and 4.32, 16.3, 16.44, 17.17, 18.42, 21.53, 22.13, 25.26, 25.80, 28.40, 28.42, 31.31.

    In restrictive context 17.15, 20.13, 24.25; *in conditional clause* 2.22, 11.9, 11.10, 12.25, 23.12, 24.3, 24.4, 26.15, 26.15, 27.12, *with condi-*

tional **qui** 25.81; *in clause introduced by* **anz que** 5.7, *introduced by* **tan que** 19.48; *in clause expressing totality* 12.29, 15.36; *in clause expressing opinion held by someone else* 15.44, 17.34, 19.42, 23.20.

Forms: **ni** 2.11, 2.22, 4.11, 4.32, 5.7, 6.8, 6.23, 6.30, 8.8, 8.9, 8.10, 9.8, 9.55, 10.4, 10.17, 11.9, 11.10, 11.48, 12.25, 12.25, 12.29, 12.63, 13.87, 14.66, 15.6, 15.10, 15.11, 15.11, 15.36, 15.44, 16.3, 17.10, 17.15, 17.17, 17.34, 18.34, 18.34, 18.35, 18.42, 19.10, 19.12, 19.20, 19.42, 19.48, 19.60, 19.60, 20.7, 20.13, 20.18, 20.19, 20.19, 20.19, 20.20, 20.21, 20.22, 20.23, 20.23, 20.24, 21.25, 21.48, 21.50, 21.51, 21.54, 21.54, 21.54, 21.75, 21.76, 22.7, 22.8, 22.11, 22.11, 22.11, 22.11, 22.12, 22.13, 22.23, 22.25, 22.26, 22.26, 22.26, 22.26, 22.26, 22.27, 22.27, 22.50, 23.10, 23.10, 23.12, 23.20, 23.28, 23.39, 23.39, 24.3, 24.4, 24.25, 24.33, 24.34, 24.34, 24.35, 24.35, 24.39, 24.40, 24.43, 25.26, 25.80, 25.81, 26.15, 26.15, 26.21, 26.22, 26.22, 26.26, 26.37, 27.12, 28.32, 28.40, 28.42, 30.15, 30.33, 30.54, 30.55, 31.31; **ne** 16.43, 16.44, 21.53, 21.54 var., 31.30.
[CL NĔC *FEW* 7: 73; It. *nè*, Sp. *ni*, Fr. *ni*]

nïẹn *n. masc.* nothing; **faire, formar de nïen** to create from nothing, *said of God* 27.3, *of a lady* 16.42; **tener a nïen** to consider as nothing, to scorn 23.33: *obl. sg.* **nïen** 23.33, 27.3, **neien** 16.42. [VL *NĔ GĔNTEM *FEW* 7: 87–88; It. *niente*, Fr. *néant*]

niers *see* **negre.**

no *see* **non.**

nọch *n. fem.* night: *nom. sg.* **nueytz** 4.5; *obl. sg.* **nuoch** 17.6, **nuoit** 8.16, 17.4, **nueyt** 4.23. [CL NŎCTEM *FEW* 7: 217; It. *notte*, Sp. *noche*, Fr. *nuit*; cf. E. *nocturnal*]

noelas *see* **novela.**

no-fes *see* **non-fe.**

noirisa *n. fem.* nurse: *obl. sg.* **noirissa** 13.12. [LL NŪTRĪCĬAM *FEW* 7: 248; Sp. *nodriza*, Fr. *nourrice*, E. *nurse*]

nọm *n. masc.* name 3.3, 30.1; signature 11.53; title 11.38, 12.31, 21.17; mere word (without substance) 16.20; (bad) name, bad reputation 13.70; **aver nom** to be called 3.3, 21.17, 30.1, to have a title 11.38: *obl. sg.* **nom** 3.3, 11.38, 12.31, 13.70, 16.20, 21.17, 30.1, **nóm** 11.53. [CL NŌMEM *FEW* 7: 177; It. *nome*, Sp. *nombre*, Fr. *nom*; cf. E. *to nominate*]

nomen (Latin) *n. neuter* name: *abl. sg.* **nomine** 12.1.

nọn *adv.* not 2.8, 2.15, 2.19, 4.12, 4.20, 4.30, 4.37, 4.41, 6.14, 6.32, 7.6, 8.25, 9.18, 11.3, 11.5, 11.8, 11.12, 11.26, 11.33, 11.42, 11.45, 11.46, 11.47, 11.69, 12.26, 12.27, 12.40, 13.19, 13.63, 13.69, 13.83, 13.86, 13.88 var., 13.91 var., 14.12, 14.17, 14.29, 14.39, 14.41, 14.45, 14.47, 14.53, 14.55, 14.72, 15.10, 15.17, 15.20, 15.49, 15.52, 16.9, 16.16, 16.19, 16.28, 16.35, 17.16, 17.18, 17.38, 18.8, 18.11, 18.15, 18.21, 18.32, 18.33, 18.40, 18.51, 18.55, 18.57, 18.58, 19.2, 19.10, 19.10, 19.12, 19.17, 19.26, 19.31, 19.33, 19.36, 19.38, 19.43, 19.44, 19.49, 19.52, 19.56, 19.60, 19.61, 19.61, 19.68, 20.1, 21.24, 21.43, 21.49, 21.67, 21.73, 21.74, 22.8, 22.12, 22.21, 22.25, 22.28, 22.31, 22.49, 23.6, 23.27, 23.29, 23.38, 23.41, 23.43, 23.44, 24.7, 24.8, 24.36, 24.41, 25.9, 25.79, 26.1, 26.13, 26.26, 26.27, 26.33, 27.6, 27.33, 27.40, 28.11, 28.17, 28.22, 28.25, 28.31, 28.40, 28.41, 28.48, 28.51, 28.64, 29.9, 29.17, 29.39, 30.26, 30.27, 30.32, 30.61, 30.73, 30.79, 30.83, 31.6, 31.13, 31.21, 31.30, 31.33; *negative answer* no 28.24, **dire de no** to say no 12.65; **non . . . ni** not . . . or 8.8, 8.9, 10.17, 12.63, 20.7, 22.23, 30.15, 30.54; **ni (. . .) non** and not, nor 4.32, 6.30,

8.10, 11.48, 14.66, 16.3, 16.44, 17.10, 17.17, 18.35, 18.42, 20.20, 23.28, 23.39, 23.39, 24.39, 28.42; **si** (. . .) **non** if not, unless 10.13, 10.17, 12.24, 14.72, 15.9, 16.2, 16.4, 16.18, 16.21, 16.32, 18.39, 19.61, 23.45, 26.9, 27.24, 27.40, 30.61; *pleonastic (may be omitted in translation)* 7.14, 14.30, 19.17, 19.40, 23.7;

with **a pauc** nearly 19.7; *with* **ab pauc** nearly 9.41, 31.46; *with* **anc** never 6.7, 9.8, 9.29, 11.67, 12.7, 14.65, 18.41, 28.30; *with* **anc mais** never 30.53, never even 18.26; *with* **anc pois** never since 14.31; *with* **de tot** not at all 11.31; *with* **gaire** scarcely 11.13, 16.1; *with* **ges** not at all 9.39, 11.48, 16.17, 17.25, 18.28, 18.57, 19.20, 22.1, 23.21, 26.20, 30.18, 30.40, 30.65, 30.72, 30.93; *with* **ja** never 11.19, 16.8, 16.10, 18.12, 18.31, 20.17, 22.14, 23.13, 27.17; *with* **ja mais** never 3.10, 15.8, 18.18, 18.36, 20.27, 21.60, 23.9, 25.27, 25.85, 30.63; *with* **mais** nothing but 6.24, 13.28, 16.20, no longer 10.3, 10.30, 17.25, 20.16, 23.34, no more 19.64, never 4.32; *with* **miga** not at all 11.11, 11.58; *with* **neis** not even 28.42; *with* **nul** no 15.45, 27.21; *with* **nulla ren** nothing 16.31, 27.21, 30.49; *with* **plus** no longer 10.31, no more 15.7; *with* **ren** nothing 16.21, 16.44, 18.15, 21.39, 21.43, 26.53, 28.26, 28.45, 30.80; *with* **ren mais** nothing else 16.43, 30.25; *with* **si tot** though 20.26; *with* **trop** not very 11.30; *with* **un** not one 18.21.

Forms: **non** 3.10, 4.41, 6.32, 7.6, 8.8, 8.9, 8.25, 9.18, 10.3, 10.17, 10.31, 11.8, 11.13, 11.19, 12.27, 12.63, 13.19, 13.63, 13.69, 13.86, 13.88 var., 13.91 var., 14.12, 14.55, 14.65, 14.66, 15.8, 15.10, 15.17, 15.49, 15.52, 16.3, 16.18, 16.19, 16.21, 16.21, 16.32, 16.43, 17.18, 17.25, 18.12, 18.26, 18.31, 18.41, 18.42, 18.51, 18.55, 18.57, 18.57, 19.17, 19.17, 19.20, 19.31, 19.44, 19.60, 20.7, 20.17, 20.20, 20.27, 21.24, 21.39, 21.43, 21.49, 22.23, 22.28, 22.31, 23.13, 23.13, 23.21, 23.29, 23.39, 23.39, 23.41, 24.7, 24.8, 24.36, 24.39, 24.41, 25.79, 25.85, 26.1, 26.9, 26.13, 26.20, 26.26, 26.27, 26.33, 27.6, 27.17, 27.21, 27.33, 27.40, 28.24, 28.40, 28.45, 28.48, 28.64, 29.17, 30.15, 30.18, 30.25, 30.27, 30.32, 30.40, 30.49, 30.54, 30.61, 30.65, 30.72, 30.73, 30.79, 30.80, 39.93; **no** 2.8, 2.15, 2.19, 4.12, 4.20, 4.30, 4.32, 4.37, 6.7, 6.14, 6.24, 6.30, 7.14, 8.10, 9.8, 9.29, 9.39, 9.41, 9.54, 9.63, 10.13, 10.30, 11.3, 11.5, 11.11, 11.12, 11.26, 11.30, 11.31, 11.33, 11.42, 11.45, 11.46, 11.47, 11.48, 11.58, 11.67, 11.69, 12.7, 12.24, 12.26, 12.40, 12.65, 13.28, 13.83, 14.17, 14.29, 14.30, 14.31, 14.39, 14.41, 14.45, 14.47, 14.53, 14.53, 14.53, 14.72, 15.7, 15.9, 15.20, 15.45, 16.1, 16.2, 16.4, 16.8, 16.9, 16.10, 16.16, 16.17, 16.20, 16.28, 16.31, 16.35, 16.44, 17.10, 17.16, 17.17, 17.38, 18.8, 18.11, 18.15, 18.18, 18.21, 18.28, 18.32, 18.33, 18.35, 18.36, 18.39, 18.40, 18.57, 18.58, 19.2, 19.7, 19.10, 19.10, 19.12, 19.26, 19.33, 19.36, 19.38, 19.40, 19.43, 19.49, 19.52, 19.56, 19.61, 19.61, 19.64, 19.68, 20.1, 20.16, 20.26, 21.60, 21.67, 21.73, 21.74, 22.1, 22.8, 22.12, 22.14, 22.21, 22.25, 22.49, 23.6, 23.7, 23.9, 23.27, 23.28, 23.34, 23.38, 23.43, 23.44, 23.45, 25.9, 25.27, 26.53, 27.24, 27.40, 28.11, 28.17, 28.22, 28.25, 28.30, 28.31, 28.41, 28.42, 28.51, 29.9, 29.39, 30.26, 30.53, 30.63, 30.83, 31.6, 31.13, 31.21, 31.30, 31.31, 31.33, 31.46; **n'** 26.27. [CL Nōn *FEW* 7: 184; It. *non*, Sp. *no*, Fr. *non*]

nǫnca *adv.* never. *Forms:* **nonca** 20.28, **nonqua** 11.14, **noqua** 30.18. [CL Nŭmquam *FEW* 7: 241; Sp. *nunca*]

non-calẹr *n. masc.* indifference: *obl. sg.* **non-chaler** 29.36. [**non** + **caler**]

non-fẹ *n. fem.* faithlessness: *nom. sg.* **no-fes** 12.19. [**non** + **fe** (1)]

nonqua *see* **nonca**.

non-saber *n. masc.* ignorance: *obl. sg.* **non-saber** 16.15. [**non** + **saber**]

noqua *see* **nonca**.

norman *adj.* Norman, of Normandy: *fem., obl. sg.* **normanda** 20.21. *See also Proper Names.* [**Normandia**]

nos *personal pron., 1st pl.* we, us: *nom.* **nos** 8.20, 8.30, 11.1, 11.1, 11.7, 12.11, 17.28, 25.85; *direct object* **nos** 11.4, 11.5, 17.44 var., 31.10, *enclitic* **·ns** 27.48 var., 29.36; *direct object reciprocal* **nos** 31.10; *indirect object* **nos** 3.3, 12.4, 12.30, 12.43, 13.88, 17.27, 17.28, 21.42, 25.26, 27.46, 29.30, 29.46, *enclitic* **·ns** 12.16, 27.17 var., 27.24, 28.65, 29.35; *object of prep.* **nos** 9.30, 9.32, 11.32, 12.6, 26.7, 29.37. [CL Nŏs *FEW* 7: 193; It. *noi,* Sp. *nos(otros),* Fr. *nous*]

nostre *possessive adj., 1st pl.* our; *with def. art. (modifying noun)* **la nostr'** 8.13, **lo nostre** 9.33, **lo nostre** 11.46: *masc., nom. sg.* **nostre** 9.17, 10.30; *obl. sg.* **nostre** 9.33, 11.46, 29.27, 29.47; *nom. pl.* **nostre** 29.40; *fem., nom. sg.* **nostr'** 8.13; *nom. pl.* **nostras** 15.18. [CL NŎSTRUM *FEW* 7: 195; It. *nostro,* Sp. *nuestro,* Fr. *notre*]

notz *see* **nozer**.

novel *adj.* new 8.1, 8.4; unusual 20.3, 27.1; **temps novel** springtime 8.1: *masc., obl. sg.* **novel** 8.1, 8.4, 27.1; *fem., obl. sg.* **novella** 20.3 ms., **novell'** 20.3. [CL NŎVĔLLUM *FEW* 7: 206; It. *novello,* Sp. *novel,* Fr. *nouveau,* E. *novel*]

novela *n. fem.* news: *obl. pl.* **noelas** 25.90. [**novel**]

novell', novella *see* **novel**.

nozer *vb. trans.* to harm: *pres. 3rd sg.* **notz** 19.19. [CL NŎCĒRE *FEW* 7: 162; It. *nuocere,* Sp. *nucir,* Fr. *nuire;* cf. E. *innocent*]

·ns *see* **nos**.

nüalhos *adj.* idle: *masc., nom. sg.* **nüallos** 11.30. [**nualh** 'laziness' (CL NŪGĀLEM 'useless' *FEW* 7: 231) + **-os**]

nuda *see* **nut**.

nueyt, nueytz *see* **noch**.

nul *adj.* any 15.11, 22.30, 23.16 var., 24.42; *with* **non** not any, no 15.45, 16.31, 27.21, 29.17, 30.49: *masc., nom. sg.* **nuls** 24.42, **nuills** 15.45, **lunhs** 29.17; *obl. sg.* **nuill** 22.30, 23.16 var.; *fem., nom. sg.* **nuilla** 16.31, 27.21; *obl. sg.* **nulla** 30.49, **nuilla** 15.11. [CL NŪLLUM *FEW* 7: 233; It. *nulla,* Sp. *nulo,* Fr. *nul,* G. *null,* E. *null*]

nuoch, nuoit *see* **noch**.

nut *adj.* naked: *masc., obl. sg.* **nut** 7.10; *fem., obl. sg.* **nuda** 19.60, 25.58. [CL NŪDUM *FEW* 7: 230; It. *nudo,* Sp. *nudo,* Fr. *nu,* E. *nude*]

o (1) *pron.* neuter, sg., *referring to a clause or phrase, may often be omitted in idiomatic English translation; refers to preceding clause* it 2.5, 10.22, 18.26, 19.14, 19.36, 19.67, 23.21, 23.27, 28.50, 30.60, 31.42, that 3.9, 4.22, 11.11, 30.24, so 9.55; *refers to a following clause* this 10.35, 23.44, it 11.8, 13.13, 19.41, 22.20, 23.44, *omitted from translation* 19.52; *refers to preceding phrase* it 30.40, 30.72, 30.73; **o que** what 3.8.

Forms: *obl.* **o** 2.5, 3.8, 3.9, 4.22, 9.55, 10.22, 10.35, 11.8, 11.11, 13.13, 18.26, 19.14, 19.36, 19.41, 19.52, 19.67, 22.20, 23.21, 23.27, 23.44, 23.44, 28.50, 30.24, 30.60, 30.72, 30.73, 31.42, **ho** 30.40.

[CL HŎC neuter 'this' *FEW* 4: 444]

o (2) *adv.* where; **lai o** *conj.* (there) where 11.61. [CL ŬBI *FEW* 14: 3; It. *ove,* Fr. *où*]

ǫ (3) *conj.* or *in contexts not marked by negation or uncertainty* (cf. **ni**): **o** 12.8, 13.23, 14.54, 14.56, 17.22, 25.30, 25.41, 25.41, **ho** 27.39; **o . . . o** whether . . . or 14.54 var., or . . . or 25.51. [CL AUT *FEW* 1: 186; It. *o*, Sp. *o*, Fr. *ou*]

obedïęn *adj.* obedient: *masc., nom. sg.* **obedïenz** 10.3. [CL ŏBOEDĬENTEM *FEW* 7: 278; It. *ubbidiente*, Sp. *obediente*, E. *obedient*]

oblidar *vb. trans.* to forget 4.30, 28.31, 29.23, 30.93; *refl.* to forget oneself, to swoon, to lose consciousness 18.3: *pres. 3rd sg.* **oblida** 18.3 ms., 28.31, **oblid'** 18.3; *imper. 2nd pl.* **oblidetz** 4.30; *pp., neuter, nom. sg.* **oblidat** 29.23; *inf.* **oblidar** 30.93. [VL *ŏBLĪTĀRE *FEW* 7: 274; Sp. *olvidar*, Fr. *oublier*]

ǫbra *n. fem.* work; woven work, cloth 26.2; created being, creature 29.43: *obl. sg.* **obra** 26.2; *obl. pl.* **obras** 29.43. [CL ŏPĔRA *FEW* 7: 363; It. *opera*, Sp. *huebra*, Fr. *oeuvre*, E. *opera*]

obrir *vb. trans.* to open (the gate of Heaven): *pres. 3rd sg.* **obre** 27.24 var., **huebre** 27.24 var., *2nd pl.* **obretz** 27.24 var., **obres** 27.24, **ubres** 27.24 var. [CL ĂPĔRĪRE VL *ŏPĔRĪRE influenced by CL COOPĔRĪRE **cobrir** *FEW* 1: 103; It. *aperire*, Sp. *abrir*, Fr. *ouvrir*]

óbs *see* **ops**.

ǫc *adv.* yes: **oc** 13.78, 28.48. [VL HŎC *FEW* 4: 443; Fr. *oui*]

ocaizonar *vb. trans.* to accuse: *inf.* **ochaisonar** 27.4. [LL ŏCCĂSĬŌNĒM *FEW* 7: 295 + **-ar** (2); It. *cagionare*, Fr. *occasionner*]

ǫch *num.* eight: **ueit** 9.62. [CL ŏCTŌ; It. *otto*, Sp. *ocho*, Fr. *huit*; cf. E. *octopus*]

ochaisonar *see* **ocaizonar**.

ofíci *n. masc.* liturgical office, the daily service of the breviary: *obl. sg.* **ofizi** 30.30. [CL ŏFFĬCĬUM *FEW* 7: 337; It. *ufficio*, Sp. *oficio*, Fr. *office*, E. *office*]

ofręnda *n. fem.* offertory, the part of the Mass in which the unconsecrated bread and wine of the Eucharist are offered to God: *obl. sg.* **uffrenda** 30.30. [ChL ŏFFĔRĔNDA 'things to be offered' *FEW* 7: 333; Fr. *offrande*]

ǫi *adv.* today. *Forms:* **huei** 25.19, 25.30, **hui** 30.61. [CL HŎDĬĒ *FEW* 4: 449; It. *oggi*, Sp. *hoy*, Fr. *(aujourd')hui*]

oills, oillz, oils, oilz, *see* **olh**.

oimais *adv.* henceforth, from now on. *Forms:* **oimais** 23.41, 25.94, **ueymay** 19.33, **hueymais** 19.45, **hueymay** 19.48. [**oi** + **mais**]

ǫlh *n. masc.* eye: *obl. sg.* **huoill** 22.19, **uelh** 12.25; *obl. pl.* **olhs** 25.71, **oilz** 30.54, **oillz** 16.7, 16.47, **oils** 30.95, **oills** 15.35, **uels** 23.28, **huoils** 12.25 var., **huoills** 7.16, 18.43, **huelhs** 18.43 var. [CL ŏCŬLUM *FEW* 7: 321; It. *occhio*, Sp. *ojo*, Fr. *oeil*; cf. E. *oculist*]

ǫli *n. masc.* olive oil: *obl. sg.* **oli** 26.20. [CL (from Gk.) ŏLĔUM *FEW* 7: 344; It. *olio*, Sp. *olio*, Fr. *huile*, E. *oil*]

ǫltra *prep.* across 11.65; **d'oltra** across 12.7, 25.102. *Forms:* **outra** 25.102, **otra** 12.7, **ultra** 11.65. [CL ŬLTRA *FEW* 14: 11; It. *oltre*, Fr. *outre*]

oltracuidat *adj.* presumptuous, reckless: *masc., obl. sg.* **outracujat** 29.32. [**oltra** + **cuidar** (1)]

om *see* **ome**.

omanatge *see* **omenatge**.

ǫme *n. masc.* man 1.1, 3.6, 5.3, 8.5, 8.6, 9.31, 11.1, 11.7, 11.20, 11.21, 11.33, 11.69, 12.38, 13.64, 14.44, 16.42, 17.31, 17.45, 19.2, 19.53, 24.25, 24.36, 24.42, 25.20, 25.105, 26.31, 26.50, 30.68; *in feudal sense* vassal 20.27; *impersonal* one 6.15, 13.61, 26.16, you 2.15, 14.50, 14.60, 17.20,

26.10, they 4.19, 29.20, people 6.30, we 21.39; *impersonal verb with* **om** *as subject may be translated with passive verb* 2.8, 13.58, 18.52, 21.49, 26.39, 30.17.

> *Forms: nom. sg.* **om** 2.8, 2.15, 4.19, 6.15, 8.5, 11.33, 11.69, 13.58, 13.61, 14.50, 17.31, 18.52, 19.2, 21.39, 26.10, 26.50, **on** 26.16, 26.39, **hom** 1.1, 3.6, 5.3, 6.30, 8.6, 9.31, 13.64, 14.60, 17.20, 17.45, 21.49, 24.42, 29.20, 30.17, **homs** 30.68; *obl. sg.* **ome** 26.31, **home** 12.38, 16.42, **om** 19.53; *vocative sg.* **hom** 24.25; *nom. pl.* **ome** 11.20, 11.21, **omne** 11.1, 11.7; *obl. pl.* **omes** 24.36, **homes** 14.44, 20.27, **homes** *used as nom. pl.* 25.20, 25.105.
>
> [CL ʜŏᴍĭɴᴇᴍ *FEW* 4: 457; It. *uomo*, Sp. *hombre*, Fr. *homme, on*; cf. E. *homicide*]

omenatge *n. masc.* homage, respect paid by ritual gesture: *obl. sg.* **omanatge** 13.66. [**ome(n)** + **-atge**]

omicidïer *adj.* murderous: *masc., nom. sg.* **homicidïers** 25.95. [**omicida** (CL ʜŏᴍĭᴄīᴅᴀᴍ *FEW* 4: 453) + **-ier**]

omnipotęnt *adj.* omnipotent, all-powerful: *masc., obl. sg.* **omnipotent** 11.16. [CL ŏᴍɴĭᴘŏᴛᴇ̆ɴᴛᴇᴍ *FEW* 7: 353; It. *onnipotente*, Sp. *omnipotente*, Fr. *omnipotent*, E. *omnipotent*]

on (1) *n. masc.* 26.16, 26.39, *see* **ome**.

ǫn (2) *interrogative adv., in direct question* where? 18.28, *in indirect question* where, in what place 18.40, 18.58; *conj.* where 2.11, 4.13, 30.48, 31.3; in whom 6.28, 10.28; to whom 10.28 var.; in which 32.16; because of which 21.79; which is why 7.7 var. (= **don** 7.7); **de lai on** from the place where 30.82; **on mais** when most 23.36; **on plus** when most 23.8; **on que** wherever 4.29; **lai on** (there) where 11.61, 13.26, 25.69, 27.48.

> *Forms:* **on** *passim;* **ont** 32.16.
>
> [CL ŭɴᴅᴇ *FEW* 14: 33; It. *onde*]

onchura *n. fem.* seasoning: *obl. sg.* **onchura** 26.20, **onchira** 26.20 var., **unchura** 26.20 var. [CL ᴜɴᴄᴛūʀᴀᴍ influenced by **ǫnher** (CL ŭɴɢŭᴇ̆ʀᴇ 'to dress [food] with oil' *FEW* 14: 29); Sp. *untura*, Fr. *ointure*]

ǫnda *n. fem.* wave, *fig.* sea, death by drowning 19.23. [CL ŭɴᴅᴀᴍ *FEW* 14: 31; It. *onda*, Sp. *onda*, Fr. *onde*]

onǫr *n. fem.* honor, personal merit 5.10; demonstration of respect 1.7; **faire onor a** to show respect (for) 5.4, 17.27; **faire onors** to confer honors, marks of respect 21.9; **portar onor a** to feel respect for 12.40; fief 10.14, 11.48; empire (in Heaven) 12.31; domain, region 11.36: *obl. sg.* **onor** 10.14, 11.36, 11.48, 17.27, **honor** 1.7, 5.4, 5.10, 12.31, 12.40; *obl. pl.* **honors** 21.9. [CL ʜŏɴōʀᴇᴍ *FEW* 4: 466; It. *onore*, Sp. *honor*, Fr. *honneur*, E. *honor*]

onransa *n. fem.* demonstration of respect: *obl. sg.* **onransa** 28.46. [**onrar** + **-ansa**]

onrar *vb. trans.* to honor, to show respect for: *pres. subj. 3rd pl.* **onren** 10.38. [CL ʜŏɴōʀāʀᴇ *FEW* 4: 464; It. *onorare*, Sp. *honrar*, Fr. *honorer*, E. *to honor*]

ont *see* **on** (2).

ǫps *n. masc.* what is necessary; **a óbs** for the benefit of, to the advantage of, for, 11.66; **aver/eser ops a** to be necessary to, **X a ops a Y** Y needs X 24.9, **X es ops a Y** Y needs X 28.15. [CL ŏᴘᴜs *FEW* 7: 381; It. *uopo*]

ǫra *n. fem.* hour of the day 31.24; moment 18.42, 19.41, 23.30; duration of time 25.45; **de l'ora en sai que** ever since 18.42; **en petida d'ora** quickly, soon 25.45: *nom. sg.* **ora** 31.24; *obl. sg.* **ora** 19.41, 23.30, 25.45,

or' 18.42. [CL (from Gk.) нōʀᴀᴍ *FEW* 4: 476; It. *ora*, Sp. *hora*, Fr. *heure*, G. *Uhr*, E. *hour*]

orba *see* **orp.**

orde *n. masc.* (monastic) order 5.15; liturgical office, ceremony, Mass; *erotic* **l'orde de san Macari** the ceremony of Saint Macareus (= Saint My Flesh-ious), fornication 31.19 note: *obl. sg.* **orde** 5.15 var., 31.19, **orden** 5.15 var., **ordre** 5.15. [CL ŏʀᴅīɴᴇᴍ *FEW* 7: 407; It. *ordine*, Sp. *órden*, Fr. *ordre*, E. *order*]

orgolh *n. masc.* pride: *obl. sg.* **orgoill** 10.34, **orguelh** 12.26, 12.58, **erguelh** 19.17, 29.25. [Frankish *ŭrgōlī FEW* 17: 414; It. *orgoglio*, Sp. *orgullo*, Fr. *orgueil*]

orgolhos *adj.* proud: *masc., nom. sg.* **orgoillos** 3.3. [**orgolh** + **-os**]

orguelh *see* **orgolh.**

ormier *n. masc.* ornament made of gold: *obl. pl.* **ormers** 25.7. [OFr. *or mier* 'pure gold' (CL ᴀᴜʀᴜᴍ ᴍᴇ̆ʀᴜᴍ *FEW* 6, part 2: 39)]

orp *adj.* blind: *fem., nom. sg.* **orba** 14.56. [CL ŏʀʙᴜᴍ *FEW* 7: 391; It. *orbo*, Fr. *(mur) orbe* 'blind wall, wall with no opening']

ort *n. masc.* garden: *obl. sg.* **ort** 22.14, 24.38; *obl. pl.* **ortz** 25.46. [CL ʜŏʀᴛᴜᴍ *FEW* 4: 490; It. *orto*, Sp. *huerto*; cf. E. *horticulture*]

ospitalier *n. masc.* Hospitaler, member of the monastic order of the Hospital of Saint John in Jerusalem: *obl. sg.* **ospitalers** 25.64. [**ospital** (CL ʜŏsᴘῐᴛᴀ̄ʟᴇᴍ *FEW* 4: 498) + **-ier**]

ostal *n. masc.* dwelling of a prince, court 21.31; home *(opposed to departure on crusade)* 12.52; priest's quarters 31.17; lodging *(for a traveler)* 15.23 var. (= **alberc** [1] 15.23): *obl. sg.* **ostal** 15.23 var., 31.17, **hostal** 21.31; *obl. pl.* **ostaus** 12.52. [CL ʜŏsᴘῐᴛᴀ̄ʟᴇᴍ *FEW* 4: 497; It. *ostello*, Fr. *hôtel*, E. *hostel, hotel*]

oste *n. masc.* innkeeper; *nom. sg.* **ostes** 30.40; *obl. sg.* **oste** 30.38, **hoste** 30.99. [CL ʜŏsᴘῐᴛᴇᴍ *FEW* 4: 492; It. *ospite*, Sp. *huésped*, Fr. *hôte*, E. *host*]

otra, outra *see* **oltra.**

outracujat *see* **oltracuidat.**

pagan *n. masc.* pagan: *nom. pl.* **payan** 12.36; *obl. pl.* **payas** 12.36 var. [CL ᴘᴀ̄ɢᴀ̄ɴᴜᴍ *FEW* 7: 466; It. *pagano*, Sp. *pagano*, Fr. *payen*, E. *pagan*]

paganor *n. masc.* of the pagans: **payanor** 12.58. [CL ᴘᴀ̄ɢᴀ̄ɴōʀᴜᴍ gen. pl. of ᴘᴀ̄ɢᴀ̄ɴᴜᴍ; cf. **pagan**]

pagar *vb. trans.* to pay for: *pp., masc., obl. sg.* **pagat** paid for 21.31. [CL ᴘᴀ̄ᴄᴀ̄ʀᴇ *FEW* 7: 458; It. *pagare*, Sp. *pagar*, Fr. *payer*, E. *to pay*]

pages *adj.* country, of the country, raised in the country: *fem., obl. sg.* **pagesza** 26.11. [LL ᴘᴀ̄ɢē(ɴ)sᴇᴍ *FEW* 7: 471; It. *paese*, Sp. *país*, Fr. *pays*; cf. E. *peasant*]

paire *n. masc.* father: *nom. sg.* **paire** 20.5, 21.18, **payre** 13.30; *obl. sg.* **paire** 27.47; *obl. pl.* **paires** 26.56. [CL ᴘᴀ̆ᴛʀᴇᴍ *FEW* 8: 11; It. *padre*, Sp. *padre*, Fr. *père*; cf. E. *paternal*]

pairin *n. masc.* godfather: *nom. sg.* **pairis** 15.48, 15.51. [LL ᴘᴀᴛʀīɴᴜᴍ *FEW* 8: 23; It. *padrino*, Sp. *padrino*, Fr. *parrain*]

pairon *n. masc.* father: *obl. pl.* **pairos** 27.47 var. [CL ᴘᴀᴛʀōɴᴜᴍ *FEW* 8: 27; It. *padrone*, Sp. *padrón*, Fr. *patron*, E. *patron, pattern*]

paisar *vb. intrans.* to eat: *pres. subj. 3rd sg.* **passe** 26.24; *pres. part., masc., obl. sg.* **paissan** 3.7. [**paiser** + **-ar** (2); see 3.7 note]

paiser *vb. trans.* to feed, to nourish: *pres. 3rd sg.* **pais** 11.5. [CL PASCĔRE *FEW* 7: 699; It. *pascere,* Sp. *pacer,* Fr. *paître*]

palaitz *see* **palatz** (2).

palatz (1) *n. masc.* palace: *nom. sg.* **palatz** 15.42. [CL PALĀTĬUM 'the Palatine hill in Rome,' later 'imperial palace' *FEW* 7: 489; It. *palazzo,* Sp. *palacio,* Fr. *palais,* E. *palace*]

palatz (2) *adj.* palatine; *occurs only in the expression* **coms palatz** 20.22, vars. **palaitz, pallatz,** *masc., nom. sg.* count palatine, count having royal prerogatives within his county. [= ML CŎMES PALĀTĬĪ 'count of the palace, count palatine' *FEW* 7: 489]

palaziṇ *n. masc.* palace: *obl. pl.* **palazins** 15.40 var. [CL PALĀTĪNUM 'the Palatine hill in Rome,' 'pertaining to the emperor' (whose palace was on the Palatine), 'imperial' *FEW* 7: 488; It. *paladino,* Sp. *paladín,* Fr. *paladin,* E. *paladin*]

pallatz *see* **palatz** (2).

paṇ (1) *n. masc.* bread: *nom. sg.* **pans** 9.27; *obl. sg.* **pan** 5.2, 9.27 var., 26.18, 32.18. [CL PĀNEM *FEW* 7: 551; It. *pane,* Sp. *pan,* Fr. *pain*]

pan (2) *n. masc.* lappet, loose flap or fold of a garment 21.22; *fig.* shred, trace 22.18: *nom. sg.* **pans** 22.18; *nom. pl.* **pan** 21.22. [CL PǍNNUM *FEW* 7: 562; It. *panno,* Sp. *paño,* Fr. *pan*]

pans (1) *n. masc.* 9.27, *see* **pan** (1).

pans (2) *n. masc.* 22.18, *see* **pan** (2).

paọr *n. fem.* fear, fright: *nom. sg.* **paors** 24.19; *obl. sg.* **paor** 10.6. [CL PAVŌREM *FEW* 8: 89; It. *paura,* Sp. *pavor,* Fr. *peur*]

papa *n. masc.* pope: *nom. sg.* **papa** 31.39. [ChL PĀPAM 'bishop' *FEW* 7: 572; It. *papa,* Sp. *papa,* Fr. *pape,* E. *pope*]

par (1) *adj.* equal, peer: *masc., obl. sg.* **par** 12.9; *nom. pl.* **par** 3.63. [CL PĀREM *FEW* 7: 601; It. *pari,* Sp. *par,* Fr. *pair,* E. *peer*]

par (2) *vb. intrans.* 19.27, 19.32, 29.30, 29.40, 30.66, *pres. 3rd sg. of* **parer,** *which see.*

par (3) *prep.* 8.18 var., *see* **per.**

parar *vb. trans.* to peel (fruit): *inf.* **parar** 15.33. [CL PARĀRE 'to make ready' *FEW* 7: 635; It. *parare,* Sp. *parar,* Fr. *parer,* E. *to pare*]

paratge *n. masc.* nobility: *nom. sg.* **paratges** 25.94. [**par** (1) + **-atge**]

paraula *n. fem.* word, speech: *obl. sg.* **paraula** 13.73; *obl. pl.* **paraulas** 8.27. [CL PARABŎLAM 'explanation' *FEW* 7: 605; It. *parola,* Sp. *palabra,* Fr. *parole,* E. *parable, parole*]

pareglia *see* **parelh.**

pareillatura *see* **parelhatura.**

parẹlh *adj.* similar, companionable: *masc., obl. sg.* **parelh** 13.19; *fem., obl. sg.* **pareglia** 13.73 var. [LL PARĬCŬLUM *FEW* 7: 650; It. *parecchio,* Sp. *parejo,* Fr. *pareil*; cf. E. *apparel*]

parelhar *vb. trans.* to prepare, to arrange, to make ready: *inf.* **perigliar** 13.73 var. [**parelh** + **-ar** (2)]

parelharia *n. fem.* companionship: *nom. sg.* **parelhayria** 13.24. [**parelh** + **-aria**]

parelhatura *n. fem.* resemblance, similarity, coupling (*erotic*): *obl. sg.* **pareillatura** 13.73 var. [**parelh** + **-atura**]

parelhayria *see* **parelharia.**

parẹn *n. masc.* kinsman: *obl. sg.* **parent** 11.8. [CL PARĔNTEM *FEW* 7: 644; It. *parenti,* Sp. *pariente,* Fr. *parent,* E. *parent*]

parẹr *vb. intrans.* to seem, to appear: *pres. 3rd sg.* **par** 19.27, 19.32, 29.30, 29.40, 30.66, *2nd pl.* **paretz** 25.18; *fut. 3rd sg.* **parra** 15.22, 15.26; *inf.* **parer** 18.49, 30.87. [CL PĀRĒRE *FEW* 7: 647; It. *parere*]

paria *n. fem.* company, companionship: *nom. sg.* **paria** 28.14; *obl. sg.* **paria** 13.19. [**par** (1) + **-ia**]

parier *adj.* partner: *fem., nom. sg.* **parieira** 28.55. [**par** (1) + **-ier**]

parla *see* **parlar**.

parlamẹn *n. masc.* speech, conversation: *nom. sg.* **parlamens** 15.26; *obl. sg.* **parlamen** 30.58. [**parlar** + **-amen** (1)]

parlar *vb. intrans.* to speak: *pres. 3rd sg.* **parla** 14.21, *1st pl.* **parllam** 11.2; *pres. subj. 1st pl.* **parlem** 13.73; *pres. part., masc., obl. sg.* **parlan** 21.5; **anar parlan** to talk unceasingly 21.12; *pp., masc., nom. sg.* **parlatz** 20.22 var. (?); *substantivized inf., masc., obl. sg.* **parlar** speech 9.32. [ChL PARABŎLĀRE *FEW* 7: 612; It. *parlare*, Sp. *parlar*, Fr. *parler*; cf. E. *parlor*]

parlier *adj.* talkative: *fem., nom. sg.* **parleyra** 19.33. [**parlar** + **-ier**]

parllam *see* **parlar**.

parra *see* **parer**.

parsonier *n. masc.* partner: *nom. sg.* **parsoniers** 22.41. [**parsọṇ** (CL PARTĪTĬŌNEM 'share,' VL *PARTĬŌNEM *FEW* 7: 693; cf. E. *partition*) + **-ier**]

part (1) *n. fem.* part, share 24.17; responsibility 29.39; side, direction 14.17, 15.11, 22.17, 25.74, 29.4; **de part** on behalf of, in the name of 11.5; **d'autra part** on the other hand 26.12: *nom. sg.* **partz** 24.17; *obl. sg.* **part** 14.17, 15.11, 25.74, 29.39; *obl. pl.* **partz** 22.17, 29.4. [CL PARTEM *FEW* 7: 672; It. *parte*, Sp. *parte*, Fr. *part*, E. *part*]

part (2) *prep.* beyond: 9.1, 20.23. [**part** (1)]

part (3) *vb. intrans. and trans.* 4.21, 12.20, 18.37, *pres. 3rd sg. of* **partir,** *which see.*

parta, partez, parti *see* **partir**.

partida *n. fem.* part, side 25.50; choice 27.37: *obl. sg.* **partia** 27.37; *obl. pl.* **partidas** 25.50. [**partir** + **-ida, -ia**]

partir *vb. intrans.* to depart 10.18, to separate 10.26; *trans.* to separate 4.21, 8.26, 12.20, 18.37, 22.19; to part, to share 26.37; to smash 25.72; *refl.* to depart 5.9, *with* **de** to depart from 4.32, 5.10, 15.3, 15.15, 30.88, to abandon 17.44.

   Forms: pres. 2nd sg. **partz** 22.19, *3rd sg.* **part** 4.21, 12.20, 18.37, *1st pl.* **partem** 10.26; *2nd pl.* **partez** 17.44, *3rd pl.* **parton** 26.37; *pres. subj. 3rd sg.* **parta** 8.26; *fut. 1st sg.* **partrai** 4.32, 15.15; *pret. 3rd sg.* **parti** 5.10, **partic** 5.10 var., 25.72, **partit** 5.10 var.; *past subj. 3rd* **partis** 5.9, 30.88; *pp., masc., nom. sg.* **partitz** 15.3, **partiz** 10.18; *substantivized inf., masc., obl. sg.* **partir** departure 13.55.

   [CL PARTĪRE *FEW* 7: 689; It. *partire*, Sp. *partir*, Fr. *partir*, E. *to part*]

partz (1) *n. fem.* 22.17, 24.17, 29.4, *see* **part** (1).

partz (2) *vb. trans.* 22.19, *see* **partir**.

parvẹn *n. masc.* appearance: *obl. sg.* **parven** 16.20. [*pres. part.* of **parer**; **-v-** from CL *pret.* PARŬĪ; cf. Adams 126]

parvẹnsa *n. fem.* opinion: *obl. sg.* **parvensa** 28.22. [**parven** + **-ensa**]

pas *n. fem.* pax ['peace' in Latin], a small tablet representing the Crucifixion, the Virgin, a saint, etc.; formerly, during the service of the Eucharist, the celebrant and worshipers kissed the tablet: *nom. sg.* **pas** 30.43; *obl. sg.* **pas** 30.37, 30.50; cf. **patz, pax**.

pasar *vb. intrans.* to pass *(of time)* 29.5, 32.16; *trans.* to pass, to cross over 11.56: *pres. subj. 3rd pl.* **passen** 11.56; *pp., masc., obl. sg.* **(temps) passat** past *(time)* 29.5; *substantivized pp., masc., obl. sg.* **·l passat** past time, the past 32.16. [VL *PASSĀRE *FEW* 7: 726; It. *passare,* Sp. *pasar,* Fr. *passer,* E. *to pass*]

pasion *n. fem.* Passion, Crucifixion: *obl. sg.* **passio** 11.24. [ChL PASSIŌNEM *FEW* 7: 733; It. *passione,* Sp. *pasión,* Fr. *passion,* E. *passion*]

passe *see* **paisar.**

passen *see* **pasar.**

passio *see* **pasion.**

pastar *vb. trans.* to knead: *pp., masc., obl. sg.* **pastat** 32.18. [**pasta** (LL PAS-TAM 'dough' *FEW* 7: 749; It. *pasta,* Sp. *pasta,* Fr. *pâte,* E. *paste*) + **-ar** (2)]

pastora *n. fem.* shepherdess: *obl. sg.* **pastora** 13.2. [**pastor** (CL PASTŌREM *FEW* 7: 760; It. *pastore,* Sp. *pastor,* Fr. *pâtre,* E. *pastor*) + **-a**]

pastorjar *vb. trans.* to pasture, to tend: *inf.* **pastorjar** 13.20. [**pastor** + **-eiar**]

pastura *n. fem.* pasture: *obl. sg.* **pastura** 13.75. [LL PASTŪRAM *FEW* 7: 765; It. *pastura,* Sp. *pastura,* Fr. *pâture,* E. *pasture*]

patena *n. fem.* paten, the plate holding the bread in the Eucharist: *obl. sg.* **patena** 30.97. [ChL (from Gk.) PATĬNAM *FEW* 8: 18; It. *patena,* Sp. *patena,* Fr. *patène,* E. *paten*]

pater (Latin) *n. masc.* father: *vocative sg.* **pater** 11.75.

patz *n. fem.* peace: *nom. sg.* **patz** 22.21; *obl. sg.* **patz** 19.48, 19.54. [CL PĀCEM *FEW* 8: 94; It. *pace,* Sp. *paz,* Fr. *paix,* E. *peace*; cf. **pas, pax**]

paubre *adj.* poor: *masc., obl. pl.* **paubres** 1.3 var., **paubre** *used as obl. pl.* 1.3 (see note); *fem., obl. sg.* **paubra** 5.2, 26.40. [CL PAUPĔREM *FEW* 8: 59, VL PAUPĔRUM; It. *povero,* Sp. *pobre,* Fr. *pauvre,* E. *poor*]

paubreza *n. fem.* poverty: *nom. sg.* **paubreza** 26.33. [**paubre** + **-eza**]

pauc (1) *adj.* little: *masc., nom. sg.* **paucs** 19.19 var.; *obl. sg.* **pauc** 28.6; *fem., obl. sg.* **pauca** little, short 4.23. [CL PAUCUM *FEW* 8: 54; It. *poco,* Sp. *poco,* Fr. *peu*]

pauc (2) *adv.* little: **pauc** 13.13, 19.19, 19.19. [**pauc** (1)]

pauc (3) *n. masc.* small amount, bit; **ab/a pauc** (. . .) **no** almost 9.41, 9.63, 19.7, 31.46; **un pauc** *adverbial* a little 13.35, 31.20: *obl. sg.* **pauc** 13.68, 19.27. [**pauc** (1)]

paus *n. masc.* rest, peace: *obl. sg.* **paus** 12.70. [CL PAUSUM; cf. *FEW* 8: 62; Sp. *poso*; cf. E. *repose*]

pausar *see* **pauzar.**

pauza *n. fem.* time; **d'esta pauza** at this time: *obl. sg.* **pauza** 31.21. [**pauzar** *FEW* 8: 62 + **-a**]

pauzar *vb. trans.* to place, put: *inf.* **pausar** 6.18. [VL PAUSĀRE *FEW* 8: 73; It. *posare,* Sp. *posar,* Fr. *poser,* E. *to pose*]

pax (Latin) *n. fem.* peace: *nom. sg.* **pax** 12.1; cf. **pas, patz.**

payan, payanor, payas, *see* **pagan-.**

payre *see* **paire.**

pazimentier *n. masc.* paving: *obl. pl.* **pazimenters** 25.100. [**pazimen, païmen** (CL PAVĪMĔNTUM; It. *pavimento,* Sp. *pavimiento,* E. *pavement*; *FEW* 8: 80, where the intrusive **-z-** is explained as a means to eliminate the hiatus in **païmen**) + **-ier**]

pe *n. masc.* foot: *obl. pl.* **pes** *used as nom. pl.* 25.12. [CL PĔDEM *FEW* 8: 305; It. *piede,* Sp. *pié,* Fr. *pied*; cf. E. *pedal*]

pebrada *n. fem.* pepper sauce; **far pebrada** to prepare with a pepper sauce: *obl. sg.* **peurada** 3.7 (see note). [VL (SALSAM) PĪPĔRĀTAM 'pepper sauce' *FEW* 8: 553; Fr. *poivrade*]

pębre *n. masc.* pepper: *nom. sg.* **peur'** 9.28 var. [CL PĬPER neuter *FEW* 8: 554; It. *pepe,* Sp. *pebre,* Fr. *poivre,* G. *Pfeffer,* E. *pepper*]

pecadọr *n. masc.* sinner: *nom. pl.* **peccador** 10.28, 11.76, 29.44. [LL PĔCCĀTŌREM *FEW* 8: 100; It. *peccatore,* Sp. *pecador,* Sp. *pécheur*]

pecat *n. masc.* sin: *nom. sg.* **pecchatz** 27.42; *obl. sg.* **pecat** 23.47. [CL PĔCCĀTUM *FEW* 8: 100; It. *peccato,* Sp. *pecado,* Fr. *péché*; cf. E. *peccadillo*]

peccador *see* **pecador.**

pecchatz *see* **pecat.**

pein *see* **penher.**

peior *see* **pejor.**

pęira *n. fem.* stone: *nom. sg.* **peira** 25.67 var., 25.69; *obl. sg.* **peira** 25.83; *obl. pl.* **peiras** 25.49, **pèiras** 32.4. [CL (from Gk.) PĔTRAM *FEW* 8: 321; It. *pietra,* Sp. *piedra,* Fr. *pierre*; cf. E. *petroleum*]

peirier *n. masc.* catapult, war machine to hurl stones: *obl. pl.* **peiriers** 25.40. [**peira** + **-ier**]

peiriera *n. fem.* catapult, war machine to hurl stones: *nom. sg.* **peireir'** 25.67; *obl. sg.* **peireira** 25.66. [LL PĔTRĀRĬA *FEW* 8: 322 note 19; It. *petraia,* Sp. *pedrera*]

peiriers *see* **peirier.**

pęis *n. masc.* fish: *obl. sg.* **peis** 26.21. [CL PĬSCEM *FEW* 8: 586; It. *pesce,* Sp. *pez,* Fr. *poisson*]

pejọr *comparative adj.* worse: *masc., nom. pl.* **peior** 11.21; *fem., obl. sg.* **peior** 17.42. [CL PĒJŌREM *FEW* 8: 156; It. *peggiore,* Sp. *peor,* Fr. *pire*; cf. E. *pejorative*]

pęl (1) *n. masc.* hair: *obl. pl.* **pels** 9.38, 31.28, 31.31. [CL PĬLUM *FEW* 8: 514; It. *pelo,* Sp. *pelo,* Fr. *poil*; cf. E. *depilatory*]

pęl (2) *enclitic* = **per lo** through the 30.43, throughout the 21.52, for the 21.45, because of the 13.34, 21.41, 30.67; cf. **pels** (2), **per.**

pelar *vb. trans.* to harvest, to reap: *inf.* **pelar** 19.28. [CL PĬLĀRE 'to pluck' *FEW* 8: 488; It. *pelare,* Sp. *pelar,* Fr. *peler,* E. *to peel*]

pelegriṇ *n. masc.* pilgrim: *nom. sg.* **pelleris** 15.33; *nom. pl.* **pellegri** 10.28 var.; *obl. pl.* **pelerins** 1.2. [CL PĔRĔGRĪNUM, LL PĔLĔGRĪNUM *FEW* 8: 234; It. *pellegrino,* Fr. *pèlerin,* E. *pilgrim*]

pelisa *n. fem.* fur-lined cloak: *obl. sg.* **pelissa** 13.5. [LL PĔLLĬCĬAM (TŪNĬCAM) *FEW* 8: 164; It. *pelliccia,* Sp. *pelliza,* Fr. *pelisse*]

pellegri, pelleris *see* **pelegrin.**

pęls (1) *n. masc.* 9.38, 31.28, 31.31, *see* **pel** (1).

pęls (2) *enclitic* = **per los** by the 15.35; cf. **pel** (2), **per.**

pęna *n. fem.* pain, suffering: *obl. sg.* **pena** 18.26; **a penas** *adverbial* scarcely, barely 29.15. [CL (from Gk.) POENAM *FEW* 9: 117; It. *pena,* Sp. *pena,* Fr. *peine,* E. *pain*]

penar *vb. refl.* to suffer in vain, to waste one's time: *pret. 3rd sg.* **penét** 11.26. [**pena** + **-ar** (2)]

penchura *n. fem.* picture, painting: *obl. sg.* **penchura** 13.89, **pintura** 13.91 var. [CL PĬCTŪRAM, VL *PĬNCTŪRAM, influenced by PĪNGĔRE 'to paint' *FEW* 8: 431; It. *pittura,* Sp. *pintura,* Fr. *peinture,* E. *picture*]

pęndre *vb. trans.* to hang: *pp., masc., nom. sg.* **pendutz** 31.5. [CL PĔNDĔRE *FEW* 8: 182; It. *pendere,* Sp. *pender,* Fr. *pendre*; cf. E. *to depend*]

penedęnsa *n. fem.* repentance, penance: *obl. sg.* **penedensa** 25.96, **pene-**
denza 11.13. [CL POENĬTĔNTĬAM *FEW* 9: 120; Sp. *penedencia,* E. *peni-*
tence]

penét *see* **penar.**

pęnher *vb. trans.* to paint: *pres. 3rd sg.* **pein** 30.17. [CL PĬNGĔRE *FEW* 8:
525; It. *pingere,* Fr. *peindre,* E. *to paint*]

pensan *see* **pezar.**

per *prep.* through 8.18; throughout 25.91; along 25.101; on, over 11.4,
13.8; **per l'aiga** on the river 25.14; through (whom), with (whose) help
11.3, 11.6, 11.25; because of 1.2, 1.7, 5.15, 6.26, 7.2, 9.17, 9.32, 12.60,
17.45, 18.4, 19.51, 21.57, 21.59, 21.77, 25.64, 28.10, 29.8, 29.25, 29.31,
29.32, 30.19, 30.53, 31.32; for fear of 20.27; by means of 20.17, 22.30,
23.37; out of 1.4, 11.2, 11.27, 11.51, 12.4, 16.15, 19.36, 29.46; for the
sake of 9.71, 15.14, 16.24, 19.66, 22.27, 24.26, 24.27, 26.7, 26.18, 26.35,
30.49; in exchange for 2.6, 13.68, 15.31, 27.44; for 13.70, 25.92; in order
to 5.2 var. (= **a** 5.2, **de** 5.2 var.), 13.17, 13.77, 21.9, 30.3, 31.7, 32.12; by
(expressing agent) 28.38, 28.63; by *(expressing means)* 11.57, 13.58,
31.34; by *(expressing manner)* 9.49; according to 14.67 (= **ab** 14.67
var.); with *(expressing manner)* 11.52, 26.45.

   Introducing expressions **per aiso** for that reason 15.20, 30.45 (cf.
pero, per so); **per dreg** by rights, deservedly 12.54, **per bon dreg**
27.14; **per fe** with trust 23.10; **per me** for myself, by my own experience 4.22; **per mort** as a dead man, as though dead 1.4, 18.38; **per o,**
see **pero; per pur tan que** provided that, if only 11.6; **per que** for
which (reason), wherefore, which is why, so (that) 2.12, 2.25, 4.40, 6.4,
6.35, 8.9, 12.59, 18.50, 26.23, 27.36, 29.9; **per que** why 17.38, 18.55,
31.13; **per so** for that reason, therefore, and that is why 16.5, **per zo**
11.47 (cf. **per aiso, pero**); **per so que** in order to 30.55; **per son vol** according to his wish, if he had his way 30.14; **per sort** by fate, in-
escapably 24.21; **per tal que** in order to 23.5, 26.32; **per tot**
everywhere 21.55; **per tot aquo** despite all that 9.53; **per totz temps**
mais forevermore 21.2; **per un mot cen** a hundred words in exchange
for (each) one 2.6; **per ver** in truth, indeed 18.25, 23.11, 26.55, 29.14;
per ver dire to tell the truth 31.8.

   In oaths **per Dieu** for God's sake 4.30, 19.9, 19.26, 19.49, 19.57 var.,
19.65; **per amor Dieu** for love of God 15.23; **per sanh Launart** by
Saint Leonard 9.6.

   Within expressions **amar per amor** to love sincerely 3.4; **aver per**
to receive as 13.54; **pregar per** to pray for 10.21, 27.45; **tan . . . (que)**
per tal so much that 13.54 (cf. **per tal que**); **tener per** to consider (as)
11.37, 15.29, 21.2, 23.9, 24.1, *refl.* to feel 7.11, 28.52, 30.52; **tolre per**
moiller to take as wife, to marry 5.13; **tot per mon grat** to please me,
for all of me 27.29.

   Forms: **per** *passim;* **par** 8.18 var.; cf. **pel** (2), **pels** (2).
   [CL PĔR *FEW* 8: 213; It. *per,* Fr. *par*]

pęra *n. fem.* pear: *obl. sg.* **pera** 14.33. [CL PĬRUM, VL PĬRA *FEW* 8: 576; It.
pera, Sp. *pera,* Fr. *poire,* E. *pear*]

perdǫn *n. masc.* pardon: *obl. sg.* **perdon** 29.48; *obl. pl.* **perdos** 31.40.
   [**perdonar**]

perdonar *vb. trans.* to pardon; *offense as direct object* 27.28 var.; *offense as*
direct object and offender as indirect object 10.22, 27.28 var.; *offender as*
indirect object and offense with **de** 27.28 var., 27.39; *offender as indirect*

object and hostility of the pardoner as direct object, to exempt 22.10; *of-fender as direct object* 27.28.

Forms: *pres. subj. 3rd sg.* **perdon** 10.22; *pres. part., masc., nom. sg.* **perdonans** 27.39; *pp., undeclined* **perdonat** 22.10; *inf.* **perdonar** 27.28.

[LL Pĕʀᴅōɴāʀᴇ *FEW* 8: 231; It. *perdonare,* Sp. *perdonar,* Fr. *pardon-ner,* E. *to pardon*]

perdos *see* **perdon.**

perdre *vb. trans.* to lose *passim; refl.* to lose oneself, to ruin oneself 18.47; **perdre lo vezer e l'auzir** to lose sight and hearing, to lose conscious-ness, to faint 3.9: *pres. 2nd sg.* **perz** 24.26, *3rd sg.* **pert** 27.13; *pres. subj. 1st sg.* **perda** 19.49; *pret. 1st sg.* **perdiei** 18.47, **perdiey** 9.41, *3rd sg.* **perdet** 3.9, 18.47, *3rd pl.* **perdero** 25.106; *pp., masc., obl. sg.* **perdut** 11.77, 21.3; *fem., nom. sg.* **perduda** 18.25, *obl. sg.* **perduda** 19.55. [CL Pĕʀᴅĕʀᴇ *FEW* 8: 225; It. *perdere,* Sp. *perder,* Fr. *perdre;* cf. E. *perdition*]

perfech *adj.* perfect: *fem., obl. sg.* **perfecha** 30.79. [CL Pĕʀꜰĕᴄᴛᴜᴍ *FEW* 8: 238; It. *perfetto,* Sp. *perfecto,* Fr. *parfait,* E. *perfect*]

perigliar *see* **parelhar.**

perilh *n. masc.* peril, danger 10.6, 25.9, 29.33; torrent 25.51: *nom. sg.* **per-ilhs** 25.51; *obl. sg.* **perilh** 29.33, **peril** 10.6; *obl. pl.* **perilhs** 25.9. [CL Pĕʀīᴄŭʟᴜᴍ *FEW* 8: 243; It. *pericolo,* Sp. *peligro,* Fr. *péril,* E. *peril*]

pero *conj.* but 11.67, 19.13, 19.27, 25.5, 28.5, 30.72; for that reason 19.43; cf. **per aiso, per so.** [**per** + **o** (1); cf. Sp. *pero*]

perponh *n. masc.* doublet, close-fitting garment for men covering the up-per body from the neck to a little below the waist: *nom. sg.* **perponz** 21.22 var.; *nom. pl.* **perpon** 21.22. [VL *ᴘᴇʀᴘŭɴᴄᴛᴜᴍ *FEW* 8: 262; Sp. *perpunte,* Fr. *pourpoint,* E. *pourpoint*]

perprendre *vb. trans.* to capture: *pres. 3rd pl.* **perprendon** 25.47. [**per-** + **prendre**]

pert, perz *see* **perdre.**

pes (1) *n. masc.* weight, burden: *obl. sg.* **pes** 32.13; *obl. pl.* **pes** 12.57. [CL ᴘēɴsᴜᴍ 'task' *FEW* 8: 206; It. *peso,* Sp. *peso,* Fr. *poids,* E. *poise*]

pes (2) *n. masc.* 25.12, *see* **pe.**

pesa (1) *n. fem.* piece (of meat or bread?): *obl. sg.* **pessa** 8.30. [Ctc. *pĕttĭa* *FEW* 8: 341; It. *pezza,* Sp. *pieza,* Fr. *pièce,* E. *piece*]

pesa (2) *vb. trans.* 16.28, **pesan** *see* **pezar.**

pesamen *n. masc.* care, concern: *obl. sg.* **pessamen** 23.24. [**pesar** + **-amen** (1)]

pesar *vb. intrans.* to think 19.54; *refl.* to believe 28.17, 28.51: *pres. 2nd pl.* **pessatz** 28.17; *pres. subj. 2nd pl.* **pessetz** 28.51; *imper. 2nd pl.* **pessatz** 19.54. [CL ᴘēɴsāʀᴇ 'to weigh, to ponder' *FEW* 8: 199; It. *pensare,* Sp. *pensar,* Fr. *penser;* cf. E. *pensive;* cf. **pezar**]

pesat *n. masc.* thought, mind: *obl. sg.* **pesat** 11.67. [**pesar**]

pescaria *n. fem.* fishpond: *obl. sg.* **pescaria** 26.21. [CL ᴘīsᴄāʀĭᴜᴍ 'of fish,' VL *ᴘīsᴄāʀɪᴀ *FEW* 8: 580; It. *pescaia,* Sp. *pesquera*]

pessa *see* **pesa** (1).

pessamen *see* **pesamen.**

pessatz, pessetz *see* **pesar.**

pestre *n. masc.* priest: *obl. sg.* **pestre** 31.2. [LL (from Gk.) ᴘʀᴇsʙўᴛĕʀᴜᴍ *FEW* 9: 359; It. *prete,* Sp. *preste,* Fr. *prêtre,* E. *priest*]

petar *vb. intrans.* to crack: *inf.* **petar** 32.9. [**pet** n. 'fart' (CL ᴘēᴅĭᴛᴜᴍ *FEW* 8: 142; It. *peto,* Fr. *pet*) + **-ar** (2)]

petit *adj.* little; *adv.* little 18.10, 24.25; **petida** *n. fem.* (*by attraction to* **ora**) **en petida d'ora** soon 25.45. [VL *PETTĪTTUM *FEW* 8: 346; Fr. *petit*, E. *petty*]

peurada, peure, *see* **pebrada, pebre.**

pezansa *n. fem.* vexation: *obl. sg.* **pezansa** 28.50. [**pezar** + **-ansa**]

pezar *vb. trans. impersonal* to grieve, to displease, to trouble: *pres. 3rd sg.* **pesa** 16.28; *pres. part., masc., obl. pl.* **pezans** vexatious 27.32; *fem., obl. sg.* **pesan** grievous 21.77, **pensan** 21.77 var. [CL PĔNSĀRE *FEW* 8: 199; It. *pesare*, Sp. *pesar*, Fr. *peser*; cf. **pesar**]

pia *see* **piu.**

pïetat *n. fem.* pity: *obl. sg.* **pïetat** 29.46. [CL PĬĔTĀTEM *FEW* 8: 441; It. *pietà*, Sp. *piedad*, Fr. *pitié*, E. *piety, pity*]

pilar *vb. trans.* to seize: *pret. 3rd pl.* **pilleron** 9.50 var. [LL PĪLĀRE 'to fix firmly' *FEW* 8: 492; It. *pilare*, Fr. *piler*]

pintura *see* **penchura.**

pitre *n. masc.* breast, chest: *obl. sg.* **pitre** 32.7. [CL PĔCTUS neuter, LL PĔCTŎREM masc. *FEW* 8: 113; It. *petto*, Sp. *pecho*]

piu *adj.* pious: *fem., vocative sg.* **pia** 13.15. [CL PĬUM *FEW* 8: 620; It. *pio*, Sp. *pio*, Fr. *pieux*, E. *pious*]

pladeramen *see* **plaideiamen.**

plag *n. masc.* conflict, quarrel 26.29; accord, pact 19.29, 19.43; reconciliation 19.54 var.: *obl. sg.* **plag** 19.29, 19.43, **plaich** 19.54 var.; *obl. pl.* **plaitz** 26.29. [CL PLACĬTUM *FEW* 9: 9; It. *piato*, Sp. *pleito*]

plaga *n. fem.* wound: *obl. sg.* **plaga** 25.64; *obl. pl.* **plaguas** 9.51. [CL PLĀGAM *FEW* 9: 11; It. *piaga*, Sp. *llaga*, Fr. *plaie*]

plagra *see* **plazer.**

plaguas *see* **plaga.**

plai *see* **plazer.**

plaich *see* **plag.**

plaideiamen *n. masc.* plea: *obl. sg.* **plaideiamen** 27.10, **plaideyamen** 27.10 var., **pladeramen** 27.10 var. [**plaideiar** + **-amen** (1)]

plaideiar *vb. intrans.* to plead: *pres. subj. 3rd sg.* **plaidei** 22.48. [**plag, plait** + **-eiar**]

plain *see* **planh.**

plaissenz *see* **plazer.**

plaitz *see* **plag.**

plaṇ (1) *adj.* flat, smooth: *masc., obl. pl.* **plans** 26.2. [CL PLĀNUM *FEW* 9: 33; It. *piano*, Sp. *llano*, Fr. *plain*, E. *plane, plain*]

plaṇ (2) *adv.* simply, well: **plan** 9.15. [CL PLĀNĒ; cf. *FEW* 9: 33]

planh *n. masc.* plaint, lamentation: *obl. sg.* **plain** 23.37; *obl. pl.* **planz** 26.5. [CL PLANCTUM *FEW* 9: 17; It. *pianto*, Sp. *llanto*, Fr. *plainte*, E. *plaint*]

planher *vb. intrans.* to lament: *inf.* **planher** 25.77, 25.78. [CL PLANGĔRE *FEW* 9: 17; It. *piangere*, Fr. *plaindre*; cf. E. *to complain*]

planisa *n. fem.* plain, field: *obl. sg.* **planissa** 13.8. [**plan** (1) + **-isa**]

plans *see* **plan** (1).

planz *see* **planh.**

plasa *n. fem.* place, square: *obl. sg.* **plassa** 25.47. [CL (from Gk.) PLATĔAM 'street' *FEW* 9: 41; It. *piazza*, Sp. *plaza*, Fr. *place*, E. *place*]

plasion *see* **plazer.**

plassa (1) *n. fem.* 25.47, *see* **plasa.**

plassa (2) *vb. intrans.* 19.15, **platz, plaz, plazen,** *see* **plazer.**

plazentier *adj.* pleasing, charming, dear: *masc., nom. sg.* **plazentiers** 25.60, 25.107; *fem., vocative sg.* **plazenteira** 28.62. [**plazer** (pres. part. **plazen**[t]) + **-ier**]

plazẹr *vb. intrans.* to please *(with* **a** *or indirect object): pres. 3rd sg.* **platz** 10.35, 15.7, 15.21, 15.24, 27.8, **plaz** 30.64, **plai** 4.14, 6.9, 6.36, 15.45, 18.44; *pres. subj. 3rd sg.* **plassa** 19.15; *imperf. 3rd pl.* **plasion** 5.11; *2nd cond. 3rd sg.* **plagra** 27.27; *pres. part., masc., obl. sg.* **plazen** 2.27; *fem., nom. sg.* **plaissenz** 3.5, *obl. sg.* **plazen** 13.19 var., 28.4, 28.14; *inf.* **plazer** 16.45, 18.35; *substantivized inf.* **plazer** pleasure 17.23. [CL PLACĒRE *FEW* 9: 4; It. *piacere,* Sp. *placer,* Fr. *plaire,* E. *to please*]

plegar *vb. trans.* to fold: *pres. 3rd sg.* **plega** 30.96. [CL PLĬCĀRE *FEW* 9: 72; It. *piegare,* Sp. *llegar,* Fr. *plier;* cf. E. *to complicate*]

plenier *adj.* general, fierce (combat): *masc., nom. sg.* **pleniers** 25.15. [**plẹn** (CL PLĒNUM *FEW* 9.61) + **-ier**]

plevir *vb. trans.* to pledge: *pres. 1st sg.* **plevisc** 13.65; *imperf. 3rd sg.* **plevia** 30.28; *pp., masc., obl. sg.* **plevit** 7.23. [Frankish **plegan FEW* 16: 634 (E. *to pledge*) + **-ir**; OFr. *plevir*]

plọia *n. fem.* rain: *nom. sg.* **ploja** 25.51; *obl. sg.* **ploia** 8.16 ms., **ploi'** 8.16. [CL PLŬVĬAM, VL *PLŎVĬA, *PLỌIA *FEW* 9: 106; It. *pioggia,* Sp. *lluvia,* Fr. *pluie;* cf. E. *pluvial*]

plọr *n. masc.* weeping: *obl. sg.* **plor** 18.21. [**plorar**]

plorar *vb. intrans.* to weep *passim; trans.* to weep for, to bewail 12.68: *pres. 1st sg.* **plor** 11.79, 29.8, *3rd sg.* **plora** 12.68, *3rd pl.* **ploron** 21.70; *pres. subj. 3rd sg.* **plor** 27.22; *substantivized inf.* **plorár** weeping 11.80, **plorar** 21.67. [CL PLŌRĀRE *FEW* 9: 78; Sp. *llorar,* Fr. *pleurer;* cf. E. *to deplore*]

plus (1) *n. masc.* the most: *obl. sg.* **plus** 18.27. [**plus** (3)]

plus (2) *adj.* greater: *masc., obl. sg.* **pus** 12.34. [**plus** (3)]

plus (3) *adv.* more 7.13, 17.32, 24.42, 30.89; *comparative of adj. or adv. modified* 13.86, 13.87, 14.23, 14.30, 14.59, 14.60, 26.2, 26.14, 27.26; most 4.2, 6.10, 8.6, 16.38, 23.8; *superlative of adj. modified* 6.3, 8.7, 12.61, 14.47, 21.46, 30.12; again 28.51;

   plus . . . **belayre** the more . . . the prettier 13.33; **al plus del tot** as much as possible 29.23; **non** . . . **plus** no longer 10.31; **non** . . . **plus que** no more than 15.7.

   Forms: **plus** *passim;* **pus** 12.61, 13.33, 13.86, 13.87, 14.23, 14.30, 14.47, 14.59, 14.60, 28.51, 29.23.

   [CL PLŪS *FEW* 9: 103; It. *più,* Fr. *plus,* E. *plus*]

pluzọr *adj.* greater; **tut li pluzor** many men, everyone 10.15, 12.22: *masc., nom. pl.* **pluzor** 12.22, **plusor** 10.15. [CL PLŪRĒS, LL PLŪRĬŌRĒS, VL *PLŪSĬŌRĒS *FEW* 9: 102; Fr. *plusieurs*]

podẹr *vb. intrans.* to be able.

   Forms: Pres. 1st sg. **puesc** 10.31, 19.17, 23.6, 23.38, **puosc** 18.11, 27.43; *3rd sg.* **pot** 2.15, 13.19, 13.61, 14.29, 16.1, 16.3, 16.17, 16.31, 18.33, 26.24, 30.20; *2nd pl.* **podez** 17.2; *3rd pl.* **podon** 25.9, 26.16, 26.56.

   Pres. subj. 1st sg. **puosca** 22.35 ms., **puosc'** 22.35; *3rd sg.* **puosca** 6.30, **pusca** 30.59; *1st pl.* **poscam** 26.8; *2nd pl.* **puscaz** 23.13; *3rd pl.* **puoscon** 26.32.

   Imperf. 3rd sg. **podia** 4.10, 26.13.

   1st cond. 1st sg. **poiria** 28.25, **poria** 27.41 var.; *3rd sg.* **poiria** 27.13, 27.30, **pori'** 23.30; *1st pl.* **poiriam** 28.61.

pret. 3rd sg. **poc** 30.94, 31.42.

2nd cond. 3rd sg. **pogra** 27.28 var.; *2nd pl.* **pogratz** 27.28, **pogras** 27.28 var.

Substantivized *inf., masc.* power: *obl. sg.* **poder** 7.18, 15.38, 16.8, 18.41, 29.32, 29.42. [CL pŏsse, VL *potēre *FEW* 9: 235; It. *potere,* Sp. *poder,* Fr. *pouvoir*; cf. E. *potent*]

pǫg *n. masc.* hill: *obl. sg.* **pueg** 19.13. [CL (from Gk.) pŏdĭum 'step, base' *FEW* 9: 113; It. *poggio,* Sp. *poyo,* Fr. *pui,* E. *podium, pew*]

poiria, poiriam *see* **poder.**

pǫis (1) *adv.* then 1.7, 14.12, 17.19, 19.5, 22.44, 30.98, 31.11, 31.28, 31.41; in that case 19.23; **pois a** *prep.* after 14.9. *Forms:* **pois** 1.7, 22.44, 30.98; **puois** 17.19; **pueus** 31.11, 31.28, 31.41; **pueys** 14.12, 19.23; **pus** 14.9, 19.5. [CL pŏst, pŏstĕa, VL *pŏstĭus (influenced by mĕlĭus) *FEW* 9: 244; It. *poi,* Sp. *pues,* Fr. *puis*]

pǫis (2) *conj.* since *(time)* 14.31, 18.45; since *(cause)* 6.5, 10.1, 10.35, 13.51, 18.21, 18.33, 20.5, 20.7, 20.15, 22.9, 22.16, 23.26, 27.30, 27.30, 28.66, 31.29, 31.36; once 6.22, **pois que** 6.20; **ja pois** . . . **non** never again 6.23. *Forms:* **pois** 6.5, 6.20, 6.22, 6.23, 18.21, 18.45, 20.5, 20.7, 22.9, 22.16; **puois** 18.33; **pueys** 14.31; **pueus** 31.29, 31.36; **pos** 10.1, 10.35, 20.15, 23.26, **pus** 13.51, 27.30, 28.66. [**pǫis** (1)]

poisan *adj.* powerful, mighty: *masc., nom. sg.* **poissans** 27.23; *nom. pl.* **poissan** 21.36. [OFr. *poisant, puisant* (CL pŏtĕntem; It. *possente,* Fr. *puissant *FEW* 9: 233); the French word is based on forms of the verb in *pois-, puis-* (Fouché, *Morphologie* 90); since such forms are exceptional in OOc **poder** (which see), OOc **poisan** must be a Gallicism]

pojar *vb. intrans.* to climb 18.56, to mount *(erotic)* 14.51: *pres. subj. 3rd sg.* **pueg** 14.51; *pret. 1st sg.* **pojei** 18.56. [**pog** + **-ar** (2)]

pǫn *n. masc.* bridge: *obl. sg.* **pon** 18.54. [CL pŏntem *FEW* 9: 171; It. *ponte,* Sp. *puente,* Fr. *pont*; E. *pontoon*]

pǫnh *n. masc.* fist: *obl. pl.* **punhs** used as *nom. pl.* 25.12. [CL pŭgnum *FEW* 9: 519; It. *pugno,* Sp. *puño,* Fr. *poing*; cf. E. *pugnacious*]

pǫnher *vb. trans.* to sting: *pres. 3rd sg.* **punh** 14.59. [CL pŭngĕre *FEW* 9: 599; It. *pungere,* Sp. *pungir,* Fr. *poindre*; cf. E. *poignant*]

popęta *n. fem.* breast, nipple: *obl. pl.* **popętas** 31.23. [**popa** (VL *pŭppam 'girl' *FEW* 9: 606; It. *poppa,* Fr. *poupe*) + **-eta**]

pori', poria *see* **poder.**

pǫrt *n. masc.* port, destination, end *(fig., death)* 22.46; pass, mountain pass 15.19; pass, transition *(fig., death)* 24.29: *obl. sg.* **port** 22.46, 24.29; *obl. pl.* **portz** 15.19. [CL pŏrtum *FEW* 9: 228; It. *porto,* Sp. *puerto,* Fr. *port,* E. *port*]

pǫrta *n. fem.* door, gate: *obl. sg.* **porta** 27.17. [CL pŏrtam *FEW* 9: 201; It. *porta,* Sp. *puerta,* Fr. *porte*]

portar *vb. trans.* to carry: *pres. 3rd sg.* **porta** 12.40, *3rd pl.* **portan** 25.86, **potan** 25.86 var., **porton** 26.37 var.; *pres. subj. 3rd sg.* **port** 24.30; *fut. 2nd sg.* **portaras** 9.68; *pret. 3rd sg.* **portet** 21.45; *past subj. 3rd sg.* **portes** 21.45 var.; *inf.* **portar** 3.7. [CL pŏrtāre *FEW* 9: 220; It. *portare,* Sp. *portar,* Fr. *porter*; cf. E. *portable*]

porters *see* **portier** (2).

portes, portet *see* **portar.**

portier (1) *n. masc.* gatekeeper: *nom. sg.* **portiers** 27.19. [LL pŏrtārĭum *FEW* 9: 223; It. *portiere,* Sp. *portero,* Fr. *portier,* E. *porter*]

portier (2) *n. masc.* gate: *obl. pl.* **porters** 25.16. [**porta** + **-ier**]

porton *see* **portar.**

portz *see* **port.**

pos *see* **pois** (2).

poscam, pot *see* **poder.**

postęla *n. fem.* sty, swelling on the eyelid: *obl. sg. (as object of implicit verb of cursing)* **pustella** 22.19 ms., **pustell'** 22.19. [CL pŭstŭlam, LL pustĕllam *FEW* 9: 621; Sp. *postilla*]

potan *see* **portar.**

prat *n. masc.* meadow: *obl. sg.* **prat** 19.28. [CL prātum *FEW* 9: 336; It. *prato,* Sp. *prado,* Fr. *pré*]

pręc *n. masc.* prayer, entreaty, plea: *nom. sg.* **precs** 18.34 var. [**pregar**]

predon *see* **prendre.**

pregar *vb. intrans.* to pray, to say a prayer 23.22; *trans.* to pray (to), to beseech *with indirect object* 10.36 *or direct object* 17.31; to court 17.28, 17.30, 19.59, 19.62, 23.19, 23.24: *pres. 1st sg.* **prec** 6.12, 6.29, 10.21, 10.36, 10.37, 23.24, 27.45, *2nd pl.* **pregatz** 19.62; *pres. subj. 3rd sg.* **prec** 10.23, 17.31, 23.19, *3rd pl.* **preguen** 17.30; *pret. 2nd pl.* **pregetz** 19.59; *2nd cond. 3rd pl.* **pregueran** 17.28; *pp., fem., nom. pl.* **pregadas** 17.25; *inf.* **pregar** 23.22 var., **prejar** 23.22; *substantivized inf., masc., obl. sg.* **prejar** prayer, entreaty 23.23. [CL prĕcārī *FEW* 9: 338, LL prĕcāre L & S; It. *pregare,* Fr. *prier,* E. *to pray*]

preichas *see* **preisa.**

preigna *see* **prendre.**

pręisa *n. fem.* throng, crowd: *obl. sg.* **preissa** 30.12; *obl. pl.* **preichas** 25.38. [**preissar** 'to press' (VL *prĕssĭāre *FEW* 9: 367); It. *pressa,* Sp. *priesa,* Fr. *presse,* E. *press*]

preiso *see* **preizon.**

preissa *see* **preisa.**

preizǫn *n. fem.* prison: *obl. sg.* **preiso** 11.27, **preso** 11.59. [LL prĕhēnsĭōnem 'arrest' *FEW* 9: 356; It. *prigione,* Sp. *prisión,* Fr. *prison,* E. *prison*]

premeyra, premieir', premieira, premier *see* **primier.**

pręndre *vb. trans.* to take; to take (profit) 16.21; to take (in marriage) 28.58; to undertake, to vow (penance) 11.14; *with complementary inf.* to begin, **lo reis lo pres de felni'a reptar** the king began to accuse him of treachery 11.64; **prendre aunimen** to suffer shame 27.18; to overcome, to befall, to strike 1.4, 16.9; *impersonal* to befall, to happen 31.35, **ni·us pren de mi sovinensa** don't you remember me 28.32, **de chantar m'es pres talenz** a desire to sing has come over me 10.1.

Forms: *pres. 3rd sg.* **pren** 11.13, 14.11, 14.37, 16.21, 20.11, 27.18, 28.32, 30.36, *3rd pl.* **prenon** 26.34, **predon** 26.34 var.; *pres. subj. 3rd sg.* **prenda** 16.9, 27.47, **prend'** 30.46, **preigna** 21.66 var., *2nd pl.* **prendatz** 27.47 var.; *fut. 3rd pl.* **prendretz** 25.19; *pret. 1st sg.* **prézi** 31.30, *3rd sg.* **pres** 1.4, 1.5, 9.19, 9.49, 11.64, 28.58, 31.12, 31.35; *pp., masc., invariable* **pres** 10.1, 30.4; *fem., obl. sg.* **presa** 11.14, **preza** 28.53.

[CL prĕhĕndĕre, prĕndĕre *FEW* 9: 352; It. *prendere,* Sp. *prender,* Fr. *prendre*; cf. E. *to comprehend*]

preǫn *adj.* profound, deep: *fem., obl. sg.* **preonda** 19.25; *substantivized n. masc., obl. sg.* **prion** the depths, deep within 18.46. [CL PRŏFŭNDUM, ML PREFUNDUM *FEW* 9: 434; It. *profondo,* Sp. *profundo,* Fr. *profond,* E. *profound*]

pręs (1) *adv.* near; **loing e pres** near and far 10.40; **ni pres ni loing** near or far 15.11; *prep.* **pres de** near to 15.25, 31.17. [CL PRĕSSĒ *FEW* 9: 367; It. *presso,* Fr. *près*]

pręs (2) *vb. trans.* 1.4, 1.5, 9.19, 9.49, 10.1, 11.64, 28.58, 30.4, 31.12, 31.35 *pret. 3rd sg. and pp. of* **prendre,** *which see.*

pręs (3) *vb. refl.* 13.13 *pres. 1st sg. of* **prezar,** *which see.*

presan, presatz, *see* **prezar.**

presen, presenssa *see* **prez-.**

preso *see* **preizon.**

pressic *see* **prezic.**

prętz (1) *n. masc.* merit 5.10, 6.17, 6.26, 15.12, 17.45, 17.48; good reputation, name 13.51, 23.6; a person of merit 12.67; price, value, as much as 22.32: *nom. sg.* **pretz** 6.26, 15.12; *obl. sg.* **pretz** 5.10, 6.17, 12.67, 13.51, 22.32, **prez** 17.45, 17.48, 23.6. [CL PRĕTĭUM *FEW* 9: 374; It. *prezzo,* Sp. *precio,* Fr. *prix,* E. *price;* cf. E. *precious*]

prętz (2) *vb. trans.* 21.74, *see* **prezar.**

preveiręsa *n. fem.* concubine of a priest: *obl. sg.* **preveyressa** 31.40. [**preveire** (LL PRĕSBŷTĕRUM *FEW* 9: 358) + **-esa**]

prez *see* **pretz** (1).

preza 28.53, *see* **prendre.**

prezar *vb. trans.* to esteem 3.2, 20.14; to care about 11.8, 21.74, *(refl.)* 13.13: *pres. 1st sg.* **pretz** 21.74, **pres** 13.13, *3rd sg.* **preza** 11.8; *pres. part., masc., obl. sg.* **prezan** (*passive sense*) esteemed, excellent 21.36 var., 21.50 var., **presan** 21.78; *pp., masc., nom. sg.* **prezatz** 3.2, **presatz** 20.24. [LL PRĕTĭĀRE *FEW* 9: 375; It. *prezzare,* Sp. *preciar,* Fr. *priser,* E. *to prize;* cf. E. *to appreciate*]

prezęn (1) *n. masc.* present (time): **prezent** 29.6. [**prezen** (2)]

prezęn (2) *adj.* present, overt; **a presen** openly, publicly: *masc., obl. sg.* **presen** 6.22. [CL PRAESENTEM *FEW* 9: 308; It. *presente,* Sp. *presente,* Fr. *présent,* E. *present*]

prezęnsa *n. fem.* presence; **a prezensa** openly, publicly: *obl. sg.* **presenssa** 6.21. [CL PRAESENTĭAM *FEW* 9: 312; It. *prezensa,* Sp. *presencia,* Fr. *présence,* E. *presence*]

prezentar *vb. trans.* to present, to offer: *pres. 1st sg.* **presen** 23.41. [CL PRAESENTĀRE *FEW* 9: 310; It. *presentare,* Sp. *presentar,* Fr. *présenter,* E. *to present*]

prezentier *adj.* which presents itself, which presses forward, imminent: *masc., nom. sg.* **prezentiers** 29.34. [**prezentar** + **-ier** *FEW* 9: 310]

prézi *see* **prendre.**

prezic *n. masc.* preaching, sermon: *obl. sg.* **pressic** 23.20. [**prezicar**]

prezicar *vb. trans. and intrans.* to preach: *pres. part., masc., nom. pl.* **prezican** 26.8, 26.47. [ChL PRAEDĭCĀRE *FEW* 9: 291; It. *predicare,* Sp. *predicar,* Fr. *prêcher,* E. *to predicate, to preach*]

prezonier *n. masc.* prisoner: *obl. pl.* **prezoners** 25.105. [**preizon** + **-ier**].

prim *adj.* delicate, elegant: *masc., obl. sg.* **prim** 26.43 var.; *obl. pl.* **prims** 26.41. [CL PRĪMUM *FEW* 9: 387; It. *primo,* Sp. *primo,* E. *prime*]

prima *n. fem.* prime, the first daylight canonical hour, usually beginning at 6 a.m. or sunrise: *obl. sg.* **prima** 30.7. [CL PRĪMAM (HŌRAM) *FEW* 9: 387]

primairaṇ *adj.* first, original: *masc., obl. sg.* **primairan** 12.38. [**primier** + **-an** (2)]

primier *adj.* first: *masc., nom. sg.* **primiers** 20.34, **primers** 25.35; *obl. sg.* **premier** 27.38, *used as nom. sg.* 12.0; *fem., nom. sg.* **premieira** 19.20, **premeyra** 19.34, **premieir'** 26.25; *obl. sg.* **primeira** 28.65. [CL PRĪMĀRĬUM *FEW* 9: 379; Sp. *primero,* Fr. *premier,* E. *primary*]

primiers *adv.* (*or adj., masc., nom. sg., see* **primier**) first, at first, the first: **primiers** 6.11. [**primier** + **-s**]

prims *see* **prim**.

prince *n. masc.* prince, lord: *nom. sg.* **princes** 1.1. [CL nom. PRĪNCEPS, acc. PRĪNCĬPEM Ernout and Meillet; *FEW* 9: 391; It. *principe,* Sp. *príncipe,* Fr. *prince,* E. *prince*]

princeps (Latin) *n. masc.* prince, lord: *nom. sg.* **princeps** 1.1 var.

princes *see* **prince**.

prion *see* **preon**.

privat *adj.* intimate, familiar; **cugey que·m fos privada** I thought she would remember me 28.9; *substantivized masc.* **privatz** intimate friend 14.24: *masc., nom. sg.* **privatz** 14.24; *fem., nom. sg.* **privada** 28.9. [CL PRĪVĀTUM *FEW* 9: 398; It. *privato,* Sp. *privado,* Fr. *privé,* E. *private*]

prǫ (1) *n. masc.,* favor 18.12, gain 29.14; **tener pro** to be worthwhile 16.31, to be helpful 18.21: *obl. sg.* **pro** 16.31, 18.12, 18.21, 29.14. [**pro** (2)]

prǫ (2) *adj.* good, noble: *masc., nom. sg.* **pros** 10.17, 17.15; *obl. sg.* **pro** 6.19, 6.25, 20.13, 21.49, **pró** 11.28; *nom. pl.* **pro** 6.23, 6.34; *obl. pl.* **pros** 21.15; *neuter, nom. sg.* **pro** 11.13. [LL PRŌDEM *FEW* 9: 420; It. *prode,* Sp. *pro,* Fr. *preux,* E. *proud*]

prǫ (3) *adv.* plenty, enough 9.56; well 31.43. [**pro** (2)]

proar *vb. trans.* to test, to examine: *inf.* **proar** 23.22 var. [CL PRŎBĀRE *FEW* 9: 407; It. *provare,* Sp. *probar,* Fr. *prouver,* G. *prüfen,* E. *to prove*]

probęt *adv.* near; **probet de** *prep.* near to 12.6, descended from 12.37. [**prop** + **-et**]

proęza *n. fem.* prowess, deeds of arms 10.25; merit 12.62, 14.5, 19.45 var.: *nom. sg.* **proesa** 19.45 var.; *obl. sg.* **proeza** 10.25, 12.62, 14.5. [**pro** (2) + **-eza**]

promęsa *n. fem.* promise: *nom. sg.* **promesa** 19.45. [LL PRŌMĬSSAM *FEW* 9: 442; It. *promessa,* Sp. *promesa,* Fr. *promesse,* E. *promise*]

promętre *vb. trans.* to promise: *pres. 3rd sg.* **promet** 13.65; *pp., masc., un-declined* **promes** 12.30. [CL PRŌMĬTTĔRE *FEW* 9: 442; It. *promettere,* Sp. *prometer,* Fr. *promettre*]

prǫp *adv.* near; *prep.* **prop de** near to 31.1. [CL PRŎPE *FEW* 9: 449]

pros *see* **pro** (2).

pudǫr *n. fem.* stench: *obl. sg.* **pudor** 13.49. [CL PŪTŌREM *FEW* 9: 639; Fr. *pueur*]

pueg (1) *n. masc.* 19.13, *see* **pǫg**.

pueg (2) *vb. intrans.* 14.51, *see* **pojar**.

puesc *see* **poder**.

pueus (1) *adv.* 31.11, 31.28, 31.41, *see* **pois** (1).

pueus (2) *conj.* 31.29, 31.36, *see* **pois** (2).

pueys (1) *adv.* 14.12, 19.23, *see* **pois** (1).

pueys (2) *conj.* 14.31, *see* **pois** (2).

punh *see* **ponher**.

punhs *see* **ponh**.

puois (1) *adv.* 17.19, *see* **pois** (1).

puois (2) *conj.* 18.33, *see* **pois** (2).

puosc, puosca, puoscon *see* **poder**.

pur (1) *adj.* pure, unmixed 26.18; unsullied, courtly 13.73: *masc., obl. sg.* **pur** 26.18; *fem., obl. sg.* **pura** 13.73. [CL PŪRUM *FEW* 9: 620; It. *puro,* Sp. *puro,* Fr. *pur,* E. *pure*]

pur (2) *adv.* yet, still 27.30 var.; **per pur tan que** if only, provided that 11.6. [**pur** (1)]

pus (1) *adj.* 12.34, *see* **plus** (2).

pus (2) *adv.* more, etc., 12.61, 13.33, 13.86, 13.87, 14.23, 14.30, 14.47, 14.59, 14.60, 28.51, 29.23, *see* **plus** (3).

pus (3) *adv.* 14.9, 19.5, *see* **pois** (1).

pus (4) *conj.* 13.51, 27.30, 28.66, *see* **pois** (2).

pusca, puscaz *see* **poder**.

pustella *see* **postela**.

putana *n. fem.* prostitute: *obl. sg.* **putaina** 13.70. [**putan** 'man who frequents prostitutes' (**put** [CL PŪTĬDUM 'rotten' *FEW* 9: 636] + **-an**) + **-a**; It. *puttana,* Sp. *puta,* Fr. *putain*]

q' *see* **que** (1), (2), (3).

qa- *see* **ca-**.

qe *see* **que** (1), (2), (3).

qecs *see* **quec**.

qerrai *see* **querre**.

qi *see* **qui** (1).

qier *see* **querre**.

qua- *see* **ca-**.

que (1) *rel. pron.* who, whom, which, that; (he) who 16.52;
    ab so que provided that 7.23; **aquel . . . que** such . . . that 16.9; **cui que** whomever 18.6; **per que** for which (reason), wherefore, which is why, so (that) 2.12, 2.25, 4.40, 6.4, 6.35, 8.9, 12.59, 18.50, 26.23, 27.36, 29.9; **per so que** in order to 30.55; **que que** whatever 4.19, 19.46; **qui que** whoever 2.18, 6.13, 13.22, 22.33; **so que** that which, what 3.11, 4.14, 5.16, 6.14, 7.24, 15.47, 15.50, 16.34, 16.35, 18.51, 18.52, 19.5, 24.44, 26.34, 27.13.
    Masc., nom. sg. (cf. **qui** [1]) 3.1, 5.2, 5.2, 5.16, 6.11, 8.28, 12.0, 12.0, 12.16, 12.28, 12.72, 13.10, 13.31, 13.92 var., 14.18, 15.31, 15.52, 16.21, 16.52, 17.33, 18.27, 18.31, 18.44, 19.21, 20.4, 20.11, 20.13, 21.4, 21.42, 21.45, 21.54, 23.21, 23.27, 23.35, 25.60, 25.70, 25.82, 25.90, 25.95, 25.102, 25.106, 27.3, 27.19, 28.7, 28.44, 28.58, 29.10, 29.34, 30.1, 30.38, 30.67, 30.68, 30.82, 31.42; *obl. sg.* 1.2, 2.2, 2.19, 6.10, 7.2, 12.36, 15.30, 17.5, 18.34, 19.15, 27.2, 29.41, 31.17; *nom. pl.* 1.2, 11.70, 12.33, 12.45, 12.63, 21.58, 21.76, 22.29, 26.17, 29.37, 32.17; *obl. pl.* 6.16, 23.28, 24.20, 30.17.
    Fem., nom. sg. 2.14, 3.3, 3.5, 5.10, 6.17, 8.15, 14.14, 14.50, 17.38, 18.3, 18.4, 18.22, 19.60, 26.22, 26.26, 26.54, 27.20, 30.21, 31.4; *obl. sg.* 1.7, 4.2, 5.6, 5.16, 16.38, 19.51, 25.66, 26.6, 28.2, 31.21; *nom. pl.* 16.24, 31.45; *obl. pl.* 5.17, 26.39, 32.14.

Forms: **que, qu', qe, q',** *passim;* **ce** 13.92 var.; **c'** 16.24, 18.4, 18.52, 19.51, 23.21, 23.27, 26.39; **ques** *masc., nom. sg.* 25.102, 30.1, 30.68; **ques** *masc., obl. pl.* 30.17.

[CL acc. QUEM (cf. nom. QUĪ) *FEW* 2, part 2: 1465; It. *che,* Sp. *quien,* Fr. *qui, que*]

que (2) *interrogative pron. in direct question* what? 4.4, 19.6, 19.22, *in indirect question* who 21.24 (= **qui** 21.24 var.), what 3.8, 9.7, 9.14, 19.26, 31.25; why 23.41; how 12.3; **per que** why 17.38, 18.55, 31.13; **que que** whatever 4.19, 19.46.

Forms: **que, qu', qe, q'** *passim.*

[CL acc. QUEM (cf. nom. QUĬS) *FEW* 2, part 2: 1465; It. *che,* Sp. *quien* Fr. *qui, que*]

que (3) *conj.* that *introducing subordinate clause* 1.6, 3.6, 4.11, 4.20, 4.38, 6.6, 6.8, 6.9, 6.10, 6.12, 6.29, 6.31, 7.5, 7.22, 8.5, 8.24, 8.26, 9.71, 10.36, 11.14, 11.33, 11.56, 11.65, 13.89, 14.48, 14.50, 14.51, 14.55, 14.68, 15.39, 15.49, 17.27, 17.30, 17.31, 18.21, 18.24, 18.30, 18.36, 19.4, 19.11, 19.13, 19.17, 19.21, 19.23, 19.24, 19.27, 19.32, 19.35, 19.37, 19.43, 19.44, 19.58, 20.2, 20.2, 21.10, 21.38, 22.28, 22.46, 23.4, 23.7, 23.14, 23.17, 23.18, 23.19, 23.20, 23.29, 23.30, 23.31, 23.34, 24.10, 24.11, 24.15, 24.23, 24.30, 24.41, 25.33, 26.24, 26.48, 26.50, 27.11, 27.30, 27.35, 27.44, 28.9, 28.11, 28.17, 28.20, 28.27, 29.8, 29.30, 29.36, 30.66, 31.4, 31.39; (the fact) that 12.22.

May, let, (I wish . . .) *introducing subjunctive of wish or command in an independent clause* 6.21, 7.19, 7.20, 10.22, 14.47, 21.14, 27.19; *in a subordinate clause* 5.9, 10.38, 21.39, 25.30, 27.46. Than *with comparative adj. or adv.* 2.21, 3.5, 12.34, 14.23, 15.7, 17.7, 17.33, 19.40, 24.10, 24.11, 24.12, 24.14, 26.2, 26.4, 28.33, 29.18; **autre . . . que** other than 28.65.

Causative meaning varies from strong (because, since) *to weak* (for) *to impalpable (may be omitted from translation)* because, since 1.6, 2.23, 4.41, 13.83, 16.6, 18.32, 19.59, 23.23, 23.38, 25.82, 27.40, 28.12, 28.53;

for 2.17, 4.5, 4.7, 4.8, 4.16, 4.17, 4.22, 4.25, 4.26, 4.31, 4.34, 4.35, 4.39, 4.43, 4.44, 6.3, 6.7, 6.15, 6.22, 7.11, 8.27, 8.29, 9.16, 9.35, 10.5, 10.39, 11.15, 12.42, 12.66, 13.14, 13.27, 13.60, 13.76, 15.10, 15.38, 16.17, 16.46, 18.19, 18.27, 18.47, 18.58, 19.2, 19.3, 19.7, 19.16, 19.50, 19.55, 21.17, 22.23, 22.51, 23.13, 23.22, 23.42, 23.44, 24.5, 25.20, 26.51, 27.7, 27.11, 27.18, 27.43, 29.15, 29.19, 29.24, 29.35, 30.93, 31.5, 31.23, 31.34;

may be omitted from translation 2.8, 2.15, 4.16, 4.25, 4.34, 4.43, 6.25, 8.25, 12.28, 14.65, 21.27, 21.43, 21.44, 22.4, 22.37, 23.15, 25.64, 29.17.

Other meanings and *(?)* 4.7, 9.57 (*or read* **entro que** . . . [entro] **que** until . . . until), 25.67, 28.57; how 19.52; if *with subjunctive* 14.39, 27.22, 27.22; so 27.15; so that *(purpose) with indicative* 11.5, *with subjunctive* 15.52; so that *(result) with indicative* 22.7, 25.54, 28.57, 29.8, *with 2nd conditional* 31.4; when 2.16, 8.17, 8.20, 8.21, 16.47, 18.43, 19.41, 25.16, 28.10, 31.18; while 13.90.

que . . . no lest 19.12, that . . . not 19.17.

ab so que provided that 7.23. **ab sol que** provided that 12.35.

aital . . . **que** such . . . that 14.9, 25.9, 25.12, 25.51. **anz que** before 5.7, 14.24, 22.48. **anz** . . . **que** rather . . . than 17.28. **avan que** before 30.47, 30.88. **dementre que** while 12.14. **enans que** before 23.22. **entro que** until 9.56. **faire que** to act like, as (**que** *conj. or prep.*) 19.61, 20.9. **mais** (. . .) **que** more than 17.9, 17.18; **mais** . . . **que** (**que**) more than that 19.28; except that 9.9, 14.41; but let 27.19. **on que** wherever 4.29. **per pur tan que** provided that, if only 11.6. **per tal que** in order to 23.5, 26.32. **pois** . . . **que** since *(time)* 14.32; once *(cause)* 6.20. **quandius que** as long as 11.1. **que** . . . **o que** either . . . or 27.38–39. **segon que** according to the way 29.40, 31.9. **si** (**bon**, etc.) . . . **que** so (good, *etc.*) . . . that 3.10. **si** (. . .) **que** so that 2.4, 5.6, 15.6, 15.34, 15.41, 25.42, 25.58, 25.59, 25.71, 26.10, 27.47, 31.10. **sol que** if only 7.12. **tal** . . . **que** such . . . that 12.7, 13.41, 14.29, 14.63, 25.44, 25.91, 29.12, [**tal**] . . . **que** 31.46; **tal que** one who 25.106; **tal** . . . **c'autre** one person . . . while another 13.90. **tan** . . . **que** so (much, many) . . . that 11.31, 12.40, 13.52, 17.18, 17.28, 21.11, 22.6, 24.37, 28.15, 29.4, 30.73; so *(adj., adv.)* . . . that 11.8, 12.27, 15.13, 15.28, 15.48, 16.49, 22.18, 22.42, 25.6; enough that 17.11, 19.47; until 8.23, 30.46; as long as 32.7. **tan tro que** until 31.24. **tro que** until 1.6, 5.14, 8.11, 14.42; as far as 2.9.

 Forms: **que, qu', qe, q'** *passim;* **c'** 2.9, 6.7, 6.15, 8.5, 8.24, 12.7, 12.27, 12.40, 12.42, 13.14, 13.41, 13.60, 13.90, 14.39, 14.50, 14.65, 15.28, 16.17, 16.46, 16.47, 16.49, 17.18, 17.31, 18.19, 18.21, 18.24, 18.30, 18.47, 19.2, 19.4, 19.7, 19.16, 19.27, 19.28, 19.52, 19.58, 19.59, 21.27, 21.38, 22.37, 22.48, 23.15, 26.2, 26.10, 26.24, 26.50, 27.30, 27.46; **ques** 30.73.

 [CL ouĭa *FEW* 2, part 2: 1466; It. *che,* Sp. *que,* Fr. *que*]

quęc *indefinite pron.* each (man) 14.11, 26.6; **us qecs** each man 24.30: *masc., nom. sg.* **qecs** 24.30, **quecx** 14.11, 26.6. [CL ouĭsoue *FEW* 2, part 2: 1490]

quęrre *vb. trans.* to seek; to ask for 6.35, 19.47: *pres. 1st sg.* **quier** 19.1, **qier** 6.35; *pres. subj. 3rd sg.* **quieira** 19.47; *fut. 1st sg.* **qerrai** 15.22, 18.28; *pres. part.* **anar queren** to go to seek 30.44, to have been seeking 9.14; *pp., fem., nom. sg.* **quesid'** 23.48. [CL ouaerĕre *FEW* 2, part 2: 1409; It. *chiedere,* Sp. *querer,* Fr. *quérir;* cf. E. *quest*]

ques (1) 25.102, 30.1, 30.17, 30.68, *see* **que** (1).

ques (2) 30.73, *see* **que** (3).

quesid' *see* **querre**.

quęza *n. fem.* quiet, calm: *obl. sg.* **quesza** 26.27. [**quezar** 'to be silent' (VL *ouĭetĭare *FEW* 2, part 2: 1470; It. *chetare,* Sp. *quedar;* cf. E. *quiet*]

qui (1) *rel. pron.* who: *masc., nom. sg.* **qui** 11.24, 15.36, 16.51, 24.15 var., 26.13, **qi** 24.8, **ki** 11.17; *obl. sg.* **qui** 28.38, **cui** 6.26, 10.14, 11.29, 11.76, 20.33, 26.6 var.; *fem., obl. sg.* **cui** 16.40, 17.45; *nom. pl.* **qui** 11.73, 11.77;
 he who **qui** 14.5, 14.37, 15.43, 17.16, 17.34, 23.25, 25.81, 27.13, 31.43, 31.43; **cel** . . . **qi** he who 16.34, **celui qui** he who 16.51;
 one which **qui** 4.21;
 whoever **qui** 12.25, 13.22, 17.46, 22.15, 26.23, 26.30; *"conditional"* **qui** [CL sī ouĭs], if someone: **qui** 9.55, 14.67, 18.29, 22.19, 30.26, **qi** 28.24; if he **qui** 26.24;
 qui que whoever, *nom. sg.* 2.18, 6.13, 22.33; *obl. sg.* **cui que** 18.6.
 [CL ouī, masc., nom. sg. and pl. *FEW* 2, part 2: 1465; It. *chi,* Fr. *qui*]

qui (2) *interrogative pron., in direct question* who?: *obl. sg.* **qui** 28.55; *in indirect question* who: *nom. sg.* **qui** 11.4, 11.5, 12.41, 21.24 var. (= **que** 21.24), 21.25; *obl. sg.* **cui** 11.3, 11.6, 16.23. [**qui** (1)]

quicǫm *indefinite pron.* something: *masc., obl. sg.* **quicòm** 32.7. [CL QUĪDAM *FEW* 2, part 2: 1469 + **com** (3)]

quieira, quier *see* **querre**.

quo *see* **com** (2).

rabinier *adj.* swift-flowing: *masc., nom. sg.* **rabiners** 25.51. [**rabina** 'impetuosity' (CL RĂPĪNAM *FEW* 10: 68) + **-ier**]

rai *n. masc.* ray (of sunlight): *obl. sg.* **rai** 18.2. [CL RĂDĬUM *FEW* 10: 25; It. *raggio,* Sp. *rayo,* Fr. *rai,* E. *ray*]

raizó *see* **razon**.

ramęl *n. masc.* branch: *obl. sg.* **ramel** 8.18. [**ram** 'branch' (CL RĀMUM *FEW* 10: 49; It. *ramo,* Sp. *ramo*) + **-el**]

randa *n. fem.* end; **a randa** at once 19.9, entirely 20.9. [Ctc. **randa* 'edge' *FEW* 10: 57; It. *randa* 'shield,' Sp. *randa* 'trimming']

rason *see* **razon**.

raustir *vb. trans.* to roast: *inf.* **raustir** 3.7. [Germ. **raustjan FEW* 16: 685 + **-ir**; It. *arrostire,* Fr. *rôtir,* E. *to roast*]

razǫn *n. fem.* reason, good sense 12.11; subject, topic 19.25; subject (for a song) 20.3, 21.3; message 11.55; words, exhortation 11.50; **aver razon** to have reason, to be right 29.8: *obl. sg.* **razon** 20.3, 29.8, **razo** 12.11, 19.25, **razó** 11.50, **rason** 21.3, **raizó** 11.55. [CL RĂTĬŌNEM *FEW* 10: 113; It. *ragione,* Sp. *razón,* Fr. *raison,* E. *reason*]

razona *see* **razonar**.

razonamęn *n. masc.* defense: *obl. sg.* **razonamen** 23.15. [**razonar** + **-amen** (1)]

razonar *vb. refl.* to speak: *pres. 3rd sg.* **razona** 25.65. [VL **RĂTĬŌNĀRE* 'to speak' *FEW* 10: 114; It. *ragionare,* Sp. *razonar,* Fr. *raisonner,* E. *to reason*]

re *see* **ren**.

rebat *n. masc.* glare, reflexion: *obl. sg.* **rebat** 32.15. [**rebatre** (**re-** + **batre**)]

rebǫndre *vb. trans.* to bury: *inf.* **rebondre** 31.46. [CL RĔPŌNĔRE *FEW* 10: 270; It. *riporre,* Sp. *reponer*]

recastenar *vb. trans.* to reproach: *pres. part., masc., nom. sg.* **recastenans** 27.43. [**re-** + ***castenar** (blend of **castejar,** a variant form of **castïar,** and **ordenar**?)]

recębre *vb. trans.* to receive: *pret. 3rd sg.* **receup** 5.11, *3rd pl.* **receubron** 25.88. [CL RECĬPĔRE *FEW* 10: 148; It. *ricevere,* Sp. *recibir,* Fr. *recevoir,* E. *to receive*]

rechinhar *vb. intrans.* to sulk: *pres. 3rd sg.* **reqinha** 14.21 var. [**re-** + Frankish *kînan* 'to twist the mouth' *FEW* 16: 324 + **-ar** (2); Fr. *rechigner*]

reclamar *vb. trans.* to invoke, to call out to: *pres. 3rd sg.* **reclama** 11.74. [CL RĔCLĀMĀRE *FEW* 10: 154; It. *richiamare,* Sp. *reclamar,* Fr. *réclamer,* E. *to reclaim*]

recobrar *vb. trans.* to recover: *pret. 3rd sg.* **recobret** 1.6. [CL RĔCŬPĔRĀRE *FEW* 10: 167; It. *ricoverare,* Sp. *recobrarse,* Fr. *recouvrer,* E. *to recover*]

recobrier *n. masc.* recovery, return to the offensive: *nom. sg.* **recobriers** 25.45. [CL RĔCŬPĔRĀRE *FEW* 10: 166 + **-ier**]

recomensar *vb. intrans.* to begin again; *pres. 3rd sg.* **recomensa** 25.4, 25.11. [**re-** + **comensar**]

recordar *vb. trans.* to remember: *pp., masc., obl. sg.* **recordat** 30.90. [CL RĔCŎRDĀRĪ *FEW* 10: 161; It. *ricordarsi*, Sp. *recordar*, E. *to record*]

recrĕire *vb. trans.* to deny 18.37; *refl.* to desist 18.59, *with* **de** to renounce 23.43: *pres. 3rd sg.* **recre** 18.37, 18.59, 23.43. [**re-** + **creire**]

rectọr *n. masc.* leader: *nom. pl.* **rector** 29.40. [CL RĒCTŌREM *FEW* 10: 163; It. *rettore*, Sp. *rector*, Fr. *recteur*, E. *rector*]

redemcịọṇ *n. fem.* redemption: *obl. sg.* **redemcio** 11.25. [ChL RĔDĔMPTĬŌNEM *FEW* 10: 177; It. *ridenzione*, Sp. *redención*, Fr. *rédemption*, E. *redemption*]

redemptọr *n. masc.* redeemer: *obl. sg.* **redemptor** 29.47. [ChL RĔDĔMPTŌREM *FEW* 10: 177; It. *redentore*, Sp. *redentor*, Fr. *rédempteur*]

redọn *adj.* round: *fem., obl. pl.* **redondas** 25.49. [CL RŎTŬNDUM, VL *RĔTŬNDUM *FEW* 10: 527; It. *rotondo*, Sp. *redondo*, Fr. *round*, E. *round*]

rẹdre *vb. trans.* to yield, to surrender 11.57; to return 19.67; *refl.* to become 1.7, *with* **a** to enter (a religious order) 5.15: *fut. 3rd sg.* **redra** 11.57; *pret. 3rd sg.* **rendet** 1.7, 5.15; *pp., fem., nom. sg.* **renduda** 19.67. [CL RĔDDĔRE; the alternative OOc root **rend-** shows influence of VL *RĔNDĔRE (= RĔDDĔRE + PRĔNDĔRE, *FEW* 10: 175); It. *rendere*, Sp. *rendir*, Fr. *rendre*, E. *to render*]

regart *n. masc.* danger: *nom. sg.* **regartz** 24.19. [**regardar** (**re-** + **gardar**)]

regẹsme *n. masc.* kingdom: *nom. sg.* **regesmes** 20.36 (see note). [CL RĔGĪMEN 'control' *FEW* 10: 209 + CL -ĬSMUM '-ism'; It. *reame*, Sp. *reino*, Fr. *royaume*, E. *realm*]

regịọṇ *n. fem.* region: *obl. sg.* **regio** 11.54. [CL RĔGĬŌNEM *FEW* 10: 214; It. *rione* 'quarter' (of a city), Fr. *région*, E. *region*]

regrẹs *n. masc.* bran: *obl. sg.* **regres** 26.18. [CL RĔGRĔSSUM 'return' *FEW* 10: 216]

rẹi *n. masc.* king; *used metaphorically* 20.8, 21.15; *used of God* 11.74, 12.5, 27.23; **joven rei** *sobriquet of Henry, son of Henry II*, 20.4, **"Reis Joves"** 21.17: *nom. sg.* **reis** 5.13, 10.14, 11.62, 11.64, 11.71, 16.40, 20.8, 20.11, 20.18, 20.31, 21.15, 21.17, 22.9, 24.35, 27.23, **reys** 12.5; *obl. sg.* **rei** 11.35, 11.74, 20.4, 21.4, 21.45, 21.78, 22.52, 24.7, **rey** 12.5 var.; *nom. pl.* **rei** 22.7; *obl. pl.* **reis** *used as nom. pl.* 32.14. [CL RĒGEM *FEW* 10: 370; It. *re*, Sp. *rey*, Fr. *roi*; cf. E. *royal*]

reisidar *vb. refl.* to awake: *pret. 1st sg.* **ressidiey** 31.29. [VL *RE- + EXCĬTĀRE *FEW* 3: 274]

religịọṇ *n. fem.* religious order: *nom. sg.* **religïons** 26.26. [ChL RĔLĬGĬŌNEM *FEW* 10: 231; It. *religione*, Sp. *religión*, Fr. *religion*, E. *religion*]

remanẹr *vb. intrans.* to remain, to stay behind 4.31, 5.14, 12.49, 17.14; to remain, to stick 25.58; to finish 21.2: *pres. 3rd sg.* **reman** 4.31; *fut. 3rd pl.* **remanran** 12.49; *pret. 3rd sg.* **remas** 5.14; *pp., masc., nom. sg.* **remazutz** 25.58; *obl. sg.* **romazut** 21.2; *nom. pl.* **remazut** 17.14, **remasu** 17.14 var. [CL RĔMĂNĒRE *FEW* 10: 235; It. *rimanere*, Sp. *remanecer*, OFr. *remaneir*, E. *to remain*]

remembrar *vb. trans.* to remember 29.5; *impersonal with* **de** to remember 15.4: *pres. 3rd sg.* **remembra** 15.4; *pres. part., masc., obl. sg.* **remembran** 29.5. [ChL RĔMĔMŎRĀRĪ *FEW* 10: 238; It. *rimembrare*, Sp. *remembrar*, E. *to remember*]

remirar *vb. trans.* to reflect: *pp., masc., nom. sg.* **remiratz** 15.35. [**re-** + **mirar**]

rẹn *n. fem.* creature 4.2, 4.4, 4.10, 4.19, 4.28, 4.37, 13.9; *(indefinite)* anything 2.22, 3.5, 9.36, 16.10, 23.11, 26.53, 27.4, 29.15; *(in negative constructions)* **nulla ren** nothing 16.31; **ren** (. . .) **non** nothing 16.21, 16.44, 18.15, 21.39, 21.43, 28.26, 28.45, 30.80; **ren mais** (. . .) **non** nothing else 16.43, 30.25; **per nulla ren non** for nothing on earth 30.49; **non** . . . **per ren** not at all 30.53.
  Forms: nom. sg. **res** 16.31, 16.44, 21.43, 28.26, 28.45, 30.80; *obl. sg.* **ren** 2.22, 16.10, 16.43, 21.39, 27.4, 29.15, 30.49, 30.53, **re** 3.5, 4.2, 16.21, 18.15, 23.11, 26.53, 30.25; *vocative sg.* **res** 4.4, 4.10, 4.19, 4.28, 4.37, **re** 13.9; *obl. pl.* **res** 9.36.
  [CL ʀĕм 'thing' *FEW* 10: 287; Fr. *rien*; cf. Latin *in re* 'regarding']

rẹnc *n. masc.* kingdom: *obl. sg.* **renc** 15.13. [CL ʀĕɢɴᴜᴍ *FEW* 10: 216; It. *regno*, Sp. *reino*, Fr. *règne*, E. *reign*]

rendet, renduda *see* **redre**.

renhar *vb. intrans.* to live, to rule: *pres. 3rd sg.* **renha** 14.67. [CL ʀĕɢɴāʀᴇ *FEW* 10: 215; It. *regnare*, Sp. *reinar*, Fr. *reigner*, E. *to reign*]

repairar *vb. intrans.* to come 25.34, to return 11.80: *pres. 3rd pl.* **repairan** 25.34, **repairen** 11.80. [CL ʀĕᴘātʀĭāʀᴇ *FEW* 10: 262; Fr. *repérer*, E. *to repair*]

repaire *n. masc.* dwelling: *obl. sg.* **repaire** 2.8. [**repairar**]

repairen *see* **repairar**.

repaus *n. masc.* repose: *nom. sg.* **repaus** 24.28. [**repauzar** (LL ʀĕᴘᴀᴜsāʀᴇ *FEW* 10: 264; It. *riposare*, Fr. *reposer*, E. *to repose*)]

repentir *vb. refl.* to repent: *pres. 3rd sg.* **repent** 11.11. [**re-** + CL ᴘᴀᴇɴĭtēʀᴇ, ᴘᴏᴇɴĭtēʀᴇ *FEW* 9: 120; It. *ripentirsi*, Fr. *se repentir*, Sp. *repentirse*, E. *to repent*]

repic *n. masc.* ringing of bells: *obl. pl.* **repics** *used as nom. pl.* 25.98. [**re-** + **picar** 'to strike' (VL *ᴘīᴋᴋāʀᴇ *FEW* 8: 470)]

reprẹndre *vb. trans.* to chide, to reproach: *pres. 3rd sg.* **repren** 16.34, 23.25. [CL ʀĕᴘʀĕʜĕɴᴅĕʀᴇ *FEW* 10: 275; It. *reprendere*, Fr. *reprendre*, E. *to reprehend*]

reprẹza *n. fem.* repetition: *obl. sg.* **represza** 26.3. [**re-** + **preza** 'taking,' pp. fem. of **prendre**]

reprovier *n. masc.* bitter words: *obl. pl.* **reproers** 25.78. [**reprovar** 'to reproach' (CL ʀĕᴘʀŏʙāʀᴇ *FEW* 10: 277; It. *riprovare*, Sp. *reprovar*, Fr. *reprouver*, E. *to reprove*) + **-ier**]

reptar *vb. trans.* to accuse: *inf.* **reptar** 11.64. [CL ʀĕᴘᴜtāʀᴇ *FEW* 10: 281; Sp. *retar*, OFr. *reter*, E. *to (be)rate*]

reqinha *see* **rechinhar**.

res *see* **ren**.

resemblar *vb. intrans.* to seem: *past subj. 3rd sg.* **resembles** 15.42. [**re-** + **semblar**]

resọrzer *vb. intrans.* to rise again: *pret. 3rd sg.* **resors** 12.72. [CL ʀĕsᴜʀɢĕʀᴇ *FEW* 10: 328; It. *risorgere*; cf. E. *resurgent*]

respọndre *vb. intrans.* to answer: *pres. 1st sg.* **respon** 18.38; *pres. subj. 1st sg.* **responda** 19.26; *pret. 1st sg.* **respozi** 9.7. [CL ʀĕsᴘŏɴᴅĕʀᴇ, VL ʀĕsᴘŏɴᴅ̆ᴇʀᴇ *FEW* 10: 314; It. *rispondere*, Sp. *responder*, Fr. *répondre*, E. *to respond*]

respọs *n. masc.* conversation: *obl. sg.* **respos** 21.30. [pp. of **respondre**]

respozi *see* **respondre.**

ressidiey *see* **reisidar.**

restar *vb. intrans. with* **en** to stick to, to cling to: *pres. 3rd sg.* **resta** 22.18. [CL RĚSTĀRE *FEW* 10: 320; It. *restare*, Sp. *restar*, Fr. *rester*, E. *to rest*]

rete, retenc *see* **retener.**

retendir *vb. intrans.* to echo, to resound: *inf.* **retendir** 25.100. [re- + VL *TĬNNĪTĪRE *FEW* 13, part 1: 346]

retener *vb. trans.* to keep 21.39; to retain 18.39; to remember 11.31; to appoint as a retainer *(said metaphorically of God)* 10.36, 27.16: *pres. 3rd sg.* **rete** 18.39; *pres. subj. 3rd sg.* **retenha** 21.39, **reteng'** 10.36; *pret. 3rd sg.* **retenc** 11.31; *inf.* **retener** 27.16. [CL RĚTĬNĒRE *FEW* 10: 336; It. *ritenere*, Sp. *retener*, Fr. *retenir*, E. *to retain*]

retornar *vb. intrans.* to return: *fut. 1st sg.* **retornarai** 4.40. [re- + **tornar**]

retraire *vb. trans.* to speak, to tell 2.4, 6.13, 6.14, 29.12; to tell, to perform *(a sirventes)* 27.2; to bring up, to say *(in reproach)* 18.50; *intrans.* to return 13.37: *pres. 1st sg.* **retrai** 18.50, **retrac** 29.12; *pres. subj. 3rd sg.* **retraia** 6.13; *fut. 1st sg.* **retrarai** 27.2; *pret. 1st sg.* **retrais** 6.14; *inf.* **retraire** 2.4, **retrayre** 13.37. [CL RĚTRĂHĚRE *FEW* 10: 344; It. *ritrarre*, Sp. *retraer*, Fr. *retraire*]

reve, reveingna *see* **revenir.**

revelhar *vb. trans.* to awaken: *pp., masc., nom. sg.* **reveillatz** 30.5. [re- + **velhar** 'to remain awake' (CL VĬGĬLĀRE *FEW* 14: 438)]

revenc *see* **revenir.**

revenimen *n. masc.* healing: *obl. sg.* **revenimen** 23.23. [revenir + -imen]

revenir *vb. intrans.* to return 13.37 var.; to regain consciousness 3.10; *trans.* to heal, to revive 21.25, 21.53, 23.35: *pres. 3rd sg.* **reve** 23.35; *pres. subj. 3rd sg.* **reveingna** 21.25, 21.53; *pret. 3rd sg.* **revenc** 3.10; *inf.* **revenir** 13.37 var. [CL RĚVĚNĪRE *FEW* 10: 353; It. *rivenire*, Sp. *revenirse*, Fr. *revenir*; cf. E. *revenue*]

reverdir *vb. intrans.* to turn green again: *inf.* **reverdir** 13.37 var. [re- + **verdir** 'to turn green' (**vert** + **-ir**)]

revertir *vb. intrans.* to go back: *pres. 3rd sg.* **revert** 13.72, **revertis** 13.72 var.; *pres. subj. 3rd sg.* **reverta** 13.72 var.; *inf.* **revertir** 13.37. [re- + **vertir** 'to turn' (CL VĚRTĚRE *FEW* 14: 320; Sp. *verter*)]

revestir *vb. refl.* to dress in *with* **ab**: *pp., masc., nom. sg.* **revestitz** 31.38. [LL RĚVĚSTĪRE L & S; cf. *FEW* 14: 355; It. *rivestire*, Sp. *revestir*, Fr. *revêtir*]

rey, reys *see* **rei.**

ri, ria *see* **rire.**

ribeira *see* **ribiera.**

riben 9.11 (see note).

ribiera *n. fem.* riverbank: *obl. sg.* **ribeira** 28.59. [CL RĪPĀRĬA adj. 'things on the riverbank,' VL *'riverbank' *FEW* 10: 416; It. *riviera*, Sp. *ribera*, Fr. *rivière*, E. *river*]

ric *adj.* rich, powerful 3.3, *(because of success in love)* 16.42; mighty 12.61, 21.28; precious 13.61; haughty 23.4: *masc., nom. sg.* **rics** 3.3; *obl. sg.* **ric** 13.61, 16.42, 21.28, 23.4; *obl. pl.* **rics** 12.61. [Frankish *rīki *FEW* 16: 714; It. *ricco*, Sp. *rico*, Fr. *riche*, E. *rich*]

ricamen *adv.* heartily: **ricamen** 30.9. [ric + -amen (2)]

rics *see* **ric.**

rire *vb. intrans.* to laugh: *pres. 3rd sg.* **ri** 8.9; *pres. subj. 3rd sg.* **ria** 27.22;

pret. 3rd pl. **rizeron** 31.39; *pres. part., masc., nom. sg.* **rizens** 27.19 var., *undeclined* **rizen** 27.19, **en rizen** 2.5; *inf.* **rire** 2.14, 31.7. [CL RĪDĒRE, LL RĪDĔRE *FEW* 10: 399; It. *ridere,* Sp. *reir,* Fr. *rire*; cf. E. *risible*]

romans *n. masc.* Romance, the vernacular language, Occitan: *obl. sg.* **romans** 10.24. [VL *RŌMĀNĬCĒ *adv.* 'in the Romance (not the Latin or German) way' *FEW* 10: 454; Fr. *roman,* E. *romance*]

romazut *see* **remaner.**

rọmpre *vb. trans.* to break: *pret. 1st sg.* **ronpei** 9.63 var., *3rd sg.* **rompet** 9.63. [CL RŬMPĔRE *FEW* 10: 573; It. *rompere,* Sp. *romper,* Fr. *rompre*]

rọs *adj.* red-haired: *masc., obl. sg.* **ros** 9.33. [CL RŬSSUM *FEW* 10: 591; It. *rosso,* Fr. *roux,* E. *russet*]

rosignol *see* **rosinhol.**

rosignolet *see* **rosinholet.**

rosinhọl *n. masc.* nightingale: *obl. sg.* **rosignol** 17.9. [CL LŬSCĬNĬAM, VL *LŬSCĬNĬŎLUM *FEW* 5: 472; It. *lusignolo,* Sp. *ruiseñor,* Fr. *rossignol*]

rosinholẹt *n. masc.* (small) nightingale: *obl. sg.* **rosignolet** 17.4. [**rosinhol** + **-ẹt**]

rotier *n. masc.* mercenary soldier: *obl. pl.* **roters** 25.63. [**rota** 'troop' (VL RŬPTAM 'small unit of men in an army' *FEW* 10: 574 {E. *rout*]) + **-ier**]

·s (1) *vb. intrans.* 25.54 = **es,** *pres. 3rd sg.* of **eser,** *which see.*

s' (2), **·s** *reflexive pron.* himself, *etc.* 2.11, 3.11, 5.4, 5.6, 5.6, 5.7, 5.8, 5.8, 5.10, 5.10, 5.10, 5.14, 5.15, 6.17, 7.11, 8.5, 8.17, 8.28, 11.8, 11.10, 11.11, 11.26, 11.68, 13.26, 14.9, 14.38, 14.41, 14.42, 17.7, 17.16, 18.3, 18.49, 19.10, 19.10, 19.12, 19.47, 19.58, 21.27, 21.52, 21.67, 22.15, 23.43, 26.14, 26.52, 27.30, 29.39, 30.18, 30.22, 30.23, 30.41, 30.43, 30.51, 30.53, 30.56, 30.74, 30.83, 30.91, 31.28, *see* **se** (1).

s' (3) *possessive pron.* his, *etc.* 6.18, 11.48, 19.68, 30.19, *see* **son** (4).

s' (4) *adv.* so, *etc.* 23.27, 31.16, *see* **si** (2).

s' (5) *conj.* if, *etc.* 2.22, 4.10, 4.37, 8.12, 10.22, 12.24, 12.65, 14.56, 15.24, 16.22, 18.39, 19.1, 19.34, 19.51, 19.52, 19.53, 19.62, 23.1, 23.12, 23.16, 26.15, 26.49, 27.4, 27.5, 27.41, 28.69, 30.61, 30.76, *see* **si** (1).

sa (1) *poss. adj., see* **son** (4).

sa (2) *adv.* 27.41, *see* **sai** (2).

sabẹr *vb. trans.* to know *passim; in preterit tense* to realize 1.6, 18.26, to learn 3.6, 5.3, to manage 16.10, 31.42; *with inf., equivalent to meaning of the inf.* 16.43.

    Forms: Pres. 1st sg. **sai** 2.22, 4.22, 6.9, 8.27, 15.10, 15.17, 16.23, 16.43, 17.38, 17.41, 18.10, 18.24, 18.40, 18.55, 18.58, 22.5, 23.17, 23.41, 26.55, **say** 12.55, 12.66, 19.26, 31.13; *3rd sg.* **sap** 2.8, 3.6, 12.28, 12.29, 14.17, 14.33, 14.63, 17.16, 23.21, 23.27; *1st pl.* **sabem** 27.30 var.; *2nd pl.* **sabetz** 12.32, 19.50, **sabez** 24.17, *3rd pl.* **saben** 6.34, 27.30.

    Pres. subj. 1st sg. **sacha** 8.11; *3rd sg.* **sapcha** 24.11.

    Imperf. 1st sg. **sabia** 16.10 ms., 18.26 var., **sabi'** 16.10.

    Pret. 1st sg. **saubi** 18.26; *3rd sg.* **saup** 1.6, 5.3, 30.29, 30.30, **saub** 1.6 var., 31.42.

    1st cond. 1st sg. **sabria** 16.10 var.; *2nd pl.* **sabriaz** 17.10.

    Imper. 2nd pl. **sapchatz** 7.21, **sapchaz** 23.34.

    Pp., masc., nom. sg. **saubutz** 9.18, **saipuz** 9.18 var., **sabutz** 9.18 var.; *neuter, modifying clause* **saubut** 7.3; *fem., obl. sg. in expression* **a saupuda** 19.59, **a saubuda** 19.59 var. openly, to the knowledge of others.

Inf. **saber** 1.5, 18.9, 26.31; *substantivized inf., masc., obl. sg.* **saber** wisdom 11.33, 29.11, knowledge 26.47, skill 29.18.

[CL sapĕre 'to taste of' *FEW* 11: 198, VL *sapēre B-W; It. *sapere*, Sp. *saber*, Fr. *savoir*; cf. E. *sapience*]

sabọr *n. fem.* savor, pleasant taste: *obl. sg.* **sabor** 29.9. [CL sapōrem *FEW* 11: 208; It. *sapore*, Sp. *sabor*, Fr. *saveur*, E. *savor*]

sabria, sabriaz *see* **saber.**

sabrier *n. masc.* sauce: *obl. sg.* **sabrier** 26.11. [**sabor** + **-ier**]

sabutz, sacha *see* **saber.**

sacrament *see* **sagramen.**

sacrifíci *n. masc.* consecration of the host in the liturgy of the Eucharist: *obl. sg.* **sacrifizi** 25.29. [ChL sacrĭfĭcĭum *FEW* 11: 43; It. *sacrifizio*, Sp. *sacrificio*, Fr. *sacrifice*, E. *sacrifice*]

sagẹl *n. masc.* seal, sealed letter: *obl. sg.* **sagel** 8.8. [CL sĭgĭllum, VL *sĭgĕllum *FEW* 11: 597; It. *suggello*, Sp. *sello*, Fr. *sceau*, E. *seal*]

sagẹta *n. fem.* arrow: *obl. pl.* **sagetas** 25.48. [CL sagĭttam *FEW* 11: 59; It. *saetta*, Sp. *saeta*]

sagnens *see* **sancnen.**

sagnós *see* **sancnos.**

sagnoses *see* **sancnos.**

sagramẹn *n. masc.* oath: *obl. sg.* **sacrament** 11.10. [CL sacrămĕntum *FEW* 1: 37; It. *sacramento*, Sp. *sacramento*, Fr. *serment*, E. *sacrament*]

sai (1) *vb. trans.* 2.22, 4.22, 6.9, 8.27, 15.10, 15.17, 16.23, 16.43, 17.38, 17.41, 18.10, 18.24, 18.40, 18.55, 18.58, 22.5, 23.17, 23.41, 26.55 *pres. 1st sg. of* **saber,** *which see.*

sai (2) *adv.* here (= with the beloved 4.31; in France 12.68, 12.71; on this side of the English Channel 5.14; in Spain, not Palestine 12.9 [see note]; in this life 24.44, 27.41); **de l'or en sai** ever since 18.42; **de sai** over here 5.14, 12.9; **sai ni lai** to either side 30.55, **sai e lai** here and there 12.36 var. *Forms:* **sai** 4.31, 5.14, 12.36 var., 12.71, 18.42, 24.44, 30.55; **say** 12.9, 12.68; **sa** 27.41. [VL ĕccĕ hāc (Fr. *ça*) influenced by **i** (2) *FEW* 4: 373]

saiat *see* **sajar.**

saint *adj.* saint; saintly, holy 26.56, 29.28: *masc., nom. sg.* **sayns** 27.18 var., **sans** 27.48; *obl. sg.* **sanh** 9.6, **sant** 29.28, **san** 21.14, 31.19, 31.36, **saint** *used as nom. sg.* 26.38, 27.18; *nom. pl.* **saint** 26.56; *obl. pl.* **sains** 26.56; *fem., vocative sg.* **sainta** 27.45. *See also Proper Names.* [CL sanctum *FEW* 11: 151; It. *santo*, Sp. *santo*, Fr. *saint*, E. *saint*]

saintorier *adj.* devout; sanctimonious 25.19: *masc., nom. sg.* **sentorers** 25.19. [**saintor** 'saint' (**saint** + **-or** *FEW* 11: 150) + **-ier**]

saipuz *see* **saber.**

sajar *vb. trans.* to test: *pp.* **saiat** 23.42. [aphetic form of **asajar**]

sal (1) *n. masc.* salt: *obl. sg.* **sal** 30.2. [CL sālem *FEW* 11: 83; It. *sale*, Sp. *sal*, Fr. *sel*]

sál (2) *vb. intrans.* 11.68, *see* **salhir.**

sal (3) *adj.* healthy, hearty 12.14; saved, redeemed 11.6; lucky, blessed 16.40; safe (place) 30.98: *masc., nom. sg.* **sals** 12.14, **saus** 16.40; *obl. sg.* **salv** 30.98; *nom. pl.* **salv** 11.6. [CL salvum *FEW* 11: 135; It. *salvo*, Sp. *salvo*, Fr. *sauf*, E. *save*]

sal (4) *prep.* except, except for; **sal tot lo tort** even if he hadn't wronged me 22.45; **sal de** except 12.7. [**sal** (3)]

salhir *vb. intrans.* to jump, to leap 25.46; **salhir en estant** to leap to one's feet, to stand up 11.68: *pres. 3rd sg.* **sál** 11.68; *pret. 3rd pl.* **salhiron** 25.46. [CL SALĪRE *FEW* 11: 97; It. *salire*, Sp. *salir*, Fr. *saillir*, E. *sally*]

salm *n. masc.* psalm: *obl. pl.* **salms** 30.87. [ChL (from Gk.) PSALMUM *FEW* 9: 500; It. *salmo*, Sp. *salmo*, Fr. *psaume*, E. *psalm*]

sals *see* **sal** (3).

salsa *n. fem.* sauce: *obl. sg.* **salsa** 26.22. [CL SALSUM 'salty,' VL SALSA 'sauce' *FEW* 11: 111; It. *salsa*, Sp. *salsa*, Fr. *sauce*, E. *sauce*]

saludar *vb. trans.* to greet: *pret. 3rd pl.* **saluderon** 9.5. [CL SALŪTĀRE *FEW* 11: 127; It. *salutare*, Sp. *saludar*, Fr. *saluer*, E. *to salute*]

salv *see* **sal** (3).

salvamen *n. masc.* safety, salvation; **a salvamen anar** to proceed to one's defense: *obl. sg.* **salvament** 11.69. [**salvar** + **-amen** (1)]

salvar *vb. trans.* to save; to defend 11.68; to redeem 27.36: *inf.* **salvar** 11.68, 27.36. [LL SALVĀRE *FEW* 11: 130; It. *salvare*, Sp. *salvar*, Fr. *sauver*, E. *to save*]

salvatge *adj.* wild, timid, savage: *masc., obl. sg.* **salvatje** 13.57. [CL SĬLVĂTĬCUM 'of the wood,' LL SALVĀTĬCUM *FEW* 11: 620; It. *salvatico*, Sp. *salvaje*, E. *sauvage*, E. *savage*]

san (1) *adj.* 21.14, 31.19, *see* **saint**.

saṇ (2) *adj.* healthy, strong; **san e sal** safe and sound 12.14: *masc., nom. sg.* **sas** 12.14; *fem., nom. sg.* **sayna** 13.14, *obl. sg.* **sana** 30.34. [CL SĀNUM *FEW* 11: 190; It. *sano*, Sp. *sano*, Fr. *sain*, E. *sane*]

sanar *vb. trans.* to cure: *pp., masc., nom. sg.* **sanatz** 14.60. [CL SANĀRE *FEW* 11: 146; It. *sanare*, Sp. *sanar*]

sanc *n. masc.* 25.13, 25.59, *fem.* 32.10, blood: *obl. sg.* **sanc** 25.13, 25.59, **sang** 32.10. [Both masc. and fem. in OOc; CL SANGUEM masc. *FEW* 11: 178; It. *sangue* masc., Sp. *sangre* fem., Fr. *sang* masc.; cf. E. *sanguine*]

sancnẹn *adj.* bloody: *masc., nom. sg.* **sagnens** 25.73. [**sancnar** (CL SANGUĪNĀRE) + **-en** (3) *FEW* 11: 163]

sancnọs *adj.* bloody: *masc., obl. pl.* **sagnós** 32.14, **sagnoses** 32.14 var. [LL SANGUĬNŌSUM *FEW* 11: 169; It. *sanguinoso*, Sp. *sanguinoso*, Fr. *saigneux*]

sanglọt *n. masc.* sigh: *obl. pl.* **sanglotz** 26.5. [OFr. *sanglot* (CL SĬNGŪLTUM, VL *SĬNGLŪTUM, influenced by GLŬTTĪRE 'to swallow' *FEW* 11: 647; It. *singhiozzo* 'hiccup,' Sp. *sollozo* 'sob']

sanh, sans, sant *see* **saint**.

sap, sapcha, sapchatz, sapchaz *see* **saber**.

sapiẹncia *n. fem.* wisdom: *obl. sg.* **sapiencia** 11.30, 11.39, 11.78. [CL SAPĬĔNTĬAM *FEW* 11: 206; It. *sapienza*, Sp. *sapiencia*, Fr. *sapience*, E. *sapience*]

saramahart 9.12 (see note).

saria *see* **eser**.

sas (1) *adj.* 12.14, *see* **san** (2).

sas (2) *possessive adj.* 3.4, 5.6, 5.6, 18.2, 27.16, 29.43, 31.23, 32.2, 32.13, *see* **son** (4).

satan *n. masc.* devil: *nom. pl.* **satan** 11.18. [ChL (from Hebrew) SATANAS, SATAN *FEW* 11: 238; It. *Satana*, Sp. *Satán*, *Satanás*, Fr. *Satan*, E. *Satan*]

saub, saubi, saubuda, saubut, saubutz *see* **saber**.

saumier *n. masc.* packhorse: *obl. pl.* **saumers** 25.103. [LL SAGMĀRĬUM *FEW* 11: 71; It. *somaro*, Sp. *somero*, Fr. *sommier*]

saup, saupuda *see* **saber.**

saus *see* **sal** (3).

saut *n. masc.* leap, hop *(erotic): obl. sg.* **saut** 14.9. [CL SALTUM *FEW* 11: 124; It. *salto,* Sp. *salto,* Fr. *saut*]

sautẹri *n. masc.* psalter, book of psalms: *obl. sg.* **sauteri** 30.70, 30.86. [ChL (from Gk.) PSALTĔRĬUM *FEW* 9: 501; It. *salterio,* Sp. *salterio,* Fr. *psautier,* E. *psalter*]

savaier *adj.* wretched, miserable: *masc., nom. sg.* **savayers** 13.30 var. [**savai** 'bad, wicked' (CL SĬLVĀTĬCUM *FEW* 11: 616, LL SALVĀTĬCUM *FEW* 11: 620) + **-ier**]

savi *adj.* wise: *masc., nom. sg.* **savis** 10.17, **savi** 14.47. [CL SAPĬDUM 'tasty' *FEW* 11: 204; It. *savio, saggio,* Sp. *sabio,* Fr. *sage,* E. *sage*]

savïẹza *n. fem.* wisdom: *obl. sg.* **savïeza** 29.42. [**savi** + **-eza**]

savis *see* **savi.**

say (1) *vb. trans.* 12.55, 12.66, 19.26, 31.13, *pres. 1st sg. of* **saber,** *which see.*

say (2) *adv.* 12.9, 12.68, *see* **sai** (2).

sayna *see* **san** (2).

sayns *see* **saint.**

scellui *see* **cel** (3).

scïẹnsa *n. fem.* knowledge: *obl. sg.* **scïensa** 2.23. [CL SCĬĒNTĬAM *FEW* 11: 310; It. *scienza,* Sp. *ciencia,* Fr. *science,* E. *science*]

scïentiers *adv.* knowingly, with care: **scïenters** 25.75. [CL SCĬĒNTER *FEW* 11: 307 + **-s**]

se (1) *refl. pron.*

Disjunctive, *masc. sg.* himself 5.8 var., 10.36, 30.92, **si mezeus** himself 18.14 var.; *fem. sg.* **si meteissa** herself 23.19.

Conjunctive, follows verb, *masc. sg.* himself 1.2, 1.4, 5.12, 5.14, 18.47, 30.23; *fem. sg.* herself 5.6 var., 5.6 var., 18.13.

Conjunctive, precedes verb, *masc. sg.* himself (etc.) 1.4, 1.4, 2.11, 5.4, 5.8, 5.8, 5.9, 5.9, 5.10, 5.10, 5.15, 6.6, 6.16, 7.11, 8.5, 8.17, 8.28, 11.8, 11.10, 11.11, 11.26, 11.68, 13.26, 13.40, 14.38, 14.41, 14.42, 17.7, 17.16, 18.3, 19.10, 19.10, 19.12, 20.28, 22.15, 23.43, 25.65, 25.101, 26.14, 26.52, 27.30, 28.37, 30.18, 30.22, 30.41, 30.43, 30.51, 30.53, 30.56, 30.74, 30.83, 30.88, 30.91; *fem. sg.* herself (etc.) 1.7, 2.21, 3.11, 3.11, 5.6, 5.6, 5.10, 6.17, 13.26, 14.9, 14.14, 18.3, 18.15, 18.49, 19.47, 19.58, 21.52, 21.67, 31.28; *masc. pl.* themselves 5.7, 8.29, 21.27, 26.32, 29.39.

Forms: **se, si,** proclitic **s'** passim, see **s'** (2); enclitic **·is** 6.6, 18.3, 20.28.

[CL SĒ *FEW* 11: 358; It. *se, si,* Sp. *se,* Fr. *se, soi*]

se (2) *conj.* if, *etc.* 14.54 var., 15.25, 16.32, *see* **si** (1)

sebẹnc *adj.* illegitimate, bastard; despicable 23.4: *masc., obl. sg.* **sebenc** 23.4, **seben** 23.4 var. [**sẹp** 'hedge' (CL SAEPEM) + **-enc** 'one from the hedge,' because an illegitimate child was thought of as conceived under a hedge *FEW* 11: 47]

sebisa *n. fem.* hedge: *obl. sg.* **sebissa** 13.1. [**sẹp** 'hedge' (CL SAEPEM *FEW* 11: 47) + **-isa**]

secrẹt *n. masc.* secret: *nom. sg.* **secretz** 9.17; *obl. sg.* **secret** *used as nom.* 9.17 var.; *obl. pl.* **sicretz** 26.31. [CL SĒCRĒTUM *FEW* 11: 378; It. *segreto,* Sp. *secreto,* Fr. *secret,* E. *secret*]

secretari *adj.* secret: *masc., obl. sg.* **cecretari** 31.16. [CL SĒCRĒTĀRĬUM 'hiding place' *FEW* 11: 374]

sega *see* **segre.**

segle *n. masc.* world: *nom. sg.* **segles** 17.23; *obl. sg.* **segle** 21.40, **siegle** 27.7. [CL saecŭlum *FEW* 11: 45; It. *secolo,* Sp. *siglo,* Fr. *siècle*; cf. E. *secular*]

segner, seign', seingner *see* **senhor.**

segon (1) *adj.* second: *fem., nom. sg.* **segonda** 19.20 note; *obl. sg.* **segonda** 19.31 note. [CL secŭndum *FEW* 11: 386; It. *secondo,* Sp. *segundo,* Fr. *second*]

segon (2) *prep.* according to: **segon** 8.4, 12.11, 13.72, 13.78, 27.42, 28.22, 31.13. **segon que** *conj.* according to the way 29.40, 31.9. [**segon** (1); It. *secondo,* Sp. *según,* Fr. *selon*]

segre *vb. trans.* to follow: *pres. subj. 3rd sg.* **sega** 14.50; *fut. 3rd pl.* **sigran** 21.26; *inf.* **segre** 11.59. [CL sĕquī, sĕquĕre *FEW* 11: 493; It. *seguire,* Sp. *seguir,* Fr. *suivre,* E. *to segue*]

segues *see* **sezer.**

segur *adj.* safe: *fem., nom. sg.* **segura** 13.76. [CL sēcūrum *FEW* 11: 390; It. *sicuro,* Sp. *seguro,* Fr. *sûr,* E. *sure*]

sei *see* **son** (4).

seign-, seingn-, *see* **senh-.**

seis *num.* six: **seis** 13.42. [CL sĕx *FEW* 11: 556; It. *sei,* Sp. *seis,* Fr. *six,* E. *six*]

seisanta *num.* sixty: **seissanta** 25.34. [CL sexagĭnta, LL sexanta *FEW* 11: 557; It. *sessanta,* Sp. *sesenta,* Fr. *soixante*]

sel, sela *see* **cel** (3).

selaray *see* **celar.**

selh *see* **cel** (3).

selis, sellis *see* **celitz.**

sellui, sels, seluy *see* **cel** (3).

semana *n. fem.* week: *obl. sg.* **semana** 30.33, **semayna** 13.42; *obl. pl.* **setmanas** 22.26. [LL sĕptĭmāna *FEW* 11: 483; It. *settimana,* Sp. *semana,* Fr. *semaine*]

sembelin *n. masc.* sable: *obl. sg.* **sembeli** 10.42. [OFr. *sembelin, sebelin* (Russian *sobol' FEW* 20: 49, Middle High German *zobelîn,* because the fur was imported from Siberia by way of Germany); It. *zibellino,* Sp. *cebellina,* Fr. *zibeline*]

sembl', sembla *see* **semblar.**

semblan *n. masc.* facial expression 21.8; **bel semblan** friendly look 16.37, agreeable prospect 21.42: *obl. sg.* **senblan** 21.8, 21.42; *obl. pl.* **semblanz** 16.37. [*pres. part of* **semblar**]

semblansa *n. fem.* semblance, appearance 31.9; comparison 14.3 (see note); **faire semblansa de** 14.6, **aver semblansa de** 28.42, to resemble: *obl. sg.* **semblansa** 14.3, 14.6, 28.42, **semlansa** 31.9. [**semblar** + **-ansa**]

semblanz *see* **semblan.**

semblar *vb. intrans.* to seem (like) 16.46, 18.29, 25.41, 25.51; *trans.* to resemble 20.12, 30.16: *pres. 3rd sg.* **sembla** 16.46, 18.29, 20.12 ms., 25.41, 25.51, **sembl'** 20.12; *pret. 3rd sg.* **semblet** 30.16. [LL sĭmĭlāre *FEW* 11: 627; It. *sembrare,* Fr. *sembler*; cf. E. *to resemble*]

semdier *n. masc.* path: *obl. pl.* **semdiers** 25.101. [CL sēmĭtārĭum adj. 'found in alleys' *FEW* 11: 441; It. *sentiero,* Sp. *sendero,* Fr. *sentier*]

semenar *vb. trans.* to sow: *pres. 3rd sg.* **semena** 17.33 var., **semen'** 17.33

var., **semn'** 17.33. [CL sēmĭnāre *FEW* 11: 438; It. *seminare*, Sp. *sembrar*, Fr. *semer*]

semlansa *see* **semblansa**.

semn' *see* **semenar**.

sęmpre *adv.* still: **sempre** 11.15. [CL sĕmper *FEW* 11: 442; It. *sempre*, Sp. *siempre*]

sęn (1) *n. masc.* mind 7.16, 16.7; wit 6.28, 13.3, 24.25, 29.13; good sense 13.23; advice 14.67; intention 11.58; **entier de sen** sensible 28.68: *nom. sg.* **sens** 6.28, **senz** 24.25, **sénz** 11.58; *obl. sg.* **sen** 7.16, 13.3, 13.23, 14.67, 16.7, 28.68, 29.13. [Germ. **sinno-*, LL sĭnnum *FEW* 17: 73; It. *senno*]

sęn (2) *n. masc.* 19.57 var., *see* **senhor**.

sęn (3) *vb. trans.* 2.2, *see* **sentir**.

senblan *see* **semblan**.

senes *see* **ses**.

senęstre *adj.* left, left-hand: *masc., obl. sg.* **senestre** 25.52. [CL sĭnĭstrum influenced by dĕxtram *FEW* 11: 649; It. *sinistro*, Sp. *siniestro*, E. *sinister*]

senestrier *adj.* left, left-hand: *masc., obl. pl.* **senestriers** 25.57. [**senestre** + **-ier**]

senhar *vb. intrans.* to make signs (flirtatiously) 14.19 var.; to make the sign of the cross over 14.21: *pres. 3rd sg.* **sinha** 14.19 var., **cinha** 14.21, **cigna** 14.21 var. [CL sĭgnāre *FEW* 11: 602; It. *segnare*, Sp. *señar*, Fr. *signer*, E. *to sign*]

senharier *n. masc.* war cry: *nom. sg.* **senharers** 25.39. [**senhal** 'banner' (VL sĭgnāle *FEW* 11: 599; It. *segnale*, Sp. *señal*, Fr. *signal*, E. *signal*) + **-ier**]

senhór, *nom. sg.* **sénher** *n. masc.* lord; feudal lord, suzerain 5.4, 11.37, 11.47, 20.24, 22.52, 24.4; **un senhor de pestre** a lord of a priest, an excellent priest (?) 31.2; *used by a woman of her husband* 3.10; *used by a shepherdess of the narrator* 13 *passim*; *used by a shepherdess of the narrator-poet* 28 *passim*; *used of God* 10.30, 12.5, 12.28, 12.69, 27.6, 27.31, 29.27, *of Christ* 12.72.

　　Forms: Nom. sg. **senher** 12.5, 12.28, 12.72, **senhers** 20.24 var., **seigner** 10.30, 12.72 var., 20.24, **seingner** 5.4.

　　Vocative sg. **senher** 13.11, 13.25, 13.36, 13.39, 13.50, 13.53, 13.67, 28.16, 28.21, 28.24, 28.28, 28.33, 28.36, 28.40, 28.45, 28.48, 28.52, 28.57, 28.60, 28.64, 28.69, 28.72, **seingner** 3.10, 21.16, 21.43, 21.57, 27.6, **segner** 19.57 var.

　　Vocative sg. in apposition **senher amics** 19.57, **senher coms** 25.18, **Dieus senher** 12.69, **bel seingner Dieus** 27.31, **segner Giraut** 19.57 var., **seign'en Giraut** 19.57 var., **sen n'amic** 19.57 var.

　　Obl. sg. **senhor** 29.27, 31.2, *used as nom. sg.* 12.5 var.; **seignor** 15.29, 22.52; **senor** 11.9, 11.37, 11.47.

　　Obl. pl. **seignors** 24.4.

　　[CL senĭōrem (nom. sĕnĭor) 'older' *FEW* 11: 458; It. *signore*, Sp. *señor*, Fr. *seigneur*, *sire*, E. *senior*, *sir*]

senhoratge *n. masc.* lordship, fief: *obl. sg.* **seignorage** 10.10. [**senhor** + **-atge**]

senhoril *adj.* lordly; *n. masc.* lord 12.5 var.: *nom. sg.* **seingnorius** 12.5 var., **seignoris** 12.5 var. [**senhor** + **-il**]

ens *see* **sen** (1).

ntir *vb. trans.* to feel: *pres. 1st sg.* **sen** 2.2; *pres. subj. 1st pl.* **sentam** 29.35; *pret. 2nd pl.* **sentis** 19.52. [CL sentīre *FEW* 11: 472; It. *sentire*, Sp. *sentir*, Fr. *sentir*; cf. E. *sentient*]

sentorer *see* **saintorier**.

senz, sénz, *see* **sen** (1).

sepelir *vb. trans.* to bury: *inf.* **sepellir** 1.7. [CL sĕpĕlīre, LL sĕpĕllīre *FEW* 11: 477; It. *seppellire*, Sp. *zambullir*, Fr. *ensevelir*]

ser *n. masc.* evening: *obl. sg.* **ser** 7.10, 7.19, 12.10. [CL sēro adv. 'late' *FEW* 11: 518; Fr. *soir*]

sera, serai, seran *see* **eser**.

serar *see* **serrar**.

serca, sercan *see* **cercar**.

serem, seretz, serez, seri', seria *see* **eser**.

sermon *n. masc.* sermon 11.23, 11.49, 13.32; insinuation 8.28: *obl. sg.* **sermon** 8.28, **sermo** 11.23, 11.49, 30.32. [CL sermōnem *FEW* 11: 516; It. *sermone*, Sp. *sermón*, Fr. *sermon*, E. *sermon*]

seror *n. fem.* sister: *vocative sg.* **sor** 9.31. [CL sŏrōrem (nom. sŏrŏr) *FEW* 12: 117; It. *suora* 'nun,' Sp. *sor* 'nun,' Fr. *soeur*; cf. E. *sorority*]

serrar *vb. trans.* to close up, to sequester: *inf.* **serrar** 5.8 var., **serar** 5.8. [CL sĕram 'bolt,' sĕrāre 'to bolt,' LL serrāre *FEW* 11: 507; It. *serrare*, Sp. *cerrar*, Fr. *serrer*; cf. E. *serried (ranks)* 'in close order']

serven *see* **sirven**.

servesa *see* **cerveza**.

servir *vb. intrans.* to serve (in court) 3.2; *trans.* to serve (God) 26.48: *inf.* **servir** 3.2, 26.48. [CL sĕrvīre *FEW* 11: 543; It. *servire*, Sp. *servir*, Fr. *servir*, E. *to serve*]

ses *prep.* without; *with noun object* 2.20, 3.7, 11.19, 13.19, 14.1, 14.44, 17.20, 21.29, 22.2, 25.96, 26.3, 28.20, 28.39, 29.10; *with pronoun object* 4.41, 18.31, 28.25; *with infinitive object* 1.2, 21.32, 26.4. *Forms:* **ses** *passim;* **senes** 3.7, 22.2. [CL sĭne *FEW* 11: 643 + **-s**; It. *senza* (influenced by CL absĕntĭa), Sp. *sin*, Fr. *sans*]

seti *n. masc.* siege: *nom. sg.* **setis** 25.101. [CL ŏbsĭdĭum 'siege,' VL *(as)sĕdĭcāre *FEW* 11: 412 + **-i**; It. *assedio*, Sp. *asedio, sitio*, Fr. *siège*, E. *siege*]

setmanas *see* **semana**.

seus *see* **son** (4).

sezer *vb. intrans.* to sit: *imperf. 3rd sg.* **sezia** 28.3, 30.38; *past subj. 3rd sg.* **segues** 26.50. [CL sēdēre *FEW* 11: 405; It. *sedere*, Sp. *ser*, Fr. *seoir*; cf. E. *sedentary*]

si (1) *conj.* if 2.22, 4.10, 4.37, 6.36, 8.12, 9.36, 10.22, 11.8, 11.9, 11.10, 11.13, 12.17, 12.24, 12.65, 13.13, 13.48, 14.48, 14.54 var., 14.56, 15.24, 16.22, 16.32, 17.19, 17.22, 17.41 var., 18.37, 19.1, 19.11, 19.13, 19.23, 19.25, 19.27, 19.27, 19.34, 19.47, 19.51, 19.52, 19.53, 19.55, 19.62, 19.65, 23.1, 23.11, 23.12, 23.16, 23.46, 24.3, 24.15, 24.26, 25.26, 26.15, 26.49, 27.4, 27.5, 27.8, 27.12, 27.41, 28.36, 28.63, 28.69, 30.18, 30.64, 30.76;

even if 12.46, 16.10, 17.41, 21.16; and 11.59; or 2.10.

Introduces clause of wishing in subjunctive 13.35.

com si as though 25.83; **si ben** although 15.25, 23.18, 30.41; **si . . . neis** even if 30.28; **si (. . .) no** if not, unless 10.13, 10.17, 12.24,

14.72, 15.9, 16.2, 16.4, 16.18, 16.21, 16.32, 18.39, 19.61, 23.45, 26.9,
27.24, 27.40, 30.61; **si sol** if only 14.36; **si tot** although 19.63, 20.26,
22.20, 27.23.

    Forms: **si** 5.8, 10.36, 18.14 var., 18.15, 26.32, 30.88; **s'** 2.22, 4.10,
4.37, 8.12, 10.22, 12.24, 12.65, 14.56, 15.24, 16.22, 18.39, 19.1, 19.34,
19.51, 19.52, 19.53, 19.62, 23.1, 23.12, 23.16, 26.15, 26.49, 27.4, 27.5,
27.41, 28.69, 30.61, 30.76; **se** 14.54 var., 15.25, 16.32; **ssi** 17.41 var.
    [CL sī *FEW* 11: 562; It. *se,* Sp. *si,* Fr. *si*]

si (2) *adv.* so; *modifies adj.* 3.10; *modifies verb* 13.66, 21.53, 25.57, 25.70;
    modifies pp. 26.10.

    Introduces verb immediately after subject 1.1, 3.1, 3.4, 4.1, 5.1, 5.5,
5.9, 5.13, 5.14; *introduces verb after remote subject* 3.5, 5.15, 5.16; *introduces verb after temporal clause* 3.10, 5.8; *introduces verb after circum-
stantial clause* 13.26; *introduces verb after complement* 18.24, 31.16;
introduces verb in subordinate clause 23.27; **e si** *introduces verb without
expressed subject (independent or coordinate)* 5.6, 5.10, 5.13, 5.13,
11.54.

    si com just as 14.69; **si** (. . .) **que** so that 2.4, 5.6, 15.6, 15.34,
15.41, 25.42, 27.47, 31.10; **si** . . . **(que)** so well *(modifying verb)* . . . that
14.33.

    Forms: **si** *passim;* **s'** 23.27, 31.16.
    [CL sīc 'thus' *FEW* 11: 577; It. *sì,* Sp. *si,* Fr. *si* 'yes']

si (3) *refl. pron.* 5.8, 10.36, 18.14 var., 18.15, 26.32, 30.88, *see* **se** (1).

sia, siais, sian, sias, siatz *see* **eser.**

sicretz *see* **secret.**

sidǫnz *n. fem.* his lady: *obl. sg.* **sidonz** 30.69, **sidons** 30.58. [modeled on
    midonz, *which see*]

siegle *see* **segle.**

siei, sieu, *see* **son** (4).

sieus *see* **son** (3), (4).

sigran *see* **segre.**

sil *see* **cel** (3).

silla 5.13 var. = **si la,** *see* **el** (1).

sillo 21.53 var. = **si lo,** *see* **lo** (2).

sincha *see* **cenchar.**

sinha *see* **senhar.**

sirvǫn *n. masc.* servant 5.2, 30.1; foot soldier 25.14, 25.47: *obl. sg.* **sirven**
    5.2, **serven** 30.1; *nom. pl.* **sirvent** 25.14; *obl. pl.* **sirvens** *used as nom. pl.*
25.47. [CL sᴇʀᴠῐᴇ̆ɴᴛᴇᴍ *FEW* 11: 534; It. *sergente,* Sp. *sargento,* Fr.
sergeant, E. *sergeant*]

sirventǫs *n. masc.* sirventes, lyric song of moral or political satire *(each
occurrence in this book refers to the song that contains it): obl. sg.*
    sirventes 20.1, 22.1, 27.1. [**sirven(t)** + **-es** *FEW* 11: 535]

sivals *adv.* at least: **sivals** 30.59, **sivaus** 16.12. [**si** (1) + CL ᴠᴇʟ 'if you wish,
or' (influenced by CL ᴠᴀʟ̄ᴇʀᴇ *FEW* 14: 216) + **-s**]

so (1) *n. masc.* song 12.0, 12.2, *see* **son** (1).

so (2) *neuter pron.* it, that, what; **so** *refers to preceding clause* 12.12, 16.48,
22.47, 26.55, 27.28 var., 30.24, *to following clause* 17.29, *to direct quotation* 9.13, 13.11, 13.25, 13.39, 13.53, 13.67, 13.84, 31.44; **so que** that
which, what 3.11, 4.14, 5.16, 6.14, 7.24, 15.47, 15.50, 16.34, 16.35,
18.51, 18.52, 19.5, 24.44, 26.34, 27.13; **ab so que** provided that 7.23;

per so for this reason 11.47, that's why 16.5; **per so que** in order to 30.55.

    Forms: **so** *passim;* **zo** 11.47, 27.28 var.; **cho** 6.14 var., 16.5 var., 16.34 var., 16.35 var., 16.48 var.

    [VL *ĕccĕ hŏc *FEW* 4: 444; It. *ciò,* Fr. *ce*]

so (3) *possessive adj.* 8.24, 9.19, 11.18, 11.23, 11.33, 11.49, 19.31, 25.60, 30.85, *see* **son** (4).

soa, soas *possessive adj., see* **son** (4).

sobeiraṇ *adj.* sovereign 27.23; superior, highly placed, on top *(erotic)* 13.49: *masc., nom. sg.* **sobeiras** 27.23; *obl. sg.* **sobiran** 13.49. [LL *supĕrānum, VL *superĭānum *FEW* 12: 435; It. *soprano,* Sp. *soberano,* Fr. *souverain,* E. *sovereign*]

sobr', sobra *see* **sobre**.

sobransier *adj.* superior: *obl. pl.* **sobrancers** *used as nom. pl.* 25.5. [LL *supĕrānum *FEW* 12: 434 + **-ansa** + **-ier**]

sobrar *vb. trans.* to conquer, to surmount: *pres. part., masc., obl. sg.* **sobran** 13.49 var. [CL sŭpĕrāre *FEW* 12: 436; Sp. *sobrar*]

sobre *prep.* on 8.15, 25.70; against 12.61; above, superior to 13.46; up to, at the discretion of 30.60; *adv.* on top 13.49 var. *Forms:* **sobre** *passim;* **sobr'** 30.60, **sobra** 13.49 var. [CL sŭper, sŭpra *FEW* 12: 433; It. *sopra,* Sp. *sobre;* cf. **sor** (2)]

sobrier *adj.* victorious 25.30, 25.94; arrogant 29.35; excessive 31.12; **a sobrier** excessively 7.4: *masc., nom. sg.* **sobrers** 25.30, 25.94; *obl. pl.* **sobriers** 29.35; *fem., obl. sg.* **sobriera** 31.12. [**sobre** + **-ier**]

socorre *vb. trans.* to help: *pres. 3rd sg.* **socor** 10.13. [CL sŭccŭrrĕre *FEW* 12: 383; It. *soccorrere,* Sp. *socorrer,* Fr. *secourir,* E. *to succor*]

socors *n. masc.* help: *obl. sg.* **socors** 23.39. [CL succŭrsum (pp. of sŭccŭrrĕre *FEW* 12: 384); It. *soccorso,* Fr. *secours,* E. *succor*]

sofers, soffrir, sofieyra *see* **sofrir**.

sofrachura *n. fem.* lack: *obl. sg.* **sofraytura** 13.82. [**sofrir** + **-atura**]

sofrir *vb. trans.* to suffer 9.59, 12.57; to bear, to endure 10.31, 19.35, 25.9; to keep from 19.17; to permit 25.80; *refl. with* **de** to keep from, to abstain from 17.2, 23.6: *pres. 2nd sg.* **sofers** 25.80, *3rd pl.* **sofron** 12.57; *pres. subj. 1st sg.* **sofieyra** 19.35; *inf.* **sofrir** 19.17, 23.6, **soffrir** 10.31, 17.2, **suffrir** 9.59, 25.9. [CL sŭffĕrre, VL *sŭffĕrīre *FEW* 12: 403; It. *soffrire,* Sp. *sufrir,* Fr. *souffrir,* E. *to suffer*]

soi (1) *vb. intrans.* 10.32, 13.14, 13.52 var., 19.8, 19.55 *pres. 1st sg. of* **eser,** *which see*.

soi (2) *possessive adj.* 11.63, *see* **son** (4).

soing *see* **sonh**.

sojorn *n. masc.* rest, repose: *obl. sg.* **sojorn** 17.8. [**sojornar** (LL *sŭbdĭŭrnāre *FEW* 12: 330; It. *soggiornare,* Fr. *séjourner,* E. *to sojourn*)]

sol (1) *n. masc.* sun: *nom. sg.* **sols** 8.17 var., **sol** *(followed by* **s'***)* 8.17. [CL sōlem *FEW* 12: 30; It. *sole,* Sp. *sol;* cf. **solelh**]

sol (2) *vb. auxiliary* 26.39, 29.22, 30.13, *see* **soler**.

sol (3) *adj.* alone 9.2, solitary 13.79 var., single 16.49; *masc., nom. sg.* **sols** 9.2, 13.79 var., 16.49. [CL sōlum *FEW* 12: 80; It. *solo,* Sp. *solo,* Fr. *seul,* E. *sole*]

sol (4) *adv.* only 14.36, 23.40; just 13.48 var.; mere 23.32; **anc sol** even 9.29; **car sol** just because 31.14. [**sol** (3)]

sǫl (5) *conj.* provided that 6.32; if only 16.45, 19.64; **sol que** if only 7.12; **ab sol que** provided that 12.35. [**sol** (3)]

solar *vb. trans.* to sole, to fit the sole to a shoe: *pp., masc., obl. sg.* **solat** 26.43 var.; *obl. pl.* **solatz** 26.43. [**sǫla** 'sole of the foot' (CL sŏlĕam, VL *sola *FEW* 12: 44) + -**ar** (2)]

solas *see* **solatz**.

solat, solatz 26.43 *see* **solar**.

solatz *n. masc.* solace 15.28, company 9.39: *nom. sg.* **solas** 9.39; *obl. sg.* **solatz** 15.28. [CL sōlācĭum *FEW* 12: 33; It. *sollazzo*, Sp. *solaz*, E. *solace*]

soldada *n. fem.* recompense, compensation: *obl. sg.* **soldada** 13.54. [**soldar** 'to pay' (**sǫlt** 'sou, penny' [CL sŏlĭdum *FEW* 12: 56] + -**ar** {2}) + -**ada**]

soldadier *n. masc.* mercenary soldier: *obl. pl.* **soldadiers** 25.21. [**soldada** + -**ier**]

soldaṇ *adj.* alone: *fem., nom. sg.* **soldayna** 13.21. [LL sōlĭtānĕum *FEW* 12: 60, VL *sōlĭtānum]

solęlh *n. masc.* sun: *obl. sg.* **soleill** 21.56. [VL *sōlĭcŭlum *FEW* 12: 30; Fr. *soleil*; cf. **sol** (1)]

solęr *vb. auxiliary* to be accustomed; **soler** *gives the meaning of the complementary inf. a durative force that may be translated* always; *the present of* **soler** *confers a durative past (imperfect) sense; the imperfect of* **soler** *confers either a durative past sense,* 11.61, 14.25, 30.85, *or a durative pluperfect sense,* 11.70: *pres. 1st sg.* **suoil** 18.19, **sueill** 10.33, *3rd sg.* **sol** 26.39, 29.22, 30.13; *imperf. 3rd sg.* **solia** 30.85, **soli'** 11.70, 14.25, *3rd pl.* **solíen** 11.61, **solient** 11.70 ms. [CL sŏlēre *FEW* 12: 45; It. *solere*, Sp. *soler*]

solers *see* **solier**.

solier *n. masc.* platform: **solers** *used as obl. sg.* 25.67. [CL sŏlārĭum 'sunlit place, terrace' *FEW* 12: 38; It. *solaio*, E. *solarium*]

sols (1) *n. masc.* 8.17, *see* **sol** (1).

sols (2) *adj.* 9.2, 13.79 var., 16.49, *see* **sol** (3).

sǫṇ (1) *n. masc.* melody, tune 1.3, 12.2, 20.25; song 12.0: *obl. sg.* **son** 20.25, **so** 12.0 *(used as nom. sg.)*, 12.2; *obl. pl.* **sons** 1.3. [CL sŏnum *FEW* 12: 103; It. *suono*, Sp. *son*, Fr. *son*, E. *sound*]

sǫṇ (2) *vb. intrans.* 11.18, 12.64, 15.1, 15.18, 16.25, 18.24, 25.5 *pres. 3rd pl. of* **eser,** *which see.*

sǫṇ (3) *possessive pron.* his, hers, its, theirs: *masc., obl. pl.* **los sieus** 27.11. [**son** (4)]

sǫṇ (4) *possessive adj., 3rd sg. and pl.* his, her, its, their.

Forms: Masc., *nom. sg.* **sos** 9.39, 14.24, 15.12, 20.5, 20.5 var. *(used as obl. sg.; see note),* 20.32, 30.48; *obl. sg.* **son** 1.5, 3.7, 5.4, 5.4, 8.22, 9.32, 9.39 ms., 10.12, 10.12 var., 10.24, 11.8, 12.20, 12.51, 13.87, 20.27, 22.19, 26.23, 30.14, 30.23, 30.24 var., 30.38, 30.44, 30.82, 30.99, 30.99, 32.1, **so** 8.24, 9.19, 11.18, 11.23, 11.33, 11.49, 19.31, 25.60, 30.85; *nom. pl.* **sei** 24.21, **siei** 10.8, **soi** 11.63; *obl. pl.* **sos** 1.5, 1.6, 5.6, 11.59, 14.57, 16.47, 18.43, 20.27, 30.54.

Fem., *nom. sg.* **sa** 19.44 var., 19.45, 21.51, 24.17, 28.34, **s'** 19.68 var.; *obl. sg.* **sa** 3.11, 5.12, 6.20, 8.22, 11.50, 11.62, 11.71, 12.4, 13.72, 13.79, 14.11, 19.4, 20.4, 20.35, 27.9, 28.7, 30.28, 30.29, 30.50, 30.54. 30.92, 31.28, **s'** 6.18, 11.48, 19.68, 30.19; *obl. pl.* **sas** 3.4, 5.6, 5.6, 18.2, 27.16,

29.43, 31.23, 32.2, 32.13, **soas** 5.6; **assa** 13.72 var., 19.59 var. = **a sa; as-sas** 29.43 var. = **a sas**.

    Possessive adj. used with def. art. followed by noun: masc., nom. sg. **lo seus** 5.4, **·l sieus** 25.36; *obl. sg.* **·l son** 10.12, **·l sieu** 2.27, 19.31 var., 29.28; *obl. pl.* **·ls sieus** 15.35, 19.31 var., 25.32; *fem., obl. sg.* **la soa** 3.3; *obl. pl.* **las soas** 5.6 var.

    [CL sŭum *FEW* 12: 482; It. *suo,* Sp. *su,* Fr. *son*]

sonar *vb. trans.* to sound, to ring 30.9; to invoke, to call upon 32.4: *fut. 1st sg.* **sonarai** 32.4; *pp., masc., obl. sg.* **sonat** 30.9. [CL sŏnāre *FEW* 12: 101; It. *sonare,* Sp. *sonar,* Fr. *sonner,* E. *to sound*]

sonęt *n. masc.* chime, ringing: *obl. pl.* **sonetz** 25.98 *used as nom. pl.* [**son** (1) + **-et**]

sǫnh, sonh *n. masc.* care: *obl. sg.* **soing** 8.25. [Frankish **sunnja,* LL sonĭum *FEW* 17: 279; Fr. *soin*]

sons *see* **son** (1).

sopleiar *vb. trans.* to supplicate, to submit to: *pres. subj. 3rd sg.* **sopplei** 24.16. [CL sŭpplĭcāre *FEW* 12: 449; It. *supplicare,* Sp. *suplicar,* Fr. *supplier,* E. *to supplicate*]

soptils *see* **sotil**.

sor (1) *n. fem.* 9.31, *see* **seror**.

sǫr (2) *prep.* on, upon: **sor** 17.6 var., **sur** 17.6 var. [CL sŭper *FEW* 12: 433; Fr. *sur;* cf. **sobre**]

sorbier *n. masc.* sorb tree, service tree *(of the apple family): nom. sg.* **sorbers** 25.67 var. [**sorba** 'sorb apple' (CL sŏrbum, VL sŏrba *FEW* 12: 107: It. *sorba,* Sp. *serba,* Fr. *sorbe,* E. *sorb*) + **-ier**]

sǫrt *n. normally fem.* (PD), *but masc.* 22.30, *of indeterminate gender in other occurrences in this book* fate 12.45, 24.21; stroke of luck 22.30; trick, stratagem 22.5: *obl. sg.* **sort** 12.45, 22.5, 22.30, 24.21. [CL sŏrtem fem. *FEW* 12: 124; It. *sorte* fem., Sp. *suerte* fem., Fr. *sort* masc.]

sos *see* **son** (4).

sospir *n. masc.* sigh: *nom. pl.* **sospir** 18.46. [**sospirar**]

sospirar *vb. intrans.* to sigh: *pres. 3rd sg.* **sospira** 25.28. [CL sŭspīrāre *FEW* 12: 475; It. *sospirare,* Sp. *suspirar,* Fr. *soupirer*]

sostenęr *vb. trans.* to sustain 1.6, 11.4, 23.34; to help 26.39; to suffer, to endure 11.24, 17.26: *pres. 3rd sg.* **soste** 11.4, 23.34; *pret. 3rd sg.* **sostenc** 11.24; *2nd cond. 3rd pl.* **sostengran** 17.26; *pp., fem., obl. sg.* **sostenguda** 1.6; *inf.* **sostener** 26.39. [**sotz** + **tener**]

sotan *adj.* low, underneath: *fem., obl. sg.* **sotana** 13.49 var. [CL sŭbtus *FEW* 12: 373 (cf. **sotz**) + **-an** (2)]

soteiran *adj.* low, underneath: *fem., obl. sg.* **soteirana** 13.49 var., **sotiraina** 13.49 var., **sotraina** 13.49, **sotrayna** 13.49 var. [CL sŭbtĕrrānĕum *FEW* 12: 364; It. *sotterraneo,* Sp. *soterraneo,* Fr. *souterrain*]

sotil *adj.* subtle: *masc., nom. sg.* **sotils** 22.3, **soptils** 22.3 var., **suptils** 22.3 var., **subtils** 22.3 var.; *obl. sg.* **soutil** 26.47; *obl. pl.* **suptils** 26.2. [CL sŭbtīlem *FEW* 12: 367; It. *sottile,* Sp. *sutil,* Fr. *subtil,* E. *subtle*]

sotiraina *see* **soteiran**.

sotlar *n. masc.* shoe: *obl. pl.* **sotlars** 13.7. [VL **sŭbtēlāre *FEW* 12: 364; Fr. *soulier*]

sotraina, sotrayna *see* **soteiran**.

sotz *prep.* under: **sotz** 9.19, 25.78, **soz** 8.24, 17.6. [CL sŭbtus *FEW* 12: 373; It. *sotto,* Fr. *sous*]

soutil *see* **sotil**.

sovẹn *adv.* often: **soven** 4.3, 27.26. [CL sŭbĭnde *FEW* 12: 334; It. *sovente,* Fr. *souvent*]

sovenir *vb. impersonal* to remember *(the agent who remembers is expressed as the indirect object): pres. 3rd sg.* **sove** 17.37, 23.3. [CL sŭbvĕnīre *FEW* 12: 378; It. *sovvenire,* Fr. *souvenir,* E. *souvenir*]

sovinẹnsa *n. fem.* memory, recollection: *nom. sg.* **sovinensa** 28.32; *obl. sg.* **sovinensa** 2.16. [**sovenir** + **-ensa**]

soy *pres. 1st sg. of* **eser,** *which see.*

soz *see* **sotz**.

ssi *see* **si** (1).

süau (1) *adj.* soft, weak: *masc., obl. pl.* **süaus** 12.50. [CL suāvem *FEW* 12: 326; It. *soave,* Fr. *suave,* E. *suave*]

süau (2) *adv.* softly, gently: **süau** 14.59. [**süau** (1)]

süavet *adv.* softly: **süavet** 30.71. [**süau** (1) + **-et**]

subtils *see* **sotil**.

sueill *see* **soler**.

sufrir *see* **sofrir**.

sui *pres. 1st sg. of* **eser,** *which see.*

suia *n. fem.* soot: *obl. sg.* **suia** 14.14. [VL *sūdĭa *FEW* 12: 397; Fr. *suie*]

sunt *pres. 3rd pl. of* **eser,** *which see.*

suoil *see* **soler**.

suptils *see* **sotil**.

sur *see* **sor** (2).

sus *adv.* up: 3.11, 13.49 var., 25.53, 31.32; *as exhortation* get up! 4.8, 4.17, 4.26, 4.35, 4.44; **de sus** on high 12.18. [CL sūrsum, sūsum *FEW* 12: 466; It. *suso,* Sp. *suso,* Fr. *sus*]

suy *pres. 1st sg. of* **eser,** *which see.*

t' (1) *personal pron.* 24.27, 24.28, 25.81, *see* **te** (1).

t' (2) *possessive adj.* 24.25, 24.26, *see* **ton**.

ta (1) *possessive adj.* 24.25 var., *see* **ton**.

ta (2) *adv.* 11.7, 11.34, 11.41, 11.49, 28.16, *see* **tan** (2).

tabọr *n. fem.* drum: *obl. pl.* **tabors** *used as nom. pl.* 25.99. [Persian *tabīr *FEW* 19: 177 + **-or;** OFr. *tabour,* E. *tabor*]

tafur *adj.* rascally: *fem., obl. sg.* **tafura** 13.86. [Armenian *thaphur* 'vagabond' *FEW* 19: 187; Sp. *tahur* 'gambler']

tahiners *see* **taïnier**.

taїṇ *n. masc.* delay: *nom. sg.* **taïs** 15.47 var. [Gothic *taheins *FEW* 17: 292]

taing *see* **tanher**.

taïnier *adj.* hesitant: *masc., nom. sg.* **tahiners** 25.18. [**taïn** + **-ier**]

tal *adj.* such 15.40 var., 25.43; such as this 12.7, 19.44 var., this 11.55; some (people) 8.29; **tal** (. . .) **com** (5) such . . . as 4.20; **tal** (. . .) **don** a . . . from which 24.29; **tal** (. . .) **c'autre** one person . . . while another 13.89; **tal** (. . .) **que** such . . . that 14.27, 14.62, 20.2, 22.4, 25.90, 29.11, **que** *implicit* 9.66, 25.55; **tal** (. . .) **que** (*rel. pron.*) some . . . who 13.40, such a one . . . who 26.54, one who 25.106, **que** *implicit* someọne . . . who 13.27; **per tal que** in order to 23.5, 26.32; **tan** . . . **per tal** so much . . . that 13.54:

Forms: *masc., nom. sg.* **tals** 12.7, 13.27, 13.40 var., 13.89, 25.43, 25.90, **tal** *before* **s-** 13.40; *obl. sg.* **tal** 9.66, 20.2, 22.4, 24.29, 25.106,

29.11; *nom. pl.* **tal** 8.29; *obl. pl.* **tals** 15.40 var., 26.55; *fem., nom. sg.* **tals** 4.20, 19.44 var., 26.54; *obl. sg.* **tal** 11.55, 14.27, 14.62; *neuter, obl. sg.* **tal** 13.54, 23.5, 26.32.

    [CL ᴛᴀ̆ʟᴇᴍ *FEW* 13, part 1: 57; It. *tale,* Sp. *tal,* Fr. *tel*]

talẹn *n. masc.* desire 10.1, 11.80, 15.5, 16.9; **a mon talen** just as I wished 9.58; **aver talen** to wish 7.21, 8.6, 19.37, 20.2: *nom. sg.* **talenz** 10.1, **talanz** 16.9; *obl. sg.* **talen** 9.58, **talan** 7.21, 8.6, 15.5, 19.37, 20.2; *nom. pl.* **talant** 11.80. [CL (from Gk.) ᴛᴀ̆ʟᴇ̆ɴᴛᴜᴍ, ᴛᴀ̆ʟᴀ̆ɴᴛᴜᴍ *FEW* 13, part 1: 38; It. *talento,* Sp. *talante,* Fr. *talent,* E. *talent*]

talọn *n. masc.* heel: *obl. sg.* **talon** 5.15 var., **talo** 9.48. [VL *ᴛᴀ̆ʟᴏ̄ɴᴇᴍ 'heel' *FEW* 13, part 1: 61; It. *tallone,* Sp. *talón,* Fr. *talon,* E. *talon* 'claw']

tals *see* **tal**.

tan (1) *adj. sg.* so much 13.20, *pl.* so many 25.77; **tan de** *with sg.* so much 17.27, 22.5; **tans de** so many 12.39, 24.36; **tan . . . que** so (much, many) . . . that 11.31, 17.10, 17.27, 22.5; **dos tans** twice as well 31.43; **tan a que** it has been so long since 28.20, 28.27: *masc., obl. sg.* **tant** 11.31, 17.10, 17.27, 22.5, 28.20, 28.27; *obl. pl.* **tans** 12.39, 31.43, **tanz** 24.36, **tant** *used as obl. pl.* 25.77; *fem., obl. sg.* **tanta** 13.20. [CL ᴛᴀ̆ɴᴛᴜᴍ *FEW* 13, part 1: 93; It. *tanto,* Sp. *tanto,* Fr. *tant;* cf. E. *tantamount*]

tan (2) *adv.* so 2.7, 8.21, 11.49, 13.21, 15.32, 19.8, 19.44, 20.3, 20.3, 20.6, 20.14, 20.16, 21.49, 21.50, 23.26, 25.19, 30.79, 31.42; such 2.11, 18.5; such a 11.32, 13.32, 14.45, 23.20;

    tan . . . com so . . . as 2.8, 30.52, as . . . as 15.45, 28.16, so much . . . as 30.80; **tan . . . que** so . . . that 11.7, 12.26, 15.12, 15.27, 16.48, 17.26, 22.17, 22.41, 25.5, 30.72, **tan . . . (que)** so . . . that 10.32, 11.34, 11.41, 22.3, 22.43; so much 11.29, 11.75, 15.50, 18.9, 21.52, **tan (. . .) que** so much (. . .) that 13.50, 14.48, 15.47, 17.17, 19.47, 21.10, 28.13, 29.3, **tan . . . per tal** so much . . . that 13.52;

    ab tan with that, then 25.17, 25.86, 30.51; **per pur tan que** if only 11.6; **tan can** as long as 11.4; **tan que** until 8.23, 30.45, as long as 32.7; **tan tro que** until 31.24.

    Forms: **tan** 2.7, 2.8, 8.21, 8.23, 11.4, 11.6, 11.29, 11.32, 12.26, 13.21, 13.32, 13.50, 13.52, 14.45, 16.48, 17.17, 17.26, 19.44, 19.47, 21.49, 21.50, 23.26, 30.45, 30.51, 30.52, 30.79, 30.80, 31.24, 31.42; **ta** 11.7, 11.34, 11.41, 11.49, 28.16; **tam** 23.20, 30.72; **tant** 2.11, 10.32, 11.75, 14.48, 15.12, 15.27, 15.32, 15.45, 15.47, 15.50, 18.5, 18.9, 19.8, 20.3, 20.3, 20.6, 20.14, 20.16, 21.10, 21.52, 22.3, 22.17, 22.41, 22.43, 25.5, 25.17, 25.19, 25.86, 28.13, 29.3, 32.7.

    [**tan** (1)]

tancar *vb. trans.* to fix; *refl.* to place oneself: *pp., masc., obl. sg.* **tancat** set, taking a stand 32.12. [VL *sᴛᴀ̆ɴᴛɪ̆ᴄᴀʀᴇ 'to bring to a halt' *FEW* 12: 235 with aphaeresis of **es-**; It. *stancare* 'to tire,' Sp. *estancar* 'to stop,' Fr. *étancher* 'to stop,' E. *to stanch*]

tanher *vb. impersonal* to be fitting, proper: *pres. 3rd sg.* **tanh** 13.26, **taing** 6.6. [CL ᴛᴀ̆ɴɢᴇ̆ʀᴇ 'to touch' *FEW* 13, part 1: 81; Sp. *tañer*]

tans *see* **tan** (1).

tant (1) *adj.* 11.31, 17.10, 17.27, 22.5, 25.77, 28.20, 28.27, *see* **tan** (1).

tant (2) *adv.* 2.11, 10.32, 11.75, 14.48, 15.12, 15.27, 15.32, 15.45, 15.47, 15.50, 18.5, 18.9, 19.8, 20.3, 20.6, 20.14, 20.16, 21.10, 21.52, 22.3, 22.17, 22.41, 22.43, 25.5, 25.17, 25.19, 25.86, 28.13, 29.3, 32.7, *see* **tan** (2).

tanta, tanz *see* tan (1).

tapi *n. masc.* (pilgrim's) cloak 15.34; a tapi in pilgrim's guise 9.2: *nom. sg.*
tapis 15.34; *obl. sg.* tapi 9.2. [Byzantine Gk. *tapition FEW* 13, part 1:
97; It. *tappeto,* Sp. *tapete,* Fr. *tapis*]

targier *n. masc.* archer or crossbowman stationed behind a rank of
shields: *obl. pl.* targiers 25.25. [targa 'shield' (Frankish **targa FEW* 17:
315) + -ier]

tarrababart 9.10 (see note).

tarzar *vb. refl.* to delay: *pres. 1st sg.* tartz 22.1. [VL **tărdĭāre FEW* 13, part
1: 116]

tavernier *n. masc.* drunkard: *obl. pl.* taverners 25.1. [CL tăbĕrnārĭum
FEW 13, part 1: 13; Sp. *tabernero,* Fr. *tavernier*]

tę (1) *personal pron.,* 2nd sg. you: *masc., nom.* tu 9.67, 25.80; *obl.* te 11.75,
18.45, t' 24.27, 24.28, 25.81. [CL tē *FEW* 13, part 1: 148; It. *te,* Sp. *te,* Fr.
te]

te (2) *vb. trans.* 12.25, 18.21, *see* tener.

té, teigna, teing, teingna *see* tener.

tęiser *vb. trans.* to weave: *pp., masc., obl. pl.* testutz 26.35. [CL tēxĕre
FEW 13, part 1: 294; It. *tessere,* Sp. *tejer,* Fr. *tisser;* cf. E. *tissue*]

temęr *vb. trans.* to fear: *pres. 1st sg.* tem 19.21, 19.23, 22.23 var.; *pres. subj.*
3rd sg. tema 24.13, temia 24.13 var.; *pres. part., masc., nom. sg.* temens
31.22 var.; *inf.* temer 16.43, 26.32, 29.33. [CL tĭmēre *FEW* 13, part 1:
331; It. *temere,* Sp. *temer;* cf. E. *timid*]

tępe *n. masc.* kettledrum: *obl. pl.* tempes *used as nom. pl.* 25.99. [CL
(from Gk.) tY̆mpănum *FEW* 13, part 2: 455; It. *timpano,* Sp. *tímpano,*
timbre, Fr. *tympan, timbre,* E. *tympanum, timbre*]

tempęsta *n. fem.* storm, commotion: *obl. sg.* tempesta 31.45. [CL
tĕmpĕstātem, VL tĕmpĕstam *FEW* 13, part 1: 178; It. *tempesta,* Sp. *tem-*
pestad, Fr. *tempête,* E. *tempest*]

tempier *n. masc.* storm: *nom. sg.* tempiers 25.41. [VL **tĕmpĕrĭum
FEW 13, part 1: 177; Sp. *tempero,* OFr. *tempier*]

tęmple *n. masc.* temple: *obl. sg.* temple 1.7, 12.56. *See also Proper Names.*
[CL tĕmplum *FEW* 13, part 1: 180; It. *tempio,* Sp. *templo,* Fr. *temple,* E.
temple]

tęmps *n. masc.* time; historical period 21.47; temps passat past 29.5; season, temps novel springtime 8.1; lonc temps for a long time 5.7, 5.12;
totz temps for all times, forever, always 7.3, 15.42, 16.12, 22.34, 23.20;
per totz temps mais forevermore 21.2: *obl. sg.* temps 5.7, 5.12, 8.1,
21.47, 29.5; *obl. pl.* temps 7.3, 15.42, 16.12, 21.2, 22.34, tems 23.20.
[CL tĕmpus *FEW* 13, part 1: 190; It. *tempo,* Sp. *tiempo,* Fr. *temps;* cf. E.
temporal]

ten, tenc *see* tener.

tęnda *n. fem.* tent: *obl. pl.* tendas 25.104. [CL **tĕndam *FEW* 13, part 1:
196; It. *tenda,* Sp. *tienda,* Fr. *tente,* E. *tent*]

tenęr *vb. trans.* to hold *lit.,* 7.10, 7.22, 28.6, 30.86, *fig.,* 7.18, 13.28; to hold
back, to keep 21.39 var.; to go with 21.38; to possess (land) 10.14, 11.48,
20.7, 20.19, to have (lodging) 31.17, to keep up (property) 21.31; to occupy (terrain) 25.102; to take (road) 4.28, 26.7, 26.7; to carry out
(penance, law) 11.14, 22.23; to deliver (sermon) 23.20;
  tener a to consider as 23.33, 24.6, 28.50; tener al latz to associate
with 14.48; tener car to hold dear 26.32 var.; tener dan a to harm, to

be held against 19.52; **tener per** to consider as 7.11, 11.37, 15.29, 21.2, 23.9, 24.1, 28.52; **tener pro** to be worthwhile 16.31, to be helpful 18.21; *refl.* **se tener** to keep oneself 22.38; **se tener ab** to persevere 17.16; **se tener de** to keep from 18.11, to cease 21.67, 29.1; **se tener per** to consider oneself 30.53.

Forms: Pres. 1st sg. **teing** 22.23, 22.38, 23.33, 24.1, **tenc** 4.28, 10.14, 15.29, 21.2, 28.50, 28.52, *3rd sg.* **ten** 20.7, **te** 12.25, 18.21, **té** 11.14, *3rd pl.* **tenon** 24.6.

Pres. subj. 3rd sg. **tenga** 19.52, 23.20, **teng'** 14.48, **teigna** 21.39 var., **teingna** 21.38, 21.67.

Imperf. 3rd sg. **tenia** 25.102, 28.6, 30.86, 31.17, *3rd pl.* **tenien** 11.37.

Fut. 1st sg. **tenrai** 7.18, 23.9, *3rd sg.* **tenra** 20.19 ms., **tenr'** 20.19.

Pret. 3rd sg. **tenc** 30.53.

Past subj. 1st sg. **tengues** 7.22.

2nd cond. 3rd sg. **tengra** 7.11.

Pp., masc., obl. sg. **tengut** 21.31.

Inf. **tener** 7.10, 11.48, 13.28, 16.31, 17.16, 18.11, 26.7, 26.7, 26.32, 29.1.

[CL TĔNĒRE *FEW* 13, part 1: 221; It. *tenere,* Sp. *tener,* Fr. *tenir*; cf. E. *tenable*]

tensa *n. fem.* dispute, insistence 21.66 var.; **ab tensa** insistently 28.29: *obl. sg.* **tensa** 21.66 var., 28.29. [**tensar** (VL *TĒNSĀRE *FEW* 13, part 1: 224)]

tercia *n. fem.* tierce, the liturgical office of the third canonical hour, about 9 a.m.: *obl. sg.* **tersa** 30.8. [ChL TĔRTĬAM (HŌRAM) 'third hour' *FEW* 13, part 1: 270; It. *terza,* Sp. *tercia,* Fr. *tierce,* E. *tierce*]

terra *n. fem.* land, real property 10.12, 20.7, 20.21, 22.42, 25.27; land, home 15.18; earth, the scene of mortal life 11.4, 25.30, 25.85; ground, surface of the earth 25.61, 25.73: *obl. sg.* **terra** 10.12, 11.4 ms., 20.7, 20.21, 22.42, 25.27, 25.30, 25.61, 25.73, 25.85, **terr'** 11.4; *nom. pl.* **terras** 15.18. [CL TĔRRAM *FEW* 13, part 1: 258; It. *terra,* Sp. *tierra,* Fr. *terre*; cf. E. *terrestrial*]

terrier *n. masc.* ground, battleground: *nom. sg.* **terriers** 25.13. [**terra** + **-ier**]

tersa *see* **tercia**.

tes *adj.* broad: *fem., obl. sg.* **tesza** 26.41. [CL TĒNSUM 'strained' *FEW* 13, part 1: 227; E. *tense*]

testa *n. fem.* head: *obl. sg.* **testa** 3.11, 30.16, 31.35. [CL TĔSTAM 'earthenware jar,' LL 'skull, head' *FEW* 13, part 1: 281; It. *testa,* Sp. *testa* 'forehead,' Fr. *tête* 'head']

testutz *see* **teiser**.

tesza *see* **tes**.

teu (1) *possessive pron., tonic, 2nd sg.* your; **los teus mezeiches** your own men: *masc., obl. pl.* **teus** 25.84. [**teu** (2)]

teu (2) *possessive adj., tonic, 2nd sg.* your; *in noun phrase with def. art.* 12.69: *masc., obl. sg.* **tieu** 12.69. [CL TŬUM *FEW* 13, part 2: 452; It. *tuo,* Sp. *tuyo,* Fr. *tien*]

tinha *n. fem.* moth: *obl. sg.* **tigna** 14.19 var. [CL TĬNĔAM *FEW* 13, part 1: 343; It. *tigna,* Sp. *tiña,* Fr. *teigne*]

tirar *vb. trans.* to draw 2.1; to yank 9.50; to shoot (a weapon) 25.56, 25.68: *pres. 1st sg.* **tir** 2.1, *3rd sg.* **tira** 9.50; *imperf. 3rd pl.* **tiravan** 25.68; *pret.*

3rd sg. **tirec** 25.56. [LL (mar)tyr(i)um *FEW* 6, part 1: 419 + **-ar** (2); It.
tirare, Sp. *tirar*, Fr. *tirer*]

tizo *see* **tuzon**.

tocar *vb. trans.* to touch, to caress: *pres. 2nd pl.* **tocatz** 14.36; *pres. subj.*
2nd pl. **toquetz** 31.21; *pres. part., masc., undeclined* **tocan** 31.23. [Ono-
matopoetic *tokk- FEW* 13, part 2: 14, VL *tŏccāre B-W; It. *toccare*, Sp.
tocar, Fr. *toucher*, E. *to touch*]

tolre *vb. trans.* to take; to take away 17.48, 18.13, 18.13, 18.15, 20.29; **tolre**
per molher to take as wife 5.13; *refl.* to deprive oneself of 19.68, to
cease 18.59 *var.: pres. 1st sg.* **tuoill** 18.59 var., *3rd sg.* **tol** 20.29; *pres.*
subj. 2nd pl. **tolatz** 19.68; *pret. 3rd sg.* **tolc** 5.13 var., 18.15, **tols** 5.13;
pp., masc., obl. sg. **tolt** 18.13, *undeclined* **tout** 17.48; *fem., undeclined*
tolt 18.13. [CL tŏllĕre *FEW* 13, part 2: 20; It. *togliere*, Sp. *toller*, OFr.
toldre]

ton *possessive adj., atonic, 2nd sg.* your: *masc., nom. sg.* **tos** 24.25, 25.81;
obl. sg. **ton** 29.47; *obl. pl.* **tos** 24.26; *fem., nom. sg.* **ta** 24.25 var., **t'** 24.25;
obl. sg. **t'** 24.26. [CL tŭum *FEW* 13, part 2: 452; It. *tuo*, Sp. *tu*, Fr. *ton*]

tondre *vb. trans.* to mow 19.28; to shave 31.27, 31.41, 31.42: *pres. subj. 3rd*
sg. **tonda** 19.28; *pret. 3rd sg.* **tondet** 31.27; *pp., masc., obl. sg.* **tondut**
31.41; *inf.* **tondre** 31.42. [CL tŏndēre *FEW* 13, part 2: 27, LL tŏndĕre L
& S; Sp. *tundir*, Fr. *tondre*]

toquetz *see* **tocar**.

tor *n. fem.* tower: *obl. sg.* **tor** 20.13. *See also Proper Names.* [CL tŭrrem
FEW 13, part 2: 436; It. *torre*, Sp. *torre*, Fr. *tour*, E. *tower*]

tormen *n. masc.* torture 9.60, 11.19; torture (in Hell) 23.47: *obl. sg.* **tor-**
ment 11.19, **turmen** 9.60, 23.47. [CL tŏrmĕntum *FEW* 13, part 2: 46; It.
tormento, Sp. *tormento*, Fr. *tourment*, E. *torment*]

tormentar *vb. trans.* to torment 27.7, to torture 27.8: *pret. 1st sg.* **tor-**
mentei 27.7; *pres. part., substantivized, masc., obl. pl.* **tormentans** tor-
menters, devils 27.8. [**tormen(t)** + **-ar** (2)]

tormentier *adj.* threatening: *masc., obl. pl.* **turmenters** 25.9. [**tormen(t)**
+ **-ier**]

torn *n. masc.* small windlass mounted on a crossbow: *obl. sg.* **torn** 25.56.
[**tornar**]

tornar *vb. intrans.* to return 17.11, 27.38; *trans.* to turn, **tornar atras** to
turn back 12.44, **tornar en jos** to overturn 10.19: *pres. 1st sg.* **torn**
17.11; *pres. subj. 1st pl.* **tornem** 12.44; *past subj. 1st sg.* **tornes** 27.38;
pp., masc., obl. sg. **tornat** 10.19. [CL tŏrnāre *FEW* 13, part 2: 76; It.
tornare, Sp. *tornar*, Fr. *tourner*, E. *to turn*]

tornei (1) *n. masc.* tournament 30.77; combat 22.39, 24.24: *obl. sg.* **tornei**
22.39, 24.24, 30.77. [**torneiar**]

tornei (2) *vb. intrans.* 20.31, *see* **torneiar**.

torneiador *n. masc.* participant in a tourney: *nom. sg.* **torneiaire** 21.46.
[**torneiar** + **-ador**]

torneiar *vb. intrans.* to participate in a tournament: *pres. subj. 3rd sg.*
tornei 20.31; *fut. 3rd pl.* **torneiaran** 21.72. [**torn** 'turn' (**tornar**) +
-eiar]

tornem, tornes *see* **tornar**.

tort (1) *n. masc.* wrong; injustice 12.35, 21.32, 22.45, 22.50, 24.5; sin
27.39, 27.42; **aver tort** to be wrong 30.18; **faire tort a** to wrong 10.22,
22.29: *nom. sg.* **tortz** 27.42; *obl. sg.* **tort** 10.22, 12.35, 21.32, 22.29,

22.45, 22.50, 24.5, 30.18; *obl. pl.* **tortz** 27.39. [**tort** (2); It. *torto*, Sp. *tuerto*, Fr. *tort*, E. *tort* 'injury']

tǫrt (2) *adj.* wrong, unjust 24.32; twisted 14.26: *masc., obl. sg.* **tort** 24.32; *obl. pl.* **tortz** 24.32 var.; *fem., nom. sg.* **torta** 14.26. [CL тŏʀтuм 'bent, crooked,' pp. of тŏʀquēʀe 'to twist' *FEW* 13, part 2: 98; see **tort** (1)]

tortz (1) *n. masc.* 27.39, 27.42, *see* **tort** (1).

tortz (2) *adj.* 24.32 var., *see* **tort** (2).

tos *see* **ton**.

toscar *vb. trans.* to polish: *pres. 3rd sg.* **tosca** 14.57. [VL тŭscuм ***'rude, rough' *FEW* 13: 439 (CL Tŭscuм 'Etruscan,' Sp. *tosco*) + -**ar** (2)]

tosir *vb. intrans.* to cough: *inf.* **tossir** 26.4. [CL тŭssīʀe *FEW* 13, part 2: 443; It. *tossire*, Sp. *toser*, Fr. *tousser*]

tǫst *adv.* soon 4.40, 29.38; quickly 9.34, 20.13 var.: **tost** 4.40, 9.34, 20.13 var., 29.38. [CL тŏsтuм 'burned,' VL ***'warmly, quickly' *FEW* 13, part 2: 121; It. *tosto*, Fr. *tôt*; cf. E. *toast*]

tostẹmps *adv.* always: **tostemps** 19.35. [**totz** + **temps**]

tǫt (1) *adj.* all 9.40, 9.53, 10.28, 10.35, 10.37, 10.38, 11.76, 11.79, 11.80, 13.52 var., 14.72, 15.21, 17.6, 17.13, 18.14, 18.23, 21.28, 21.38, 21.44, 21.58, 21.79, 22.45, 23.7, 25.33, 25.38, 25.92, 25.109, 26.40, 27.7, 27.27, 29.8, 30.11, 30.60, 31.39; whole 11.36, 11.37, 25.91, 27.9, 29.24, 31.7, 31.27; any 22.2; every 13.46, 13.71, 20.30, 22.17, 23.33, 27.20, 29.4, 30.68, 30.81; *masc., nom. pl.* everyone 22.44, 23.18, 27.30;

    tot (. . .) **cant** whatever 2.3, 2.26, 10.33, 12.28, 12.29, 15.36, 29.22; **tot jorn** all day, always 14.50, 31.10; **tot so** everything 7.24; **totz temps** forever 7.3, 15.42, always 16.12, 22.34, 23.20; **tut li pluzor** many men, everyone 10.15, 12.22; **al pus del tot** as much as possible 29.23; **de tót no** not at all 11.31; **del tot** completely 29.38; **per totz temps mais** forever 21.2.

    Forms: Masc., nom. sg. **totz** 9.2, 9.40, 15.51, 21.44, 30.14, 30.68; *obl. sg.* **tot** 14.50, 18.14, 22.45, 30.81, 31.7, 31.10, **tót** 11.37; *nom. pl.* **tut** 10.15, 10.28, 10.38, 21.28, 21.58, **tuit** 11.76, 11.80, 21.79, 25.33, **tuich** 17.13, 22.44, **tuig** 23.18, **tug** 12.22, 14.72, 27.30, 31.39; *obl. pl.* **totz** 7.3, 15.42, 20.30, 21.2, 21.37, 22.2, 22.34, 23.20, 25.38, 25.92, 25.109, 27.7, 29.8, **toz** 10.37, 16.12.

    Fem., nom. sg. **tota** 13.71, 27.20, 30.11; *obl. sg.* **tota** 11.36, 11.79, 17.6, 23.7, 25.91, 27.9, 27.27, **tot'** 13.46, 23.33, **tuta** 13.52 var.; *obl. pl.* **totas** 18.23, 22.17, 26.40, 29.4.

    Neuter, nom. sg. **tot** 2.3, 15.21, 21.38, 29.22; *obl. sg.* **tot** 2.26, 7.24, 9.53, 10.33, 10.35, 11.31, 12.28, 12.29, 15.36, 29.23, 29.38, 30.60.

    [CL тōтuм, LL тōттuм by affective duplication *FEW* 13, part 2: 128; It. *tutto*, Sp. *todo*, Fr. *tout*]

tǫt (2) *adv.* all 19.9, 32.4; quite 9.15, 11.50, 19.59, 25.69; completely 11.17, 15.47 var.; just 27.29; **tot** *adv., declined like the adj. it modifies* **totz derrers** last of all 30.14, **totz los meillors** the best of all 21.37, **totz . . . mauditz** utterly cursed 15.51, **totz sols** all alone 9.2; **per tot** everywhere 21.55; **si tot** although 19.63, 20.26, 22.20, 27.23. [**tot** (1)]

tout *see* **tolre**.

toz *see* **tot** (1).

tǫza *n. fem.* girl, young woman: *nom. sg.* **toza** 13.18; *obl. sg.* **toza** 13.60, 31.14; *vocative sg.* **toza** 13.9, 13.15, 13.29, 13.43, 13.57, 13.71, 28.13,

28.19, 28.23, 28.25, 28.31, 28.35, 28.37, 28.43, 28.49, 28.55, 28.59, 28.62, 28.67, 28.71, toz' 28.47; *nom. pl.* **tozas** 25.68. [**tǫs** 'young man' (CL tōnsum 'shaved' *FEW* 13, part 2: 32) + **-a**]

tozęta *n. fem.* young girl: *vocative sg.* **tozeta** 13.74. [**toza** + **-eta**]

tozoirętas *n. fem., pl.* pair of scissors: *obl. pl.* **tozoyretas** 31.26. [**tozoiras** (CL tǒnsōrǐum 'of a barber,' LL *tonsoria 'scissors' *FEW* 13, part 2: 31) + **-eta**]

traazo *see* **traïcion.**

trachar *vb. trans.* to apply oneself to, to negotiate, to scheme 22.28; *refl.* to become worried 5.8: *pres. subj. 1st sg.* **tracte** 22.28; *pret. 3rd sg.* **trachet** 5.8 var. [CL trăctāre *FEW* 13, part 2: 143; It. *trattare,* Sp. *trechar,* Fr. *traiter,* E. *to treat*]

tradar *vb. trans.* to betray 11.8, to surrender 11.66: *pres. 3rd sg.* **trada** 11.8; *inf.* **tradár** 11.66. [CL trādĕre *FEW* 13, part 2: 151 (It. *tradire,* Fr. *trahir,* E. *to betray*) + **-ar** (2) by change of conjugation; cf. **traïr**]

trafęi *n. masc.* intrigue: *obl. sg.* **trafei** 24.31. [*trafegar by dissimilation from VL *transfrǐcāre 'to rub repeatedly,' Corominas and Pascual 4: 609]

trag, traga *see* **traire.**

trahida *see* **traïr.**

traïciǫn *n. fem.* treachery: *obl. sg.* **traazo** 11.57. [CL trădǐtiōnem *FEW* 13, part 2: 151; Sp. *traición,* Fr. *trahison,* E. *treason*]

traidoręsa *n. fem.* traitress: *obl. sg.* **traydoressa** 31.44. [**traïdor** (**traïr** + **-idor**) + **-esa**]

traïr *vb. trans.* to betray: *pp., masc., nom. sg.* **trays** 15.47 var.; *fem., nom. sg.* **trahida** 7.5. [CL trădĕre *FEW* 13, part 2: 151 + **-ir**; cf. **tradar**]

traire *vb. trans.* to pull 25.67; to take 5.13; to take out 3.7; to lure, to lead on 19.34; *refl.* to go 8.10, 19.23; **mal traire** to suffer 2.15: *pres. subj. 1st sg.* **traga** 19.23; *pret. 3rd sg.* **trais** 3.7, 5.13; *pp., masc., obl. sg.* **trag** 19.34; *fem., nom. sg.* **traita** 25.67; *inf.* **traire** 2.15, 8.10. [CL trăhĕre *FEW* 13, part 2: viii; It. *trarre,* Sp. *traer,* Fr. *traire* 'to milk'; cf. E. *tractor*]

tramętre *vb. trans.* to send: *pres. 3rd sg.* **tramét** 11.54; *imperf. 3rd sg.* **trametía** 11.65. [CL trămǐttĕre *FEW* 13, part 2: 211; It. *tramettere;* cf. E. *to transmit*]

trap *n. masc.* pavilion: *obl. pl.* **traps** 25.104. [Frankish *trabo 'fringe' *FEW* 17: 640; OFr. *tref* 'tent,' It. *trevo* 'sail,' Sp. *treo* 'sail']

traspasar *vb. intrans.* to pass; to die 27.16; *pres. part., fem., obl. pl.* **tres-passans** 27.16. [**tras-** + **pasar**]

traspasatge *n. masc.* passing acquaintance: *obl. sg.* **trespassatje** 13.59. [**tras-** + **pasatge** (**pasar** + **-atge**)]

traspasemęn *n. masc.* death: *obl. sg.* **trespassemen** 27.35. [**tras-** + **pasamen** 'passage, death' (**pasar** + **-amen** [1])]

trastǫt *adj.* all *(intensive):* *masc., nom. pl.* **trastút** 11.25; *obl. pl.* **trastotz** 25.101, 27.29. [**tras-** + **tot** (1)]

traydoressa *see* **traidoresa.**

trays *see* **traïr.**

trebalh *n. masc.* ordeal: *nom. sg.* **trebalhs** 25.4. [**trebalhar** (VL *trǐpăliāre *FEW* 13, part 2: 291; Sp. *trabajar,* Fr. *travailler*)]

trefaṇ *adj.* faithless, deceptive: *fem., obl. sg.* **trefayna** 13.87. [Hebrew ṭerēfā *FEW* 20: 28 (Sp. *trefe*) + **-an** (2)]

trega *n. fem.* truce: *obl. sg.* **tregua** 14.53, **treva** 19.48; *obl. pl.* **tregas** 22.12.
[Frankish **treuwa FEW* 17: 361; It. *tregua,* Sp. *tregua,* Fr. *trève,* E. *truce*]

trei *see* **tres.**

tremblar *vb. intrans.* to tremble: *pres. 3rd sg.* **trembla** 25.28 ms., 25.42,
trembl' 25.28; *pres. part., fem., undeclined* **tremblan** 8.15 var. [VL
*TRĔMŬLĀRE FEW 13, part 2: 244; It. *tremolare,* Sp. *temblar,* Fr. *trembler,*
E. *to tremble*]

tremer *vb. intrans.* to tremble: *pres. part., fem., undeclined* **treman** 8.15
var. [CL TRĔMĔRE *FEW* 13, part 2: 240; cf. E. *tremor*]

tres *num.* three: *masc., nom. pl.* **trei** 22.31; *obl. pl.* **tres** 9.30, 17.22; *fem.,*
obl. pl. **tres** 28.10, 28.44. [CL TRĒS *FEW* 13, part 2: 249; It. *tre,* Sp. *tres,*
Fr. *trois*]

treslitz *adj.* made of coarse canvas cloth; *fem., obl. sg.* **treslissa** 13.6. [CL
TRĪLĪCEM, VL **TRĪLĪCĬUM FEW* 13, part 2: 274; It. *traliccio,* Sp. *terliz,* Fr.
treillis, E. *trellis*]

tresp- *see* **trasp-.**

treu *n. masc.* strife: *obl. sg.* **trieu** 26.26. [*masc. of* **trega, treva** *FEW* 17:
361]

treva *see* **trega.**

triar *vb. trans.* to separate: *pret. 3rd sg.* **triet** 14.32. [LL TRĪTĀRE *FEW* 13,
part 2: 307; It. *tritare,* Fr. *trier;* cf. E. *triage*]

tric *adj.* deceptive: *masc., obl. sg.* **tric** 23.4 var. [**trichar**]

trichairitz *n. fem.* deceiving woman: *nom. pl.* **trichariz** 17.47. [**trichar** +
-airitz]

trichar *vb. intrans.* to deceive: *pres. 3rd sg.* **tricha** 14.19 var. [VL **TRĪCCĀRE
FEW* 13, part 2: 261; Fr. *tricher,* E. *to trick*]

trichariz *see* **trichairitz.**

triet *see* **triar.**

trieu *see* **treu.**

trist *adj.* sad: *masc., nom. sg.* **tristz** 5.14, **trist** 25.28. [CL TRĪSTEM *FEW* 13,
part 2: 303; It. *triste,* Sp. *triste,* Fr. *triste*]

tristeza *n. fem.* sadness: *nom. sg.* **tristeza** 18.57 var., **tristesa** 18.57 var.
[CL TRĪSTĬTĬAM; It. *tristezza,* Sp. *tristeza,* Fr. *tristesse*]

tro (1) *prep.* until 8.17, 28.66, as far as 21.56, 21.66, 25.16; **tro a** as far as
9.48, 21.56 var., **troc a** 21.56 var.; **tro en** until 28.21; **tro que** as far as
2.9. [CL (ĬN)TER HŎC *FEW* 4.749]

tro (2) *conj.* until 28.11; **tro que** until 1.6, 5.14, 8.11, 14.42; **tan tro que**
until 31.24. [**tro** (1)]

trob, troba, trobada *see* **trobar.**

trobador *n. masc.* troubadour, Occitan lyric poet of the 12th and 13th
centuries: *obl. sg.* **trobador** *used as nom. sg.* 12.0. [**trobar** + **-ador**]

trobar *vb. trans.* to find 3.7, 6.32, 9.3, 9.14, 10.28, 12.27, 12.53, 13.2, 17.42,
23.1, 23.4, 28.1, 28.2, 28.68; to compose poetry 5.3.
> *Forms: Pres. 1st sg.* **trop** 23.4, **trob** 6.32, **truep** 28.68; *3rd sg.* **troba**
> 3.7; *3rd pl.* **troban** 10.28.
> *Pres. subj. 3rd sg.* **truep** 12.27.
> *Imperf. 1st sg.* **trobava** 17.42 var.
> *Fut. 3rd pl.* **trobaran** 12.53.
> *1st cond. 1st sg.* **trobaria** 17.42 var.

Pret. 1st sg. **trobei** 28.1, **trobey** 9.3, 13.2.

Past subj. 1st sg. **trobes** 23.1.

2nd cond. 1st sg. **trobera** 17.42.

Pp., masc., obl. sg. **trobat** 9.14; *fem., obl. sg.* **trobada** 28.2.

Inf. **trobar** 5.3; *substantivized, masc., obl. sg.* **trobar** composition of poetry 29.19, manner of composition 5.4.

[Gk. *trópos* 'figurative usage of a word' + **-ar** (2), ChL *ᴛʀŏᴘāʀᴇ 'to compose a liturgical trope' *FEW* 13, part 2: 321; for a hypothetical Arabic etymon (*trob* 'song' + **-ar** [2]), see Menocal 137–48; It. *trovare,* Sp. *trovar,* Fr. *trouver,* E. *(treasure) trove*]

troc *see* **tro** (1).

trompa *n. fem.* trumpet: *nom. pl.* **trompas** 25.97, **trumpas** 25.39. [Frankish *trŭmba FEW* 17: 380; It. *tromba,* Sp. *trompa,* Fr. *trompa,* E. *trump*]

tron *n. masc.* throne; Heaven 10.23: *obl. sg.* **tron** 10.23. [CL (from Gk.) ᴛʜʀŏɴᴜᴍ *FEW* 13, part 1: 316; It. *trono,* Sp. *trono,* Fr. *trône,* E. *throne*]

troneire *n. masc.* thunder: *nom. sg.* **troneire** 25.41. [CL ᴛŏɴīᴛʀᴜᴍ, VL *ᴛʀŏɴīᴛᴜᴍ *FEW* 13, part 2: 28; Sp. *tronido,* Fr. *tonnerre*]

trop (1) *vb. trans.* 23.4, *see* **trobar.**

trop (2) *adj.* many: *masc., obl. pl.* **trops** 14.44. [**trop** (3)]

trop (3) *adv.* too, more than enough 18.56, 19.33, 25.18, 26.36; too long 30.66; too much 31.34; too often 28.35; very 9.65, 11.30, 15.18, 31.3, 31.12, 31.22; **trop . . . als deriers** too late 29.16; **trop de** too much 28.46; **trop melhs** very well, deservedly 31.5. [Frankish *thorp* 'village,' later 'herd,' hence adv. 'much, very' *FEW* 17: 399; It. *troppo,* Fr. *trop*]

tropelada *n. fem.* a dance: *obl. sg.* **tropellada** 13.48 var. [**trepar** 'to leap' (Germ. *tʀĭᴘᴘōɴ *FEW* 17: 365; Sp. *trepar* 'to crawl,' E. *to trip*) + **-elada**]

trops *see* **trop** (2).

truan *adj.* wretched, treacherous: *masc., obl. sg.* **truan** 21.40; *fem., nom. sg.* **truanda** 19.3. [Ctc. *tʀūɢᴀɴᴛ- 'beggar' *FEW* 13, part 2: 332; Sp. *truhán,* Fr. *truand,* E. *truant*]

truandar *vb. intrans.* to act treacherously: *pres. 3rd sg.* **truanda** 20.15. [**truan(t)** + **-ar** (2)]

truep *see* **trobar.**

trufa *n. fem.* trifle: *obl. sg.* **truffa** 31.0. [CL ᴛūʙᴇʀ 'excrescence; truffle' *FEW* 13, part 2: 385; Sp. *trufa,* Fr. *truffe,* E. *truffle, trifle*]

trumpas *see* **trompa.**

tu *see* **te** (1).

tug, tuich, tuig, tuit *see* **tot** (1).

tuoill *see* **tolre.**

turc *adj.* Turkish: *fem., nom. sg.* **turqua** 26.54 var. [Persian *Türk FEW* 19: 193; It. *turco,* Sp. *turco,* Fr. *turc,* E. *Turk*]

turga *adj. fem.* sterile: *nom. sg.* **turgua** 26.54. [LL *ᴛᴀᴜʀĭᴄᴀᴍ 'sterile cow' *FEW* 13, part 1: 133]

turmen *see* **tormen.**

turmenters *see* **tormentier.**

turqua *see* **turc.**

tut, tuta *see* **tot** (1).

tuzon *n. masc.* coal, ember: *obl. sg.* **tuzo** 12.47, **tizo** 12.47 var. [CL ᴛīᴛĭŏɴᴇᴍ *FEW* 13, part 1: 359; It. *tizzone,* Sp. *tizón,* Fr. *tison*]

u *see* **un.**

ubres *see* **obrir.**

ueit *see* **och.**

uelh, uels *see* **olh.**

ueymay *see* **oimais.**

ufana *n. fem.* show, outward appearance: *obl. sg.* **ufayna** 13.28. [Ono-matopoetic *ŭf- FEW* 14: 4 + **-ana;** It. *ufo,* Sp. *ufo*]

uffrenda *see* **ofrenda.**

ultra *see* **oltra.**

uman̦ *adj.* human, not divine 32.17; humane, kind 13.35: *fem., nom. sg.* **humayna** 13.35; *obl. sg.* **umana** 32.17. [CL ʜūᴍāɴᴜᴍ *FEW* 4: 509; It. *umano,* Sp. *humano,* Fr. *humain,* E. *human*]

umil *adj.* humble: *masc., nom. sg.* **humils** 23.2 ms., 30.74; *obl. sg.* **umil** 21.8, **humil** 23.2. [CL ʜŭᴍīʟᴇᴍ *FEW* 4: 512; It. *umile,* Sp. *humilde,* Fr. *humble,* E. *humble*]

un̦ *indef. art.* a, an 1.4, 3.1, 3.3, 3.7, 4.1, 5.2, 6.19, 7.2, 7.20, 8.21, 8.28, 10.2, 11.38, 11.52, 12.6, 13.1, 13.35, 13.45, 13.68, 15.4, 17.37, 18.44, 20.1, 21.74, 21.75, 22.32, 24.38, 25.17, 25.52, 25.55, 25.66, 25.66, 25.76, 25.83, 25.89, 26.42, 27.1, 27.37, 28.6, 30.77, 31.2, 31.3, 31.14, 31.16, 31.20, 31.26, 32.7, 32.10, 32.12, 32.13; *numerical adj.* one 2.6, 8.19, 11.38, 13.48 var., 15.31, 16.49, 27.44, 30.59; **un dia** one day 3.7, **una dia** 3.7 var.; **un jorn** 31.11, 31.15; **un ser** one evening 7.10, 7.19; **una vegada** just once 13.48, the same 26.51; *pron.* un 6.25, 11.8, 12.26, 12.40, 14.65, 18.21, *with def. art.* **l'un** one man 11.10, 13.63, 19.11, 27.22, **la una** one of them 9.19; **un quec** each man 24.30; **un . . . autre** one . . . another 11.10, 13.63, 19.11; **una . . . non** not one 18.21.

Forms: *masc., nom. sg.* **uns** 3.1, 16.49, 27.22, **us** 4.1, 11.8, 11.10, 12.40, 13.63, 19.11, 24.30, 25.17, 25.52, 25.55, 25.66, 25.89, **un** *before* **s-** 16.49 var.; *obl. sg.* **un** 1.4, 2.6, 3.7, 3.7, 5.2, 6.19, 6.25, 7.2, 7.10, 7.19, 7.20, 8.19, 8.21, 8.28, 10.2, 12.6, 12.26, 13.35, 13.68, 15.31, 18.44, 20.1, 21.74, 22.32, 24.38, 26.42, 27.1, 27.44, 28.6, 30.77, 31.2, 31.11, 31.15, 31.16, 31.20, 32.10, 32.12, 32.13, **u** 11.38 var., 11.52, 30.59; *obl. pl.* **us** 12.26 ms.;

fem., nom. sg. **una** 9.19, 18.21; *obl. sg.* **una** 3.3, 3.7 var., 11.38, 13.1, 13.45, 13.48, 13.48 var., 14.65, 17.37, 25.66, 25.76, 25.83, 27.37, 31.3, 32.7, **un'** 15.4, 21.75, 26.51, 31.14; *obl. pl.* **unas** 31.26.

[CL ūɴᴜᴍ *FEW* 14: 56; It. *uno,* Sp. *uno,* Fr. *un*]

unitat *n. fem.* unity, an attribute of God: *obl. sg.* **unitat** 29.41. [CL ūɴĭᴛāᴛᴇᴍ *FEW* 14: 49; It. *unità,* Sp. *unidad,* Fr. *unité,* E. *unity*]

uns *see* **un.**

·us (1) *personal pron.* 4.37, 6.36, 7.18, 7.20, 7.22, 13.10, 13.31, 13.47, 13.65, 13.65, 14.35, 14.53, 14.53, 14.54, 17.17, 19.1, 19.2, 19.15, 19.19, 19.26, 19.27, 19.36, 19.37, 19.38, 19.41, 19.43, 19.46, 19.61, 19.63, 19.64, 19.68, 21.58, 21.73, 22.6, 22.30, 22.47, 23.1, 23.3, 23.4, 23.7, 23.9, 23.10, 23.12, 23.12, 23.28, 23.41, 23.44, 23.44, 23.44, 23.44, 25.2, 26.53, 27.8, 27.45, 28.17, 28.20, 28.22, 28.31, 28.32, 28.44, 28.49, 28.51, 28.59, 28.67, 28.72, *see* **vos** (2).

us (2) *indef. art.* 4.1, 11.8, 11.10, 12.26, 12.40, 13.63, 16.49 var., 19.11, 25.17, 25.52, 25.55, 25.66, 25.89, *see* **un.**

usatje *see* **uzatge.**

uzansa *n. fem.* custom: *obl. sg.* **uzansa** 28.60. [**uzar** 'to use' (LL ŪSĀRE *FEW* 14: 72) + **-ansa**]

uzatge *n. masc.* custom 14.49; patience 13.58: *obl. sg.* **uzatje** 13.58, **usatje** 14.49. [LL ŪSĀGĬUM *FEW* 14: 85; Sp. *usaje,* Fr. *usage,* E. *usage*]

va, vai *see* **anar.**

vailla, vaillatz *see* **valer.**

vair *n. masc.* vair, fur of a gray-and-white squirrel, used to trim and line clothing: *obl. sg.* **vair** 10.42. [CL VĂRĬUM 'variegated' *FEW* 14: 186; It. *vaio,* Fr. *vair*]

vaire *adj.* fickle, inconstant: *masc., obl. sg.* **vaire** 21.29. [**vair** with support vowel]

val *see* **valer.**

valat *n. masc.* ditch: *obl. pl.* **valats** 32.5. [**val** 'valley' (CL VALLEM *FEW* 14: 137) + **-at**]

valen (1) *n. masc.* value: *obl. sg.* **valen** 24.38. [**valen** (2)]

valen (2) *adj.* noble, worthy: *masc., obl. sg.* **valen** 6.19, 23.9; *nom. pl.* **valen** 6.23, 6.34. [*pres. part.* of **valer**]

valensa *n. fem.* worth 6.20, 6.33; aid 28.15: *nom. sg.* **valensa** 28.15; *obl. sg.* **valenssa** 6.20, 6.33. [**valer** + **-ensa**]

valer *vb. trans.* to be worth 6.9, 12.71 var., 17.18, 24.25; to be the equal of 19.60; to help 18.33, 19.63, 23.11, 27.35; to be good 16.1: *pres. 3rd sg.* **val** 6.9, 19.60, 24.25; *pres. subj. 3rd sg.* **valha** 12.71 var., **vailla** 17.18, *2nd pl.* **vaillatz** 27.35; *fut. 1st sg.* **valray** 19.63; *1st cond. 3rd sg.* **valria** 23.11; *inf.* **valer** 16.1, 18.33. [CL VĂLĒRE *FEW* 14: 134; It. *valere,* Sp. *valer,* Fr. *valoir;* cf. E. *valiant*]

valor *n. fem.* merit; valor 9.41 var.; **aver valor aprob** to be esteemed by 11.34: *obl. sg.* **valor** 5.6, 5.10, 11.34, 12.67, 17.34, 17.45, 17.48; *obl. pl.* **valors** 9.41 var. [LL VĂLŌREM *FEW* 14: 153; It. *valore,* Sp. *valor,* Fr. *valeur,* E. *valor*]

valray, valria *see* **valer.**

van *see* **anar.**

vas (1) *n. masc.* sepulcher, tomb: *obl. sg.* **vas** 12.72. [CL VĂSUM 'container' (for foods, etc.) *FEW* 14: 189; It. *vaso,* Sp. *vaso,* Fr. *vase,* E. *vase*]

vas (2) *prep.* toward 2.1, 6.31, 11.10, 12.36, 13.8, 19.23, 23.4, 23.14, 23.16, 25.17, 25.91, 27.11, 30.56; regarding, in a matter of 14.5; with, in the eyes of 18.22; **en vas** toward 12.8; *with* **part** in *(direction)* 14.17, 15.11. *Forms:* **vas** 2.1, 6.31, 12.8, 14.17, 15.11, 18.22, 19.23, 25.17, **vaus** 30.56, **ves** 12.36, 13.8, 14.5, 23.4, 23.14, 23.16, 25.91, 27.11; **vel = ves lo** 11.10 (see note). [CL VĔRSUS *FEW* 14: 314; It. *verso,* Fr. *vers;* cf. E. *versus*]

vau, vauc *see* **anar.**

vaus *see* **vas.**

vay *see* **anar.**

ve (1) *vb. intrans.* 4.5, 15.36, 18.5, 30.22, *see* **venir.**

ve (2) *vb. trans.* 18.29, 30.21, *see* **vezer.**

ve (3) *interj.* 22.6, *see* **vec.**

vec *interj.* behold: **vec** 22.6 var., **ve** 22.6. [**vezer** + **ec** 'behold']

vedar *vb. trans.* to deny: *imper. 2nd pl.* **vedetz** 19.2; *inf.* vedar 27.17. [CL VĔTĀRE *FEW* 14: 358; It. *vietare,* Sp. *vedar;* cf. E. *veto*]

vegada *n. fem.* time, occasion; **una vegada** *adv.* once; *obl. sg.* **vegada** 13.48. [VL *VĬCĀTAM *FEW* 14: 409; Sp. *vegada*]

vei, veia *see* **vezer.**

veigna *see* **venir.**

veirai, veiran, veirei, vejatz *see* **vezer.**

vel *see* **vas** (2).

vẹn (1) *n. masc.* wind: *nom. sg.* **vens** 13.13, 25.51, **venz** 13.13 var.; *obl. sg.* **ven** 13.10, 13.13 var., **vent** *used as nom. sg.* 32.1. [CL vĕntum *FEW* 14: 268; It. *vento,* Sp. *viento,* Fr. *vent*; cf. E. *ventilator*]

ven (2) *vb. intrans.* 5.3 var., 18.35, 23.36, 28.36, 30.82, *see* **venir.**

venal *adj.* venal, corrupt: *fem., nom. pl.* **venaus** 16.25. [CL vēnālem *FEW* 14: 230; It. *venale,* Sp. *venal,* Fr. *vénal,* E. *venal*]

venc *see* **venir.**

vencuda *see* **venser.**

veng, vengan, vengau *see* **venir.**

venguem *see* **venjar.**

vengutz, venguen, vengut, vengues *see* **venir.**

venir *vb. intrans.* to come *passim*; to become 5.3; *impersonal (a feeling or experience comes to a person = a person has the feeling or experience)* 9.65, 11.41, 14.71, 16.11, 18.5, 22.28, 23.36, 25.8, 25.43, 31.11; **venir a plazer a** to please 16.45, 18.35; **venir sobre** to come against, to oppose 12.61; **ben vengut** welcome 21.30; *refl.* **s'en venir** to come along 5.14, 30.22, 31.16.

    Forms: Pres. 2nd sg. **ves** 24.29; *3rd sg.* **ven** 5.3 var., 18.35, 23.36, 28.36, 30.82, **ve** 4.5, 15.36, 18.5, 30.22.

    Pres. subj. 3rd sg. **venha** 14.71, **veigna** 22.28; *3rd pl.* **vengan** 10.38, **vengau** 25.33.

    Fut. 3rd sg. **venra** 12.61, 22.47, 24.24; *3rd pl.* **venran** 12.54.

    Pret. 3rd sg. **venc** 1.5, 3.7, 5.3, 5.3, 5.14, 9.65, 11.41, 11.67, 25.8, 25.17, 25.35, 25.43, 25.60, 25.69, 30.11, 30.14, 31.11, 31.16, **veng** 11.40, 11.62; *3rd pl.* **venguen** 1.2.

    Past subj. 1st sg. **vengues** 16.45; *3rd sg.* **vengues** 16.11.

    Pp., masc., nom. sg. **vengutz** 29.16, 30.47; *obl. sg.* **vengut** 9.37; *nom. pl.* **vengut** 21.30.

    Inf. **venir** 2.2, 4.9, 4.18, 4.27, 4.36, 4.45, **veni** 2.2 var.

    [CL vĕnīre *FEW* 14: 245; It. *venire,* Sp. *venir,* Fr. *venir*]

venjansa *n. fem.* revenge: *obl. sg.* **venjansa** 28.53, 31.12. [**venjar** + **-ansa**; Sp. *venganza,* Fr. *vengeance,* E. *vengeance*]

venjar *vb. trans.* to avenge: *pres. subj. 1st pl.* **venguem** 12.35. [CL vĭndĭcāre *FEW* 14: 470; It. *vendicare,* Sp. *vengar,* Fr. *venger,* E. *to avenge*]

venra, venran *see* **venir.**

vens *see* **ven** (1).

vẹnser *vb. trans.* to surpass 17.21, to win over 28.36: *pres. 3rd sg.* **venz** 17.21; *pres. subj. 3rd sg.* **vensa** 28.36; *pp., fem., nom. sg.* **vencuda** conquered, subservient 19.61. [CL vĭncĕre *FEW* 14: 463; It. *vincere,* Sp. *vencer,* Fr. *vaincre,* E. *to vanquish*]

vent *see* **ven** (1).

venz (1) *n. masc.* 13.13 var., *see* **ven** (1).

venz (2) *vb. trans.* 17.21, *see* **venser.**

vẹr (1) *n. masc.* truth 15.43, 16.22, 17.24; **per ver** in truth 18.25, 23.11, 26.55, 29.14; **per ver dire** to tell the truth 31.8: *obl. sg.* **ver** 16.22, 17.24, 18.25, 23.11, 26.55, 29.14, 31.8. [**ver** (2)]

ver (2) *adj.* true, accurate 3.6; true, faithful 14.31: *masc., nom. sg.* **vers** 3.6; *fem., nom. sg.* **vera** 14.31. [CL vᴇ̄ʀᴜᴍ *FEW* 14: 331; It. *vero*; cf. E. *to verify*]

verai *adj.* true, loyal 6.5, 6.6, 15.29; reliable, certain 12.16; real 15.12: *masc., nom. sg.* **verais** 6.6, 12.16 var., 15.12, **vrais** 12.16 var., **veray** *used as nom. sg.* 12.16 note; *obl. sg.* **verai** 15.29; *fem., nom. sg.* **veraia** 6.5. [OFr. *verai* (VL *vᴇ̄ʀᴀ̄ᴄᴜᴍ *FEW* 14: 274); Fr. *vrai*]

veraiamen *adv.* truly, in truth: **veraiamen** 15.40. [verai + -amen (2)]

verais, veray *see* **verai.**

verga *n. fem.* rod, switch: *nom. sg.* **verga** 14.39. [CL vɪ̆ʀɢᴀᴍ *FEW* 14: 499; It. *verga*, Sp. *verga*, Fr. *verge*]

vergier *n. masc.* orchard: *obl. pl.* **vergers** 25.46. [CL vɪ̆ʀɪ̆ᴅɪ̄ᴀ̄ʀɪᴜᴍ *FEW* 14: 506; It. *verziere*, Sp. *vergel*, Fr. *vergier*]

vergonhos *adj.* ashamed: *fem., nom. sg.* **vergonjoza** 31.20. [vergonha (CL vᴇ̆ʀᴇ̄ᴄᴜ̆ɴᴅɪ̆ᴀᴍ *FEW* 14: 282; It. *vergogna*, Sp. *vergüenza*, Fr. *vergogne*) + -os]

veritat *see* **vertat.**

vermelh *adj.* red: *masc., nom. sg.* **vermelhs** 25.13, 25.59. [CL vᴇ̆ʀᴍɪ̆ᴄᴜ̆ʟᴜᴍ *FEW* 14: 290; It. *vermiglio*, Sp. *bermejo*, Fr. *vermeil*; cf. E. *vermilion*]

vers (1) *n. masc.* song 1.3, 5.6, 5.11, 9.68, 10.2, 14.2, 16.50, 29.0; measure, rhythmic structure 8.4, 12.2: *nom. sg.* **vers** 16.50, 29.0; *obl. sg.* **vers** 8.4, 9.68, 10.2, 12.2, 14.2; *nom. pl.* **vers** 5.11; *obl. pl.* **vers** 1.3, 5.6. [CL vᴇ̆ʀsᴜᴍ *FEW* 14: 316; It. *verso*, Sp. *verso*, Fr. *vers*. E. *verse*]

vers (2) *adj.* 3.6, *see* **ver** (2).

vert *adj.* green: *fem., obl. sg.* **vert** 8.18. [CL vɪ̆ʀɪ̆ᴅᴇᴍ *FEW* 14: 515; It. *verde*, Sp. *verde*, Fr. *vert*]

vertat *n. fem.* truth: *obl. sg.* **vertat** 16.27, **veritat** 9.35. [CL vᴇ̆ʀɪ̆ᴛᴀ̄ᴛᴇᴍ *FEW* 14: 288; It. *verità*, Sp. *verdad*, Fr. *vérité*, E. *verity*]

vertut *n. fem.* virtue, power: *obl. sg.* **vertut** 12.42. [CL vɪ̆ʀᴛᴜ̄ᴛᴇᴍ *FEW* 14: 519; It. *virtù*, Sp. *virtud*, Fr. *vertu*, E. *virtue*]

ves (1) *n. fem.* 9.52, 30.89, *see* **vetz.**

ves (2) *vb. intrans.* 24.29, *see* **anar.**

ves (3) *prep.* 12.36, 13.8, 14.5, 23.4, 23.14, 23.16, 25.91, 27.11, *see* **vas** (2).

vescomte *n. masc.* viscount, a nobleman below a count: *nom. sg.* **vescoms** 5.16, **vescons** 5.4, 5.5, 5.7, 5.8. [ML vɪ̆ᴄᴇ̆ᴄᴏ̆ᴍɪ̆ᴛᴇᴍ *FEW* 2: 941; It. *visconte*, Sp. *visconde*, Fr. *vicomte*, E. *viscount*]

vescomtesa *n. fem.* viscountess: *nom. sg.* **vescomtessa** 5.16. [vescomte + -esa]

vescons *see* **vescomte.**

vescut *see* **viure.**

vest, vestida *see* **vestir** (2).

vestir (1) *n. masc.* article of clothing 26.41; vestment, garment worn by officiant at Mass 30.96: *obl. sg.* **vestir** 30.96; *obl. pl.* **vestirs** 26.41. [vestir (2)]

vestir (2) *vb. trans.* to wear 13.6; to dress 7.8, 19.60: *pres. 3rd sg.* **vest** 13.6; *pp., fem., nom. sg.* **vestida** 7.8, 19.60. [CL vᴇ̆sᴛɪ̄ʀᴇ *FEW* 14: 355; It. *vestire*, Sp. *vestir*, Fr. *vêtir*; cf. E. *to invest*]

vestirs *see* **vestir** (1).

vetz *n. fem.* time: *obl. sg.* **vetz** 28.65, **ves** 9.52; *obl. pl.* **vetz** 6.15, 9.62, 19.34, 28.2, 28.10, 28.44, **ves** 30.89. [CL vɪ̆ᴄᴇᴍ *FEW* 14: 412; It. *vece*, Sp. *vez*, Fr. *fois*, E. *vice (president)*] vey, veyrem *see* vezer.

vezer *vb. trans.* to see; to foresee 19.41.
    Forms: pres. 1st sg. vei 7.5, 8.8, 18.1, 18.21, vey 4.8, 4.17, 4.26, 4.35,
    4.44, 13.37, 19.41, *3rd sg.* ve 18.29, 30.21; *pres. subj. 1st sg.* veia 15.39,
    18.6, *2nd pl. (= imper. 2nd pl.)* vejatz 31.27; *imperf. 1st sg.* vezia 4.37,
    13.48 ms., vezi' 13.48; *fut. 1st sg.* veirai 15.16, 15.17, 15.30, veirei
    23.11, *1st pl.* veyrem 12.41, *3rd pl.* veiran 10.20, 21.73; *pret. 1st sg.* vi
    9.37, 13.86, 28.11, 28.22, 31.18, 31.30, 31.44, vic 23.28, *3rd sg.* vi 21.49,
    23.28, 31.14; *past subj. 3rd sg.* vis 30.87; *pp., masc., obl. sg.* vist 28.10,
    vezut 21.58; *fem., obl. sg.* vista 1.6; *neuter, obl. sg.* vist 30.24; *inf.* vezer
    1.2, 1.4, 16.38, 18.43, 29.19; *substantivized inf.* vezer power of sight 3.9.
    [CL vĭdēre *FEW* 14: 428; It. *vedere*, Sp. *ver*, Fr. *voir*; cf. E. *video*]

vezi (1) *n. masc.* 8.26, *see* vezin (1).

vezi' (2) *vb. trans.* 13.48, vezia *see* vezer.

veziṇ (1) *n. masc.* neighbor: *obl. sg.* vezi 8.26; *nom. pl.* vezin 10.8. [vezin
    (2)]

veziṇ (2) *adj.* near: *masc., nom. sg.* vezis 15.27. [CL vīcīnum, VL *vēcīnum
    FEW 14: 416; It. *vicino*, Sp. *vecino*, Fr. *voisin*]

vezọch *n. masc.* billhook, thick knife with a hooked point, used to prune
    shrubs: *obl. sg.* vezoich 13.38. [LL (from Ctc.) vĭdŭbĭum *FEW* 14: 434;
    Fr. *vouge*]

vezut *see* vezer.

vi (1) *n. masc.* 26.28, *see* vin.

vi (2) *vb. trans.* 9.37, 13.86, 21.49, 23.28, 28.11, 28.22, 31.14, 31.18, 31.30,
    31.44, *see* vezer.

via (1) *n. fem.* road 4.28, 13.16, 13.38 var.; way *(of Christ)* 26.5; dar via a to
    dismiss 31.18: *obl. sg.* via 4.28, 13.16, 13.38 var., 26.5, 31.18. [CL vĭam
    FEW 14: 379; It. *via*, Sp. *via*, Fr. *voie*; cf. E. *via* prep.]

via (2) *interj.* away! 4.8, 4.17, 4.26, 4.35, 4.44. [via (1)]

viandier *adj.* going away, running, in retreat: *masc., obl. pl.* vianders
    25.44. [viandan, *pres. part. of* vianar 'to go away' (via + anar) + -ier]

viatz *adv.* quickly: vias 10.19. [CL vīvācĭus adv. 'more quickly' *FEW* 14:
    575; cf. Fr. *vivace*, E. *vivacious*]

vic *see* vezer.

vida *n. fem.* life, the state of being alive 1.6, 4.41; the length of time one
    lives 7.16, 28.41: *obl. sg.* vida 1.6, 4.41, 7.16, 28.41. [CL vītam *FEW* 14:
    543; It. *vita*, Sp. *vida*, Fr. *vie*; cf. E. *vital*]

vieus *see* viu (2).

vil *adj.* vile, wretched: *fem., nom. sg.* vils 31.25. [CL vīlem *FEW* 14: 448; It.
    vile, Sp. *vil*, Fr. *vil*, E. *vile*]

vila *n. fem.* town: *nom. sg.* vila 25.42; *obl. sg.* vila 25.5, 25.91, 25.100,
    25.105, 25.109. [CL vīllam 'farm, manor' *FEW* 14: 451; It. *villa*, Sp.
    villa, Fr. *ville*]

vilaṇ *n. masc.* peasant: *nom. sg.* vilas 13.81. [LL vīllānum *FEW* 14: 455; It.
    villano, Sp. *villano*, Fr. *vilain*, E. *villain*]

vilana *n. fem.* peasant woman: *nom. sg.* vilaina 13.25, vilayna 13.11,
    13.18, 13.32, 13.39, 13.53, 13.67; *obl. sg.* vilaina 13.4, vilayna 13.46,
    13.60, 13.81; *vocative sg.* vilayna 13.74. [vilan + -a]

vilanamęn *adv.* in coarse language 16.27; severely 23.48 var. [**vilan** *adj.* 'rustic' + **-amen** (2)]

vilas *see* **vilan**.

vilayna *see* **vilana**.

vils *see* **vil**.

viltat *n. fem.* abundance, plenty: *obl. sg.* **viutat** 27.14. [CL vīlĭtātem 'worthlessness' *FEW* 14: 499; It. *viltà*, Sp. *vildad*]

vĩn *n. masc.* wine: *nom. sg.* **vins** 9.27; *obl. sg.* **vin** 26.13, **vi** 26.28. [CL vīnum *FEW* 14: 483; It. *vino*, Sp. *vino*, Fr. *vin*, G. *Wein*, E. *wine*]

vint *num.* twenty: **vint** 9.62. [CL vīgĭnti *FEW* 14: 444; It. *venti*, Sp. *veinte*, Fr. *vingt*]

viola *n. fem.* viol, a stringed instrument: *obl. sg.* **viol'** 21.34. [Two syllables (**io** is a diphthong), but the position of the **o** is uncertain; onomatopoetic *vi-*, *viol-* *FEW* 14: 370; It. *viola*, Sp. *viola*, Fr. *viole*, E. *viola*]

virar *vb. intrans.* to turn: *pres. 3rd sg.* **vira** 25.55. [CL vībrāre 'to brandish,' VL *vīrāre (influenced by lībrāre 'to throw' *FEW* 14: 402); Sp. *virar*, Fr. *virer*]

vis, vist *see* **vezer**.

vista (1) *n. fem.* sight; **sa vista** the sight of him 28.34; meeting 28.54: *nom. sg.* **vista** 28.34; *obl. sg.* **vista** 28.54. [*pp., fem. of* **vezer**]

viu (1) *vb. intrans.* 20.9, *see* **viure**.

viu (2) *adj.* alive 14.42, 31.46; living 11.17: *masc., nom. sg.* **vieus** 14.42; *obl. sg.* **viu** 31.46; *obl. pl.* **vius** 11.17. [CL vīvum *FEW* 14: 585; It. *vivo*, Sp. *vivo*, Fr. *vif*; cf. E. *vivid*]

viure *vb. intrans.* to live 8.23, 20.9, 21.16; to live eternally (in Heaven) 11.3: *pres. 3rd sg.* **viu** 20.9; *pp., masc., undeclined* **vescut** 21.16; *inf.* **viure** 8.23, **viuri** 11.3 ms., **viur'** 11.3; *substantivized inf., masc., obl. sg.* **bel viure** living well 26.15. [CL vīvĕre *FEW* 14: 580; It. *vivere*, Sp. *vivir*, Fr. *vivre*]

vius *see* **viu** (2).

viutat *see* **viltat**.

vivęn *adj.* living: *masc., obl. pl.* **vivents** 32.16. [*pres. part. of* **viure**]

voill *see* **voler**.

vǫl (1) *n. masc.* wish: *obl. sg.* **vol** 30.14. [**voler**]

vol (2) *vb. trans.* 10.30, 12.50, 14.50, 14.54 var., 16.34, 18.51, 22.15, 22.42, 24.15, 27.5, 29.20, 30.49, 30.93, *see* **voler**.

volar *vb. intrans.* to fly: *pres. 3rd pl.* **volan** 25.12. [CL vŏlāre *FEW* 14: 607; It. *volare*, Sp. *volar*, Fr. *voler*; cf. E. *volley*]

volc *see* **voler**.

volentos *see* **volontos**.

volęr *vb. trans.* to want *passim*; to want (to go) 12.22; to be willing 23.45, 26.7, 30.49; to intend 11.66, 12.50, 13.69, 30.93; to love 4.2; to try 27.5; *in pret.* to try 3.11, 11.22, 11.51, to choose 26.7; **voler ben** (**a**) to love, **voler ben major** (**a**) to love (someone) better 3.5; **voler mais** to prefer 9.59, 19.28, 29.20.

    Forms: Pres. 1st sg. **voill** 16.38, 21.38, 21.57, 22.23 var., 27.1, 27.33, **vuoil** 7.3, **vuoill** 15.47, 15.50, 20.25, 22.43, **vuelh** 13.69, 14.1, 19.28, **vueil** 23.22, **vueill** 23.13; *3rd sg.* **vol** 10.30, 12.50, 14.50, 16.34, 18.51, 22.15, 22.42, 24.15, 27.5, 29.20, 30.93; *2nd pl.* **volez** 23.45; *3rd pl.* **volon** 12.22, 24.3, 26.20, 26.31, 26.40; *imperf. 3rd sg.* **volia** 4.2, 11.66,

voli' 3.5; *1st cond. 1st sg.* **volria** 7.9, 7.24; *pret. 1st sg.* **vuelc** 9.59; *3rd sg.* **volc** 3.11, 26.7, **volg** 11.22, 11.45, 11.47, 11.48, 11.51; *past subj. 1st sg.* **volgues** 16.22; *3rd sg.* **volgues** 26.26, 27.20; *2nd cond. 1st sg.* **volgra** 20.34, 31.4; *pp., fem., obl. sg.* **volguda** 19.57; *inf.* **voler** 18.51.
  Substantivized inf., masc. will 29.31, yearning 16.29, wish 19.10: *nom. sg.* **volers** 19.10; *obl. sg.* **voler** 16.29, 29.31.
  [CL vĕlle, VL *vŏlēre *FEW* 14: 219; It. *volere,* Sp. *voler,* Fr. *vouloir*]
volon *adj.* yearning: *masc., obl. sg.* **volon** 18.16. [**voler** + **-on** (2)]
volontat *n. fem.* desire: *nom. sg.* **voluntaz** 16.32; *obl. sg.* **voluntat** 1.4, 9.44. [CL vŏlŭntātem *FEW* 14: 616; It. *volontà,* Sp. *voluntad,* Fr. *volonté;* cf. E. *voluntary*]
volontiers *adv.* gladly 9.23. [**volontier** 'willing' (CL vŏlŭntārĭum *FEW* 14: 614) + **-s**]
volontos *adj.* eager, avid: *masc., nom. sg.* **volentos** 9.26. [**volontier** + **-os**]
vos (1) *n. fem.* 30.34, *see* **votz.**
vos (2) *personal pron., 2nd pl.* you; **vos mezeis** you yourself 27.28; *impersonal reference (like Fr. nom.* on, *obl.* vous) 13.65, 13.65.
  Forms: **vos** *masc., nom.* 5.17, 17.13, 19.14, 27.28, 28.70; *obl., direct object* 7.19, 10.18, 12.9, 12.12, 17.7, 17.43, 19.29, 21.26, 21.27, 21.38, 21.43, 21.44, 21.57, 21.59, 23.14, 23.16, 23.26, 23.28, 23.38, 27.28, 27.33, 27.34, 28.33; *obl., indirect object* 6.35, 11.44, 11.72, 13.17, 14.1, 14.19, 14.20, 14.21, 14.71, 17.24, 19.15, 19.47, 19.67, 27.24, 27.37, 27.43, 31.7, 31.25, 31.35;
  vos *fem., nom.* 19.18, 19.40; *obl., direct object* 4.32, 4.41, 13.33, 13.44, 13.49, 28.25, 28.51, 28.68; *obl., indirect object* 4.19, 19.19, 19.55, 28.23;
  vos *refl., masc., obl., direct object* 14.72, 17.2, 17.44; *obl., indirect object* 28.46;
  ·us *enclitic form (joins a preceding vowel, has no syllabic value): masc., nom.* 14.54 var., 19.46; *obl., direct object* 7.18, 7.22, 17.17, 19.61, 21.58, 21.73, 23.1, 23.3, 23.4, 23.7, 23.9, 23.10, 23.28, 28.22; *obl., indirect object* 6.36, 7.20, 13.65, 13.65, 14.35, 14.53, 19.15, 19.26, 19.41, 19.43, 19.63, 22.6, 22.47, 23.12, 23.41, 23.44, 25.2, 26.53, 27.8, **·eus** 19.13, 19.27;
  ·us *fem., obl., direct object* 4.37, 13.10, 13.31, 19.37, 28.20, 28.31, 28.49, 28.59, 28.67; *obl., indirect object* 13.47, 19.1, 19.2, 19.19, 27.45, 28.32, 28.44;
  ·us *refl., masc., obl., direct object* 19.64, 28.72; *obl., indirect object* 19.36, 19.68, 28.17; *fem., obl., direct object* 19.38; *obl., indirect object* 28.51.
  [CL vōs *FEW* 14: 635; It. *voi,* Sp. *vos(otros),* Fr. *vous*]
vostre (1) *possessive adj., 2nd pl.* your; *with def. art. (modifying noun)* **·l vostre** 13.34, **la vostra** 6.33, 13.24, 28.14, **las vostras** 25.21: *masc., nom. sg.* **vostre** 13.30, **vostres** 4.29; *obl. sg.* **vostre** 13.34, 23.6, 23.43, 27.46; *fem., nom. sg.* **vostra** 13.24, 19.3, 28.14, 28.15, **vostr'** 13.52; *obl. sg.* **vostra** 6.33, 6.36, 13.85, 27.17, **vostr'** 19.49; *obl. pl.* **vostras** 25.21.
  [CL vĕstrum, VL vŏstrum *FEW* 14: 350; It. *vostro,* Sp. *vuestro,* Fr. *votre*]

vǫstre (2) *possessive pron., 2nd pl.* yours; *with def. art.* **lo vostre** 23.35: *masc., obl. sg.* **vostre** 23.35. [**vostre** (1)]

vǫtz *n. fem.* voice: *obl. sg.* **votz** 25.79, 26.1, 32.7, **vos** 30.34. [CL vōcem *FEW* 14: 639; It. *voce,* Sp. *voz,* Fr. *voix,* E. *voice*]

vrais *see* **verai**.

vueil, vueill, vuelc, vuelh, vuoil, vuoill, *see* **voler**.

y *see* **i** (1).

yeu *see* **eu** (1).

ylh *see* **el** (1).

yrascuda *see* **iraiser**.

yssit, yssitz *see* **eisir**.

zo *see* **so** (2).

Prefixes, Infixes, Suffixes

a-, ad-, as-, az- *prefix* already present in CL etyma of **abatre, aduire, aitz** (s.v. **aizinar**), **ajudar, apelar, aportar, aprendre, aprochar, atendre, atraire, avenir, aventura, aversier** (2); in LL etyma of **acaptar, acordar, apres** (2); in VL etyma of **ades, adreisar, afaire, afanar** (s.v. **afan**), **alumnar, aora, asatz, asetar, atras, aturar, azirar, azolhar** (s.v. **azolh**);

    used in OOc to create verbs **abelir, abenar, abrandar, abrivar, acoatar, acolhir, acostumar, adastrar, adomesgar, afizar, aflamar, agaitar, agarar, agensar, agradar, amenar, apaisar, apercebre, apezar, aplanar, arandar, asajar, asenar, aterrar**; in double prefix, in pp. **dezadordenat**;

    used in OOc to create adverbs **adenan, adonc, amon, aprop**;

    used in OOc to create adjective **adrech**.

    [CL AD- 'to']

-a *n. suffix, fem.* in nouns for female persons based on masc. nouns, etymological in **filha**; analogical in **bergiera, druda, garsa, mercadanda, pastora, putana, toza, vilana,** in words designating things or abstractions based on masc. nouns or adjectives such as **camina, corsa, dia, maniera**, in deverbals such as **aizina, barata, bauza, comanda, crida, deça, demanda, ganda, garda, guida, pauza.** [CL -AM]

-ada *n. suffix, fem.* added to verb roots and nouns, designates abstractions: **encontrada, jornada, soldada, tropelada.** [CL -ĀTAM]

-ador (*nom.* **-aire**) *n. suffix, masc.* added to verb roots, designates agent: **cantador, cavalgador, ensenhador, torneiador, trobador.** [CL -ĀTŌREM, nom. -ĀTOR; **-a-** is the theme vowel of the verb; see -TŌREM *Oxf.*; cf. **-idor**]

-ai *adj. suffix* added to adj., etymological in **verai**, analogical in **lecai**. [VL -ĀCUM]

-airia *see* **-aria**.

-airitz *n. suffix, fem. of* **-ador** added to verb roots, designates agent: **cambiairitz, trichairitz.** [CL -ATRĪCEM; **-a-** is the theme vowel of the verb; see -TRĪCEM *Oxf.*]

-al *adj. or n. suffix, masc.* added to nouns, originally adjectival and still so in **cabal, celestial, coral, gauzinal;** adjectival force has been lost in nouns **bocal** (viz., **loc bocal** 'entryway'), **caisal** (viz., **dent caisal** 'tooth in the jaw, molar'), **costal** 'flank, side.' [CL -ālem]

-alhar *vb. suffix* added to verb stem, seems to express frequent repetition with connotation of contempt: **baralhar** (s.v. **baralha**). [CL -acŭlāre Adams 349]

-amẹn (1) *n. suffix, masc.* added to verb stems, expresses abstraction, the action described by the verb, or the result of such action: **aziramen, emendamen, esperamen, jutjamen, mandamen, parlamen, pasamen** (s.v. **traspasemen**), **pesamen, plaideiamen, razonamen, salvamen, traspasemen.** [CL -ā-mĕntum; **-a-** is the theme vowel of the verb; see -mentum *Oxf.*; cf. **-imen**]

-amẹn (2) *adv. suffix* added to fem. adjectives: **apertamen, aspramen, certanamen, eisamen, finamen, francamen, malamen, ricamen, veraiamen, vilanamen.** [LL -āmentĕ ablative 'with an ... (*adjective*) mind'; cf. **-men**]

-an (1) *n. suffix, masc.* added to nouns, names agent (**mercadan**) or action (**mazan**). [CL -āntem ending of pres. part.]

-aṇ (2) *adj. or n. suffix* added to adjectives, extends form without changing meaning: **certan** (s.v. **certanamen**), **dousan, primairan, sotan, trefan;** added to noun, produces noun **bocaran.** [CL -ānum]

-ana *n. suffix, fem.* **ufana.** [CL -ānam Adams 112–13]

-anda *n. suffix, fem.* added to verb roots, designates abstraction (**garanda**), collective (**liuranda**), or product (**Garlanda**). [CL -anda ending of fut. passive part., 1st conjugation, neuter pl.; 2nd conjugation, fut. passive part. -enda is etymological in **fazenda, legenda** (s.v. **legendier**), **ofrenda**]

-ansa *n. suffix, fem.* added to verb roots, expresses the action of the verb (**comensansa, onransa, venjansa**) or, most frequently, the result of such action, either a state (**alegransa, amistansa, doptansa, esperansa, membransa, pezansa, semblansa, sobransa** [s.v. **sobransier**]), a condition (**acordansa**), or a thing (**uzansa**); Adams 116–17. [CL -antĭam = -ā-nt-ĭa-m; **-a-** is the theme vowel of the verb to which the suffix is added; cf. **-ẹnsa;** in CL the suffix -ĭam was added to the pres. part. -ntem]

-anta *n. suffix, fem.* **garganta.** [perhaps CL -āntem ending of pres. part. + **a** (1); Corominas and Pascual 3: 95]

-ar (1) *n. suffix, masc.* added to nouns, designates articles of dress: **causar.** [CL -āre n. suffix; Adams 128]

-ar (2) *vb. suffix* added to nouns and adjectives, gives meanings such as 'to have (the root noun),' 'to use ... ,' 'to equip with ... ,' 'to put on ... ,' 'to fill with ... ,' 'to cover with ... ' (Adams 333): **abenar, abrandar, abrivar, acostumar, adastrar, adomesgar, agaitar, agradar, aizinar, albergar, alegrar, arandar, asajar, asenar, aterrar, balaiar, balansar, baratar** (s.v. **barata**), **bauzar** (s.v. **bauza**), **capdelar, carbonar** (s.v. **carbonada**), **cenchar, confinar, cornar** (s.v. **corna-vin**), **crozar, definar, deglazïar, degrunar, derocar, desenar, desviar, doblar, enamorar, enansar, endeutar, enfernar, enveiar, escaldar, esperonar, estranhar, fadar, folhar, gabar, garandar, gardar, gazanhar, gensar,**

gratar, guidar, guinhar, linhar, lonhar, mazantar (s.v. **mazan**), **mer-avelhar, muzar** (s.v. **muza** [2]), **nafrar, ocaizonar, paisar, parelhar, pastar, penar, petar, pojar, rechinhar, solar, soldar** (s.v. **soldada**), **tirar, tormentar, toscar, tradar, trobar, truandar.** [CL -ĀRE inf. suffix]

-aria, -airia *n. suffix, fem.* added to nouns and adjectives to form abstract nouns: **cavalaria, draparia, drudaria, parelharia.** [CL -ĀRĬUM + -ĬAM Adams 130]

-art *adj. suffix* added to noun: **galhart.** [Germ. *-ard* or *-hard* Adams 297]

-ás (1) *n. suffix, masc.* added to noun; augmentative in size or depreciative in value: **brazás.** [CL -ACĔUM Adams 140]

-ás (2) *n. suffix, masc.* **bartás.** [Ctc. *-at* 'measure, content'; *FEW* 1: 263 s.v. **barros*]

-asier *n. suffix, masc.* added to noun, names person who works with object identified by noun (Adams 401): **dardasier.** [**-ás** (1) + **-ier**]

-astron *n. suffix, masc.* depreciative, added to noun: **cogastron.** [**-astre** (CL -ASTRUM Adams 146–47) + **-on** (1)]

-at *pp. suffix* forms past participles: **desbraiat, desnaturat;** added to noun with no change in meaning (Adams 153): **valat;** added to noun within verb: **acoatar.** [CL -ĀTUM pp.]

-atge *n. suffix, masc.* added to nouns, adjectives, or verb roots, expresses collective or abstract sense; etymological in **salvatge;** analogical in **auratge, companhatge, coratge, damnatge, despiuselatge, entratge, folatge, linhatge, mesatge** (s.v. **mesatgier**), **omenatge, paratge, senhoratge, traspasatge, uzatge.** [CL -ĀTĬCUM]

-atura *n. suffix, fem.* added to verb roots, expresses abstract or collective sense (**-adura** Adams 57): **folatura, parelhatura, sofrachura.** [CL -ATŪRAM; **-a-** is the theme vowel of the verb and **-t/d-** is from pp.; cf. -ŪRAM *Oxf.*]

-azor (*nom.* **-áire**) *adj. suffix* added to adjectives, creates synthetic comparative: **belazor.** [CL -ĀTĬŌREM acc., -ĀTĬOR nom.; cf. **-sor**]

bis- *vb. prefix* **bistensar.** [CL BĬS 'twice'; Adams 419, 465]

de- *vb. and adv. prefix* added to verbs, confers intensive meaning, as in **definar** 'to die' (cf. **finar** 'to cease'), **deglazïar** 'to cut to pieces' (cf. **glazi** 'sword'), **devedar** 'to forbid' (cf. **vedar** 'to deny'); privative meaning, as in **degrunar** 'to fall from the husk' (cf. **grun** 'husk'); or the same meaning as the root, as in **demenar, departir, derocar;** added to adverbs, shows no difference from the meaning of the root, as in **dedins, desempre, desobre, desotz, devas.** [CL DĒ-]

des- *n., vb., and adj. prefix* added to verbs, negates the meaning of the verb root in **deserrar, descaptener, descobrir, desconvenir, desviar, dezeretar, dezesperar;** makes little difference in meaning in verbs **desliurar, destolre, destrigar** (s.v. **destric**); used with **-ar** (2) to create a verb from a noun, negating the meaning of the noun root in **desenar;** added to nouns, negates the meaning of the root in **deservitor, desplazer, dezonor;** used with **-atge** to create a noun from a noun, negating meaning of the root in **despiuselatge;** added to adjectives, negates meaning of the root in **dezavinen;** used with pp., negates root in **dezadordenat, desbraiat, desnaturat.** [CL DĬS-]

dezad- *double prefix:* **dezadordenat.** See **des-, a-.**

-ec *n. suffix, masc.* added to nouns; diminutive (Adams 21–22): **cavec**. [LL *-ĕccum*]

-edat *n. suffix, fem.* added to adjectives, designates abstraction: **escarsedat, foledat**. [CL -ĭtātem; cf. **-tat**]

-eiar *vb. suffix* added to nouns and adjectives, expresses same senses as **-ar** (2): **barreiar** (s.v. **barrei**), **carreiar** (s.v. **carrei**), **domneiar** (s.v. **domnei**), **guerreiar, pastorjar, plaideiar, torneiar**. [Gk. *-izein*, introduced during the Christian period as VL -ĭdĭāre Adams 357]

-eira *see* **-iera**.

-el *n. suffix, masc.* diminutive: **fornel, gonel, mantel, ramel, tropelada**. [CL -ĕllum]

-ela *n. suffix, fem.* diminutive: **gonela**. [CL -ĕllam]

-elada *n. suffix, fem.* added to verb root, names action of the verb: **tropelada**. [**-el** + **-ada**]

en- (1) *prefix* added to verbs, adds privative meaning of **en** (2): **emportar**. [CL ĭnde]

en- (2) *prefix* added to nouns, verbs, adjectives, adverbs, or prepositions, imparts various meanings of **en** (3): forming nouns **encombre** (s.v. **encombrier**), **endeman**; forming verbs **embrugir, emprendre, enamorar, endeutar, endevenir, endreisar, enrogir**; forming adjective **embronc;** forming adverbs **empero, enaisi, enapres;** forming preposition **enivers**. [CL ĭn-]

-en (3) *adj. suffix* added to verb root, creates present participle: **sancnen**. [CL -entem]

-ena *n. suffix, fem.* added to numerals, expresses collective meaning: **carantena**. [CL -ēnum, -ēnam Adams 176–77]

-enc *adj. suffix* added to nouns, confers adjectival force: **sebenc**. [Germanic *-inc* Adams 178–79]

-ensa *n. suffix, fem.* added to verb roots, expresses action of the verb or the result of such action; etymological in **crezensa, sapiencia;** analogical in **avinensa, conoisensa, entendensa, falhensa, guirensa, mantenensa, parvensa, sovinensa, valensa**. [CL -ĕntĭam; **-e-** is the theme vowel of the verb to which the suffix is added; cf. **-ansa**]

es- (1) *vb. prefix* added to verbs, confers meaning of separation, as in **esduire;** of intensification, as in **esbaudir, esperdre;** causes little change in meaning, as in **escaldar, escoisendre, escridar, esdevenir** (s.v. **endevenir**), **escercar, esgardar**. [CL ĕx 'out of']

-es (2) *adj. suffix* added to nouns, means 'pertaining to': **borges, cortes, engles, frances, marques, marselhes, sirventes;** proper nouns **Albeges, Narbones, Polhes, Vianes**. [CL -ēnsem influenced by Germ. *-isk*]

-esa *n. suffix, fem.* added to masc. nouns, especially those denoting rank, designates feminine: **comtesa, duchesa, preveiresa, traidoresa, vescomtesa**. [Gk. *-issa*, VL *-ĭssam Adams 185]

-et *n., adj., or adv. suffix* added to nouns, adjectives, or adverbs, expresses diminutive in masc. nouns **broet, rosinholet, sonet,** proper nouns **Aimeriguet, Monet;** adj. **alegret, coindet;** adv. **probet, süavet**. [CL -ĭttum Adams 188–89]

-eta *n. or adj. suffix, fem. of* **-et:** **lauzeta, popeta, tozeta, tozoiretas**. [CL -ĭttam Adams 188–89]

-eza *n. suffix, fem.* added to adjectives to form abstract nouns; etymological in **tristeza;** analogical in **ampleza, fereza, paubreza, proeza, savïeza.** [CL -ĭtĭam Adams 195]

-i- *infix, fem.* indicates feminine gender in **il** 'she,' fem. nom. sg. of **el** (1); **li** 'the,' fem. nom. sg. of **lo** (2); fem. nom. sg. demonstrative pronouns such as **cil** from **cel** (3); and forms not included in the texts in this book such as **cist** from **cest, aquil** from **aquel, aquist** from **aquest.** Also in **midonz, sidonz.** [CL ĭllī dat.]

-i *n. suffix, masc.* etymological, from CL -ĭum, in **emperi, glazi, martiri, ofíci, sacrifíci, sauteri, secretari,** proper nouns **Capitoli, Flori;** etymological, from CL -ĕum, in **ciri,** proper noun **Macari;** analogical in **avi, calici, seti;** cf. proper noun **Tripoli.** [CL -ĭum *Oxf.*]

-ia *n. suffix, fem.* added to nouns, adjectives, or verb stems to form abstract nouns: **bailia, companhia, cortezia, diablia, falsia, felnia, folhia, maïstria, malautia, paria, partia** (cf. **-ida**). [CL -ĭam, -īam influenced by Gk. -*ía*]

-ida *n. suffix, fem.* added to verb roots to express abstraction or result: **bruida, partida** (cf. **-ia**). [CL -ītam Adams 24; **-i-** is the theme vowel of the verb]

-idọr, -itor *n. suffix, masc.* added to verb roots, creates noun designating agent in **deservitor, felpidor, folpidor, traidor** (s.v. **traidoresa**); creates adjective that may be used as a noun: **avenidor.** [CL -ītōrem; **-i-** is the theme vowel of the verb; see -tōrem *Oxf.*; cf. **-ador**]

-ieira *see* **-iera.**

-ier *n. and adj. suffix, masc.* added to nouns, adjectives, or verb roots, denotes the agent of an action, place or instrument, or abstraction; etymological in **acier, aversier, candelier, carpentier, cartier, cavalier, denier, fornier, manier, mercenier, mestier, mostier, portier** (1), **primier, saumier, scïentiers, semdier, solier** (1), **tavernier, tempier, vergier;** analogical in **alegrier, arquier, aventurier, balestier, bordonier, braguier, caplier, castïer, clamadier, cloquier, cominalier, companhier, consirier, corsier, costaliers, dardasier, derier, destrier, desturbier, dezirier, doblier, domengier, drechurier, egalier, encombrier, eretier, escudier, encensier, espaventier, estremier, flamier, glazier** (1), **glazier** (2), **gonfanonier, gravier, grosier, legendier, logadier, mainadier, marvier, meitadier, mensongier, menudier, mercadier, mesatgier, milier, murtrier, nautonier, omicidïer, ospitalier, parier, parlier, parsonier, pazimentier, peirier, plazentier, plenier, portier** (2), **prezentier, prezonier, rabinier, recobrier, reprovier, rotier, sabrier, saintorier, savaier, senestrier, senharier, sobransier, sobrier, soldadier, sorbier, taïnier, targier, terrier, tormentier, viandier, volontiers.** [CL -ārĭum influenced by -ĕrĭum Adams 207–10; regular development of -ārĭum according to Fouché, *Phonètique* 2: 413–14]

-iera, -ieira, -eira *n. suffix, fem.* of **-ier;** etymological in nouns **carriera, neciera, peiriera, ribiera;** analogical in **bergiera** and in feminine adjectives **parieira** (s.v. **parier**), **parleyra** (s.v. **parlier**). [CL -ārĭam influenced by -ĕrĭam, etc.; Adams 207–10]

-il *adj. suffix* added to nouns denoting persons, forms adjective **senhoril.** [CL -īlem]

-imẹn *n. suffix, masc.* added to verb roots, expresses abstraction, as in **ardimen, falhimen;** or the result of the action described by the verb, as in **aunimen, jauzimen, revenimen.** [CL -ī-mĕntum; cf. **-amen** (1)]

-iṇ *n. and adj. suffix* added to noun, forms nouns of similar meaning such as **borsin, jardin;** added to adjective, forms verb root as in **aizinar.** [CL -īnum]

-ir *vb. suffix* creates infinitives from Germanic roots: **aunir** (s.v. **aunimen**), **cauzir, cropir** (s.v. **crup-en-cami**), **esbaudir, escarnir, fromir, garnir, gequir, marrir** (s.v. **marrit**), **marvir** (s.v. **marvier**), **murtrir, plevir, raustir;** or from Latin or Romance roots: **abelir, brugir** (s.v. **bruida**), **complir, convertir, embrugir, enrogir, falhir, grazir, reverdir, traïr.** [CL -īre]

-is *adj. suffix* added to verb root: **aïs;** or to noun: **masis.** [CL -ĭcĭum]

-isa *n. suffix, fem.* added to nouns, lacks well-defined meaning; etymological in **pelisa;** analogical in **calmisa, cambisa, planisa, sebisa.** [CL -ĭcĭam, -īcĭam *Oxf.;* Adams 143]

-it *adj. suffix:* **arabit, ardit.** [CL -ītum pp.]

-itọr *n. suffix, masc.* added to verb root, designates agent: **deservitor.** [CL -ītōrem; cf. **-ador**]

-mẹn *adv. suffix* added to feminine adjectives: **breumens, leumen.** [CL mĕnte 'with a mind, in a manner'; cf. **-amẹn** (2)]

mes- *vb. prefix* added to verbs, adds depreciative or negative force: **mescreire.** [Frankish *missi-* Gamillscheg 610]

-ọṇ (1) *n. suffix, masc.* added to nouns; sometimes diminutive: **balcon, baron, cogastron, esperon** (s.v. **esperonar**), **felon, garson, gonfanon, guinhon.** [CL -ōnem]

-ọṇ (2) *adj. suffix* added to verb roots; etymological in **jauzion;** analogical in **deziron, volon.** [CL -bŭndum *Oxf.*]

-ọr *n. suffix, fem.* added to adjectives, forms abstract nouns: **dousor, folhor, lauzor, lezor, saintor** (s.v. **saintorier**); or name of a thing: **tabor.** [CL -ōrem]

-ọs *adj. suffix* added to nouns, designates quality or abundance; etymological in **enveios;** analogical in **angoisos, cochos, enojos, joios, nüalhos, orgolhos, vergonhos, volontos.** [CL -ōsum]

per- *vb. prefix* added to verbs, adds meaning of 'thoroughly, through and through, completely': **perprendre.** [CL prefix pĕr-; cf. prep. pĕr 'through']

re- *vb. prefix* added to verbs or nouns, adds meaning of 'again', etc.; etymological in **rebondre, recebre, reclamar, recobrar, recobrier, retener, revestir;** analogical in **rebatre** (s.v. **rebat**), **recastenar, rechinhar, recomensar, recreire, regardar** (s.v. **regart**), **reisidar, remirar, repic, repreza, resemblar, retornar, revelhar, reverdir, revertir.** [CL rĕ-]

-s *adv. suffix* etymological in **alhors, fors, inz, jos, mais, mens, plus** (3), **sotz, sus;** analogical in **adoncs, alhons, anz, aras, breumens, can-**

dius, coras, costaliers, doncs, enans (2), ensems, eras (2), loncs (s.v. lonc [2]), primiers, scïentiers, ses, sivals, volontiers; substantivized in pron. als (1). [CL -s in fŏrīs, ĭntŭs, dĕōrsum, măgis, mĭnus, plūs, sŭbtus, sūsum]

-sǫr (*nom.* ´-ser) *adj. suffix* added to adjectives, creates synthetic comparative: gensor. [CL -tĭōrem acc., -tĭŏr nom.; cf. -azor]

-tat *n. suffix, fem.* added to adjectives, forms abstract nouns: etymological in amistat, bontat; analogical in alegretat, beltat, malvestat. [CL -tātem; cf. -edat]

tras- *adj., n., or vb. prefix* etymological sense 'over': traspasar, traspasatge, traspasemen; intensifies meaning of root trastot. [CL trăns-]

-uc *adj. suffix* added to noun: malastruc. [CL -ūcum Adams 279]

-ura *n. suffix, fem.* added to adjective, creates abstract noun drechura. [CL -ūram]

-zero (1) *n. suffix* verb root used as noun; verbs with infinitives in -ar: aiziṇ (1) [aizinar], albẹrc (1) [albergar], barat [baratar], cẹl (2) [celar], conǫrt [conortar], consir [consirar], crit [cridar], deman (1) [demandar], dezerẹt [dezeretar], dezir [dezirar], engan [enganar], espẹr [esperar], gazanh [gazanhar], man (1) [mandar], perdǫn [perdonar], plǫr [plorar], prẹc [pregar], prezic [prezicar], repaire [repairar], sospir [sospirar], tǫrn [tornar], tornẹi [torneiar], tric [trichar]; verbs with infinitives in -ẹr: captẹnh [captener], vǫl (1) [voler]; verbs with infinitives in -ir: escarn [escarnir].

-zero (2) *adj. suffix* verb root used as adj.: aiziṇ (2) [aizinar].

Proper Names

Aenrics *see* **Enric** (2).

Agnęs *n. fem.* Female character, apparently wife of **Garin**: *nom. sg.* **n'Agnes** 9.13. [ChL Agnes < Gk. *agnē* 'pure'; Dauzat 3]

Agolant *n. masc.* Brother of Marsile, coregent of Castile in the *Vida de Sant Honorat: nom. sg.* **Agolanz** 24.34 note. [OOc **aguilen, aigolentier** 'wild rose' < VL *aquīlĕntum; *FEW* 1: 118]

Aimars *see* **Azemar**.

Aimer *n. masc.* Follower of Simon de Montfort, perhaps Aimery de Blèves (normally **Aimeri,** here shortened for meter?—Martin-Chabot 2: 209, note 2): *nom. sg.* **n'Aimers** 25.74. [**Aimeric**]

Aimeric *n. masc.* Unidentified variant reading: *nom. sg.* **Aimerics** 20.7 var. [Germ. *Haim-rīc: haim* 'home,' *rīc* 'powerful'; Dauzat 4]

Aimeriguęt *n. masc.* Follower of the count of Toulouse: *obl. sg.* **n'Aimeriguet lo jove** 25.107. [**Aimeric** + **-et**]

Aimǫṇ *n. masc.* Follower of Simon de Montfort, perhaps Aimery de Blèves (normally **Aimeri,** here shortened for meter, but cf. **Aimer** above; Martin-Chabot 2: 203, note 6): *nom. sg.* **n'Aymes** 25.24. [Germ. *Haimon: haim* 'home'; Dauzat 4]

Ainrics *see* **Enric** (2).

Alaman *n. masc.* Man from Germany: *nom. pl.* **Aleman** 21.70; *obl. pl.* **Alamanz** 24.2. [Germ. tribal name *Alamann-,* al 'foreign' + *mann* 'man'; the dental in obl. pl. **Alamanz,** fem. **Alamanda** derives from a substitution of the suffix **-an** (1), CL -āntem]

Alamanda *n. fem.* Interlocutor, perhaps fictional, perhaps real, of Giraut de Bornelh in a **tenso:** *obl. sg.* **n'Alamanda** 20.25; *vocative sg.* **bel'ami'Alamanda** 19.1. [fem. of **Alaman**]

Albeges *n. masc.* The Albigeois, region around Albi (Tarn): *obl. sg.* **Albeges** 31.1. [CL Albius, name of a clan + **-g-** uncertain; cf. city name *Albige* (Nègre 10568) + **-es** (2)]

Aleman *see* **Alaman**.

Alvęrnhe *n. fem.* Auvergne, region of France in the center of the Massif Central: *obl. sg.* **Alvernhe** 9.1. [Provĭncĭa Alvĕrnĭa: Ctc. tribal name *Arverni* + CL -ĭa; Nègre 2437]

Amblart *n. masc.* Perhaps Amblardus d'Ans, vassal of Bertran de Born: *nom. sg.* **n'Amblarz** 22.11 (see note). [Germ. *Amal-hard: Amal* uncertain, *hard* 'strong'; Dauzat 8]

Angeviṇ *n. masc.* Man from Anjou: *nom. pl.* **Angevi** 10.16. [Ctc. tribal name *Andicavi*; Nègre 2430]

Angiẹus *n. masc.* Angers (Maine-et-Loire), capital of Anjou: *obl. sg.* **Angieus** 10.11, 10.13, 20.19. *See also* **Folcon d'Angieus**. [Ctc. tribal name *Andicavi*; Nègre 2429]

Angleterra *see* **Englaterra**.

Antiọcha *n. fem.* Antioch (Syria): *obl. sg.* **Antiocha** 1.2, 12.67. [CL Aɴᴛĭŏᴄʜĩᴀᴍ (*Oxf.*), with substitution of suffix **-a**]

Archimbaut *n. masc.* Husband of Flamenca: *nom. sg.* **ens Archimbautz** 30.13, **en Archimbautz** 30.91; *obl. sg.* **en Archimbaut** 30.46, **n'Archimbaut** 30.50. [Germ. *Ercan-bald: ercan* 'natural, excellent,' *bald* 'bold'; Dauzat 11]

Arnaut *n. masc.* Grandfather of Guillaume d'Orange in the OFr. epic: *obl. sg.* **Arnaut, lo marques de Belanda** 20.12. *See also* **Belanda**. [Germ. *Arn-wald: arn* 'ern, eagle,' *waldan* 'to govern'; Dauzat 12]

Audoart *n. masc.* Unidentified variant reading ('Edward'): *nom. sg.* **Audoartz** 22.11 var. [Germ. *Aldo-ward: alda* 'old,' *wardan* 'to keep'; Dauzat 15]

Autafọrt *n. fem.* Castle that belonged to the troubadour Bertran de Born, now in the town of Hautefort (arrondissement of Périgueux, Dordogne): *obl. sg.* **Autafort** 22.13, 22.49. [OOc **auta** + **fort**, fem., 'high and strong' (implicit **forsa** 'fortification'); Nègre 26963]

Aymes *see* **Aimon**.

Azemar *n. masc.* Aimar V, viscount of Limoges (1148–98): *nom. sg.* **n'Azemars** 22.11, **n'Aimars** 22.11 var. [Germ. *Ade-mar: adal* 'noble,' *mar* 'famous'; Dauzat 2]

Barnartz *see* **Bernart** (2).

Bartas *n. masc.* Pierre-Guillaume Bartas, follower of the count of Toulouse: *nom. sg.* **en Bartas** 25.16. [OOc **bartás** 'thicket' < Ctc. **barros* (*FEW* 1: 262) + **-as** (2); cf. Dauzat 28]

Basatz *n. masc.* Bazas (Gironde): *obl. sg.* **Basatz** 20.24. [LL Vᴀsᴀᴛᴇs, name of an Aquitanian people; Aquitanian (Pre-Ctc.) *basa* 'town' + Ctc. *-ates* 'inhabitants of a town'; Nègre 1205]

Beguina *n. fem.* Beguine, member of a lay sisterhood: *obl. pl.* **Beguinas** 26.53 (see note). [Lambert le Bègue, d. 1177, priest of Liège who founded the first house of Beguines; Fr. *bègue* 'stammering' < Dutch **beggen* 'to chatter, to talk excessively'; B-W]

Belanda *n. fem.* City in the OFr. epic *Girart de Vienne*, possibly equivalent to Nice: **Belanda** 20.12. *See also* **Arnaut**. [OFr. *Beaulande*, possibly a back-formation from Beaulandais (Orne): *beau* 'handsome' + *landier* 'furze, gorse'; Nègre 4027]

Bẹl Depọrt *n. masc.* **Senhal** for an unidentified lady: *nom. sg.* **Belhs Deportz** 28.43 (see note). [OOc **bel, deport**]

Berenguiera *n. fem.* Proverbial giver of bad advice: *nom. sg.* **na Berenguieira** 19.39 (see note). [Germ. *Beren-gari: beren* 'bear,' *gari* 'lance'; Dauzat 37]

Bernart (1) *n. masc.* Husband of a female character: *obl. sg.* **en Bernart** 9.4, **en Bernat** 9.70. [Germ. *Bern-hard: bern* 'bear,' *hard* 'strong'; Dauzat 38]

Bernart (2) **de Ventadǫrn** *n. masc.* The troubadour (**vida,** reading 1; poems 16–18): *nom. sg.* **Bernartz de Ventedorn** 5.1, **Bernarz del Ventador** 16.53, **en Bernartz** 5.15, 5.16, **Bernatz** 5.15 var., **en Barnartz** 5.14; *obl. sg.* **en Bernart** 5.6, 5.9, 5.11; *vocative sg.* **Amics Bernarz del Ventadorn** 17.1, **Bernarz** 17.15, 17.29, 17.43. *See also* **Ventadorn.** [See **Bernart** (1), **Ventadorn**]

Bernat 9.70, *see* **Bernart** (1).

Bernatz 5.15 var., *see* **Bernart** (2).

Bersilianda *n. fem.* Brocéliande, forest in Brittany frequently used as setting in Arthurian romance: *nom. sg.* **Bersilianda** 20.33. [Uncertain; perhaps Ctc. *Bré-killien* 'shelters in the mountains of *Bré*']

Bertran *n. masc.* The troubadour Bertran de Born (poems 20–22): *nom. sg.* **en Bertrans** 22.44. [Germ. *Berht-hramn: berht* 'bright,' *hramn* 'raven'; Dauzat 40]

Blaia *n. fem.* Blaye (Gironde): *obl. sg.* **Blaia** 1.1. *See also* **Jaufre** (2). [CL man's name Bᴀʟᴀʙɪᴜs, *Bʟᴀʙɪᴜs + -ᴀ; Nègre 10163]

Blanchaflǫr *n. fem.* Heroine of the romance *Floire et Blanchefleur;* see 7.14 note: *obl. sg.* **Blanchaflor** 7.14. [OOc blanc, flǫr]

Boǫci *n. masc.* Author of the *Consolation of Philosophy: nom. sg.* **Boecis** 11.22, 11.28, 11.47, 11.63; *obl. sg.* **Boeci** 11.41, 11.53, 11.67, 11.72, *with genitive sense* **Boeci** 11.55. [CL Bŏ̄ᴛʜɪ̆ᴜᴍ]

Bordǫls *n. masc.* Bordeaux (Gironde): *obl. sg.* (*etymologically pl.*) **Bordels** 20.23. [*Bourdigala* in a Gk. inscription, 1st century A.D.; Pre-Celtic place-name of uncertain meaning; Nègre 1137]

Braiman *n. masc.* Man from Brabant: *nom. pl.* **Braiman** 21.71. [*Brabant:* perhaps Ctc. *bracu 'mud' + *bani 'region'; Nègre 2308]

Bretǫn *n. masc.* Man from Brittany: *nom. pl.* **Breton** 21.61. [CL Bʀɪᴛᴀɴɴɪ̄ (*Oxf.*); Bʀɪᴛᴛᴀɴɴɪ̄, name of the people of Britain; Nègre 6327]

Brezi *n. masc.* Berzy-le-Sec, arrondissement of Soissons (Aisne). *See* **Joan de Brezi** (Martin-Chabot 3: 347). [Germ. man's name *Berisius* + CL -ɪᴀ̄ᴄᴜᴍ; Nègre 12866]

Caïn̥ *n. masc.* Cain, who slew Abel: *obl. sg.* **Caï** 12.37, **Caïm** 12.37 var. [ChL Cᴀɪɴ]

Caire *n. masc.* Perhaps Le Caire (Basses-Alpes). *See* **Simonet del Caire.** [OOc **caire** 'cut stone, fortress' (Nègre 26577); CL ǫᴜᴀᴅʀᴜᴍ 'square' (*FEW* 2, part 2: 1400)]

Campeyna *see* **Compeingna.**

Canda *n. fem.* Candes-Saint-Martin (Indre-et-Loire), at the confluence of the Loire and Vienne Rivers in Anjou: *obl. sg.* **Canda** 10.19, **Ganda** 20.19 var., **Glanda** 20.19 var. [Ctc. *cóndate* 'confluence of two rivers,' influenced by CL cᴀɴᴅɪ̆ᴅᴜs 'gleaming white'; Nègre 2090]

Capestanh *n. masc.* Capestany (arrondissement of Perpignan, Pyrénées-Orientales): *obl. sg.* **Capestaing** 3.1, 3.4, 3.8. *See also* **Guilhem** (1). [CL cᴀᴘᴜᴛ sᴛᴀɢɴɪ̄ 'the end of the pond'; Nègre 5152]

Capitǫli *n. masc.* The Capitoline hill in Rome: *obl. sg.* **Capitoli** 11.60. [CL Cᴀᴘɪᴛᴏ̄ʟɪ̆ᴜᴍ; E. *Capitol*]

Castęl Rossillọn *n. masc.* Castel-Roussillon (arrondissement of Perpignan, Pyrénées-Orientales): *obl. sg.* **·l Castel Rossillon** 3.7, **·l Castel
de Rossillon** 3.3, **·l Castel de Rossiglon** 3.6. *See also* **Raimon** (1),
Rosilhon. [OOc **castel** + **Rosilhon**]

Catalonha *n. fem.* Catalonia: *obl. sg.* **Cataloingna** 3.1. [Perhaps CL
Lācētānĭa 'a district in the extreme northeast of Spain' (*Oxf.*),
*Cātēlānĭa by metathesis, influenced by Vascŏnĭa 'the region of the
Basques' (L & S); for discussion of this and other hypotheses, see Ud-
ina i Martorell 37–40]

Cerni *see* **Saint Cerni**.

Charle Martęl *n. masc.* Charles Martel, lived c. A.D. 685–741, character in
the epic *Girart de Roussillon: nom. sg.* **Charles Martels** 24.33 (see
note). [Germ. *carl* 'man,' ML Carŏlus (Dauzat 112); VL *martĕllus, CL
martŭlus, marcŭlus 'small hammer']

Circ *see* **Saint Circ**.

Coberlanda *n. fem.* Cumberland (England): *obl. sg.* **Coberlanda** 20.17.
[Old E. *Cumbraland*, from Welsh *Cymry* 'the Welsh' + Germ. *land:* 'land
of the Cumbrians'; Ekwall]

Compęingna *n. fem.* Compiègne (Oise): *obl. sg.* **Compeingna** 21.66,
Compeigna 21.66 var., **Campeyna** 21.66 var. [CL compĕndĭa neuter pl.
'short cut'; Nègre 5714]

Corberan *n. masc.* Persian commander in the battle before Antioch, in
the *Chanson d'Antioche: nom. sg.* **Corberanz** 24.12 (see note). [Cf. Fr.
name *Courbrant*, contraction of *courberand* (cf. *tisserant*) 'one who
bends bows, bowmaker'; Dauzat 154]

Cornęt *n. masc.* Family name of **Raimon de Cornet;** *obl. sg.* **31.0**. [OOc
cornet 'small horn,' merchant's surname; Dauzat 148]

Crist *n. masc.* Christ: *nom. sg.* **Crist** 12.60; *obl. sg.* **Jhesu Crist** 26.6; *vocative sg.* (*in prayer*) **Jhesu Crist** 25.29. *See also* **Jhesu**. [ChL cristus,
from Greek *khristos*, 'anointed,' translating Hebrew *masiah*,
'anointed,' whence 'messiah.']

Dalọn *n. masc.* Cistercian abbey near Bertran de Born's castle: *obl. sg.*
Dalon 5.15 (see note). [Germ. man's name *Tallo(n)*; Nègre 14575]

Deportz *see* **Bel Deport**.

Dęu *n. masc.* God; *in oath* **per Deu** 4.30, 19.9, 19.26, 19.49, 19.57 var.,
19.65: *nom. sg.* **Deus** 16.8, 25.93, **Dieus** 8.23, 12.50, 14.45, 15.36,
18.34, 25.63, 29.11, 29.36, 30.51; *obl. sg.* **Deu** 11.12, 11.16, 11.24, 11.46,
11.74, 19.57 var., 26.8, **Dieu** 1.6, 4.30, 6.12, 10.35, 12.35, 12.40, 12.65,
13.12, 15.21, 17.12, 19.9, 19.26, 19.49, 19.65, 21.13, 26.16, 26.18, 26.23,
26.48, 30.64, 31.33, **Deus** 31.33 var., *obl. sg. in gen. sense* **Deu** 11.19,
11.45, **Dieu** 15.23; *vocative sg.* **Dieus** 12.69, 25.79, 27.31. [CL dĕum]

Dĕus (Latin) *n. masc.* God; *gen. sg.* **Dei** 30.36.

Domás *n.masc.* Damascus (Syria): *obl.sg.* **Domas** 12.36. [CL Damascus; *Oxf.*]

Duręnsa *n. fem.* The river Durance, which rises in the southern French
Alps and flows westward, joining the Rhône south of Avignon: *nom. sg.*
Durensa 2.10. [Pre-Celtic river name *dora; Nègre 1042]

Ęble de Ventadorn *n. masc.* Eble IV, viscount of Ventadorn, active
1169–84: *nom. sg.* **lo vescoms n'Ebles de Ventedorn** 5.16. [Germ.
Ebulo, ML Ebalus: *eber* 'boar'; Dauzat 231; see **Ventadorn**]

Englaterra *n. fem.* England: *obl. sg.* **Engletera** 5.13, **Angleterra** 5.13.
[Old E. *Engle* 'Anglians' (Ekwall) + CL těRRAM]

Engles *n. masc.* Englishman: *obl. sg.* **Engles** 26.2; *nom. pl.* **Engles** 21.62;
obl. pl. **Engles** 20.18. *See also Glossary.* [Old E. *Englĭsc* 'English'; Ek-
wall]

Enric (1) *n. masc.* Henry II Plantagenet, king of England 1154–89: *nom.
sg.* **lo reis Enrics d'Engletera** 5.13. [Germ. *Haim-rīc: haim* 'home,' *rīc*
'powerful'; Dauzat 324]

Enric (2) *n. masc.* Henry Curtmantle, called the Young King (died 1183),
son of Henry II Plantagenet: *nom. sg.* **n'Aenrics** 20.7, **n'Ainrics** 20.7
var., **Enrics** 20.7 var., **nai Henrics** 20.7 var. [See **Enric** (1)]

Ermessen *n. fem.* Female character, apparently wife of **Bernart** (1): *nom.
sg.* **Ermessen** 9.13, 9.49. [OOc *ermes* 'inhabitant of an **erm**, waste-
land' (LL ĚRĚMUS; *FEW* 3: 237) + **-en** (Adams 305)]

Espanha *n. fem.* Spain: *obl. sg.* **Espanha** 12.55. [CL HĬSPĀNĬA; *Oxf.*]

Flamenca *n. fem.* Heroine of the romance; the name is the feminine of
the adjective **flamenc** 'Flemish': *nom. sg.* **Flamenca** 30.19; *obl. sg.*
Flamenca 30.56. [Germ. tribal name *Vlamingen* 'natives of Flanders'
+ **-a**]

Flándres *n. masc.* Flanders: *nom. sg.* **Flandres** 21.68. [Flemish *Vloen-
deren*]

Flori *n. masc.* Hero of the romance *Floire et Blanchefleur: nom. sg.* **Floris**
7.14 (see note); *voc. sg.* **Floris** 6.33 var. [CL FLŌRĬUM]

Folcaut *n. masc.* Follower of Simon de Montfort: *nom. sg.* **·l Folcautz**
25.37. [Germ. *Folc-wald: folc* 'folk,' *waldan* 'to govern'; Dauzat 263]

Folcon d'Angieus *n. masc.* Folque V, count of Anjou 1109–42: *nom. sg.*
Folcos d'Angieus 10.13; *obl. sg.* **Folcon d'Angieus** 10.11. *See also*
Angieus. [Germ. *Folco: folc* 'folk'; Dauzat 263]

Forquer *n. masc.* Folquet de Marselha, troubadour, then monk and
bishop of Toulouse: *nom. sg.* **l'evesques Forquers** 25.87 note. [Germ.
Folco (see **Folcon**); the derivative with suffix **-ier** is substituted for the
sake of rhyme; cf. **Folquer** in charters]

Frances *n. masc.* Frenchman: *masc., nom. sg.* **Fransses** 26.14; *nom. pl.*
Franses 12.64; *obl. pl.* **Frances** 24.3. *See also Glossary.* [**Fransa** + **-es**
(2)]

Fransa *n. fem.* France: *nom. sg.* **Fransa** 21.66; *obl. sg.* **Fransa** 25.32.
[Germ. tribal name *Frank* + CL -ĬA, 'land of the Franks'; Nègre 12415]

Gan *n. masc.* Ghent (Belgium): *obl. sg.* **Gan** 21.68. [LL GANTUM; Ctc.
Ganda < *cóndate* 'confluence of two rivers'; cf. **Canda**]

Ganda *see* **Canda.**

Garin *n. masc.* Husband of **Agnes**, a female character: *obl. sg.* **en Guari**
9.3, 9.69. [Germ. *Warino: waran* 'to shelter'; Dauzat 312]

Garlanda *n. fem.* A fief in or near Paris: *obl. sg.* **Guarlanda** 20.31 (see
note), **Guislanda** 20.31 var. [Doubtful; possibly Frankish **wiarōn* 'to
adorn' + **-el** + **-anda;** *FEW* 17: 575]

Garnier *n. masc.* Follower of Simon de Montfort: *nom. sg.* **Garniers**
25.22. [Germ. *Warin-hari; wara* 'shelter,' *hari* 'army'; Dauzat 279]

Gascon *n. masc.* Man from Gascony: *nom. pl.* **Gascon** 10.16, **Gasco**
21.63; *obl. pl.* **Gascos** 20.23. [CL tribal name VASCONES; Nègre 6346]

Gaucelin *n. masc.* Follower of Simon de Montfort: *nom. sg.* **Gaucelis** 25.74. [Germ. *Walho: walh-* 'foreigner' (Dauzat 282) + diminutive **-el** + **-in**]

Gauter *n. masc.* Follower of Simon de Montfort; possibly Gautier de Langton, but the name was used in a general sense by the Toulousains for the followers of Simon de Montfort (Martin-Chabot 2: 366); *nom. sg.* **Gauters** 25.23. [Germ. *Waldo* (*waldan* 'to govern' {Dauzat 282}) + *hari* 'army']

German *n. masc.* Man from Germany: *nom. pl.* **German** 21.63 var. [CL GERMĀNUS; *Oxf.*]

Giena *see* **Guiana**.

Girart *n. masc.* Character in the epic *Girart de Roussillon: nom. sg.* **Girartz** 24.33. [Germ. *Ger-hard: gari* 'lance,' *hard* 'strong'; Dauzat 288]

Giraut (1) *n. masc.* The troubadour Giraut de Bornelh as a character in his **tenso** with Alamanda: *vocative sg.* **Giraut** 19.9, 19.26, 19.41, **Seign'en Giraut** 19.57 var., **Segner Giraut** 19.57 var. [Germ. *Ger-wald: gari* 'lance,' *waldan* 'to govern'; Dauzat 288]

Giraut (2) *n. masc.* The troubadour Giraut Riquier: *nom. sg.* **en Guirautz Riqiers** 28.29, **·n Guirautz** 28.31; *obl. sg.* **en Giraut Riquier** 29.0. [See **Giraut** (1)]

Giraut (3) *n. masc.* Unidentified variant reading: *nom. sg.* **Guirautz** 22.11 var. [See **Giraut** (1)]

Glanda *see* **Canda**.

Gormont *n. masc.* Saracen king in the OFr. epic *Gormond et Isembart: nom. sg.* **·l reis Gormonz** 24.35. [Perhaps OFr. *Gourmon* 'scrofula; nickname of a scrofulous man' (Dauzat 302; cf. *T-L* 4: 454), from Frankish **worm* (*FEW* 17: 609), influenced by Germ. *mund* 'protection']

Grec *n. masc.* Greek man: *obl. pl.* **Grécx** 11.66. [CL GRAECUM]

Grecia *n. fem. (2 syllables)* Greece: *obl. sg.* **Grecia la regio** 11.54. [CL GRAECĬAM]

Guari *see* **Garin**.

Guarlanda *see* **Garlanda**.

Gui *n. masc.* Guy, count of Montfort, brother of Simon de Montfort: *nom. sg.* **en Guis** 25.65; *obl. sg.* **Gui lo comte** 25.53, **en Gui** 25.57. [Germ. *Wido: wid-* 'wood, forest'; Dauzat 316]

Guian *n. masc.* Man from Aquitaine: *nom. sg.* **Guians** 21.63 var.; *nom. pl.* **Guian** 21.63. [CL AQUĪTĀNUS (*Oxf.*), by aphaeresis and lenition; cf. **Guiana**]

Guiana *n. fem.* Aquitaine (Guyenne), province of France, capital Bordeaux: *nom. sg.* **Guiana** 12.68 var., 21.63 var., **Giena** 21.63 var. [CL AQUĪTĀNĬAM; *Oxf.*]

Guians *see* **Guian**.

Guilhem (1) *n. masc.* The troubadour Guilhem de Cabestanh: *nom. sg.* **Guillems de Capestaing** 3.1, 3.4; *obl. sg.* **Guillem** 3.7, **en Guillem de Capestaing** 3.8. [Germ. *Wil-helm: wil-* 'willpower,' *helm* 'helmet'; Dauzat 314]

Guilhem (2) *n. masc.* The character Guilhem de Nevers, lover of Flamenca: *nom. sg.* **Guillems** 30.24, 30.29, 30.34, 30.44, 30.69, 30.74, 30.86, 30.95. [See **Guilhem** (1)]

Guilhem (3) *n. masc.* Guillaume d'Orange, hero of the OFr. epic *Chanson de Guillaume: obl. sg.* **Guillem** 20.13. [See **Guilhem** (1)]

Guilhęm (4) *n. masc.* Follower of Simon de Montfort: *nom. sg.* **Wilelmes** 25.22. [See **Guilhem** (1)]

Guiraut *see* **Giraut.**

Guis *see* **Gui.**

Guislanda *see* **Garlanda.**

Guizan *n. masc.* Wissant (Pas-de-Calais), a port: *obl. sg.* **Guizan** 21.69. [Flemish *wit* 'white,' *zand* 'sand'; Nègre 18516]

Henrics *see* **Enric.**

Insebart *n. masc.* Isembart, Christian prince who converts to paganism in the OFr. epic *Gormond et Isembart: nom. sg.* **Insebartz** 24.35. [OFr. *Isembart,* Germ. *Isan-bard: īs* 'ice,' *bard* 'giant'; Dauzat 337]

Irlan *n. masc.* Irishman: *nom. pl.* **Irlan** 21.61. [back-formation from OOc **Irlanda**]

Irlanda *n. fem.* Ireland: *obl. sg.* **Yrlanda** 20.18. [Germ. *Irland* < Old Irish *Eriu* 'Ireland' + Germ. *land*]

Jacopiṇ *n. masc.* Jacobin monk, member of the Dominican order: *nom. pl.* **Jacopi** 26.27. [ML JACŎBUS < the first Dominican convent, founded in 1229 on the rue Saint-Jacques, Paris]

Jaufrę (1) *n. masc.* Geoffrey, count of Brittany, son of Henry II Plantagenet, younger brother of Henry Curtmantle and Richard Lionheart: *nom. sg.* **lo coms Jaufres cui es Bersilianda** 20.33. [Germ. *Gaut-frid: Gaut* 'name of a divinity,' *frid* 'peace'; Dauzat 288]

Jaufrę (2) *n. masc.* The troubadour Jaufre Rudel (**vida,** reading 1; poem 15): *nom. sg.* **Jaufres Rudels de Blaia** 1.1. *See also* **Blaia.** [**Rudel** < OOc **ruda** 'rue, a medicinal plant' (CL RŪTAM; *FEW* 10: 540) + diminutive **-el;** less likely < CL RŬDEM 'rude, coarse, ignorant,' because OOc **rude** is attested only from the 14th century; cf. Dauzat 531]

Jhesu *n. masc.* Jesus: *nom. sg.* **Jhesus** 12.43; *obl. sg.* **en Jezu** 10.23, **Jhesu Crist** 26.6; *vocative sg. (in prayer)* **Jhesu Crist** 25.29. *See also* **Crist.** [ChL JĒSUS, a Hebrew name; L & S]

Joan (1) *n. masc.* Saint John the Apostle; see 21.14 note: *nom. sg.* **Sans Johans** 27.48; *obl. sg. with gen. meaning* **San Joan** 21.14. [ChL JŌANNES; L & S]

Joan (2) **de Brezi** *n. masc.* Follower of Simon de Montfort: *nom. sg.* **·n Joans de Brezi** 25.37. [See **Joan** (1)]

Jozafat *n. masc.* The valley of Jehoshaphat in the Holy Land (Joel 3.2): *obl. sg.* **Jozafat** 12.8 (see note). [ChL IOSAPHAT]

Landa *n. fem.* The Landes, coastal region south of Bordeaux: *obl. sg.* **Landa** 20.23. [OOc **landa** (Ctc. **landa* 'meadow'; *FEW* 5: 158); Nègre 4026]

Launart *n. masc.* Saint Leonard, patron of prisoners: *obl. sg.* **Sanh Launart** 9.6. [Germ. *Leon-hard; Leon* 'lion' (borrowed from CL), *hard* 'strong'; Dauzat 382]

Lemoziṇ *n. masc.* The Limousin, region around Limoges (Haute-Vienne): *obl. sg.* **Lemozi** 9.1, 10.4, **Limozin** 5.1. [OOc **Lemoge** (Ctc. *lemo-* 'elm' + Ctc. suffix *-odius*; Nègre 2333) + **-in**]

Loirenc *n. masc.* Man from Lorraine: *nom. pl.* **Loirenc** 21.71, **Loairenc** 21.71 var., **Loiarenc** 21.71 var., **Lorench** 21.71 var., **Lorenchs** 21.71 var., **Loier** 21.71 var. [Germ. man's name *Lotharius* + Germ. suffix *-ing* 'man of'; Nègre 12430]

Lombart *n. masc.* Lombard, man from northern Italy: *obl. pl.* **Lombartz** 24.1 (see note). [It. *Lombardo,* CL Longobardus (L & S), Germ. tribal name *Langobardi: lang* 'long,' *bart* 'beard']

Longobart *n. masc.* Longobard, man from southern Italy: *obl. pl.* **Longobartz** 24.2 (see note 24.1). [CL Longobardus (L & S), Germ. tribal name *Langobardi: lang* 'long,' *bart* 'beard']

Lorench, Lorenchs *see* **Loirenc.**

Lormandia *see* **Normandia.**

Macári *n. masc.* Saint Macaire: *obl. sg.* **San Macari** 31.19 (see note). [CL Măcărĕum; *Oxf.*]

Maines *n. masc.* Le Maine, region of France, capital Le Mans: *nom. sg.* **·l Maines** 21.65. [Ctc. tribal name *Cenomani,* *Cenomana (regio) '(region) of the Cenomani,' thence *Cemaine; initial *Ce-* interpreted as demonstrative adj. and replaced by def. art.; Nègre 2463]

Mallio *n. masc.* Fictional emperor of Rome, see 11.29 note: *nom. sg.* **Torquator Mallios** 11.29, **Mallios Torquator** 11.43; *obl. sg.* **Mallio lo rei emperador** 11.35, **Mallio Torquator** 11.40. [CL Manlĭus, name of a Roman gens (*Oxf.*); **torquator,** deformation of CL torquātus 'wearing a collar or necklace,' as in the cognomen of T. Manlius Torquatus, dictator 353 B.C. (*Oxf.*)]

Marcabru *n. masc.* The troubadour Marcabru (readings 12–14): *nom. sg.* **Marcebrus** 12.2, 14.61; *obl. sg.* **Marcebru** 12.0. [Perhaps a backformation from **Marcabruna,** *which see*]

Marcabruna *n. fem.* Mother of the troubadour: *obl. sg. in gen. sense* **Marcebruna** 14.61. [OOc **marca bruna** 'brown mark' < Germ. *merki,* *brūn]

Marcebrus *see* **Marcabru.**

Marcilis, Marcilius *see* **Marsili.**

Maria *n. fem.* The Virgin Mary: *vocative sg.* **Sainta Maria** 27.45. [ChL Maria < Hebrew *Miriam,* influenced by CL Marĭus; Dauzat 416]

Marsel *see* **Saint Marsel.**

Marsili *n. masc.* Saracen ruler in the OFr. epic *Song of Roland: nom. sg.* **Marcilis** 24.34 (see note), **Marcilius** 24.34 var., **Marsilis** 24.34 var., **Marsili** 24.34 var., **Marsilles** 24.34 var., **Marseles** 24.34 var. [CL Marcĭlĭus, name of a gens; Dauzat 419]

Martels *see* **Charle Martel.**

Martin *n. masc.* Saint Martin of Tours (4th century): *nom. sg.* **Saint Martin** 26.38 (see note). [LL Martīnus < CL Mars, god of war; Dauzat 420]

Miquel *n. masc.* Saint Michael the archangel: *obl. sg.* **San Miquel** 31.36. [ChL Michael < Hebrew *Michaël* 'who is like God'; Dauzat 433]

Mirmanda *n. fem.* Castle in the city of Orange (Vaucluse): *obl. sg.* **Tor Mirmanda** 20.13 (see note). [Germ. personal name *Mirmanda*; Nègre 14948]

Monet *n. masc.* Joglar in the service of Guilhem IX: *vocative sg.* **Monet** 9.67. [Aphaeresis of **Aimonet** < **Aimon** + diminutive **-et;** Dauzat 439]

Monfort *see* **Montfort.**

Monsaurel *n. masc.* Montsoreau (Maine-et-Loire), on the Loire River in Anjou: *obl. sg.* **Monsaurel** 20.19. [OFr. *mont* 'mountain' + *sorel, soreau* 'reddish'; Nègre 21678]

Montaut *n. masc.* Montaut (canton of Carbonne, arrondissement of Muret, Haute-Garonne): *see* **Sicart de Montaut**. [CL MONTEM 'mountain' + ALTUM 'high'; Nègre 5275]

Montfọrt *n. masc.* Montfort (arrondissement of Rambouillet, Seine-et-Oise): *see* **Simon de Montfort**. [OFr. *mont* 'mountain' + *fort* 'strong, fortified'; cf. Nègre 21665]

Montoliu *n. masc.* One of the gates of Toulouse: *obl. sg.* **Montoliu** 25.15. [ChL MONTEM OLIVĀRUM 'Mount of Olives,' treated as MONTEM OLĪVUM; Nègre 30488]

Narbonẹs *n. masc.* The region around Narbonne: *obl. sg.* **Narbones** 3.1. [Pre-Celtic **narbon*, of uncertain origin and meaning; Nègre 1171]

Narcisus *n. masc.* Narcissus, who fell in love with his reflection: *nom. sg.* **Narcisus** 18.48 (see note). [CL NĂRCĬSSUS; *Oxf.*]

Nil *n. masc.* The Nile River: *obl. sg.* **·l Nill** 21.56. [CL NĪLUS; *Oxf.*]

Niort *n. masc.* Niort (Deux-Sèvres): *nom. sg.* **Niortz** 12.71 var.; *obl. sg.* **Niort** 12.71. [Ctc. *novio-* 'new' + *-ó-ritum* 'ford'; Nègre 3089]

Norman *n. masc.* Man from Normandy 21.62: *nom. pl.* **Norman** 21.62. *See also Glossary.* [Germ. tribal name *Nortmanni* 'men of the north'; Nègre 12436]

Normandia *n. fem.* Normandy: *obl. sg.* **Normandia** 5.10, 5.13, **Lormandia** 5.10 var. [Germ. tribal name *Nortmanni* 'men of the north' + **-ía**; Nègre 12436]

Pẹire (1) *n. masc.* Saint Peter, guardian of the gate of Heaven: *nom. sg.* **Saint Peire** 27.18, **Sayns Peires** 27.18 var. [ChL PĔTRUS, from Hebrew 'rock'; Dauzat 482]

Pẹire (2) *n. masc.* Interlocutor of Bernart de Ventadorn in a *tenso*: *vocative sg.* **Peire** 17.8, 17.22, 17.36, 17.46. [See **Peire** (1)]

Peire (3) **de Vezis** *n. masc.* Follower of Simon de Montfort: *nom. sg.* **·n Peire de Vezis** 25.24. *See also* **Vezis**. [See **Peire** (1)]

Peires *see* **Peire** (1).

Peitau *n. masc.* Poitou, region of France, capital Poitiers: *nom. sg.* **Peitaus** 12.68, **Peitou** 21.64; *obl. sg.* **Peitau** 10.4, 20.15. [Ctc. tribal name *Pictavi*; *-avus* gives *-au, -ou*; Nègre 2501]

Peitẹus *n. masc.* Poitiers (Vienne), capital of the region of Poitou: *nom. sg.* **Peiteus** 12.71 var.; *obl. sg.* **Peiteus** 20.20, **Peitieus** 10.10, 12.71. [Ctc. tribal name *Pictavi* treated as *Pictavis*, locative pl., with influence of ending **-iers;** Nègre 2500]

Peitou *see* **Peitau**.

Picart *n. masc.* Man from Picardy: *obl. pl.* **Picartz** 24.3. [OFr. *Picart* 'man from Picardy' < Middle Dutch *pickaert* 'soldier armed with a pike'; *FEW* 16: 622]

Polhẹs *n. masc.* Man from Apulia: *obl. pl.* **Poilhes** 24.1, **Polles** 24.1 var. [Aphaeresis of CL APŪLĬA (*Oxf.*) + **-ẹs**]

Proẹnsa *n. fem.* Provence, region of France, capital Aix-en-Provence: *obl. sg.* **Proensa** 2.2. [CL PROVĬNCĬA 'province,' comprising all southern Gaul from the Alps to Toulouse after the conquest by Caesar; after the Germanic migrations, Provincia designated the eastern region from the Rhône to the Alps; Nègre 6332]

Raimǫn (1) **del Castel de Rossillon** *n. masc.* Raimon de Castel-Roussillon; see 3.3 note: *nom. sg.* **Raimon del Castel Rossillon** 3.7, **en Raimon** 3.8; *obl. sg.* **en Raimon del Castel de Rossillon** 3.3, **Raimon del Castel de Rossiglon** 3.6. [Germ. *Ragin-mund: ragin* 'counsel,' *mund* 'protection'; Dauzat 507]

Raimǫn (2) **de Cornǫt** *n. masc.* Author of reading 31: **Frayre Ramon de Cornet** 31.0. [See **Raimon** (1), **Cornet**]

Raimǫn (3) **Izarn** *n. masc.* Follower of Simon de Montfort: *nom. sg.* **En Ramons Yzarns** 25.1. [See **Raimon** (1); Germ. *Is-arn: īs* 'ice, hardness,' *arn* 'ern, eagle'; Dauzat 337]

Raimǫn (4) **de Tolǫza** *n. masc.* Count Raymond V of Toulouse (1148–94): *obl. sg.* **comte Raimon de Tollosa** 5.14. *See also* **Toloza**. [See **Raimon** (1)]

Rayner *n. masc.* Follower of Simon de Montfort, perhaps Renaud d'Aubusson (Martin-Chabot 2: 203, note 6): *nom. sg.* **·n Rayners** 25.24. [Germ. *Ragin-hari: ragin* 'counsel,' *hari* 'army'; Dauzat 514]

Renart *n. masc.* The wily fox, protagonist of the *Roman de Renart: nom. sg.* **Renartz** 24.11. [Germ. *Ragin-hard: ragin* 'counsel,' *hard* 'strong'; Dauzat 515]

Richart *n. masc.* Richard Lionheart, son of Henry II Plantagenet, count of Poitiers and duke of Aquitaine, king of England 1189–99: *nom. sg.* **·l coms Richartz** 22.9, **Richartz** 22.11 var.; *nom. sg. form used for obl. sg. function* **son frair Richartz** 20.5, **sos frairs Richarz** 20.5 var.; *obl. sg.* **Richart** 20.5 var., **·n Richart** 20.26. [Germ. *Rīc-hard: rīc* 'powerful,' *hard* 'strong'; Dauzat 520]

Riqiers *see* **Giraut** (2).

Riquer *n. masc.* Follower of Simon de Montfort; since the name, normally **Riquier,** is Occitan but not French, Martin-Chabot (3: 204, note 3) speculates that it may represent **Ricartz,** Fr. *Richard,* modified for the sake of rhyme: *nom. sg.* **·n Riquers** 25.37. [Germ. *Rīc-hari: rīc* 'powerful,' *hari* 'army'; Dauzat 520]

Riquier *see* **Giraut** (2).

Roine *see* **Rozer**.

Rolan *see* **Rotlan**.

Rǫma *n. fem.* Rome: *obl. sg.* **Roma** 11.33, 11.34, 11.44, 11.57, 11.66. [CL Rōma]

Rosilhǫn *n. masc.* Roussillon, region of France, capital Perpignan: *obl. sg.* **Rossiglon** 3.6, **Rossillon** 3.1, 3.3, 3.7. *See also* **Castel Rossillon, Raimon** (1). [Perhaps Phoenician (Nègre 4526), from Semitic *rus, ros* 'head, chief, capital' + Pre-Celtic **kin,* of uncertain origin and meaning; Nègre 1177]

Rotlan *n. masc.* Roland, the hero who died at Roncevaux: *nom. sg.* **Rotlanz** 24.10; *obl. sg. with gen. sense* **Rolan** 21.47. [Germ. *Hrod-land: hrod* 'glory,' *land* 'land'; Dauzat 525]

Rǫzer *n. masc.* The Rhône River: *obl. sg.* **Rozer** 2.9, **Roine** 2.9 var. [CL Rhŏdănum in Caesar, from Pre-Celtic river name **rod* 'to flow, wetness' + Ctc. suffix *-ano;* Nègre 1063]

Rudels *see* **Jaufre** (2).

Saint Cerniṇ *n. masc.* Saint-Sernin, abbey in Toulouse: *obl. sg.* **Sent Cerni** 25.67. [CL Sᴀᴛᴜʀɴɪ̄ɴᴜꜱ < Sᴀᴛᴜʀɴᴜꜱ, the god; Dauzat 541; cf. Nègre 28329]

Saint Circ *n. masc.* Saint-Circ-d'Alzon, once a village (now disappeared) near Rocamadour (arrondissement of Gourdon, Lot): *obl. sg.* **Saint Circ** 5.16. *See also* **Ugon de Saint Circ**. [ChL Cʏʀɪ̆ᴄᴜꜱ; Dauzat 132; cf. Nègre 28346]

Saint Marsel *n. masc.* Saint-Marcel, commune in the canton of Cordes, arrondissement of Gaillac, Tarn: *obl. sg.* **San Marsel** 31.1 (see note). [ChL Mᴀʀᴄᴇ̆ʟʟᴜꜱ (CL Mᴀʀᴄᴜꜱ + diminutive -ᴇ̆ʟʟᴜᴍ); Dauzat 414; cf. Nègre 28470]

Salamoṇ *n. masc.* Solomon: *obl. sg. in gen. sense* **Salamo** 12.56. *See also* **Temple**. [ChL < Hebrew *shalom* 'peace'; Dauzat 537]

Salas *n. fem.* Salles (Tarn): *obl. sg. (etymologically pl.)* **Salas** 31.1. [OOc **sala** 'residence of a lord'; Nègre 27134]

San Marsel *see* **Saint Marsel**.

Sarraziṇ *n. masc.* Saracen, Muslim: *obl. pl.* **Sarrazis** 15.13, 29.35. [LL ꜱᴀʀʀᴀᴄᴇ̄ɴᴜꜱ, name of a nomadic people in Arabia (B-W); < Byzantine Gk. *Saraceni; FEW* 11: 217]

Sent Cerni *see* **Saint Cernin**.

Sermoṇda *n. fem.* Wife of **Raimon del Castel de Rossillon**, beloved of the troubadour Guillem de Cabestanh in the **vida**: *obl. sg.* **Sermonda** 3.3 (see note). [Reduction of **Seremonda**, dissimilation (like ꜱᴏʀᴏ̄ʀᴇᴍ > OOc **seror**) of **Soremonda** (see variants); the ML form of the same individual's name, Sᴀᴜʀɪᴍᴜɴᴅᴀ, is preserved in a document (see 3.3 note). Frankish **saur* 'yellow-brown' (*FEW* 17: 18) + Germ. *mund* 'protection, ward' + **-a**]

Sicart de Montaut *n. masc.* Follower of Simon de Montfort: *nom. sg.* •**n Sicartz de Montaut** 25.36. *See also* **Montaut**. [Germ. *Sig-hard: sig* 'victory,' *hard* 'strong'; Dauzat 551]

Simon de Montfort *n. masc.* Leader of the crusade against the Albigensians (died 1218): *nom. sg.* •**l cons de Monfort** 24.14 (see note), **le comte de Montfort** 25.55 var.; *vocative sg.* **Senher coms de Montfort** 25.18. *See also* **Montfort**. [ChL < Hebrew 'hearkening']

Simonet del Caire *n. masc.* Follower of Simon de Montfort, not identified historically (Martin-Chabot 3: 203, note): *nom. sg.* •**n Simonetz del Caire** 25.23. [**Simon** + diminutive **-et**]

Talairan *n. masc.* Elias VI Talairan, count of Périgord (1166–1205): *nom. sg.* **Talairans** 22.12. [Surname of counts of Périgord: 'the destroyer' = **talar** 'to destroy' (Dauzat 562) + **-airan;** Adams 402]

Teiric *n. masc.* Theodoric the Great (A.D. 455–526), king of the Ostrogoths, then king of Italy: *nom. sg.* **Teiríx** 11.50; *obl. sg.* **Teiric** 11.44, *with gen. sense* **Teiric** 11.58. [Germ. *Theud-rīc: theud* 'people,' *rīc* 'powerful'; Dauzat 569]

Temple *n. masc.* The military and monastic order of Knights Templars, or Brethren of the Temple of Solomon at Jerusalem, founded in 1119: *obl. sg.* (**la maion del**) **Temple** 1.7, (**sels del**) **temple Salamo** 12.56. [OOc **temple**]

Tholoza *see* **Toloza**.

Thomas *n. masc.* Follower of Simon de Montfort: *nom. sg.* **Thomas** 25.22. [ChL Tʜᴏᴍᴀs < Hebrew 'twin'; Dauzat 569]

Toloza *n. fem.* Toulouse (Haute-Garonne): *obl. sg.* **Toloza** 25.43, 25.89, **Tollosa** 5.14, **Tholoza** 25.20. [CL Tᴏʟᴏsᴀ in Caesar; Pre-Celtic **tolosa* or **tolossa*, of uncertain origin and meaning; Nègre 1189]

Torquator *see* **Mallio.**

Tors *n. fem.* Tours (Indre-et-Loire): *obl. sg. (etymologically pl.)* **Tors** 21.65. [Ctc. tribal name of the *Turones*, which became the name of their capital; Nègre 2533]

Toscan *n. masc.* Man from Tuscany: *obl. pl.* **Toscans** 24.1 var. [CL Tᴜsᴄᴀɴᴜs; L & S]

Trípol *n. fem.* Tripoli (Lebanon): *obl. sg.* **Tripoli** 1.2 (see note), 1.4, **Tripol** 1.2 var. [CL nom. sg. Tʀɪ̆ᴘᴏ̆ʟɪs, acc. sg. Tʀɪ̆ᴘᴏ̆ʟᴇᴍ; L & S]

Tristan *n. masc.* Senhal for a friend or patron, alluding to the lover of Iseut: *vocative sg.* **Tristan** 18.57. [Welsh *Dristan, Tristan*; Dauzat 578]

Ugon de Saint Circ *n. masc.* Troubadour who flourished 1217–53, apparently the author of the **vida** of Bernart de Ventadorn and of **razos** on Savaric de Mauléon, perhaps of others (but see 5.16 note): *nom. sg.* **n'Ucs de Saint Circ** 5.16. *See also* **Saint Circ.** [Germ. *Hugo,* acc. *Hugōnem: hūg-* 'understanding'; Dauzat 333]

Vaudes *n. masc.* Waldensian, follower of the twelfth-century heretic Waldo: *nom. sg.* **Vaudes** 26.30. [Germ. *Waldo: waldan* 'to govern' + **-es** (2)]

Vensa *n. fem.* Vence (Alpes-Maritimes): *obl. sg.* **Vensa** 2.9. [Ctc. man's name *Venucius* + **-a;** Nègre 3624]

Ventadorn *n. masc.* Fr. Ventadour, one of the four viscounties of the Limousin; the ruins of the castle are near Moustier-Ventadour (canton of Egletons, Corrèze): *obl. sg.* **Ventadorn** 17.1, **Ventador** 16.53, **Ventedorn** 5.1, 5.1, 5.4, 5.5, 5.16. *See also* **Bernart (2) de Ventadorn, Eble de Ventadorn.** [Possibly from Ctc. personal name *Venetus,* source of place-name *Venteigeol* (Corrèze) etc. (Nègre 2959); *-dorn* perhaps from Pre-Celtic river name **dora* (Nègre 1042)]

Vezis *n. masc.* Voisins (canton of Chevreuse, arrondissement of Rambouillet, Seine-et-Oise): *obl. pl.* **Vezis** 25.24. *See also* **Peire de Vezis.** [OOc **vezin** (1) 'neighbor'; cf. LL ᴠɪᴄɪɴᴏ̄s 'neighbors, village'; Nègre 5957]

Viana *n. fem.* The Vienne River, which rises in Corrèze, flows past Limoges, and joins the Loire: *nom. sg.* **Vian'** 12.68. [Pre-Celtic river name **vig* + Pre-Celtic or Celtic *-enna*; Nègre 1078]

Vianes *n. masc.* Le Viennois, the region of Vienne (Isère): *nom. sg.* **Vianes** 21.63 var. [Perhaps Ctc., uncertain meaning; Nègre 3653]

Vidal *n. masc.* Servant of Guilhem of Nevers in *Flamenca: obl. sg.* **Vidal** 30.1. [ChL ᴠɪᴛᴀ̄ʟɪs, name of several saints: 'relating to (eternal) life'; Dauzat 593]

Wilelmes *see* **Guilhem** (4).

Yrlanda *see* **Irlanda.**

Yzarns *see* **Raimon Izarn.**

Translations

Reading 1: Vida of Jaufre Rudel

(1) Jaufre Rudel of Blaye was a very noble man, and he was lord of Blaye. (2) He fell in love with the countess of Tripoli sight unseen, because of the good that he heard tell of her by the pilgrims who were coming back from Antioch. (3) And he made about her many songs with good melodies, [but] with poor words.

(4) Out of desire to see her he took the cross and set to sea; and sickness took him in the ship, and he was brought to Tripoli to an inn near death. (5) [This] was made known to the countess, and she came to him, to his bed, and took him in her arms. (6) And he realized that she was the countess, and at once he recovered the power of hearing and smell, and he praised God, who had sustained his life until he had seen her; and thus he died in her arms.

(7) And she had him buried with great honor in the house of the Templars, and then on the same day she became a nun, for the grief that she felt over his death.

Reading 2: Peire Vidal, "Ab l'alen tir vas me l'aire"

1
With my breath I draw toward myself the breeze
that I feel coming from Provence;
all that is from there pleases me,
so that when I hear [people] speaking well of it
I hear it with a smile,   5
and in exchange for one word I ask for a hundred;
I am so happy when I hear [people] speak well of it.

2
No one knows as sweet a place
as from the Rhône as far as Vence,
or as the sea and the Durance enclose,   10

517

or where such pure joy shines;
which is why among the noble people
I have left my heart rejoicing
with her who makes the sad ones laugh.

3
One cannot suffer on the day   15
that one has memory of her;
for in her joy is born and begins,
and whoever may praise her
does not lie in any good thing that he may say.
She is better (without debate!)   20
and nobler than [any other woman] who may be seen in the world.

4
So if I know how to say or do anything,
may she have thanks for it, for knowledge
she has given me, and understanding;
which is why I am joyful and full of song.   25
And everything I do that is pleasing
I get from her beautiful, charming person,
even when I reflect sincerely.

Reading 3: Vida of Guilhem de Cabestanh

(1) Guilhem de Cabestanh was a knight from the region of Roussillon, which bordered on Catalonia and the region of Narbonne. (2) He was very charming and esteemed in arms and service and courtesy.

(3) And there was in his region a lady who was called my lady Sermonda, wife of Sir Raimon of Castel de Roussillon, who was very wealthy and noble and wicked and harsh and proud. (4) And Guilhem de Cabestanh loved her (the lady) with true love and sang of her and made his songs about her. (5) And the lady, who was young and noble and beautiful and pleasing, loved him more than any creature in the world. (6) And [this] was told to Raimon of Castel de Roussillon, and he, like a wrathful and jealous man, investigated the situation and learned that it was true, and had his wife closely guarded.

(7) And when one day came, Raimon of Castel Roussillon found Guilhem eating without much company, and killed him and drew his heart out of his body; and he had it carried by a squire to his lodging, and had it roasted and prepared with a pepper sauce, and had it given to eat to his wife. (8) And when the lady had eaten it, the heart of Sir Guilhem de Cabestanh, Sir Raimon told her what it was. (9) And when she heard it, she lost sight and hearing. (10) And when she regained consciousness, she said, "Sir, you have indeed given me such good food that I shall never eat any other." (11) And when he heard what she had said, he ran to his sword and tried to strike her on the head; but she fled to the balcony and let herself fall down, and she died.

1
A knight was lying
with the creature he most loved.
Often kissing [her], he was saying to her,
"Sweet creature, what shall I do?
For the day comes and the night goes,   5
    Oh!
And I hear that the watch is crying,
'Away! Up! For I see the day
   coming after the dawn.'

2
"Sweet creature, if it could be   10
that never there were dawn or day,
a great mercy it would be,
at least in the place where there is
a true lover with what pleases him.
    Oh!   15
I hear that the watch is crying,
'Away! Up! For I see the day
   coming after the dawn.'

3
"Sweet creature, whatever they tell you,
I do not believe there is such a grief   20
as [one] that parts a lover from a beloved,
for I know it for myself;
alas, how little night is left!
    Oh!
I hear that the watch is crying,   25
'Away! Up! For I see the day
   coming after the dawn.'

4
"Sweet creature, I take my road.
I am yours wherever I may be;
for God's sake, don't forget me at all,   30
for the heart in my body remains here
and I shall never leave you.
    Oh!
I hear that the watch is crying,
'Away! Up! For I see the day   35
   coming after the dawn.'

5
"Sweet creature, if I didn't see you
soon, believe that I would die,

for my great desire would kill me;
which is why I shall return soon, 40
since without you I have no life.
     Oh!
I hear that the watch is crying,
'Away! Up! For I see the day
     coming after the dawn.'"

Reading 5: Vida of Bernart de Ventadorn

(1) Bernart de Ventadorn was from the Limousin, from the castle of Ventadorn. (2) He was of poor birth; he was the son of a servant who was a baker, who would heat the furnace to cook the bread of the castle. (3) And he became a handsome man and clever, and learned how to sing well and to compose, and he became courtly and well educated. (4) And the viscount of Ventadorn, his lord, was greatly pleased by him and his manner of composition and his singing, and did him great honor.

(5) Now the viscount of Ventadorn had a wife, young and noble and joyful. (6) And she was pleased by Sir Bernart and by his songs, and fell in love with him and he with the lady, so that he made his songs about her, about the love that he had for her and about her merit. (7) Their love lasted a long time before the viscount or anyone else became aware of it. (8) And when the viscount became aware of it, he became aloof from him, and had his wife closed up and guarded. (9) And he made the lady dismiss Sir Bernart, to depart and go far away from that region.

(10) And he departed and went to the duchess of Normandy, who was young and of great merit and very keen on reputation and honor and well-expressed praise. (11) And the songs of Sir Bernart pleased her greatly, so she received him and welcomed him very warmly. (12) For a long time he stayed in her court, and he fell in love with her and she with him, and he made many good songs about her. (13) And while he was with her, King Henry of England took her as his wife, and took her away from Normandy and took her to England. (14) Sir Bernart remained over here sad and grieving, and went to the good Count Raymond of Toulouse, and stayed with him until the count died. (15) And because of that grief, Sir Bernart entered the order of Dalon, and there he died.

(16) And what I, Sir Uc de Saint Circ, have written about him Viscount Eble de Ventadorn told me, who was son of the viscountess whom Sir Bernart loved. (17) And he made these songs that you will hear, written below.

Reading 6: Comtessa de Dia, "Ab joi et ab joven m'apais"

1
I nourish myself on joy and youth
     and joy and youth nourish me,
for my lover is the most joyful,
     so that I am charming and joyful;
     and since I am true to him, 5

it is quite fitting for him to be true to me;
for I never have ceased loving him,
  nor have I any intention to cease.

2
I am very pleased, for I know he is worth most,
  the one that I most desire to have me,   10
and as for the one who first brought him to me,
  I pray God to bring him great joy;
  and whoever may tell him evil about him,
let him not believe it, except what I have told him;
for a man often picks the rods   15
  with which he himself is beaten.

3
So a lady who cares for good reputation
  must surely put her affection
on a worthy, noble knight,
  once she recognizes his worth.   20
  Let her dare to love him openly,
for once a lady loves openly,
never again will the worthy or the valiant
  say anything but praise of her.

4
I have chosen one [who is] worthy and noble   25
  by whom merit improves and is ennobled,
generous and adroit and discerning,
  in whom there is wit and wisdom.
  I pray him to believe me,
and not to let people make him believe   30
that I would commit a disloyalty toward him—
  provided that I not find disloyalty in him.

5
  Lover, the worthy and valiant
recognize your valor;
and for this reason, I ask at once,   35
  if you please, your support.

Reading 7: Comtessa de Dia, "Estat ai en greu cossirier"

1
I have been in heavy grief
for a knight that I have had,
and I want it to be known forever
how excessively I have loved him;
  now I see that I am betrayed   5
since I did not give him my love,
which is why I have been in great bewilderment
  in bed and when I am dressed.

2
I would like very much to hold
my knight one evening naked in my arms,   10
for he would feel ecstatic
if only I served as his pillow.
    Since I am fonder of him
than Floris was of Blanchefleur,
I give him my heart and my love,   15
    my mind, my eyes, for my life.

3
Handsome lover, charming and good,
when shall I hold you in my power?
[I wish] I could lie with you one evening
and give you a loving kiss!   20
    Know that I would like very much
to hold you as my husband,
provided that you had promised
    to do everything I would want.

Reading 8: Guilhem IX, "Ab la dolchor del temps novel"

1
In the sweetness of the new season
the woods leaf out, and the birds
sing, each one in its language,
following the measure of the new song;
then it is well for a man to enjoy   5
what he most desires.

2
From the place from which I am most pleased and delighted
I see no messenger or sealed letter,
and so my heart neither sleeps nor laughs
nor dare I to advance   10
until I know for sure about our pact,
if it is as I ask.

3
Our love goes just like
the branch of the hawthorn bush
that remains on the tree   15
at night, in the rain and the frost,
until the next morning, when the sun spreads
through the green leaves and the branches.

4
I still remember one morning
when we made an end to war,   20
and when she gave me so great a gift,
her loving and her ring.

God let me live until
I can get my hands beneath her cloak again!

5
I have no care for their words   25
that would part me from my good neighbor,
for I know about words, how they go
with a short insinuation that spreads abroad;
some people go around boasting of love,
but we have the piece [of bread or meat?] and the knife.   30

Reading 9: Guilhem IX, "En Alvernhe part Lemozi"

1
In Auvergne beyond the Limousin
I went all alone [dressed] in a pilgrim's cloak;
I found the wife of Sir Guari
   and [the wife] of Sir Bernart;
they greeted me heartily   5
   by Saint Leonard.

2
Hear what I answered them:
I never mentioned iron or wood,
but I spoke to them these words:
   "Tarrababart,   10
marrababelio riben
   saramahart."

3
Lady Agnes and Lady Ermessen said,
"We've found what we have been seeking!
Let's put him up, simply and nicely,   15
   for he cannot speak,
and through him our secret
   will never be known."

4
The one took me under her cloak
and [that] was just fine with me;   20
they led me to their hearth,
   and I liked the fire,
and I warmed myself gladly
   by the great coals.

5
To eat they gave me capons,   25
and I dined avidly,
and the bread was hot, and the wine was good,
   strong and abundant;
and there was not even a scullion,
   just us three.   30

6

"Sister, this man is deceptive
and has stopped his speaking because of us.
Bring out our red cat
    quick and snappy,
for it will make him tell the truth,   35
    if he's lying at all."

7

When I saw the awful creature coming
(his fur was long, his whiskers ferocious,
I didn't like his company at all!),
    I was thoroughly frightened;   40
I nearly lost my desire
    and my courage.

8

When we had drunk and eaten,
I undressed according to their desire;
behind me they brought the cat,   45
    mean and nasty;
and they flayed me from my head
    down to my heel.

9

Lady Ermessen took it by the tail
and yanks, and the cat scratches;   50
they gave me more than a hundred wounds
    that time;
he seared me, but for all of that
    I didn't move at all.

10

Nor would I have even if someone had killed me,   55
until I had fucked them both
a lot, and it happened
    just as I wished;
I preferred to suffer the pain
    and the grievous torment.   60

11

I fucked as much as you will hear:
a hundred eighty-eight times!
My belt nearly broke
    and my harness;
and very great discomfort came to me,   65
    it hurt so bad.

12

Monet, you will go for me in the morning,
and carry my song in your pack
straight to the wife of Sir Guari
    and [to the wife] of Sir Bernart,   70

and tell them, for love of me,
    to kill the cat!

Reading 10: Guilhem IX, "Pos de chantar m'es pres talenz"

1
Since a desire to sing has come over me,
I shall make a song about what I am sad about;
no more shall I be obedient
in Poitou or in Limousin,

2
For now I shall go into exile;   5
in great fear and in great peril,
in war I shall leave my son,
and his neighbors will do him harm.

3
Departure is very difficult for me
from the lordship of Poitiers;   10
in protection of Foulque of Angers
I leave the land and his cousin.

4
If Foulque of Angers doesn't help him,
and the king from whom I hold my fief,
many men will do him harm,   15
treacherous Gascons and Angevins.

5
If he is not very wise and worthy
when I shall have left you,
soon they will have overturned him,
for they will see [that he is] young and weak.   20

6
For mercy I beg my companion;
if ever I wronged him (her), let him (her) pardon me
and pray to Sir Jesus of heaven
in vernacular and in his Latin.

7
I have been of prowess and joy,   25
but now we both do part;
and I shall go away to him
in whom all sinners find peace.

8
I have been very pleasant and joyful,
but our Lord wants it no more.   30
Now I can no longer bear the burden,
so near I have come to the end.

9

I have given up all I used to love,
chivalry and pride,
and since it pleases God, I accept it all,   35
and pray him to retain me with him.

10

All my friends I pray at my death
to come [where I am], all [of them], and honor me well;
for I have had joy and pleasure
far and near and in my domain.   40

11

Thus I give up joy and pleasure
and vair and gray [fur] and sable.

Reading 11: *Boeci*

1

As long as we are young men,
we speak with great folly, out of foolishness,
because we do not remember through whom we hope to live [eternally],
who sustains us as long as we walk on earth
and who nourishes us so that we do not die of hunger,   5
by whom we are saved if only we call out to him.

2

As young men we spend our youth so badly
that not a one cares if he betrays his kinsman,
if he mistreats his lord or his peer,
nor if one swears a false oath to another.   10
When he has done that, he repents not at all,
nor makes amends toward God.
It is scarcely noble if he undertakes to do penance:
he says he has undertaken it, but he never keeps it at all,
for he still does the same wicked deeds all the same.   15
So he leaves God, the great all-powerful,
who has the dead [man] and the living [men] completely in judgment.
Even the devils are in his power:
without God's permission they will never perform torture.

3

In earlier days men were wicked;   20
men used to be bad, now they are worse.
Boethius tried to chastise them;
in the hearing of the people he would make his sermon,
that they should believe in God who endured Crucifixion,
and that they would all gain redemption through him.   25
He suffered greatly, for he did not harvest abundance;
instead, out of envy they put him in prison.

4

Boethius was a lordly man, he had a good and noble person,
whom Manlius Torquator loved so much.
In wisdom he was not very idle;   30
he retained so much of it that he was not lacking at all.
Such a good example he left among us
[that] I do not believe there was a man of his wisdom in Rome.

5

He was count of Rome and was so esteemed
by Manlius, the emperor-king,   35
[that] he was the most highly regarded of all the domain;
they considered him the lord of all the empire.
But he had more noble renown for one reason:
they called him a teacher of wisdom.

6

When the end came to Manlius Torquator,   40
then such great grief came to Boethius's heart
[that] I do not believe that in comparison any other grief remained for
    him.

7

Dead was Manlius Torquator, of whom I speak.
Behold the emperor Theodoric in Rome;
he did not wish to make a friend of the [man] faithful to God.   45

8

He did not believe in God, our creator.
For this reason Boethius did not want him as his lord,
nor did he wish at all to hold his fief from him.

9

He chastises him so well with his sermon,
but Theodoric takes his words amiss;   50
out of great hatred he tried to make a criminal of him.
He had a letter made with great deception,
and had the name of Boethius written,
and sent it to the region of Greece.
On Boethius's behalf he told them this message: 55
that they should cross the sea equipped for battle,
he will surrender Rome to them by treachery.
Theodoric's intention was not at all good:
he had his messengers followed, and had them put in prison.

10

On the Capitoline hill the next day at dawn,   60
where they would decide the other punishments,
there came the king to carry out his plot;
Boethius was there, and his peers were there.
The king began to accuse him of treachery,
that he had sent the letters across the sea,   65

[that] he wanted to surrender Rome to the advantage of the Greeks.
But [such an idea] had never come into Boethius's mind.
He leaps to his feet and tried to defend himself;
the man did not let him proceed to his defense.
Those whom he had aided before failed him;   70
the king had him thrown into his prison.

11

Behold Boethius fallen into grief,
in great chains that weigh upon him;
he calls out to God, the king of Heaven, the great:
"*Domine pater,* I trusted so much in you,   75
in whose mercy are all sinners!
My poems, which have lost their song,
I had written about wisdom;
I weep all day, I follow the custom of a child,
all my desires return to weeping."   80

Reading 12: Marcabru, "Pax in nomine Domini!"

Here begins a song of Marcabru, who was the first troubadour who ever was.

1

Peace in the name of the Lord!
Marcabru made the measure and the melody.
    Hear how I tell
how the heavenly lord king
has made for us, in his mercy,   5
near us, a washing place
such that there has never been one like it except across the sea
toward Jehoshaphat, or here,
and I exhort you about this one here.

2

We should wash ourselves   10
evening and morning according to reason,
    I assure you.
Each of us has the opportunity to wash;
while he is hale and hearty
he should go to the washing place   15
which is a true remedy for us.
And if we go to death first,
we shall have a low dwelling instead of a high one on high.

3

But stinginess and faithlessness
divide youth from its companion.   20
    That is a grief
that everyone wants [to go] where
the gain will be infernal,
unless we run first to the washing place;

whoever keeps his mouth or eye closed,   25
there is not a one so fat with pride
that he will not find an enemy when he dies.

4
For the lord who knows all that is
and knows all that will be or ever was
    has promised us   30
honor and the title of emperor;
and the beauty (do you know what?)
of those who go to the washing place
will be greater than the morning star,
provided that we avenge God for the wrong   35
that pagans do him there toward Damascus.

5
Descended from the lineage of Cain,
of the first wicked man,
    there are so many now
that not a one bears honor to God.   40
We shall see who will be his heartfelt friend,
for by the virtue of the washing place
Jesus will be shared among us;
so let us turn the rascals back
who believe in augury and in fate!   45

6
Even if the lecherous wine tooters,
eager to dine by the fire,
    swaybacks on the road,
will remain in savage stench,
God intends to test the brave and the soft   50
at his washing place;
and those ones will watch over the lodgings,
so they will find a strong enemy.
By right they will come to such a guilty deed!

7
I know the marquis [is] in Spain   55
and those of the temple of Solomon;
    they suffer the weight
and the burden of the pride of the pagans,
which is why youth gains bad reputation.
And Christ, because of this washing place,   60
will come against the most mighty captains,
broken failures, weary of prowess,
who do not love joy or delight.

8
The French are degenerate
if they say no to the work of God,   65
    for I know how it is
about Antioch. Here the Vienne

and Poitou bewail merit and valor;
Lord God, in your washing place
put the soul of the count to rest,   70
and here may the Lord who rose from the sepulcher
protect Poitiers and Niort!

Reading 13: Marcabru, "L'autrier just'una sebissa"

1
The other day beside a hedge
I found a half-breed shepherdess
brimful of joy and wit,
and she was a daughter of a peasant woman;
cape and skirt, fur-lined cloak   5
she wore, and a shirt of canvas,
shoes and woolen hose.

2
Toward her I went over the field.
"Girl," I said, "you pretty thing,
I'm terribly worried that the wind will sting you."   10
"Sir," said the peasant girl,
"thanks to God and to my nurse,
I care little if the wind blows my hair,
for I am cheerful and healthy."

3
"Girl," I said, "you pious creature,   15
I have turned off the road
to keep you company,
for such a peasant girl
cannot, without companionable companionship,
pasture so much livestock   20
in such a place, so alone."

4
"Sir," she said, "whoever I am,
I can tell good sense from folly;
as for your companionship,
sir," said the peasant girl,   25
"let it stay where it belongs,
for someone thinks she has it
in her power who has only the show."

5
"Girl of noble conduct,
your father was a knight   30
who begot you, and your mother
was such a courtly peasant girl.
When I look at you more, you are prettier to me,
and for joy of you I brighten up;
if only you were a little humane!"   35

6

"Sir, my conduct and my family
I see go back and return
to the billhook and the plow,
sir," said the peasant girl;
"but some people pretend to be horsemen   40
who ought to do the same
six [working] days of the week!"

7

"Girl," I said, "a noble fairy
endowed you when you were born
with a refined beauty   45
above every other peasant girl;
and it would surely be doubled,
if I saw myself just once
on top, and you beneath."

8

"Sir, you have praised me so much   50
since you have raised me in merit
that now your love pleases me so much,
sir," said the peasant girl,
"[that] you will get in recompense
when you depart, 'Gape, fool, gape!'   55
and an idle wait at noon."

9

"Girl, a wild and savage heart
one tames by patience;
I can tell from passing acquaintance
that with such a peasant girl   60
one can make precious company
with friendship of the heart,
when one does not deceive the other."

10

"Sir, a man driven by folly
makes you promises and pledges payment;   65
thus you would do me homage,
sir," said the peasant girl,
"but never, for a little entrance fee,
do I intend to trade my deflowering
for the name of whore!"   70

11

"Girl, every creature
returns according to its nature.
Let us speak with pure words,"
I said, "little peasant girl,
in the shelter beside the pasture,   75
for you will be safer
to do the sweet thing."

12
"Sir, yes—but according to what's right
a fool seeks his folly,
a courtly man [seeks] a courtly adventure,   80
and the peasant [seeks an adventure] with the peasant girl;
'In many places there is a lack
because they don't take heed of measure,'
say the ancient folk."

13
"Pretty one, I have never seen   85
a more rascally girl with a face like yours
or more faithless in her heart."

14
"Sir, the owl augurs to us
that one person gapes at a painting
while another hopes for manna."   90

Reading 14: Marcabru, "Dire vos vuelh ses duptansa"

1
I want to tell you without doubt
the purpose of this song;
the words make many a comparison.
    Listen!
He who hesitates regarding prowess   5
makes semblance of a bad [man].

2
Youth fails and breaks and shatters,
and love is of such a kind
that it is begun after the hop [*erotic*];
    listen!   10
Each one takes some as he wants,
so then he won't be indebted.

3
Love goes like the spark
that mixes with the soot,
burns the wood and the straw   15
    (listen!),
and he doesn't know which way to flee
who is damaged by the fire.

4
I'll tell you how love destroys:
to you it sings, at him it peeps,   20
to you it speaks, to the other it makes the sign of the cross,
    listen!
It will be straighter than a line
before you are its intimate.

5
Love used to be straight,   25
but now it is twisted and notched,
and it has acquired such a flaw
    (listen!)
that when it cannot bite, it licks
more roughly than does a cat.   30

6
Never has love been true
since it separated the wax from the honey,
rather it knows so well how to peel the pear
    (listen!)
[that] it will be as sweet to you as the song of a lyre,   35
if only you touch your tail to it [*or*: touch its tail].

7
He who strikes a bargain with love
ties his tail to the devil;
he doesn't care if another rod beats him.
    Listen!   40
There's no solution but to scratch himself
until he has skinned himself alive.

8
Love is from a very wicked lineage;
it has slain many men without a sword.
God has not created a teacher so good   45
    (listen!)
that [love] can't make a fool of the wisest,
if it is true that [love] can catch him in his trap.

9
Love has the custom of a mare
that wants a man to follow it all day   50
and to mount from league to league.
    Listen!
And it won't ask you for a truce
whether you are fasting or have feasted.

10
Do you think that I don't know   55
if love is blind or one-eyed?
It smooths and polishes its deeds
    (listen!),
and stings more softly than a fly—
but a man is cured with greater difficulty.   60

11
Marcabru, son of Marcabruna,
was engendered under such a moon
that he knows how love falls [like a seed] from the husk.
    Listen!

He never loved any [woman] sincerely,   65
nor has he been loved by another.

12

If someone lives according to a woman's wit
it is right that harm should befall him,
just as the letter teaches.
    Listen!   70
May bad luck come your way,
if you don't all watch out!

Reading 15: Jaufre Rudel, "Lanqan li jorn son lonc en mai"

1

When the days are long in May
I like a sweet song of birds from afar;
and when I have gone away from there,
I remember a love from afar.
I go bent and bowed with desire,   5
so that neither song nor hawthorn flower
pleases me more than frozen winter.

2

Never shall I enjoy love
if I do not enjoy this love from afar,
for neither fairer nor better do I know   10
anywhere, neither near nor far.
Her merit is so true and fine
that there in the kingdom of the Saracens
[I wish] I were called, for her sake, a captive.

3

Saddened and rejoicing will I depart   15
when I see this love from afar;
but I do not know when I shall see her,
for our lands are very distant.
There are many passes and roads,
and for this reason I am not a prophet;   20
but let all be as it pleases God.

4

Joy will surely appear to me when I seek there,
for the love of God, lodging from afar;
and if it pleases her, I shall lodge
near her, though I am from afar.   25
Then will conversation seem noble,
when I, a distant lover, shall be so near
that with gracious words I shall enjoy solace.

5

I hold indeed the Lord to be true
through whom I shall see the love from afar.   30

But for one good thing that befalls me,
I have two harms, because it is so far from me.
Oh! [I wish] I were a pilgrim there
so that my staff and my cloak
would be reflected in her beautiful eyes! 35

6
May God, who made all that comes and goes
and formed this love from afar,
give me power, for I have the intention,
to see soon the love from afar
truly in agreeable places, 40
so that the chamber and the garden
might forever seem a palace to me.

7
He speaks the truth who calls me covetous
and desirous of love from afar,
for no other joy pleases me as much 45
as enjoyment of love from afar.
But what I want hates me so much
that my godfather fated me
to love but not to be loved.

8
But what I want hates me so much . . . ; 50
a curse on the godfather
who fated me not to be loved!

Reading 16: Bernart de Ventadorn, "Chantars no·m pot gaires valer"

1
Singing, for me, cannot be good
unless the song comes from the heart;
and song cannot come from the heart
unless there is true, sincere love there.
That's why my singing is best, 5
for I engage and devote to joy of love
my mouth and eyes and heart and mind.

2
May God never give me such power
that desire for love would not strike me;
even if I could never manage to get any of it 10
but every day sorrow would come to me,
I'll always have a good heart, at least;
and I have much more enjoyment,
for I have a good heart from it, and am attentive to it.

3
They criticize love out of ignorance, 15
foolish people, but there is no harm [to love];

for love can scarcely decline,
unless it is vulgar love.
That is not love; that
has only the name of it and the appearance,   20
which loves nothing unless it takes [profit].

4
If I wanted to tell the truth,
I know well from whom the deception comes:
from [women] who love for money,
and they are venal merchants.   25
[I wish] I were a liar and false!
I tell the truth in coarse language,
and I'm sorry that I'm not lying.

5
In pleasing and in yearning
is the love of two true lovers;   30
nothing can do any good
unless the desire is mutual.
And he is surely a fool since birth
who chides her for what she wants
and advises her what is not fitting.   35

6
I have placed my good hope very well,
since she shows me friendly looks
whom I most desire and want to see,
noble and sweet, true and loyal,
with whom the king would be blessed.   40
Pretty and graceful, with a lovely body,
she has made me a rich man from nothing.

7
I neither love nor fear anything else,
and nothing would be a hardship for me
if only I could please my lady,   45
for that day seems like Christmas to me
when she looks at me with her pretty,
spirited eyes—but she does it so slowly
that just one day lasts a hundred to me.

8
My verse is true and natural,   50
and good [is] he who understands it well;
and better he who awaits the joy.

9
Bernart de Ventadorn understands it,
and says it and makes it, and awaits the joy!

1
Friend Bernart de Ventadorn,
how can you keep yourself from song
when you hear the nightingale
rejoicing this way, night and day?
   Listen to the joy he expresses;   5
he sings all night beneath the flower.
He understands love better than you!

2
Peire, I like sleep and rest
better than listening to a nightingale;
and you could never say enough   10
to make me go back to madness.
   Praise to God, I am free from the chain,
and you and all the other lovers
have stayed behind in madness.

3
Bernart, he can scarcely be worthy or courtly   15
who cannot persevere in love;
and it can never make you suffer so much
that it isn't worth more than anything else,
   for if it causes pain, later on it compensates.
A man can scarcely get a great good without suffering,   20
but the joy always surpasses the weeping.

4
Peire, if the world were made
to please me for two years or three,
I tell you the truth about ladies:
they would never be wooed again at all,   25
   but would suffer such great pain
that they would do us such great honor
that they would woo us, not we them.

5
Bernart, it is improper
for ladies to woo; rather men   30
should woo them and beg their mercy.
And he is more foolish, in my opinion,
   than one who sows in sand,
who criticizes them or their merit;
and he is prompted by a bad teacher.   35

6
Peire, my heart is very sad
when I remember a false [woman]

who has killed me, and I don't know why,
except because I loved her truly.
 I have done a long penance,   40
and I know, even if I made it longer,
I'd find her still worse.

7

 Bernart, madness drives you
to separate this way from love,
by which a man gains merit and valor.   45

8

 Peire, he who loves goes mad,
because deceiving [women] among themselves
have stolen joy and merit and valor.

Reading 18: Bernart de Ventadorn, "Qan vei la lauzeta mover"

1

When I see the lark beat
his wings with joy in the [sun's] ray,
that forgets himself and lets himself fall
for the warmth that goes to his heart,
Oh! Such great envy comes to me   5
of anyone I see rejoicing
[that] I'm amazed that right away
my heart doesn't melt with desire.

2

Alas, I thought I knew so much
of love, and how little I know!   10
Since I cannot keep from loving
her, from whom I shall never get favor,
she has taken my heart and taken herself
and me myself and all the world,
and when she took herself she left me nothing   15
but desire and a yearning heart.

3

I despair of the ladies;
never again will I trust them,
for just as I have always defended them
so I shall stop defending them.   20
Since I see that not one of them does me good
with her who destroys me and confounds me,
I fear them all and distrust them,
for I just know they are all the same.

4

Love is lost for sure,   25
and I never even knew it;
for she who should have had the most

has none at all, so where shall I seek it?
Oh! how bad it looks to anyone who sees her,
that she lets this yearning wretch,   30
who will never have any good without her,
die, since she won't help him.

5
Since with my lady God helps me not,
nor mercy, nor the right I have,
and it does not please her   35
to love me, I shall never tell her;
and if she casts me off and denies me,
she has killed me, and I answer her as a dead man;
so I'll go away, if she doesn't keep me,
a wretch, in exile, I know not where.   40

6
I have never had power over myself
or been my own, ever since
she let me look into her eyes,
in a mirror that pleases me greatly.
Mirror, since I saw myself in you,   45
sighs from deep down have killed me;
for I lost myself, just as handsome Narcissus
lost himself in the fountain.

7
My lady looks just like a woman
for this, and so I reproach her,   50
for she doesn't want what she should want,
and she does what she is forbidden to do.
I have fallen into ill favor,
and I have acted just like the fool on the bridge;
and I don't know why it happens to me,   55
except because I climbed too high.

8
Tristan, you'll get nothing [no news] from me,
for I'm going away, grief-stricken, I know not where.
I cease and desist from singing,
and conceal myself from joy and from love.   60

Reading 19: Giraut de Bornelh, "S'ie·us quier cosselh, bel'ami'Alamanda"

1
"If I ask you for advice, beautiful friend Alamanda,
don't deny it to me, for a troubled man asks you for it;
for now your treacherous lady has told me
that I have been far away, gone out of her control;
what she gave me then, now she takes back and asks for.   5
    What do you advise me?

For my heart almost burns inside with anger,
  so strongly I am grieved."

2

"For God's sake, Giraut, a lover's wish
is scarcely accomplished or granted thus, all at once; 10
for if the one is false, the other should pardon,
lest their torment grow or expand.
But if she tells you that a high hill is a plain,
  you believe it
and let the good and the bad she sends you please you, 15
. for that way you will be loved."

3

"I cannot keep from scolding against pride,
even though you are a pretty maiden and blond;
a little anger upsets you and joy affects you little,
but you are neither the first nor the second! 20
But as for me, who fear that sadness will overhelm me,
  what do you advise me?
If I am afraid to die, that I should draw toward the wave?
  I think you advise me badly."

4

"If you ask me about such a deep subject, 25
by God, Giraut, I don't know what to answer;
but if it seems to you that I should be joyful for little [reason],
I prefer to harvest my meadow than that another should clip it.
Shall I conceal you [your infidelity] out of desire to make a pact?
  Now you are seeking 30
a way for her not to remove her good self, [even though she is] in second
    place!
  It seems quite clear that you are troubled."

5

"Maiden, from now on don't be too talkative!
If she has lured me more than a hundred times first,
do you advise me then to put up with it always? 35
Wouldn't you think I was doing it out of lack
of another friendship? Now I want to strike you;
  why don't you be quiet?
Lady Berenguieira would have given better counsel
  than you give me." 40

6

"I see the time, Giraut, when she will repay you
because you call her fickle and frivolous;
do you think for that reason I won't ask about the pact for you?
But I don't think she is so tame,
rather from now on her promise will be final, 45
  whatever you say,
if she tempers herself enough to seek from you
  from now on a truce or a peace."

7

"Beautiful one, for God's sake let me not lose your help,
for you well know how it was promised me;   50
if I have failed because of the anger I had,
don't let it harm me; if you have felt how easily changes
the heart of an angry man in love, if ever you have been a sweetheart [i.e.,
  in love],
    think about this peace,
for I tell you truly, I am as good as dead if I have lost her—   55
    but don't reveal this to her!"

8

"Sir friend, I would have already wanted an end to it,
but she told me she was right to be angry,
because you wooed another quite openly, like a fool,
who is not her equal either dressed or naked.   60
Will she not act, then, if she does not throw you over, like a conquered
  woman,
    if you woo another?
I'll surely help you, although I have supported her [before],
    if only you don't get involved anymore [with the other woman]."

9

"Beautiful one, for God's sake, if you are believed by her,   65
    for my sake, assure her of it."

10

"I shall do it, but when she is returned to you,
    don't deprive yourself of her love!"

Reading 20: Bertran de Born,
"D'un sirventes no·m cal far loignor ganda"

1

It doesn't concern me to make longer delay with a sirventes,
such desire I have to say it and spread it;
I have a subject so unusual and so great
about the Young King, who has dropped his claim
on his brother Richard, because his father commands it.   5
    He is so compelled!
Since Sir Henry neither holds nor governs land,
    let him be king of the fools!

2

He acts like a fool since he lives this way, entirely
on an allowance, by count and by measure.   10
A crowned king who takes food from another
scarcely resembles Arnaut, the marquis of Beaulande,
or brave Guillaume, who conquered Mirmanda Tower.
    How he was esteemed!
Since in Poitou [Sir Henry] lies to [his men] and cheats them,   15
    he will never be loved there as much.

3

Never by sleeping will he be king
of the English of Cumberland, or conquer Ireland,
or hold Angers or Montsoreau or Candes,
nor will he have the watchtower of Poitiers,   20
or be duke of the Norman land,
    or count palatine
either of Bordeaux or of the Gascons beyond the Landes,
    or lord of Bazas.

4

I want to give some advice to Richard, there,   25
to the tune of Lady Alamanda, though he doesn't ask me for it:
no more should he flatter his men because of his brother.
He never does anyway; instead he besieges them and keeps them on the
     run,
steals their castles, and destroys and burns
    on all sides!   30
And let the [Young] King tourney there with the men of Guarlanda,
    and the other one, too, [who is] his brother-in-law.

5

I wish Count Geoffrey, to whom Brocéliande belongs,
    had been the first born,

6

for he is courtly, and I wish the kingdom   35
    and the duchy were in his command.

Reading 21: Bertran de Born, "Mon chan fenis ab dol et ab maltraire"

1

I end my song in grief and suffering
for evermore and think it finished,
for I have lost my subject and my joy
and the best king that was ever born of a mother,
    generous and well-spoken,   5
    and a good horseman,
    of friendly appearance
    and humble manner
    to do great honors.
    I believe that grief torments me   10
    so much that it will kill me,
    for I go about talking about it.
    I commend him to God;
  may He put him in the place of Saint John.

2

You would have been king of the courtly and emperor of the noble,   15
lord, if you had lived longer;
for you had gained the name "Young King,"

and you were the guide and father of youth.
    And hauberks and swords,
    and beautiful buckram,   20
    helmets and gonfalons,
    doublets and lappets,
    and joy and love
    have no one to maintain them
    or to bring them back.   25
    They will follow you there;
    for they will disappear with you,
  and [so will] all mighty, honorable deeds.

3
Noble hospitality and giving without a fickle heart,
and fair conversation and warm welcome,   30
and a great court, well paid and well kept up,
gifts and equipment and living without doing wrong,
    eating to the sound
    of viol and song,
    with many a companion   35
    bold and mighty
    among all the best—
    I want it all to go with you,
    let nothing be kept
    in this vile world   40
    after this ill-starred year
  that showed us an agreeable prospect.

4
Lord, in you there was nothing to change:
the whole world had chosen you
for the best king who ever bore a shield,   45
and the bravest one and the best tourney goer.
    Since the time of Roland
    and even before,
    a man never saw so noble [a king]
    or one so skilled in war,   50
    or one whose fame
    so spread through the world
    and gave it new life,
    one who sought fame,
    looking for it everywhere   55
  from the Nile to the setting sun.

5
Lord, because of you I want to renounce joy,
and all those who had seen you
must be grieved and mute because of you—
and may joy never shine on me—   60
    Bretons and Irish,
    English and Normans,
    Aquitanians and Gascons.
    And Poitou suffers,

and Maine and Tours. 65
Let France weep without ceasing
as far as Compiègne,
and Flanders from Ghent
as far as Wissant.
Even the Germans weep! 70

6

When the Lorrainers and the Brabançons
go tourneying,
they will mourn when they don't see you.

7

I care not a penny
or the blow of an acorn 75
for the world or those who are in it,

8

because of the grievous death
of the good, worthy king,
in which we must all suffer.

Reading 22: Bertran de Born, "Ges de far sirventes no·m tartz"

1

I don't delay at all to make a sirventes,
rather I do it without any effort,
so subtle are my wit and my art.
I got such a head start,
and I know so many tricks 5
that behold! I have escaped;
for neither counts nor kings
have power over me, nor cares.

2

And since the king and Count Richard
have exempted me from their ill will, 10
let Sir Aimar or Sir Amblart
never give me peace, or Sir Talairan.
Of Autafort,
I won't give him a garden!
Whoever wants to may attack me, 15
for have it I must!

3

I'm so strong on every side
that the shreds of war cling to me.
A sty in his eye, if you part me from it!
Even if I started it first, 20
peace gives me no comfort.

To war I'm attuned,
for I do not keep or believe in
any other law!

4
I don't observe Monday or Tuesday   25
or weeks or months or years;
not even for April or March do I stop
scheming how harm may come
   to those who wrong me.
   But never by any stroke of luck   30
   will the three of them conquer
   as much as a strap!

5
Whoever makes cleared fields from woods,
I've always been getting in trouble
over how to get bolts and spears,   35
helmets and hauberks, horses and swords.
   I comfort myself
   and keep myself amused—
   with war and the tourney,
   giving and flirting.   40

6
My partner is so outrageous
that he wants my children's land,
and I'm such a dupe I'm willing to give it to him.
Then they'll all say, "Flabby Sir Bertran!"
   But even if he hadn't wronged me so much,   45
   I believe he will come
   to a bad port, I assure you,
   before he'll talk to me.

7
   I don't care anymore
   about doing right or wrong about Autafort,   50
   for I accept the decision
   of my lord, the king.

Reading 23: Castelloza, "Amics, s'ie·us trobes avinen"

1
   Friend, if I had found you charming,
humble, open, and compassionate,
I would have loved you indeed—since now I realize
that I find you wicked, despicable, and haughty toward me,
yet I make songs to make   5
your good name heard; which is why I cannot keep
from making everyone praise you
when most you cause me harm and anger.

2

Never shall I consider you worthy,
nor shall I love you from the heart or with trust;   10
in truth I'll see if ever it would do me any good
if I showed you a cruel and hostile heart.
—I will never do it, for I don't want you to be able to say
that I ever had an intention to be false to you;
you would have some defense,   15
if I had committed disloyalty toward you.

3

I know well that it pleases me,
even though everyone says that it's very improper
for a lady to court a knight herself
or make him so long a sermon all the time.   20
But whoever says that doesn't know how to discern well at all,
for I want to court before I let myself die,
since in courting I find much sweet healing,
when I court the one from whom I get great care.

4

He is quite a fool who reproaches me   25
for loving you, since it is so very pleasing to me;
and he who says it doesn't know how it is with me,
nor has he seen you with the eyes I saw you with
when you told me not to worry,
that at any time it could happen   30
that I would again have joy.
From your mere word I have a rejoicing heart.

5

All other love I consider nothing—
so know well that joy no longer sustains me,
but for yours that delights me and heals me   35
when most pain and distress come to me.
By my lamentation and lays I always hope
to enjoy you, friend, because I cannot convert;
I have no joy, nor do I expect help,
except only as much as I'll get while sleeping.   40

6

From now on I don't know why I present myself to you,
for I've tested with evil and with good
your hard heart—which my own doesn't renounce.
And I don't send you this, for I say it to you myself:
I shall die unless you are willing to make me rejoice   45
with whatever joy. And if you let me die,
you will commit a sin, and you'll be in torment for it,
and I'll be more sought after at Judgment.

1

I consider fools the Apulians and North Italians
and South Italians and Germans,
if they want French or Picards
as lords or as interpreters,
    for murder and wrong   5
    they consider amusement,
    and I do not praise a king
    who does not obey the law.

2

And he will need a good standard
and to strike better than Roland   10
and to know more than Renard
and to have more than Corbaran
    and to fear death less
    than the count of Monfort,
    if he wants by means of violence   15
    [to make] the world submit to him.

3

And do you know what will be his share
in the wars and in the tumult?
The apprehension and fear and danger
that he will have caused, and the torment and harm   20
    will be his by fate;
    this much I advise him,
    that with such booty
    he will come from the tourney.

4

Man, little is worth your wit and skill   25
if you lose your soul for the sake of your children,
if you burn yourself for someone else's grilled meat
and if his repose becomes your grief,
    and for this reason you come to a pass
    from which I believe each man carries   30
    the deception and intrigue
    and the wicked deeds that he ever committed.

5

Never did Charles Martel or Girart
or Marcilius or Agolanz
or King Gormond or Isembart   35
kill so many men
    that they got from it

the price of a garden,
nor do I envy them
wealth or adornment.   40

6

I do not believe that at death
any man takes with him more
wealth or adornment
than what he did here.

Reading 25: *Chanson de la Croisade albigeoise*

Sir Ramon Yzarn cried out, "Let's give [it] to these drunkards!
Knights, to arms! Remember the plan!"
The battle of swords and lances and heavy bolts
begins again, and the ordeal and the slaughter.
But those of the town were so superior to them   5
that inside the wattle shelters they were their equal in combat,
and, striking, they knock down their crystals and their golden ornaments
        [of their helmets].
But to the men from the outside there came such disarray
that they could not endure the threatening perils,
so they left the shelters; but [once they were] on their chargers,   10
the slaughter began again with such carnage
that feet and fists and arms flew in pieces,
and the ground was red with blood and brains.
Even on the river, foot soldiers and boatmen fight them.
Outside at Montoulieu there was general combat,   15
when Sir Bartas spurred right up to the entryway of the gates.
Then a squire came toward the count, shouting,
"Lord Count de Montfort, you seem too hesitant;
today you will take great loss, since you are so sanctimonious!
For the men of Toulouse have killed the knights   20
and your troops and the best mercenaries,
and Wilelme has died there and Thomas and Garnier
and Sir Simonet del Caire, and Gauter is wounded.
And Sir Peire de Vezis and Sir Ayme and Sir Rayner
are resisting the attacks and defending the men behind the shields.   25
And if this slaughter and torment last any longer,
you will never be the inheritor of this land!"
And the count trembled and sighed and became sad and somber,
and said at the [moment of the] consecration, "Righteous Jesus Christ,
grant me death today on earth, or to be victorious!"   30
After that he sent to tell the troops
and the barons of France and his mercenaries
to come all together on their Arabian coursers;
with that, fully sixty thousand come.
And the count came swiftly, first before the others,   35
and Sir Sicart de Montaut and his standard-bearer
and Sir Joan de Brezi and Folcaut and Sir Riquer,
and after [them] the great throngs of all the pilgrims.

And the outcry and the trumpets, and the blast and the war cries,
the slaughter of the catapults and the carnage of the slings   40
seemed snow or wind, thunder or storm,
so that the town trembled and the river and the bank.
To the men of Toulouse there came such fright
that [the French] felled many of them running in the trenches.
But soon the recovery was made,   45
for they leapt out through the gardens and the orchards,
and foot soldiers and lancers captured the square.
Of slender arrows and thick quarrels
and round stones and great, rapid blows
on both sides there was such a blaze   50
that it seemed like wind or rain or a swift-running torrent.
But an archer shot from the parapet on the left
and wounded Count Guy in the head of his charger,
and the bolt was halfway in his brain.
And when the horse turned, another crossbowman   55
with a [cross]bow equipped with a windlass shot at him from the side
and hit Sir Guy in the left side
so that the steel remained in his naked flesh,
and his side and his breeches were red with blood.
The count came to his brother, who was dear to him,   60
and dismounted and said impious words:
"Fair brother," said the count, "me and my companions
God has visited with wrath, and he is protecting the mercenaries;
because of this wound I shall become a Hospitaler!"
While Sir Guy spoke and complained,   65
there was on the inside [of the town] a catapult that a carpenter made,
and the catapult had been drawn from Saint-Sernin onto the platform,
and ladies, both girls and wives, were shooting it.
And the stone came straight where it was needed
and struck the count on the helmet, which was of steel,   70
so that it smashed to pieces his eyes and brains
and back teeth and forehead and jaws;
and the count fell to the ground dead and bleeding and discolored.
Gaucelin and Sir Aimer spurred in that direction
and covered the count, with haste and care,   75
with a blue cape, and panic spread.
Then you could have heard so many knight-barons lament,
lamenting under their helmets and saying bitter words.
Aloud they cried, "God! You are not just,
since you allow the death of the count and this loss;   80
he is surely a fool who defends you or is your vassal,
since the count, who was benevolent and enterprising,
has died by a stone, as though he were a devil.
And since you cut to pieces and strike your very own men,
no more shall we serve in this land!"   85
With that they carry the count to the clerks, who knew how to read;
and the cardinal and the abbot and Bishop Folquet
received him with grief, with crosses and censers.
And a messenger entered Toulouse

who told them the news; and there was such rejoicing   90
that throughout the city they ran to the churches
and lighted the candles in all the candle stands;
and they shouted, "What joy! For God is merciful,
since Nobility burns bright and will henceforth be victorious.
And the count, who was wicked and murderous,   95
has died without penance, because he was bloodthirsty."
But the horns and the trumpets and the communal joy,
the ringing and the peals and the chimes of bells
and the drums and kettledrums and the slender bugles
make the town and the pavings echo.   100
Then the siege is raised ([the men depart] along all the paths)
which was across the river and occupied the banks.
But nevertheless they left their possessions and the packhorses
and their pavilions and tents and their harness and their money;
and the men of the town took many prisoners.   105
But on the inside [of the town] they lost one who was useful,
young Sir Aimeriguet, courtly and pleasant,
in whom the loss was great, and harm and unhappiness
    for all those of the town.

Reading 26: Peire Cardenal, "Ab votz d'angel, lengu'esperta, non blesza"

1

With the voice of an angel, with a skilled tongue, not stammering,
with subtle words, smoother than the work of an English [weaver],
well placed, well said, and without repetition,
better heard, without coughing, than learned,
    with groans, sighs, they show the way   5
    of Jesus Christ, which each man should
take, as he chose to take it for our sake;
they go about preaching how we can have God . . .

2

. . . Unless, like them, we eat good shelled beans
and soup so well beaten that a man could drink it,   10
with rich sauce from a country hen,
and on the other hand, fresh verjuice with beets,
    and wine that could not [be] better,
    on which a Frenchman gets drunk the more easily.
If by living well and eating and lying around   15
a man conquers God, they may well conquer him . . .

3

. . . Just like those who drink beer
and eat bread of pure bran for [love of] God,
and the broth of the fat ox gives them great revulsion
and they don't want seasoning of oil at all   20
    or a fresh, fat fish from a fishpond
    or soup or sauce that fries.

For this reason I advise whoever has his hope in God
to eat of their feasts, if he can get some.

4
The first religious order was founded   25
by people who did not want strife or noise,
but Dominicans have no calm after eating,
rather they argue over the wine, which one is better.
    And they have established a court of conflicts,
       and anyone who deters them from it is [considered] a Waldensian;   30
and they want to know the secrets of a man
the better to make themselves feared.

5
Their poverty is not spiritual;
they keep what is theirs, they take what is mine.
For soft robes woven with English wool   35
they leave a hair shirt, because it is too harsh for them.
    Nor do they part their garment,
      as Saint Martin did;
but they want to have all the alms
with which one used to help poor people.   40

6
With elegant clothing, ample, with a broad hood,
of woolen cloth in summer, thick in winter,
with strong shoes soled in the French style
when it is very cold, of fine Marseille leather,
    quite strongly sewn with skill   45
    (for poor sewing is a great folly),
they go about preaching with their subtle knowledge,
that we should put our heart and wealth in serving God.

7
If I were a husband, I would have great displeasure
that a man with no pants should sit beside my wife;   50
for women and they have skirts of the same breadth,
and fire catches very easily from grease.
    I wouldn't say a thing to you about Beguines;
    such a one is sterile who bears fruit,
they do such miracles, I know this for truth;   55
of holy fathers, holy may be the heirs.

Reading 27: Peire Cardenal, "Un sirventes novel voill comensar"

1
I want to begin an unusual sirventes
that I shall perform on the day of judgment
to him who made me and formed me from nothing.
If he intends to accuse me of anything
and tries to put me in Hell,   5

I shall tell him, "Lord, mercy, let it not be,
for I tormented the wicked world all my years;
so protect me, please, from the torturers."

2
I shall make all his court marvel
when they hear my plea,   10
for I say he commits a wrong toward his own
if he intends to destroy them and send them to Hell;
for he who loses what he could win
by rights has lack instead of abundance,
so he should be kind and generous   15
in appointing his dying souls [as retainers].

3
You should never refuse your gate,
for Saint Peter takes great shame by that,
who is the gatekeeper; but let every soul
enter smiling that wants to enter there,   20
for no court is ever quite perfect
if one man weeps and if the other laughs;
so even though you are a sovereign and powerful king,
if you don't open to us, a complaint will be made to you.

4
You ought to disinherit the devils,   25
and you would get more souls and [get them] more often,
and the disinheritance would please everybody;
and you could pardon yourself yourself.
(For all of me he would destroy them all,
since they all know he could absolve himself.)   30
Fair Lord God, please disinherit
the envious and vexatious enemies!

5
I do not wish to despair of you,
rather I have in you my good hope
that you will help me at my death,   35
which is why you must save my soul and my body.
So I shall offer you an attractive choice:
either I return to where I started on the first day,
or you pardon me for my wrongs—
since I would not have committed them, if I had not been born first.   40

6
If I have harm here and had it in Hell,
by my faith, it would be a wrong and a sin;
for I can surely reproach you
that for one good thing, I have a thousand times more bad.

7
For mercy I beg you, lady Saint Mary,   45
to be a good guide for us with your son
so that he will take the father and the children
and put them where Saint John is.

The fourth *pastorela* of Sir Guiraut Riquier, in the year 1267.

1
The other day I found the shepherdess
that I found at other times
watching lambs, and she was sitting,
and she was of a pleasing manner;
but she was greatly changed,   5
for she was holding a little child
that was sleeping in her lap,
and she was spinning like a sensible woman.
I thought that she would remember me
because of the three times she had seen me   10
until I saw that she did not recognize me,
for she said, "You there, are you leaving the road?"

2
"Girl," I said, "your pleasing company
delights me so
that now I need your aid."   15
She told me, "Sir, I am not as silly
as you think I am,
for my attention is on something else."
"Girl, you are making a great mistake,
since I have loved you for so long without infidelity."   20
"Sir, until this very day
I never saw you, so it seems to me."
"Girl, is your memory failing?"
"No, sir, if you understand me."

3
"Girl, without you nothing could   25
give me a cure of this illness,
it has been so long since you [first] pleased me."
"Sir, Guiraut Riquier
used to tell me the same thing insistently,
but he never put me to shame."   30
"Girl, Sir Guiraut hasn't forgotten you;
don't you remember me?"
"Sir, he and the pleasant sight of him
please me more than you!"
"Girl, you have escaped him too often."   35
"Sir, if he comes, I really think he will conquer me."

4
"Girl, my joy begins,
for I am surely he because of whom
you are renowned in song."
"Sir, you are not, and I wouldn't   40
believe it ever in my life;
you don't even resemble him."

"Girl, Good Conduct brings me forward,
who has been your guide three times."
"Sir, rumor is nothing;   45
you hope to give yourself too much honor."
"Girl, do you have any memory of me?"
"Yes, sir, but not complete."

5
"Girl, I have made you famous,
but I think it a great vexation;   50
don't think I'll ask you again."
"Sir, I am quite satisfied,
since now I have taken vengeance
for that last meeting."
"Girl, with whom are you a partner   55
in this child? Was it [a moment] of pleasure?"
"Sir, with [a man with whom] I hope to have more,
for he took me [as his wife] in church."
"Girl, why does he leave you on a riverbank?"
"Sir, because it is my custom."   60

6
"Could we reach an agreement
together, charming girl,
if I concealed your part in it?"
"Sir, not of any other friendship
than we formed on that first occasion,   65
since I have kept myself [from you] until now."
"Girl, I have tested you well,
and I find you thoroughly sensible."
"Sir, if I had been frivolous,
you would scarcely have made me sensible."   70
"Girl, I go to do my day's work."
"Sir, take to your road!"

Reading 29: Guiraut Riquier, "Be·m degra de chantar tener"

The twenty-seventh *vers* of Sir Guiraut de Riquier, in the year 1292.

1
I should indeed cease to sing,
for happiness befits a song
but distress so torments me
that it makes me ache on every side,
remembering my unpleasant past,   5
looking at the cramped present
and considering the future,
so that for all [three] I have reason to weep.

2

For this [reason] my song cannot have
savor for me, since it is without happiness,   10
since God has given me such wisdom
that as I sing I tell my folly,
my wit, my joy, my displeasure,
both my loss and my gain, in truth;
for I scarcely say anything well otherwise,   15
since I have come too late.

3

Now no craft is welcomed
less in court than [the craft] of pleasing skill
in composition; for they prefer there
to hear and see frivolous behavior   20
and cries mixed with dishonor;
for everything that used to give praise
has been forgotten as much as possible,
for almost the whole world has fallen into fraud.

4

Because of the pride and the wickedness   25
of so-called Christians, far from love
and from the commands of our Lord
we are driven from his holy place
with many other woes,
so that it seems that he is hostile toward us   30
because of [our] disordered will
and reckless power.

5

We must fear the dire peril
of double death, which is near:
to feel the Saracens arrogant toward us,   35
and that God becomes indifferent toward us;
and since we are angry among ourselves,
we soon will be completely brought low,
and our leaders, as it seems to me,
do not consider their responsibilities.   40

6

May he whom we profess in unity,
power, wisdom, goodness,
grant to his creatures light
by which sinners may be cleansed.

7

Lady, mother of charity,   45
grant us out of pity
from your son, our redeemer,
grace, pardon, and love.

Reading 30: *Flamenca*

He had the servant, whose name was Vidal,
bring water and salt
to make holy water,
and when he had taken some to wash his hands,
the chaplain was awakened.   5
He gave him some water for his hands
and they began their prime,
and when they had sung tierce
and heartily sounded their peal,
as was customary,   10
all the people came to Mass.
After the densest crowd
came Sir Archimbaut, as he usually did,
last of all, and according to his wish,
it would not have been Sunday or a feast day.   15
He looked like a devil with his head,
one of those that are painted with shaggy hair;
if Flamenca never pretends
[to be] joyful in his love, she is not at all wrong,
for a lady who sees such a devil   20
can be very frightened;
nevertheless, after him she comes
and enters his box.
Guilhem had seen it, I believe,
for he was thinking of nothing else;   25
if someone did not agree with me about this opinion,
I would not agree with him very well
even if he pledged me his faith.
Guilhem knew his business very well,
knew the office well, and the offertory   30
by heart, and the communion.
The chaplain made no sermon,
nor announced a feast for that week.
Guilhem had a clear, hearty voice,
and sang with full throat   35
at the Agnus Dei, and he took
the Peace just as he was supposed to do,
and gave some at once to his landlord,
who was sitting in the choir.
The innkeeper did not hide it away,   40
although he was within the choir,
for he gave it out to the burghers,
and the peace went its way through the church.
Guilhem sought his book,
and to do so he delayed until   45
Sir Archimbaut took some, before
he had come outside the place
where his joy was hidden.

For nothing on earth would he kiss
Sir Archimbaut or give him his peace;   50
with that he went on, and God help him!
For never had he felt so distraught
for any reason as he did now.
He did not raise his eyes or his face
to look to either side.   55
Toward Flamenca he went at once,
and thought that he would certainly
have a word with his lady
and be able to say to her at least one word,
but he left it all up to Love   60
and said, "If Love does not lead me today
from my desire to some light,
I shall never trust in it;
but if it please God, I shall surely succeed.
Love never fails in pressing need,   65
but it seems to me that it delays too long
for the great desire that burns in my heart."
And such is every man who loves.
Guilhem stood before his lady;
when she kissed the psalter,   70
he said to her softly, "Alas!"
But he surely did not say it so low
that she could not hear it very well.
Guilhem went on, humble and bowed,
and thought that he had made great progress;   75
[that] if he had just unhorsed
a hundred knights in a tourney
and won five hundred chargers,
he would not have such perfect joy,
for nothing in the world so delights   80
every true lover as does the joy
that comes from the place where he has his heart.
The chaplain did not hesitate,
after Mass he began
his sext, as he always did.   85
Guilhem was holding the psalter
and made it appear that he was looking at the psalms;
but before he left it,
he kissed the page more than a hundred times,
and remembered that word "Alas!"   90
Sir Archimbaut went out at once
and took his wife with him,
for he certainly did not want to forget her.
As long as he could follow her,
Guilhem followed her with eyes of the heart.   95
He folded the vestments and put them away,
the chalice and the paten

he put in a safe place, and then led away
his landlord and his chaplain.

Reading 31: Raimon de Cornet, "A San Marsel d'Albeges, prop de Salas"

Friar Raimon de Cornet, "Trifle"

1
At Saint-Marcel d'Albigeois, near Salles,
I was lodged with a lord of a priest
where I was harmed by a very pretty girl
who played a trick on me, so that I wished she had been burned
and I hanged, for I very well deserved it,   5
since I did not watch out for such bad business;
and I shall tell you the whole trick to make you laugh.

2
I loved her sincerely, to tell the truth,
and she me, as she made appearance,
so that all day we kissed with true love;   10
but then one day when she got the opportunity,
she took excessive vengeance on me,
I don't know why, but (in my opinion)
just because she saw me kiss another girl.

3
A day later, with very joyful look   15
she came to me in a secret place,
in my room, which I had taken near her [home];
when I saw her, I sent my clerk away,
for I hoped to do the order of Saint Macarius;
but she said, "I'm a little ashamed;   20
faith you owe me, don't touch me at this time."

4
I was aggrieved for a very disagreeable reason,
for, kissing her and fondling her breasts,
I fell asleep until the hour was late;
and I'll tell you what the wretched slut did to me.   25
With snip and snap, with a pair of scissors
she shaved my whole head—see what a trick!
Then she went away with my hair in her purse.

5
I awoke, then thought in haste
I'd do the deed, but I did not see or catch her,   30
nor did I realize the loss of my hair;
but for great grief I hit myself on the cheek,
and thanked God for not giving me a knife,
for with it I would have been put in damnation.
Now I shall tell you what happened to me because of my head.   35

6
Since the next day was the feast of Saint Michael,
I intended to say High Mass to the people,
but when I had put on my cope,
they all laughed, and said the pope
should give pardon to a priest's concubine,   40
since she had shaved me; then they made their inquiry
who could have done it, who managed to shave me so well.

7
"He who walks away does well, and twice as well who escapes,"
I thought, when I saw the traitress
and the other people who raised such a storm   45
that for grief I almost tried to bury myself alive.

Reading 32: Martí, "Cridarai!"

"I Shall Cry"

Let the wind help me and its breath from a forge,
let the sea help me with its angry waves;

    I shall cry!
All along the road I shall call upon the stones,
the thickets, the ditches, the trees and the woods.   5
    I shall cry
as long as I have a voice and something in my chest,
    I shall cry
to crack the flesh of my throat,
and to make my blood spurt in a mad shout: 10

I shall cry, I shall cry, I shall cry, I shall cry,
like a man taking a stand to survey the horizon,
a man freed of the weight of his chains
which the mad kings forged, and the bloody barons,
and the monks reddened by the glare of the fire   15
in which they burned alive my brothers of the past
who had sung of love and of human friendship,
and eaten white bread kneaded with freedom.

I shall cry, I shall cry, I shall cry, I shall cry!

Musical Examples

10. Guilhem IX, "Pos de chantar m'es pres talenz"
Music from *Jeu de sainte Agnès*; text from ms. *D*ᵃ fol. 190v

1. Pos   de   chan - tar—   m'es   pres—   ta - lenz,———

1. fa - rai   un   vers   don   sui   dolenz. . . .

12. Marcabru, "Pax in nomine Domini!"
Music from ms. *W* fol. 194; text from ms. *R* fol. 5

1. Pax   in   no - mi - ne——   Do - mi - ni!
2. La - var   de   ser   e——   de   ma - ti
3. Mas   es - cha - se - tatz—   e   no - fes
4. Que·l   se - nher   que   sap—   tot   cant   es
5. Pro - bet   del   li - nha - tje   Ca - ï,
6. Si·l   lu - xu - ri - os ——   cor - no - vi,
7. En   Es - pa - nha   say——   lo   mar - ques
8. Des - na - tu - rat   son——   li   Fran - ses

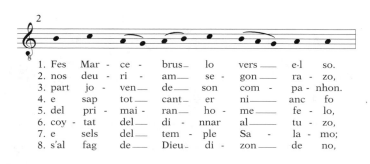

2

1. Fes Mar - ce - brus— lo vers —— e·l so.
2. nos deu - ri - am— se - gon —— ra - zo,
3. part jo - ven— de— son com - pa - nhon.
4. e sap tot — cant— er ni—— anc fo
5. del pri - mai - ran— ho - me —— fe - lo,
6. coy - tat del— di - nnar al—— tu - zo,
7. e sels del— tem - ple Sa - la - mo;
8. s'al fag de — Dieu— di - zon—— de no,

3

1. Au - jatz que — di——
2. so —— vos a - fi. ——
3. A - quel dols — es——
4. nos—— i pro - mes—
5. a —— tans ay - si ——
6. com—— e·l ca - mi, ——
7. so - fron los — pes—
8. qu'ieu— say com— es——

4

1. com nos a fat, per sa—— do - ssor,—
2. Cas - cus a de la - var— le - zor;—
3. que tug vo - lon lai li—— plu - zor—
4. ho - nor e nom d'em - pe - ra - dor;—
5. c'us a Dieu no por - ta— ho - nor.—
6. re - man - ran en fe - ra—— pu - dor,—
7. e·l fays de l'or - guelh pa - ya - nor,——
8. d'An - ti - o - cha. Pretz ab— va - lor——

5

1. lo se - nher reys ce - les - ti - als ——
2. de - men - tre qu'el es sas—— e—— sals—
3. don lo ga - zanhs er i - fer - naus,
4. e·l beu - tatz se - ra (sa - betz—— cals?)
5. Vey - rem qui l'er a - mics— co - raus,—
6. Dieus vol los ar - ditz e·ls sü - aus—
7. per que jo - vens cuelh a - vol—— laus.
8. say plo - ra Vi - an' e—— Pei - taus;—

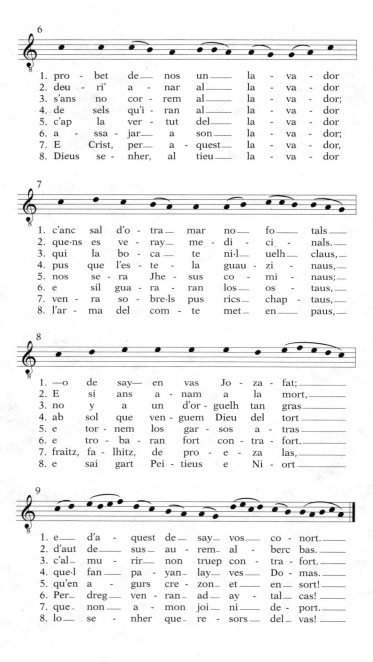

6

1. pro - bet de— nos un—— la - va - dor
2. deu - ri' a - nar al—— la - va - dor
3. s'ans no cor - rem al—— la - va - dor;
4. de sels qu'i - ran al—— la - va - dor
5. c'ap la ver - tut del—— la - va - dor
6. a - ssa - jar— a son—— la - va - dor;
7. E Crist, per— a - quest— la - va - dor,
8. Dieus se - nher, al tieu—— la - va - dor

7

1. c'anc sal d'o - tra— mar no—— fo—— tals——
2. que·ns es ve - ray— me - di - ci - nals.—
3. qui la bo - ca— te ni·l uelh— claus,—
4. pus que l'es - te - la guau - zi - naus,—
5. nos se - ra Jhe - sus co - mi - naus;—
6. e sil gua - ra - ran los - os — taus,—
7. ven - ra so - bre·ls pus rics— chap - taus,—
8. l'ar - ma del com - te met— en—— paus,—

8

1. —o de say— en vas Jo - za - fat;——
2. E si ans a - nam a la mort,——
3. no y a un d'or - guelh tan gras——
4. ab sol que ven - guem Dieu del tort——
5. e tor - nem los gar - sos a - tras——
6. e tro - ba - ran fort con - tra - fort.——
7. fraitz, fa - lhitz, de pro - e - za las,——
8. e sai gart Pei - tieus e Ni - ort——

9

1. e—— d'a - quest de— say vos—— co - nort.
2. d'aut de—— sus— au - rem— al - berc bas.——
3. c'al mu - rir— non truep con - tra - fort.——
4. que·l fan—— pa - yan- lay— ves—— Do - mas.——
5. qu'en a - gurs cre - zon— et —— en— sort!—
6. Per— dreg— ven - ran— ad— ay - tal— cas!—
7. que— non a - mon joi— ni— de - port.——
8. lo— se - nher que— re - sors— del— vas!——

13. Marcabru, "L'autrier just'una sebissa"
Music and text from ms. *R* fol. 5

1

1. L'au -	trier	just'	u -	na	se -	bi -	ssa
2. Ves	lieys	vau	per	la	pla -	ni -	ssa;
3. "To -	za,"	fi	m'ieu,	"cau -	za	pi -	a,
4. "Don,"	fay	se -	la,	"qui	que	si -	a,
5. "To -	za	de	gen -	til	a -	fay -	re,
6. "Se -	nher,	mon	genh	e	mon	ay -	re
7. "To -	za,"	fi	m'ieu,	"gen -	til	fa -	da
8. "Se -	nher,	tan	m'a -	vetz	lau -	za -	da
9. "To -	za,	fel	cor	e	sal -	va -	tje
10. "Don,	hom	co -	chat	de	fo -	la -	tje
11. "To -	za,	to -	ta	cri -	a -	tu -	ra
12. "Don,	oc—	mas	se -	gon	dre -	chu -	ra

2

1. tro -	bey	pas -	to -	ra	mes -	ti -	ssa
2. "To -	za,"	fi	m'ieu,	"re	fay -	ti -	ssa,
3. des -	toutz	me	soy	de	la	vi -	a
4. ben	co -	nosc	sen	o	fu -	li -	a;
5. ca -	va -	yers	fo	vos -	tre	pay -	re
6. vey	re -	ver -	tir	et	re -	tray -	re
7. vos	a -	das -	trec	can	fos	na -	da
8. pus	en	pretz	m'a -	vetz	le -	va -	da
9. a -	do -	mes -	g'om	per	u -	za -	tje;
10. e·us	pro -	met	e·us	ple -	visc	ga -	tje;
11. re -	vert	se -	gon	sa	na -	tu -	ra.
12. ser -	ca	fol	sa	fo -	la -	tu -	ra,

3

1. de	joi	e	de	sen	ma -	ssi -	ssa,"
2. dol	ay	gran	del	ven	que·us	fi -	ssa."
3. per	far	a	vos	com -	pa -	nhi -	a,
4. la	vos -	tra	pa -	re -	lhay -	ri -	a,
5. que·us	en -	gen -	ret,	e	la	may -	re
6. al	ve -	zoich	et	a	l'a -	ray -	re,
7. d'u -	na	beu -	tat	es -	me -	ra -	da
8. qu'ar	vos -	tr'a -	mor	tan	m'a -	gra -	da
9. ben	co -	nosc	al	tres -	pa -	ssa -	tje
10. si·m	fa -	ri -	atz	o -	ma -	na -	tge,
11. Par -	lem	ab	pa -	rau -	la	pu -	ra,"
12. cor -	tes	cor -	tez'	a -	ven -	tu -	ra,

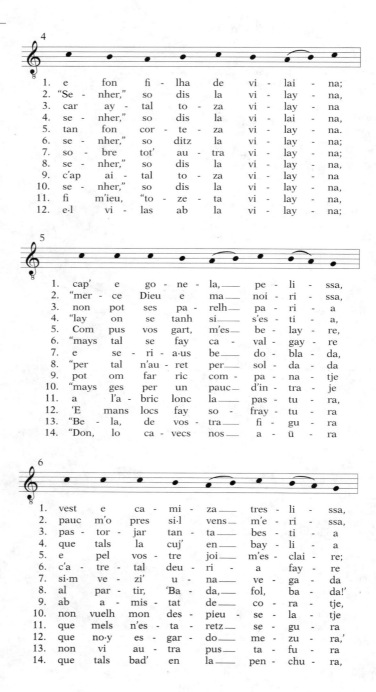

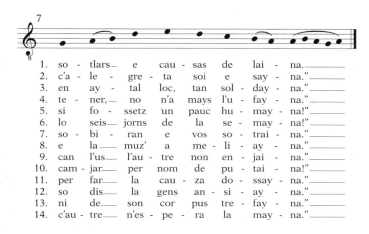

1.	so - tlars	e	cau - sas	de	lai -	na.	
2.	c'a - le -	gre - ta	soi	e	say -	na."	
3.	en	ay - tal	loc,	tan	sol - day -	na."	
4.	te -	ner,	no	n'a	mays l'u - fay -	na."	
5.	si	fo - ssetz	'un	pauc	hu - may -	na!"	
6.	lo	seis	jorns	de	la	se - may -	na!"
7.	so -	bi - ran	e	vos	so - trai -	na."	
8.	e	la	muz'	a	me - li - ay -	na."	
9.	can	l'us	l'au - tre	non	en - jai -	na."	
10.	cam - jar	per	nom	de	pu - tai -	na!"	
11.	per	far	la	cau - za	do - ssay -	na."	
12.	so	dis	la	gens	an - si - ay -	na."	
13.	ni	de	son	cor	pus	tre - fay -	na."
14.	c'au - tre	n'es - pe - ra	la	may -	na."		

14. Marcabru, "Dire vos vuelh ses duptansa"
Music and text from ms. *R* fol. 5

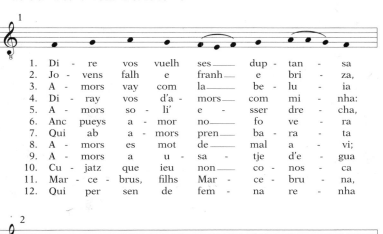

1.	Di - re	vos	vuelh	ses	dup -	tan -	sa
2.	Jo - vens	falh	e	franh	e	bri -	za,
3.	A - mors	vay	com	la	be -	lu -	ia
4.	Di - ray	vos	d'a -	mors	com	mi -	nha:
5.	A - mors	so - li'	e -	sser	dre -	cha,	
6.	Anc	pueys	a - mor	no	fo	ve -	ra
7.	Qui	ab	a - mors	pren	ba -	ra -	ta
8.	A - mors	es	mot	de	mal	a -	vi;
9.	A - mors	a	u - sa -	tje	d'e -	gua	
10.	Cu - jatz	que	ieu	non	co -	nos -	ca
11.	Mar - ce - brus,	filhs	Mar -	ce -	bru -	na,	
12.	Qui	per	sen	de	fem - na	re -	nha

1.	d'a - quest	vers	la	co -	men -	san -	sa;
2.	et	a - mors	es	d'ay -	tal	gui -	za
3.	que	se	mes - cla	en	la	su -	ia,
4.	a	vos	can - ta,	se -	luy	gui -	nha,
5.	mas	er	es	tor -	ta	e	bre - cha,
6.	que	tri - et	del	mel	la	ce -	ra,
7.	ab	di - a -	ble	s'a -	co -	a -	ta;
8.	trops	ho - mes	a	mortz	ses	gla -	vi.
9.	que	tot	jorn	vol	c'om	la	se - ga
10.	d'a - mors	s'es	or -	ba	o	los -	ca?
11.	fon	en - gen -	ratz	en	tal	lu -	na
12.	dretz	es	que	mals	li·n	a - ve -	nha,

3

	1	2	3	4	5	6	7
1.	li—	mot	fan	man - ta	sem - blan - sa.—
2.	que—	pus	al	saut	s'es	em - pri - za;—
3.	art—	lo	fust	e	la	fes - tu - ia—
4.	a—	vos	par - la,	l'au - tre	ci - nha,—
5.	e—	a - cu - lhid'	a	tal	de - cha—
6.	ans—	sap	si	pa - rar	la	-pe - ra—
7.	no·l—	cal	c'au - tra	ver - ga·l	ba - ta—
8.	Dieus	no	fes	tan	bon	gra - ma - vi—
9.	e—	que	pueg	de	legu'	en	le - ga.—
10.	Sos—	fatz	a - pla - na	e	tos - ca—
11.	que—	sap	a - mors	com	de - gru - na.—
12.	si—	com	la	le - tra	en - se - nha.—

4

1.	Es - co - tatz!
2.	es - co - tatz!
3.	(es - co - tatz!),
4.	es - co - tatz!
5.	(es - co - tatz!)
6.	(es - co - tatz!)
7.	Es - co - tatz!
8.	(es - co - tatz!)
9.	Es - co - tatz!
10.	(es - co - tatz!),
11.	Es - co - tatz!
12.	Es - co - tatz!

5

1.	Qui	ves	pro - e - za	ba - lan - sa
2.	Quecx	en	pren	a	sa	de - vi - za,
3.	e	no	sap	vas	cal	part	fu - ia
4.	Pus	se - ra	drei - ta	que	li - nha
5.	que	can	no	pot	mor - dre,	le - cha
6.	do - sa·us	er	com	chans	de	le - ra,
7.	No·y	a	co - sselh	mas	que·s	gra - ta
8.	que	fol	no	fa - sa·l	pus	sa - vi,
9.	E	no·us	de - man - da - ra	tre - gua
10.	e	punh	pus	sü - au	de	mos - ca—
11.	C'anc	de	cor	non	a - met	u - na,
12.	Mal'	a - ven - tu - ra	vos	ve - nha,

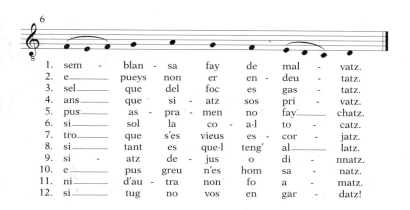

1.	sem -	blan -	sa	fay	de	mal -	vatz.
2.	e—	pueys	non	er	en -	deu -	tatz.
3.	sel—	que	del	foc	es	gas -	tatz.
4.	ans—	que	si -	atz	sos	pri -	vatz.
5.	pus—	as -	pra -	men	no	fay—	chatz.
6.	si—	sol	la	co -	a·l	to -	catz.
7.	tro—	que	s'es	vieus	es -	cor -	jatz.
8.	si—	tant	es	que·l	teng'	al—	latz.
9.	si -	atz	de -	jus	o	di -	nnatz.
10.	e—	pus	greu	n'es	hom	sa -	natz.
11.	ni—	d'au -	tra	non	fo	a -	matz.
12.	si—	tug	no	vos	en	gar -	datz!

15. Jaufre Rudel, "Lanqan li jorn son lonc en mai"
Music from ms. *X* fol. 81; text from ms. *A* fol. 127

1.	Lan -	qan	li	jorn	son—	lonc—	en	mai—
2.	Ja	mais	d'a -	mor	non	gau -	zi -	rai—
3.	I -	ratz	e	gau -	zens—	m'en	par -	trai—
4.	Be·m	par -	ra	jois	qan—	li—	qer -	rai,—
5.	Ben	tenc	lo	sei -	gnor—	per—	ve -	rai—
6.	Dieus	qui	fetz	tot	cant—	ve—	ni	vai—
7.	Ver	ditz	qui	m'a -	pe -	lla—	le -	chai—

1.	m'es	bels	doutz—	chans	d'au -	zels —	de—	loing;—
2.	si	no·m	gau—	d'est'—	a -	mor—	de—	loing,—
3.	qan	vei -	rai—	cest'—	a -	mor—	de—	loing;—
4.	per	a -	mor—	Dieus,—	l'al -	berc—	de—	loing;—
5.	per	qu'eu	vei -	rai—	l'a -	mor—	de—	loing.—
6.	e	for -	met—	cest'—	a -	mor—	de—	loing —
7.	ni	de -	si -	ron—	d'a -	mor—	de—	loing,—

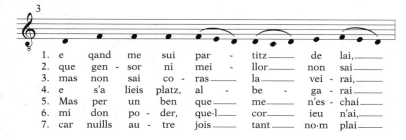

1.	e	qand	me	sui	par -	titz—	de	lai,—
2.	que	gen -	sor	ni	mei -	llor—	non	sai—
3.	mas	non	sai	co -	ras—	la—	vei -	rai,—
4.	e	s'a	lieis	platz,	al -	be -	ga -	rai—
5.	Mas	per	un	ben	que	me—	n'es -	chai—
6.	mi	don	po -	der,	que·l	cor—	ieu	n'ai,—
7.	car	nuills	au -	tre	jois —	tant—	no·m	plai—

17. Bernart de Ventadorn and Peire, "Amics Bernarz del Ventadorn"
Music from ms. *W* fol. 190; text from ms. *D* fol. 143

569

*Musical
Examples*

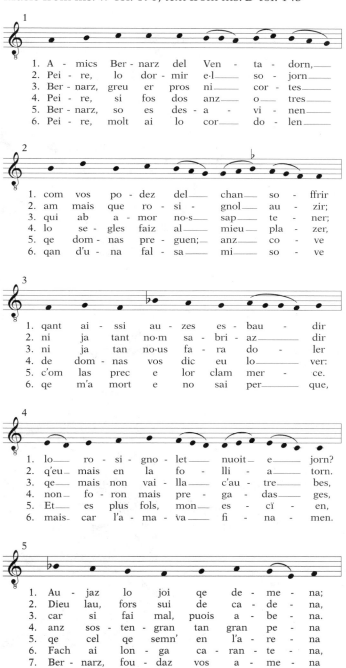

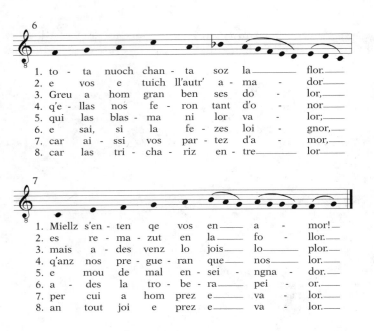

6

1. to - ta nuoch chan - ta soz la———— flor.——
2. e vos e tuich ll'autr' a - ma - dor——
3. Greu a hom gran ben ses do - lor,
4. q'e - llas nos fe - ron tant d'o - nor——
5. qui las blas - ma ni lor va - lor;——
6. e sai, si la fe - zes loi - gnor,——
7. car ai - ssi vos par - tez d'a - mor,——
8. car las tri - cha - riz en - tre——— lor.——

7

1. Miellz s'en - ten qe vos en—— a - mor!—
2. es re - ma - zut en la—— fo - llor.——
3. mais a - des venz lo jois—— lo—— plor.——
4. q'anz nos pre - gue - ran que—— nos—— lor.——
5. e mou de mal en - sei - ngna - dor.——
6. a - des la tro - be - ra—— pei - or.——
7. per cui a hom prez e——— va - lor.——
8. an tout joi e prez e——— va - lor.——

18. Bernart de Ventadorn, "Qan vei la lauzeta mover"
Music from ms. *W* fol. 190; text from ms. *A* fol. 90

1

1. Qan vei la lau - ze - ta——— mo - ver
2. Ai las, tant cu - ja - va——— sa - ber
3. De las domp - nas mi des - es - per;
4. A - mors es per - du - da—— per— ver,
5. Puois ab mi - donz no·m pot—— va - ler
6. Anc non a - gui de mi—— po - der,
7. D'ai - sso·s fai ben fem - na——— pa - rer

2

1. de joi sas a - las——— con - tra·l— rai,
2. d'a - mor, e qant pe - tit—— en—— sai!
3. ja mais en lor no·m—— fi - a - rai,
4. et ieu non o sau - bi—— anc— mai;
5. Dieus ni mer - ces ni·l—— dreitz q'ieu— ai,
6. ni non fui mieus de—— l'or'— en— sai
7. ma domp - na, per q'ieu—— lo—— re - trai

3

1. que   s'o - blid'___ e·is___ lai - ssa___ ca - zer
2. Car   ieu   d'a - mar___ no·m___ puosc   te - ner
3. c'ai - ssi   cum   las___ suoil___ cap - te - ner,
4. que   cil   que___ plus___ en___ degr'___ a - ver
5. ni   a   lieis___ no___ ven___ a___ pla - zer
6. qe·m   lai - sset___ en___ sos___ huoills   ve - zer
7. car   non   vol___ so___ que___ deu___ vo - ler

4

1. per   la   dou - ssor   c'al   cor   li   vai,_____
2. ce - lei   don   ja   pro   non   au - rai,_____
3. en - ai - ssi   las   des - cap - ten - rai._____
4. no   n'a   jes,   et   on   la   qer - rai?_____
5. qu'il   m'am,   ja   mais   no   lo   di - rai;_____
6. en   un   mi - raill   que   mout   mi   plai.
7. e   so   c'om   li   de - ve - da,   fai._____

5

1. ai!_____ Tant   grans   en - vei - a   m'en   ve
2. tolt_____ m'a   mon   cor   e   tolt   m'a   se
3. Pois_____ vei   c'u - na   pro   no   m'en   te
4. Ai,_____ cum   mal   sem - bla   qui   la   ve
5. e_____ si·m   part   de   lieis   re - cre,
6. Mi - raills,   pois   me   mi - riei   en - te,
7. Ca - zutz   sui   e   ma - la   mer - ce,
8. Tri - stan,   no·n   au - retz   jes   de   me,

6

1. de   cui   que   vei - a_____ jau - zi - on,
2. e   mi   me - teus   e_____ tot   lo_____ mon,
3. vas   lieis   qe·m   des - trui___ e·m   co - fon,
4. c'az   a - quest   cai - tiu___ de - si - ron,
5. mort   m'a   e   per   mort___ li   res - pon;
6. m'ant   mort   li   sos - pir___ de   pri - on;
7. et   ai   ben   faich   co·l___ fols   e·l___ pon;
8. que   vau   m'en,   mar - ritz,_____ no   sai - on.

7

1. me - ra - vi - llas   ai   car   de - sse_____
2. e   qan   si·m   tolc   no·m   lai - set   re_____
3. to - tas   las   dopt'   e   las   mes - cre,_____
4. que   ja   ses   lieis   non   au - ra   be,_____
5. e   vau   m'en,   s'e - lla   no·m   re - te,_____
6. c'ai - ssi·m   per - diei   cum   per - det   se_____
7. e   non   sai   per   que   m'es - de - ve,_____
8. De   chan - tar   mi   lais   e·m   re - cre,_____

1. lo cors de de - si - rier— no·m· fon.
2. mas de - si - rier— e— cor— vo - lon.
3. car ben sai c'a - tre - tals— si— son.
4. lai - sse mo - rir— que— no·il— a — on.
5. cai - tius, en i - ssill,— no— sai — on.
6. lo bels Nar - ci - sus— en— la— fon.
7. mas car po - jei— trop— contr' a — mon.
8. e de joi e— d'a - mor— m'es - con.

19. Giraut de Bornelh, "S'ie·us quier cosselh, bel'ami'Alamanda"
Music and text from ms. *R* fol. 8

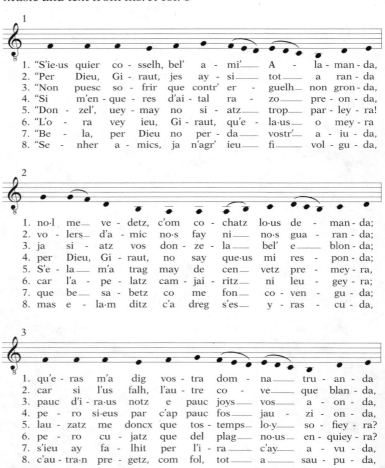

1. "S'ie·us quier co - sselh, bel' a - mi'— A - la - man - da,
2. "Per Dieu, Gi - raut, jes ay - si— tot— a ran - da
3. "Non puesc so - frir que contr' er - guelh— non gron - da,
4. "Si m'en - que - res d'ai - tal ra - zo— pre - on - da,
5. "Don - zel', uey - may no si - atz— trop— par - ley - ra!
6. "L'o - ra vey ieu, Gi - raut, qu'e - la·us— o mey - ra
7. "Be - la, per Dieu no per - da— vostr'— a - iu - da,
8. "Se - nher a - mics, ja n'agr' ieu— fi— vol - gu - da,

1. no·l me— ve - detz, c'om co - chatz lo·us de - man - da;
2. vo - lers— d'a - mic no·s fay ni— no·s gua - ran - da;
3. ja si - atz vos don - ze - la bel' e - blon - da,
4. per Dieu, Gi - raut, no say que·us mi res - pon - da;
5. S'e - la— m'a trag may de cen - vetz pre - mey - ra,
6. car l'a - pe - latz cam - jai - ritz— ni leu - gey - ra;
7. que be— sa - betz co me fon— co - ven - gu - da;
8. mas e - la·m ditz c'a dreg s'es— y - ras - cu - da,

1. qu'e - ras m'a dig vos - tra dom - na— tru - an - da
2. car si l'us falh, l'au - tre co - ve— que blan - da,
3. pauc d'i - ra·us notz e pauc joys— vos - a - on - da,
4. pe - ro si·eus par c'ap pauc fos— jau - zi - on - da,
5. lau - zatz me doncx que tos - temps - lo·y— so - fiey - ra?
6. pe - ro cu - jatz que del plag— no·us— en - quiey - ra?
7. s'ieu ay fa - lhit per l'i - ra— c'ay— a - vu - da,
8. c'au - tra·n pre - getz, com fol, tot— a— sau - pu - da,

4
1. c'a - lhons fuy, fors y - ssitz de— sa co - man - da;
2. que lur— de - streg no cres - ca— ni s'es - pan - da.
3. mas ges— non es pre - miei - ra— ni se - gon - da!
4. may vuelh pe - lar mon prat c'au - tre·l mi— ton - da.
5. No·us cu - ja - ratz o fe - zes— per ne - ssiey - ra
6. Mas ieu— non cug que si - a— tan ma - niey - ra,
7. no·m ten - ga dan; s'o sen - tis— c'a leu— mu - da
8. que non— la val ni ves - ti - da ni— nu - da.

5
1. pus so que·m det, er m'es - tra— e·m de - man - da.
2. Pe - ro si·eus ditz d'aut pueg que— si - a lan - da,
3. Mas yeu que tem de l'i - ra— que·m co - fon - da,
4. Vos se - la - ray, del plag far— de - si - ron - da?
5. d'autr' a - mis - tat? Ar ay ta - lan que·us fiey - ra;
6. ans er huey - mais sa pro - me - sa de - riei - ra,
7. cor d'om i - rat a - mo - ros,— s'anc fos dru - da,
8. No fa - ra doncs, si no·us giec,— que ven - cu - da

6
1. Que·m co - sse - lhatz?—
2. vos o— cre - zatz—
3. que m'en lau - zatz?—
4. Ja l'e - sser - catz—
5. co no·us— ca - latz?—
6. que que·us di - atz, —
7. del patz— pe - ssatz,—
8. s'au - tra·n— pre - gatz?—

7
1. C'a pauc lo cor d'i - ra dins no m'a - bran - da,—
2. e pla - ssa vos lo bes e·l mals que·us man - da,—
3. Si tem mu - rir, que·m tra - ga pueys vas l'on - da?—
4. com so bo cors non es - duy', en se - gon - da!—
5. Me - lhor co - sselh de - ra na Be - ren - guiei - ra—
6. si s'en des - trenh tan qu'e - la ja vos quiei - ra—
7. que be vos dic, mort soi si l'ai per - du - da—
8. Be·us en val - ray, si tot l'ay man - ten - gu - da,—
9. "Be - la, per Dieu, si d'e - la n'es cre - zu - da,—
10. "Ben o fa - ray, mays can vos er ren - du - da,—

1. tant fort___ en soi___ i - ratz."___
2. c'ay - si___ se - retz___ a - matz."___
3. Mal cug___ que·m cap - de - latz."___
4. Ben par___ que n'es___ co - chatz."___
5. que vos___ no mi___ do - natz."___
6. huey - may___ tre - va___ ni___ patz."___
7. may no___ lo·y des - co - bratz!"___
8. sol mays___ no·us i___ mes - clatz."___
9. per mi___ lo·y a - fi___ atz."___
10. s'a - mor___ no la·us___ to - latz!"___

20. Bertran de Born, "D'un sirventes no·m cal far loignor ganda" Music from ms. *R* fol. 8 (Giraut de Bornelh, "S'ie·us quier cosselh"); text from ms. *A* fol. 195

1. D'un sir - ven - tes no·m cal far___ loi - gnor gan - da,
2. Que mal - vatz fai, car ai - ssi___ viu___ a ran - da
3. Ja per dor - mir non er de___ Co - ber - lan - da
4. Con - seill vuoill dar e·l son de___ n'A - la - man - da

1. tal ta - lan ai qe·l dig' e___ qe l'es - pan - da;
2. de liu - ra - zon a comt' et___ a ga - ran - da.
3. reis dels_ En - gles, ni con - quer - ra Yr - lan - da,
4. lai a·n_ Ri - chart, si tot no___ lo·m de - man - da:

1. car n'ai ra - zon tant no - vell'___ e___ tant gran - da
2. Reis co - ro - natz que d'au - trui___ pren___ liu - ran - da
3. ni tenr' An - gieus ni Mon - sau - rel___ ni Can - da,
4. ja per son frair mais sos ho - mes___ non blan - da.

1. del jo - ven rei q'a fe - nit___ sa de - man - da
2. mal sembl' Ar - naut, lo mar - ques_ de Be - lan - da,
3. ni de___ Pei - teus non au - ra___ la mi - ran - da,
4. Non - ca·is_ fai el, anz a - setg'_ e·ls a - ran - da,

5

1. son frair Ri - chartz, pois sos pai - re·l co - man - da.
2. ni·l pro Gui - llem que con - quis___ Tor Mir - man - da.
3. ni se - ra ducs de la ter - ra nor - man - da,
4. tol lor cha - stels e der - roc'___ et a - bran - da

6

1. Tant es___ for - satz!___
2. Tant fon___ pre - satz!___
3. ni coms___ pa - latz___
4. de - vas___ totz latz!___

7

1. Pois n'A - en - rics ter - ra non ten ni man - da,___
2. Pos en Pei - tau lor ment e lor tru - an - da,___
3. ni de Bor - dels ni dels Gas - cos part Lan - da,___
4. E·l reis tor - nei lai ab cels de Guar - lan - da___
5. Lo coms Jau - fres cui es Ber - si - li - an - da___
6. car es cor - tes, e fos en sa co - man - da___

8

1. si - a___ reis dels___ mal - vatz!___
2. no·i er___ mais tant___ a - matz.___
3. sei - gner___ ni de___ Ba - satz.___
4. e l'au - tre, sos___ coi - gnatz.·
5. vol - gra___ fos pri - miers___ natz,___
6. re - ges - mes e·l___ du - chatz.··

27. Peire Cardenal, "Un sirventes novel voill comensar"
Music from ms. *R* fol. 69; text from ms. *I* fol. 169

1

1. Un sir - ven - tes no - vel voill___ co - men - sar___
2. To - ta sa cort fa - rai mi - ra - vi - llar___
3. Vos - tra por - ta non de - gratz___ ja ve - dar,___
4. Los di - a - bles de - gratz dez - e - re - tar___
5. Heu non mi voill de vos dez - es - pe - rar,___

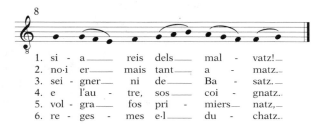

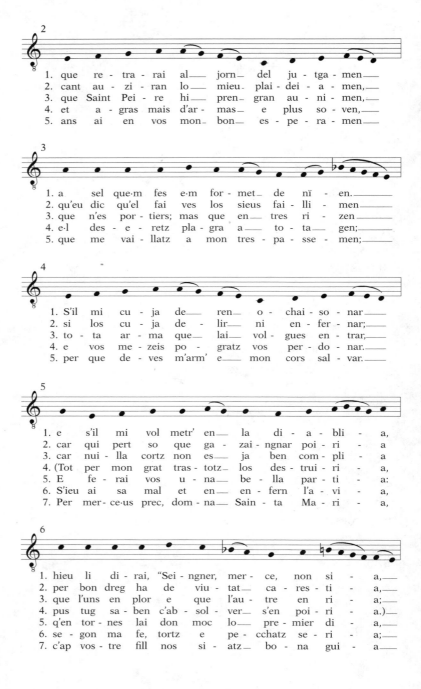

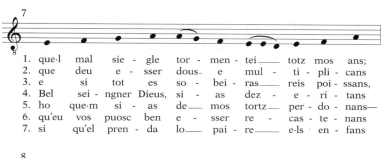

1. que·l   mal   sie - gle   tor - men - tei___ totz mos   ans;
2. que   deu   e - sser   dous_   e   mul - ti - pli - cans
3. e   si   tot   es   so - bei - ras___ reis poi - ssans,
4. Bel   sei - ngner Dieus, si - as   dez - e - ri - tans
5. ho   que·m   si - as   de___ mos   tortz___ per - do - nans—
6. qu'eu   vos   puosc   ben   e - sser   re - cas - te - nans
7. si   qu'el   pren - da   lo___ pai - re___ e·ls   en - fans

1. e   gar - das   mi,   si·us___ platz,   dels   tor - men - tans."___
2. de   re - te - ner   sas___ ar - mas   tres - pa - ssans.___
3. si   no·ns   o - bres,   er___ vos___ en   faitz   de - mans.___
4. dels   e - ne - mics   en - vei - os   e   pe - zans!
5. qu'eu   no·ls   fei - ra   si___ non_   fos   natz   e - nans.___
6. que   per   un   ben   ai___ de___ mal   mil   ai - tans.___
7. e·ls   me - ta   lay   on___ es - tai   Sans   Jo - hans.___

The Accompanying Compact Disk:
The Music of the Troubadours

Elizabeth Aubrey

At some time after the troubadours created their songs, the poems may have been read aloud or silently. But the troubadours themselves almost certainly *sang* their songs. Many of the melodies the troubadours composed for their poems were written down in the thirteenth century, and about 250 of them have survived.[1] They are monophonic (i.e., made up of a single musical line) and are often unified by short motives that recur and develop as the song proceeds. Some of the melodies include repeated phrases, clear pitch goals, and predictable contours, while others embody striking contrasts of leaping intervals, dramatic gestures, and unexpected cadential turns. The sparse preservation of the music in comparison to the rich transmission of the poems and the many variants among extant versions of the melodies that do survive suggest a dynamic tradition of improvisation and spontaneous creation and re-creation. Many of the melodies flow so freely that today's performer is tempted to embellish or reinterpret the notes—a practice that is probably not inappropriate in the light of the flexible performing practices of the twelfth and thirteenth centuries.

Singing a troubadour's poem adds a dimension that is not present when the work is read silently or recited. A complete *song* is text and music together; the troubadour used both the poem and the melody, each in its own way, to express the song's theme, whether love, lamentation, satire, or playful dialogue. A musical performance brings the song to life. The poem develops the theme linearly, the words progressing in time through various arguments, topoi, and figures, and often through changing rhymes; each stanza addresses the overall theme in a distinct way, adding layer upon layer of meaning. The music, far from being a mere vehicle

[1] For a comprehensive study of the melodies, see Aubrey.

for the poem, has the power to express the song's theme in a way that transcends the words, appealing to the heart and mind, unbound by the specificity of the words.

The melody, which is repeated for each stanza of the poem, provides the song with unity, while the music takes on new meaning itself as it is sounded over and over with the evolving text. The recurrence of the melody in performance while the poem develops creates a tension, as poem and melody present their materials at different speeds and in different realms of human perception, helping propel the song forward. The strophic repetition of the melody, overlaid on the single iteration of the stanzas, creates a multilayered texture that reinforces the thematic material (poetic and musical) and foreshadows a sense of completion, even while the poem continues through its emotional journey, providing both singer and listener with new perspective in each stanza.

Our knowledge of many aspects of the performance of the troubadours' songs is limited. The notation in which the melodies were recorded is the barest sketch of what a performance would have entailed: much of the written music conveys no clear indication of the rhythms of the notes, and it is completely silent on the question of who performed the songs or how—whether a single singer or more than one, with instruments or without. These issues have generated heated debate among scholars, and none of the theories that have been proposed can be either proved or disproved. While there is unequivocal evidence that instruments were common in the Midi, clues to their use (or nonuse) during the performance of the courtly songs of the troubadours are lacking. Although it has not been our intention to avoid the question of the use of instruments, the songs on the compact disk that accompany this book are sung entirely without accompaniment. This practice is somewhat unusual among modern performances, which tend to rely on instruments to help make the medieval songs more appealing and interesting to a modern audience. However, an unaccompanied performance can be both entertaining and moving, especially if the singer is attentive to the meaning of the text and if the listeners can understand the words, as one hopes that the readers of this book will now be able to do.

The question of rhythm is equally insoluble. Hypotheses range from the imposition on the notes of strict patterns similar to the meters of classical poetry (iambic, trochaic, etc.), to a loosely measured style, to an almost completely free declamatory style of delivery. While it is tempting to believe that the words themselves give some sort of rhythm to the notes, it is not always easy to apply the idea, since the words and phrases move with a sonic (and syntactic) fluidity that is constrained only by the syllable count and rhyme scheme of the verses; similarly, the melodies often flow with a freedom that defies any constraint of regularity. Faced with this uncertainty, the singer today must rely largely on musical instincts that are informed by a sensitivity to the style and structure of the poem, instincts that can only approximate those of a medieval musician. As a singer performs the several stanzas of a song, the melody almost unavoidably takes on a sort of "macrorhythm" common to all the stanzas, even if the words of each stanza call forth different rhythmic nuances in detail. Repeated music (phrases, motives, stanzas) surely had more or less the same rhythm, regardless of the change of words.

On our compact disk the singer exercises a great deal of liberty, both within a song and among the different songs, not adhering to any single approach but allowing the song itself (both its text and its melody) to generate its own rhythm. For the **pastorela** by Marcabru, the relatively unadorned melody, with its several internal repetitions—together with the raucous text, short verses, and persistent paroxytonic rhyme sounds—demands a quick, metrical performance. The narrative, which alternates between the voices of the lord and of the peasant girl, requires a storytelling style that differentiates between the two voices—the song would be most entertaining sung by a man and a woman, although it can be equally amusing if sung by one singer who switches back and forth between a "male" voice and a "female" one.

A similar shift of voice seems appropriate for the **tenso** between Giraut de Bornelh and the Lady Alamanda; the distinction between the two is here obtained less by a change in voice quality than by a subtle change in mood or tone, from pleading, demanding, and complaining (Giraut) to bemusement and solicitude (Alamanda). The melody of this song is unsettled and unpredictable in its motion, evoking somewhat more freedom in delivery than the **pastorela**.

The melody of the **tenso** between Giraut and Alamanda is used also on the CD for the **sirventes** by Bertran de Born, who disclosed in the final stanza his intention to use the preexisting melody, although the poem is not given music in any surviving medieval manuscript (see Paden, Sankovitch, and Stäblein 50–51, 184–89). Because the two poems have an identical poetic structure, the melody fits both perfectly, and the same "macrorhythm" seems appropriate. But because the theme and spirit of Bertran's satire differ fundamentally from those of Giraut's **tenso,** a performance of the **sirventes** calls for more vigor and intensity.

The recording's two **cansos**, perhaps the most famous in the entire repertoire of troubadour song, have melodies of sharply contrasting styles. Jaufre Rudel's song of the distant lover is filled with short-lived motives, florid figures, and repeated phrases. The composer stretches the refrain word **loing**, which recurs at the end of verses 2 and 4 of every stanza, by setting it to a melisma of four lengthened notes; this performance deliberately exaggerates the duration of these notes, to highlight the obvious word painting (a relatively rare device in troubadour song).

In contrast to Jaufre's straightfoward melody, Bernart de Ventadorn's song of the lark achieves an equally expressive effect by quite different musical means. His melody has only a small amount of internal repetition, few ornaments, and phrases that avoid resolution until the final cadence. This melody was far more widely disseminated during the Middle Ages than any other troubadour melody—and, in a way impossible to explain, the melody is as moving and memorable today as it must have been to its medieval singers and listeners.

TRACK LISTING OF THE COMPACT DISK

Lessons and readings delivered by William D. Paden

1.	General introduction	[1:41]
2.	Reading in chapter 1	[1:03]
3.	Introduction to reading in chapter 2	[1:44]
4.	Reading in chapter 2	[1:09]
5.	Introduction to reading in chapter 3	[4:40]
6.	Reading in chapter 3	[1:50]
7.	Introduction to reading in chapter 4	[0:33]
8.	Reading in chapter 4	[1:27]

Songs performed by Elizabeth Aubrey

9. Marcabru, *L'autrier just'una sebissa* (ch. 13)   [5:26]
10. Jaufre Rudel, *Lanqan li jorn son lonc en mai* (ch. 15)   [7:11]
11. Bernart de Ventadorn, *Qan vei la lauzeta mover* (ch. 18)   [6:09]
12. Giraut de Bornelh, *S'ie·us quier cosselh, bel'ami'Alamanda* (ch. 19)   [5:52]
13. Bertran de Born, *D'un sirventes no·m cal far loignor ganda* (ch. 20)   [3:04]

[Total CD time: 42:41]

Works Cited

Adams, Edward L. *Word-Formation in Provençal.* New York: Macmillan, 1913.

Akehurst, F. R. P., and Judith M. Davis, eds. *A Handbook of the Troubadours.* Berkeley: U of California P, 1995.

Alibert, Louis. *Gramatica occitana segon los parlars lengadocians.* Toulouse: Societat d'Estudis Occitans, 1935.

Anglade, Joseph. *Grammaire de l'ancien provençal.* Paris: Klincksieck, 1921.

———, ed. *Las leys d'amors: Manuscrit de l'Académie des Jeux Floraux.* Bibliothèque Méridionale. Première série, 17–20. 4 vols. Toulouse: Privat, 1919–20.

Appel, Carl, ed. *Bernart von Ventadorn: Seine Lieder.* Halle: Niemeyer, 1915.

———, ed. *Provenzalische Chrestomathie mit Abriss der Formenlehre und Glossar.* 1930. 6th ed. Leipzig: Reisland. Hildesheim: Georg Olms, 1971.

Association Internationale d'Etudes Occitanes. *Bulletin de l'Association Internationale d'Etudes Occitanes.* London: Westfield Coll., 1985–.

Aston, S. C., ed. *Peirol, Troubadour of Auvergne.* Cambridge: Cambridge UP, 1953.

Aubrey, Elizabeth. *The Music of the Troubadours.* Bloomington: Indiana UP, 1996.

Audiau, Jean, ed. *La pastourelle dans la poésie occitane du Moyen Age.* 1923. Paris: De Boccard. Genève: Droz, 1973. Marseille: Laffitte, 1980.

Avalle, D'Arco Silvio. *La letteratura medievale in lingua d'oc nella sua tradizione manoscritta: Problemi di critica testuale.* Torino: Einaudi, 1961.

———, ed. *Peire Vidal, Poesie.* 2 vols. Milano: Ricciardi, 1960.

Baldinger, Kurt. *Complément bibliographique au* Provenzalisches Supplementwörterbuch *de Emil Levy: Sources—Datations.* Genève: Slatkine, 1983.

———, ed. *Dictionnaire onomasiologique de l'ancien gascon (DAG).* Tübingen: Niemeyer, 1975–.

———, ed. *Dictionnaire onomasiologique de l'ancien occitan (DAO).* Tübingen: Niemeyer, 1975–.

Banniard, Michel. "La voix et l'écriture: Émergences médiévales." *Médiévales* 25 (1993): 5–16.

Barbieri, Giammaria. *Dell'origine della poesia rimata.* Ed. Girolamo Tiraboschi. Modena: Società Tipografica, 1790.

Barthès, Henri. *Etudes historiques sur la "langue occitane."* Saint-Geniès-de-Fontédit: Barthès, 1987.

Bartsch, Karl. *Chrestomathie provençale (Xe–XVe siècles).* 1904. Rev. Eduard Koschwitz. 6th ed. Marburg: Elwert. New York: AMS, 1973.

Bec, Pierre. *Chants d'amour des femmes-troubadours: Trobairitz et "chansons de femme."* Paris: Stock, 1995.

———. *La langue occitane.* Que sais-je? 1059. 2nd ed. Paris: PU de France, 1967.

Benedict, Saint. *The Rule of Benedict: A Guide to Christian Living.* Dublin: Four Courts P, 1994.

Bennett, William H. *An Introduction to the Gothic Language.* New York: MLA, 1980.

Bertolucci Pizzorusso, Valeria. "Il grado zero della retorica nella *vida* di Jaufre Rudel." *Studi mediolatini e volgari* 18 (1970): 7–26.

Bickerton, David M., and Peter V. Davies, directors. *La batalha de la lenga: Documentaire sur la langue occitane.* Glasgow: Univ. of Glasgow Language Centre, 1991.

Blaise, Albert. *Le vocabulaire latin des principaux thèmes liturgiques.* Turnhout: Brepols, 1966.

Bloch, Oscar, and Walther von Wartburg. *Dictionnaire étymologique de la langue française.* 5th ed. Paris: PU de France, 1968.

Boase, Roger. *The Origin and Meaning of Courtly Love: A Critical Study of European Scholarship.* Manchester: Manchester UP, 1977.

Bond, Gerald A., ed. *The Poetry of William VII, Count of Poitiers, IX Duke of Aquitaine.* Garland Library of Medieval Literature 4A. New York: Garland, 1982.

Bossuat, Robert. *Le roman de Renart.* Paris: Hatier-Boivin, 1957.

Boutière, Jean, and Alexander Herman Schutz, eds. *Biographies des troubadours.* 1964. Rev. Jean Boutière and Irénée-Marcel Cluzel. 2nd ed. Paris: Nizet, 1973.

Branca, Vittore, ed. *Giovanni Boccaccio: Decameron.* 2nd ed. Firenze: Le Monnier, 1960.

Bruckner, Matilda Tomaryn, Laurie Shepard, and Sarah White. *Songs of the Women Troubadours.* Garland Library of Medieval Literature 97A. New York: Garland, 1995.

Brun, Auguste. *Recherches historiques sur l'introduction du français dans les provinces du Midi.* Paris: Champion, 1923.

Brunel, Clovis Félix. *Bibliographie des manuscrits littéraires en ancien provençal.* Paris: Droz, 1935.

———, ed. *Les plus anciennes chartes en langue provençale: Recueil des pièces originales antérieures au XIIIe siècle. Supplément.* Paris: Picard, 1926–52.

Buffum, Douglas Labaree, ed. *Gerbert de Montreuil:* Le roman de la violette ou de Gérart de Nevers. Société des Anciens Textes Français 124. Paris: Champion, 1928.

Calzolari, Monica, ed. *Il trovatore Guillem Augier Novella*. Subsidia al Corpus des Troubadours 11. Istituto di Filologia Romanza dell'Università di Roma, Studi, Testi e Manuali 13. Modena: Mucchi, 1986.

Il Canzoniere provenzale estense, riprodotto per il centenario della nascita di Giulio Bertoni. Presentazione di Aurelio Roncaglia; introduzione di D'Arco Silvio Avalle e Emanuele Casamassima. 2 vols. Modena: STEM Mucchi, 1979–82.

Cerquiglini, Bernard. *La parole médiévale: Discours, syntaxe, texte*. Paris: Editions de Minuit, 1981.

Chambers, Frank M. *An Introduction to Old Provençal Versification*. Philadelphia: American Philosophical Soc., 1985.

———. *Proper Names in the Lyrics of the Troubadours*. Univ. of North Carolina Studies in the Romance Languages and Literatures 113. Chapel Hill: U of North Carolina P, 1971.

Chiarini, Giorgio, ed. *Il canzoniere di Jaufre Rudel*. Romanica Vulgaria 5. Roma: Japadre, 1985.

Cichon, Peter. *Spracherziehung in der Diglossiesituation: Zum Sprachbewusstsein von Okzitanischlehrern*. Dissertationen der Universität Wien 160. Wien: Verband der wissenschaftlichen Gesellschaften Österreichs, 1988.

Cnyrim, Eugen. *Sprichwörter, sprichwörtliche Redensarten und Sentenzen bei den provenzalischen Lyrikern*. Marburg: Elwert, 1888.

Cornicelius, Max, ed. *Raimon Vidal: So fo e·l temps c'om era iays*. Berlin: Feicht, 1888.

Corominas, Joan, and José A. Pascual. *Diccionario crítico etimológico castellano e hispánico*. 5 vols. Madrid: Gredos, 1980–83.

Coupier, Jules. *Dictionnaire français-provençal*. Marseille: Edition de l'Association Dictionnaire français-provençal, 1995.

Cremonesi, Carla. *Nozioni di grammatica storica provenzale*. 3rd ed. Varese: Istituto Editoriale Cisalpino, 1967.

Crescini, Vincenzo. "Del canzoniere provenzale V (Marc. App. XI)." *Atti della R. Accademia dei Lincei*. Serie 4. *Rendiconti* 6.2 (1890): 39–49.

———. *Manualetto provenzale per uso degli alunni delle facoltà di lettere*. 2nd ed. Verona: Drucker, 1905.

Cropp, Glynnis M. "L'ancien provençal *retener*: Son sens et son emploi dans la poésie des troubadours." *Mélanges d'histoire littéraire, de linguistique et de philologie romanes offerts à Charles Rostaing*. Liège: Association des Romanistes de l'Université de Liège. 1 (1974): 179–200.

———. *Le vocabulaire courtois des troubadours de l'époque classique*. Publications Romanes et Françaises 135. Genève: Droz, 1975.

Dante Alighieri. *Il convivio*. Ed. G. Busnelli and G. Vandelli. 2nd ed. 2 vols. Firenze: Le Monnier, 1964.

———. *De vulgari eloquentia*. Ed. Aristide Marigo. 3rd ed. Firenze: Le Monnier, 1957.

Dauzat, Albert. *Dictionnaire étymologique des noms de famille et prénoms de France*. Rev. Marie-Thérèse Morlet. Paris: Larousse, 1980.

Dejeanne, Jean-Marie-Lucien, ed. *Poésies complètes du troubadour Marcabru*. Toulouse: Privat, 1909. New York: Johnson, 1971.

Delbouille, Maurice. "Les 'senhals' littéraires désignant Raimbaut d'Orange et la chronologie de ces témoignages." *Cultura neolatina* 17 (1957): 49–73.

Dictionary of the Middle Ages. Ed. Joseph R. Strayer. 13 vols. New York: Scribner, 1982–89.

Dictionnaire d'archéologie chrétienne et de liturgie. Ed. Fernand Cabrol, Henri Leclercq, and Henri Marrou. 15 vols. Paris: Letouzey et Ané, 1907–51.

Dictionnaire des lettres françaises: Le Moyen Age. 2nd ed. Ed. Geneviève Hasenohr and Michel Zink. Paris: Fayard, 1992.

Diez, Friedrich. *Die Poesie der Troubadours.* Zwickau: Schumann, 1826. 2nd ed. Ed. Karl Bartsch. Leipzig: Barth, 1883. French trans. by Ferdinand de Roisin. *La poésie des troubadours.* Paris: Labitte, 1845.

Di Girolamo, Costanzo. *I trovatori.* Torino: Bollati Boringhieri, 1989.

Duby, Georges. "Le modèle courtois." *Histoire des femmes en Occident: Le Moyen Age.* Ed. Christiane Klapisch-Zuber. Paris: Plon, 1991. 261–76.

———. "Les origines de la chevalerie." *Hommes et structures du Moyen Age.* Paris: Mouton, 1973. 325–42.

———. *William Marshal, the Flower of Chivalry.* Trans. Richard Howard. New York: Pantheon, 1985.

Du Cange, Charles du Fresne. *Glossarium mediae et infimae latinitatis.* New ed. 10 vols. Niort: Favre, 1883–87.

Duparc-Quioc, Suzanne, ed. *La chanson d'Antioche.* Documents Relatifs à l'Histoire des Croisades 11. 2 vols. Paris: Geuthner, 1976.

Ekwall, Eilert. *The Concise Oxford Dictionary of English Place-Names.* 4th ed. Oxford: Clarendon, 1960.

Elcock, W. D. *The Romance Languages.* Rev. John N. Green. London: Faber, 1975.

Enciclopedia cattolica. 12 vols. Città del Vaticano: Ente per l'Enciclopedia Cattolica e per il Libro Cattolico, 1949–54.

Enciclopedia dantesca. Ed. Umberto Bosco. 6 vols. Roma: Istituto della Enciclopedia Italiana, 1970–78.

Ernout, A., and A. Meillet. *Dictionnaire étymologique de la langue latine.* 4th ed. 2 vols. Paris: Klincksieck, 1959–60.

Fernández de la Cuesta, Ismael, and Robert Lafont, eds. *Las cançons dels trobadors.* Tolosa: Institut d'Estudis Occitans, 1979.

Fernández González, José Ramón. *Gramática histórica provenzal.* Oviedo: Universidad de Oviedo, Servicio de Publicaciones, 1985.

Ferrante, Joan M. "*Cortes'Amor* in Medieval Texts." *Speculum* 55 (1980): 686–95.

Field, Thomas. Rev. of *Etudes historiques,* by Henri Barthès. *Romance Philology* 47 (1993): 229–36.

Fleischman, Suzanne. *Tense and Narrativity: From Medieval Performance to Modern Fiction.* Austin: U of Texas P, 1990.

Fouché, Pierre. *Morphologie historique du français: Le verbe.* 2nd ed. Paris: Klincksieck, 1967.

———. *Phonétique historique du français.* 3 vols. Paris: Klincksieck, 1952–61.

Frank, István. *Répertoire métrique de la poésie des troubadours.* 2 vols. Paris: Champion, 1953–57.

Frappier, Jean. *Amour courtois et table ronde.* Publications Romanes et Françaises 126. Genève: Droz, 1973.

Fukumoto, Naoyuki, Noboru Harano, and Satoru Suzuki, eds. *Le roman de Renart édité d'après les manuscrits C et M.* Tokyo: France Tosho, 1983.

Gamillscheg, Ernst. *Etymologisches Wörterbuch der französischen Sprache.* 2nd ed. Heidelberg: Winter, 1969.

Gatien-Arnoult, Adolphe Félix, ed. *Monumens de la littérature romane.* 4 vols. Toulouse: Paya, 1841–49.

Gay-Crosier, Raymond. *Religious Elements in the Secular Lyrics of the Troubadours.* Chapel Hill: U of North Carolina P, 1971.

Glare, P. G. W. *Oxford Latin Dictionary.* Oxford: Clarendon, 1982.

Gonfroy, Gérard. "Les grammairiens occitano-catalans du Moyen Age et la dénomination de leur langue." *La licorne* no. 4 (1980): 47–76.

Gougaud, Henri, trans. *Guillaume de Tudèle et l'Anonyme:* La chanson de la Croisade albigeoise. *Reproduction en fac-similé du manuscrit intégral.* Paris: Berg, 1984.

Gouiran, Gérard, ed. *L'amour et la guerre: L'oeuvre de Bertran de Born.* 2 vols. Aix-en-Provence: Université de Provence, 1985.

———. Rev. of *The Syntax of Medieval Occitan,* by Frede Jensen. *Revue de linguistique romane* 51 (1987): 202–09.

———, ed. *Le seigneur-troubadour d'Hautefort: L'oeuvre de Bertran de Born.* Aix-en-Provence: Université de Provence, 1987.

Grafström, Åke. *Etude sur la graphie des plus anciennes chartes languedociennes avec un essai d'interprétation phonétique.* Uppsala: Almqvist & Wiksell, 1958.

———. *Etude sur la morphologie des plus anciennes chartes languedociennes.* Acta Universitatis Stockholmiensis: Romanica Stockholmiensia 4. Stockholm: Almqvist & Wiksell, 1968.

Grandgent, C. H. *An Outline of the Phonology and Morphology of Old Provençal.* Rev. ed. Boston: Heath, 1905.

Grundriss der romanischen Literaturen des Mittelalters. Ed. Hans Robert Jauss and Erich Köhler. 11 vols. to date. Heidelberg: Winter, 1968–.

Gschwind, Ulrich, ed. *Le roman de* Flamenca. 2 vols. Romanica Helvetica 86A–86B. Berne: Francke, 1976.

Guiraud, Pierre. "Les structures étymologiques du trobar." *Poétique* 7 (1971): 416–26.

Gumbrecht, Hans Ulrich. "'Un souffle d'Allemagne ayant passé': Friedrich Diez, Gaston Paris, and the Genesis of National Philologies." *Romance Philology* 40 (1986): 1–37.

Hackett, W. Mary, ed. *Girart de Roussillon, chanson de geste.* Société des Anciens Textes Français 141. 2 vols. Paris: Picard, 1953.

Hall, Robert A., Jr. *External History of the Romance Languages.* New York: Elsevier, 1974.

Hamlin, Frank R., Peter T. Ricketts, and John Hathaway, eds. *Introduction à l'étude de l'ancien provençal: Textes d'étude.* Publications Romanes et Françaises 96. 2nd ed. Genève: Droz, 1985.

Harris, Marvyn Roy. *Index inverse du* Petit dictionnaire provençal-français. Heidelberg: Winter, 1981.

Hill, R. T., and T. G. Bergin, eds. *Anthology of the Provençal Troubadours.* Rev. Thomas G. Bergin, with the collaboration of Susan Olson, William D. Paden Jr., and Nathaniel Smith. 2nd ed. 2 vols. New Haven: Yale UP, 1973.

Hitchcock, Richard. The *"Kharjas": A Critical Bibliography*. London: Grant and Cutler, 1977.

Holtus, Günter, Michael Metzeltin, and Christian Schmitt, eds. *Lexikon der romanistischen Linguistik*. Vol. 5, part 2: *Okzitanisch, Katalanisch*. Tübingen: Niemeyer, 1991.

Honnorat, S. J. *Dictionnaire provençal-français: ou, Dictionnaire de la langue d'oc, ancienne et moderne*. 3 vols. Digne, 1846–47. Marseille: Lafitte, 1971.

Hoppin, Richard H., ed. *Anthology of Medieval Music*. New York: Norton, 1978.

———. *Medieval Music*. New York: Norton, 1978.

International Medieval Bibliography. Leeds: Univ. of Leeds, 1967–.

Isambert, F.-A., et al., eds. *Recueil général des anciennes lois françaises*. 29 vols. Paris, 1827–33.

Jeanroy, Alfred. *Bibliographie sommaire des chansonniers provençaux (manuscrits et éditions)*. Classiques Français du Moyen Age 16. Paris: Champion, 1916.

———. *La poésie lyrique des troubadours*. 2 vols. Toulouse: Privat, 1934.

Jensen, Frede. *From Vulgar Latin to Old Provençal*. Univ. of North Carolina Studies in the Romance Languages and Literatures 120. Chapel Hill: U of North Carolina P, 1972.

———. *The Old Provençal Noun and Adjective Declension*. Etudes Romanes de l'Université d'Odense 9. Odense: Odense UP, 1976.

———. *Provençal Philology and the Poetry of Guillaume of Poitiers*. Etudes Romanes de l'Université d'Odense 14. Odense: Odense UP, 1983.

———. *The Syntax of Medieval Occitan*. Beihefte zur Zeitschrift für romanische Philologie 208. Tübingen: Niemeyer, 1986.

———. "A True Dilemma: Is Occitan *verai* Domestic or Foreign?" *Romance Notes* 32 (1992): 209–13.

Kay, Sarah. "Derivation, Derived Rhyme, and the Trobairitz." Paden, *The Voice of the Trobairitz*. 157–82.

Kent, Roland G. *The Forms of Latin: A Descriptive and Historical Morphology*. Baltimore: Linguistic Soc. of America, 1946.

Kibler, William W. *An Introduction to Old French*. New York: MLA, 1984.

Klingebiel, Kathryn. *Bibliographie linguistique de l'ancien occitan (1960–1982)*. Romanistik in Geschichte und Gegenwart 19. Hamburg: Buske, 1986.

———. Rev. of *Spracherziehung*, by Peter Cichon. *Romance Philology* 46 (1993): 487–89.

Kloss, Heinz, and Grant D. McConnell. *Linguistic Composition of the Nations of the World*. 5 vols. Quèbec: P de U Laval, 1974–84.

Knecht, R. J. *Francis I*. Cambridge: Cambridge UP, 1982.

Kolsen, Adolf, ed. *Sämtliche Lieder des Trobadors Giraut de Bornelh*. 2 vols. Halle: Niemeyer, 1910–35. Genève: Slatkine, 1976.

Körner, Josef. "François-Juste-Marie Raynouard" [sic]. *Germanisch-Romanische Monatsschrift* 5 (1913): 456–88.

Kremnitz, Georg. *Das Okzitanische: Sprachgeschichte und Soziologie*. Romanistische Arbeitshefte 23. Tübingen: Niemeyer, 1981.

Kussler-Ratyé, Gabrielle. "Les chansons de la Comtesse Béatrix de Dia." *Archivum Romanicum* 1 (1917): 161–82.

Lafont, Robert. *Eléments de phonétique de l'occitan*. Enèrgas: Vent Terral, 1983.

Lafont, Robert, and Christian Anatole. *Nouvelle histoire de la littérature occitane.* 2 vols. Paris: P U de France, 1970.

Långfors, A., ed. *Les chansons de Guilhem de Cabestanh.* Classiques Français du Moyen Age 42. Paris: Champion, 1924.

Lavaud, René, ed. *Poésies complètes du troubadour Peire Cardenal.* Toulouse: Privat, 1957.

Lavaud, René, and Georges Machicot, eds. *Boecis: Poème sur Boèce (fragment).* Toulouse: Institut d'Etudes Occitanes, 1950.

Lazar, Moshé, ed. *Bernard de Ventadour: Chansons d'amour.* Paris: Klincksieck, 1966.

Leclercq, J. *Initiation aux auteurs monastiques du Moyen Age.* Paris: Cerf, 1957.

Lecoy, Félix, ed. *Jean Renart:* Le roman de la rose ou de Guillaume de Dole. Classiques Français du Moyen Age 91. Paris: Champion, 1962.

Lejeune, Rita. "La chanson de l'amour de loin de Jaufré Rudel." *Studi in onore di Angelo Monteverdi.* Modena: Società Tipografica Editrice Modenese. 1 (1959): 403–42.

———. "L'extraordinaire insolence du troubadour Guillaume IX d'Aquitaine." *Mélanges de langue et de littérature médiévales offerts à Perre Le Gentil.* Ed. Jean Dufournet and Daniel Poirion. Paris: SEDES, 1973. 485–503.

———. "Le nom de Bernart de Ventadour." *Mittelalterstudien: Erich Köhler zum Gedenken.* Ed. Henning Krauss and Dietmar Rieger. Heidelberg: Winter, 1984. 157–65.

Le Roy Ladurie, Emmanuel. *Montaillou: The Promised Land of Error.* Trans. Barbara Bray. New York: Vintage, 1978.

Levy, Emil. *Petit dictionnaire provençal-français.* 1909. 4th ed. Heidelberg: Winter, 1966.

Levy, Emil, and Carl Appel. *Provenzalisches Supplement-Wörterbuch, Berichtigungen und Ergänzungen zu Raynouards* Lexique Roman. 8 vols. Leipzig: Reisland, 1894–1924.

Lewis, Archibald R. "Patterns of Economic Development in Southern France, 1050–1271 A.D." 1980. Rpt. in *Medieval Society in Southern France and Catalonia.* London: Variorum, 1984. Sec. 13.

Lewis, C. S. *The Allegory of Love: A Study in Medieval Tradition.* Oxford: Clarendon, 1936.

Lewis, Charlton T., and Charles Short. *A Latin Dictionary.* Oxford: Clarendon, 1879.

Lexikon des Mittelalters. Ed. Robert Auty et al. München: Artemis, 1980–.

Löfstedt, Bengt. "Spätes Vulgärlatein—ein abgegrastes Feld?" *Indogermanische Forschungen* 75 (1970): 107–30.

Lo Nigro, Sebastiano, ed. *Novellino e conti del duecento.* Torino: Classici Italiani UTET, 1963.

Marchello-Nizia, Christiane. *Dire le vrai: L'adverbe "si" en français médiéval. Essai de linguistique historique.* Genève: Droz, 1985.

Marrou, Henri-Irénée. *Les troubadours.* 2nd ed. Paris: Seuil, 1971.

Marshall, J. H., ed. *The* Razos de trobar *of Raimon Vidal and Associated Texts.* London: Oxford UP, 1972.

Martin-Chabot, Eugène, ed. *La chanson de la Croisade albigeoise.* 3 vols. Paris: Belles Lettres, 1957–61.

Medieval France: An Encyclopedia. Ed. William W. Kibler and Grover A. Zinn. New York: Garland, 1995.

Menocal, María Rosa. "The Etymology of Old Provençal *trobar, trobador:* A Return to the 'Third Solution.'" *Romance Philology* 36 (1982): 137–48.

Meyer, Paul, ed. *La chanson de la Croisade contre les albigeois.* 2 vols. Paris: Renouard, 1875–79.

———. "Fragment d'une *Chanson d'Antioche* en provençal." *Archives de l'orient latin* 2, no. 2 (1884): 467–509.

Meyer-Lübke, W. *Romanisches etymologisches Wörterbuch.* Heidelberg: Winter, 1935.

Miquel, Pierre. *Le vocabulaire latin de l'expérience spirituelle dans la tradition monastique et canoniale de 1050 à 1250.* Paris: Beauchesne, 1989.

Mistral, Frédéric. *Lou tresor dóu Felibrige: ou, Dictionnaire provençal-français, embrassant les divers dialectes de la langue d'oc moderne.* 2 vols. Aix-en-Provence, 1879–87. Barcelona: Berenguié, 1968.

Mölk, Ulrich. *Guiraut Riquier: Las cansos, kritischer Text und Kommentar.* Studia Romanica 2. Heidelberg: Winter, 1962.

———. *Trobadorlyrik.* München: Artemis, 1982. Italian trans. by Gabriella Klein and Elda Morlicchio. *La lirica dei trovatori.* Bologna: Il Mulino, 1986.

Mok, Q. I. M. *Manuel pratique de morphologie d'ancien occitan.* Muiderberg: Coutinho, 1977.

Monier, Janine. "Essai d'identification de la comtesse de Die." *Bulletin de la Société d'Archéologie et de Statistique de la Drôme* 75 (1962): 265–78.

Mouzat, Jean, ed. *Les poèmes de Gaucelm Faidit, troubadour du XIIe siècle.* Paris: Nizet, 1965.

Mundy, John Hine. "Le mariage et les femmes à Toulouse au temps des Cathares." *Annales: Economies, sociétés, civilisations* 42 (1987): 117–34.

———. "Urban Society and Culture: Toulouse and Its Region." *Renaissance and Renewal in the Twelfth Century.* Ed. Robert L. Benson and Giles Constable, with Carol D. Lanham. Cambridge: Harvard UP, 1982. 229–47.

Mussafia, Adolf. "Ueber die provenzalischen Liederhandschriften des Giovanni Maria Barbieri." *Österreichische Akademie der Wissenschaften, Philosophisch-historische Classe (Wien): Sitzungsberichte* 76 (1874): 201–66.

Nègre, Ernest. *Toponymie générale de la France.* 3 vols. Genève: Droz, 1990–91.

Nichols, Stephen G., Jr., and John A. Galm, with A. Bartlett Giamatti, Roger J. Porter, Seth L. Wolitz, and Claudette M. Charbonneau, eds. *The Songs of Bernart de Ventadorn.* Univ. of North Carolina Studies in the Romance Languages and Literatures 39. Chapel Hill: U of North Carolina P, 1962.

Nicholson, Derek E. T., ed. *The Poems of the Troubadour Peire Rogier.* Manchester: Manchester UP, 1976.

Niermeyer, J. F., and C. van de Kieft. *Mediae latinitatis lexicon minus.* Leiden: Brill, 1976.

Nolhac, Pierre de. *Ronsard et l'humanisme.* Paris: Champion, 1921.

Noulet, Jean-B., and Camille Chabaneau, eds. *Deux manuscrits provençaux du XIVe siècle contenant des poésies de Raimon de Cornet, de Peire de Ladils, et d'autres poètes de l'école toulousaine.* Publications Spéciales 13. Montpellier: Société pour l'Etude des Langues Romanes, 1888.

Oxford English Dictionary. Prep. J. A. Simpson and E. S. C. Weiner. 2nd ed. 20 vols. Oxford: Clarendon, 1989.

Paden, William D. "Bernart de Ventadour le troubadour devint-il abbé de Tulle?" *Mélanges de langue et de littérature occitanes en hommage à Pierre Bec.* Poitiers: Centre d'Études Supérieures de Civilisation Médiévale, 1991. 401–13.

―――. "De l'identité historique de Bertran de Born." *Romania* 101 (1980): 192–224.

―――. "L'emploi vicaire du présent verbal dans les plus anciens textes narratifs romans." *14th Congresso Internazionale di Linguistica e Filologia Romanza: Atti* 4. Napoli: Macchiaròli, 1977. 545–57.

―――. "*Et ai be faih co·l fols en pon:* Bernart de Ventadorn, Jacques de Vitry, and Q. Horatius Flaccus." *Studia occitanica in memoriam Paul Rémy* 1. Kalamazoo: Medieval Inst. Pubs., 1986. 181–91.

―――. "The Etymology of *Midons.*" *Studies in Honor of Hans-Erich Keller: Medieval French and Occitan Literature and Romance Linguistics.* Ed. Rupert T. Pickens. Kalamazoo: Medieval Inst. Pubs., 1993. 311–35.

―――, ed. *The Medieval Pastourelle.* 2 vols. Garland Library of Medieval Literature 34–35A. New York: Garland, 1987.

―――. "Old Occitan as a Lyric Language: The Insertions from Occitan in Three Thirteenth-Century French Romances." *Speculum* 68 (1993): 36–53.

―――. "Pound's Use of Troubadour Manuscripts." *Comparative Literature* 32 (1980): 402–12.

―――. "Reading Pastourelles." *Tenso* 4 (1988): 1–21.

―――. "The Troubadours and the Albigensian Crusade: A Long View." *Romance Philology* 49 (1995): 168–91.

―――, ed. *The Voice of the Trobairitz: Perspectives on the Women Troubadours.* Philadelphia: U of Pennsylvania P, 1989.

Paden, William D., with Julia C. Hayes, Georgina M. Mahoney, Barbara J. O'Neill, Edward J. Samuelson, Jeri L. Snyder, Edwina Spodark, Julie A. Storme, and Scott D. Westrem, eds. "The Poems of the Trobairitz Na Castelloza." *Romance Philology* 35 (1981): 158–82.

Paden, William, D., Tilde Sankovitch, and Patricia H. Stäblein, eds. *The Poems of the Troubadour Bertran de Born.* Berkeley: U of California P, 1986.

Paris, Gaston. "Lancelot du Lac, II: *Le Conte de la Charrette.*" *Romania* 12 (1883): 459–534.

Pasero, Nicolò, ed. *Guglielmo IX d'Aquitania: Poesie.* Unione Accademica Nazionale, Roma: Subsidia al Corpus des Troubadours 1. Istituto di Filologia Romanza dell'Università di Roma, Studi, Testi e Manuali 1. Modena: STEM-Mucchi, 1973.

Paterson, Linda M. *The World of the Troubadours: Medieval Occitan Society, c. 1100–c.1300.* Cambridge: Cambridge UP, 1993.

Pécout, Roland. *Claude Martí: Edition bilingue.* Poésie et Chansons 27. Paris: Seghers, 1975.

Pellegrini, Silvio. "Frammento inedito di canzoniere provenzale." *Studi mediolatini e volgari* 15–16 (1968): 89–99.

Pfaff, S. L., ed. *Guiraut Riquier. Die Werke der Troubadours in provenzalischer Sprache.* Ed. Carl A. Mahn. Vol. 4. Berlin, 1853. Genève: Slatkine, 1977.

Pfister, Max. *Lexikalische Untersuchungen zu Girart de Roussillon.* Beihefte zur Zeitschrift für romanische Philologie 122. Tübingen: Niemeyer, 1970.

Pickens, Rupert T., ed. *The Songs of Jaufre Rudel.* Studies and Texts 41. Toronto: Pontifical Institute of Medieval Studies, 1978.

Pillet, Alfred, and Henry Carstens, eds. *Bibliographie der Troubadours.* Halle: Niemeyer, 1933.

Pirot, François. *Recherches sur les connaissances littéraires des troubadours occitans et catalans des XIIe et XIIIe siècles.* Barcelona: Real Academia de Buenas Letras, 1972.

Quemada, B. *Matériaux pour l'histoire du vocabulaire français.* Vol. 24: *Datations et documents lexicographiques.* Paris: Klincksieck, 1984.

Rajna, P. "Varietà provenzali IV: Bertran de Born nelle bricciche di un canzoniere provenzale." *Romania* 50 (1924): 233–46.

Raynouard, François-Just-Marie, ed. *Choix des poésies originales des troubadours.* 6 vols. Paris: Didot, 1816–21. 1966.

———. *Lexique roman: ou, Dictionnaire de la langue des troubadours comparée avec les autres langues de l'Europe latine, précédé de nouvelles recherches historiques et philologiques, d'un résumé de la grammaire romane, d'un nouveau choix des poésies originales des troubadours, et d'extraits de poèmes divers.* 6 vols. Paris: Silvestre, 1844.

Renzi, Lorenzo, with Giampaolo Salvi. *Nuova introduzione alla filologia romanza.* 2nd ed. Bologna: Il Mulino, 1987.

Richter, Reinhilt, ed. *Die Troubadourzitate im "Breviari d'amor."* Modena: STEM-Mucchi, 1976.

Ricketts, Peter T., ed. *Le "Breviari d'amor" de Matfre Ermengaud.* Vol. 5. Leiden: Brill, 1976.

Ricketts, Peter T., and E. J. Hathaway. "Le 'vers del lavador' de Marcabrun: Édition critique, traduction et commentaire." *Revue des langues romanes* 77 (1966): 1–11.

Rieger, Angelica, ed. *Trobairitz: Der Beitrag der Frau in der altokzitanischen höfischen Lyrik. Edition des Gesamtkorpus.* Beihefte zur Zeitschrift für romanische Philologie 233. Tübingen: Niemeyer, 1991.

Riquer, Martín de, ed. *Los trovadores: Historia literaria y textos.* 3 vols. Barcelona: Planeta, 1975.

Rochegude, Henri-Pascal de. *Le Parnasse occitanien.* Toulouse: Benichet cadet, 1819. 1977.

Rohlfs, Gerhard. *From Vulgar Latin to Old French.* Trans. Vincent Almazan and Lillian McCarthy. Detroit: Wayne State UP, 1970.

Romanische Bibliographie. Tübingen: Niemeyer, 1961–.

Roncaglia, Aurelio, ed. "Cortesamen vuoill comensar." *Rivista di cultura classica e medioevale* 7 (1965): 948–61.

———. *La lingua dei trovatori: Profilo di grammatica storica del provenzale antico.* Roma: Ateneo, 1965.

————. "Obediens." *Mélanges de linguistique romane et de philologie médiévale offerts à M. Maurice Delbouille*. Ed. Jean Renson and Madeleine Tyssens. 2 vols. Gembloux: Duculot, 1964. 2: 597–614.

————. "Valore et giuoco dell'interpretazione nella critica testuale." *Studi e problemi di critica testuale*. Bologna: Commissione per i Testi di Lingua, 1961. 45–62.

Ronjat, Jules. *Grammaire istorique des parlers provençaux modernes*. 4 vols. Montpellier: Société des Langues Romanes, 1930–41.

Rosenstein, Roy. "Les années d'apprentissage du troubadour Jaufre Rudel: De *l'escola n'Eblo* à la *segura escola*." *Annales du Midi* 100 (1988): 7–15.

Rychner, Jean, ed. *Les lais de Marie de France*. Classiques Français du Moyen Age 93. Paris: Champion, 1968.

Schultz-Gora, O. *Altprovenzalisches Elementarbuch*. Sammlung romanischer Elementar- und Handbücher 1. Reihe: Grammatiken 3. 6th ed. Heidelberg: Winter, 1973.

Schwarze, Christoph, ed. *Der altprovenzalische "Boeci."* Forschungen zur romanischen Philologie 12. Münster: Aschendorff, 1963.

Sharman, Ruth Verity. *The Cansos and Sirventes of the Troubadour Giraut de Borneil: A Critical Edition*. Cambridge: Cambridge UP, 1989.

Simons, Marlise. "Provençal Leading a Revival of Europe's Local Languages." *New York Times*, 3 May 1993. A1, A8.

Smith, Nathaniel B., and Thomas G. Bergin. *An Old Provençal Primer*. New York: Garland, 1984.

Société Guilhem IX. *Tenso*. Louisville, 1985–.

Stern, S. M. "Les vers finaux en espagnol dans les muwaššaḥs hispano-hebraïques: Une contribution à l'histoire du muwaššaḥ et à l'étude du vieux dialecte espagnol 'mozarabe.'" *Al-Andalus* 13 (1948): 299–346.
"The Final Lines of Hebrew Muwashshaḥs from Spain: A Contribution to the History of the Muwashshaḥ and of the Mozarabic Dialect of Old Spanish." *Hispano-Arabic Strophic Poetry: Studies by Samuel Miklos Stern*. Ed. L. P. Harvey. Oxford: Clarendon, 1974. 123–60.

Stimm, Helmut, and Wolf-Dieter Stempel. *Dictionnaire de l'occitan médiéval*. Fasc. 1. A-acceptar. Tübingen: Niemeyer, 1996–.

Strayer, Joseph R. *The Albigensian Crusades*. New York: Dial, 1971.

Stroński, Stanislaw. *La légende amoureuse de Bertran de Born*. Paris: Champion, 1914.

Sturtevant, Edgar H. *The Pronunciation of Greek and Latin*. 2nd ed. Philadelphia: Linguistic Soc. of America, 1940.

Sutherland, Dorothy R. "Flexions and Categories in Old Provençal." *Transactions of the Philological Society* (1959): 25–70.

————. "The Language of the Troubadours and the Problem of Origins." *French Studies* 10 (1956): 199–215.

Suttina, L. "Frammento di un nuovo canzoniere provenzale del sec. XIII." *Romania* 54 (1928): 1–10.

Switten, Margaret L. *Music and Poetry in the Middle Ages: A Guide to Research on French and Occitan Song, 1100–1400*. New York: Garland, 1995.

Switten, Margaret, and Howell Chickering. *The Medieval Lyric: Anthologies and Cassettes for Teaching. A Project Supported by the National Endowment for the Humanities and Mount Holyoke College*. 4 vols., 5 cassettes. South Hadley: Mount Holyoke Coll., 1988–89.

Taylor, Robert A. *La littérature occitane du Moyen Age: Bibliographie sélective et critique.* Toronto: U of Toronto P, 1977.

Tobler, Adolf, and Erhard Lommatzsch. *Tobler-Lommatzsch altfranzösisches Wörterbuch.* 10 vols. to date. Berlin: Weidmann, 1925–.

Trésor de la langue française: Dictionnaire de la langue du XIXe et du XXe siècle (1789–1960). Ed. Paul Imbs. 16 vols. Paris: Editions du CNRS, 1971–94.

Udina i Martorell, Frederic. *Nom de Catalunya.* Barcelona: Dalmau, 1961.

Väänänen, Veikko. *Introduction au latin vulgaire.* 3rd ed. Paris: Klincksieck, 1981.

van der Werf, Hendrik. *The Chansons of the Troubadours and Trouvères: A Study of the Melodies and Their Relation to the Poems.* Utrecht: Oosthoek, 1972.

van der Werf, Hendrik, and Gerald A. Bond. *The Extant Troubadour Melodies: Transcriptions and Essays for Performers and Scholars.* Rochester: Publ. by the author, 1984.

Vincenti, Eleonora. *Bibliografia antica dei trovatori.* Milano: Ricciardi, 1963.

Walsh, Thomas J. "Two Problems in Gallo-Romance Etymology" (OOc **gens** [3] and **faduc**). *Romance Philology* 35 (1981): 89–104.

Wartburg, Walther von. *Französisches etymologisches Wörterbuch.* 25 vols. to date. Bonn: Klopp, 1928–.

Wheeler, Max N. "Occitan." *The Romance Languages.* Ed. Martin Harris and Nigel Vincent. New York: Oxford UP, 1988. 246–77.

Wiacek, Wilhelmina M. *Lexique des noms géographiques et ethniques dans les poésies des troubadours des XIIe et XIIIe siècles.* Paris: Nizet, 1968.

Wilhelm, James J., ed. *The Poetry of Sordello.* Garland Library of Medieval Literature 42A. New York: Garland, 1987.

Wolf, George, and Roy Rosenstein, eds. *The Poetry of Cercamon and Jaufre Rudel.* Garland Library of Medieval Literature 5A. New York: Garland, 1983.

Zeitschrift für romanische Philologie. Supplementheft: Bibliographie. Halle: Niemeyer, 1878–1943. Tübingen: Niemeyer, 1957–64.

Zenker, R., ed. "Peire von Auvergne." *Romanische Forschungen* 12 (1900): 653–924.

Zufferey, François. *Bibliographie des poètes provençaux des XIVe et XVe siècles.* Genève: Droz, 1981.

———. *Recherches linguistiques sur les chansonniers provençaux.* Publications Romanes et Françaises 176. Genève: Droz, 1987.

Index of Occitan Words

Indexed here are words discussed in the text, not simply adduced to illustrate a point. For terms and concepts, see Subject Index; for words in the readings, see Glossary (app. B).

Subject Index

This index includes terms concerning language, literature, and history. Names of authors or titles of works are indexed if they are discussed, but not if they are merely cited.